I

The Formative Centuries

A NAVAL HISTORY OF ENGLAND

I

The Formative Centuries

G. J. MARCUS

An Atlantic Monthly Press Book
Little, Brown and Company
BOSTON   TORONTO

ATLANTIC–LITTLE, BROWN BOOKS
ARE PUBLISHED BY
LITTLE, BROWN AND COMPANY
IN ASSOCIATION WITH
THE ATLANTIC MONTHLY PRESS

PRINTED IN GREAT BRITAIN

To J. A. Williamson

To the question, ' What shall we do to be saved in this world? ' there is no other answer but this – Looke to your Moate. The first article of an Englishman's political creed must be, that he believeth in the sea. HALIFAX, *Rough Draught of a New Model at Sea* (1694).

CONTENTS

MAPS

ACKNOWLEDGMENTS

We are indebted to the following for permission to quote copyright material:

Hollis & Carter Ltd. and Henry C. Taylor for material from *The Art of Navigation in Tudor and Early Stuart Times* by D. W. Waters; Houghton Mifflin Co. for material from *A Naval History of the American Revolution* by G. W. Allen and from *Maritime History of Massachusetts* by S. E. Morison; Little, Brown & Co. for material from *Influence of Sea Power upon History* and *Sea Power in its Relation to the War of 1812* by Mahan; Macmillan & Co. Ltd. for material from *Lloyd's of London* by D. E. W. Gibb; The Navy Records Society for extracts from various publications; The Syndics of the University Press, Cambridge, for material from *Select Naval Documents* edited by Hodges and Hughes.

INTRODUCTION

'Naval history', Sir Lewis Namier once observed, 'is a vast subject which requires highly specialized knowledge.' Herein lies what is probably the true explanation of the long-standing neglect of naval history in this country, and also of the fact that, in consequence, in the average general history, whether of England, Europe, or the Commonwealth, the maritime sections are almost invariably the weakest part of the work. The last full-scale naval history of England was compiled, nearly sixty years ago, by Sir William Laird Clowes, assisted by a distinguished band which included A. T. Mahan and Theodore Roosevelt; since then a number of both short and outline naval histories have been published from time to time, with greater or lesser success; but it is evidently too much to expect that a general naval history, on approximately the same scale as, say, Sir John Fortescue's *A History of the British Army*, will ever appear in future.

The present work is in certain respects a compromise between the short and the full-scale naval history. It embraces the whole of the formative period between the nascent English maritime expansion of the later Middle Ages and the outbreak of the French Revolutionary War. In a general naval history of such a length anything like detailed documentation is naturally impossible; but where it has been considered desirable the necessary references have been supplied *ad hoc* in the form of footnotes or by inference in the text (e.g. when some admiral or captain is quoted reference may be made to the appropriate In-Letter or Captain's Journal among the Admiralty Papers preserved in the Public Record Office).

My grateful thanks are due to the following for advice and assistance on particular points: Captains A. G. Course, Edwin Jones, and H. L. Lang, Rear-Admiral S. E. Morison, U.S.N.R., Captain Carl V. Sölver, Lieut.-Commander D. W. Waters, R.N.; Professors C. R. Boxer, G. S. Graham, M. A. Lewis, and C. C. Lloyd, the late Sir Alan Moore, Bt., Messrs. A. B. Rodger, Anthony Ryan, R. A. Skelton,

Björn Thorsteinsson, and E. W. White, Drs. J. A. Williamson and Charles Wilson. I have also to thank the Staffs of the Admiralty Library, the Bodleian, the Reading Room, Manuscript Room, and Map Department of the British Museum, the Institute of Historical Research, the Manchester Central Library, the National Maritime Museum, the Public Record Office, the University of London Library, and the West Sussex County Library, for their kind and unfailing help. Finally I should like to thank the Editors for allowing me to reproduce certain material which had previously appeared in the following journals: *Economic History Review, History, Journal of the Royal United Service Institution,* and *The Mariner's Mirror.*

Two books that I was commissioned to write on particular subjects, *Quiberon Bay: The campaign in home waters, 1759* (Hollis & Carter, 1960) and *The Great Armada* (in preparation), have been largely laid under contribution in the present work, which originated in a series of lectures delivered in H.M.S. *Gosling,* in the latter half of the War, to successive classes of Officers under Training.

I

The mediaeval prelude

I

The successive stages by which this country rose to become the greatest maritime nation in history belong for the most part to the modern age, namely, from the sixteenth century onwards. It was the first part of this period which saw the foundation of the battle fleet, the organization of a permanent, effective naval administration, and a true shipping policy. In the ensuing centuries the growth of England's sea power was fostered by a supremely favourable geographical situation, a sufficiency of good natural harbours, an adequate territory and population, the national character and aptitudes of her people, and the wisdom and foresight of their rulers.

The origins of English maritime enterprise are to be found, in an earlier era, in those towns and ports whose population of merchants and mariners, together with craftsmen concerned in kindred callings, were engaged in activities far removed from the normal agricultural round of Englishmen. This mercantile element, at first very small in comparison with the total population, was practically outside the feudal régime. Throughout the whole of the mediaeval era, indeed, the expansion of English shipping and of the English seafaring and commercial community generally, represented the main and vital thread in our naval history.

About the year 1380 the English seaman was still for the most part tied to the coast, a ' rock-dodger ', steering from ' view to view ', and dependent upon the rough, rule-of-thumb methods of navigation gained by long experience of seafaring, and the knowledge handed down to him from his fathers. Chaucer, in the Prologue to the *Canterbury Tales*, has sketched for us an unforgettable picture of the typical coasting skipper of his day.

A shipman was ther, woning fer by weste;
For aught I woot, he was of Dertemouthe. . . .
The hoote somer had maad his hew al brown;
And certainly he was a good felawe.
Ful many a draughte of wyn had he y-drawe
From Burdeux-ward, whyl that the Chapman sleepe.
Of nyce conscience took he no keep.
If that he faught, and hadde the hyer hond,
By water he sente hem hoom to every lond.
But of his craft to rekene wel his tydes,
His stremes and his daungers hym bisydes,
His herberwe and his mone, his lodemenage,
Ther nas noon swich from Hulle to Cartage.
Hardy he was, and wys to undertake;
With many a tempest hadde his berd ben shake.
He knew wel alle the havenes, as they were,
From Gootland to the cape of Finistere,
And every cryke in Britayne and in Spayne;
His barge y-cleped was the Maudelayne.

During the period under survey a few modest lights and beacons
(as at Spurn Head, Yarmouth, and Winchelsea) began to be maintained
on the coast. There was a gradual expansion of trade, and, owing to
the lack of good inland communications, a great deal of it went by
water. Year by year, in fair weather and in foul, sturdy coasting
skippers of the type of Chaucer's *Shipman* navigated their cogs, barges,
or balingers around the long, indented coasts of the British Isles or
fared forth across the narrow seas to the ports of Holland and Flanders.
Others were fishermen who followed the herring shoals in their
seasonal migrations down the east coast of Scotland and England, or
worked the lesser fisheries of the English and Bristol Channels. They
acquired in these activities a familiar knowledge of the intricate
coastal navigation which could only come from the accumulated
experience of generations. They learned to find their position in mist
or darkness by taking note of the varying sound of the sea on cliffs,
rocks, sands, and beaches, and by keeping careful watch for such
adventitious aids to navigation as passing seabirds, seals, fishes, sea-
weed, and the colour and run of the seas. They learned to work the
tides, to take advantage of short cuts, and to know the signs of the
weather. As a rule a fisherman does not depend on charts or sailing
directions—he carries such knowledge in his head. So it was with the

coasting skippers of Chaucer's time. For long this knowledge was neither written nor read: but was passed down by hand and mouth from generation to generation; and was to stand their descendants in good stead when, at a later date, they struck out across the ocean. The coasting trade bred seamen.

In the later mediaeval era these seafaring folk were increasing steadily in numbers and importance: a tough, truculent, highly individualistic fraternity, evidently regarded by the landsman as a race apart, with a distinctive kind of dress (rough jackets and long loose trousers), clumsy rolling gait, and conversing in an argot of their own. The crew was subject to the master: but the master's authority was in many ways hedged about by the law and custom of the sea. The master, for instance, was accustomed to consult the crew before sailing, if the signs of the weather were unpromising (just as in fishing vessels in our own time); and he was expected to abide by the majority opinion. The composition of a ship's company varied according to the needs of the voyage. The crew for a Channel crossing would not be the same as for a distant trading or fishing venture. Mention is made of the master's mate; of the boatswain and his mate; of the lodesman, or pilot; also of the purser, steward, cook, and ship's boy. We may read of the *clamor nauticus*, of mariners straining at the halliards to the cry of ' howe! hissa! y howe taylia! ' Across the centuries, we may catch a snatch of what sounds very like some sea-shanty in embryo:

hale and howe Rumbylowe
stire well the gode ship and lete the wynde blowe.[1]

2

Down to the close of the Middle Ages, the richer part of our overseas trade remained in foreign hands. The Italians were sailing regularly to the North Sea for more than two centuries before any English merchantman entered the Mediterranean. The products of central and southern Asia were transported to the Black Sea and the Levant by caravan and by Arab shipping plying in the Red Sea and Persian Gulf; from the termini of the eastern trade-routes they were brought to England and the neighbouring lands by way of the long sea-route

[1] Q. E. M. Carus-Wilson, *The Overseas Trade of Bristol* (1937).

through the Straits of Gibraltar. Amalfi, Pisa, Genoa, and Venice successively contested the mastery of the Mediterranean. In the latter half of the fourteenth century the Genoese were predominant in the Italian trade with England. They brought to this country the produce of their extensive alum mines at Foglia in Asia Minor, returning, as a rule, with cargoes of English wool. Eventually Venice succeeded in gaining the lion's share of the trade. In 1317 the Venetian Council first sent out a State trading fleet, ' the Flanders Galleys ', consisting of a few merchantmen of the largest size, which every year from this time on sailed in company to the English Channel, and there separated, part of the fleet calling at Bruges and other Flemish ports and part at Southampton, Sandwich, and London. London was the centre of the Venetian trade to England. (Galley Wharf, near the Tower, derived its name from the Venetian galleasses that used to lie there.) The Genoese and Catalan shipping went mostly to Southampton. The Italians enjoyed the privilege of being permitted to transport English wool direct to the Mediterranean, instead of having to traffic through the Staple at Calais.

The seaborne commerce of the north was controlled in the main by the Hanseatic League. This was an alliance of trading towns situated along the North Sea and Baltic coasts. The Hanse were essentially carriers, not manufacturers. The towns lived on, and by, the great trade-route of the north which extended from Novgorod in the east to the ports of the Peninsula in the west. In the second half of the fourteenth century the Hanse twice went to war with Denmark in defence of the rights they had acquired over the herring fishery of Skania, upon which the prosperity of the north German towns largely depended. From this struggle the Hanse had emerged as an organiza-tion of city-states united for mutual support in defence of the trade-routes and commercial interests generally. Throughout the greater part of the fourteenth, fifteenth, and sixteenth centuries the Hanse were dominated by a strong combination of Wendish towns under the leadership of Lübeck. It was this group which controlled the herring trade of Skania, and in Bergen gained a virtual monopoly of Norway's foreign trade.

At the same time a small but gradually increasing proportion of the shipping used in foreign trade was English-owned. Wool, hides, and fells of the best quality were regularly dispatched to the Staple at

Calais in trading-fleets from London, Boston, Ipswich, and Hull; while large quantities of woollen cloth were sent overseas from most of our east coast ports. In 1407 the merchants in the various ports exporting cloth to the great marts of the Netherlands were combined into a regulated company, known as the Merchant Adventurers, which enjoyed a prosperous existence throughout the fifteenth century. A great deal of English cloth was also exported, in the first half of the century, to Prussia and the Baltic.

The Gascony wine trade was another of these foreign trades in which English shipping was now predominant. Every autumn the wine fleet would assemble, generally at Dartmouth or Plymouth, and sail to Bordeaux to bring home the new vintage. The trade was carried on for the most part by the western ports, especially Bristol, Dartmouth, and Fowey; but there were also large trading fleets from Hull and Lynn. The trade consisted in the main of the exchange of English cloth for Gascony wines and woad. Gascony also imported varying quantities of corn, and occasionally fish from Cornwall. The English wine ships were accustomed to sail in large fleets, for mutual protection, both on the outward and homeward passages. The Gascony wine trade, in that it demanded vessels of substantial tonnage, was one of the leading factors in the expansion of English shipping during the fifteenth century. Between the years 1400 and 1450 the average tonnage of Bristol ships sailing to Bordeaux nearly doubled. The Gascony trade survived all the vicissitudes, and even the final eclipse, of English fortunes in the Hundred Years War. Long after the time when the entire province had been reconquered by the King of France, it is recorded that, in the vintage season, the streets of Bordeaux would be thronged with thousands of English merchants and mariners.

The first half of the fifteenth century also saw a substantial increase in the English trade with the Peninsula. English shipping called principally at San Sebastian, Bilbao, Fuenterrabia, Pasajes, Santander, Coruna, and Ferrol on the north Spanish coast, Cadiz and San Lucar in Andalusia, and Lisbon in Portugal. To Spain and Portugal our merchants dispatched large quantities of cloth and imported a wide variety of products, but more especially wine, fruit, oil, salt, leather, iron and iron goods. The pilgrim traffic to Santiago de Compostella, on the north-west coast of Spain, now attained its greatest prosperity. In 1437 licences were granted to 27 pilgrim packets, and in 1433–34 to 65. Our wine fleets from Spain, like those from Gascony, were accustomed to sail in convoy for protection. Most of the English shipping employed in this Peninsular traffic hailed from the western ports, especially Bristol.

In 1412 the English sailings to Iceland began. The first arrival was a single fishing craft, probably from one of the east coast ports. Next year the fishermen were followed by traders; and that summer there sailed out from England ' 30 fishing doggers and more '. Despite the strong opposition of the Danish officials in Iceland, the commerce rapidly increased. It would appear from an anonymous rhyming poem of 1435 or 1436, entitled *The Libelle of Englyshe Polycye*, that Bristol began to engage in the Iceland trade from about 1425.

> Of Yseland to wryte is lytill nede
> Save of stokfische; yit for sothe in dede
> Out of Bristow and costis many one
> Men have practised by nedle and stone
> Thiderwardes wythine a lytel whylle,
> Wythine xij yeres, and wythoute parille,
> Gone and comen, as men were wonte of olde
> Of Scarborowgh, unto the costes colde.

For more than sixty years the bulk of the Iceland trade remained in English hands. The visitors gave good prices for Iceland's principal article of export, the ' comodius stokfysshe '; the goods they brought out with them were hardly less welcome. From England the Icelanders obtained what they needed most of all: namely, corn and cloth. They exported in return immense quantities of cod, together with other fish. Though the direct trade to Iceland continued to be illegal, it was nevertheless possible for our merchants to obtain a licence either from the King of England or from the King of Denmark, or from both, and thereby to by-pass the Staple at Bergen. Moreover, judging from the numerous cases of arrest, forfeiture of ship and cargo, imprisonment, etc., that we meet with in the national archives during the next decade or so, there must have been many who determined to dispense with the formality of a licence, and to follow the more economical, if riskier, course of sailing direct to Iceland. At any rate, by 1436 it is said that there were so many of them that not a few were unable to get a cargo and had to return home with empty holds.

And now so fele shippes thys yere there were
That moche loss for unfraught they bare.
Yselond myght not make hem to be fraught
Unto the hawys; this moche harme they caught.[1]

No precise statistics as to the total volume of trade, or even of the sailings from any one port over a lengthy period, are available. There exists, however, more than sufficient evidence to enable one to say with confidence that the voyage to Iceland was regularly made, by vessels of various types and sizes, from all over the British Isles.[2] During the same period a number of voyages were also made to the Faeroe Islands. In this way a substantial proportion of the seafaring population of the kingdom gradually gained experience of ocean navigation. The importance of the commerce with Iceland, as a factor in English maritime expansion, can scarcely be set too high; these were the first real deep-sea ventures in our history. The Iceland traffic may in fact be regarded as marking the half-way stage between the purely coastal navigation of Chaucer's *Shipman* and the transoceanic ventures of the Cabots and their successors.

Another major factor in English maritime development was the fisheries. The important confederation of the Cinque Ports were essentially fishing-ports. Besides engaging in the lesser fisheries of the Channel, they sent a large fleet each year to the North Sea for the autumn herring fishery and assisted at the ancient fish-fair of Yarmouth, the overlordship of which belonged to the ports. Certain fishing ports had a particular reputation for a certain fish. We hear, for instance, of the *Haraung de Gernemue* (Yarmouth), *Playz de Wychelsee*, and *Merlyng de la Rye*. The opening years of the fifteenth century saw the eclipse of the rich herring fishery at Skania—whose salted and smoked herrings were famed throughout Europe, and which had contributed in such large measure to the strength and prosperity of the Hanse—as the herring shoals moved out of the Baltic into the North Sea. From this time onward the herring fishery off the east coast of Britain became the most important in Europe. It was worked about equally by the English and the Dutch. Another highly important fishery in home waters was that off the south and west coasts of

---

[1] *Fele:* many; *unfraught:* without a freight; *hawys:* havens.
[2] For details of the English traffic to Iceland in the fifthteenth century, see *Diplomatarium Islandicum*, Vol. XVI, Parts 1–6, ed. Bj. Thorsteinason.

Ireland, which was much frequented by ships from our western ports. The rich cod fishery off the south-west coast of Iceland, in the vicinity of the Vestmannaeyjar, was systematically exploited by the English, chiefly from the east coast ports, throughout the fifteenth century.[1]

3

The progress and promise of the first half of the fifteenth century were scarcely maintained in the second half. This must be attributed to a variety of causes; but more especially to the Wars of the Roses, the opposition of the Hanse, the increase of piracy, and, above all, ' lack of governance '. Hence political, rather than economic, causes were mainly responsible. The history of the following half-century presents, indeed, a confused and contradictory pattern of events. It is now beginning to be recognized that what was happening was not so much retrogression, as slowing down in the rate of commercial and maritime expansion. None the less, the powerful mercantile interest and enterprising seafaring population of England were too strong to be held permanently in check; and, notwithstanding the manifold disorders engendered by baronial faction and the endemic weakness of the central government, our merchants and mariners were still, at any rate in some directions, able to make headway.

A significant development of the fifteenth century was the increasing importance in the North Sea traffic of our great trade rivals of the future, the Dutch. During this period the latter secured the Newcastle coal trade to the Netherlands, and also captured the bulk of the traffic in Sussex firewood. The Low Countries were now becoming the great entrepôt of northern Europe; and their ships brought to our shores not only local products, but valuable cargoes of goods from the Baltic and the south. Their shipping competed with our own in the Channel, as well as in the North Sea.

It was symptomatic of the situation in the North Sea in the mid-fifteenth century that a good many of the east coast merchants who had formerly trafficked with the Hanse now took to privateering. Privateering was in fact greatly on the increase, alike in the North Sea, the Channel, and Atlantic. The most thorough-going freebooters of

[1] For the Iceland fishery, see the present writer in the *Mariner's Mirror*, XL, pp. 294–6 and XLII, pp. 313–8.

all were the mariners of the West Country—men like John Mixtow of Fowey, William Kidd of Exmouth, and Hankyn Seelander and John Fresshowe of Falmouth. In their depredations in the English and Bristol Channels the men of Fowey, the far-famed ' Fowey gallants ', took the lead; but Dartmouth and most of the other ports lying along the south-west coast were involved, and, as English ships increased in number and size, extended their operations to more distant waters, working off the Atlantic coasts of France and Spain.

In the western ports, where the conditions governing foreign trading were different and a more individualistic outlook prevailed, no such large-scale chartered associations as the Merchant Adventurers ever took root. Bristol, the second port in the kingdom, had built up a thriving trade on the Atlantic, principally with Ireland, Gascony, the Peninsula, and Iceland. In the later fifteenth century, notwithstanding the disorders of the times, the town became a centre of overseas enterprise; the merchants, shipowners, and pilots of Bristol gradually acquiring an oceanic outlook and experience which were destined to play a vital role in the maritime development of the future. Most prosperous of all appear to have been the ports of Devon and Cornwall. Situated on one of the busiest thoroughfares in the world, most of these ports—but especially Exeter and Dartmouth—continued to flourish throughout the century. Even in the worst times their shipping was still expanding, and their trade was still brisk: there is little sign here of the retrogression that had set in on other parts of the coast.

The latter half of the fifteenth century witnessed a series of remarkable English ventures southward to the Mediterranean, and westward into the Atlantic. In 1446 the *Cog Anne*, with a cargo of wool and tin and 160 pilgrims aboard, sailed from Bristol to the Levant: she landed her pilgrims at Jaffa, but on the return passage was wrecked off the coast of Greece and was there lost with all hands. In 1457 Robert Sturmy, ' a ful notable worshipful marchaunt ' of Bristol, who had fitted out the ill-fated venture of 1446, went out in person in the *Katherine Sturmy*, with a large cargo and two attendant caravels. He traded in various parts of the Levant; but on the return passage his vessel was boarded and sacked, near Malta, by hostile Genoese. There were also a number of English voyages to the Mediterranean in the reign of Edward IV.

Still seeking new outlets for their trade, English mariners pushed far out into the Atlantic in search of the legendary isle of Brasil, believed to lie somewhere to the west of Ireland. In the summer of 1480 a substantial merchant of Bristol, John Jay the Younger,[1] dispatched an 80-ton ship to search for this island. Two months later the news reached Bristol that this ship had been compelled by stress of weather to abandon the quest, and had put back into an Irish port. The following year a second expedition, consisting of two small vessels named the *Trinity* and *George*, was sent out ' to serche & fynde a certain Isle called the Isle of Brasil '. In view of the fact that these vessels carried with them a large quantity of salt there is a likelihood that one of the principal objects of the enterprise was the discovery of new fishing grounds.

Nothing is known of the result of the expedition, nor is there any record of further attempt at Atlantic exploration during the same decade. But it would appear from a letter written in 1498 by the Spanish envoy in London to Ferdinand and Isabella that, during the 1490s, the search for the mythical isle continued. This evidence has been confirmed by a most interesting and important document recently discovered in the Archivo de Simancas, containing not only a detailed account of John Cabot's expedition in 1497 but also a reference to a transatlantic voyage made by some vessel from Bristol several years earlier. The truth is that a good deal of uncertainty surrounds the whole matter of English ventures into the Atlantic towards the close of the mediaeval era.[2]

4

The expansion of English maritime enterprise went hand in hand with technical progress. The first half of the fifteenth century ushered in a new era in shipbuilding. Apparently as a result of Mediterranean influence, the bluff-bowed, broad-beamed, single-masted cog, or round ship, of northern Europe was, within a comparatively short space of time, supplanted by vessels fitted with two and three masts.

---

[1] The Jays, with the Thornes and Elyots, belonged to that enterprising group of Bristol merchants who traded to Spain, Portugal, and Iceland; some of them helped to finance John Cabot's expedition and subsequent ventures to the New World.

[2] See the present writer in *Economic History Review*, 2nd Series, VII (1955), 79–80, and L. A. Vigneras in the *Hispanic American Historical Review*, XXXVI (1956), pp. 503–9.

The earliest two-masted ships began to appear in the reign of Henry IV. There is a remarkably fine carving of such a two-master on a stall-end (dating back to about 1419), formerly in St. Nicholas's chapel at Lynn, and now in the Victoria and Albert Museum. The vessel depicted therein, with its finer lines and sharp, sturdy bows, shows a distinct advance on the old, basin-shaped cog. The carving reveals that the mainmast was square-rigged as of old, but the mizen was fitted with a lateen, or fore-and-aft sail. But the day of the two-master (fitted with either a fore or mizen mast) was soon ended. It is apparent from a variety of sources that the earliest types of three-masted ships were evolved well before the middle of the century. In continental Europe also the advent of the three-master appears to have occurred at about the same time.

In the matter of detail, this development of an improved sail-plan and rigging is exceedingly obscure. But the general outline was probably as follows. The introduction of the two-masted ship, very early in the century, was followed soon after by that of the three-master: the mainmast carried a topmast as well as a course: and some time later the foremast, too, was fitted with a top and a topsail. Towards the middle of the century, a spritsail was spread under the bowsprit. Thus the mediaeval round ship—with its short keel, bowl-like hull, and all its canvas amidships—had developed into a two- and three-masted vessel, square-rigged except for its lateen mizen, with greatly improved lines, and sturdy, high bows capable of standing up to Atlantic seas—altogether an immense improvement on the cog, able to sail nearer to the wind, and fitted for longer voyages, such as those to the Levant and Iceland.[1]

The introduction of a second and third mast made possible a substantial increase in the size of ships. The steady progress in shipbuilding during this period is also revealed in the increasing number of voyages made in early spring and winter, not only to Bordeaux and the Peninsula, but also across the ocean to Iceland. Ships which had sailed to Iceland early in the year would sometimes make a second voyage to Gascony, the Peninsula, or the Netherlands. Occasionally vessels which had spent the summer in Iceland would sail thence to Finmark in northern Norway—another great fishing centre—instead

[1] The leading authority on sail-plan and rigging is the late Sir Alan Moore, Bt.: in particular, see his *Rig in Northern Europe*.

of returning direct to their home ports. Seaborne trade was now being carried on on a scale unheard of during the previous century. Ships were increasing both in size and number; as shipbuilding progressed larger cargoes could be carried, and longer voyages became practicable; all this meant that an ever-increasing proportion of our seamen were now deep-water sailors, rather than mere coasters. At the same time the fifteenth century saw the emergence of a specialized class of ship-owners, each possessing a small fleet of ships of his own, and drawing his profits from the carrying trade. Wealthy shipowners like John Hawley of Dartmouth, William Soper of London, and, above all, William Canynges, five times mayor of Bristol—who is recorded to have had as many as eight hundred men employed in his shipping for eight years—were the predecessors of the great Tudor merchants.

In the mid-fifteenth century the first sailing directions, or rutter, in the English language appeared. This old manuscript, which was copied down in the reign of Edward IV in the neat, clear hand of one William Ebesham, a professional scribe—the original would appear to date from the opening years of the century: but much of it is based upon earlier information—with its recital of familiar place-names and marks and graphic description, ' At the Londis ende lieth Raynoldis stone . . . Lesarde is grete stone as it were benys [beans] and it is raggyd stoon. . . . Opyn of Dudman in xl fadome there is rede sande and whit shellis and small blak stonys. . . . And the name of the Rok is called the Kep ', and he lieth undir the watir but it brekith upon hym And the breche [breaker] shewith '—is, in fact, the prototype of a long succession of sailing directions for the waters around the British Isles whose latest representative is the current Admiralty *Pilot*. From it we learn that in addition to the mariner's compass[1] the navigational instruments then in use were the sounding-line and lead, for discovering the depth and nature of the bottom, and the hour-glass, for timing the length of the tacks. The rutter clearly shows that the mariner's compass was used on most of the trade-routes frequented by our shipping, including the highly important traffic with Gascony

---

[1] The early history of the magnetic compass is very obscure. In its primitive form it is known to have been in use in British waters towards the close of the twelfth century; it is possible that its introduction, together with certain important developments in ship design, may have been due to the influence of the Crusades; the compass rose came in about two hundred years later. For the influence of the mariner's compass upon practical navigation in the later mediaeval age, see the present writer in *History*, N.S., XLI, pp. 16–24.

and the Peninsula. Of outstanding interest are the two direct courses across the Bay of Biscay from Finisterre to the entrances of the Bristol and English Channels, showing as they do how the compass was used in conjunction with the sounding-line and lead.[1] The direct navigation across the Bay to Gascony, Santiago and other Peninsular ports—in the same way as the English traffic to Iceland—was certainly made possible by the advent of the mariner's compass. There is no record of these particular passages in the pre-compass era.

No evidence exists as to the use of any astrolabe or quadrant on board English vessels of the time; nor is there any reason to suppose that such instruments were ever used at all in the mediaeval era. All this goes to show that the methods of navigation practised by English masters and pilots were not based on general scientific principles but on personal experience and observation, and on the traditional, rule-of-thumb methods and expedients handed down to them from their forefathers.

5

During the Plantagenet era, the King possessed a number of ships and galleys of his own placed under the superintendence of an official called the Clerk or Keeper of the King's Ships. The first to bear this title appears to have been a cleric, William of Wrotham (later Archdeacon of Taunton), in the reign of King John. In this Clerk or Keeper of the King's Ships, together with his subordinate officials, is to be found the germ of the future Admiralty organization.

However, as the royal ships alone were too few to constitute a fleet, recourse was had in an emergency to two other sources. First, there

[1] ' And ye come oute of Spayne. And ye bee at capfenister go your cours north northest. And ye gesse [reckon] you ij. parties ovir the see and be bounde into sebarne [Severn] ye must north and by est till ye come into Sowdyng [Soundings]. And yif ye have an C. fadome depe or els iiij.x. then ye shall go north in till the sonde ayen [again] in lxxij. fadome in feir grey sonde. And that is the Rigge [Nymphe Bank] that lieth betwene clere [Cape Clear] and Cille [Scilly] than go north till ye come into sowdyng of woyse [ooze]. and than go your cours est north est or els est and by north. . . . And yif ye be three parties ovir the see and ye be bounde into the narowe see and ye go north northest and by north till ye come into sowdyng of an hundrith fadom depe than go your cours north est till ye come into iiij fadome depe. And yif it be stremy grounde it is betwene Huschaunt and cille in the entry in the Chanell of Flaundres [English Channel]. And so go your cours till ye have lx. fadome depe. than go est northest along the see. . . .' (British Museum: *Lansdowne Ms.*, 285, ff.139–40).

13

were the Cinque Ports. The early history of this renowned confederacy is somewhat obscure; but its origins date back to before the Conquest. The Cinque Ports proper were Hastings, Romney, Hythe, Dover, and Sandwich, together with the two Ancient Towns of Winchelsea and Rye, to which were presently added the 'limbs', or member ports, of Seaford, Pevensey, Northeye, Lydd, Folkestone, Margate, and various others. In return for certain privileges and immunities the Portsmen were required by the terms of their charters to serve the King with a fleet of fifty-seven ships, each carrying a master, twenty men and a boy, for fifteen days every year, free of charge. Each of the original Cinque Ports was a 'head port', which from time to time had acquired 'limbs'. The latter shared its privileges in return for contributing towards its quota of ships for the King's service. The confederation eventually included all the ports and fishing villages in the vicinity of the Straits. Situated as they were along the bottle-neck of the Channel, the Ports exercised something like a monopoly of shipping there and effective control of cross-Channel communications. For two centuries and more after the Conquest the fleet provided by the Cinque Ports was capable of performing all the normal sea-business of the crown.

It is always to be borne in mind that the navigational conditions which then obtained on the south-east coast were very different from what they are today. The Kent and Sussex coastline, which at the present time is straight or smoothly curving, was deeply indented and broken into numerous bays and creeks which are now dry land. The Sussex Ouse was a broad estuary, and Hastings possessed a good harbour within the shelter of its cliffs. To the east of Beachy Head lay a line of lagoons, protected by a chain of islands and sandbanks. The flat sandy country which now stretches for miles to the south of Winchelsea and Rye then formed part of the estuary of the Rother. Winchelsea, Rye, Lydd, Romney, and Sandwich all stood on islands. At Hythe a broad haven was protected from the open sea by a shingle bank. Dover also possessed a good natural harbour. The promontory of Dungeness did not exist.

During the civil and foreign wars of the thirteenth century, following the loss of Normandy, the Cinque Ports were a factor of crucial importance. It was largely the support of the Portsmen which enabled John to hold out against his enemies and secured the succession of his son, Henry III. In Edward I's expeditions against Wales in 1277 and 1283, most of the fighting ships were provided by the Cinque Ports, the other ships being mostly transports and supply ships.

On occasions when larger fleets were required they were composed of vessels from all parts of the kingdom. An embargo would be laid on all shipping in the ports; and orders would be issued for all masters with their ships to proceed forthwith to a specified port. As early as the reign of John, the right of the Crown to impress both shipping and men was strictly enforced. It was with such large composite fleets that Henry II invaded Ireland in 1171; that the King of England's contingents left Dartmouth in 1147 and 1190 for the Crusades; and that Edward III overthrew a French invading force at Sluys in 1340, blockaded the port of Calais in 1347, and defeated a large Spanish force which had been pillaging in the Channel in 1350. (It was his victory in this last action of *Espagnols sur Mer* which gained for Edward III the title of ' Lord of the Sea '.) The shipping engaged in the Bordeaux wine trade formed a valued reservoir of naval strength in time of need. The importance of this trade was fully recognized by contemporaries as ' gret plesur to all estatez and degreez, grete richesse and by the myght of such Nave [Navy], gret defence for all this lond '. In short, in the mediaeval era, and for long afterwards, the navy comprised both the relatively small number of fighting ships which were the personal property of the King and the whole mass of mercantile shipping.

The title of Admiral came in at the close of the thirteenth century. A few years later, in September 1300, Gervase Alard, in command of the Cinque Ports' contingent in Edward I's expedition against Scotland, is described as ' Admiral of the Fleet of the Cinque Ports '. From this time on the title continually recurs. The Admirals who were given command of these fighting fleets were assisted in the duties of administration by groups of clerks assigned to particular regions. They arrested all ships in the ports within their areas of a specified tonnage; prepared the ships for war (sometimes fitting them with fore- and summer-castles), and supervised the mustering of mariners and soldiers, and the provision of all kinds of victuals, stores, and weapons. In the office of Admiral was vested the authority to impress both ships and mariners.

The Court of Admiralty was apparently a later development. Its origin can be traced to the period following the battle of Sluys, in

1340, when the Admiral's powers were extended to include jurisdiction in mercantile shipping cases outside the sphere of common law, especially those concerned with piracies and spoils.

In the fourteenth century—and still more in the fifteenth—the small fishing and coastal vessels of the Cinque Ports were increasingly outclassed by the broad roomy cogs of the rising eastern and western ports, able to carry large numbers of fighting men and fitted fore and aft with lofty superstructures for the accommodation of archers. From this time onward the Ports gradually but surely dropped out of the running. It is significant that in the naval expeditions of the Hundred Years War the Ports contributed only a small fraction of the whole fleet. Their misfortunes at the hands of the enemy had left them unable either to build up to the standard of the rivals which were now ousting them from their old position of leadership, or to keep open their own havens, which, owing to the continual action of the eastward drift, were rapidly filling with sand and shingle.

6

At no time during the mediaeval period, properly speaking, was there anything like a true naval policy, which, in fact, only came in with the Tudors. ' Sea warfare was soldiers' warfare,' Williamson declares, ' as it had been from the days of Greece and Rome, and a fleet was quite correctly designated an " army by sea ", for such was its fundamental nature.'[1] All attempts to discern significant developments in the strategy and tactics of sea warfare during this period are likely to prove unfruitful: for these and other reasons it has been found impossible to treat naval history in the Middle Ages as it will be treated in succeeding chapters of the present work.

In spite of his vaunted sovereignty of the sea, there was no sign or suggestion in the policy of Edward III of any perception of the use and importance of naval power as it came to be understood in later centuries. The King claimed to be the lawful owner of both sides of the English Channel and of the sea between. It was a claim—and nothing more. The navy operated for the most part as a subsidiary of the army. Fleets were assembled to carry the King and his men across the sea; to transport horses, victuals, and other supplies for the army;

[1] J. A. Williamson, Sir John Hawkins (1927), p. 313.

to engage an enemy already at sea, and to keep open communications. Once the King's army had been transported safely across the Channel, or the enemy's fleet had been disposed of, the navy made no attempt to keep the sea.

In the reign of Henry IV, though a nominal truce existed between England and France and there was no formal declaration of war, ' cross-ravaging ' continued at intervals until the King's death; and there was a marked increase in piracy. With the renewal of the Hundred Years War in the reigns of Henry V and Henry VI large fleets were assembled to carry the invading armies across to France and to deal with the enemy's naval forces. A number of engagements were fought in the Channel, the most important of which were those off Harfleur[1] and off the Brittany coast.

Under Henry V the mediaeval navy may be said to have reached its apogee, including as it did ships of a size and strength formerly unheard of, such as the *Jesus*, 1,000 tons, *Holy Ghost*, 760, *George* and *Christopher of Spayne*, 600, *Marie Sandwich*, 550, *Trinity Royal*, 540, and *Mary Hampton*, 500. (Another great craft, the *Grace Dieu*, proved a failure from the start and never got to sea.) Henry V possessed in all fourteen large ships of between 300 and 1,000 tons and twenty-four smaller ones. The royal fleet now contained a number of carracks and at least two balingers which were fitted with a second mast. Small guns of a primitive type had been introduced in the previous reign. Henry V's *Holy Ghost* seems to have carried six guns, his *George* three. Pumps were now in use on shipboard. The compass was housed in a lead-covered binnacle. From this time onwards, it is important to observe, the King's ships were substantially larger and stronger than merchantmen: nevertheless, the bulk of the fleet was composed as usual of merchant vessels impressed for service—and this continued to be the normal practice for more than two centuries to come.

Though in the reign of Henry V the navy effectually established and maintained its ascendancy over the enemy's forces in the Channel,

---

[1] In his account of the action off Harfleur in 1416, Wylie sums up the tactics of mediaeval sea warfare generally in the following graphic passage: ' The object of a sea fight in those days was to ram and scuttle your enemy, or to manoeuvre him into shallow water with your galleys and throw him out of action at the mercy of the sea or to get alongside and disable his tack and tackle, cut his halliards and cordage with shearhooks mounted on long poles and then grapple and board at the waist for a hand-to-hand encounter ' (J. H. Wylie, *History of England under Henry IV*).

and though there was a significant diminution in complaints of piracy, it must never be overlooked that all this was achieved at a ruinous cost to merchants and shipowners. The same abuses associated with impressment flourished in this as in earlier reigns. The truth is, in the mediaeval era there were only sufficient seamen and shipping available in this country either for normal trade or for war; it followed that trade and war could not be carried on simultaneously.

On Henry V's death in 1422, one of the first orders of the Council was to direct the sale of most of the royal fleet to pay off the late King's debts. One after another nearly all the ships owned by Henry V were bought up by merchants from different parts of the kingdom; the anchors and other gear were similarly disposed of; and in the end all that remained of Henry V's once fine fleet were the hulls of the *Holy Ghost* and the *Trinity* rotting in the Hamble. Some idea of the grievous neglect and ruin which had overtaken the royal fleet by the middle of Henry VI's reign can be gathered from the fact that, in the two years ending 31 August 1439, the sum total of all the moneys expended upon the navy was only £8 9s. 7d. The famous gold noble coined by Edward III, bearing the effigy of the King—crowned, and sword in hand—standing in a ship, had by this time become an object of derision to foreigners, who bade the English take away the ship from the noble and put a sheep there instead:

> Where bene oure shippes, where bene oure swerdes become?
> Oure enmyes bid for the shippe sette a shepe.

This retrograde state of affairs was the main theme of *The Libelle of Englyshe Polycye*, which reveals a remarkably clear understanding of the importance of sea power, and of the political and commercial advantages to be gained from the King's possession of Dover and Calais, enabling him to control the great trade focal through the English Channel. The author of the *Libelle* recalls with regret the spacious days of Henry V:

> Henry the Fifte, what was hys purposynge,
> Whan at Hampton he made the grete dromons,
> Which passed other grete ships of all the Commons,
> The *Trinitie*, the *Grace Dieu*, the *Holy Ghost*,
> And other moo whiche as now be lost.

He laments that English shipping now lay open to continual attack by foreigners, especially the Flemings; and he points out that, as the latter were dependent upon their foreign trade, were the King of England indeed master of the narrow seas, both these and other foreigners would eagerly seek his friendship. He argues that it is upon the navy that the peace and prosperity of the kingdom chiefly depend. Towards the end of the *Libelle*, the writer compares England to a city and the sea to its encircling wall; and he declares that this land would be safe from all danger of foreign attack, if only the sea were strongly guarded.

> Kepe than the see, that is the walle of Englond,
> And than is Englond kepte by Goddes honde.

Nevertheless, it is always to be remembered that the author of the *Libelle* was far in advance of the statesmanship of his day—his was a voice crying in the wilderness. What the *Libelle* set out to describe were not things as they were, but rather as the author believed that they ought to be.

During the first part of the reign of Henry VI there was no sea fighting of any consequence. The war was fought out on the soil of France, and the role of the navy was simply that of ferry. Thus 10,000 men were transported across the Channel to reinforce the Duke of Bedford in 1423, and another 5,000 accompanied the Duke of Gloucester to Calais in 1424. From time to time certain magnates contracted with the Council to keep the sea with a naval force raised and maintained by themselves; but this guard of the sea by contract was intermittent and, as a rule, inadequate. During these years the French raids on the south coast began anew. Piracy was rife in the Channel, Bay, and North Sea. The sea-passages became increasingly insecure. The bad sea-keeping was, in fact, one of the main contributory factors in the situation which finally resulted in the overthrow of the Lancastrian dynasty in 1460; for the severe and widespread injury to our seaborne commerce had helped to swing the mercantile class as a whole to the side of the Yorkists.

The same period saw this country engage in a sporadic, confused and unsatisfactory struggle with the Hanse. In such a quarrel the Council lay under a heavy handicap. For political reasons it was hazardous during the troublous times of the baronial wars, when the English throne was the prize of contending factions, to offend the all-powerful League, by means of whose assistance Henry IV had landed to dispossess Richard III in 1399, and Edward IV had made his bid for the throne in 1471. Furthermore, on the breakdown of the Lancastrian government English merchants could expect no support against their enemies, and, in any case, English acts of piracy on the high seas had played into the hands of the Hanse. Piracy in fact became the central issue in Anglo-Hanseatic relations, in consequence of which Lübeck and other Wendish towns joined in the struggle against England. The result was the closing of many lucrative channels of north European trade to English merchants and the retention of their privileges by the Hanse till the latter part of the Tudor era.

Under the House of York the work of naval restoration was at last set in train. For Edward IV's expedition against Scotland in 1480, not only was there the usual impressment of merchant shipping, but four fair-sized vessels were also purchased from English and foreign owners. In the reign of Richard III the fleet consisted of seven ships— the *Nicholas, Governor, Grace Dieu, Mary of the Tower, Martin Garcia, Falcon,* and *Trinity*; and the King of England once more possessed the nucleus of a fighting fleet.

To sum up: the late mediaeval era witnessed the advent of certain developments of the highest significance in our maritime history. It saw the evolution of the modern sailing ship—larger, stronger, more weatherly, and better rigged than the old mediaeval cog; the common use, in Northern waters, of the mariner's compass; the awakening of the national consciousness to the importance of sea power; the rise in England of a substantial merchant class which, as early as the reign of Richard II, was beginning to assert itself; the steady expansion of native industries, especially the cloth trade, demanding new outlets; the inauguration of an important traffic to Iceland and the Faeroes; the beginning of direct trade to the Mediterranean; and at last, in the early 1480s, the fitting-out of certain oceanic ventures which were the precursors of the English voyages of discovery in the reigns of Henry VII and Henry VIII. The seaborne trade of the realm, notwithstanding later setbacks and reverses, had continued, on the whole, to expand. In the England of the late Plantagenets an altogether new spirit of enterprise was stirring. The whole of this epoch may properly be regarded as a time of transition during which the foundations were laid of the large-scale maritime and commercial expansion of the Tudor age.

II

The early Tudor Navy

I

The close of an era of baronial anarchy and bloodshed was brought appreciably nearer by the overthrow of Richard III on Bosworth Field in 1485. His successor was the representative of a dynasty which proved itself capable of providing the firm governance, efficient administration, and political stability necessary for the protection and expansion of trade; at the same time the growth of internal peace and prosperity, which, throughout most of England, was a characteristic of the Tudor age, made possible the maintenance of a large standing navy.

On the accession of Henry VII the overseas trade of England entered on a new phase. In the famous words of Francis Bacon, the new King ' could not endure to see trade sick '. Accordingly, after the safety of his throne—which caused him to renew the privileges of the Hanse and to invite the friendship of Spain—the aggrandizement of commerce by trade negotiations, tariff reprisals, and diplomatic bargaining was Henry VII's main objective. To this end he initiated the pivotal alliance with Spain and secured the vital trade with the Netherlands; negotiated a treaty with the King of Denmark and restored the lucrative Iceland traffic; and protected and fostered the new Mediterranean trade, which was destined to become one of the major factors in our maritime expansion.

At the beginning of the reign the richer part of English trade was still in foreign hands. The former traffic with Prussia and the Baltic was practically at an end, and English commerce with northern Europe restricted to the Netherlands. On a number of other leading trade-routes our shipping was losing headway. In Henry VII's first Parliament a Navigation Act was passed, the purpose of which was to reserve the Bordeaux wine trade to English shipping. This was followed by a series of Navigation Acts, to the general effect that goods imported into England should be brought over only by English, Irish, or Welsh crews. Similarly for the encouragement of shipbuilding Henry VII instituted a system of bounties for the construction of merchantmen of 100 tons and over, ' to make ships for the increase of the Navy of this our Realm '. The success of these measures was reflected in the steady expansion of English shipping, especially at London, Ipswich, and Hull. From this time on the customs accounts show a substantial increase in the number of English ships and the value of the cargoes carried.

In most of our ports the period 1495–1520 was a time of mounting prosperity. In almost every port the ratio of English entries to foreign was markedly increasing. The returns of the bounty payments show that London throughout this period was making rapid progress as a shipowning centre. During the reigns of Henry VII and Henry VIII, as the customs accounts reveal, the city's general trade more than doubled in value. In the latter reign the throng of shipping in the Pool was such that the trade of London was almost equal to that of all the rest of England. This gain was partly at the expense of the smaller ports which were now declining as the result of the increase in the size and draught of merchantmen.

2

At the outset of the Tudor period and for a good many years after-wards the Mediterranean trade was still largely monopolized by Venice and Genoa. In the second half of the fifteenth century first the Floren-tines and later the Genoese had dropped behind their wealthier and more powerful rivals. The Genoese had lost their rich colony at Pera, as well as the alum mines of Foglia and certain of the trading-stations along the Black Sea coast, to the Ottoman Turks; and their commerce was gravely affected by their long-drawn-out maritime war with the Catalans. Meanwhile, under the paternal despotism of the Doge and the Council of Ten, Venice had prospered. By an energetically applied and consistent fiscal policy she had made herself the principal maritime and commercial power of the Mediterranean—all her strength lay in her ships and trade. Secure behind her lagoons, the city could neither be beleaguered nor starved out. No enemy could challenge her formidable fleet of war galleys. Her depots and trading-stations were established throughout the Mediterranean; she had lately acquired substantial territories on the Italian mainland; and, so long as Venice continued to ' hold the gorgeous East in fee ', her rich revenues were assured. Year by year two or more of the galleys from her Flanders Fleet would arrive in English waters, bringing with them large cargoes of costly luxury goods—oriental spices, drugs, and perfumes; velvets, satins, and damasks; Mediterranean wines and fruits, and all manner of exotic pets: and (as the anonymous author of the *Libelle of Englyshe Polycye* had reason to complain) draining this land of good English cloth, wool, and tin.

> The great galleys of Venice and Florence
> Be well laden with things of complacence,
> All spicery and of grocer's ware,
> With sweet wines, all manner of chaffaire.
> Apes and japes and marmusettes tailed,
> Nifles, trifles that little have availed.
> And things with which they fetely blear our eye.
> With things not enduring that we buy. . . .
> Thus these galleys for this liking ware
> And eating ware, bear hence our best chaffaire,
> Cloth, wool, and tin.[1]

But in extending her dominion to the mainland and in acquiring trading stations over so wide an area the Republic had given hostages to fortune. As the disastrous struggle against the League of Cambrai had revealed, her territories in northern Italy were not defensible by ships; and many of her distant depots, too, were all too vulnerable to attack. In the latter half of the century the springs of her prosperity were gravely menaced by the gradual advance of the Ottoman Turks along the shores of the Mediterranean. Not only was her trade thereby directly assailed, but she could no longer draw upon the communities of mixed Greek descent in the eastern Mediterranean for the crews with which to man her galleys. Two other factors also seriously undermined her trade—first, the opening of the sea-route to India, round the Cape of Good Hope, and, second, the progress of ship-building in western Europe. The overland traffic of Venice to the East was by no means destroyed by the discovery of the sea-route;

---

[1] *Chaffaire* = merchandise; *fetely* = cleverly.

but it was seriously undermined. About this time the revolutionary improvement in the design and rigging of the sailing merchantman deprived the galleass of the superiority in speed and safety which in the past had enabled her owners to demand and receive far higher freight charges. The galleass had attained the zenith of its fame in the last quarter of the fifteenth century—an era when the wealth and splendour of the Venetian Republic were the envy of Christendom. But now the conditions governing the Mediterranean traffic were changing. By the accession of Henry VIII it was apparent that the days of the Flanders galleys were numbered.

Henry VII's efforts to increase the range and volume of English trade were seriously circumscribed by the need to propitiate the Hanse —a useful friend, but a dangerous enemy. The same considerations governed the policy of his son and successor, Henry VIII, who, at the time of the Third French War, purchased from the League several vessels for the royal fleet, including the *Jesus of Lübeck* of future fame.

More important even to England than the ships were the Baltic spars, hemp, tar, and other naval stores which the Hanse could supply or cut off at will. Though for generations to come the extensive oak groves of southern England were able to provide ample supplies of timber for shipbuilding, the indispensable naval stores could be obtained only from Norway and the Baltic. Masts from the Baltic countries were also replacing the oaken masts of a bygone era. As early as 1540 the King's agent was importing great masts from Danzig for the royal fleet. Throughout the early half of the sixteenth century the Hanse continued to dominate the trade with Germany and the Baltic. On the death of Henry VIII the prosperity of their London factory, the Steel-yard, had never stood higher. But in 1552 the privileges of the Hanse were abruptly revoked and they were reduced to the status of alien merchants. Thereafter the power and prosperity of the Steel-yard began to decline.

3

Towards the close of the fifteenth century English shipping frequented various trade-routes, such as the wool traffic to Calais, the Bordeaux wine trade, and the cloth trade to the Netherlands (especially Antwerp) and Germany, and secondarily to Spain and Portugal. Besides these there were other more distant trades which, though on a far smaller scale, constituted an important factor in English maritime enterprise. The first tentative attempts by English merchants, in the reign of Henry VI, to trade direct with Italy and the Levant were never entirely abandoned; they were followed up, as we have seen, in the reign of Edward IV; and, under the early Tudors, the Mediterranean trade was set on a firm basis. The English success in penetrating the Mediterranean was due in part to the continued support of the Tudor kings, and in part to political conditions in Italy at the outset of the sixteenth century, when Venice was involved in a desperate struggle for existence against the League of Cambrai. Henceforward ' divers tall ships of London ' began to voyage more or less regularly to Sicily, Crete, Chios, Tripoli, and Beirut. These ventures were financed by wealthy syndicates, for the cost of fitting out the ships was considerable. Southampton also took a leading part in the trade. Owing to the length and hazards of the voyage the Mediterranean traffic called for large and heavily armed vessels. In the early Tudor period the warships of the royal fleet occasionally engaged in this trade. Thus the *Mary de la Towre* went to the Mediterranean in 1486 and again in 1491, and the *Sovereign* in 1494, 1497, and 1504. In the reign of Henry VIII the sailings of the Flanders galleys ceased altogether; and the English merchants had this lucrative commerce to themselves until 1553, when, owing to the activities of Turkish pirates in the Mediterranean, the trade languished for some twenty-five years. It is worth noticing that Chancellor and Jenkinson, the pioneers of the direct trade to Russia, engaged in this Mediterranean trade in their youth.

From the purely maritime point of view, the English traffic with Iceland was of outstanding importance. The trade with Iceland had reached its peak towards the middle of the fifteenth century, the most prosperous years probably being those between 1430 and 1460, and Hull, Bristol, and Lynn the principal ports involved. In the two final decades of the century the German Hanse had secured the lion's share of the Iceland trade, though not of the fisheries. These continued to be worked by the English. Year by year a large fishing fleet—drawn principally from our east-coast ports—made the long voyage to Iceland. It is stated that they would sail from England early in the year —in April, March, or even February—fish for about three months off Iceland, and return home again in July, August, or September. Some of them fished off the north coast in the Skagafjörd; but more frequently they worked the great flat which fringes the whole west coast of Iceland—their chief centre, perhaps, at any rate in the early years of the traffic, was the Vestmannaeyjar, a group of islands situated off the south-west coast: there was said to be 'the best fishing in all Iceland'. The small fishing doggers had always formed a fairly substantial proportion of our Iceland fleets; towards the end of the century they monopolized the English share of the traffic entirely. Even though the large German trading fleets absorbed most of the commerce of the island, the English could still exploit the fisheries, and so fill their holds.

The traffic increased to such an extent that, in 1500, the Althing had occasion to complain that the English, lying in the offing with their large vessels and their long-lines streaming down the tide, were ruining the inshore fishing for the Icelandic fishermen in their small craft. The Iceland fishery flourished exceedingly during the fifteenth and early sixteenth centuries, reaching its peak period, perhaps, in the decade 1520–30. In 1528 there were nearly one hundred and fifty English craft of the dogger type engaged in the Iceland traffic, the great majority of which belonged to the east coast ports, especially to East Anglia. Though in time of war arrangements were made to 'waft', or convoy, the fishing fleet on its outward and homeward passage, no adequate protection was forthcoming in Icelandic waters, where English craft were frequently attacked by the German Hanse.[1] That the doggers engaged in trade as well as in fishing is apparent from the nature of the cargoes they carried. Firkins of butter, bales of woollen cloth and linen, copper kettles, caps, knives, 'gerdelles et pynnes', 'poyntes nedilles et laces' were among the goods they transported to Iceland, and these, in the aggregate, in considerable

---

[1] In spite of these attacks the fishery seems to have remained almost exclusively in English hands. A far more serious handicap, indeed, in the case of many of our east-coast fishing-ports than the competition of the Hanse and the raids of foreign and home-bred pirates appears to have been the condition of their havens and channels, which were in continual danger of silting up. Several of the most flourishing havens of East Anglia were now threatened with a fate similar to that of the Cinque Ports. During the fifteenth century repeated, but in the long run unavailing, attempts were made to keep open the harbour of Dunwich, which was continually filling with shingle. Southwold and Walberswick were destined in this way to lose both their haven and their livelihood. A local jingle puts the matter in a nutshell:

> Dunwich, Sowl and Walderswick
> All go in at a lowsy crick.

quantities. It is stated that some of these doggers carried between 40 and 50 tuns of Gascony wine, which gives us some idea of their approximate tonnage. On the other hand some were much larger than this, while others were a good deal smaller.

At the same time the migration of the herring in the early fifteenth century from the Baltic into our own waters had made the North Sea fishery by far the most important in Europe. 'These herrings,' observed Camden, 'which in the times of our grandfathers swarmed only in Norway, now in our times by the bounty of Providence swim in great shoals round our coasts every year.'[1] The increase of deep-sea fishing under the early Tudors was one of the prime contributory factors in English maritime expansion. As will later be seen, the English fisheries continued to be held in high esteem by the government as the breeding-ground of experienced seamen, who were available, in time of emergency, for the Navy. During the French war of 1544–6 the men were impressed for the king's service in such numbers that, it is said, only women were left to man the fishing fleets.

The expansion of trade which had been a main objective of Henry VII's foreign and domestic policy was well maintained in the following reign, with the result that, by the middle of the sixteenth century, most of the branches of our overseas commerce were in English hands. More and more ships were being built; larger and richer cargoes were being carried. The early Tudor era saw the increasing prosperity and influence of the English merchant class, the Thornes, the Gonsons, the Hawkinses, the Greshams, and their associates. During this time the leading sea-ports of the kingdom after London were Southampton and Bristol.

4

Five years after Christopher Columbus's arrival in the New World a small craft of Bristol, named the *Matthew*, manned by a crew of eighteen men and led by the Genoese navigator, John Cabot, sailed out into the Atlantic and, after a six weeks' passage, sighted land at some point fairly high up the North American coast (this land was formerly supposed to have been Newfoundland but is now considered more probably to have been Nova Scotia). An important result of this voyage was the discovery of the rich cod fishery off the banks of

[1] *Q.* G. M. Trevelyan, *English Social History*, p. 135n.

Newfoundland. In the summer of 1498 another expedition, likewise led by John Cabot, was fitted out by the merchants of Bristol and London, with some assistance from Henry VII. The outcome of this other voyage is not directly known, but it would appear from the world-map drawn by the Spanish pilot, Juan de la Cosa, in the year 1500 that the expedition coasted southward for a considerable distance down the North American littoral. The men of Bristol, in conjunction with certain Portuguese colonists of the Azores, followed up this enterprise with further voyages to the north-west during the period 1501 to 1505, and possibly still later; and towards the end of 1502 a syndicate which became known as ' The Company Adventurers to the New Found Land ' was formed. The newly discovered fisheries off the Grand Banks also began to be worked by fishing vessels from the west coast ports (those from the east coast, however, continued to voyage to Iceland); though the English contingent in the cosmopolitan Newfoundland fleet was by no means large until fairly late in the sixteenth century.

Though little enough is known of Cabot's venture of 1497 it would appear that the new methods of navigation, which had been developed by the seamen and scholars of Italy and the Peninsula, were now introduced in northern waters. We hear for the first time of a globe and chart in an English ship. The course shaped by Cabot in the little *Matthew* is similarly suggestive. ' After leaving Bristol the explorers passed the south of Ireland, and then steered northwards for an indeterminate time—" a few days "—Cabot's intention apparently being to reach a certain parallel of latitude, and then to follow it westwards.'[1]

The arrival of shipping from Bristol in the New World marks a milestone in the maritime history of England: for it was then that the mediaeval era may be said to have ended and modern times to have begun. This is by no means to belittle the English achievement. In the field of shipbuilding and seamanship the progress achieved had been considerable. A substantial number of seafaring communities all around the coasts of England had by now acquired a valuable stock of ocean experience. Already the foundations of that future English prowess at sea, which was to earn the unstinted respect of those shrewd observers of maritime affairs, the Venetians—were being well and truly laid.

[1] J. A. Williamson, *Maritime Enterprise, 1485-1558*, p. 75.

5

The naval revival begun in the reign of Edward IV was continued under the first of the Tudors. The progress of shipbuilding was reflected in four important additions to the royal fleet. These were the *Regent, Sovereign, Sweepstake,* and *Mary Fortune.* The *Regent* was a large four-master, carrying topsails above her courses and a top-gallantsail above her main topsail. Even the *Sweepstake* and *Mary Fortune,* which were comparatively small vessels, had three lower masts, a main topmast, and a spritsail on the bowsprit. Like the Navy of Henry V, that of Henry VII was still essentially mediaeval in character. Despite the improvements embodied in the *Regent,* she was an armed transport rather than a fighting ship, designed not for ' off-fighting ' but for ' in-fighting ', i.e. boarding and taking; and the governing factor in an engagement would not be gunfire, but the hand-to-hand mêlée. The *Regent* mounted a multiplicity of small breech-loading guns but no heavy ordnance. The principal gun on board was the serpentine, which was merely a man-killer. The upper deck served as the gun deck; and below this no guns were mounted. The ship's sides were lined with pavesses or wooden shields painted in different colours and emblazoned with coats of arms and other devices. Prominent among the standards and streamers flying from the rigging were the favourite Tudor colours, white and green, and the cross of St. George. These warships of the royal fleet formed the permanent nucleus round which the King might gather a far larger naval force composed of merchantmen impressed for the occasion. Conversely, in time of peace he might hire out his fighting ships to merchants who had need of their services. The warships of the Tudor monarchs were much in demand for the long and perilous voyage to the Levant.

The reign of Henry VII also saw the inauguration of an important ancillary service. In 1496 the first dry dock of which there is any record in English history was constructed by Brygandine at Portsmouth. It was built of wood except for the dockhead, which was ' fortifyed ', or strengthened, with stone and gravel; it was enclosed by a wall and provided with wharves and storehouses. Here were accommodated, first, the *Sovereign,* and, later, the *Regent.* From the accession of Henry VII a storehouse was hired at Greenwich for the use of the

King's ships lying in the Thames. But down to the middle of the sixteenth century Portsmouth was our leading naval port; and later on, in the Commonwealth era, after a lengthy period of eclipse, it was once again to become, as it has ever since remained, the principal naval base of the kingdom.

The accession of the young King Henry VIII, in 1509, ushered in the first great era in English maritime history. To this period, indeed, may be traced the true beginnings of the fighting navy. From the outset of his reign the King was keenly interested in the ' sea affair ', as is shown by his frequent inquiries about the sailing and other qualities of new ships; and he is known also to have had some technical knowledge of artillery.

The reign of Henry VIII lasted for nearly thirty-eight years, and was a time of sustained and unprecedented expansion of our naval forces. To quote the leading authority on the early period of our naval administration:

> That his action was due to a settled policy . . . is shown by the fact that it commenced with his accession and was still progressing at his decease. For almost thirty-eight years nearly every year marked some advance in construction and administration, some plan calculated to make the Navy a more effective fighting instrument. . . . Regulations for the management of fleets and the discipline of their crews were due to him. He discarded the one mediaeval officer of the crown and organized an administration so broadly planned that, in an extended form, it remains in existence today. Ministers might come and go, but the work of naval extension, done under his personal supervision and direction, went on methodically and unceasingly.[1]

For the first time the dependence of England upon the sea was officially recognized. In the opening words of the preamble to the Navigation Act of 1540 it was laid down that ' the Navy or multitude of ships of this Realm ' was ' a great defence and surety in time of war, as well for offence and defence and also the maintenance of many masters, mariners and seamen, making them expert in the art and science of shipmen and sailing '.[2]

To the seven ships which he inherited from his father Henry VIII added, by purchase and construction, no less than twenty-four within

---

[1] Oppenheim, *A History of the Administration of the Royal Navy, 1509–1660* (1896)
[2] *Q.* H. W. Richmond, *Statesmen and Sea Power* (1946).

five years of his succession.[1] Those newly built for the fleet revealed no change in design but carried heavy ordnance of unprecedented power. Thus in 1509 the *Mary Rose* and *Sovereign* were armed with five and four brass muzzle-loading curtalls, each weighing about 3,000 lbs. respectively (the *Sovereign* also carried three demi-curtalls and three brass culverins).[2] Henry VIII's shipwrights followed the Italian innovation of mounting heavy guns low down in the waists of their ships—only they used bigger guns than the Italians—and piercing the sides of the ships with gun-ports; thus was evolved the broadside. Throughout the sixteenth century the cannon cast by English gun-founders were unsurpassed in Europe. Moreover, they were specially designed and mounted, for the first time, for shipboard use. This brought about a fundamental change in naval warfare. With the advent of the great gun it became possible to smash and sink at a distance, and ' in-fighting ' in course of time gave place to ' off-fighting '. As a natural corollary, as the close connection between gunnery and sea-manship was gradually recognized the seaman began to oust the soldier on shipboard, and the sailor-captain to supplant the military commander. The transition to an armament of fewer but more powerful guns progressed rapidly in the middle of the sixteenth century.

It is from these new sailing battleships, armed with heavy guns and firing on the broadside, that the modern Fleet directly descends; and in this sense it is permissible to speak of Henry VIII as the founder of the Royal Navy.

6

In the opening phase of the Tudor era the kingdom was amply pro-vided with the most vital of the raw materials of sea power, namely, timber for shipbuilding. A great part of England was as yet covered with virgin forest. Much of the land was so densely wooded that, in the words of the old jingle—

---

[1] The largest of the King's ships was the *Henri Grace à Dieu* or *Great Harry*, a huge four-master of 1,500 tons, with a very lofty poop and forecastle. A number of other ships were likewise ' built loftie ' in the *Great Harry* tradition; but they were found to be so expensive to maintain that they were never put into commission unless the whole royal fleet were mobilized.

[2] A number of these early brass cannon, which early in the last century were recovered from the wreck of Henry VIII's *Mary Rose* at Spithead, are to be seen, in a remarkably good state of preservation, in the Tower of London.

From Blacon Point to Hillbree
A squirrel may jump from tree to tree.

Most of the timber for naval construction was obtained from the great oak region situated between the Thames and the Channel. The chief timber-producing counties were Kent, Surrey, Hampshire, and, above all, Sussex. The Kentish Weald was the usual source of supply for Chatham, the New Forest and the Forest of Bere for Portsmouth; and the timber from Alice Holt—also in Hampshire—was conveyed, by way of the Thames, to Deptford. The woodlands of southern England produced timber admirably suited for naval purposes. Unlike the straight, slender trunks of the oak woods of the Continent, our English oaks, as Charnock observes, ' often assumed a great variety of forms, especially the rugged oaks growing in hedgerows, which had ample room to develop the branches essential for compass timbers. It was believed that English oaks acquired a toughness from constant buffeting with the winds, which gave them strange shapes while it toughened their timber.'[1] From these gnarled and crooked hedgerow oaks were fashioned the curved frame timbers indispensable to the construction of wooden ships. The great and compass timbers were shaped from oak-trees at least one hundred and fifty years old; and for want of such timbers the construction of ships might be held up for months.

The reign of Henry VIII witnessed the first wholesale felling of trees for timber purposes. Throughout the Tudor era there was a great and ever-increasing demand for oak in domestic as well as in naval architecture. In the years following the dissolution of the monasteries there was a particularly heavy felling of trees. Lord Lisle, then Lord Admiral, traded extensively in oak from monastic lands. In the reign of Elizabeth, heavy inroads were made on Ashdown and St. Leonard's Forests. Notwithstanding the fact that the country was still heavily timbered, already there arose fears for the future. In 1543 it was enacted that, in felling, a specified number of mature trees must be left standing; shortly before the year of the Armada an Act was passed ' for the preservation of Tymber in the Wildes of the Counties of Sussex, Surrey, and Kent '. At the same time there was a significant allusion in Holinshed's *Description of England* to the ' great sales

---

[1] Charnock, *History of Marine Architecture*, III, p. 172.

yearlie made of wood, whereby an infinit quantitie hath bin destroied within these last few years '.

In the ground beneath the great Wealden forest lay extensive deposits of iron ore. These deposits were widely diffused throughout the whole geological district known as the Hastings sands, stretching across the greater part of Sussex. The iron in this region had, indeed, been worked as far back as the time of the Romans; but the large-scale exploitation of its resources only came in with the Tudors. Throughout the Weald, in the close proximity of the ironfields, the streams threading the narrow ghylls were dammed up in order to furnish a good head of water to provide the power to operate the heavy drop-hammers employed for crushing the ironstone. In the heyday of the Sussex iron industry there were nearly 150 of these ' hammer ponds ', as they were called; a large number of which have survived to the present day. In St. Leonard's Forest and certain other wooded regions the pits from which the miners extracted the ironstone may still be seen; and the ancient ironworks are commemorated in numerous place-names like Crooked Cinder Lane, Hammer Hill, Minepit Wood, and Furnace Farm. During the reign of Henry VIII the Wealden ironworks multiplied so fast that they assumed the proportions of a national industry. A steadily increasing percentage of the ordnance supplied to the Navy was cast in the south country. According to an old tradition, the first of the Sussex gunfounders was one Master Huggett:

> Master Huggett and his man John
> They did cast the first cannon.

In 1543, according to Holinshed, another Sussex gunfounder, Ralph Hogge of Buxted, began to cast guns for the Navy, and continued to do so for the next thirty years. In the reign of Edward VI Sir Edward Seymour's iron-mills in Worth Forest were occupied in turning out culverins and lesser pieces. Under Elizabeth the Wealden iron industry reached the zenith of its prosperity; great landowners like the Carylls and Pelhams amassed fortunes; a number of the Sussex yeomanry founded county families. The principal centres of the industry were situated in Ashburnham, Mayfield, Buxted, Ashdown Forest, Sheffield, Worth and St. Leonard's Forests. The chief ports for the export of iron goods were Lewes and Rye. The opening years of the Spanish war saw a rapid increase in the production of ordnance. About this time the Council endeavoured, though with only limited success, to prevent these guns from falling into unfriendly hands. Thus, in 1573, Ralph Hogge had complained that his rivals were exporting cannon overseas, so that ' yor enimie is better fourneshed with them than or owne country ships ar'. Following the defeat of the Spanish Armada,

34

the Lord Admiral, Lord Charles Howard, ordered all foundries to cease casting cannon.

7

In 1491 the union of the Duchy of Brittany with the French crown, which had long been maturing, became an accomplished fact. France now gained possession of the Duchy's important Atlantic ports and with them some of the finest mariners in Europe. French warships were transferred from the Mediterranean to the Channel. The new situation threatened the traditional claim of the Kings of England to the sovereignty of the narrow seas: henceforward, across the Channel, they were faced by a potentially formidable rival. Over against Portsmouth the new port of Havre de Grace was arising. From the opposite coast, from Dieppe to St. Malo, there presently came forth a race of tough, fighting seamen to contest the mastery of the Channel.

When the First French War broke out in 1512, with Ferdinand of Spain and Henry VIII ranged against Louis XII of France, the English fleet was at first successful, but was seriously handicapped by defective organization and tactical weakness. In the opening year of the war the Lord High Admiral, Sir Edward Howard, swept the Channel unopposed, and after a brisk action in the approaches to Brest drove the enemy into port. The following year Howard blockaded Brest and lost his life in a daring attempt to cut out a squadron of Mediterranean galleys which were lying in Conquet Bay. Close 'infighting' was as yet the rule. The action off Brest in 1512, with the desperate duel between the *Regent* and *Cordelie*, was fought out in the traditional way and has been described by Williamson as ' the last of the mediaeval sea-fights ' in our history. No attempt was made to exploit the broadside, though in the revolutionary advance in naval armament already referred to England took and kept the lead. After the blockade of Brest had been raised, the naval war degenerated into the usual ' cross-ravaging '. In the spring of 1514 the French galleys burned Brighthelmstone on the Sussex coast. By way of reprisals Sir John Wallop attacked the shores of Normandy, destroying both towns and shipping. These raids had no material effect on the course of the war. In the meantime, in the summer of 1513, while Henry VIII was away fighting in France, the Scots had swept over the border under the leadership of their King, James IV, but were heavily defeated by the Earl of Surrey, on 9 September, at Flodden Field. Peace was restored in the following year.

In the 1520s the dominating issue in European affairs was the rivalry of Henry VIII's nephew, the young Emperor Charles V, and Francis I of France; in the mutual antagonism of these two monarchs was England's salvation. When in 1519 Charles V became possessed of immense territories on both sides of the Atlantic, only the King of France, with his strong and compact realm, stood between the House of Habsburg and the hegemony of Europe; and the balance was so critical, and the rivalry between the two so keen, that the support of Henry VIII and his great minister, Cardinal Wolsey, was anxiously invited. In general the English government inclined towards the Habsburg group, including as it did Spain, Burgundy, and the Empire, traditionally the friends and allies of England.

In the Second French War (1522–5) Henry VIII's fleet, joined to that of his ally, Charles V, showed itself so superior to the French that the enemy avoided decisive action and kept their battle fleet laid up in port. On land, the French army in Italy was conclusively defeated at Pavia in 1524. But Henry VIII and the Emperor having quarrelled, the interests of England were disregarded at the peace.

The later 1520s witnessed the crisis of the reign. As a result partly of the successful campaigns of the First French War, partly of the lavish expenditure of the treasure accumulated by Henry VII, but principally of Wolsey's genius for diplomacy and administration, English prestige had been raised for a time higher in Europe than it had stood since the death of Henry V. The last and greatest of all the ecclesiastical statesmen to hold the Great Seal, Wolsey during his seventeen years' tenure of power had gained for this country a weight and influence in the councils of nations that was out of all proportion to its actual resources. Then, following the Second French War and the fiasco of Wolsey's international manoeuvres, the hollowness of his pretensions to stand forth as the arbiter of the fate of Europe was finally made manifest.

During the first ten years of the reign, Henry VIII had taken little part in the government of his kingdom. Preoccupied for the most part with the New Learning, his Navy, and his sports and pleasures, the young King had left the details of administration first to his Council and later to Wolsey. ' He devotes himself ', noted Chieregati [the papal envoy], 'to accomplishments and amusements day and night, is intent on nothing else, and leaves business to Wolsey, who rules everything.' The Cardinal, however, had never possessed any hold over the nation, but only over the King. Now that hold was ominously weakening.

On top of the failure of Wolsey's foreign policy and the serious discontent excited by his heavy taxation came the decisive issue of the marriage suit between Henry VIII and his Queen, Catherine of Aragon, who was Charles V's aunt. For years the Cardinal had endeavoured by every means in his power to secure the long-desired annulment for his master. His failure to do so occasioned not only his own downfall but also that of his order. Wolsey's disgrace and dismissal from office were followed by his death in November 1530. Meanwhile the Pope—at this time virtually a prisoner in the power of Charles V—had revoked the King's suit to Rome. While the papal curia parleyed and procrastinated, Henry VIII, with the aid of his new minister, Thomas Cromwell, and the general approbation of Parliament, successively sundered every link of the chain which for centuries had bound England to Christendom.

Appealing successfully to the swiftly mounting anti-papal, anti-sacerdotal feeling abroad in the land, Cromwell in 1529 launched the campaign in the House of Commons with a wholesale attack on ecclesiastical rights and privileges, following this up with an Act to abolish the payment of annates, or first-fruits, to Rome. In the spring of 1532 the English clergy made complete and abject submission to Henry VIII, acknowledging him as Supreme Head of the Church. In 1533 appeals to Rome were forbidden by law; 1534 saw the passage of the Act of Supremacy and the Act of Succession; at the same time Cromwell was preparing to put down the monasteries; in 1536 the lesser houses, and in 1539 the great abbeys, were summarily dissolved. A dangerous insurrection, known as the Pilgrimage of Grace, which broke out in the northern counties in the autumn of 1536, was mercilessly repressed. With the suppression of the mendicant orders, the Knights of St. John, and a certain number of colleges and hospitals, the Henrician Reformation was complete.

In the following decade the fate of the dynasty hung in the balance. The breach with Rome and the dissolution of the monasteries had jeopardized the alliance with the Emperor without in any way assuaging the ancient enmity with France. On more than one occasion, indeed, it appeared possible that Charles V and Francis I would sink their differences and make common cause against England. Henry VIII had shocked the conscience of all Catholic Europe. He had put away the Emperor's aunt; he had flouted the Holy See; he had profaned and plundered the shrines, renowned throughout Europe, of Our Lady of Walsingham and St. Thomas of Canterbury. The heads of a lord chancellor and a cardinal had rolled on the scaffold. The inhuman treatment meted out to the heroic Carthusians had excited horror and revulsion throughout Christendom. Ireland was in revolt; Scotland, as ever, was hostile; even in England, popular sympathy showed itself unmistakably on the side of the injured Queen.

Relations between England and Spain progressively worsened. In 1533 the Council sent orders for the defences of the realm to be hurriedly overhauled against the risk of a Spanish descent; two years later the menace of a Catholic coalition against this country rose stark on the horizon; and in 1539, with a *rapprochement* apparently pending between the Emperor and Francis I, England was again in peril.

Despite all the forces ranged against him, Henry VIII held on his ruthless course. The Pope had excommunicated him—Henry told the Imperial envoy that he cared not a jot for ten thousand excommunications. The banishment of Catherine of Aragon from his court was a flagrant insult to Spain. Henry did not fear the Spaniards. Was not his kingdom guarded by a moat? They might come, declared the King with prophetic truth: but perhaps they might not return. Nor, when it came to the point, could Charles V afford to add England to his other enemies. The safety of his communications through the Channel and Straits of Dover was vital to the continued existence of the Hapsburg empire. The aggression of the Ottoman Turks on his southern frontier and in the Mediterranean was, after all, a matter of graver concern to the Emperor than the plight of Queen Catherine, Henry VIII's breach with Rome, and the spoliation of the English Church. Such discontent as existed among Henry VIII's own subjects was never strong enough to disrupt the united front which his kingdom presented at the threat of foreign intervention. The rising spirit of nationality responded whole-heartedly to the King's appeal; the musters were taken in every shire, and the people turned out as one man to defend their coasts against the invader. Between England and the armies of the Continent rolled the hazardous waters of the Channel and the North Sea. In our southern ports lay the strongest fighting fleet in western Europe. Henry had once boasted that he would show the princes of Europe how small was the power of the Pope; and he had kept his word. The Tudor monarchy stood four-square against the storm. The spring of 1539 passed peacefully away; and the threatened invasion had not come.

8

Spurred on by the threat of a possible continental coalition against him, Henry VIII continued to enlarge his fleet. Not only were new ships built, but a number of vessels were also purchased from Italian and Hanseatic powers. At the same time steps were taken to strengthen the coastal defences against the risk of invasion. From the Scottish border to the Thames estuary, and thence southward round the North Foreland to the Lizard, commissioners were hard at work overhauling the fortifications of the ports and coastal towns. At Pendennis, St. Mawes, Camber, and elsewhere along our southern and eastern ports Henry VIII's forts are still to be seen. The heavy cost of the naval expansion and of the coastal defences was met, during the period 1536 to 1543, out of the spoils of the Dissolution.

It is significant that the new ships which were constructed at this time mounted far more of the heavy guns than did those built earlier in the reign: besides a complete lower tier of guns, there was now a rudimentary upper tier also. In 1540 the *Great Harry* was rebuilt as a vessel of 1,000 tons, with a double tier of gunports and was very heavily armed. In 1546 even comparatively small vessels like the *Swallow* (240 tons) carried one demi-curtall and two demi-culverins, and the *Greyhound* (200 tons), one culverin and one demi-culverin. The presence of a large number of heavy pieces along the vessel's sides brought about a considerable change in ship-construction. By the middle of the reign clincher-built vessels were giving place to ships constructed carvelwise and with square instead of round sterns; also the tumble-home was increased to bring the heavy ordnance nearer the centre line. These developments provided the needful extra strength and facilitated the piercing of the ship's sides with gun-ports.

Although to the end of his reign Henry VIII continued to build great ships of the 'high-charged' type—vessels of increased beam and depth, with towering poops and forecastles, designed essentially for boarding and hand-to-hand fighting—he also created a squadron of fast-sailing galleons. These were of moderate size and their length was greater in proportion to their beam; they were fitted with a beak-head like that of a galley, and they had low poops and forecastles: indeed, the last four vessels built in the reign—the *Hart*, *Antelope*, *Tiger*, and *Bull*—were almost flush-decked. They were handier and far more weatherly than their predecessors, relying for victory upon gun-power and speed.

Side by side with the expansion of the fleet went the growth of the royal dockyards at Portsmouth, Woolwich, Deptford, and Erith for the building, repair, and accommodation of the King's ships. In 1509 Portsmouth dockyard was the only one in existence. It was considerably enlarged in the course of the reign; but later it was eclipsed by Woolwich and Deptford, and was not restored to its old importance until the Commonwealth era. The dockyard at Woolwich grew up round the King's great ship, *Henry Grace à Dieu*, which was built in 1514; that at Deptford was founded a few years later, in 1517, when John Hopton, the comptroller of the King's ships, contracted for 600 marks to 'make and cast a pond' near the existing storehouse and to build 'a good hable and suffycient hed for the same pond and also certyn hable sleysis through which the water may have entre and course into the foresaid ponde as well at spryng tydes as at nepetydes'.[1] The dockyard at Erith, of rather earlier construction, fell into disuse before the end of the reign. It is to be noted that Henry VIII was the first monarch in Europe to possess such a system of dockyards.

In his latter years the King's energies were directed chiefly towards the severance of the Franco-Scottish alliance and the enforcement of the old claim of suzerainty over Scotland, rather than towards any scheme of continental aggrandizement. Scotland at this time was almost an appanage of France; and every recrudescence of hostilities saw the Scots linked in close alliance with the historic enemy across the Channel. Despite all his endeavours, however, the King's design proved abortive. His policy only exacerbated Scottish national feeling; and at the end of the reign Scotland was as fully and as firmly independent of England as it had been at the beginning.

[1] Oppenheim, *op. cit.*, p. 70.

On the eve of the Third French War (1544–6) Henry VIII prepared to secure his rear by a well-planned amphibious attack on Edinburgh. On 1 May 1544 a fleet of transports carrying an army of 12,000 foot, escorted by a squadron of warships under Lord Lisle, sailed from the northern ports, while a force of 4,000 cavalry invaded Scotland from Berwick. On 4 May the infantry and guns under Lord Hertford made an unopposed landing up the Firth of Forth about two miles west of Leith. The Scots were taken completely by surprise. Leith was stormed and sacked, after which Hertford and the main body of the army pushed on to Edinburgh. There they were joined by the cavalry; and, after a fierce fight at the Canongate, the whole city, with the exception of the castle, was plundered and set on fire. Meanwhile Lisle's squadron had swept up the shipping in the Forth and captured two Scottish warships. When Hertford returned to Leith, the enemy's guns and equipment were put on board the fleet, and the general and his men set out for the border, ravaging as they went. In rather less than three weeks from the expedition it was back at Berwick, its object successfully achieved with a remarkable economy of force.

The same good staff-work marked the passage of the English forces to France. Detachments of the army were rapidly embarked at all the ports of the eastern and southern coasts between Harwich and Winchelsea, and were conveyed across the Channel under convoy of the fighting fleet. Boulogne was presently taken and held against every assault of the enemy. Then Henry VIII's ally, Charles V, made a separate peace with the King of France; and during the winter of 1544–5 the situation became increasingly perilous. The Emperor was alienated by the depredations of the English privateers as well as by the recent suppression of the religious houses. Francis I was resolved to avenge the seizure of Boulogne; and the Pope, alarmed and angered by Henry VIII's anti-ecclesiastical policy, offered him moral and material aid. In 1545, after the Scots had worsted the English at Ancrum Moor, the kingdom was threatened by a formidable French invasion directed against Portsmouth and the Isle of Wight. The council thereupon ordered the castles and forts around the coasts to be manned and put into good repair; arrangements were made for calling out the militia; a system of fire-beacons was set in train, and the beacons and buoys marking the intricate channels in the Thames estuary were removed.

On the night of 19 July the chains of warning fires carried the news of the enemy's approach across the length and breadth of England.[1] The French fleet entered the Solent and disembarked their troops at Bembridge on the eastern side of the Isle of Wight. The English fleet, once more under the command of Lord Lisle, remained within the cover of the batteries in Portsmouth harbour, where the enemy dared not follow, but contented themselves with a distant cannonade. The English military forces, with Henry VIII himself in command, were quickly concentrated around Portsmouth before the French could reach the mainland. The bridgehead that the enemy had established on the Isle of Wight lasted less than twenty-four hours. There was some skirmishing in the wooded country between the shore and Bembridge Down; then, in the face of mounting odds, the enemy hurriedly embarked on board their fleet again. A westerly breeze having sprung up, they dropped down before it along the Sussex coast, and the English followed. A French descent at Seaford was easily repelled. The enemy retired across the Channel. Later in the summer they reappeared off the English coast. Lisle sailed round to meet them: in a minor action off Shoreham the French galleys suffered some damage. By this time, moreover, the usual epidemic had broken out on the crowded decks and the hostile army was a spent force; and the enemy finally withdrew to Havre.

Across the Channel the French had been defeated outside Boulogne, and in the north Hertford had ravaged the Scottish borders. Meanwhile light and handy privateers from the western ports scoured the Channel and the Bay of Biscay. Though the royal fleet had had comparatively little serious battle experience, these bold privateers of the Channel and Atlantic were already becoming adept in the new art of naval gunnery. It is to be observed that large-scale professional privateering may, in fact, be said to date from the Third French War.

A portentous development of this privateering warfare was the seizure off Cape St. Vincent, in March 1545, of a Spanish treasure-ship, the *San Sebastian*, by one Robert Reneger of Southampton. The Reneger incident effectually opened the eyes of English mariners

---

[1] ' From the coast the beacon system spread inland from hill to hill to the most distant recesses of the country. So efficient was it that the men of Worcester were on the march within a very short time after the approach of the French was signalled at Portsmouth ' (J. A. Williamson, ' A Tudor Army ', *Blackwood's Magazine*, September 1914).

to the impotence of Spain in the face of such attacks; and from this time on the English depredations increased both in numbers and audacity. As a result of the recent political and religious trends in this country, a new spirit of animosity towards the Spaniards was arising among our merchants and mariners, some of whom had lately suffered imprisonment and torture at the hands of the Spanish Inquisition. In the final phase of the reign the lucrative and long-established traffic with Spain was visibly declining and privateering and piracy took its place.[1]

' Of all others,' Corbett declares, ' the year 1545 marks the birth of English naval power; it is the year that most clearly displays the transition from oars to sails, and it was probably in this very year the first great sailing Admiral the world ever saw came obscurely into being.'[2]

It is nevertheless to be noted that, though the reign of Henry VIII saw the construction of a true fighting fleet, naval power played but a limited role in the three French wars. In the words of the late Sir Herbert Richmond, ' The army was the instrument of offence, the navy the bridge by means of which it reached its destination, and the main defence against invasion on a large scale. In the war of 1544, it was not the loss of his subjects' ships or their commerce which caused the French King to make overtures to the Emperor. It was the Allied advance on Paris.'[3]

When peace was restored in 1546 Henry VIII set up an organization of supply, later to be known as the Navy Board, which was made responsible for the administrative work of the Fleet under the Lord Admiral. This new organization had become necessary on account of the immense expansion of the Fleet in Henry VIII's reign. The administration was supervised by the Lieutenant of the Admiralty, the Treasurer, Comptroller, Surveyor, Clerk of the Ships, and Master of the Ordnance for the Ships. The office of the Lieutenant of the Admiralty, however, soon lapsed; and the Treasurership became the chief administrative office. The Clerk of the Ships eventually became the Clerk of the Acts; his functions were now to be mainly secretarial.

[1] For the Reneger incident and its consequences, see Connell-Smith, *Forerunners of Drake* (1947) and Rowse, *Tudor Cornwall* (1941).
[2] Francis Drake was born on a farm called Crowndale, on the outskirts of Dartmoor in or about 1545.
[3] H. W. Richmond, *The Navy as an Instrument of Policy* (1953).

These reforms were of great and lasting significance. The creation of the Navy Board was one of the main foundations of English sea power; forty years later it rendered possible the swift and efficacious action of the Elizabethan navy against Spain and the West Indies: no other European State possessed such a simple, efficient, and unified system of naval administration, the essential features of which were to remain until the early nineteenth century.

III

The age of expansion

I

It was no coincidence that the great voyages of discovery, at the conclusion of the fifteenth century and at the beginning of the sixteenth, took place when and where they did. The success and continuance of these ventures were dependent upon factors which were operative then and which were not operative in earlier periods of the world's history. Hitherto neither the ships nor the navigation of our ancestors had been equal to such undertakings. Towards the close of the fifteenth century, however, the situation was changing. At this stage a revolutionary advance had been brought about, not only in the structure and rigging of ships, but also—among the Latins—in the knowledge and practice of navigation.

In the forefront of this advance were the mariners of the Italian city states, and of Portugal and Spain. Columbus, Vespucci, and John and Sebastian Cabot were all Italians. Portugal, in the course of the fifteenth century, had become the leading maritime Power in Europe; she had a long seaboard and a fine natural harbour in Lisbon, her capital; and though small in territory and population, she had early attained national unity. Under the inspiration of Prince Henry she had begun to send out successive expeditions to the southward; these ventures were continued by his brother and successor, John, with the object of discovering the sea-route to Asia, the riches of which, portrayed with glowing detail in the *Travels* of Marco Polo, had long served as a lure to the explorer. The nautical school founded by the Prince at Sagres in 1419 applied the study of astronomy and mathematics to the problems of ocean navigation. The work of learned Jews, such as James of Mallorca, played a major part in these calculations. Before Prince Henry's death in 1460 the Portuguese had visited, surveyed, and charted the west coast of Africa as far south as the vicinity of Sierra Leone, and colonized the Madeira, Azores, and Cape

Verde Islands. In the fast-sailing and handy caravel they had evolved a type of craft which was admirably adapted to their purpose. Pioneers of scientific navigation, they were accustomed to determine their position, first, from the *altura*, or elevation, of the Pole-star, and presently (the latter being no longer visible after they had crossed the equator) from the meridian altitude of the sun. The quadrant and Jacob's Staff were used to determine the altitude of the Pole-star, while the astrolabe was employed for observing the meridian altitude of the sun. It would appear that the quadrant was coming into use by about 1450, and the mariner's astrolabe in the last two decades of the century. The Portuguese ventures had culminated in the great voyage of Vasco de Gama round the Cape of Good Hope to India (1497-9). The accuracy of da Gama's observations and reckoning marked an era in the progress of scientific navigation. The outward passage of his voyage may well be reckoned the finest feat of navigation yet recorded. With the expedition of 1497-9 began the lucrative Portuguese traffic to the Indies.

Early in the following century the conquests of Albuquerque established the Portuguese empire of the East, based on the command of the sea and a network of factories and fortresses set up along the trade-routes. For the navigation between Lisbon and Goa, by far the furthest and most formidable passage known to Christendom, the Portuguese employed squadrons of large merchantmen called carracks; some of the best of which were constructed at Goa and other eastern ports. Lisbon thereafter supplanted Venice as the principal European mart for eastern produce.

While the Portuguese thus discovered and exploited the long sea-route round the Cape, the Spaniards endeavoured to find a short cut across the North Atlantic to the eastern seaboard of Asia. In 1492 a squadron of three caravels, led by Christopher Columbus, sailing westward along the 28th parallel, had reached the New World; and the Spaniards began to colonize the West Indies. In 1519 Fernando Magellan, a Portuguese in Spanish service, discovered and successfully passed through those Straits ever afterwards known by his name; after which he crossed the Pacific and reached the Moluccas. Magellan himself perished in a fight with some natives; but the only surviving ship of his squadron, the *Victoria*, rounded the Cape of Good Hope and in 1522 returned safely to Europe—the first vessel ever to encompass the globe. The explorers were succeeded by the Conquista-dores. In 1521 Hernando Cortés at the head of a few hundred Euro-pean foot and a handful of cavalry overthrew, in one swift and brilliant campaign, the ancient Aztec empire and conquered Mexico. In 1537 another of the Conquistadores, Francisco Pizarro, invaded Peru with a still smaller force and added the territories of the Incas to the already immense possessions of the Spanish Crown. During the long reign of Charles V the hispanization of the Americas went rapidly ahead. The vast extent of the territories controlled and administered by the Spanish bureaucracy was out of all proportion to the actual number of the Spanish settlers. The ordinary day-to-day business of government was carried on, with remarkable efficiency, by a system of councils. It may safely be said that no other race in Europe could have accomplished this work. The colonial empires acquired by the Peninsular Powers brought, for the time being, immense wealth to their fortunate possessors.

In the second half of the sixteenth century Spain was unquestion-ably the first power in Europe. The military strength of the monarchy was based on the magnificent Spanish infantry, with its imposing roll of victories, to which other States could show no equal. At the battle of Lepanto, in 1571, the King's half-brother, Don John of Austria, overthrew, in the last great galley action in history, the Sultan's fleet in the Mediterranean. In the following decade the victories gained by his squadrons in the Azores still further enhanced the renown of the Spanish fleet. The power and prestige of Spain perhaps attained their zenith in the early 1580s, when, following upon the annexation of Portugal and her overseas possessions, the empire of Philip II became by far the most extensive that the world had ever known; and the poet Hernando de Acuño looked forward to the universal monarchy of Spain—' un Monarca, un Imperio y una Espada '.

While Europe was ringing with the exploits of the Conquistadores and a steady stream of gold and silver from the mines of Central and South America flowed eastward, year by year, into the Spanish treasury, the English ventures had yielded hardly anything of value except the cod fisheries of Newfoundland; and these were exploited by foreigners rather than by Englishmen. In point of fact, the Peninsu-lar States were ripe for expansion, while England was not. The England of the early Tudors could never have fitted out such an expedition as that with which Cabral voyaged to India, in 1500, carrying with him the most skilful pilots and cosmographers of his day: nor that led by Magellan a couple of decades later. Even in the mid-sixteenth century few Englishmen could shape a course across the Western Ocean; and none could navigate to the Orient. The reasons for this were various. England's geographical position was considerably less favourable than that of the Peninsular Powers. The richer share of her overseas commerce, in the early half of the Tudor period, was still in foreign hands. The volume of shipping which frequented London River could not compare with that lying in the docks of Antwerp—the great emporium of the Continent. English merchants as yet lacked fluid capital, business technique, and organization. English shipbuilding was backward in comparison with that of the Italians, Portuguese, and Spaniards. English mariners were still far behind the Latins in the knowledge and practice of scientific naviga-tion. English crews had little experience of oceanic ventures and voyages of exploration. Leadership, too, was wanting—no galaxy of brilliant names had appeared in England comparable with those of Diaz, Columbus, Vasco da Gama, Cabral, Vespucci, and Magellan. Little interest had been shown by the English public in the news of the great discoveries. Moreover, during the early Tudor period England was distracted by grave political and religious problems at home, and, externally, by the threat of Scotland and Ireland. At the same time the Anglo-Spanish alliance was for long a deterrent to English enterprise in the Atlantic. England, beset with many difficulties and dangers, was in no position to risk a head-on collision with Spain. Last but not least, the missionary fervour which had operated as a major factor in the Peninsular expeditions was wholly lacking in those fitted out from England.

2

The continuous rise in commercial prosperity that marked the reigns of the two Henries, the accumulation of floating capital, and the steadily increasing experience of business practices and devices were the conditions precedent of English maritime expansion. After the middle of the sixteenth century these new ventures began under the patronage of Northumberland. A variety of causes combined to pro-duce an urgent demand for new outlets for English trade; even in the inauspicious reign of Philip and Mary the strong uncontrollable urge of the mercantile interest towards ocean trade manifested itself in voyages to Morocco, to the Guinea coast, and to Russia. Side by side with the discovery and exploitation of new markets went the advance of shipbuilding and navigation; of mathematics and astronomy; of geography and cartography. And eventually, in the reign of Elizabeth, overseas enterprise was taken up on an unprecedented scale and became a factor in State policy.

In the new oceanic era that was now opening out London, greatly preponderant in wealth and population as compared with the rest of the country, gave the lead to all England. The 1530s witnessed the eclipse of Southampton as a major port. Bristol also had entered on a period of retrogression. Trade and shipping tended to concentrate to an increasing degree in the Thames. English ships trading to the Mediterranean, in the reign of Henry VIII, sailed more and more to London, less often to Southampton. A list of 1560 shows that London owned something like a third of all the ships of 100 tons and over in the kingdom; and this proportion tended to increase as the century advanced. After the mid-century London outstripped the West Country in the general leadership of transoceanic enterprise. It was London that initiated the new ocean trades of the 1550s which infringed the colonial monopolies of the Peninsular States and ultimately led to the rupture of the Spanish alliance. The same set of City merchants was to be found over and over again in the syndicates financing these ventures; and in the reign of Elizabeth, Camden described the multitude of vessels congregated in London River as ' a very wood of trees, disbranched to make glades and to let in light: so shaded is it with masts and sails '.

Compared with that of London, the shipping of the West Country was of small tonnage, but more numerous. The maritime population of the western ports was very large—in 1582 the seamen of Devon and Cornwall alone numbered more than one-third of the total for all the ports in the kingdom; and from the ranks of the West Country gentry presently emerged leaders, like Grenville and Ralegh, who took the lead in the fight against Spain. Upon the solid foundations of maritime enterprise laid in the previous century was reared the splendid achievement of the Elizabethan era. Plymouth—mainly owing to the successful exertions of three generations of the Hawkins family and the world-famed ventures of Francis Drake—now came rapidly to the fore. What Bristol had been in the fifteenth century, Plymouth became in the sixteenth, and more: the great arsenal of the West; a centre of oceanic enterprise; the rendezvous of some of the boldest spirits of the age; the base from which voyage after voyage was made to trade, to explore, to colonize, and to wage war; wholly overshadowing Dartmouth, Fowey, and other ports of the West Country.

As a result of the depression that set in towards the middle of the sixteenth century and the decline of many of our old European connections, the opening up of new trades became a national necessity. It was in these circumstances that a series of oceanic ventures was begun. In 1530 William Hawkins, sailing from Plymouth, made the first of a series of voyages to the Ivory coast of Africa and Brazil, which brought wealth to himself and his native town. In 1551 a syndicate of London merchants fitted out an expedition which was the beginning of a long and profitable English connection with Morocco. Two years later, financed by substantially the same set of investors, Wyndham sailed to the Guinea coast. This voyage, notwithstanding severe casualties among the crew due to disease, yielded an immense profit to the subscribers and played no inconsiderable part in determining the characteristically individualist form of English maritime expansion. Wyndham was followed by a host of others: connived at by the Council under Mary, openly encouraged under Elizabeth, the Guinea trade flourished exceedingly, and ultimately provoked hostilities with Portugal.

There were also important developments in the north. In 1553, after careful consultation with Sebastian Cabot, now an old man of vast and varied experience, and John Dee, the great geographer and mathematician, an expedition led by Sir Hugh Willoughby, with Richard Chancellor as his second in command and chief pilot, sailed in search of the North-East Passage to Asia. A storm separated the two leaders; wintering on the Lapland coast, Willoughby perished with all his men, while Chancellor discovered the entrance to the White Sea, landed at Archangel, and journeyed overland to Moscow. With the discovery of the northern sea-route was begun the direct trade to Russia. Year by year the newly formed Muscovy Company sent a small fleet to the White Sea, enjoying several years of great prosperity. The trade secured a much desired outlet for English cloth, and the imports included essential naval stores like cordage, pitch, tar, and hemp.[1] Naval stores were also imported by the Eastland Company, formed in 1579, which traded to the Baltic.

The large and well-armed vessels employed by the Turkey Company (1581) on the long sea-route to the Levant formed a substantial addition to the naval reserves of the kingdom. Off Pantelaria in 1586 eleven of the King of Spain's Sicilian galleys and frigates were routed and driven back to port by the guns of the Turkey Company's *Merchant Royal* and her four consorts. The Venice Company (1583) traded with Venice and her possessions in the eastern Mediterranean. The Levant Company was formed in 1592 by the amalgamation of the Turkey and Venice Companies. A high proportion of the largest ocean-going vessels in the kingdom either belonged to, or were hired by, these corporations. Thus in 1581 the Levant Company possessed fourteen ships of between 200 and 350 tons; and by 1600 the tonnage belonging to the Company had greatly increased.

Finally, at the turn of the century there was formed the greatest of all these trading-companies. The various attempts to reach the Indies by way of the North-East and North-West Passages had failed: but the lure of the richest trade in the world still drew them on. The main stages on the road to Eastern expansion were the voyages of Drake, Cavendish, Lancaster, and Wood; the appearance of the Dutch pilot Linschoten's sailing directions for the Eastern voyage; John Davis's voyage to the East Indies with the Hollanders in 1598–1600 to learn the navigation; the publication of an enlarged edition of Hakluyt's *Principal Navigations*, containing much new material concerning the East; and the capture in 1587 and 1592 of two Portuguese Indiamen which yielded up, in addition to a rich lading, documents and charts which had further whetted the appetite of the captors. On the basis of the experience gained in these ventures the East India Company was formed, and in 1601 the first trading fleet was dispatched to the Indies with Sir James Lancaster in command and John Davis as pilot-major.

Another important factor in English maritime expansion was the successive attempts of Elizabethan mariners to penetrate the North-East and North-West Passages to Asia. These, though unsuccessful, stimulated in no small degree the progress of English seamanship and

---

[1] The fleet that defeated the Great Armada in 1588 was largely rigged with Russian cordage and cables.

navigation. Owing to the convergence of the meridians and the variation of the compass in the high latitudes new methods of navigation had to be worked out by experienced scholars like the learned Dr. Dee and practical seamen like William Borough. The influence of the former can scarcely be set too high: Dee was in close and constant touch with some of the highest personages in the land, from the Queen downwards; he was the friend of famous continental scholars like Gemma Frisius and Gerard Mercator; he was the valued guide and counsellor of a long succession of skilful mariners, beginning with Richard Chancellor and ending with John Davis. In 1556 the Muscovy Company sent out an expedition under Stephen Borough to search for the North-East Passage. Borough discovered the entrance to the Kara Sea and explored the coast of Nova Zembla. In 1576, notwithstanding the Muscovy Company's protests, Frobisher was sent by Lok and other London merchants to search for the North-West Passage and discovered Frobisher Sound. Frobisher made two further voyages in 1577–8; but apart from the chance discovery of the sound later known as Hudson Strait his second and third voyages were barren of results. In 1585–7 John Davis thrice visited the seas between Greenland and Canada and accurately charted the adjacent coasts. On his third voyage to the North-West, in a 20-ton pinnace, he penetrated as high as the 73rd parallel, the ' furthest north ' of the era.

Mention must also be made of English attempts at colonization on the eastern seaboard of North America. In 1583 an expedition led by Sir Humphrey Gilbert sailed to North America to plant a colony. But Gilbert lost all the necessary stores for this settlement while on the way to Nova Scotia; and on the return passage he was himself lost with all hands in the little 10-ton *Squirrel*. In 1585 and 1587 two successive expeditions were sent out by Sir Walter Ralegh to plant a settlement in the southern region of the same coast. The new colony received the name of Virginia in honour of the Queen. In 1586 the first batch of colonists abandoned the settlement and returned to England. The fate of the second is a mystery which, in all probability, will never be solved.

Since the last French war of Henry VIII's reign privateering in the Channel had become almost endemic. In the second half of the sixteenth century it spread to the Azores and Canaries, and thence to the Caribbean, serving as a school of seamanship and fighting experience that was of inestimable value in the development of Tudor sea power. In 1557 one French and one English privateer were in action with five Portuguese ships; and ten years later Fenner in the *Castle of Comfort*, in action for two long days with seven Portuguese ships near Terceira in the Azores, beat off every attack by her overwhelming gunfire. The news of this victory was received in England with enthusiasm. It was a striking demonstration of the power of the broadside. In the following decade the Spaniards, too, were made aware of the new and formidable English tactics—broadsides aimed low at the enemy vessel's hull. Gradually these privateersmen appear to have discovered what types of cannon were best suited to this method of attack. In the hard school of privateering, on both sides of the Atlantic, the new form of sea warfare was being evolved which was to make of the fighting seamen of the Elizabethan era past-masters of naval gunnery and of what nowadays would be called ' shock tactics '. Thus most of the actual fighting experience in the pre-Armada era was gained, not by the crews of the royal fleet, but by the English privateersmen. The latter became sufficiently adept, indeed, in ship-to-ship fighting, but were lacking in organization and anything like fleet tactics. Between these adventurers and the rulers of the royal fleet there was a close, though more or less concealed, connection from the reign of Henry VIII onwards. It is now known that the same family groups were in control both of these trading and privateering ventures and of the affairs of the royal fleet.[1]

During the first decade of Elizabeth's reign the increasingly aggressive trading ventures of John Hawkins in the New World heralded the breakdown of the traditional alliance with Spain. These ventures had originated in the negro slave traffic. Owing to the extermination of the indigenous population of the West Indies it had become necessary for the Spanish colonists to import negro slaves from Africa. As the Spanish settlements across the Atlantic increased, the demand for negroes increased proportionately. The dearth of slaves in the Spanish plantations became known to the English and French sea-captains who trafficked to the African coast. On his slaving voyage in 1562–3 Hawkins secured a cargo of slaves from the Guinea coast and sailed to

---

[1] ' The conception of a party, a solid connection of brains, courage and capital . . . emerges with increasing clearness from the researches of the past half-century ' (J. A. Williamson, *Hawkins of Plymouth* (1949), p. 194).

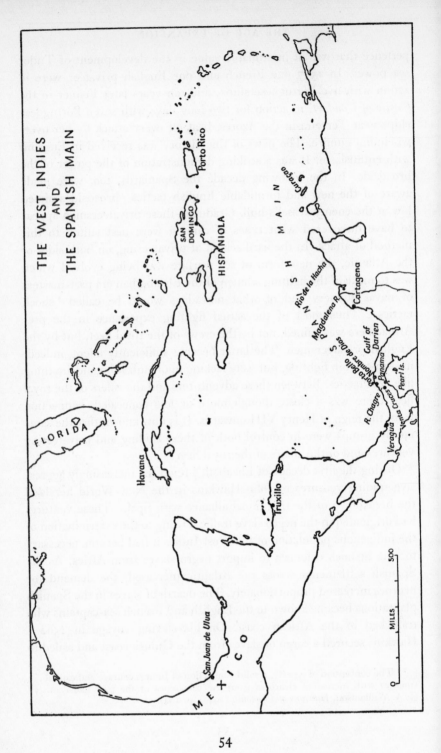

THE WEST INDIES
AND
THE SPANISH MAIN

FLORIDA

Havana

Truxillo

San Juan de Ulua

MEXICO

Porto Rico

SAN DOMINGO

HISPAÑIOLA

Curacao

SPANISH MAIN

Rio de la Hacha

Cartagena

Magdalena R.

Gulf of
Darien

Nombre de Dios

Porto Bello

Panama

Veragua

R. Chagre

Venta Cruces

Pearl Is.

MILES

0   500

Hispaniola, where, contrary to the laws of Spain, he sold the slaves at a very large profit. On his second slaving voyage (1564–5), with the backing of the Queen, four of her Council, and various London merchants, Hawkins sailed to the Guinea coast, captured his negroes as before, and crossed to the Spanish Main, where he disposed of his cargo. On his third slaving voyage (1567–9), Hawkins, with a well-armed squadron, including two ships of the Queen's, sailed to the Guinea coast and, after attacking Portuguese shipping, collected his slaves and stood across to the Spanish Main, where, not without serious opposition, he disposed of the cargo. But bad weather having forced him to put into San Juan de Ulua, he was treacherously attacked by a strong Spanish squadron escorting the Viceroy of Mexico. Hawkins sank two of the Spanish ships and eventually escaped, with the loss of most of his force, to England. The action afforded another striking illustration of the power of the broadside and confirmed the lesson of Fenner's recent fight in the Azores. The injury suffered by Hawkins and his followers at San Juan de Ulua led to an unofficial war of reprisals and greatly intensified English feeling against Spain.

It has lately been established that these trading ventures to the Caribbean did not end with the affair at San Juan de Ulua. From time to time English vessels still made the passage to the forbidden shores of Spanish America; and in the 1570s the expeditions fitted out by the Hawkins brothers and Francis Drake brought abounding wealth to Plymouth.

From the Queen's accession the coastwise trade and fisheries of the realm formed a most important element of its total maritime resources. The coastal traffic, which was already considerable, had increased, before the end of the reign, to about four times the growing export trade. A major item in this coastal traffic was the Newcastle coal trade. The rapid expansion of the coal industry towards the close of the sixteenth century created an increasing demand for craft of substantial tonnage to transport the produce of the north country mines to towns and villages on the east and south coasts, and, above all, to London and its environs. The coal trade was valued by the government as the ' true nursery and seminary for English seamen ', who, in time of war, could be readily impressed for the fleet.

At the same time Sir William Cecil (later Lord Burghley) took steps to revive the fisheries. The religious changes of Edward VI's reign had substantially diminished the consumption of fish in England. The Catholic revival under Mary reversed this tendency and infused fresh life into our fisheries. But with the resurgence of Protestantism in the next reign the fisheries had once more fallen on evil days. Lynn, which had once supplied three hundred seamen for the royal fleet, was now unable to furnish more than two or three dozen. The neighbouring ports of Cromer and Yarmouth were also in decline. The formerly flourishing Iceland fishery was threatened with extinction. In 1553 there were only 43 ships sailing to Iceland in place of the 149 which had voyaged there in 1528. By the middle of the sixteenth century the King of Denmark had secured complete control of Iceland and Icelandic waters, and the English were expelled from their trading and fishing stations in the island; their last foothold, the important fishing post in the outlying Vestmannaeyjar group, being finally lost in 1559. To the ' recovery of the Isles of Island [Iceland] into the possession of the Kyng of Denmark ' Cecil attributed the disastrous decay of the Iceland fishery.[1]

' Let the old course of fishing be maintained by the straitest observation of fish-days,' declared Cecil on his return to power, ' for policy's sake; so the sea-coasts should be strong with men and habitations and the fleet flourish more than ever '. In the reign of Elizabeth legislation was accordingly introduced to the end that the population was compelled henceforth to abstain from flesh on certain days of the year— not, as was carefully pointed out, for religious reasons: but for the good of the fisheries and the greater strength of the fleet.[2] These and other measures taken about the same time (1563) to encourage the fisheries appear to have been effective. A certificate sent in by the Corporation of Trinity House in 1581 shows a substantial increase in the number of fishing vessels. The Newfoundland fishery now began to bulk large in the national economy. As has already been said, though it was an English expedition which had originally discovered the rich cod fishery off Newfoundland it was not until well on in the reign of Elizabeth that the English contingent formed any considerable part of the heterogeneous fishing fleet which sailed every year for the

---

[1] For the decline of the Iceland fishery, see Thorsteinsson in the *Saga Book of the Viking Society*, XV, pp. 98–101.

[2] It was said that this Act was passed ' for the preservation of the navy and the maintenance of convenient numbers of seafaring men, both of which would otherwise decrease if some means were not found whereby they might be increased '.

Grand Banks. Between 1574 and 1578 the numbers of English ships resorting to the Grand Banks had increased from thirty to fifty. These ships were between forty and fifty tons, manned by a crew of about twenty, of whom a dozen would fish while the rest looked after the curing ashore. They would sail for Newfoundland at the beginning of March, returning home about six months later. Dartmouth and most of the other western ports assisted in the Banks fishery, which was later described by Ralegh as ' the mainstay and support of the West '. In the final decade of the century the English secured the first place in the Newfoundland fishery, supplying vast quantities of dried cod to France and the Mediterranean countries. The Iceland fishery was also prospering. About the same time English whalers began to frequent the northern seas visited by the vessels of the Muscovy Company and also the coasts of Greenland. Early in the next century they were to exploit the rich whale-fishery off Spitzbergen.

3

The remarkable progress in ship-design in the later Elizabethan era can be seen in a set of draughts, believed to be the work of the great shipwright, Matthew Baker, about the year 1586. These draughts reveal that the larger warships of the period were designed with finer lines than those of an earlier era. They were all galleon-built, with a long projecting beak, and a square or transom stern. As in all Elizabethan craft, the sheer, or upward curve of the hull towards the bow and stern, was very pronounced.

The larger Elizabethan vessels were frequently four-masters; for the use of the bonaventure mizen continued down to the end of the century. The normal sail-plan, therefore, comprised a square spritsail under the bowsprit: square foresail and topsail: square mainsail and main-topsail: and main and bonaventure mizen. The topsails increased in hoist as the century advanced, and the courses became shallower. A method of striking topmasts was introduced in the Navy by John Hawkins. Towards the end of the reign many of the larger ships carried topgallant sails.

Early in the seventeenth century Ralegh thus summarized the more important of the improvements in shipping and shipbuilding which had been brought in during this era.

In my own time the shape of our English ships hath been greatly bettered. It is not long since the striking of the topmasts (a wonderful ease to great ships, both at sea and in harbour) hath been devised, together with the chain-pump, which takes up twice as much water as the ordinary did; we have lately added the bonnet and the drabbler. To the courses we have devised studding-sails, top-gallant-sails, sprit-sails, top-sails;[1] the weighing of anchors by the capstan is also new. We have fallen into consideration of the length of cables, and by it we resist the malice of the greatest winds that can blow . . . for true it is, that the length of the cable is the life of the ship in all extremities; and the reason is, because it makes so many bendings and waves, as the ship riding at that length is not able to stretch it, and nothing breaks that is not stretched. . . . We carry our ordnance better than we were wont, because our nether over-loops are raised commonly from the water, to wit, between the lower part of the port and the sea. We have also raised our second decks, and given more vent thereby to our ordnance, tying on our nether overloop. We have added crosspillars in our royal ships to strengthen them, which being fastened from the keelson to the beams of the second deck, keep them from settling, or from giving way in all distresses.[2]

The simple three-masted sail-plan continued unchanged in small merchantmen down to the end of the seventeenth century. Through-out this period, for the smaller trading craft the normal rig was three masts and six sails (viz. spritsail, foresail and fore-topsail, mainsail and main-topsail, and mizen).

The effect of the steady advance of English shipbuilding in the period under survey made possible the development of the ocean-going type of vessel fitted for the voyages of Chancellor, Frobisher, Davis, Drake, and Cavendish. The growth of the Levant trade, as we have seen, served as a powerful stimulus to English shipbuilding. Another leading factor was the demand for private warships of the type of the *Castle of Comfort* and *Golden Hind*. In the 1580s a regular boom in privateering set in and continued throughout the war. Privateers like Cumberland's *Malice Scourge*, a fine galleon of 500 tons, were virtually equal in strength to the royal ships of the same tonnage.

The shipbuilding bounty was regularly paid and the returns show a continued increase in the size and number of English merchantmen. Between 1592 and 1595 the number of newly built ships of 100 tons

---

[1] This is an error. Spritsails and bonnets had come in long before.
[2] *Works of Sir Walter Ralegh*, ed. Oldys and Birch, VIII, pp. 323–4.

and over was 48. A few years later, in a single year (September 1596 –September 1597), it was 57.

4

It has already been observed that one of the major factors militating against English maritime expansion was the backwardness of English mariners in the new nautical science that was being developed in the era of the great discoveries. As late as the 1570s there was nothing in this country comparable with the School for Navigators which had been established in Portugal early in the fifteenth century; or with the similar institution which had been set up in Spain a century or so later.[1] The French had rapidly acquired the technique of the new navigation. Not so the English. Stephen Borough said truly, ' We have to go to Spain and France for pilots '; in England, down to the middle of the sixteenth century, there were no nautical treatises, instruments, or sea-charts like those which had been produced in considerable numbers in the Peninsular States and France. Englishmen had yet to learn ' the art of the astrolabe '. Hitherto, in such oceanic ventures as they had accomplished, English mariners had nearly always been obliged to avail themselves of the services of foreign-born pilots, like John and Sebastian Cabot. By the last decade of the century, however, they frequently sailed the ocean unaided, and even acted as pilots for the Dutch on many of their enterprises. (When in 1598 three Dutch trading fleets sailed for the East Indies, one by way of the Cape and the other two via the Magellan Straits, the Chief Pilot in each case was an Englishman.)

Sebastian Cabot, who had passed the greater part of his long life in Spanish service, was induced, in 1548, to transfer his allegiance, and the vast store of knowledge and experience he had acquired at the Casa de Contratación, to England, where he lived until his death in 1558. During his old age he occupied himself with the instruction of navigators and with the production of charts and navigational instruments.

First of a line of English master-navigators was Richard Chancellor,[2] who discovered the Arctic route to Russia—a line which included

[1] The renowned Casa de Contratación at Seville, where navigators were instructed, examined, and approved.

[2] Chancellor was one of the first English mariners to receive a thorough training, under the supervision of Sebastian Cabot and the learned Dr. Dee, in the new nautical science.

Stephen Borough, another mariner of the new school, and his brother, William, who succeeded Chancellor as the chief pilots of the Muscovy Company, and surveyed and charted the White Sea and the adjacent coasts; and John Davis, the greatest scientific navigator of his day, who, before the close of the century, could justly testify to the skill of Englishmen in navigation and hydrography and who could claim that in seamanship also ' wee are not to be matched by any nation of the earth.'

At the same time the growing interest of the English in the arts of astronomy, mathematics, geography, navigation, hydrography, and cartography were evidenced by a steady stream of original English treatises which formed a substantial contribution to the advance of nautical science. In the last half of the sixteenth century skilled and experienced instrument-makers, like Humphrey Cole, Emery Molyneux, and Robert Norman, were producing really excellent work; and the standard chart used at sea today owes much to the patient labours of two English mathematicians.[1]

At the beginning of the Elizabethan era English mariners still depended upon translations of Spanish works like the well-known *Arte de Navegar* by Martin Cortes which was in 1561 translated into English by Richard Eden and published at the expense of the Muscovy Company. In 1574, however, there appeared William Bourne's *Regiment of the Sea*: a manual of navigation which was essentially practical and supplemented Cortes' in many important respects; and like Cortes' was destined to pass through many editions. The *Regiment* contained simpler tables of the sun's declination than those given by Cortes and also the earliest known description of the means whereby a vessel's speed was estimated with the aid of a log and line. In 1581 the publication of the *New Attractive*, by Robert Norman, and the *Variation of the Compass*, by William Borough, represented a solid advance in the study of terrestrial magnetism. Norman and Borough were recognized authorities on the mariner's compass abroad as well as at home. Above all, there were two works published towards the end of the period which testify to the steady progress that had been achieved in the theory and practice of navigation during the last two decades of the century. The *Tractatus de Globis*, written by Robert Hues, a travelled and distinguished mathematician, and Captain

[1] See *infra*, p. 64.

John Davis's *The Seaman's Secrets* were both published in 1594. This latter work, arranged in the then customary form of a dialogue, was a practical and comprehensive manual of navigation, which embodied the lifelong experience of the greatest of all the Elizabethan navigators. In this connection it is worthy of notice that Davis's traverse book for his third voyage of discovery, included in *The Seaman's Secrets*, is set out in substantially the same form which ships' log-books have followed ever since.

One of the principal contributory factors towards the English westward expansion of the seventeenth century was the publication, in 1600, by Richard Hakluyt in his *Principal Navigations, Voyages and Discoveries of the English Nation* of two Spanish rutters of the North Atlantic, which in this way made accessible to his countrymen the hard-bought experience of successive generations of Spanish navigators.

By the 1570s the astrolabe and cross-staff were in fairly common use among seamen of north-western Europe engaged on long voyages as they had been for generations among mariners of the Peninsula. The earliest known reference to a quadrant and cross-staff carried in an English vessel was in 1533. In the *Regiment for the Sea* the need for the new methods of navigation was emphasized. ' And also he that taketh charge for long voyages ', observed William Bourne, ' ought to haue knowledge in plats or cardes [charts], and also in such instruments, as he meete to take the heighth of the Sunne or any Starre.' Though the astrolabe was commonly used for observations in the tropics, it was found by experience that the cross-staff was the better instrument for measuring the altitude of the sun in the highest latitudes; and it was also handier in heavy weather. Towards the close of the sixteenth century the back-staff, or Davis's Quadrant, which was an improved form of the cross-staff, largely superseded the older instruments. As afterwards improved by Flamsteed, the back-staff was the forerunner of the modern method of taking angles by reflection, by superimposing upon the direct image of the heavenly body the reflection of the horizon.

It is to be remembered that latitude sailing by celestial observation was the underlying principle of all ocean navigation down to the introduction of the chronometer.[1] In such standard works as Martin

[1] See C. V. Sölver and G. J. Marcus in *The Mariner's Mirror*, XLIV, pp. 22–5.

Cortes' *Arte de Navegar* this was taken for granted. Because they knew that they could not safely trust their reckoning, mariners were accustomed to steer for the latitude of their destination, and then alter course to the eastward or westward, as the case might be, until they made their landfall. Latitude sailing was practised by the Portuguese in the second half of the fifteenth century. It was practised by Christopher Columbus on his homeward passage from the Caribbean in 1493. It was practised by Vasco de Gama and his successors sailing to the East: in 1500, in the sailing directions which Pedro Cabral had from Vasco da Gama, the former was advised to steer to the southward until he arrived in the latitude of the Cape and then shape an easterly course for the Indian Ocean. Half a century or so later vessels from north European ports bound for Lisbon or Cadiz were accustomed to shape a southerly course across the Bay until they reached the latitude of the Rock of Lisbon or Cape St. Vincent and then alter course to the eastward until they made their landfall. On his return from the North-West in 1577 Frobisher made his southing until he arrived in the latitude of Scilly and then steered an easterly course along the parallel of latitude of his intended landfall.[1] That great Elizabethan navigator,

[1] The narrative of Frobisher's return passage furnishes an admirable illustration of the use of the new nautical science in conjunction with the old traditional methods of navigation, e.g. latitude sailing by celestial observation outside soundings, combined with lead and look-out when within the 100-fathom line:—' Having spent foure or five dayes in traverse of the seas with contrarye winde, making oure souther way good as neare as we could, to raise our degrees to bring ourselves with the latitude of Sylley, we tooke the heighth the tenth of September, and founde ourselves in the latitude of [*cypher*] degrees and ten minutes. The eleaventh of September about sixe a clocke at night the wind came good southwest, we verde [*veered*] short and sette oure course southest. And upon Thursday, the twelfth day of September, taking the height, we were in the latitude of [*cypher*] and a halfe, and reckoned oure selves not paste one hundred and fiftie leagues short of Sylley, the weather faire, the winde large at west-south-west, we kepte our course southest. The thirteenth daye the height [latitude] being taken, we founde ourselves to be in the latitude of [*cypher*] degrees, the wind west-south-west, then being in the height of Sylley, and we kept our course east, to run in with the sleeve or channel so called, being our narrow seas, and reckoned as shorte of Sylley twelve leagues. Sonday, the fifteenth of September, about foure of the clocke, wee began to sounde with oure lead, and hadde grounde at sixty-one fadome depth, white small sandie grounde, and reckned us upon the backe of Sylley, and set our course easte and by north, easte north-easte, and north-east away. The sixteenth of September, about eight of the clocke in the morning sounding, we had sixty-five fadome osey sande, and thought ourselves athwart of Saint Georges Channel a little within the bankes. And bearing a small saile all nighte, we made many soundings, whiche were aboute fortie fadome, and so shallowe that we coulde not well tell where we were. The seaventeenth of September we sounded, and had fortie fadome, and were not farre off the landes end, branded sande with small worms and cockle-shells, and were shotte beteene Sylley and the landes ende,

John Davis, returning from his voyage to the North-West in 1587, like Frobisher before him, sailed down to the latitude of the Channel and then shaped an easterly course until he made the Lizard. Similarly Cavendish, returning from his voyage round the world in 1586-8, sailed north from St. Helena until he was in the latitude of the northernmost Azores and then 'haled est, and east and by south' until he sighted Flores and Corvo. The Earl of Cumberland, bound for the Azores in 1589, first sailed down to lat. 39° N. (which was the latitude of his destination), and then steered east for the Azores.

Various attempts were made in the course of the sixteenth and seventeenth centuries to discover a method of calculating the longitude from the variation of the compass. Columbus had endeavoured by this means to ascertain his approximate longitude on his later voyages; and during the seventeenth century the masters of English merchantmen sailing to the East Indies were accustomed to record their position by latitude and variation; but by the middle of that century it was generally realized that the laws governing the variation of the compass were very little understood, and the problem of longitude determination was not finally solved till the invention of the chronometer.

A factor of prime importance in the progress of navigation during the Elizabethan era was the influence of mathematicians like Recorde, Hues, Hariot, and Wright; the result of their labours was that during the next reign navigation was becoming largely a mathematical science. One of the most interesting and important works on this subject was the mathematical text-book, *The Whetstone of Witte*, dedicated by its author, Dr. Robert Recorde, to the Governors of the Muscovy Company. 'Robert Recorde's work may have been popular, elementary, instructional,' says Waters, 'but it was invaluable for just that reason. It brought mathematics out of the scholar's closet into the merchant's counting-house and into the sea-captain's cabin.'[1]

and being within the baye, we were not able to double the pointe wyth a south and by east way, but were fayne to make another boorde [*tack*], the wynde beeyng at southwest, and by weast, and yet could not double the poynte, to come cleere of the landes ende, to beare along the Channell: and the weather cleered up when we were hard aboorde the shore, and we made the landes ende perfite, and so put up alongst Sainte Georges Channell: and the weather beeyng very foule at sea, we coveted some harborough, bycause our steerage was broken, and so came to anker in Padstowe roade in Cornewall.'

[1] D. W. Waters, *The Art of Navigation in England in Elizabethan and Early Stuart Times* (1958), p. 95.

The remarkable progress that had been achieved in the knowledge and practice of navigation in this age was shown in the significant increase of English trade and colonization in the early seventeenth century; more especially in the ventures of the Chartered Companies to the East Indies and to North America, as well as in the many private and clandestine ventures to Central and South America.

This new nautical science, however, did not go unchallenged. That some of the older shipmasters remained unconvinced by the march of progress is to be surmised from a significant observation made by William Bourne in the *Regiment for the Sea*,

> for I haue knowen within this 20 yeares that them that wer auncient masters of shippes hath derided and mocked them that haue occupied their cardes and plattes; and also the obseruation of the altitude of the Pole, saying: that they care not for their sheepes skinnes, for he could keepe a better account vpon a boord.[1] And when that they dyd take the latitude, they would call them starre shooters and sunne shooters; and would aske if they had striken it.

The first recorded chart of the Thames estuary dates back to about 1547. Later in the sixteenth century William Borough, one of the earliest English hydrographers, drew charts of north European waters for the Muscovy Company. In 1569 the appearance of Gerard Mercator's great chart of the world marked an era in the history of cartography. Mercator himself was a Fleming and cosmographer to the Duke of Cleves; but the mathematical principle of his new projection was worked out independently by two Englishmen, Edward Wright, a well-known lecturer on navigation, and Thomas Hariot, who was navigational adviser to Sir Walter Ralegh. The projection was generally adopted for the construction of charts and was in common use for ocean navigation by about 1630. The importance of Mercator's projection to navigation was that on it rhumb lines were represented by straight lines. Courses and bearings could therefore be laid down by using a ruler and protractor. Though distances were distorted the bearings of places on the chart were correctly represented and distances could be measured off accurately. The advantages of the new projection greatly outweighed the disadvantages; and on it practically all ocean charts were, and ever since have been, drawn.

The sixteenth century also saw the rapid development of the

[1] The daily reckoning of course and distance made good was noted on a traverse board.

Corporation of Trinity House. In the Middle Ages there seems to have been some kind of seamen's guild at Deptford. This was now reorganized as a guild of pilots and entrusted with certain rights and responsibilities. Incorporated by Henry VIII in the year 1514, in response to a petition from the Thames shipmasters, the Corporation of Trinity House of ' Deptford Strond ' was empowered ' to make, erect, and set up such and so many Beacons, Marks, and Signs for the Sea, in such place or places of the Sea shores and up lands near the Sea-Coasts or Forelands of the Sea, only for Sea Marks, as to them shall deem most meet, needful, and requisite, whereby the Dangers may be avoided and escaped, and Ships the better come into their Ports without peril.' Similar corporations were set up, during the same reign, at Newcastle and Hull; though the one at Deptford was always the most important. These measures were presently supplemented by the Act of 1565, which empowered Trinity House to establish as many marks and beacons along the coasts, as well as in the approaches to ports, throughout England and Wales, as might be deemed necessary: the cost of their erection and maintenance to be met out of the shipping dues which the Corporation was entitled to levy. The destruction of steeples and conspicuous trees used as marks was prohibited under penalty of £100 fine. The certification of masters and pilots competent to undertake overseas and oceanic voyages was also regulated by this Act.

Though from its foundation London had always been the chief port in the realm, its expansion had been to some extent handicapped by the navigational difficulties in the approaches and passage of the Thames. Vessels had unloaded or discharged at Southampton and other Channel ports in order to avoid the doubling of the North Foreland, the changeable winds and strong tidal-streams in the Straits of Dover, and the intricate navigation of the Thames estuary. The revolutionary advance in the design and rigging of ships during the period under review had made the passage a far less formidable undertaking than it had been in the past; and the provision of an adequate supply of skilled and experienced pilots and of buoys and beacons, together with the buoying, beaconing, and dredging of the channels in the estuary, was a major factor in the immense expansion of London's trade and shipping during the later Tudor era. Another step forward was the abandonment by the Lord Admiral, in 1593, of certain offices and dues in respect of shipping, which were then made over by the Crown to Trinity House. Towards the close of the century, Edward Wright testified to the good work done by the Corporation in doing away with ' many gross and dangerous enormities '.

5

Compared with the Spanish system, with its pronounced emphasis on governmental control, regular instruction at an official school of navigation, and careful regimentation, the English approach to the problems of the new age was flexible and individualistic. It was in fact admirably suited to the needs and temper of the Elizabethan seamen; and the Council for its part made certain of a sufficient ' store of skylful Pilotes '.

' After seeing to the provision of ships and seamen ', the historian of English navigation has observed, ' this was its chief concern. By itself participating in overseas ventures, and by encouraging individual adventurers of outstanding merit, such as Hawkins, Drake, and Frobisher, to take well educated young gentlemen to sea with them, to learn the art of navigation, the Crown began at the same time to ensure that there should also be a sufficiency of men qualified by navigational skill and experience as well as by birth and education to command its ships in the event of war.'[1]

The English had been slow off the mark, indeed; for it was not until the 1570s that their maritime expansion really got under way. But after that the speed of their advance was almost miraculous. In the course of only a few decades they had overhauled the pioneer maritime peoples of the Renaissance, the Italians, the Portuguese, and the Spaniards, and were making their own important and distinctive contribution to the science of navigation.

From the sun-baked ports of Spanish America to the palaces and pagodas of southern Asia; from the fogs of the Grand Banks to the crystalline waters of the Aegean archipelago; from the stormy track around the Horn to the ice-bound shores of Greenland and Lapland: our national flag, the red cross of St. George, presently proclaimed the advent of the future lords of the seven seas.

Well might Hakluyt, in his preface to *The Principal Navigations*,

[1] Waters, *op. cit.*, p. 114.

Voyages and Discoveries of the English Nation, observe in a celebrated passage that in years past his countrymen had been reproached for their ' sluggish security ' and reluctance to attempt ' discoveries and notable enterprises by sea ': whereas now (he declared) the English

in searching the most opposite corners and quarters of the world and, to speak plainly, in compassing the vast globe of the earth more than once, have excelled all the nations and people of the earth. For which of the kings of this land before her Majesty had their banners ever seen in the Caspian Sea? Which of them hath ever dealt with the Emperor of Persia, as her Majesty hath done, and obtained for her merchants large and loving privileges? Who ever saw before this regimen an English lieger [ambassador] in the stately porch of the Grand Signior at Constantinople? Who ever found English consuls and agents at Tripolis in Syria, at Aleppo, at Babylon, at Basra and, what is more, who ever heard of Englishmen at Goa before now? What English ships did heretofore ever anchor in the mighty river of Pale? Pass and repass the unpassable (in former opinion) strait of Magellan, range along the coast of Chile, Peru and all the backside of Nova Hispania, further than any Christian ever passed, traverse the mighty breadth of the South Sea, land upon the Luçones [Philippines] in despite of the enemy, enter into alliance, amity and traffic with the princes of the Moluccas and the Isle of Java, double the famous Cape of Bona Speranza, arrive at the Isle of St. Helena, and last of all return home most richly laden with the commodities of China, as the subjects of this now flourishing monarchy have done?

IV

The Spanish War

I

At the opening of the Elizabethan era it was France—with her ally, Scotland—and not Spain, that was the greater peril to England. This was the crucial fact that governed Elizabeth's first moves on the European chessboard. France, still a formidable Power, was accounted the national enemy; and so long as ' the postern gate of the North ' remained ajar her small realm was liable to be ground between the upper and lower millstones. The Queen's position was a hazardous one: the kingdom was weak and divided, the crown heavily in debt. To the judicious support of Philip II in the early years of her reign Elizabeth probably owed her throne. In the ensuing decade the national economy steadily improved. Each year saw the country stronger and more prosperous. The religious settlement imposed by the Queen and her ministers was apparently achieving outward uniformity, as large numbers of Catholics were gradually weaned from the old faith and quietly absorbed into the established church. France, fast drifting into civil war, had ceased to be an urgent problem. At the other end of the kingdom the postern gate was finally slammed to by the triumph of Scottish Calvinism under John Knox, which put a period to the ancient alliance with France. The Treaty of Edinburgh, which the English Council in July 1560 concluded with the Scottish government, was one of the decisive achievements of the reign. It provided for the withdrawal of the French troops from Scotland and the demolition of the fortress of Leith.

The long-standing alliance between England and Spain had been mutually advantageous to both countries, being based upon common interests; it had lasted until well on in the sixteenth century, when the break-up of the rival Valois-Hapsburg combinations and the advance of the Counter-Reformation eventually brought about a re-alignment of forces, as a result of which the growing hegemony of Spain was

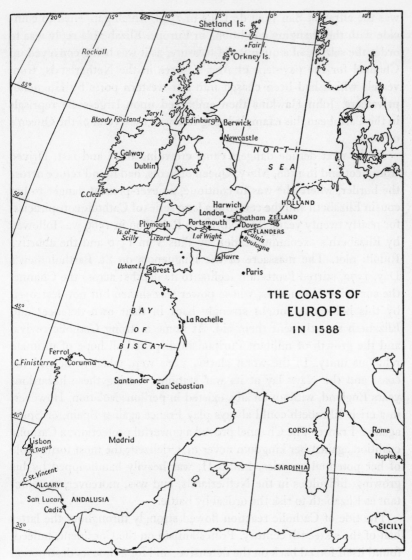

THE COASTS OF
EUROPE
IN 1588

confronted by a Protestant group, headed by England. Another determining factor was the serious clash of economic interests consequent
upon the expansion of English overseas trade. The increasingly
aggressive ventures of John Hawkins, together with the high-handed
commercial policy of England in the Netherlands, had engendered a
dangerous friction. The turning-point in Anglo-Spanish relations

was the affray at San Juan de Ulua in 1568, which happened to coincide with the changing conditions in Europe. Elizabeth's reply was to order the seizure of a quantity of treasure, as it was being conveyed up Channel for the payment of Alva's forces in the Netherlands, from vessels which had been chased into our western ports by Huguenot privateers. John Hawkins then embarked upon large-scale reprisals in the Caribbean, his example being followed by several of the Queen's officers.

In the next decade dangers came crowding thick and fast. Driven from Scotland in 1568, Mary, Queen of Scots, had found refuge across the border, where she was to continue, an ever-present danger to her cousin Elizabeth and the centre of a long series of Catholic conspiracies, for nearly twenty years. The Northern Rebellion in 1569 was followed by Elizabeth's excommunication by Pius V in 1570 and the abortive Ridolfi plot. The massacre of the Huguenots on St. Bartholomew's Day, 1572, stirred Protestant feeling to its depths: across the Channel the surviving Huguenots, whose power was shaken but not destroyed by this holocaust, fought strongly back in their own defence; and Elizabeth secretly sent them aid. At home a strong Catholic revival and the growth of militant Puritanism dispelled all hope of ultimate religious unity. In the worst alarms steps were taken to defend the coast and the Navy lay at its war stations. During these hazardous years England, without an ally, existed in perilous isolation. However, in a crisis Elizabeth could always play France against Spain, or Spain against France. The Channel proved a powerful protection; a Catholic coalition against her kingdom never materialized; the most formidable of her potential enemies, Philip II, was heavily handicapped by his growing difficulties in the Netherlands, and was, moreover, as reluctant as Elizabeth to risk the ordeal by battle.

The tide of Catholic reaction flowed strongly throughout the latter half of the sixteenth century. Protestantism on the Continent, indeed, found itself forced back on the defensive: and for a time its destruction seemed imminent. But the forces of the Counter-Reformation stopped short at the water's edge. Beyond the reach of the incomparable Spanish *tertios* the Channel and the narrow seas swarmed with the Protestant privateers of three nations. French Protestants under Coligny's flag, assisted—with Elizabeth's connivance—by their English co-religionists, preyed unceasingly on the busy traffic passing between Spain and the Netherlands. Between the great Huguenot stronghold of La Rochelle and Protestant Plymouth there existed strong and enduring ties of friendship and common interests. It was for the most part at Plymouth that the freebooters were accustomed to dispose of their booty and replenish their supplies; the proceeds of this warfare financed the Huguenot armies on land. Presently Dutch Calvinists, fleeing from the wrath of Alva and the Council of Blood, followed the example of the Rochellois. In the autumn of 1569 there were 18 Dutch privateers at sea; by the following spring the number had increased to over 100. On 1 April 1572, the town of Brill, commanding the entry into the lower Rhine, was seized and held by the Beggars of the Sea under William de la Marck. Soon after Flushing and Enkhuizen were taken in the same way. In June and July the *Gueux*, sallying forth from these three bases, brought most of the towns of Zeeland and Holland under the authority of William of Orange.

The Spanish troops advancing to recapture Brill were forced to beat a hurried retreat when the Beggars cut the sluices and let in the sea; and the surrounding polder was engulfed in a rapidly rising flood. Shortly after the flotilla which the Spaniards had assembled in Antwerp, with the object of breaking up the blockade of Walcheren, was heavily defeated by the Dutch under their admiral, Boisot; and Middelburg surrendered to the insurgents. In 1573 Alva was summarily recalled.

The siege of Leyden in 1574 marked a turning-point in the progress of the revolt. The Spaniards, moving out from Amsterdam, had occupied a wide area of the adjacent countryside; once more the Dutch opened the sluices and cut the dykes, and the water flowed in to within a short distance of the city: but the dykes were still strongly held by the Spaniards, as were also the roads to Utrecht and The Hague. Weeks went by while the garrison, sick with hope deferred, awaited the long-expected relief. At last, on 20 September, with a strong spring-tide and the angry wrack of a full nor'-wester tearing across the sky, the swollen Maas burst through the sluices and breaches in the dykes; suddenly the flood-water, which for long had risen no higher than twelve inches, deepened to thirty-six, and the Dutch flotilla sailed in. Hauling and shoving the galleys by main force across the shallows, their crews at last approached the beleaguered city.

F 2

Early in October the Spaniards were obliged to abandon their positions on the dykes before Leyden, and fled in panic haste before the onset of the dreaded *Gueux*. In the nick of time two supply-ships sailed up to the city walls and the starving garrison was saved.

The revolt of the Dutch Calvinists proved a much more serious affair than the insurrection of the Rochellois. In secure possession of the entire complex of estuaries, islands, rivers, lakes, and canals of Zeeland and Holland, which provided an ideal theatre for the kind of amphibious warfare in which they excelled, the Dutch successfully flouted the foremost military Power in Europe. Neither Philip nor Alva possessed a navy capable of dealing with these freebooters. In the shoal waters in which their light craft usually operated the Beggars had things all their own way. The capture of Brill ushered in the long-drawn-out war of sieges and blockades that was slowly but inexorably to sap the vital strength of Spain. The revolt of the Netherlands forms one of the most striking and significant examples in history of the influence of sea power upon the fortunes of nations.

2

After the disastrous affray at San Juan de Ulua the era of aggressive commerce had been followed by a period of what might be described as private hostilities against Spain, varying from plain piracy to more or less authorized privateering. As early as the 1530s French corsairs had been active off the Azores and in the Caribbean. Since then almost every place of consequence in the West Indies had been stormed and sacked, some of them several times over. The activities of the corsairs exacted a severe toll from Spanish trade. To check these depredations the Spaniards presently had recourse to a convoy system which effectually protected their commerce on the high sea; their settlements and shipping in the Caribbean and on the Main, however, for long remained vulnerable to attack.

In the second half of the century English freebooters in increasing numbers joined in these operations. Their daring incursions into the close preserves of Spanish trade and settlement across the ocean constitute one of the most dramatic and potent factors in the maritime enterprise of the Elizabethan age. These ventures—the majority of which are little known—appear to have followed the same general pattern. Ship after ship sailed westward on the track of richer loot than was likely to be won in home waters. Hard tack, salt junk, and stinking water or sour beer was their lot on many an outward passage. To the reckless youngsters comprising the bulk of these crews the first prospect of the New World, with its luxuriant vegetation, exotic perfumes, and luscious tropical fruits, must have seemed like a vision of paradise. On arrival at their destination it was their custom to conceal, and sometimes even to burn, the vessel in which they had crossed the Atlantic, in full confidence that when the time came for them to return homeward they would be able to seize some ocean-going craft from the Spaniards. For their operations in American waters they usually relied on small, light, handy pinnaces equipped with oars as well as sails. The secret of their success lay in their skilful exploitation of the kindred factors of speed and surprise.

It was during this time that Francis Drake began to win undying fame as a master-corsair 'beyond the Line'. He was then in his middle twenties: a short, sturdy, thick-set man with keen blue eyes and a ruddy beard; a commander of lightning decision, iron will, and inexhaustible resource; a fervent Protestant, and a born leader of men. In Spanish eyes Drake was simply a pirate. In his own view, however, he regarded himself as at war with the King of Spain—a war which had begun with the treacherous attack at San Juan de Ulua. The wonder of it is that as the years went by and the feud developed not merely his own countrymen but Europe generally began to share Drake's view of the matter. It is probable, though not proven, that he assisted in a French venture to the West Indies in 1569. In that year, apparently for the first time, corsairs lay at the mouth of the Chagre River, and began to prey on the rich traffic between Spain and South America.

In 1570 Drake was back in the Caribbean, probably engaged in illicit trading; and in the following year he sailed to the Spanish Main in the 25-ton *Swan*. Waylaying the coastal traffic near Nombre de Dios, he secured a good many prizes, including a ship of 180 tons, which he carried off to a secluded anchorage in the Gulf of Darien—a good natural harbour with some ten fathoms of water, abounding in fish and game—to which he gave the name of Port Pheasant. During part of this time he co-operated with a crew of Frenchmen led by one Leyerre. In their attacks on Spanish shipping Drake and Leyerre trusted to swift and flexible tactics. The commander of the *flota* lying at Nombre de Dios, Don Diego de Valdes, chased the intruders with two armed galleons. But the corsairs in their light and handy craft eluded him with ease, using sweeps in calms and in a good sailing breeze standing in for shoal waters where the Spaniards dared not follow.

The significance of these developments lay in the threat to the vital line of communications, at its weakest and most vulnerable point, between Spain and her South American possessions. During the period under survey the bulk of the traffic proceeded to Nombre de Dios on the northern coast of the Isthmus, where the cargoes were loaded into barks for the passage up the Chagre River to the post of Venta Cruces, after which the merchandise was conveyed by pack-train to Panama. Both by land and sea this commerce lay open to attack. In the mountainous, densely wooded interior dwelt the warlike Cimaroons, a mixed tribe of runaway negro slaves and Indians, whose sporadic assaults on their land-communications were already beginning to trouble the Spaniards. If, over and above, the intruders from across the ocean were to develop their offensive against the communications of the Isthmus, Spain's hold on the riches of the New World would be gravely imperilled. Already her officials in the danger zone were alive to the perturbing situation that was arising. ' As to danger ', one of them observed in May 1571, ' and the damage and destruction done by corsairs along the coast, and by outlaw negroes on land, the situation grows worse daily, for neither the barks of the Chagre River trade to the House at Cruces nor the overland pack-trains have been able to make their journeys without being assaulted and robbed.'[1]

Drake's next voyage to the Spanish Main was his first major venture in independent command, and one—to quote his own word—which ' made ' him. Accompanied by two of his brothers and John Oxenham, he sailed from Plymouth on 24 May 1572 in the *Pascoe* (70 tons) and the *Swan*, and, making for his former refuge on the Darien coast, there assembled three pinnaces which he had brought out in sections from England. At Port Pheasant he was joined by another English vessel with a crew of thirty men, bringing his forces up to a total of just over seventy; after which, stealing westward in the pinnaces up the coast, he launched a sudden night attack on Nombre de Dios. The attack

[1] *Documents concerning English Voyages to the Spanish Main*, 1569–1580, ed. I. A. Wright (Hakluyt Society, 1932), p. 25.

74

was brilliantly successful. The town was carried by storm and most of its defenders fled. But before the ' mouth of the Treasure House of the World ', Drake, who had been badly wounded in the affray, fainted through loss of blood; whereupon his men insisted on abandoning the town and bearing back their leader to the boats.

This was the first of a heartbreaking series of failures and defeats. For a time it seemed as if the stars in their courses were fighting against them. In August Drake appeared off Cartagena on the Main; but warning of their approach had already gone out, and they found the garrison too strong for them. In September Drake set up his camp by the Magdalena River, where he obtained food and supplies, and later got in touch with the Cimaroons. He filled in his time harrying the coastal trade, and also gathered much valuable information about the conveyance of the Peruvian treasure across the Isthmus. In this retreat he and his followers passed the rainy season.

At last in January 1573, the *flota* again arrived off Nombre de Dios to lade the treasure for Spain. Shortly after Drake, in concert with the Cimaroons, prepared plans to ambush the treasure-train at the start of its journey across the Isthmus. Accompanied by a chosen band of Englishmen and friendly Indians, with Oxenham as his lieutenant, Drake slowly ascended the densely forested slopes of the Cordilleras and arrived, after four days' march, on the highest ridge, where the Cimaroons led him to ' a goodly and great high tree ', from the upper branches of which it was possible to view both the Atlantic and Pacific Oceans. Drake and Oxenham climbed the tree in turn, and gazed southward over the myriad tree-trops towards the distant blue line of the Pacific; and the former ' besought Almightie God of his goodnesse to give him life and leave to sayle once in an English Ship in that sea.' Another two days' march brought them down into the open pampas country between the mountains and Panama. Hidden in the tall grass near the post of Venta Cruces, on the Chagre River, they prepared to attack the mule-train. Owing to the imprudence of a drunken seaman, however, the attempt miscarried. Drake then returned by forced marches to the north coast to secure the safety of his rearguard.

With his forces re-united, he next made a pact with a Huguenot captain, Le Testu, and his men. It was then decided to make a last attempt to win the treasure. With a picked force of Englishmen,

Frenchmen, and Cimaroons, Drake pushed up-river in the pinnaces, and then took to the jungle; after a march of twenty miles or so, the party emerged by the Panama road at the back of Nombre de Dios; at which point they could hear the hammering of the carpenters as they worked about the *flota* in the harbour below. For hours the party lay in hiding. At last the deep-toned mule bells could be heard in the distance and they braced themselves for the attack. This time there was no mischance. Allowing the head of the cavalcade to pass un-molested, the men suddenly burst from their hiding-place as the mules bearing the gold and silver approached, and seized the treasure. Then, with as much gold as they could carry (they were obliged to bury most of the bar-silver), they raced for the ships. Thus had Drake, at the eleventh hour, snatched victory out of the jaws of defeat. In mid-April they finally stood out to sea, ' passing hard by Cartagena with a Flag of Saint George in the maine top of our Fregat ': worked over to Cuba, where, in desperate need of water, they got ' a good store of raine ', enabling them to sail for England by the shortest and speediest route—23 days from the Cape of Florida to the Isles of Scilly: ' and so arrived at *Plimouth* on Sunday about Sermon-time, August the ninth 1573 '.[1]

About this time many other English privateers raided the Caribbean. The most important of these ventures was that of John Oxenham in 1576.[2] It was Oxenham who conceived the idea of seizing and per-manently holding the Isthmus against the Spanish settlers. The project appears to have been entirely feasible. The Isthmus at this time was only weakly held; a force of two or three hundred was the most that the Spaniards could expect to put into the field against an invader. Even so, Oxenham's force was too small for the work: when he arrived on the Main he had hardly more than fifty men. He ran his vessel ashore up a small creek, covered her with ' boughes of trees ', buried her guns and stores, and then marched across the Isthmus. As in the raid of 1572–3, the English entered into an alliance with the Cimaroon Indians. On the banks of a river flowing southward to the Gulf of Panama Oxenham and his men constructed a pinnace ' five and fortie foote by the keele ', and rowed her downstream to the Pacific. There

[1] *Ibid.*, p. 326.
[2] The chapter entitled ' The True and Tragical History of Mr. John Oxenham ' in Charles Kingsley's *Westward Ho !* is based upon this episode.

they captured two treasure-ships and raided the Pearl Islands. Oxenham's irruption threw the whole western coast of South America into a panic. The threat to the treasure-route across the Isthmus, represented by the pact between the English and Cimaroons, was clearly understood. Unless vigorous measures were taken at once the whole Spanish economy would be undermined. ' Corsairs have been more numerous this year than in any since I came to the Indies,' wrote a Spanish Officer from Veragua in 1576. ' Five have appeared off this port, the least formidable with eighty men.'[1] But the Audencia at Panama rose to the occasion, and the Spanish troops were well led. A strong force, sailing northward from Peru, hurried up to their support. In the ensuing weeks the small band of English raiders was remorselessly hunted down. During Oxenham's absence on the other side of the Isthmus, his shipping on the northern coast was discovered by the Spaniards; and most of his guns, munitions, and trade goods were captured. Moreover, the party which had been raiding in the Gulf of Panama had imprudently left traces of their passage, whereby the enemy were presently able to track them. Most of the booty which they had taken was recaptured. The Spanish arquebusiers advancing through the jungle came suddenly upon Oxenham's lair, and most of the band were made prisoners. The pursuers pressed on into the wilds of Vallona where the survivors were believed to be in hiding. There they discovered and destroyed the Cimaroon stronghold of Ronconcholon, and fired their crops and banana-groves. About a dozen of the English shook off the pursuit and, constructing a canoe, got away to sea off the north coast and took a coasting vessel in which they sailed for England (whether they ever got there is unknown). Most of the prisoners were dispatched out of hand at Panama. Oxenham and his lieutenants were taken to Lima. There, unable to produce any kind of licence or commission, they were eventually hanged as pirates.

The semi-piratical ventures of the Elizabethan sea-dogs culminated in Drake's great voyage of 1577-80. This had originated in the project of Sir Richard Grenville and others for the discovery and colonization of a vast Southern Continent, *Terra Australis Incognita* (of which Tierro del Fuego was believed to form part), which was supposed to lie in the South Pacific. With the Queen's connivance and approval the object of the voyage was presently changed to a raid on the treasure

[1] Wright, *op cit.*, p. 100.

of Spanish America. Drake sailed out of Plymouth Sound in the late autumn of 1577 with the *Pelican*, 120 tons, *Elizabeth*, 80, and *Marigold*, 30, and two auxiliary vessels. He stood southward to the Cape Verde Islands and thence sailed to South America. The following summer at Port St. Julian, near the entrance to the Straits of Magellan, he destroyed his two shore-ships, and had one of his chief officers, Thomas Doughty, tried and beheaded on a charge of mutiny. A few weeks later he delivered the well-known discourse in which he laid down the rules of discipline to be observed in the hazardous venture that lay before them and founded a new tradition in naval leadership. After passing in seventeen days through the Straits the *Marigold* was lost, the *Elizabeth* forced back into the Straits, and the *Pelican* driven as far south as the 57th parallel by a series of violent westerly and north-westerly gales. There they discovered that, contrary to common belief, there was ' no maine nor Island to be seene to the southwards, but that the Atlanticke Ocean and the South Sea meete in a most large and free scope '. For the first time in recorded history civilized man beheld the gale-lashed waters off Cape Horn. Eventually the weather moderated, and Drake was able to stand to the northward in the *Pelican* (which he had renamed the *Golden Hind*); and then with his armament of eighteen guns fell like a bolt from the blue upon the defenceless shipping and settlements along the west coast of South America.

As yet no warning of his approach had reached the Spaniards. It was this factor of *surprise*, combined with the formidable armament he carried, that enabled Drake to work such havoc with so small a force. On 5 December 1578, entering the small port of Valparaiso by moon-light, he surprised and captured a local craft, whose crew ' thinking us to have bene Spaniards and their friends, welcomed us with a drumme, and made ready a *bottija* of wine of *Chili* to drinke to us '. There were no more than half a dozen Spaniards on board and these were quickly overpowered. The inhabitants of Valparaiso fled to the mountains and the raiders looted the warehouses stored with wine and provisions.

In January 1579 they careened and tallowed the *Golden Hind* in the lonely bay of Salada, and hauled up their heavy guns from the hold. On 4 and 5 February, they seized some bar-silver at Tarapaca and Arica. On the 13th they cut the cables of the shipping in the roads of

Callao and set it adrift. On 1 March, about 150 leagues from Panama, there occurred the crowning achievement of this cruise, the capture after long pursuit of a treasure-ship known as the *Cacafuego*, and the transference to the hold of her captor of her rich lading, including such items as ' thirteene chests full of riyals of plate, four score pound weighte of golde, and sixe and twentie tunne of siluer '. Their prize also provided them with food-stuffs and ship's stores. They stood on up the North American coast and searched in vain for the North-West Passage; later they came southward to careen, and then, ballasted with Peruvian silver, sailed westward across the Pacific to the Moluccas, where they laded spices and entered into trade negotiations with a local sultan; then, early in January 1580, running before the trade wind in the perilous passage of the archipelago, they ' stuck fast upon a desperate shoale ' for some twenty hours, narrowly escaping ship-wreck; in the face of baffling winds it took them several more weeks to get clear of the Celebes, after which the *Golden Hind* sailed on to Java, whence in March course was shaped for the Cape of Good Hope; and then northward, by way of Sierra Leone, to England.

On 26 September they arrived ' safely with joyfull minds and thank-ful hearts to God ' in Plymouth Sound, having completed the first English circumnavigation of the globe. The following April, when his ship had been brought round to Deptford, the Queen visited Drake on board the *Golden Hind* and had him knighted by the Duc d'Alençon's ambassador. The booty he had brought home from the ends of the earth represented a sum considerably in excess of Eliza-beth's annual revenue and substantially increased the fluid capital of the kingdom. The great voyage of 1577–80 marked another milestone towards the eventual breach with Spain.

Drake was now a national hero—the first English sailor ever to become so: an inspiration to his countrymen, the terror of the Dons, and the focus and centre of the anti-Spanish feeling in England. The Queen kept him ever at her side, and was seen to converse with him ' as often as nine times a day '. ' The people generally ', observed Stowe, ' applauded his wonderful long adventures and rich prizes. His name and fame became admirable in all places, the people swarm-ing daily in the streets to behold him, vowing hatred to all that mis-liked him. . . . Books, pictures, and ballads were published in his praise; his opinion and judgment concerning marine affairs stood current.' In the years that followed the famous exploits of the great sea-captain were told and sung all over the kingdom.

Eight years later Thomas Cavendish achieved the second English circumnavigation (1586–8). Following in Drake's track, he crossed the Atlantic, passed through the Straits of Magellan, and sailed up the west coast of South America, destroying the enemy's shipping, burning his settlements, and levying a heavy toll of booty. He continued northward to the coast of California, where he waylaid and pursued the yearly galleon from the Philippines, the *Santa Ana*, laden with gold, silks, satins, damask, spices, and perfumes. ' We gave them chase some 3 or 4 houres ', records the narrator of this voyage, ' standing with our best advantage and working for the winde. In the afternoon we got up unto them, giving them the broad side with our great ordinance and a volee of small shot and presently layed the ship aboord.' After a stiff fight the *Santa Ana* surrendered, and Cavendish's men transferred to their own vessel as much of her rich lading as they could find room for. They sailed across the Pacific to the East Indies, and returned home round the Cape. It was, perhaps, symbolical of our country's emergence as an oceanic Power that Cavendish made his triumphant appearance in Plymouth Sound in the self-same week that Medina Sidonia's storm-tossed galleon struggled into Santander.

3

In the decade following the death of Henry VIII the effective strength of the royal fleet was not greatly reduced, though a good many of the smaller craft—among them thirteen 20-ton rowing barges—disappeared from the Navy list. Also the work of reorganization begun by Henry VIII was continued under his son and successor, Edward VI. Through the action of the Council the construction of a large dockyard at Chatham on the Medway was set in train, and a separate responsible organization for victualling inaugurated. The young King, who had inherited his father's interest in the sea, was a frequent visitor to Deptford, ' to se the buylding of his Highnes shippes '. Corruption was nevertheless rife during this reign; and though after the accession of Edward VI's half-sister, Mary, in 1522, the government of the kingdom was in the hands of a more reputable set of ministers, the conduct of the Navy was still far from satisfactory.

The year 1557 witnessed a grave national humiliation. England had lately been drawn into the Franco-Spanish quarrel through the influence of the Queen's husband, Philip II of Spain. An Allied success at St. Quentin, coupled with the approach of winter, had lulled both Spaniards and English into a false sense of security. The Spanish army was disbanded and the English fleet laid up. In December of that year, there being no winter squadron to guard the Channel, the French, under the Duke of Guise, appeared suddenly within the Pale in overwhelming strength and laid siege to Calais, where the English flag had flown for more than two centuries. The fortifications of Calais were obsolete, the leadership of our troops was inadequate; too late the Council sent orders for the relief of the garrison. On 10 January ' the heavy news came to England that the French had won Calais, the which was the heaviest tidings that ever was heard of.'[1] As a result of this disaster several large ships (of the old ' high-charged ' type) were laid down; and during the first twenty years of the reign of Elizabeth, though the fleet was maintained at barely half the strength of her father's, there was a significant improvement in quality, and the Queen's ships did their work efficiently, as in the winter of 1559–60, when a squadron under Winter helped to destroy the French hold on Scotland.

The general direction of naval affairs in the early part of Elizabeth's reign was in the hands of Sir William Cecil, later Lord Burghley. Cecil's steps to restore the English fisheries have already been noted. At the same time he strove, by various Acts, ' for the maintenance and increase of the Navy and mariners ' to encourage English shipping generally; to restrict the coastwise traffic to English vessels; to preserve the great oak forests of our southern counties, which yielded the chief part of the finest ship timber of the realm, from the consuming maw of the iron industry; to assure an adequate supply of naval stores, and to prohibit the export of English ordnance. In 1563 mariners were exempted from service with the militia. Throughout the reign the mercantile marine was periodically surveyed for the information of the Council. ' The strength of England on the seas,' says Waters, ' the skill and ability of her seamen were the conscious products of a national policy as carefully nurtured as it was deliberately begotten. The preparations for the Armada campaign

[1] Q. H. M. Prescott, *Spanish Tudor*, p. 483.

may be said to date from the accession of Elizabeth to the throne.'[1]

It is probable that the lessons learnt in the action at San Juan de Ulua had some bearing on naval construction during the middle part of the reign. In 1570 appeared the first true galleon of the Elizabethan era, the *Foresight*, 300 tons. This was followed in 1575 by the *Revenge*, 450 tons, described by Monson as ' low and snug in the water, like a galliasse ' and considered by Drake to be the finest fighting galleon of his day. The improvement in shipbuilding was gradual rather than sudden; but progress was steady and the later Elizabethan ships were designed on finer lines.

For twenty years the personnel of the Navy Board had been almost unchanged, with Sir William Winter and his brother George occupying three out of the five seats on it.[2] The squadrons which it periodically equipped and sent to sea appear to have been reasonably sound, well-found, and efficient. On the other hand, the administration was riddled with jobbery, graft, and waste. The Treasurer of the Navy, Benjamin Gonson, now old and failing, though aware of these abuses, was manifestly unable to prevent them. As Hawkins revealed to Burghley towards the end of 1577, the Queen was being constantly defrauded by her servants. The sum charged for building the *Revenge*, for example, had amounted to nearly double what the ship had actually cost. ' The Queen's work was done,' Williamson declares, ' but it was done at an excessive cost; and the surplus went into the pockets of a group of officials.'

Following upon these disclosures, Hawkins was presently appointed Treasurer of the Navy in succession to Gonson. In 1579, with a view to effecting certain reforms and economies he had in mind, the new Treasurer proposed a contract (known as ' the first bargain ') whereby the two master-shipwrights, Matthew Baker and Peter Pett, and himself were to undertake most of the ordinary care and maintenance of the Queen's ships in return for fixed sums yearly. The dry-docking and heavy repairs, or ' extraordinary ' expenditure, were to go on as before.

Like Admiral Sir John Fisher early in the present century, Hawkins in the ensuing years demonstrated how increased efficiency might be

[1] D. W. Waters in *Mariner's Mirror*, XXXV (1949), p. 91.
[2] Sir William Winter was Master of the Ordnance and also Surveyor of the Ships.

achieved at reduced cost. 'I have endeavoured', he afterwards declared, 'with all fidelity and painful travail to reduce the whole course of this office into such order as the same might be safe, sure, and bountifully provided, and performed with an easy and convenient charge, so that Her Majesty thereby should not be discouraged to maintain so necessary a defence for her royal state and country.' During the next few years, though there was little new construction, many of the Queen's ships were virtually rebuilt. The old type of warships, 'built loftie' and short in proportion to their beam, were lengthened and had their towering superstructures fore and aft drastically reduced. In the period 1581–4 three middle-sized ships, the *Antelope*, *Golden Lion*, and *Nonpareil*, were reconstructed in this way; and in 1584 the *Bull*, *Tiger*, and *Hope* are stated to have been 're-formed'. It was these new galleon-built ships which were used most continuously in the naval operations of the era. 'We find by experience', Ralegh testified many years later, 'that the greatest ships are least serviceable, go very deep to water, and of marvellous charge and fearful cumber, . . . besides, they are less nimble, less mainable, and very seldom employed. . . . A ship of 600 tons will carry as good ordnance as a ship of 1,200 tons; and though the greater have double her number of guns, the lesser will turn her broadsides twice before the greater can wind once, and so no advance in that overplus of ordnance.'

A bitter and protracted struggle now arose. It was complained by Borough, Winter, and other opponents of the Hawkins régime that the new Treasurer had thrust himself into office 'for the better filling of his purse' and that the ships under his charge had fallen into such decay as to be unfit for service. 'In the passing of these great things,' Hawkins avowed to Burghley, 'the adversaries of the work have continually opposed themselves against me and the service so far as they durst be seen in it, so that a number of trifling crossings and slanders the very walls of the realm have been brought in question.'

Later attacks on Hawkins centred on his new constructional policy. Both Sir William Winter and the new Clerk of the Ships, William Borough, strongly criticized the recent changes in ship-design. Hawkins was charged with having cut down the high and imposing superstructures of the Queen's ships, 'the romthes and commodious fights', so that they looked like galleasses. The truth was that Winter and Borough favoured a force of strongly manned, 'high-charged' floating fortresses—in fact, a Narrow Seas navy of the Henrician kind: what Hawkins and the new school wanted were ocean-going ships of the galleon type—long in proportion to their beam, low-built, weatherly and seaworthy, and heavily gunned. The old type of 'high-charged' warship, though sufficiently imposing in appearance, was liable in bad weather to develop strains and leaks, as Hawkins had learned to his cost in the ill-fated venture of 1569—and as the Spaniards were also to discover in the far more disastrous experience of 1588. Once again the opposition failed to prove its case; and in 1585 Burghley showed his confidence in Hawkins by agreeing to ' the second bargain ', whereby, in return for a fixed yearly sum, the latter was to undertake not merely a part, but the whole, of the work of building, equipping, and repairing the ships of the Navy.

In the early phase of the Spanish War a number of important new warships were added to the Navy. In 1586 the *Ark Ralegh* was built, and shortly after bought into the Navy and re-named the *Ark Royal*. In 1587 two galleons of the *Revenge* type, the *Vanguard*, 500 tons, and the *Rainbow*, 400 tons, were built by Baker and Pett respectively.

About this time there was a significant change in the cut of the sails, which in English craft were made flatter, so that the ships were faster, handier, and more weatherly. The superior sailing qualities of our ships were destined to be a factor of crucial importance in the naval war that lay ahead.

The high standard of English shipbuilding and seamanship may, perhaps, be gauged from the fact that, during the whole of the reign, not a single English warship was lost through shipwreck; while, over the same term of years, entire squadrons of Spaniards were overwhelmed by the sea. ' The ships ', William Hawkins observed from Plymouth, in February 1588, to his brother John, ' sit aground so strongly and are so staunch as if they were made of a whole tree.' ' I have been aboard of every ship that goeth out with me,' wrote Lord Charles Howard to Burghley about the same time, '. . . and I do thank God that they be in the estate they be in; and there is never a one of them that knows what a leak means.' He later declared that ' what false and villainous reports have soever been made of them ', the Queen had ' the strongest ships that any prince in Christendom hath '.

The largest class of galleons, like the *Triumph*, were 40 to 45-gun ships; the second-class galleons, like the *Lion* and *Revenge*, were

30 to 34-gun ships; and the third-class galleons, like the *Tiger*, were 20-gun ships. All the Queen's ships possessed, in addition to their heavy guns firing on the broadside, a secondary armament of small breech-loading guns mounted upon the superstructure and tops. It has been estimated by Professor Lewis that, of the heavy guns carried in the Queen's ships, rather more than 86 per cent. were of culverin types (i.e. for ' off-fighting ') in the campaign of 1588.

In the development of ship's guns, especially in the use of the truck carriage, the English were ahead of other nations. English ordnance had become famous throughout Europe. The Spaniards themselves constantly endeavoured to obtain guns from this country. The first to realize the potentialities of the broadside, the English had exploited this great new instrument of war for upwards of a generation in armed trade and privateering throughout the world; and the art of modern naval warfare was gradually taking shape in the hands of the forward school of English seamen under the leadership of Hawkins, Drake, Grenville, Fenner, and Frobisher.

Another important service of Hawkins was the creation of a large force of pinnaces. ' In 1588 the fleet had eighteen ocean-going ones. English naval intelligence was as efficient as Walsingham's political intelligence, the Navy never took its eyes off the coast of Spain, every movement was at once reported.'[1] These pinnaces were also used for inshore work and subsidiary services generally.

The high level of efficiency to which the royal fleet had been raised in these years on but slender means gives testimony of Hawkins' devotion and skill. He took steps to restrain the endemic dishonesty of the Tudor era. ' I think it would be meet there were a provost master attendant upon the Lord Admiral and Officers of the Navy to do such present execution aboard the ships upon the offenders as should be appointed.'[2] In the past the Queen's ships had been grossly overcrowded. In 1586 Hawkins had reduced the size of the crews and substantially raised the scale of pay—measures which, as he had already told Burghley, ' no doubt would greatly strengthen and benefit the service and nothing at all increase the charge '. The success of this policy was shown in the Armada campaign. In 1588 the Lord Admiral could claim with justice that his ships were manned

[1] A. L. Rowse, *Expansion of Elizabethan England*, p. 252.
[2] *Q*. J. A. Williamson, *Sir John Hawkins* (1927), p. 371.

with ' a very sufficient and able company of sailors as ever were seen ' and Burghley could boast that our ships were ' both in number, in strength, in able Captains Mariners, stronger than ever they were in the memory of man '.

4

For close on a generation the consummate statecraft of Queen Elizabeth and Burghley, her great minister, had kept England inviolate in the midst of increasing tension and continually recurring crises. While the immensely wealthy and highly industrialized Netherlands were harassed by the religious wars and the excesses of the unpaid Spanish soldiery, and the commerce of Antwerp was practically ruined, her kingdom had enjoyed long years of peace and prosperity. But England and Spain were rapidly falling apart; and in the course of the 1580s the drift to war became manifest. By the absorption of Portugal in 1580, entailing a vast accession to Spanish strength, Spain became what she had not been before, an important naval Power. France, as a counterpoise to Spain, had almost ceased to count. The assassination at Philip II's instigation of William of Orange in 1584 was followed by the sustained, methodical, remorseless advance of Parma across the southern Netherlands. Bruges, Ghent, and other important places were successively recaptured. With the surrender on 17 August 1585, of Antwerp, greatest of all the cities of the Netherlands, virtually the whole of the southern provinces fell once again under the authority of the Spanish governor. The Wars of Religion effectively kept France from assisting the Dutch. It appeared as if the revolt of the Netherlands would finally collapse and the northern as well as the southern provinces be brought again under Spanish rule. The imminent hazard to England forced Elizabeth to come into the open; and she sent over a small army commanded by Leicester to defend the seven Dutch provinces. With this meagre reinforcement, the rebels staved off defeat. Though the odds were formidable, geography favoured the Dutch. The extensive lakes and marshlands of Friesland secured their frontier in the north almost as effectively as did the great rivers in the south. Parma's advance was not halted; but its tempo was sensibly slackened.

Because of the threat to national security represented by the presence of a great military Power in the Netherlands, the Queen and her

Council constantly strove to keep alive resistance to Spain there. The truth was that both Huguenots and Dutch were Elizabeth's first line of defence, and helped to keep the war away from England. For his part Philip II aided and encouraged the malcontents among Elizabeth's subjects. The cumulative effect of these developments was to produce something like official war between the two States, although no formal declaration was made by either side. The actual commencement of hostilities is generally ascribed to 1585, when English corn-ships in Spanish harbours were seized by Philip's order and Drake was commissioned by the Queen to conduct a retaliatory raid against the enemy's sea-ports in Europe and the New World.

The naval expedition of 1585–6, like the trading and exploration ventures of earlier years, took the form of a joint-stock enterprise to which the London merchants contributed two-thirds and Elizabeth one-sixth. With Martin Frobisher as his vice-admiral, Drake sailed from Plymouth with a composite squadron of privateers, armed merchantmen, and two warships of the Queen's; he plundered Vigo and raided the Canary and Cape Verde Islands, then stood away across the Atlantic for Hispaniola and San Domingo, the capital of the Indies. The assault presented formidable difficulties. The harbour of San Domingo was protected by a dangerous bar and commanded by a strong castle. While Drake sailed close in, as though to disembark his forces under the castle walls, the real landing was made about ten miles further off. Swiftly and silently, 1,000 soldiers were landed from the pinnaces and ships' boats. Presently the assailants, advancing in two columns along the coast, attacked the Spaniards so fiercely that the latter were driven back in desperate hand-to-hand combat through the gates and streets of the city until the two columns re-united in the central square. Soon after the castle of San Domingo surrendered, and Drake was able to occupy the harbour and seize all the shipping therein, revictualling his own squadron with the enemy's supplies. He then shaped a course for Cartagena, the strongest city of the Spanish Main, and the principal commercial centre of the New World. Cartagena, like San Domingo, was difficult of approach. The English method of attack was most skilfully devised and entirely successful. Once again the assailants mastered the difficulties of the terrain, fought their way in through the city gates, and, storming the barricades thrown up in the streets, halted, breathless but triumphant, in the *plaza*, while the Spanish soldiery fled to the hills. Both San Domingo and Cartagena yielded a substantial ransom. Later, however, the recrudescence of a disease which the squadron had contracted in the Cape Verde Islands forced Drake to abandon his intended enterprise against Nombre de Dios and Panama, ' where we should have strucken the stroke for the treasure, and full recompense of our tedious travails'.

The raid of 1585–6 came as a revelation to Europe of the aggressive power of Elizabethan England and dealt a damaging blow to the Spanish finances. Above all, as Waters has truly said, ' The bubble of Spanish invincibility had been pricked.'[1]

Meanwhile the situation in Europe had been rapidly deteriorating. In January 1586 Philip ordered the Marquis of Santa Cruz to prepare plans for the invasion of England. Later in the year a small English force crossed the Atlantic and captured the Spanish and Portuguese fishermen working the Newfoundland Banks, and thereby disorganized the Spanish victualling arrangements. In 1587 the plots against Elizabeth's life culminated in the Babington conspiracy. This was followed by the trial and execution of Mary, Queen of Scots, which hardened Philip's resolve to undertake the ' Enterprise of England ', as the invasion project was called. In the new alignment of forces in Europe the Protestant cause was personified in Elizabeth and the Catholic in Philip. England formed, in fact, the keystone of the Protestant arch; and while this stood the Netherlands could not be subdued. This in brief outline was the situation as 1588, the ' Climacterical Yeare of the World ', foretold of the sages and astronomers, *annus mirabilis, mundi climacterium*, approached.

Though Elizabeth still hoped for peace, Philip now was determined on war. His resources had lately been increased by a promise of financial aid from the Papacy and by the safe arrival of a rich West Indian *flota*. In England, prompt preparations were made to meet the crisis. Hawkins was dispatched to ply up and down the Channel with a small squadron; orders were sent out for the mustering of the militia and for the erection and watching of the beacons. In the winter of 1586–7 the Council began to receive, both from their secret agents abroad and from their pinnaces hovering off the enemy's coast, alarming reports of the preparations in the Spanish ports, in con-

[1] *The True and Perfect Newes*, ed. D. W. Waters (1957).

sequence of which it was decided to send Drake on an expedition ' to impeach the joining together of the King of Spain's fleet out of their several ports ', to cut off their supplies, and ' to distress the ships within the havens themselves '.

On 2 April 1587 Drake left Plymouth Sound with a powerful squadron of privateers, fighting merchantmen, and four of the Queen's galleons. Three days later, off Cape Finisterre, his force was dispersed by a gale, but re-united off the Rock of Lisbon. He sailed for Cadiz, where part of the Armada was assembling, and, taking the Spaniards by surprise, immediately entered the harbour between the batteries on either side, driving off a division of galleys by the raking fire of his broadsides; by nightfall all the shipping which had not managed to escape was in his hands, and the city was in a state of panic; next morning in his barge accompanied by the boats and pinnaces of the squadron and supported by one of the armed merchant-men, the *Merchant Royal*, Drake stood in on the flood and fell upon the shipping in the inner harbour; for thirty-six hours he remained within the harbour, repulsed the repeated attacks of the galleys and fireships, destroyed and captured thousands of tons of shipping—including a 1,500-ton galleon belonging to the Spanish commander, Santa Cruz—and practically annihilated the Cadiz division of the Armada, besides working considerable havoc in the storehouses and dockyards, and revictualling his entire squadron with the captured supplies. The stroke against Cadiz amply demonstrated the conclusive superiority of the sailing warship over the galley even in landlocked waters and under the most favourable conditions. Next, storming the fortress of Sagres, Drake took up his station off Cape St. Vincent, whence he raided the coastal trade and effectually prevented the Spaniards from concentrating their scattered squadrons. ' We hold this cape so greatly to our benefit and so much to their disadvantage ', wrote Fenner to Walsingham, ' as it is a great blessing the obtaining thereof; for the rendezvous is at Lisbon. . . . [As for] the rest,' he added, ' we lie between home and them, so as the body is without the members, and they cannot come together.' Among the stores inter-cepted by the English pinnaces was an immense quantity of barrel-staves; for want of these seasoned staves the Armada was to sail next year with leaking casks. ' We burned also some 50 or 60 fisher-boats,' Fenner declared, ' and great store of nets, to their great damage '.

The destruction of the Andalusian and Port Algarve fisheries, upon which the Armada mainly depended for its supply of salt fish, was not the least of the services performed by Drake's squadron in 1587. Lisbon was found too strong to be attempted in like manner to Cadiz; and, returning to the anchorage off Sagres, Drake had his ships cleaned and fumigated and pumped dry and many of his men given a spell ashore. Finally he sailed to the Azores where he waylaid and captured a rich East Indiaman, the *San Felipe*, whose lading more than covered the cost of the expedition. The effect of these activities was completely to dislocate the timetable for the assembly of the Armada; for Santa Cruz, ignorant of Drake's whereabouts after he had quitted Cape St. Vincent, sent out a squadron to the Azores to secure the safety of the homecoming *flota*.

The expedition of 1587, like that of the year before, served as a triumphant vindication of the privateering technique and organization developed by Drake and his contemporaries. Well might old Burghley exclaim, 'Truly Sir Francis Drake is a fearful man to the King of Spain!' This brilliant campaign in the enemy's waters was his finest achievement and marks the zenith of his career. 'The truth is,' observed the Venetian ambassador, 'that he has done so much damage on these coasts of Spain alone, that though the King were to obtain a most signal victory against him he would not recover one half the loss he has suffered.' Within the space of a few weeks he had so damaged and disorganized the enemy's preparations that the 'Enterprise of England', notwithstanding all Philip's remonstrances, had to be called off until the following year. In January the experienced Santa Cruz died and the command was entrusted to the far less capable Duke of Medina Sidonia.

Still clinging to the hope of peace, Elizabeth had suspended all hostile operations against Spain and had sent over commissioners to treat with Parma. But she might as well have hoped to hold back the tide. Day by day the preparations for the 'Enterprise of England' went steadily forward; shipping was assembling in all the Atlantic ports of the Peninsula and stores were arriving from every part of the Mediterranean littoral that lay within the Spanish zone of influence; across the Channel, the star of the Guise was again in the ascendant, and Henry III had fled from Paris. Parma's flank, and that of Medina Sidonia, was thereby rendered secure. In the Netherlands, the citadel of Dutch resistance had been imperilled in January 1587 by the loss of Deventer, as a result of which the line of the Ysel was pierced, and seven months later by the surrender of Sluys, whereby Parma gained another North Sea port.

In December, Walsingham having warned the Queen that the Spanish descent was imminent, all the vessels in the Thames estuary were hurriedly mobilized. Lying in the Medway was the Lord Admiral in the *Ark*, with Hawkins and Frobisher and the bulk of the royal fleet. At Plymouth, covering the entrance of the Channel, lay Drake in the *Revenge* with a small squadron. Sir Henry Palmer in the *Rainbow* with another small squadron cruised off the Flanders coast, watching the enemy ports. A few weeks later, on the arrival of reassuring intelligence, half these crews were discharged; but the work of cleaning and refitting went on. In the spring tides of January and February 1588, all the ships lying at Chatham and Plymouth were careened and tallowed; the work went on throughout the night, ' by torchlight and cressets ', declared William Hawkins, ' and in extreme gale of wind '. By the summer the Queen's ships had been raised to the highest pitch of efficiency and had proved their seaworthiness. ' Sir,' wrote Howard to Walsingham, ' I think there were never so many of the prince's ships so long abroad, and in such seas, and with such weather as these have had, with so few leaks.'

In sure and certain hope of the Armada's approaching triumph, Cardinal Allen presently issued his historic manifesto against Queen Elizabeth, whom he denounced as ' an infamous, depriuved, accursed, excommunicate heretike; the very shame of her sexe, and princely name; the chiefe spectacle of sinne and abomination in this our age; And the onely poison calamitie and destruction of our noble Churche and Cuntrie.' The Cardinal's broadside was a complete fiasco. It served merely to increase the swelling tide of hatred and contempt for Spain and Rome. About this time Sir John Arundell and a number of other leading Catholics signed a declaration of loyalty to the Queen, pledging themselves to venture their lives and all their possessions in defence of her person and realm. But the Council were taking no risks. As the crisis approached, they sent orders for all the leading recusants to be disarmed and taken into custody. There was never the slightest chance of a general Catholic rising, upon which Cardinal Allen and his fellow-exiles had confidently reckoned, materializing.

5

In order to arrive at a proper understanding of the course of the Armada campaign it is necessary to bear in mind that the true object of Spanish strategy in 1588 was the *military* conquest of England, to be achieved by a composite force drawn partly from Parma's army in the Netherlands and partly from the troops carried on board the fleet. Medina Sidonia's instructions were to proceed up Channel to the North Foreland, seize a suitable landing-place, and convoy Parma's flotilla to England. For a good many months preparations for the invasion had been pressing on in Flanders. Parma had constructed or improved water-communications between Ghent, Sluys, Nieuport, and Dunkirk; and an adequate fleet of transports, together with munitions and supplies, had been gradually assembled on the coast. There his men were practised in embarking and disembarking with order and rapidity. Parma's army, once safely landed in England, was to march directly on London. On this side of the water, there were no large regular forces or well-planned system of fortresses to obstruct the advance of the first general and the finest troops in Europe. In organization, training, and equipment the English military forces were at least half a century behind the Continent. The train-bands were the jest of the London wits. Some of the county levies still clung to the long-bow. In influential Spanish circles the English powers of resistance were regarded with contempt.

What the Spanish plan of campaign, however, altogether failed to take into account was the necessity for a safe port of assembly on Parma's coast: such a port was not available. Because of the Dutch blockade, Parma could not get out from either Antwerp or Sluys. The rebel cruisers swarmed in the Scheldt, and in the shallow waters off Nieuport and Dunkirk. Parma's vessels were merely light transports, powerless in the face of an enemy attack. They could never make the passage in a seaway, or without the protection of Medina Sidonia's fleet. In his voluminous dispatches to Parma, Philip II showed a total disregard of navigational conditions and of the realities of the situation in Flanders. He even went so far as to suggest that Parma should attempt the crossing without waiting for the Armada at all. The Flanders coast was, in fact, the strategic centre of the whole campaign. A strong squadron—nearly one-fourth of the entire English

Navy—was disposed near the Straits of Dover to blockade Parma's ports in Flanders; and what in future centuries would have been called the advanced, or inshore, squadron was represented by the numerous Dutch flyboats mentioned above. It followed that Parma had no possible chance of getting his veterans across the narrow seas until the Armada should arrive to break the blockade.

On the other hand, there has been a tendency among British historians seriously to underestimate the strength of the Spanish fleet. It has sometimes been argued that the Armada was not so much a fighting fleet as an assemblage of armed transports. This is an exaggeration which needs to be corrected in the light of recent research.[1] In point of fact, the lessons of the past decade had not gone unheeded by the Spaniards. When the Armada sailed it was accompanied by only four galleys instead of the forty proposed by Santa Cruz the year before. Again, the Spaniards had been steadily increasing the proportion of long-range guns in their vessels, so that in the early phase of the Armada campaign the English had scarcely any superiority in armament. Also the Armada was well supplied with powder and ammunition. Lastly, the proportion of sailors carried in the Spanish fleet was amply sufficient to work the ships; nor, in the actual accounts of the fighting, is there any evidence to suggest that these Spanish seamen were lacking in skill.

The number of true fighting ships on each side was roughly the same, about forty. But the English were superior in leadership and the sailing quality of their ships; also their crews were more skilled in seamanship and gunnery. The English tactics were new and revolutionary. In the van of naval progress, they had broken away from the traditional usages of sea-warfare: grappling and boarding. Instead, as at San Juan de Ulua, Pantelaria, and Cadiz, they had trusted to the deadly broadsides of the ' off-fight ', the long-range fire of culverins and demi-culverins. They were, perhaps, the best naval gunners in Europe. In 1588 the English fleet was dominated by the school of Hawkins and Drake: though the supreme command had gone to the Lord Admiral, Lord Howard of Effingham, the latter was a follower of the new school, and the naval element was predominant in his council.

[1] See M. A. Lewis in *The Mariner's Mirror*, XXVIII, XXIX, and D. W. Waters, *ibid.*, XXXV.

It was an altogether different matter with the Duke of Medina Sidonia. ' This nobleman is the first grandee of Spain,' wrote the Venetian ambassador in Spain on 19 February 1588; ' he has excellent qualities, and is generally beloved. . . . Only one might desire in him a wider experience of the sea, but all other possible appointments present greater difficulties.' Medina Sidonia himself had no illusions about his own deficiencies. From the outset he had shown great unwillingness to accept the command: but the King paid no heed to his protests and bade him go forward in all confidence.

Meanwhile in the Netherlands Parma completed his preparations for the descent. Decade after decade the Spanish army in Flanders had been advancing steadily in experience, skill, and warlike prowess. Seasoned by long years of active service, trained to the highest pitch of discipline and morale, equipped with the best and latest weapons of the age, imbued with boundless confidence in themselves and their great commander, these troops were to be accounted beyond compare the most formidable under arms. Their ranks were constantly being augmented by the arrival of reinforcements from other parts of Philip's far-flung empire. With them, too, were a number of English Catholic noblemen and gentry, including the recreant Sir William Stanley, formerly one of Elizabeth's most trusted and skilful generals: who, lately subverted from his duty and allegiance by Jesuit wiles, had early in 1588 betrayed Deventer to the Spaniards and gone over, body and soul, to the enemy.

On the eve of the Armada's departure the spiritual exercises of King Philip and his people were redoubled. Throughout the Peninsula fervent prayers were offered up to heaven for the success of the Enterprise of England with ' processions, austerities, fasting, and devotion '. ' The litany of the forty hours is recited in each parish,' the Venetian ambassador reported to the Senate, '. . . . and in all the churches they make constant prayers; and the King is on his knees every day before the Sacrament.' Once again the Papal thunders rolled out against the heretic Elizabeth; and on 30 April, ' with pomp and many salvoes of artillery ', the blessing of the Standard was performed.

Despite his misgivings, the Duke was ordered to hasten his prepara-tions. On 20 May the Armada left Lisbon, only to be driven back by bad weather into Corunna to refit; it finally got away with a light south-westerly breeze on 12 July. For three days it ran before a fresh southerly wind. ' No better weather could have been desired,' wrote Medina Sidonia to the King. On the 17th it freshened to a gale, with heavy rain squalls and a high sea. Soon the galleys were in difficulties. They had not enough freeboard for the steep Biscay seas, and were obliged to part company. On the 18th it moderated and the sea went down. There was presently vouchsafed to Medina Sidonia twelve days of the most perfect weather for his purpose.

Since the last week of May the main English fleet had been lying at Plymouth, with a squadron under Sir William Winter and Lord Henry Seymour blockading the hostile ports in Flanders. In those fateful weeks neither Drake nor Howard succeeded in gaining intelligence of the enemy's movements. Howard and his admirals wished to sail for Spain and attack the Armada in its home waters; but the Council refused permission. In the end, however, the naval view prevailed; and they were almost within sight of the Spanish coast when the wind came south and drove them back and brought the Armada, hot upon their heels, to the entrance of the Channel.

At four o'clock in the afternoon of Friday, 19 July, the Spanish fleet came in sight of the Lizard. The gale had died away and the sea was calm, with a light westerly breeze. Medina Sidonia's pilots had done their work well. The great Armada had arrived safely and swiftly at its destination. Westward in the summer sunlight lay St. Michael's Mount and the broad recesses of Mounts Bay; northward rose up the dark, beetling cliffs of the most notable landfall on the English coast. It was the supreme moment for which their priests had prayed and of which their poets had sung. Before them lay the heretic realm and its infamous Queen, *reina infame; reina no, más loba Libidinosa y fiera!*

In the evening the Duke reduced sail and waited for his ships which had been dispersed by the gale to come up with the rest; and then the whole fleet, comprising 120 sail in all, closed up in the rigid military formation which it effectively preserved throughout the vicissitudes of the next nine days. In the van was Medina Sidonia himself with the best of the fighting galleons sailing in line abreast. After them came the hulks (transports and supply ships), disposed in close order, and protected against attack from flanks and rear by several other squadrons of warships. It was unquestionably the most formidable force that had ever appeared in northern waters.

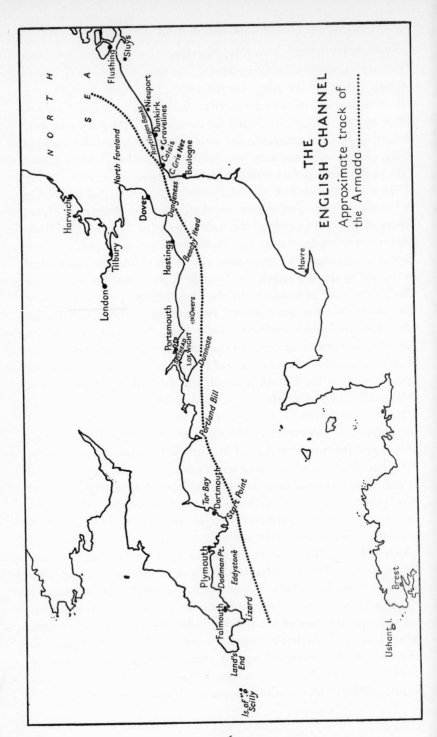

THE
ENGLISH CHANNEL
Approximate track of
the Armada ....

Map labels:

NORTH SEA

Flushing
Sluys
Nieuport
Ruytingen Banks
Dunkirk
Gravelines
Calais
C. Gris Nez
Boulogne
North Foreland
Dungeness
Dover
Hastings
Beachy Head
Harwich
Tilbury
London
Havre
Portsmouth
Owers
I. OF WIGHT
Dunnose
Portland Bill
Tor Bay
Dartmouth
Start Point
Plymouth
Dodman Pt.
Eddystone
Falmouth
Lizard
Land's End
Is. of Scilly
Ushant I.
Brest

At daybreak next morning, the Spaniards, closing the land, saw the beacons blazing on the Cornish hills. During Friday and Saturday crowds of country folk came hurrying out to the Lizard, Pendennis, and other vantage-points to watch the great fleet sail by. The Duke had hoisted to the main-top of his flagship, the *San Martin*, the Standard portraying on one side our Lord on the cross and on the other His Blessed Mother; whereupon every man in the fleet knelt down and prayed God to give them victory over the enemies of His faith. The Armada sailed on slowly past the Dodman. Medina Sidonia was urged by some of his officers to attack the English in Plymouth Sound; but the Duke rejected this advice on the grounds that it was contrary to the King's orders.

Since his return to Plymouth after the southerly gale Howard had been refitting and revictualling his ships. On Friday afternoon he received intelligence from a pinnace he had left scouting in the entrance of the Channel that the Armada was approaching the Lizard. (According to tradition, Drake and a number of others were playing bowls on Plymouth Hoe when the news arrived.) During the night and morning of the 19th-20th the English fleet, taken by surprise, was warping out of harbour and beating out of the Sound.[1] With the help of the tidal streams and by skilful manœuvring during the evening and night of the 20th-21st Howard's captains gradually worked their ships up to westward of the Armada and thus gained the weather-gauge. It was a superb feat of seamanship, which, as Ubaldino remarked, ' could not have happened without the long experience of naval discipline among the English seamen '.[2] On the morning of Sunday, the 21st, off Plymouth, sailing in line ahead, the English opened fire at long range on the Spanish rear. Their long culverins, however, were not powerful enough at this range to damage the enemy in any vital spot. The somewhat cautious approach of the English warships may be ascribed to the unexpected strength of the Spanish artillery. ' We made some of them to bear room to stop their leaks,' observed Howard to Walsingham; ' notwithstanding we durst not adventure to put in among them, their fleet being so strong.' It was then that he dispatched an urgent appeal—the first of many—for

---

[1] From 3 p.m. to 9 p.m. on the 19th the flood stream was flowing into Plymouth Sound, and Howard could not get out in the face of the westerly wind.

[2] Petruccio Ubaldino, a Florentine long resident in England, is believed to reflect the views of Drake.

ammunition. ' Sir,' he exhorted Walsingham, ' for the love of God and our country, let us have with some speed some great shot sent us of all bigness; for this service will continue long; and some powder with it.' The enemy sailed in good order with the mass of hulks in their midst closely guarded by warships. ' They . . . do keep such excellent order in their fight,' wrote one of Walsingham's secret agents, who was with Drake that day in the *Revenge*, ' that if God do not miraculously work, we shall have wherein to employ ourselves for many days.' The action of the 21st was indecisive. It appears, however, that the sailing qualities of the English ships in this first encounter between the rival fleets came as a revelation to the Spaniards—' their ships being very nimble and of such good steerage as they did with them whatsoever they desired ', and ' the speediest ship in the Armada . . . seemed in comparison . . . to be standing still '.

In the meantime the alarm had gone out from the west and messengers were speeding to and fro between the Council and the naval and military commanders on the coast. As the beacons flared from hill-top to hill-top across the length and breadth of the kingdom, there was a feverish mustering of train-bands, distribution of arms and armour, and jailing of recusants. Court gallants hurried down to the Channel ports to join the fleet. In Cornwall and Devon Grenville and Ralegh were hard at work overhauling the western levies; Sir George Carey was in command of the troops encamped about Carisbrooke Castle in the Isle of Wight; the Earl of Sussex directed operations at Portsmouth, and Lord Buckhurst was in charge of the forces assembled along the threatened south-east coast; in London the magistrates had the principal streets barred with chains, stationed guards at the cross-roads, and kept a close watch on all foreigners. During the ensuing campaign Burghley and Walsingham worked wonders with but exiguous resources and a wholly inadequate administrative machine. Powder, victuals, and reinforcements were hurriedly dispatched to the fleet. Forts were put in readiness with ammunition and supplies. Forces were assembled to guard Portsmouth, Harwich, and other seaports. One large army was gathering at Tilbury, and another was slowly forming in the capital.

In fine summer weather, with a favouring wind, the Armada held on its course. Slowly and majestically, with barely steerage way, it passed up the Channel. On the night of the 21st the Spanish fleet with a freshening breeze was close in with Start Point and early next day off Berry Head. During the 22nd the red cliffs of Dawlish and Sidmouth gave place to the white chalk headland at Beer and the yellowish cliffs of Dorset. In the evening the Duke sent the ensign-bearer, Juan Gil, in a pinnace to Parma to warn him of the Armada's approach. On the same day the English gained possession of two large galleons, the *San Salvador* and *Neustra Señora del Rosario*, which had become disabled and fallen astern; but they failed altogether to make any impression on the close fighting order of the Armada. At daybreak on the 23rd—with the wind, for the first and only time in the long running fight up Channel, at north-east—the Spaniards discovered Frobisher in the *Triumph* with a number of merchantmen well to leeward of the main body of the English fleet, near Portland Bill. That he managed to get away from them may have been due in part at least to the Race, which, perhaps, broke up the formation of the enemy fleet. Meanwhile, further out to sea, as the wind suddenly veered from north-east to south-west, the English attacked the Spanish rear and Medina Sidonia's flagship in groups, sailing in line ahead, while Recalde, Leyva, and Oquendo rallied to the Duke's support; upon which they put up their helms and stood out to sea. It is impossible to ascertain exactly what happened during the Portland fight. ' It was managed with confusion enough,' as Camden truly says. Some of the Spanish ships (notably the *San Martin*, which had been closely engaged with Howard's flagship) suffered a good deal of damage; their rigging was badly cut up, and they were taking in water through numerous shot-holes. Once again the Spaniards found themselves out-manœuvred by the superior sailing qualities of the English warships and the superior seamanship of the English crews. After the action Medina Sidonia strengthened his rearguard, and Howard sent boats and pinnaces to the shore for ammunition.

From Portland to St. Catherine's Point ' the fleets drifted rather than sailed at an average speed of little more than one knot.'[1] At the news of their approach Carey rode westward from Carisbrooke Castle to defend the southern beaches against a hostile landing. At daybreak on the 25th the Armada lay becalmed off Dunnose, so close in as to be in full view of Carey's troops and a great crowd of spectators gathered on the southward cliffs. With their fleet now reinforced and

[1] J. A. Williamson, *Hawkins of Plymouth* (1949), p. 308.

divided into squadrons under the Lord Admiral, Drake, Lord Thomas Howard, and Frobisher, the English again bore down on the enemy. Hawkins at this stage had sighted, lying somewhat to leeward of the main body of the Armada, one of their best galleons, the *Santa Ana*, ' which ', said he, ' we hoped to have cut off.' The English attack was, however, repelled, largely by the enemy's galleasses[1]: and out of this manœuvre ' there grew a hot fray ', in which the Spanish galleasses were so badly mauled that they ' were never seen to fight any more ', as Howard remarked, ' so bad was their entertainment in this encounter '. Medina Sidonia, with some of his strongest ships, endeavoured unsuccessfully to close with the swift English galleons, which continued to elude him and fight at long range. Once again the *Triumph* found herself hard beset by the Spaniards (' so as it appeared certain that we would that day succeed in boarding them ', said Medina Sidonia, ' wherein was the only way to victory '), when a lucky slant enabled Frobisher to escape. To seaward the squadrons of Howard and Drake were closely engaged with Recalde and Oquendo. Carey, watching from the cliffs, declared that the fight ' continued from five of the clock until ten, with so great expense of powder and bullet, that during the said time the shot continued so thick together that it might rather have been judged a skirmish with small shot on land than a fight with great shot on sea '. He and his men looking down from the hills of Wight that morning were beholding something unprecedented in history—a general action between two great fleets of sailing warships. To and fro on the sunlit water below moved the brightly painted vessels as on some immense stage: the swift bursts of smoke from hundreds of open ports were followed, several seconds later, by the reverberation of the guns, echoing for miles along the high chalk cliffs and rousing the seabirds in clamorous clouds from their ledges; countless spouts of foam rose, dazzling white in the sun, against the blue sea. All this time the flood was setting towards the Owers banks, off Selsey Bill; on which, in the opinion of Corbett and other leading authorities, the English may have been hoping to drive their opponents. If so, they did not succeed.

Once again the fighting was inconclusive. But when it ended the

[1] The four galleasses of Naples, under the command of Hugo de Moncada, were regarded by the Spaniards as the most powerful vessels in the Armada. They were fast, heavily gunned ships, half galleon and half galley, propelled both by sails and by oars.

Armada had been manœuvred safely past the Isle of Wight. With Howard doggedly pursuing, the Armada resumed its easterly course; and by about three o'clock in the afternoon (according to Carey) had disappeared in the distance. An important consequence of the action off Dunnose was that it had used up much of the ammunition on both sides; but whereas the English could replenish their supplies from their southern ports Medina Sidonia would get none until he made the junction with Parma. That night the *Santa Ana*, which had been so badly damaged in the recent fighting that she was unable to keep the sea, fell out of the Armada and stood over to Havre.

The Spanish fleet stood on slowly up Channel, past the Seven Sisters and the great chalk *massif* of Beachy Head and across Pevensey Bay: to the no small alarm of the citizens of Hastings, many of whose mariners (as the Mayor declared) were away at sea with the Lord Admiral. Off Fairlight, Medina Sidonia dispatched another pinnace to Dunkirk, urging Parma to join him at the earliest opportunity. At ten o'clock in the morning of Saturday, the 27th, the Spaniards saw the coast of France near Boulogne and the following evening anchored off Calais. The Armada had lost but three vessels and was still in very good order. In accordance with the instructions laid down for them by the King, the time had come for Medina Sidonia to join hands with Parma and to ferry their combined forces across to England. The same day Lord Henry Seymour, with the English blockading squadron which had been lying in the Downs, crossed the Straits and joined Howard, then anchored ' within culverin-shot ' to the windward of the Armada. Seymour had under his command fifteen of the Queen's ships and about as many merchant vessels. The English fleet thereby reached its maximum strength. Medina Sidonia waited for Parma to make some move, and waited in vain.

The inherent weakness of the Spanish plan of campaign was now made manifest: their great ships, drawing over twenty feet of water, could not get anywhere near the shallow ports of Nieuport and Dunkirk—nor could Parma's flotilla, ' for feare of five and thirtie warrelike ships of Holland and Zeland, which there kept watch and warde under the conduct of the Admirall Justin of Nassau ', come out to join them, or dispatch any of the munitions and supplies so badly needed by Medina Sidonia. The only suitable port for the junction was Flushing; but Flushing was in Dutch territory, and held by an English garrison.

The Duke addressed a final appeal to Parma to come out with his flat-bottoms. His words fell on deaf ears: unless and until Justin's blockading squadron was driven away, Parma and his army dared not put to sea. Disquiet and foreboding lay heavy upon the officers of the Armada. The Governor of Calais presently sent his nephew to warn Medina Sidonia of the perils of the roadstead in which they were lying; already there were ominous signs of a change in the weather. But to quit the anchorage was to give up all hope of a junction with Parma.

During the evening of the 27th, and throughout the following day, the Armada lay off the Calais cliffs under the lee of the hostile fleet; and the initiative passed to the English. The crisis of the campaign had arrived. At a council of war held by Howard and his officers on Sunday morning it was resolved to seek a decision. Towards midnight eight large fireships, with loaded guns, were suddenly launched on the flood against the anchored Armada; impelled by wind, tide, and current, they bore swiftly down on the crowded lines of shipping in the roads: by the Spaniards they were taken for explosion vessels, similar to those which had shattered the boom at Antwerp in 1585. In sudden panic the crews slipped or cut their cables and drifted away to the eastward. In the haste and confusion of that midnight débâcle the flagship of the galleasses, the *San Lorenzo*, had her rudder broken by another vessel's cable and went aground close to Calais. The following morning found the greater part of the Armada scattered for miles, far down to leeward, along the Flanders coast.

There was still no sign of Parma's flotilla. During the 29th and 30th his troops were actually embarking at Nieuport and Dunkirk. But it was impossible for the flat-bottomed transports to get out except under the most favourable conditions of weather and sea. During the period in question such conditions did not obtain.

The scene of the final and decisive engagement between the rival forces was the hazardous shoal water off Gravelines, about half-way between Calais and Dunkirk. Away in the background lay the low mono-tonous Flanders coastline, with here and there a spire or a windmill lifting above the long line of dunes. To outward appearance defence-less against attack, this shore was in reality amply protected from the great ships of the Armada by navigational conditions; extending for many miles to seaward lay an immense and complicated congeries of banks and sands—for the most part submerged, but with a few small patches drying at low water. The fine summer weather had at last broken up; and the sky was overcast and threatening, the wind freshening at south-south-west.

It had been Medina Sidonia's intention, as soon as the fireships had passed, to return at once to his anchorage. But though he and a few of his captains brought up a little to the east of Calais and anchored again, the bulk of the fleet was hopelessly scattered and in danger of running ashore. The Duke therefore weighed and sent pinnaces to warn those ships to leeward to haul their wind before they drove on the sands. He then bore away with the handful of ships that were with him to cover their retreat.

Instead of falling straightway on the flanks of the dispersed and demoralized enemy, according to plan, Howard had turned aside to attack the stranded galleass, leaving Drake, followed by Fenner in the *Nonpareil*, ' to lead the first charge upon the Spanish admiral '. Next Frobisher in the *Triumph* and Hawkins in the *Victory* engaged Medina Sidonia's flagship. The Duke, at first with but five ships of the squadron of Portugal, and then with a gradually increasing force, fought a bold and skilful rearguard action to cover his scattered squadrons and so enabled them to get into close fighting order again. As before, the power of the Spanish gunfire checked the English attack. The *Revenge*, ' riddled with every kind of shot ' and ' pierced with shot above forty times ' was forced to retire. Then, as Medina Sidonia's best ships were running out of ammunition, Drake was joined by Howard's and Seymour's squadrons: and the English closed the range.

The English superiority in long-range runs at this stage was nearly two to one. Recent research, however, tends to establish the important fact that it was not so much superiority in armament, as fine seamanship and the superior sailing qualities of the ships, that gave the English fleet the victory at Gravelines. Howard's ships were clearly reluctant to fight at close range. ' It was not convenient to attack them thus together and in close order,' observed an eye-witness aboard the *Ark*; ' but . . . if any ship was beaten out of their fleet she was surrounded and suddenly separated from the rest.' The Lord Admiral summed up the English tactics in this, as well as in the former actions, in a famous passage: ' Their force is wonderfully great and strong; and yet we pluck their feathers by little and little.'

During the ensuing action the two fleets moved eastward along the Flanders coast with the water gradually shoaling as they drew closer to the outlying banks. The English concentrated their attack on certain selected, isolated victims. A hail of shot crashed into the hulls and rigging of a number of the enemy's vessels which by now were almost invisible behind heavy banks of smoke: masts and yards came toppling down: sails, rigging, and tackle were slashed and rent: a great many of the enemy were killed and wounded: several shattered hulls drifted astern. Burghley's son, Robert Cecil, watching that day from the hills above Dover, could see far away across the water the dense pall of smoke that cloaked the contending fleets and heard the sullen roar of the guns. In this latter phase of the action Medina Sidonia's flagship, with fifteen or sixteen other ships, was cut off from the rest of the Armada. The *San Martin* was badly damaged aloft and leaking from holes below her waterline. With the sea running high, her people were unable to repair the injuries to her hull. Certain other ships, notably two Portuguese galleons, the *San Felipe* and *San Mateo*, and also the *San Juan de Sicilia*—all three of which had been closely engaged with the English—were in even worse case. The *San Felipe* was practically a wreck, with her upper deck shattered and her rigging severely damaged. With his cordage cut to pieces, water pouring into the hold through shot-holes, his crew decimated, and his guns dismounted, the captain of the *San Mateo* fought on with arquebuses. The two galleons were surrounded by enemies and smothered in powder-smoke: but their masts having been sighted from the tops of the *San Martin*, Medina Sidonia came to their rescue with several of his strongest ships, and, for the time being, they were saved. The *San Juan de Sicilia* managed to keep up with the fleet. But the *San Felipe* and *San Mateo*, though they struggled on through the night in a half-sinking condition, were early next morning obliged to run ashore before they foundered and were captured by the Dutch. It was said of the *Regazona*, the flagship of the Levant squadron, that her scuppers were running with blood.

' God', wrote Drake to Walsingham at the end of the fighting, ' hath given us so good a day in forcing the enemy so far to leeward as I hope in God the Prince of Parma and the Duke of Sidonia shall not shake hands this few days.' In vain Medina Sidonia, forgetful of the navigational conditions, desired to turn on the English with the whole

Armada, so as not to leave the Channel. His Flemish pilots assured him that it was absolutely necessary to stand out into the North Sea or the entire fleet would be upon the sands.

Late in the afternoon a heavy squall of wind and rain stopped the fighting; the wind suddenly flew to the north-west; the English abandoned their prey, the hands swarming aloft to shorten sail; while the Spaniards were obliged to bear away. In the midst of the squall a ship of Recalde's squadron, the *Maria Juan*, went down with most of her hands. The Armada was now on a dead lee shore and driving on the Ruytingen banks.

That night the wind and sea increased until, shortly after midnight, the gale reached its height. The *San Martin* and seven of her consorts, steering north-east under shortened sail, were being forced steadily to leeward. 'Hardly a man slept that night,' observed Father Jerónimo, one of the chaplains on board the fleet; 'we went along all wondering when we should strike one of those banks'.

At daybreak on Tuesday the wind moderated; but the sea still ran high and the wind blew from the north-west. 'Our *capitana* [flagship] remained in the rear with Juan Martinez de Recalde and Don Alonso de Leyva, and the galleasses, and the galleons *San Marcos* and *San Juan* of Diego Flores,' related the Duke, 'the rest of our fleet being far to leeward. The enemy's ships stood towards our *capitana*, which lay-to; the galleasses also abode their coming, as also did the other ships which were in the rear; whereupon the enemy brought-to.' But the Armada was now confronted with a greater peril than the English guns. Away to windward stretched the sullen, storm-speckled grey of the North Sea; out there lay deep water and safety; but to leeward, where strong tide-rips, lines and patches of foam, and the discolouration of the water marked the hidden sands, the Spaniards could see the sea rising and breaking over the outer banks, where leeway and the ebb stream were inexorably carrying them. His pilots warned Medina Sidonia that the fleet was lost, 'for that with the wind as it was, in the north-west, they must all needs go on the banks of Zeeland; and that God alone could prevent it.' 'It was the most terrible day in the world,' wrote Don Luis de Miranda, 'for all of us had now abandoned hope and stood waiting for the end.' The water shoaled until the soundings gave but $6\frac{1}{2}$ fathoms. (The galleass *Patrona*, which sailed to leeward of the *San Martin*, had only 5.) The English followed astern and to seaward of the Spaniards, keeping out of range. Then, early in the morning, the wind suddenly shifted to south-south-west, which enabled the Armada to haul off to the northward.

The wind continuing in the south-west quadrant, the fateful decision was taken on board the Spanish flagship to return home by the long hazardous route north-about. With the exception of Seymour's squadron, which was now sent back to guard the Thames estuary against Parma, the English followed in pursuit. Two days after Drake could write exultantly to Walsingham: ' There was never anything pleased me better than seeing the enemy flying with a southerly wind to the northwards. God grant you have a good eye to the Duke of Parma; for with the grace of God, if we live, I doubt it not but ere it be long so to handle the matter with the Duke of Sidonia as he shall wish himself at St. Mary Port among his orange trees.'

Only the sudden shift of wind had in fact saved the Spanish fleet from complete destruction: in the second half of the action, on the arrival of Howard and Seymour, the Duke's galleons had been cruelly mauled: by this stage of the campaign the latter had lost seven or eight of his best ships, and the battered remnant of his fighting force was in full retreat. But the powder and shot of the English were now exhausted and their supplies were running low; and soon their ships stood southward again after seeing the Spaniards safely out of our waters.

The Armada, passing on 9th–10th August between the Orkneys and Shetlands, with a following wind, ran into bad weather. With the wind shifting and veering between north-west and south, the fleet struggled for weeks against head-winds, gales, and fogs. Many of the ships had sustained serious damage alow and aloft in the recent fighting, and there was a grievous shortage of fresh water and provisions. On 15th August, when Medina Sidonia was some seventy miles to the north-west of Rockall, there were about eighty ships in company with him. The Armada continued steering to the south as best the wind allowed. The plight of the crews grew daily worse. On the 23rd a southerly gale arose which dispersed the fleet; and on the 26th the noonday sun shone down on a number of these storm-tossed galleons labouring in the long Atlantic seas as far north as the 63rd parallel—the latitude of southern Iceland. ' I pray that God in His mercy will grant us fine weather ', Medina Sidonia wrote in his dispatch to the King, ' so that the Armada may soon enter port; for we are so short of provisions that if for our sins we be long delayed, all will be irretrievably lost.' The Armada once more stood to the south. On 1 September the wind began to blow fresh from the south-west. Early in the evening of the 2nd it hauled to the southward and rapidly increased, till at nightfall it was blowing a gale, with a heavy head sea. Some of the vessels that sighted Ireland about this time stood to the north-west and gained an offing before the wind veered, and so escaped. On the 5th it blew hard again from the south-west. Recalde's squadron, accompanied by a number of other ships, had some time before fallen away from the main body of the fleet—and, though most of the latter, with their pumps continually at work, and the crews dying daily in hundreds of disease, hunger, and thirst, did eventually struggle home to Spain— many of the former ships, approaching too close to the Irish coast, became embayed. In batches of twos and threes they presently piled up all along the long lee shore, whereupon most of the survivors were sporadically slaughtered by the ' wild Irish ', or methodically executed by the English.

The heaviest toll of all was exacted in the north-westerly gale of 10 September, when, according to the clerk of the Council of Con-nacht, ' There blew a most extreme wind and cruel storm, the like whereof hath not been seen or heard a long time.' On that day of wrath the wind, which throughout the past week or so had been variable but for the most part westerly, finally veered to north-west and blew with redoubled force. From Bloody Foreland to Rathlin O'Birne the great ocean swell broke violently over the sunken ledges and banks and encircled with heavy surf the outlying islands, shoals, reefs, and skerries that fringe the irregular, broken coastline of western Donegal. Further south, in the deep bight between the Donegal shore and the northern coast of Mayo and Sligo were entrapped no fewer than nine of Medina Sidonia's vessels, most of which were wrecked in different parts of the bay. The worst of these disasters occurred in the vicinity of Sligo. Three great ships, which in the south-westerly gale of 2 September had failed to weather the westernmost point of Mayo, gradually became embayed. Day after day the heavy western swell, rolling in from the Atlantic, sent them reeling to leeward. Eventually the three ships anchored, on the 5th, scarcely more than half a league off the long line of surf thundering on the Streedagh strand. The

Malin Head
Tory I.
Inishowen
Dunluce
Bloody Foreland
O'DOHERTIE
MACDONNELL
Aranmore I.
MACSWEENY
O'DONNELL
MACSWEENY
Donegal
Bay
O'ROURKE
Broad Haven
Blacksod
Bay
O'MALLEY
Clare I.
Slyne Hd.
O'FLAHERTY
Galway
Dublin
Aran Is.
Liscannor Bay
Mal Bay
Limerick
Loop Hd.
R. Shannon
Blasket
DESMOND
Dingle Bay
MACCARTHY

**IRELAND
AND THE
ARMADA**

Sites of known shipwrecks X

C. Clear

north-westerly gale of the 10th sealed their fate. They were now on a dead lee shore. Dragging their anchors, the ships, one after the other, drove on the strand and broke to pieces within an hour, strewing the sands for miles with immense quantities of wreck and many hundreds of corpses.[1] Two other large ships were lost in Mal Bay, and the

[1] According to tradition, the largest of the galleons struck on Carraig na Spáinneach, situated off a small island called Derninish at the eastern end of Streedagh strand.

Nuestra Señora de la Rosa and *San Juan* of Ragusa foundered in Blasket Sound. *La Rata Santa Maria Encoronada*, with the lieutenant-general of the Armada, Don Alonso de Leyva, on board, and many other high-born young officers, ran aground, on the 11th, off Ballycroy in Blacksod Bay. About the same time another great galleon, *El Gran Grin*, struck on a rock off Clare Island and went down with a loss of 700 men.

During this time vague and conflicting rumours continued to spread across England and Europe. Not for weeks, indeed, was the full truth known even to the Council, which anxiously awaited intelligence from Ireland, where the small English garrison, manifestly inadequate in this crisis, must be overwhelmed by a landing in force. News arrived of large numbers of Spanish ships standing in to the western coast. Word was told of noble captains coming ashore ' with chains of gold about their necks '. The danger zone was around the littoral of Donegal Bay, where the old Gaelic order was still unsubdued and the power of the chieftains unbroken. Here on the borders of Tirconnell and Connacht was the *bearna baoghail*[1] of the English defences in Ireland; here was the real threat to Elizabeth's power. It seemed that that danger had indeed materialized when news reached London that de Leyva with 2,000 of his men had arrived in the MacSweeney country in south Donegal and had there established a strong armed camp, from which he presently sent out messengers to the neighbouring chieftains. But the Spaniards, it appeared, were landing through distress and not design: later de Leyva with the best of his company got away to the northward: as to the rest, though considerable numbers of Spaniards managed to struggle ashore, they soon revealed themselves, not as an organized force, but ' miserable and ragged creatures utterly spoiled by the Irishry '. A great many more of the Spanish crews never reached the land alive, but were cast up by the waves, in the midst of planks and timbers and variegated wreckage, as bruised and battered corpses.

In some cases the Gaelic names of ill-omen, commemorating these tragedies, have survived to this day. Mention has already been made of Carraig na Spáinneach off Streedagh strand. A small rocky cove in the

---

On a map of the Sligo coast (A.D. 1609) opposite Derninish are the words, ' Three Spanish ships here cast away in A.D. 1588.' Bones and cannon-balls have been cast up in storms along Streedagh strand almost to this day.

[1] The Gap of Danger (*Gaelic*).

vicinity of Dunluce Castle, near the Giant's Causeway, where the galleass *Girona* (in which de Leyva and his company were attempting to reach Scotland) was wrecked, is called Port na Spáinneach. The site of another wreck, near Aranmore Island, bears the name of Carraig na Spáinneach. The promontory where one of the ships wrecked in Mal Bay took the ground is known as Rinn na Spáinneach; and the mound in which lie the remains of the survivors of yet another wreck, after their execution at the hands of the Sheriff of Clare, is called Tuaim na Spáinneach.

It has often been stated that the Spaniards had neither pilots nor charts for the voyage. This is to some degree erroneous. Certainly experienced pilots were carried in some of the Spanish ships. It is significant that in a number of cases their vessels found safe anchorages and were eventually able to continue their voyage. The *Duquesa Santa Ana* lay for a while in the best anchorage in Blacksod Bay; the *Zuñiga* anchored for a week in the north-east corner of Liscannor Bay, repairing her rudder; four galleons and three smaller vessels lay in Scattery Roads, the safest anchorage in the lower Shannon; and Recalde in the *San Juan* rode out the gales of 5 and 10 September in a good anchorage under the lee of the Blasket. On the other hand, it is probably true that the Spanish charts, through failing to portray the long westward projection of the Connacht coast, contributed largely to the many shipwrecks in Donegal Bay and further south.

Meanwhile Medina Sidonia, with the bulk of the fleet, now comprising about sixty vessels, was sailing down the Bay of Biscay. The *San Martin* herself had passed, far out in the Atlantic, without so much as sighting the Irish coast. The main body of the survivors held fairly well together until, on the 8th, they were again scattered by a gale in latitude 45°N. The Duke then continued on his course with a westerly wind. On 13 September Don Balthasar de Zuñiga arrived at the Escurial with the dispatch Medina Sidonia had sent off after rounding the north of Scotland on 10 August. ' The Armada begins to reach the coast of Spain,' wrote the Venetian ambassador in Madrid on the 15th; ' it is in a very bad plight, to say the truth, with the result of the enemy's attacks and the long voyage.' ' Half the ships of the Armada,' he went on a week later, ' are still missing.' Of the miserable survivors among the crews, a substantial proportion continued to sicken and die. Not until the winter was the full extent of the catastrophe learned in Spain. Altogether about two dozen vessels are known for certain to have been lost off the west coast of Ireland, and four others off the Devon coast, the Inner Hebrides, Fair Isle, and the Faeroes; many more must have gone down with all hands, unobserved and unrecorded, in the open sea. In the end rather less than a half of the vessels, and about a third of the crews, ever returned to Spain.

Disease also took a grievous toll of the English fleet. Though remarkably few casualties had been sustained in the actual fighting, soon after the ships returned to port the men were dying in hundreds. ' Sickness and mortality begins wonderfully to grow amongst us,' Howard informed Burghley on 10th August; ' and it is a most pitiful sight to see, here at Margate, how the men, having no place to receive them into here, die in the streets. . . . It would grieve any man's heart, to see them that have served so valiantly to die so miserably.' ' The companies do fall sick daily,' wrote Hawkins several weeks later. But the government could do little enough to relieve them; for the unprecedented demands of the campaign of 1588, both by land and by sea, had drained the treasury almost to the bottom.

The dramatic dénouement of the Armada campaign was a damaging blow at the prestige of Catholic Spain and correspondingly raised the morale of the Protestant peoples. The wound to Spanish pride was deep and lasting. It is said that even the young students at the English College in Rome—many of them destined to lay down their lives for the Faith—burst into cheers at the news of the Armada's overthrow. The Pope, Sixtus V, made no attempt to conceal his poor opinion of the King of Spain and his admiration for Queen Elizabeth and Drake. The Spanish ambassador in France, Bernadino de Mendoza, was followed about the streets of Paris by a jeering rabble. On his arrival at Santander, on 10 September, the unfortunate Medina Sidonia found himself the object of merciless contempt and scorn. Crowds of mocking urchins dogged his heels, with cries of, ' Drake is coming! Drake is coming! ' Four days later one of his admirals, Miguel de Oquendo, entering San Sebastian, refused so much as to look on his wife and children; and, forthwith taking to his bed, turned his face to the wall and died of grief. Recalde likewise perished at Corunna within two days of his arrival there. Philip II shut himself up in his closet in the Escurial and would speak to no one but his confessor.

On their side the Protestant adversaries of Spain hastened to attribute the victory to Divine intervention. Joyfully they gave thanks for the downfall and discomfiture of their foes, and Ralegh recalled with satisfaction ' how their Navy, which they deemed invincible ' was put to utter rout and confusion, and ' how with all their great terrible ostentation they did not, in all their sailing round about England, so much as burn so much as one sheepcote on this land '. Caricatures of the Armada were published with the legend, ' She came, she saw, she fled.' Ballads were composed celebrating the attack on the stranded galleass at Calais, the Queen's visit to her troops at Tilbury, and the other highlights of the campaign. In commemoration of their deliverance, the Estates of Zeeland presently ordered medals to be struck with the inscription, ' *Flavit Jehova et dissipati sunt, 1588* ': the reverse depicted the Protestant Church founded on a rock in the midst of the sea. On 20 August a great thanksgiving service was held at St. Paul's, which was attended by the Mayor and Corporation. Tuesday, 19 November, was appointed ' a solemne festivall day ' throughout the kingdom with sermons, psalms, and bonfires. On the following Sunday the Queen rode in state ' from her Palace unto the Cathedrall Church of Saint Paul, out of the which the ensignes and colours of the vanquished Spaniards hung displayed. And all the Citizens of London in their Liveries stood on either side the street, by their severall Companies, with their ensignes and banners; and the streets were hanged on both sides with Blue cloth, which, together with the foresayd banners, yielded a very stately and gallant prospect.'[1]

The closing lines of Shakespeare's *King John*, published not very long afterwards, admirably reflect the soaring spirit of pride and exaltation that possessed this nation on the overthrow of the Armada.

> Come the three corners of the world in arms,
> And we will shock them. Nought shall make us rue,
> If England to herself do rest but true.

Faint and distant echoes of the Armada campaign are also to be discovered here and there in English folk-lore: notably in the ' Hal-an-Tow ' song, sung on 8 May, Furry Day, at Helston in Cornwall, and in one of the best-known of our South Country harvest songs, ' Founder of the Feast '.

[1] Camden, Q. Hakluyt, *Voyages*, IV, 233–4.

The defeat and destruction of the *Invencible Armada* is one of the great decisive events of history. It was the supreme calamity of King Philip's reign, and presaged the passing of the golden age of Spain. It halted the advance of the Counter-Reformation and dispelled for ever the legend of Spanish invincibility. It disposed once and for all of the mediaeval pretensions of the Papacy (never again was the Pope to pronounce sentence of deposition against a sovereign prince). It caused the Spanish advance in the Low Countries to waver at the crucial moment: after the débâcle of 1588 the Spaniards had no possible chance of recapturing the seven Dutch provinces; it thereby secured the independence, and the rapid maritime, commercial, and colonial expansion, of the northern Netherlands; it firmly established the Anglo-Dutch alliance. It heralded the rise of England as a great maritime Power, and made possible, in the next decade, her eastward expansion. It enormously enhanced the personal prestige of Queen Elizabeth. It marked, with the first great victory of the sailing battle-ship, the beginning of a new era in naval warfare. Last but not least, it implanted in the national consciousness an imperishable tradition.

6

The latter phase of the war, which occupied the remainder of Eliza-beth's reign, was hardly so successful as the first. As was to be expected, the governing consideration was always finance. The heavy cost of military intervention in the Netherlands and France, combined with the doubts and reservations of the Queen, effectively prevented the naval offensive from being pressed home with vigour. The result was that the royal fleet was for the most part laid up and took a gradually diminishing share in the war, which was largely left to private enter-prise and privateers.

In the wave of enthusiasm that swept over the country in the hour of victory a combined naval and military expedition, under the leader-ship of Sir Francis Drake and Sir John Norris, was launched, in 1589, against Spain as a counterpoise to the Armada. Like the expeditions of 1585 and 1587 it was financed on a joint-stock basis, but on a far greater scale. The royal fleet contributed six strong ships, with the *Revenge* as flagship, and there were, in addition, more than a hundred merchantmen and privateers. What was originally proposed by the

Queen's ministers was, first and foremost, to destroy the remnants of the Armada sheltering in Santander.[1] Afterwards it was intended to seize and hold the great port of Lisbon as a base for the fleet; to foment a Portuguese rising in favour of the pretender, Don Antonio; and, if possible, to occupy some islands in the Azores. But in the event the Queen's instructions were not followed. Drake and Norris proceeded to attack, not Santander, but Corunna. Moreover, all but a small fraction of the troops sent out were without discipline or training; and they were badly equipped and ill-fed. Undermined from the first by interminable delays, confused objectives, and a divided command, the expedition was foredoomed to failure. The attack on the enemy's shipping at Corunna not only failed to achieve its object, but also lost the English the incalculable advantage of surprise. The raid was followed by a drunken orgy which demoralized and undermined the health of the troops. When the expedition finally sailed southward the Spaniards were forewarned and ready. No help was forthcoming from the Portuguese. Norris's troops disembarked at Peniche, about fifty miles distant from Lisbon. To reach the city took Norris seven days, in the course of which he lost touch with the fleet. He found Lisbon strongly held and his siege-guns were still aboard his ships. In the end he retreated to the coast and was taken off by Drake. The health of the men had now so deteriorated that any attempt to establish a base in the Azores was plainly out of the question. The fleet returned to England. The fiasco of 1589 revealed the weakness, as the achievements of 1585 and 1587 had demonstrated the strength, of this type of composite expedition. As a result of the failure Drake was discredited and was appointed to no command during the next six years.

With the object of stopping the indispensable Baltic stores from

---

[1] Professor Wernham makes out a strong case for this strategy (*English Historical Review*, LXVI, pp. 199 *et seq.*). He argues that the plight of Philip's warships, during the critical months which followed the overthrow of the Armada, was England's golden opportunity. 'Battered and decayed, they rode defenceless, forty huddled together in Santander and another dozen or so at San Sebastian. The whole remaining navy of Spain lay helpless in those two ports. For months they must be there, powerless to move or fight. Their destruction would complete the work of 1588 and crush Spanish naval power past hope of recovery. It had taken Philip seven years to prepare the '88 Armada. Half of it was already lost. Were this remaining half now burned in the Biscayan ports, he must start upon his seven years' labour all over again and with much less hope of success. For during these years the English would be able to keep their squadrons—fleets would now hardly be required—at the Azores in perfect safety.'

reaching the Spanish navy, Elizabeth in July 1589 issued a decree warning neutral States that certain commodities were to be treated as contraband and liable—together with the vessels carrying them—to confiscation. But as the means for putting a stop to the traffic were wanting the English endeavours to prevent Hanse merchants from supplying the enemy with these naval stores were largely ineffective.

A different strategy now came under consideration. The new proposals came from Sir John Hawkins, who had outlined his plan in a letter to Burghley. ' In the continuance of this war ', Hawkins observed, ' I wish it to be ordered in this sort; that first we have as little to do in foreign countries as may be but of mere necessity, for that breedeth great charge and no profit at all.' He proposed instead to hold the seas between the coast of Spain and the Azores with a small squadron of Queen's ships maintained there permanently by a system of reliefs, and by this means to prevent the passage of the *flotas*, or treasure fleets from the Indies, on the safe arrival of which depended the government and armament of Philip's empire. According to Hawkins' plan there should always be ' six principal good ships of Her Majesty's upon the coast of Spain victualled for four months and accompanied with some six small vessels which shall haunt the coast of Spain and the islands and be a sufficient company to distress anything that goeth through that sea: and when these must return there would be six other good ships, likewise accompanied, so that they be never unsucceeded.' It had long been appreciated in this our country that Spain was peculiarly vulnerable to economic pressure of this kind. Even the temporary interruption of the flow of bullion would be a serious matter for King Philip. What Hawkins was aiming at above all was the capture of the Spanish treasure fleet, ' which if we might once strike, our peace were made with honour, safety and profit'. Since the treasure from the Indies was the life-blood of the Spanish empire, he believed that, deprived of her overseas revenues, Spain would be unable to carry on the war. It was part of the plan that, while the blockade was thus throttling the seaborne trade of Spain, the Channel would be defended by twelve warships and six pinnaces, and also (during most of the time) by whichever of the cruising squadrons happened to be at home undergoing its refit.[1]

[1] For an accurate and lucid presentation of the Blue Water strategy proposed by Hawkins, see J. A. Williamson, *Hawkins of Plymouth* (1949).

Hawkins's plan was a good one; but the difficulties were immense, and not even for a single year was it ever put into continuous operation. Instead there was a series of isolated cruises at infrequent intervals, which altogether failed to stop the passage of the *flotas*. Not one squadron was ever sent out to relieve another. In 1589, when Spain was unable to get a fleet to sea at all to convoy the threatened trade, Cumberland cruised in the Azores during the summer and early autumn with a few of his own warships. If a squadron had arrived in time to relieve him, it must either have taken the *flota* or kept it locked up indefinitely in the Azores. Early next year Hawkins was hurriedly preparing for sea when the Council took alarm at a Spanish concentration in Corunna; and Hawkins, now in the depths of despair, as he informed Burghley, that he should ever ' perform any royal thing ', was ordered to stay in port. Meanwhile the *flota* slipped home. When at last Hawkins was allowed to depart in May, his instructions were that with one division he was to cruise off the coast of Spain to watch for the Brittany expedition preparing in the Spanish ports, while Frobisher with the other was to proceed to the Azores, where he arrived just too late to intercept the West Indies treasure.

In the meantime Philip, profiting by the lessons of 1588, began gradually but surely to build up an ocean navy which was to prove more formidable than the Armada and effectively kept open his communications. Notwithstanding Elizabeth's attempts at a blockade, shipbuilding materials continued to reach the Spanish shipyards in sufficient quantity. Philip gave orders for twelve galleons on the English model (they were later known as ' the Twelve Apostles ') to be laid down in the Biscayan ports, and nine more on the Portuguese model in Lisbon; the following year he also secured the services of twelve Ragusan galleons. The naval rearmament of Spain was pressed forward under the aegis of Bazan, brother of the illustrious Santa Cruz and himself an experienced admiral, who was responsible for the construction of a small fleet of heavily armed, fast-sailing frigates called *gallizabras* to carry the treasure.

The efficacy of these measures was dramatically justified in 1591. In that year a small squadron of six Queen's ships—the *Defiance*, *Revenge*, *Bonaventure*, *Lion*, *Foresight*, and *Crane*—accompanied by a number of victuallers and pinnaces, was sent out to the Azores under the command of Lord Thomas Howard, with Sir Richard Grenville as his vice-admiral. To protect the homecoming *flota* Philip II dispatched Alonso de Bazan to the islands with twenty warships as well as many lesser vessels. The English squadron, heavily outnumbered, and with a high proportion of its crews incapacitated through disease, received warning from Cumberland, then cruising off the coast of Spain, of the approach of this formidable force.

In the actual encounter Howard seems to have been taken by surprise; ' our ships had scarce time to weigh anchor,' says Ralegh, ' but some of them were driven to slip their cables and set sail.' Led by Howard in the flagship, they tacked in order to get to windward of the Spanish fleet. This they all succeeded in doing, except the *Revenge*, which was the last of the squadron to get under way. Grenville was therefore faced with the necessity of bearing up and running before the wind or else standing on unsupported through the midst of the enemy. The fact that the *Revenge* was the best sailer in the squadron may very well have induced him to choose the latter course— 'persuading his company that he would pass through the two squadrons, in despite of them: and enforce those of Castile to give him way '.

The *Revenge* appears to have been in action from about 3 p.m. onwards. Later in the afternoon the Seville squadron exchanged shots with Howard. Bazan followed with the rest of the Spanish fleet; and the *San Felipe* and the *San Barnabe* attempted unsuccessfully to board, first, the *Defiance*, and then the *Revenge*. The *Defiance* and the other English ships got away under cover of dusk, but the *Revenge* became entangled with the *San Barnabe*: firing continued throughout the night: as often as some of the enemy ships were beaten off, Ralegh declares, ' so always others came in their places, she having never less than two mighty galleons by her sides, and aboard her.' In the course of this memorable action the *Revenge* engaged no less than fifteen of the Spaniards, actually sinking four of them and repulsing every attempt to board.

And the night went down, and the sun smiled out far over the summer sea,
And the Spanish fleet, with broken sides lay round us all in a ring.

But at daybreak the *Revenge* was like a shambles, ' filled with the blood and bodies of dead and wounded men '; and Grenville himself was desperately wounded. At this stage his master-gunner and he would gladly have blown up their ship. But they were overborne by those others of the crew that survived, who thereupon surrendered to the enemy on honourable terms. Shortly after a storm arose, and the shattered *Revenge* filled and sank.

The last great fight of the *Revenge*, in a still higher degree than the defeat of the Armada, was a supreme example of the fighting value of the newer type of English galleon. On the other hand, it is not to be forgotten that the expedition had wholly failed to achieve its object, but had been obliged to retire before the far superior Spanish force that had been sent out to protect the trade.

On account of her alarm at the revival of Spanish sea power the Queen kept the Navy in home waters for the next three years and sent only one warship to cruise off Spain and another off the Azores. The Azores station henceforth became the preserve of privateers. The damage to Spanish shipping thereby was considerable. Though no success was ever scored against the western *flota*, in August 1592, a joint-stock enterprise in which Elizabeth was a partner succeeded in capturing a Portuguese East Indiaman, the *Madre de Dios*, off Flores. In 1593 a squadron under Cumberland was sent to the Azores, but found the new heavily armed *gallizabras* too strong to attack. The English squadronal warfare failed to interfere to any material degree with the passage of the *flotas*, and the much-needed cargoes of bullion continued to reach the mother-country in an increasing flow. Above all, Spain had been able to rebuild her navy. Twelve galleons at Lisbon and another twelve at San Lucar were kept in readiness to escort the outward and homeward-bound convoys to and from the Azores. The Spanish convoys were assisted by a highly efficient intelligence system operated by swift pinnaces. Meanwhile a powerful squadron stationed at Ferrol was an ever-present threat to England and Holland.

The last few years had witnessed a significant reduction in the English forces at sea. The average annual expenditure on the fleet fell from about £66,000 in 1590 to £44,000 in 1594. Meanwhile England was concentrating her chief energies on the war on land. This was due partly to the new danger across the Channel, where Henry IV of France was hard-pressed by his Spanish and domestic foes. A conjunct English expedition of 4,000 men, with a smaller French force, succeeded in saving Brest. But by and large it is difficult to resist the conclusion that much of the money swallowed up in military operations on the Continent during the later years of the war would have been far more profitably expended on a vigorous naval offensive, perhaps on the lines of John Hawkins's plan.

In 1595 it was determined to strike once more at the Spanish colonies across the Atlantic. A composite expedition similar to that of 1585–6, consisting of six royal ships and twenty-one merchantmen, under the leadership of Drake and Hawkins, with a force of 2,500 troops on board, under the command of Sir Thomas Baskerville, sailed from Plymouth, at the end of August, to attack the western treasure at its source. But the situation in Spanish America was now very different from what it had been in the previous decade; as a result of Drake's great raid of 1586, the principal ports had been strongly fortified and the transport of the treasure reorganized. As Waters has observed, ' The Indies became invincible, their treasure unattainable. Ten years after his victory in the Caribbean Drake was to be defeated by the defences he had caused to be erected. In the hour of his triumph he had sown the seeds of his death.'[1] Moreover, the expedition was mismanaged from the start: in the significant words of Sir Thomas Maynarde, the two leaders were ' men of so different natures and dispositions, that what the one desireth the other would commonly oppose against ', and at ' many times was it very doubtfull whether the jorney should proceed.' Through a succession of disastrous delays the vital advantage of surprise was lost; Drake's stroke in the Canaries miscarried, the Spanish colonists received timely warning of the impending assault; and, the hostile defences proving unexpectedly formidable, all attempts on the treasure in Puerto Rico failed; whereupon Hawkins sickened and died, and Baskerville's ill-fated march across the Isthmus was repulsed with heavy loss. This last reverse weighed heavily on the spirits of the surviving leader; ' since our returne from Panama,' says Maynarde, ' he never caried mirth nor joy in his face.'[2] The fleet then took refuge some thirty leagues to the westward of Puerto Rico in Porto Bello Bay, which bore an evil reputation as a breeding-ground of sickness. The original intention had been to sail against Trujillo; but the westerlies held them for weeks inactive in this pestilential retreat, where a large number of them

---

[1] *The True and Perfecte Newes*, ed. D. W. Waters (1957).
[2] Thomas Maynarde, *Sir Francis Drake, His Voyage, 1595*, ed. W. D. Cooley.

died of disease, among them their great commander. Finally Basker-ville led the discomfited fleet back to England after repulsing a Spanish attack off Cuba.

Meanwhile an expedition was being fitted out to attack the enemy's shipping in his home ports. The great raid on Cadiz in 1596 represents the one outstanding success on our side in the post-Armada era. It was carried out by a well-found expedition of seventeen ships of the royal fleet, forty-seven other vessels, and a Dutch squadron of eighteen, with six to eight thousand troops, under the command of the Lord Admiral, Essex, Lord Thomas Howard, and Ralegh. The two last attacked the shipping, while Essex with the army landed and stormed the city. In the harbour of Cadiz were lying four great galleons of 1,000 tons and over, belonging to the newly built ' Twelve Apostles ', eighteen galleys, and between forty and fifty merchantmen. The four galleons were anchored, broadside on, across the narrow part of the harbour, with the galleys in support; the merchantmen had retired to the inner harbour. The Spaniards put up a stubborn resistance. ' Volleys of cannons and culverins ', says Ralegh, ' came as thick as if it had been a skirmish of musketeers.' After a fierce fight the issue was decided by the superiority of the English gunnery. As the assailants were about to board, the galleons cut their cables and withdrew; in attempting to evade the English attack they ran aground, and the *San Felipe* and the *San Tomas* were presently set fire to by their commanders; the *San Mateo* and the *San Andrés* were captured, and later taken to England and added to the royal fleet. The merchantmen lying in the inner harbour were set on fire apparently by order of the Governor of Andalusia, Medina Sidonia. The holocaust raged for three days and three nights, to the total disorganization of the American trade and the ruinous loss of the merchants. The damage to Spain was colossal. Meanwhile Cadiz had been sacked and given up to the flames, after which the raiders sailed for home. Though a fine opportu-nity had been let slip by the English (soon after their departure from Cadiz the homecoming *flota* and the Portuguese East Indiamen arrived safely in port), the operation was a brilliant achievement.

Strategically, however, the raid was of small account and had practically no effect on the course of the war. It did not destroy the Spanish navy; nor did it cripple Spain financially: the *flotas* continued to arrive, and the damage, great as it was, could be made good—in point of fact, the flow of treasure to Spain reached its peak in the period 1590–1600.

Stung to action by the disgrace of Cadiz, Philip II by feverish exertions assembled a fleet of a hundred sail, and, once more aiming at the invasion of England, ordered it to sea in the stormy autumn season. This second Armada, which was put under the command of Don Martin de Padilla, did not get so far as the first. The ships were ill-found, the crews raw and untrained, and the officers discouraged. For four days the force stood slowly to the northward. Then off Finisterre on 17 October it ran into a gale. When the gale had passed the fleet was shattered and dispersed; about a third of the vessels, including some of the best warships, had foundered or gone to pieces on the neighbouring sands; and thousands of Spaniards had perished. That was well for England; for, in point of fact, with her fleet laid up at Chatham, our country was in no condition to meet a winter attack.

In 1597 Philip II, now dying but still resolved on revenge, dispatched his third—and last—Armada against England. Its objective, Falmouth, was kept a profound secret; it was instructed to seize and fortify the peninsula on which Pendennis castle stands, after which it was to lie in wait, off the Isles of Scilly, for the return of an English squadron under Essex which had been sent to the Azores. Following the arrival of reinforcements from Spain, it was further to capture and garrison Plymouth. In the autumn the Council received the disturbing news that the Spanish fleet was off the western coast and began hurriedly to mobilize. Then, at the height of the alarm, the news reached London that Essex had returned. Actually there had been nothing to fear. Once again ' Jehova blew with His winds and they were scattered.' Off Blavet in Brittany the enemy fleet had been dispersed by a hard north-easter. Only a few of the ships, holding on for the rendezvous off the Lizard, had come within sight of our shores. Most of the enemy got away before the Lord Admiral could put to sea; and by the middle of November almost the whole Armada was safely back in its home ports.

It was only too clear, however, that the frustration of the enemy's plans had been due to bad weather and bad seamanship on the part of the Spaniards. English strategy could claim no possible credit for the overthrow of the second and third Armadas. To that extent Elizabeth's mistrust of the navalists was justified. In 1599 yet another attempt at invasion was abandoned because the Dutch were threatening the *flota* and the Azores. Again, when in 1601 the Spaniards invaded Ireland the English fleet made no attempt to strike at the hostile naval forces. Only at the end of the reign was our Navy again put to a proper use. In 1602 an English squadron attacked the enemy in his home waters and did him so much damage as effectively to remove any danger of invasion that year. In 1603 there was also to be a return to a sound and comprehensive strategy. It was proposed to maintain a continuous blockade of the enemy's coast from February to November by two strong squadrons, the one relieving the other, with the object of forcing the Spaniards to decisive action or of cutting off the vital flow of treasure. But in March the old Queen died; and peace negotiations were at once begun by her successor, James I.

V

England and Holland

I

Even before the death of Queen Elizabeth in 1603 signs had not been lacking of the grave deterioration of the Navy. It would scarcely be too much to say that England, in those early years of the seventeenth century, was, in fact, living upon her prestige. The cost of the Navy had been continually increasing while its effective strength was fast declining. Sir John Hawkins and his brethren were dead; ineptitude, waste, graft, and peculation had appeared in every department of the administration; the once proud ships lay rotting in harbour, and their crews were disbanded; nepotism was rampant, and the Lord Admiral (the Earl of Nottingham, formerly Lord Howard of Effingham) in his dotage.

Under the administration of Sir Robert Mansell, Treasurer of the Navy from 1604 to 1618, the Fleet may be considered to have reached its nadir. There were frequently recurring cases of violation of English territorial waters, and even of English ports, by the Dunkirkers and Dutch; the traditional right of the flag could no longer be enforced; and pirates abounded all about the British Isles. The truth was, that while England's merchant shipping was expanding year by year, her fighting Navy was in a state of decay.[1]

In 1604 the long Spanish War was at last brought to an end through the combined efforts of James I and his chief minister, Robert Cecil. Henceforth, by the King's order, privateering was forbidden. The consequence was that mariners like John Ward, who had formerly obtained letters of marque, now found their occupation gone. The prohibition, however, was to some extent nominal, rather than

---

[1] ' Now it numbers only 37 ships,' the Venetian Ambassador informed the Senate, in 1607, ' many of them old and rotten, and barely fit for service '. Yet England, he added, was ' full of sailors and men fit for service at sea '. By 1618 the total strength of the Navy had shrunk to about 27 ships.

actual. For many of the craft which in the previous reign had engaged in privateering now turned over to plain piracy, which—in default of a strong Navy—proved a highly lucrative calling.

But it was all to the good that the cessation of hostilities enabled the national energies, which for close on twenty years had been largely absorbed in the long-drawn-out struggle with Spain, to be directed once more to commerce, colonization, and exploration. The successful outcome of the maritime war now rendered possible the peaceful expansion which marked the early decades of the seventeenth century. The English continued to work the deep-sea fisheries in the North Atlantic; the Newfoundland and Iceland fisheries employed about 150 and 120 ships respectively. The first permanent English colony in America—Virginia—was founded in 1607. The occupation of Bermuda dates from 1609. The year 1620 saw the voyage of the Pilgrim Fathers in the *Mayflower*. Other plantations followed at brief intervals: St. Kitt's (1624), Barbados (1627), Massachusetts (1628), Rhode Island (1630), Antigua (1632), Connecticut, and Maryland (1633). During the same era the search for the North-West Passage was resumed with the voyages of Henry Hudson and William Baffin. On the other side of the globe the East India Company had begun to establish itself in the East Indian archipelago; thither they made successive voyages on an ever-increasing scale; but, being inferior in numbers, resources, and organization to their Dutch rivals, they presently abandoned the islands for the Indian mainland. English depots were set up at Surat (1607), Madras (1639), Hugli (1650), and Bombay (1668).

The reign of James I witnessed the first manifestations of the coming rift with Holland. Under the Tudor monarchs the rich herring fishery off the east coast of Britain had been open to foreigners, who actually outnumbered the native fishermen. James I now reserved the exclusive rights of fishing in English waters for his own subjects. The exploitation of the herring fishery was not an issue where compromise was easy or perhaps even possible. The naval power of both peoples was closely linked up with these hardy North Sea fishing crews: the Dutch regarded the fisheries as the foundation of their shipping, prosperity, and power; our statesmen and economists considered the rapid expansion of the Dutch fishing fleets as a menace to the wealth and strength of England; and from this time onward the fierce rivalry which was to culminate half a century later in three great maritime wars began to manifest itself in a variety of directions.

At the same time complaints poured into the Council concerning the depredations of the pirates and privateers who infested the waters around the British Isles. Throughout the whole Stuart period the light and speedy lateen-rigged pirate craft from the Barbary ports of northern Africa harassed our seaborne trade and raided our ports and fishing villages. The reign of James I witnessed the rapid rise of Salee as a pirate stronghold, rivalling and surpassing those older centres of piracy, Tunis and Algiers. The activities of the Moors soon embraced both sides of the Atlantic. In 1615 some pirates from Salee appeared off the Newfoundland banks. In 1617 the Algerines pillaged Madeira, carrying off 1,200 prisoners and much plunder. In 1634 they abducted 800 persons from Iceland. In 1617 one of these Moorish pirates was actually taken in the Thames. In 1625 three others surprised and captured Lundy Island. In the same year no less than a thousand English seamen were taken and enslaved by the Moors. On the night of 31 June 1631, Murad Reis seized and sacked Baltimore, a flourishing fishing port on the south coast of Ireland, carrying off more than two hundred of its inhabitants into slavery. In 1640 a similar raid was made on Penzance. Pirates ranged the Channel, and matters at last reached such a pass that Trinity House desired that the light on the Lizard should be extinguished for fear that it should assist the Moors.

A high percentage of these pirates were European renegades, including Englishmen who had once been privateersmen and had found themselves put out of business by the peace of 1604. They had thrown in their lot with the Moors of the Barbary coast and in not a few cases had prospered exceedingly. Two of the most celebrated renegades were John Ward and Simon Danzer, who had established themselves at Tunis and Algiers respectively. There were also Captain Richard Giffard of the *Fortune*, and Sir Francis Verney, who is even said to have adopted the costume of the country. Some of the renegades returned to England in 1612 upon the proffer of pardon for life and goods; but the majority chose to remain in the country of their adoption. From Ward, Danzer, Giffard, Verney, and their fellows the Moorish crews learned the art of sailing men-of-war in northern seas. These Barbary corsairs were admirably adapted for their work. To lighten the ships many of their knees were cut away, which, as Monson remarked, resulted in a notable increase of speed, ' like a man that is tight trussed and hath his doublet buttoned, that by loos'ning it he is able to run the faster '. Since the practice of the Moors was to board, they did not need to carry many guns; and when pursued by warships, their superior speed generally enabled them to escape. The Barbary ports were essentially pirate strongholds. ' Their one function was to prey upon commerce, and for this purpose not only the fleet but the whole state was organized.'[1]

Meanwhile privateers from Dunkirk swarmed in the North Sea, and other pirates—many of them home-bred—cruised off the coasts of Scotland and Ireland. Bristol was the port most seriously affected as much of its trade followed the Atlantic coasts which lay furthest from protection. During the period 1604–16 Sir William Monson was employed as Admiral of the Narrow Seas for the purpose of putting down piracy and privateering. But his ships were poor sailers, and they were at sea only for comparatively short periods. English merchants, finding that they could look for little protection from the Navy, were obliged to arm several of their own vessels for the defence of commerce. The operations of the pirates continued on an ever-increasing scale, in spite of spasmodic attempts to curb them, until the revival of English sea power in the days of the Commonwealth.

The graft and peculation which flourished under the administration of Sir Robert Mansell finally attained such dimensions that, in 1618, a long and searching inquiry was instituted into the condition of the Navy. These investigations were entrusted to a Commission presided over by a leading London merchant, Sir Lionel Cranfield, and revealed grave and widespread abuses, for which they suggested certain remedies and reforms. The Commission set about its work in a thoroughly determined and businesslike way; and, when Nottingham and his party resisted, the old Admiral was pensioned—in point of fact, bought out. He was replaced by the King's favourite, the Duke of Buckingham, whose powerful influence and support were thereby secured. Mansell was got rid of in much the same way. The Cranfield Commission did much to deal with the more glaring examples of corruption and fraud. Thenceforward things were never so bad as before.

[1] G. N. Clark, ' The Barbary Corsairs in the Seventeenth Century ', *Cambridge Historical Journal*, Vol. VIII (1944), p. 25.

Despite the decline of England's naval power her Fleet was still a factor to be reckoned with in the politics of Europe. Alarmed by the threat to their interests, and even independence, of a Habsburg hegemony of Europe, France, Holland, Venice, and Genoa, together with certain other States, began to draw together in opposition to the recombination of the Spanish and Austrian branches of the House of Habsburg. In the new political situation that was arising the control of sea-communications between Spain and Austria was of prime importance, and the alliance of England was sought by the opponents of the Habsburg power.

On the outbreak of the Thirty Years War in 1618 and the eviction of James I's son-in-law, the Elector Palatine, from his hereditary dominions, James I sought to effect his restoration by developing a friendly understanding with Spain, whose ambassador, Gondomar, exercised at this time a powerful influence upon English policy. To placate the Spaniards, the King in 1618 had Ralegh executed on a false charge of treason, and later attempted to marry his son Charles, Prince of Wales, to a Spanish Infanta. The marriage negotiations, however, proved abortive; and the Prince of Wales and his companion, Buckingham, returned to England. James I's foreign policy was, in fact, both weak and vacillating. The truth was that England, in the early half of the seventeenth century, was of small account in European affairs; and Buckingham—the trusted friend and counsellor of both James I and his son—was regarded with special aversion by the Commons, who refused to support his grandiose schemes of a coalition against the Habsburgs.

The latter part of the reign was notable for a venture of great future consequence. The first beginnings of English naval action in the Mediterranean may be traced back to James I's consent to the hiring out of certain English merchantmen to assist the Venetian Republic in its impending struggle with Spain. This was soon followed by a much more important development. In 1620 James I sent a powerful squadron under the leadership of Sir Robert Mansell into the Mediterranean, ostensibly to coerce the Barbary pirates, but actually to serve as a check on Spanish aggression. Mansell's operations against Algiers were unsuccessful; and the expedition soon afterwards retired through the Straits without achieving any material success. Nevertheless, it marked a beginning. The weapon was clumsily wielded and promising opportunities had been missed. But, for the first time in history, an English fleet had appeared as a political force in the Mediterranean. The presence of this squadron of Mansell's in the waters hitherto dominated by the galleys of Spain and her tributaries made a profound impression on the surrounding States and came as a severe shock to the Spanish government; the lesson was not forgotten.

2

In the reign of Charles I the condition of the Navy continued, though slowly, to improve. The new King, like all his House, was keenly interested in the Service, and desired to increase its strength. By exacting the payment of Ship-Money, he was able to keep in being the nucleus of a permanent, professional fighting Fleet. This in years to come was destined to expand into the immense Navy of the Commonwealth and Protectorate. Moreover, the Ship-Money squadrons—unlike the heterogeneous expeditions of earlier years—were composed of warships only: there were no merchantmen. But, largely owing to Charles I's failure to come to terms with Parliament, he never had enough money to maintain the Navy in a reasonable state of efficiency.

On Charles I's accession, in 1625, Buckingham had continued in control of English policy. His endeavours, however, to act the parts of a great diplomatist or an inspired commander were uniformly unsuccessful. Reversing his former policy, Charles I declared war on Spain. What was now envisaged by the English government was the total overthrow of Spanish sea power through the seizure of Cadiz and the destruction of the Spanish fleet. After this Spain was to be blockaded by our naval forces based on Cadiz and the whole flow of treasure, upon which both Spain and her Empire depended for the successful prosecution of the war, intercepted. A great naval and military force, under the command of Lord Wimbledon, was in 1625 dispatched against Cadiz. The fleet was a very large one, numbering over a hundred sail. But most of the vessels were small merchantmen; and the captains were principally concerned with keeping themselves and their craft out of harm's way. The vessels were ill-found, the crews diseased and half-starving, the troops but raw levies; the commander-in-chief was wholly ignorant of sea affairs, and the expedition was mismanaged from start to finish. Wimbledon's main object was supposed to be the destruction of Spanish shipping. This he wholly failed to achieve. Instead he resolved to attack the city. But, halting at a village *en route*, his troops looted the wine stored for the West India trade and speedily drank themselves into a state which precluded any such attempt. A half-hearted attempt to waylay the homecoming treasure ships was likewise abandoned, and the expedition straggled back to England.

Having failed to achieve anything against Spain, Buckingham proceeded to quarrel with Richelieu: all hope of waging war effectively against Spain or Austria was now at an end, since only by developing the understanding with France would it have been in any way possible for England to make headway against the Habsburg power and thus to restore the Elector Palatine. Buckingham took command of the large but ill-organized naval and military force fitted out against France. It was his object to relieve the beleaguered Huguenots in La Rochelle; and to that end it was necessary to seize and use as a base the neighbouring island of Rhé. The expedition proved a calamitous failure; and the fleet did not distinguish itself. The English overran Rhé but were unable to secure the citadel. Large French forces were landed on the island, and the besiegers in their turn were besieged. In the end, after fighting a desperate rearguard action, the English were compelled to withdraw with heavy losses; and the wretched remnant of the expedition returned to port. A second attempt to relieve the Huguenots had also to be given up. Buckingham was preparing a third expedition when he was murdered in the High Street of Portsmouth by a fanatic named Fenton.

The condition of the Navy now went from bad to worse. In January 1628 Sir John Mervyn, commanding in the narrow seas, reported from Plymouth that there were no hammocks in the vessels and that ' the men lodge on the bare decks . . . their condition miserable beyond relation; many are so naked and exposed to the weather in doing their duties that their toes and feet miserably rot and fall away piecemeal, being mortified with extreme cold.' In the following year Mervyn further declared that ' Foul winter weather, naked bodies, and empty bellies make the men voice the King's service worse than a galley slavery.'

As a result of the growth of the Dutch and French navies and the formidable numbers of the Barbary corsairs a new situation was developing, for which the English naval forces of the early Stuart era were plainly inadequate. A substantial addition to the English Navy was the outcome. In his endeavours to govern without a Parliament Charles I in 1634 had recourse to the expedient of Ship-Money. According to ancient precedent writs were sent out to the sea-ports of the realm, requiring them to contribute to the upkeep of the Fleet (only instead of the vessels they had formerly supplied, these were now expected to pay Ship-Money). The first Ship-Money Fleet, comprising the *Merhonour* (flagship), *James, Swiftsure, St. George, St. Andrew, Henrietta Maria, Vanguard, Rainbow, Red Lion, Reformation, Antelope, Leopard, Swallow, Mary Rose, Adventure*, and a number of pinnaces, cruised in the Channel between May and October 1633, under the command of the Earl of Lindsey, with instructions that part of the force was to be dispatched ' to such places in the Narrow Seas where you shall hear or learn any pirates, sea rovers, or picaroons frequent, and to use all possible means to suppress or apprehend them '.

Next year the Ship-Money writs were issued to inland as well as to maritime towns and counties; and on this occasion there was determined and widespread opposition. The Ship-Money controversy became, in fact, part of the great constitutional struggle which finally terminated in Charles I's downfall and execution. Nor, from the naval point of view, did the experiment achieve any marked success. The great ships of war, comparatively few in number, were quite unable to cope with the swarms of small and nimble privateers. The Ship-Money Fleets, it is true, did something to restore the English supremacy in the narrow seas and forced the Dutch to pay for the right of fishing in English waters; and Rainborow won a well-deserved success, in 1637, in his expedition against the Salee rovers. But the moral effect of this parade of strength was for the most part lost, as will presently appear, through the débâcle in the Downs in 1639, which revealed the essential weakness of Charles I's Navy.

In the struggle between King and Parliament (1642–8) naval power played a decisive part. The support of the Navy, indeed, was vitally important to Parliament; since London, which was the principal stronghold and arsenal of the Parliamentary cause, might well have been blockaded and starved into submission, had the Fleet declared for the King. As it was, the Earl of Northumberland, the Lord High Admiral, went over to the side of Parliament; and the mass of the seamen, who were strongly Puritan in outlook, followed his lead. The principal command was given to the Earl of Warwick. In the Civil War the Fleet assisted the Parliamentary Army, patrolled the coasts and prevented foreign intervention, helped to relieve the Parliamentary garrisons, cut off the Royalist areas of the country from traffic with the outside world, and protected that of the Parliamentarians. The homage of the flag—the traditional English claim that in the Channel and narrow seas all other craft should strike their flags and lower their topsails on meeting English warships—was strictly enforced.

3

So strong was the English tradition of hostility to Spain that it was long before either the government or people awoke to the fact that, while our old enemy, Spain, was visibly weakening, a new and formidable rival was arising across the North Sea.

The defeat and destruction of the Armada in 1588 had given the Dutch a superb opportunity, of which they had taken full advantage. The following decade saw the rapid and sustained expansion of Dutch maritime and colonial enterprise. At the same time religion gave place to commerce as the matrix of wars. In place of the decadent Spanish monarchy, our ancestors found themselves confronted by the virile, industrious, and immensely wealthy Dutch Republic, or United Provinces, now the leading maritime and commercial Power of the Continent. The principal barrier to English maritime expansion was no longer Catholic Spain, but Protestant Holland.

The Dutch represented the first example in history of a true Sea Power, in the modern sense of the term. Holland was nothing if not a maritime Power. Her soil, indeed, would support only a fraction of her population: for the rest she must look to her commerce and fisheries. The very existence of Holland as a nation depended upon the sea. Her people had become rich, first, by the fisheries, and, in later centuries, by the carrying-trade. In the reign of Elizabeth (' to their immeasurable wealth and our shame,' as Monson declared) they had begun to work the fertile fishery on the British side of the North Sea. Year after year an immense Dutch fleet of busses, schuyts, doggers, and other craft sailed for the fishing grounds to the north of the

British Isles.[1] Thence they worked gradually down the east coast of Britain, from the Shetlands to Yarmouth, barrelling the catch by day and shipping it home to Holland, from the end of June to early autumn. By the middle of the seventeenth century the Dutch possessed some two thousand fishing vessels, about one-half of which were good-sized herring busses of 80 tons or over. Their smoked herrings were exported to all parts of the Continent. Amsterdam, according to the old Dutch saying, was ' built on herrings'. Their busses went long-lining for cod on the Dogger Bank both before and after the herring season. They were also predominant in the whale fisheries of the Arctic. The Hollanders were the greatest shipbuilders and shipowners that the world had ever seen. Shipbuilding was cheaper by a third or even a half than in England. Throughout the century their shipyards drove a roaring trade. The vessels they turned out were better-rigged and designed to be worked by far smaller crews than the average; and, in consequence, their running costs were much lower than those of their English rivals. The bulkiest European cargoes were almost invariably shipped in Dutch bottoms. About 1650 they developed a type of barque called the fluyt, which was especially adapted for the carriage of merchandise. The Dutch were in fact the pioneers of large-scale ocean commerce.[2] They had no less than eight hundred vessels engaged in the West Indian trade alone. An even more important factor in the development of their shipbuilding was the traffic to the East. Early in the seventeenth century the Dutch had begun to follow a new and better track on the long voyage to Batavia. On rounding the Cape they would now run their easting down in about latitude 40°S. before turning north for the Straits of Sunda. On this wild passage through the ' roaring forties ' stout ships were needed.

History could show nothing to compare with the range and volume of Dutch commerce. It was one of the prime factors in seventeenth-

---

[1] ' The Hollander busses are greate and strong and able to brooke foul weather whereas our cobles, crayers, and boats, being small and thin-sided, are easily swallowed by rough seas, not daring to adventure far in fair weather by reason of their weaknesse for feare of stormes ': Tobias Gentleman, *Englands Way to Win Wealth*, (1614), p. 111.

[2] ' The desiderata for merchantmen were cheap but seaworthy construction, good burthen with convenience of stowage suited to the cargo, simplicity of rigging so that a small crew would suffice, a low wage for seamen, cheap victualling ': V. Barbour in *Economic History Review*, 1st Series, II, p. 273.

century politics. The more virile and industrious Protestant elements in the south had abandoned their homes and migrated to the north. Amsterdam had succeeded Antwerp as the leading entrepôt of Europe. The wealth of the northern provinces was concentrated in Amsterdam, which had outstripped Genoa and Venice as the international money-market; its warehouses were crammed with goods from all over the globe. Not only had the Dutch secured the commerce formerly carried on by the Hanse and the rich Italian trade of the Mediter-ranean, but they had also extended their traffic far beyond the limits of either. Within seven short years they had built up a great empire in the orient on the ruins of the Portuguese. They had established themselves on the Indian mainland, and in Malacca, the Moluccas, and various other parts of the East Indian archipelago. They had extended their trade to China and Japan. In 1603 the Dutch East India Company was formed, with the then enormous capital of over £$\frac{1}{2}$ million, and backed by the State. The initial capital of the English East India Company was only £30,000. For upwards of fifty years the Dutch practically monopolized the bulk of the Eastern trade. Under their able and unscrupulous leader, Jan Pieterszoon Coen, they dominated the Indian Ocean and made Batavia the great entrepôt of the East Indian archipelago. The English were then obliged to retire to the mainland. On the other side of the globe the Dutch had seized extensive territories in Brazil, and had founded the township of New Amsterdam in North America. From their settlements in St. Eustatius and Curaçao they largely controlled the export and import trade of the West Indies. By their capture of all the Portuguese strongholds on the West African coast, by the middle of the century they gained what was practically a monopoly of the supply of negro slaves to the West Indian sugar islands. ' In short,' declared the Grand Pensionary, John de Witt, ' the Hollanders have well nigh beaten all nations, by traffic, out of the seas, and become the only carrier of goods throughout the world.'

In the first half of the seventeenth century the Dutch republic had attained the summit of its prosperity. Its cities and towns were enlarged, and new harbours dug. By the skilful reclamation of swamps and lakes its inhabitants turned vast areas of submerged soil into fertile farmland, and erected dykes, or artificial embankments, to keep back the sea; the power from countless windmills forced the water out of their sluices. ' The country has become rich by the force of industry ', Sir William Temple declared in 1668, ' by being the general magazine of Europe, and furnishing all parts with whatever the market wants and invites, and being as they are very properly called, the common carriers of the world.' In seaborne trade, in commercial organization and finance, in literature and scientific knowledge, the Dutch were in the forefront of European nations. It was from Holland that the finest mathematical and astronomical instruments could be procured. The Dutch had also discovered the art of cutting and polishing diamonds and for centuries Amsterdam possessed a monopoly of this art. The earliest newspapers appeared in Holland. The Bank of Amsterdam was founded many decades before the Bank of England. The early seventeenth century was also the golden age of Dutch painting. The solid comfort and prosperity of the burgher aristocracy of the republic are superbly reflected in the rich canvases of Rubens, Rembrandt, and Hobbema.

In 1635 the understanding between France and the United Provinces developed into a formal alliance. The Dutch struggle for independence now merged with the wider issues of the Thirty Years War. In the autumn of 1639 a great Spanish fleet, comprising about seventy sail, with a considerable force of troops on board, commanded by Antonio de Oquendo, passed up Channel on its way to the Spanish Netherlands. On 16–18 September it was attacked off Beachy Head by a handful of ships under Martin Tromp, who presently caused it to seek refuge in the Downs. For several weeks the two fleets lay watching each other in these neutral waters; until at daybreak on the misty morning of 21 October Tromp, who by this time had been substantially reinforced, bore down on the enemy, and, despite the presence in the Downs of an English fleet under Pennington, engaged Oquendo to such effect that all but a dozen of his ships were either taken or destroyed. Oquendo arrived home with the remnant of his force in March 1640, only to die of a broken heart like his father before him half a century before. This action in the Downs, together with the equally decisive four days' fight off the coast of Brazil, resulted in the annihilation of the Spanish navy, and marked the culminating point of the long and desperate struggle waged by the Dutch against the historic enemy. It also revealed, in the clearest possible manner, the present impotence of the English Navy, even in its own waters.

4

The naval problem confronting the leaders of the Parliamentary party after the execution of Charles I in 1649 was a formidable one. The Civil War had by now spread from the land to the sea. A number of ships which had broken away from the rest of the Fleet during the previous year had sailed over to Holland and were now under the command of Prince Rupert. Scotland and Ireland were still unconquered. A number of outlying islands, including the Isles of Scilly, were held by the Royalists. Several of the English settlements in North America and the West Indies were hostile to the new government, as were all the States of the Continent.

The Parliamentary leaders took prompt and effective action to deal with the situation. The office of the Lord High Admiral was executed by the Council of State. The principles of the Parliamentary Army were similarly applied to the Parliamentary Navy; and the officers appointed by the new government began to exhibit the same vigour and efficiency in naval affairs as they had previously displayed in military. Three colonels of the New Model Army—Edward Popham, Robert Blake, and Richard Deane—were appointed to command the Fleet with the rank of 'Generals at Sea'. Sir Harry Vane presided over the Navy Commissioners, who were made responsible for the work of administration and reorganization. These measures were taken primarily for the purpose of securing the Navy firmly under the control of the Parliamentary party.

To uphold its rights and to protect the trade-routes, the Council of State sent a squadron to hunt down Rupert. The latter, who was on the way to becoming a highly successful commerce-raider, was blockaded at Kinsale by a strong force commanded, first, by Sir George Ayscue, and, later, by Blake and Deane. Blake, however, was presently forced off his station by a gale; whereupon the Prince managed to escape and sought refuge in Lisbon. Blake followed in pursuit, and, lying off that port, assailed Portuguese shipping until their government changed its policy and required Rupert to leave. The Prince then entered the Mediterranean, with Blake still in pursuit. Near Cartagena one of the Royalist warships was taken, while several others were driven ashore and wrecked. The Council of State then dispatched Penn with a squadron to reinforce Blake, who, towards the close of 1651, returned to England. Rupert in the meantime had sought shelter in Toulon, then got away into the Atlantic, where, for a period, he preyed on English and Spanish shipping. But the Royalist squadron was doomed. In no condition to keep the sea, it eventually wasted away; there followed an unprofitable, semi-piratical cruise in the West Indies; and finally, in the spring of 1653, Rupert returned to Europe, in the only warship left to him, and took refuge in a French port. Meanwhile, the Royalist bases in Scilly, the Isle of Man, Jersey, and Guernsey had been successively reduced; the Navy played a vital role in Oliver Cromwell's victorious campaigns in Scotland; and Ayscue led a squadron across the Atlantic to subdue the English colonies in the West Indies and North America. The final triumph of the Parliamentary cause was, therefore, in great part owing to the assistance and support of the Navy.

The appearance of Blake's strong squadron within the Straits in the period 1650–1 was destined to have consequences of the highest importance. First, it served to counter the French design to dominate the Mediterranean. Second, it secured the diplomatic recognition of the Commonwealth Government by Spain; its recognition by Portugal also quickly followed. Third, it marked a new departure in English naval policy. Henceforward the task of trade protection came to be regarded as one of the first duties of the fighting Navy. Hitherto the Levant trade had had to look to its own defence: now a regular service of convoys was organized. Early in 1651 William Penn arrived within the Straits with the outward-bound Smyrna fleet, while Blake escorted back the homeward-bound Levant trade. Thus English commerce with the Mediterranean was protected, French privateering repressed, and Rupert driven out of the Straits. The following January Badiley came out with another squadron, convoying the Levant trade, to relieve Penn, who then returned to England. In these vigorous measures for commerce protection within the Straits may be traced the germ of the future Mediterranean Fleet.

In 1650 the Commonwealth government passed a Convoy Act for the better protection of 'the Trade of this nation'. It is to be noted that this measure was followed by a series of later Acts and Orders in Council.

Between 1649 and 1651 the strength of the Fleet was virtually doubled. No less than forty-one new vessels were added to the Navy

List. Nothing on anything like the same scale had ever existed before. For the first time in our history a large standing Navy was kept continuously in being and efficiently administered. The remarkable success achieved by the Parliamentary leaders in naval affairs is largely to be ascribed to the ample financial reserves at their disposal, derived from the sequestration of the estates of the Cavaliers. Under the new government the nation expended more than half of its income on the Navy. The money was on the whole well and wisely spent. During the Interregnum over two hundred vessels of various sizes were added to the Fleet.[1] Many of these vessels were built by Phineas Pett and his numerous relations established in the dockyards. Nevertheless, it is always to be borne in mind that the Protectorate was living largely on capital, and bequeathed a heavy debt to the succeeding government.

5

The antagonism between the English and Dutch, which developed during the second quarter of the century and finally came to a head in the time of the Commonwealth, sprang from maritime and commercial jealousy. The two peoples were natural and inevitable rivals—rivals alike for the herring fisheries of the North Sea and the whale fisheries of Spitzbergen; for the traffic with Russia and the Baltic; for the West African trade, and, above all, the rich East Indies trade. From the Brazils to Batavia the English found the struggle going against them and their commercial and colonial expansion held in check by these stronger and more experienced competitors. After twenty years of strife the rivalry of the English and Dutch East India Companies had culminated in the terrible Amboyna massacre of 1623 and the expulsion of all the English factors from the Spice Islands: in the ensuing decades ' the foule and bloody act ' of Amboyna was neither forgotten nor forgiven in this country. As the century advanced there was a similar conflict of interests on the other side of the globe—in North America, in the West Indies, and in Guiana. A major factor in these developments was the English insistence upon the right of search during the war of reprisals then being waged against France and the consequent injury

---

[1] In view of the serious inroad upon the oak groves occasioned by the vast ship-building programme of this era, the supply of suitable timber was henceforward of paramount importance to the Fleet. In this connection the main authority is R. G. Albion, *Forests and Sea Power* (1926).

to Dutch interests. Another fruitful cause of quarrel lay in the demand that all other craft should strike their flags and lower their topsails on encountering English warships. The Dutch were further incensed by the news that Ayscue in the West Indies had captured twenty-seven of their ships that had been trading with the Royalists.

On top of all the existing causes of conflict came the Navigation Act passed by the Council of State in 1651, prohibiting the import into England of all colonial goods, save in English ships, or those of the producing country. The preamble to the Act made it plain that its ultimate object was the increase of the Navy. It was stated that the Act was made ' for the increase of the shipping and the encouragement of the Navigation of the Nation, which, under the good providence and protection of God is so great a means of the welfare and safety of the Commonwealth '. This was seen as a direct threat to the enormous carrying trade on which the prosperity of Holland chiefly depended. Though the effect of the Navigation Act had been somewhat exaggerated, it did, nevertheless, accelerate the drift to war. The angry feeling on both sides of the North Sea was exacerbated by the outpourings of the pamphleteers. In the end hostilities were precipitated by a quarrel off Dover in May 1652 between Blake and Tromp over the salute, from which the latter had to retire with the loss of two of his ships. The declaration of war followed soon afterwards.

From the beginning of the war it was apparent that the odds were heavily against the Dutch. Though the latter possessed far more ships and seamen, the Dutch navy was comparatively small. Few of the Dutch ships mounted as many as forty guns; nor had they nearly as many seamen available for war. The Dutch vessels, being flat-bottomed on account of their shallow and sandy coasts, were less weatherly than the English, which were faster when sailing on a wind and better adapted for tacking and manœuvring; from which it followed that the English were more often successful in securing the weather-gauge. The fine battleships lately constructed by the Pett family were greatly superior to anything which Holland could produce. Moreover, the proportion of merchantmen to fighting ships in the Dutch navy was much higher than in the English; and the former carried only a few small guns. The average Dutch sailor was a first-class seaman, but an indifferent officer. The Dutch crews were, on the whole, inferior to the English in training, discipline, and morale.

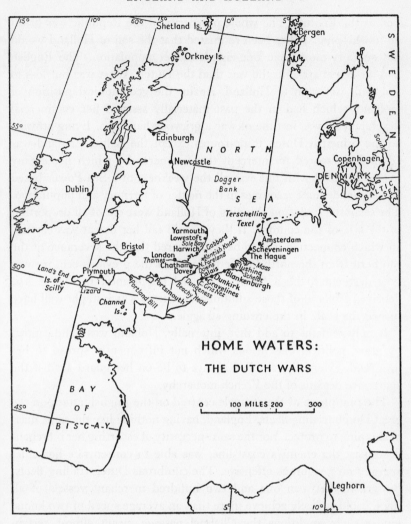

HOME WATERS:

THE DUTCH WARS

0   100 MILES 200   300

To the high organizing ability of the Navy Commissioners was largely
due the rapid and efficient fitting out of the English fleets.[1] For their
part the Dutch were handicapped by the fact that the naval power of
the Republic was administered by no less than five admiralties.

Economically, the Dutch were in nothing like as favourable a posi-

---

[1] 'Never, before or since, were the combatant branches of the Navy so well
supported. As a rule our seamen have had to beat the enemy afloat in spite of the
Admiralty ashore, but here they had every assistance that foresight and earnestness
could give '. Oppenheim, *History of the Administration of the Royal Navy* (1896),
p. 111.

tion as the English. The whole prosperity of the Republic was based on its shipping. It has been estimated that the soil of Holland would not support more than one-eighth of her population. The English had far less at stake in the war than the Dutch. What was but loss to England, was ruin to Holland. Again, the geographical position of Holland, which had in the past materially assisted her commercial development, was in time of war a grievous handicap. Lying athwart all the principal Dutch trade-routes except the Baltic, England was admirably situated to intercept the commerce by which her enemy lived.[1] Coupled with this was all the weakness of a Sea Power based on very inadequate resources in the matter of territory and population. The seaborne trade and shipping of Holland were out of all proportion to the size of the country. If they should fail her defeat was certain. In which connection it is to be remembered that the severance of the southern from the northern Netherlands in the previous century was now destined to be a factor of crucial importance, in that it had deprived Holland of those additional resources which might well have turned the scale in the ensuing struggle.

It only remains to add that, internally, Holland was handicapped by grave political dissensions which not infrequently spread to her fleet, and, externally, she had always to be on her guard against the aggressive designs of the French monarchy.

The first phase of the struggle centred on the English attack on the great Dutch trading fleets. England, having nothing like the same mass of shipping to protect, nor the same necessity of escorting her merchant fleets past the enemy's coast-line, was able to concentrate her chief energies on a vigorous offensive. The cumbrous Dutch trading-fleets, comprising between one and two hundred merchant vessels of all sizes, could scarcely achieve more than an average speed of two knots. Under such conditions the Channel passage meant almost certain destruction except with the most powerful protection. The Dutch were therefore compelled to use their battle fleet to cover the outward and homeward sailings of their trade. Thus in the summer of 1652 Blake with the main force was ordered to intercept the enemy's Baltic commerce and to destroy his fishing fleet and its escorts off the

---

[1] It has been estimated that no less than 1,500 prizes were taken from the Dutch in the course of the war—a number more than double the total merchant tonnage of England.

north of Scotland. Meanwhile Ayscue succeeded in intercepting a Dutch trading fleet near Calais, and captured or destroyed every vessel. Thereafter fortune continued to smile on the English. Tromp with a great fleet of 100 sail was prevented from sailing northward to attack Blake by strong northerly winds; and Ayscue, left to cover the Thames estuary with his small force, was saved from certain destruction at the hands of Tromp's vastly superior fleet by a sudden shift of the wind. Tromp now sailed northward and on 25 July sighted the main English fleet off the Shetland Islands. But a heavy north-west gale arose, from the full force of which Blake, lying in the lee of the Shetlands, was protected, while Tromp's vessels were caught and scattered over a wide area, with the result that he was compelled to return to port to refit. Soon afterwards he was superseded in his command by de Witt.

Later in the same season Ayscue and de Ruyter, sailing to the westward to convoy their respective trading fleets through the Channel, joined action, on 16 August, off Plymouth; Ayscue—though somewhat superior in numbers—was worsted and compelled to retire into Plymouth to refit, while de Ruyter, with the outward-bound trade, continued his voyage. On his return, with the homecoming trade, de Ruyter adroitly out-manœuvred the superior English forces waiting for him in the Channel.

The English Council had now begun to realize that the destruction of the enemy's fighting fleet was the essential preliminary to the destruction of the enemy's seaborne commerce. Not until the hostile fleet had been decisively defeated and disabled, in fact, would an effective blockade of the enemy's coast become possible. By the early autumn of 1652 the second phase of the war, the period of concentration and battle for the command of the sea, had begun.

The next encounter took place on 28 September at the Kentish Knock, a shoal lying off the mouth of the Thames, when a heavy gunnery duel was fought between a force of sixty-eight English ships under Blake, and another fifty-seven Dutch under de Witt: the rival fleets sailing slowly past each other close-hauled in line ahead and can-nonading at close range—the action terminating in the defeat of the Dutch. After this final attempt to secure a decision, the Dutch returned .to their former policy of trade protection.

Elated with their success, the English thought that there would be no further fighting until the spring. In the Mediterranean, the Dutch were markedly the stronger. A small English squadron had been defeated and driven into the refuge of the neutral port of Leghorn by a superior Dutch force under Van Galen; and the English traffic with the Mediterranean had been brought to a standstill. Blake was therefore instructed by the Council to detach a squadron of twenty sail for service in the Mediterranean. But the campaign of 1652 was *not* ended. The Dutch rapidly repaired their fleet, which presently put to sea under Tromp, eighty-five strong. In November he received orders to escort a convoy of 450 merchantmen through the Channel, while the bulk of the English Fleet was laid up for the winter—Blake being left with no more than forty-two ships in the Downs. Leaving his convoy with an escort off the Flanders coast, Tromp worked round behind the Goodwins; and Blake, despite the disparity of numbers, elected to fight. The ensuing action lasted until nightfall, when the English, heavily defeated, retired under cover of darkness into Dover roads. The battle of Dungeness had given the Dutch the command of the Channel. Van Galen's victory off Leghorn had likewise confirmed the Dutch control of the Mediterranean. The consequence was that Dutch commerce flowed freely once more, and the English suffered correspondingly. At the same time the enemy had induced Denmark to close the Sound against English shipping. The effect of this measure was to deprive our Fleet of Baltic timber, tar, hemp, and other naval stores. The loss was a very serious one for the Navy. But the English government at once took energetic steps to explore new sources of supply.

Following his defeat off Dungeness Blake complained to the Council that 'there was much baseness of spirit, not among the merchant men only, but many of the state's ships.' A number of improvements were therefore determined on, which had the effect of materially strengthening the Fleet.

An innovation of considerable significance was the establishment, in December 1652, of the Articles of War. These provisions, thirty-nine in number, formed the groundwork of all the succeeding Articles of War down to the present day. For the future masters of merchantmen were no longer allowed to command their own vessels in action. Vane and his fellow-commissioners also initiated a series of sweeping reforms affecting food, pay, prize money, and the care of the sick

nd wounded. The results of these measures were immediate and
ffective.[1]

Every effort was now made to increase the effective strength of the
leet with a view to intercepting Tromp on his homeward passage.
By the middle of February 1653 a force of nearly eighty sail had been
ssembled at Portsmouth, and, under the command of Blake, shortly
fter cruised to the westward. It was known in England that Tromp
vas approaching the entrance of the Channel with a fleet of approxi-
nately equal numbers and a convoy of over 150 merchantmen. The
Dutch fleet was brought to action off Portland Bill on the 18th. The
ong running action which followed is known as the Three Days'
Battle and was destined to be the turning-point of the war. The Dutch
vere short of stores and ammunition, and were, moreover, weakened
by the defection of some twenty of their ships.[2] The rival fleets were
closely engaged until nightfall; then Tromp, seeing his convoy in
langer of attack, drew off to its support. Under cover of darkness,
Tromp, together with all his convoy, slipped past the English. During
he 19th and 20th the chase continued. Stationing his warships astern
of the merchantmen, Tromp fought a series of masterly rearguard
actions. The decisive day of the fighting was the 20th, when, many of
he Dutch having run out of powder, the English broke through the
enemy's line of battle off Cape Gris Nez, and captured and sank many
of the convoy. The Dutch then ' bore directly in for the French shore,
so near that we durst not follow them, it being nigh a lee-shore,' and
he rigging of most of the heavy English ships being badly damaged.
With the wind at N.W. and the French coast under his lee, and the
English to windward, Tromp's situation appeared desperate. Assured
by his pilots that the Dutch fleet ' could not weather the French shore,
is the tide and wind then was, to get home,' Blake anchored a few
eagues off Cape Gris Nez. That night the wind increased. Neverthe-
ess, by his daring and skilful seamanship Tromp accomplished the
eat which the English pilots had pronounced impossible. He success-
ully shepherded what was left of the convoy round Cape Gris Nez, and

[1] In the contemporary sources, observes Oppenheim in his *A History of the Adminis-
ration of the Royal Navy*, ' there are very few indications of the existence of Puritan
ervour or even of ordinary religious feeling; the great mass of men and officers
imed at pay and prize money, gave strenuous service when the former was punctual
nd the latter plentiful, and became heedless and indifferent when they failed.'

[2] Tromp was badly supported by many of his captains both in the Three Days
Battle and the later action off the Gabbard.

on the following morning anchored inside the Polders off Gravelines. In the meantime the English had retired to their own coast.[1]

As has already been said, the Dutch strategy had hitherto centred on the protection of their convoys in the Channel and North Sea. Thus in 1652 de Ruyter in the summer and Tromp in the autumn had succeeded in escorting large outward-bound convoys safely down the Channel; and the following February Tromp brought back up the Channel another huge fleet of merchantmen. In May Tromp sailed with his convoy before Monck and Deane arrived off the Texel; having escorted the outward-bound convoy safely through the danger zone, he met the homecoming convoy and returned with it to the Texel on the 20th. Later in the year, as will presently be seen, the Channel route was closed to the Dutch. The weakness of their strategy was then made manifest. ' I could wish ', Tromp declared in the autumn of 1652, ' to be so fortunate as to have only one of the two duties, to seek out the enemy or to give convoy: for to do both is attended by great difficulties.' That the destruction of the English fleet was the only means of preserving their seaborne commerce from ruin was finally recognized by the Dutch government. Henceforward the Dutch as well as the English concentrated on the destruction of the enemy's fighting fleet.

It was shortly after the Three Days' Battle that the Generals at Sea issued the first Fighting Instructions, whereby the formation of the ' line ahead ' was made obligatory. This formation, which enabled a fleet to develop its maximum fire, was by no means an innovation; it was now formally enjoined as the normal tactics of attack and defence. The general adoption by the Navy of the line ahead was a tactical development of the highest importance. From the first it appears to have made a strong impression on the Dutch. It also rendered inevitable the disappearance of the armed merchant vessel from the line of battle. The value of the tactics inculcated in the new Fighting Instructions was conclusively demonstrated in the next action of the war.[2]

---

[1] ' Blake and Monck, great fighting men but not seamen, find themselves unexpectedly baulked at critical moments by sands, tides, shifts of wind and other difficulties which Tromp foresaw and used, and they did not. As the Army would say, he made good use of ground ' (A. H. Taylor in *The Mariner's Mirror*, XL, p. 234).

[2] It is clear from the evidence of eye-witnesses that the English fought in line ahead at the Gabbard: '. . . and when they [the English] approached them, they stayed upon

Realizing the impossibility of protecting their trade through the Channel, the Dutch now diverted their mercantile shipping to the long and hazardous route north-about round the British Isles. Tromp successfully escorted two large convoys on the new route, the English admirals failing to intercept him. But on 2 June he was brought to action by Monck and Deane off the Gabbard. Each fleet comprised about a hundred sail; but the Dutch vessels were far inferior to the English in point of size, strength, and weight of metal. For two days the fight was stubbornly and fiercely contested. But on the arrival of Blake with thirteen fresh ships the Dutch were decisively defeated, with a loss of some twenty vessels. Tromp then saved his fleet from complete destruction by leading it within the banks of the Wielings, where the heavier English ships ' for fear of sands and shoal water in the night ' dared not follow.

For a full month after the action of the Gabbard Blake and Monck ' held the coast of Holland as 'twere besieged '; and the trade and fisheries upon which the Dutch depended were brought to a standstill. The loss to the Netherlands was immense.[1] It is said that the Zuyder Zee was a forest of masts; workshops were closed down, and grass grew in the streets of the principal ports. Amsterdam was faced with ruin. The food and clothing of the Netherlanders, the raw materials for their manufactures, the very timber, masts, and hemp for the construction of their ships, were for the most part brought to them from overseas. All these had now been cut off. The sufferings of the inhabitants were such that it became urgently necessary to break the blockade.

The Dutch admiralties strained every nerve to refit and reinforce their fleet, which was lying in two squadrons—the larger, under Tromp, comprising eighty-five sail, and the smaller, under de Witt, comprising thirty-one—in the Maas and Texel respectively. Meanwhile Monck lay off the Texel with a strong force of a hundred ships to prevent their junction. By skilful manœuvring, however, Tromp

a tack, having the wind, within twice cannon shot about half an hour, to put themselves in their order they intended to fight in, which was in file at half cannon shot, from whence they battered the Hollanders furiously all that day. . . . The second day the English battered them in file.' (*Navy Records Society*, XLI, p. 109)

[1] The Dutch fisheries suffered their first serious check in this war. The herring fishery was forbidden in 1653, and thereafter continued to go downhill; it was forbidden again in 1665 and 1666, and later in the War of the Spanish Succession. In 1736 the once immense Dutch herring fleet had shrunk to only 300 sail.

managed to draw Monck southward in pursuit of himself while de Witt escaped from the Texel. Then, unseen by the English, he tacked under cover of night and joined de Witt on 30 July. On the following day, off Scheveningen, the combined Dutch squadrons gave battle to the English. The latter were numerically the weaker fleet: but they had the advantage of more skilful crews, stronger ships, and superior gun-power; and this proved the deciding factor. Once again it would appear from the contemporary evidence that the English formed themselves in a single line close-hauled.

That night their Texel fleet and this [Tromp's force in the Maas] met and joined; the 31st the weather was seasonably fair, in the morning both standing off to sea, we tacked upon them and went through their whole fleet, leaving part on one side and part on the other side of us; in passing through we lamed then several ships and sunk some; as soon as we had passed them we tacked again upon them and they on us, passed by each other very near.[1]

The Dutch manœuvred to keep the weather-gauge but eventually lost it. No sooner had battle been joined than Tromp was killed. Like most of the actions between Dutch and English, this fight was long and fiercely contested. It is vividly related how ' two of their Admirals coming up close to the *Resolution* [Monck's flagship] and had much ado to weather her, at which time the very heavens were obscured by smoke, the air rent with the thundering noise, the sea all in a breach with the shot that fell, the ships even trembling and we hearing everywhere messengers of death flying.' By nightfall the Dutch fleet was decisively defeated and flying for the Texel. Monck's force also was in so crippled a state that it could no longer keep the sea and had to return to port—' night drawing on ', as Monck wrote to the Lord President of the Council, ' and the Dutch making directly for the Texel with what sail they could, so that it was not fit to be bold on that shore, not knowing how the wind may take us, many of our ships being much disabled '.

In so far as the Dutch with their smaller ships, inferior gun-power, and weaker crews had been able to contest the mastery of the sea with the English, the credit must largely lie with Tromp's leadership. He was an able strategist, a skilful tactician, and, as a seaman, without

[1] *Ibid.*, p. 372.

qual on either side. The fighting retreat of the Dutch fleet up Channel
the Three Days' Battle has been acclaimed by Professor Boxer as
one of the most masterly delaying actions in recorded history '. Both
this action, and subsequently after the Gabbard, Tromp had
natched his fleet out of the jaws of destruction by his skill as a seaman.
o finer feat of seamanship was performed by either side in this war
an Tromp's manœuvre on the eve of Scheveningen. Now he was
ead, and there was no commander of comparable stature to succeed
im. When the news of their admiral's death reached The Hague it
as said ' if they should cast twenty Jan Evertsens and twenty de
uyters into one, they could not make one Tromp, and to make him
ive again they would yet once more fight the last fight.'[1]

A few weeks after Monck returned to port, Lawson took his place
f the Texel with a squadron of forty-eight sail which remained on
e station until reinforced by Monck and his force. Minor trade
as, however, still carried on from the other Dutch ports. Then in
e autumn the English blockade was raised, and a homecoming
onvoy of about 400 ships entered the Texel at the end of October
nder the escort of de Witt.

Tromp was succeeded by Opdam, and the Dutch refitted their fleet.
ut because of the grievous injury to their trade caused by the war
ey were far more exhausted than their opponents, and were forced
come to terms. The result was that all the old disputes were settled
favour of England. By the treaty signed at Westminster on 5th April
654 the Dutch agreed to pay compensation for the Amboyna mas-
cre, to acquiesce in the Navigation Act, to make an annual payment
r the right of fishing in English waters, and to recognize the English
ght of the flag.

6

Ieanwhile on the Continent the long-drawn-out struggle between
rance and Spain was still in progress. But Spain was patently
eakening. The Protector for some time hesitated at the cross-roads.
ventually, true to his ideology, he resolved to make war on Spain—
e traditional enemy of Protestantism. He concealed his intentions,
owever, until the last possible moment; and, in the meantime, the
avy could make use of the Spanish ports.

The Journal of Maarten Harpertszoon Tromp, Anno, Anno 1639, ed. C. R. Boxer.

During the First Dutch War, as a result of the action off Leghorn, the nascent English power in the Mediterranean had been completely destroyed; and it was not until the Treaty of Westminster put a term to hostilities that England was free to re-assert herself within the Straits. The strong squadron which, under Blake's command, Cromwell in 1654 sent into the Mediterranean to protect our Levant trade, to checkmate the designs of Mazarin, and to restore English prestige generally, marked a further advance in our Mediterranean policy. For several weeks the English squadron lay in the Straits of Gibraltar, thereby preventing the junction of the two French squadrons, and defeating the enemy's strategy in the Mediterranean. Blake's fleet then sailed triumphantly from port to port, ' showing the flag '. After this he crossed to the Barbary coast, and attacked a squadron of Tunisian warships lying in the harbour of Porto Farino. Silencing the guns of both port and castle, he sent ' boats of execution ' against the pirate men-of-war, which were promptly set on fire and destroyed; after which the English fleet warped out again. Blake went on to visit Tripoli and Algiers, from whose rulers he managed to extort a satisfactory settlement. In 1656 he was succeeded in the Mediterranean by Captain John Stokes, who two years later successfully negotiated a treaty with Tunis which rendered English commerce immune from attack.

The joint naval and military expedition under Admiral Penn and General Venables, which Cromwell in 1655 sent out to the West Indies, formed part of the Protector's wider designs of conquest in Spanish America. Its first objective was the island of Hispaniola. But the expedition was heavily handicapped by bad leadership and very inadequate equipment. The attempt to capture San Domingo, the island capital, having failed—with the loss of several hundred men slaughtered by the Spaniards and an even greater number who fell victims to the ' fluxes and fevers' born of the pestilential climate—the English troops re-embarked and landed in Jamaica, situated about one hundred miles to the west of Hispaniola, which they successfully occupied. Our country thus gained permanent possession of an invaluable base in the West Indies.

The war now spread to Europe. Blake received orders to blockade Cadiz: to intercept the homecoming Plate fleet, and to prevent the dispatch of reinforcements to the West Indies. In the autumn of 1655 he returned to England. In consequence of the friendly understanding with Portugal, secured by Cromwell's treaty of 1654, our fleet was able to make use of Lisbon's fine harbour as a base. Early in 1656 Blake, accompanied by Montagu, was sent out to waylay a Peruvian treasure fleet. But they arrived too late, and the attempt failed. Later in the same year, while Blake was refitting in Lisbon, his Rear-Admiral, Richard Stayner, attacked another Plate fleet off Cadiz, capturing two of the ships and destroying four others. The booty taken on this occasion was valued at over £2 millions. Montague and Stayner, with several of the larger vessels, then returned to England; but Blake, based on Lisbon, supplied by means of store ships from home, remained through the winter of 1656-7 off the enemy's coast, blockading Cadiz. It was an achievement hitherto unexampled in naval war. Hearing next spring that a treasure fleet was lying in the Canaries, he sailed in pursuit. The treasure, however, had been landed, and the ships lay under the guns of Santa Cruz. Nevertheless, on 20 April 1657, Blake stood into the harbour on the flood, silenced the batteries, and destroyed all the ships, and then—though the wind was contrary—drew off on the ebb; after achieving one of the finest feats of arms ever seen in this or, indeed, any other century. It was destined to be Blake's last triumph; for he died on the homeward passage, on 7 August, within sight of Plymouth.

In the middle of the seventeenth century the Baltic was becoming a prime and integral factor in English foreign policy. As has already been said, during the First Dutch War the enemy had virtually cut off the vital naval stores from the Baltic. The government thereupon set to work to develop new sources of supply—particularly of masts[1]—in our North American colonies. Despite their efforts, however, the colonial supply proved insufficient to meet the full needs of our shipping. The Baltic still remained the main source of supply; and the highly organized timber trade of the surrounding forests had clearly been seen to lie at the mercy of the Northern Powers. Because of our vital interests in this area, Cromwell protected Sweden against Holland, and Denmark against Sweden. 'If they can shut us out of the Baltic', said Cromwell, 'and make themselves masters of that, where is your trade? where are the materials to preserve your shipping?' For the

---

[1] Between 1653 and 1775 nearly all the great masts for the Navy were imported either from Portsmouth, New Hampshire, or from Falmouth, Maine.

future it became a cardinal object of English policy to maintain the balance of power in the Baltic.

The ultimate effect of the Dutch and Spanish Wars was to ruin English trade, which had begun to revive after the ravages of the Civil War. The narrow seas at this time swarmed with privateers working from Dunkirk and Ostend; and, notwithstanding the extension of the convoy system, the English merchant marine suffered severely. Under Cromwell England had become a great military power, but at ruinous cost. At the Protector's death the State was rapidly heading for bankruptcy; and this was among the determining factors which inclined public opinion in this country towards the Restoration.

VI

The Restoration Navy

I

The Restoration ushered in one of the great formative periods in the history of the Navy, completing the system of administration set up by Henry VIII. The powerful Fleet built up during the Interregnum was maintained at full strength by the new government, which from the outset showed itself fully alive to the importance of sea power. The Restoration era also witnessed the birth of a conscious Service tradition and *esprit de corps*. Charles II himself was keenly interested in shipbuilding and all that appertained to the business of the sea. ' 'Tis certain ', declared Buckingham, ' no prince was ever more fitted by nature for his country's interest than he was in all his maritime inclinations.' The King was no less insistent than his father on the homage of the flag; in spite of French and Spanish pressure he refused to give up Nova Scotia, Jamaica, and Dunkirk to their former owners; and he firmly supported colonial expansion for the strengthening of British trade and sea power.

One of the first steps taken by Charles II on his accession was to make his brother, James, Duke of York, Lord High Admiral. Under the energetic administration of the Duke of York, assisted by a Board of highly skilled and experienced officials—including the gifted young Clerk of the Acts, Samuel Pepys—an immense improvement was effected in the discipline and efficiency of the Service.

During these early years of the reign various attempts were made to grapple with the evil traditions of waste and dishonesty which had grown up in the Navy. To this end regulations were made to forbid the excessive employment of pilots; to check the wasteful expenditure of powder by ' unusuall salutes '; and to enforce the discharge of redundant workmen from the dockyards. Another important innovation was the introduction, in 1668, of half-pay for senior captains, which was afterwards extended to lieutenants and masters.

A significant development of the Restoration era was the replacement of the older type of captain, bred from his youth up to the service of the sea, by ' gentlemen captains ' having influence at Court —' to the great discouragement ', as Pepys observed in 1679, ' of tarpaulins of Wapping and Blackwell, from whence . . . the good commanders all used to be chosen.' It was Pepys' experience that many of these new arrivals were by no means amenable to discipline, ' thinking themselves above the necessity of obeying orders and conforming themselves to the rules and discipline of the navy, in reliance upon the protection secured to them therein through the quality of their friends at court '. It was largely through the courage and resolution of Sir William Coventry that the Navy, in the Second Dutch War, retained the services of the good sea-officers of the Interregnum era; for, regardless of his popularity at Court, Coventry steadfastly supported and promoted able professional seamen like Sir Christopher Myngs, whom the fine ' gentlemen captains ' of the Restoration affected to despise. ' Who is it ', Pepys wrote in his diary on 6 July 1666, ' that the weight of the war depends upon? that it is only Sir William Coventry.' On the other hand, it is to be remembered that the entry into the Navy of large numbers of officers of birth and breeding did much in the long run to improve the tone and fighting spirit of the Service.

' There were gentlemen and there were seamen in the navy of Charles the Second,' Macaulay has recorded in a celebrated passage. ' But the seamen were not gentlemen; and the gentlemen were not seamen.' The Duke of York applied himself wholeheartedly to the task of training and disciplining these officers. ' In other words,' as Tedder observes, ' James was determined that since gentlemen must join the Navy they should as far as possible be properly trained to the sea, and from that determination dates the birth of the modern naval officer.'[1] Thus on 7 May 1661 a certain young Mr. Thomas Darcy, under royal patronage, entered the Navy with the pay of a midshipman;[2] a title which had hitherto been borne by a non-com-

---

[1] A. W. Tedder, *The Navy of the Restoration* (1916), p. 60.
[2] ' Sir Richard Stayner,—His Royal Highness being desirous to give Encouragement to such young Gentlemen as are willing to apply themselves to the learning of Navigation, and fitting themselves to the Service of the Sea, hath determined, that one Volunteer shall be entered on every Ship now going forth; and for his Encouragement, that he shall have the Pay of a Midshipman, and one Man less shall be borne

missioned officer serving under the boatswain, but gradually came to be given to young gentlemen such as Mr. Thomas Darcy, who were first termed 'Volunteers', and later 'King's Letter Boys'.

The long-standing jobbery and malversation of the dockyards reached new heights during the Restoration period. Official honesty was a thing as yet unknown: everyone as a matter of course cheated the King, and Pepys could not but regretfully recall the better management of things 'in the late rebellious times, when men, some for fear, and some for religion, minded their business, which none do now, by being void of both'. But the main and fundamental reason for the eventual breakdown of naval administration in the reign of Charles II was lack of money. The whole system of finance was, in fact, antiquated, chaotic, and inadequate to the needs of the day. Parliament was unwilling to grant the King sufficient supplies, and, in any case, the administration was encumbered with the huge debt inherited from the Protectorate, amounting to more than £1¼ million. In February 1660 the wages due to the seamen alone amounted to nearly half a million; some of the crews had gone unpaid for several years. 'God knows!' Pepys recorded on 28 June 1662, 'the King is not able to set out five ships at this present without great difficulty, we neither having money, credit, nor stores.' In the last years of the Commonwealth the victualling had gone from bad to worse. Bad victualling was the inevitable consequence of bad finance, and seriously affected the morale of the fleet. 'Englishmen,' Pepys observed sapiently in his *Naval Minutes*, 'and more especially seamen, love their bellies above everything else, and therefore it must always be remembered, in the management of the victualling of the navy, that to make any abatement from them in the quantity or agreeableness of the victuals is to discourage and provoke them in the tenderest point, and will sooner render them disgusted with the King's service than any one other hardship that can be put upon them.' It was not only the seamen who suffered. The unfortunate tradesmen who supplied the

on the Ship: In prosecuting of this Resolution, I am to recommend to you the Bearer Mr. Tho. Darcy; and to desire you that you would receive him according to the Intentions of His Royal Highness, as I have acquainted you; and that you would shew him such kindness, as you shall judge fit for a Gentleman, both in the accommodating him in your Ship, and in farthering his Improvement.—I am, Your affectionate Friend,

W. Coventry.'

(*Select Naval Documents*, ed. Hodges and Hughes, pp. 71–2.)

Service, being similarly unpaid, now found themselves faced with ruin. A certain Captain Heaton thus described the straits to which some of the townsmen of Plymouth had been reduced by the failure of the Government to pay its debts—' One cries, " For God's sake spare me £20 to keep me out of prison "; another begs for money to buy his family meat to eat, and today I saw a poor woman beg of Mr. Addis ten shillings of her due, to buy her four poor children bread, as for alms.' As the years went by merchants refused to supply the government except for ready money. Commissioner Middleton wrote from Portsmouth that he was ' put to his wits' end for want of masts and money: he cannot procure broom, candles, timber, oars or any necessaries '. The same Commissioner was probably not far wrong when he declared that " reddy money " would save the King ' 2/6 att least in ye pound '.

With the withdrawal of the English fleet from the Mediterranean after the cruises of Blake and Penn, the Barbary pirates had returned to their old courses; on 19 January 1661 Pepys recorded in his diary the ominous increase of these activities: ' I am troubled to hear that the Turks do take more and more of our ships in the Straights, and that our merchants here in London do daily break, and are still likely to do so.' One of the earliest tasks undertaken by the new administration was to detach a squadron for service in the Mediterranean. The steps taken by Sir John Lawson, who was entrusted with the command of this detachment, against the corsairs achieved but a limited success; by April 1662 he had succeeded in getting them to consent to a treaty, ' they agreeing not to search our ships,' and at the end of the year Lawson led his squadron home ' with great renown among all men, and mightily esteemed at Court by all '; but the memory of the pirates was short. The result was that throughout the Restoration era successive squadrons had to be maintained within the Straits for the protection of British trade. Perhaps the most successful of the operations against the Barbary corsairs was that of Sir Edward Spragge (1670–2). The latter had previously seen service in the Mediterranean as second-in-command under Sir Thomas Allin who, in 1669, had destroyed and captured large numbers of the pirate cruisers. Spragge's operations against the Moors culminated in an audacious attack on the Algerine warships lying in Bugia Bay on 8 May 1671; some of his ships broke through the boom by which they were protected and destroyed the whole squadron, while Spragge lay in the offing, watching with satisfaction the ' lovely bonfires which in my opinion was the best sight that I ever saw '. This stroke so alarmed the Algerines that they presently executed their Dey and forced his successor to come to terms with the English. In 1675 Sir John Narbrough blockaded Tripoli and, having destroyed most of its warships, extorted a satisfactory treaty from its Dey; following which he likewise coerced Salee. In the summer of 1677 he had, however, to re-enter the Mediterranean to deal in a similar manner with Algiers, returning home in the spring of 1679, leaving a detachment under Arthur Herbert. It is worth noticing that an English expedition to Algiers in 1687 was based, not on Lisbon, but on the Spanish port of Gibraltar.

2

In the war of 1652–4 the naval power of Holland was weakened, not destroyed. After the war her recovery had been rapid, and, under the wise leadership of John de Witt, she remained well in the forefront of European Powers. By her successful intervention in Northern affairs she had secured, through the Treaty of Oliva in 1660, her access to the Baltic and its indispensable naval stores. On the other hand, the English government of the Restoration showed plainly that it intended to persevere in the strong maritime and commercial policy of the Commonwealth and Protectorate by renewing and strengthening the Navigation Act in 1660. The old causes of dispute still remained. ' The Dutch,' observed Shaftesbury in 1663, were ' England's eternal enemy, both by interest and inclination.' The quarrel centred on the carrying trade of Europe, which the Dutch had come to regard as their own cherished monopoly. 'What matters this or that reason?' asked Monck. 'What we want is more of the trade which the Dutch now have.' 'The trade of the world is too little for us two,' an English sea-captain told Pepys in 1664, ' therefore one must down.'

Once again the mariners of the two nations were at odds beyond the line, and the English jealousy and hatred of the Dutch was intensified by the close connection of the Court with the great chartered companies, such as the East India Company and Royal Africa Company, which were becoming increasingly embroiled with their Dutch rivals. Throughout the year 1664 the war-feeling in England rapidly increased. Sir Robert Holmes was ordered to attack the Dutch trading stations on the west coast of Africa; after which he stood across the Atlantic and assisted the English settlers to seize the Dutch colony of New Amsterdam. The Dutch retaliated by assailing the English stations in West Africa. Hostilities spread to European waters in December when Sir Thomas Allin attacked the homeward-bound Dutch Smyrna fleet in the Straits of Gibraltar. This was followed by the seizure of Dutch ships lying in English ports and the confiscation of their cargoes. War was formally declared by England on 4 March 1665.

The outbreak of hostilities found the Dutch far better prepared for a struggle against the superior resources of their English rivals than had been the case thirteen years earlier. With the strong support of Jan de Witt de Ruyter had built up a powerful battle fleet which no longer needed to be reinforced by large numbers of armed merchantmen. The new Dutch warships were far more homogeneous than the old, and de Ruyter had done much to make good the deficiency of trained officers; the Dutch victualling arrangements were also markedly improved. The superior organization, discipline, and fighting efficiency of de Ruyter's fleet were soon to be demonstrated in the Four Days' Battle. Holland was also financially the stronger of the two Powers at the outset of the war. In other respects, however, the advantage still lay with England.

The English followed the same general strategy as in the First Dutch War. The safety of their commerce being of paramount importance to the enemy, the object of the English admirals was to force the Dutch to decisive action by threatening them with the stoppage of their inward and outward trade. Cut off from the seaborne commerce that was the lifeblood of the State, the ruin of the Provinces would not long be delayed. Their great trading fleets must sail or the Republic would perish; as Edward Montagu (now Earl of Sandwich) declared: 'Methought the hindering of their trade to come home the best provocation to make the enemy's fleet come out.'

To that end a large English fleet of a hundred sail, under the command of the Duke of York, assisted by Prince Rupert and the Earl of Sandwich, was concentrated off the enemy's principal base at the Texel, where the bulk of the Dutch navy was lying, cutting it off from the smaller Zeeland division. In this position the English were well placed to block the commerce of Amsterdam and thus oblige the

Dutch either to fight at a disadvantage or suffer the loss of their vital convoys. Everything now depended on whether they could remain in full strength on this station for a long enough period to force a decision. The governing factor, in short, was the endurance of the blockading force. Eventually they were compelled to cross over to Southwold Bay to revictual, with the result that the separated Dutch divisions were able to unite under Opdam and follow in pursuit. After some unsuccessful manœuvring on the part of the Dutch to secure the weather-gauge, action was joined off Lowestoft in the early morning of 3 June. The two fleets, each sailing close-hauled in line ahead, passed each other on opposite tacks. The Dutch were heavily defeated, with a loss of more than twenty of the line; Opdam being blown up with his flagship. Though the Dutch were indeed much stronger than they had been in the previous war, their weakness in tactics, discipline, and morale was still very marked. A striking example of this was seen in the conduct of a dozen or so of the vessels of Opdam's own squadron, which suddenly broke off the action and withdrew, leaving a great gap in the Dutch line. The close-hauled line of battle was now the established formation in both fleets.

The English advantage was not pressed home. The Dutch fire had so damaged the masts and rigging of their opponents that they were unable to pursue their beaten foe, who now fled for the shelter of their shoals. The English fleet likewise returned to port to refit.

In July the Duke of York was transferred to the Admiralty, while the command of the fleet was given to the Earl of Sandwich. The victory of Lowestoft had left the English masters of the sea; but, owing to administrative deficiencies and shortage of supplies, they were unable fully to exploit their success. Sandwich made an unsuccessful attempt to intercept a homecoming Dutch East Indies fleet which had taken refuge in the neutral port of Bergen. While the English were thus occupied in the North de Ruyter, returning with his squadron from the Mediterranean, seized the opportunity to get home through the unguarded Channel. He was then appointed to the chief command, and succeeded in getting the bulk of the East Indies convoy safely back from Bergen to Holland. In the Mediterranean, English trade was paralysed through the presence of a Dutch squadron at Cadiz, blocking the Straits, while another hostile force blockaded Tangier.

Charles II's government was heavily handicapped by having entered upon the struggle saddled with a debt amounting to about one year's parliamentary revenue. Under the exceptional strain of the Second Dutch War the national finances were stretched to breaking-point. With the spread of the Plague, in the hot summer of 1665, the administration broke down altogether.[1] Trade was stagnant, and the taxes were yielding practically nothing. The government's credit was gone, and no one would lend it money. The seamen's pay was months, and even years, in arrear; the dockyards were empty of workmen and destitute of stores; the bakers refused flatly to supply any more biscuit, and the slop-sellers any more clothes, until the existing debts were met; and the contractors—being unpaid themselves—were unable to satisfy these employees. The procedure then customary was to give the seamen, in lieu of pay, certificates or 'tickets'. These, during the periods of gravest financial stress, could be cashed only in London. Great hardship was thereby inflicted on the unfortunate seamen. The evils of the ticket system reached a climax in the autumn of 1665 when the Navy Office was obliged to suspend payment, which led to scenes of disorder and distress graphically recorded in Pepys's *Diary*: ' Up and to the office. Did business, though not much, because of the horrible crowd and lamentable moan of the poor seamen that lie starving in the streets for lack of money, which do trouble and perplex me to the heart; and more at noon when we were to go through them, for then a whole hundred of them followed us, some cursing, some swearing, and some praying to us.' It was through the collapse of the victualling service that the fleet had been obliged to return home, and the opportunity of destroying the Dutch after the victory of 3 June had been allowed to pass.[2]

The fleet fitted out next spring by the United Provinces, under the

[1] Throughout that terrible time when many hundreds died daily in the City and the solitude and stillness of the streets was broken only by the rumble of the pest-cart making its rounds and the dreadful tolling of the death-bell, Pepys remained doggedly at his post in the Navy Office. ' The sickness in general thickens round us, and particularly upon our neighbourhood. You, Sir,' he wrote to Sir William Coventry, then serving with the fleet, ' took your turn of the sword; I must not therefore grudge to take mine of the pestilence.' ' But, Lord!' he recorded later in his diary, ' what a sad time it is to see no boats upon the River; and grass grows all up and down White Hall court.'

[2] ' The want of victuals being the whole overthrow of this yeare both at sea, and now at the Nore here and Portsmouth where the fleete lies ' (Pepys's *Diary*, 24 October 1665). But 1666 saw a marked improvement in the victualling.

command of Michael de Ruyter, was the strongest which the English had ever had to face. In January France also had declared war. At this juncture, by a major strategical error, the English fleet was divided to cope with the double danger: the main body of the fleet, under Albemarle, lying in the North Sea, while a squadron of thirty ships, under Rupert, secured the Channel against a French squadron which was believed to be approaching from the Mediterranean. The consequence was that when on 1 June Albemarle engaged the Dutch in the Straits of Dover he was hopelessly outnumbered. After four days' desperate fighting the English were heavily defeated. Only the timely appearance of Rupert and his squadron, on the third day of the battle, saved Albemarle from complete destruction. Though Rupert succeeded in breaking through the Dutch fleet, the enemy's fire had so damaged his masts and rigging that his ships were out-manœuvred by their opponents; and Albemarle and he were unable to prevent the separated hostile squadrons from re-uniting, and bearing down on the English fleet.

The Four Days' Battle, which was one of the most fiercely contested and bloodiest ever fought at sea, marked an important advance in naval tactics. In this action the component squadrons of the two fleets manœuvred skilfully and effectively. A French tribute to the English line of battle is worth quoting:

> Nothing equals the beautiful order of the English at sea. Never was a line drawn straighter than that formed by their ships; thus they bring all their fire to bear upon those who draw near them. . . . They fight like a line of cavalry which is handled according to rule, and applies itself solely to force back those who oppose; whereas the Dutch advance like cavalry whose squadrons leave their ranks and come separately to the charge.[1]

De Ruyter blockaded the Thames, and England was threatened by a French invasion. The country, however, rallied valiantly to the task of defence, reliant on ' the oak and courage of England ' to settle the business. Within seven weeks the fleet was refitted; and Rupert and Albemarle—working out of the Swin in a single tide—attacked the Dutch, on 25 July, off the North Foreland. In the afternoon the English began to have the best of it, and the enemy's van and centre retired. The following day the Dutch took refuge in the shoals off Flushing, while the English anchored outside.

[1] De Guiche, *Mémoires*, p. 249.

The victory off the North Foreland had secured for the English the mastery of the sea. Our fleet now sailed triumphantly up the whole coast of Holland, and lay for a time in the Schooneveld. In August Sir Robert Holmes led a small squadron into the Zuyder Zee, and, after destroying their escort, set fire to some 150 Dutch merchantmen in Terschelling roads, besides burning an enormous quantity of naval stores ashore (in after years the affair was succinctly referred to as ' Sir Robert Holmes, His bonfire '). This, however, marked the end of the English operations in 1666; for Rupert and Albemarle were obliged, through lack of victuals, to return to port.

At this stage both sides were distracted from the naval war by the pressure of exterior events. On the one hand, the Great Fire of London, in September 1666, destroying the greater part of the City in which was housed more than one-half of our country's total wealth, paralysed the English war effort; on the other, Louis XIV's aggressive designs on the Spanish Netherlands obliged the Dutch to look to their land defences. In Turenne's victorious campaign of 1667 Charleroi, Tournai, Douai, Lille, and other frontier towns passed permanently into French keeping.

In the autumn of 1666 the Dutch established a limited blockade of the English ports. The Newcastle coal trade was severely harassed, and the vital supplies of masts and naval stores from the Baltic were gravely imperilled; December saw the arrival of four mast-ships from New England, which, noted Pepys, ' is a blessing mightily unexpected, and without which, if for nothing else, we must have failed the next year.' At the end of the month the long-awaited Baltic fleet at last came home. ' To the office,' wrote Pepys on the 29th, ' and have the news brought us of Captain Robinson's coming with his fleet from Gottenburgh: dispersed, though, by foul weather.'

In May 1667 negotiations for peace were opened at Breda. Charles II's government was faced with bankruptcy; the treasury was practically empty, and the fleet could no longer be kept at sea. The truth was that Parliament, by its obstinate and persistent refusal to vote sufficient supplies, had hamstrung the fleet. The Dutch were actually spending more than double on the costly maritime war than were the English.

In the winter of 1666–7 a squadron of twenty ships had been detached to the Mediterranean, and the following spring the decision was taken to lay up the battle fleet. As the late Sir Herbert Richmond has declared, ' It was an attempt to gather the fruits of victory before the victory had been won.' Meanwhile the peace negotiations at Breda hung fire. The old questions at issue were raised anew. De Witt was well aware that the English were disarmed and unprepared. He now determined on a daring stroke to secure peace—and a favourable peace—for Holland.

On 4 June de Ruyter left the Texel with a fleet of over eighty ships. He arrived off the Firth of Forth, and sailed southward down the east coast to the mouth of the Thames. On the 10th a Dutch landing-party stormed Sheerness and captured the magazines and store-houses; on the 11th, while the main body of the enemy's fleet lay out in the estuary, a detached division under Lieutenant-Admiral Van Ghent entered the Medway with a favouring north-west breeze, broke through the boom at Gillingham and forced the way up to Chatham, and there fell upon the deserted and defenceless warships moored in the stream, what time Commissioner Pett—' in a very fearful stink for fear of the Dutch '—hurriedly removed himself and his gear to a place of safety, while the roar of the enemy's guns was heard afar off in London, striking fear and dismay into the hearts of the inhabitants. An English flagship, the *Royal Charles*, was taken and six large ships were destroyed by fire; after which, to the derisive strains of ' Joan's Placket is Torn '—played by an exultant Dutch trumpeter on the quarter-deck of the *Royal Charles*—the enemy, retiring in good order with their prize in tow, dropped down the Medway on the ebb.

' On the 28th,' John Evelyn observed in his *Diary*, ' I went to *Chattham*, and thence to view not onely what Mischiefe the Dutch had don, but how triumphantly their whole Fleete, lay within the very mouth of the Thames, all from North-foreland, Margate, even to the Buoy of the Noore, a Dreadfull Spectacle as ever any English men saw, & a dishonour never to be wiped off.'

The Dutch attack on Chatham must be accounted one of the most brilliant, audacious, and completely successful strokes in the annals of naval warfare. From start to finish the operation was conducted with consummate skill. The navigation of the Thames estuary by so large a fleet, and, still more, the orderly retreat down the Medway, spoke volumes for the fine seamanship of the Dutch officers and crews. In spite of himself Pepys was moved to ungrudging admiration for the enemy's prowess and observed how 'they managed their retreat down this difficult passage, with all their fear, better than we could do ourselves in the main sea, when the Duke of Albemarle run away from the Dutch, when the *Prince* was lost, and the *Royal Charles* and the other great ships come on ground on the Galloper. Thus, in all things, in wisdom, courage, force, knowledge of our own streams, and success, the Dutch have the best of us, and do end the war with victory on their side.'[1]

For several weeks de Ruyter, with a great fleet of a hundred sail, blockaded the Thames estuary and strangled the seaborne trade of London. The price of coal in the capital rose from 15s. to 140s. a ton. English commerce was virtually brought to a standstill. That of the enemy moved freely about the seas without let or hindrance. During this period a Dutch East Indies fleet of immense value passed up the Channel unopposed, protected by only a small escort.

De Ruyter's success had the effect desired by his countrymen. Soon afterwards England was forced to make peace on very disadvantageous terms. The summer before her admirals, to all appearances, had secured the control of the sea. Now the position was reversed. On 21 July 1667 was signed the Treaty of Breda, the English yielding up Surinam in Guiana to the Dutch, and Acadia to the French, while the Dutch gave up their colonies on the North American coast; at the same time the Navigation Act was somewhat modified in favour of Holland, which also received various commercial concessions.

By the Treaty of Breda the Dutch Republic may be said to have attained the summit of its fortunes, with John de Witt, the Council Pensionary, firmly established at the head of the government. But already the position of both Holland and de Witt was gravely endangered. In the late summer of 1667 the armies of Louis XIV were

---

[1] It is clear that the discontent of the English seamen, whose wages in many cases had been for so long grievously in arrears, was an important factor in the situation. This is evident from various entries in Pepys's *Diary*. ' And indeed the hearts as well as the affections of the seamen are turned away; and in the open streets of Wapping, and up and down, the wives have cried publickly, " This comes of your not paying our husbands." ' Not a few of these malcontents had even gone over to the Dutch. Pepys relates that one of his acquaintances ' did hear many Englishmen on board the Dutch ships speak to one another in English; and that they did cry and say, " We did heretofore fight for tickets; now we fight for dollars!" and did ask how such and such a one did, and would commend themselves to them: which is a sad consideration.'

rapidly over-running the Spanish Netherlands and menacing the integrity of the Republic. In the present impotence of Spain, the only hope of stopping him lay in the formation of a coalition.

Louis XIV's invasion of the southern Netherlands had also excited profound alarm in England. There was an increasing tendency on this side of the Channel to regard France, rather than Holland, as our rival and enemy of the future. Now as always the occupation of the Rhine delta by a great military Power constituted a standing threat to our national security. There was also the fear that the French and the Dutch might come to an understanding. Faced by the possibility of a Franco-Dutch partition of the Spanish Empire, which would not only give France the hegemony of Europe, but would also make the Dutch all-powerful on the sea, Charles II dispatched Sir William Temple to The Hague to conclude a treaty of alliance with Holland—to which Sweden later adhered. Under the pressure of the Triple Alliance the Peace of Aix-la-Chapelle was signed between France and Spain in 1668. Louis XIV was forced to evacuate the Rhine delta.

3

The real and underlying causes of the Third Dutch War were essentially political—the perennial commercial and colonial grievances being merely worked up anew to excite popular feeling in England against the Dutch. Moreover, a strong desire existed in this country to avenge the disgrace of the Medway. Louis XIV, determined once and for all to destroy Holland, which in 1667 had effectually defeated his designs on the Spanish Netherlands, now strove to break up the Triple Alliance and thus to isolate Holland. He accordingly detached Sweden and afterwards sent over Charles II's favourite sister, Minette, Duchess of Orleans, to win over her brother to the French king's *grand design*.

On 22 May 1670, by the Secret Treaty of Dover, the two monarchs prepared to launch a concerted attack on the Dutch Republic. France was to provide the military force, and England the fleet, with the addition of a strong French squadron. The plan was for the French to conquer the coast, and the English the Zeeland islands. During the course of the struggle Charles II was assured of an annual war subsidy from France. Over and above all this there was a religious compact, under the terms of which Charles II was to get a further sum of £150,000 to enable him to declare his conversion to the Catholic faith. Closely associated with Charles II's new policy was his intimate circle of ministers, popularly known as the Cabal—Clifford, Arlington, Buckingham, Ashley, and Lauderdale.

In 1672 this scheme of conquest was put to the test. In the early spring of that year Louis XIV after a long and careful preparation launched his armies against the United Provinces. One hundred and twenty-thousand troops under Condé, Turenne, and Luxembourg suddenly crossed the southern frontier, and within a few weeks overran the greater part of the Dutch Netherlands; at the same time a further army of 30,000 men from Munster and Cologne, the allies of France, attacked the northern provinces. The English had already surprised the Hollanders by sea. On 13 March Sir Robert Holmes's squadron made a treacherous attack on the Dutch Smyrna fleet lying off the Isle of Wight, the declaration of war following a few days later.

The general design of Allied strategy envisaged a large-scale invasion of Holland over her land frontiers, combined with a descent from the sea by a smaller English force. Before this seaborne invasion could be launched, the Dutch fleet must first be dealt with; it was accordingly proposed that the combined English and French fleets should proceed to the Dogger Bank and lie there in the track of the homecoming Dutch trade, in the expectation of forcing the enemy fleet well out to sea, where it could be brought to decisive action. The crucial theatre of the naval war was, therefore, the North Sea; there the main forces of both belligerents were concentrated; and huge convoys of merchantmen no longer figured in the struggle.

At the outbreak of the war de Ruyter had come down into the Channel to prevent the junction of the English and French fleets. But the Duke of York got clear of the Thames in time and, joining hands with the French force from Brest, lay in Sole Bay on the Suffolk coast to revictual, before proceeding to his appointed station on the Dogger Bank. The wind suddenly shifting from west to north-east gave de Ruyter his opportunity. The disposition of the Allied squadrons had become known to him through his scouts. He sailed from the Maas, and, on 28 May, with a force somewhat inferior to that of the English and French, he fell upon the two English divisions before the Allied line was properly formed, while the French were contained by the Zeeland squadron under Bankert. In the close-range fighting which followed, lasting from midday till dusk, the losses on either side were severe. The French fleet was as yet but new and inexperienced. The brunt of the battle was borne by the English, who, in fact, afterwards accused their French Allies of having purposely held back from the fight. The Hollanders' fireships wrought great havoc among their opponents. The English flagship *Royal James* was destroyed by fire, and the Duke of York was three times forced to shift his flag. At nightfall the Dutch retired. The Allied fleet was obliged to return to port to refit, and, owing to the deficiencies of the victualling department, was not ready for sea again until the end of June. During the remainder of the summer and autumn de Ruyter, with some sixty vessels, kept watch along the coasts of Holland and Zeeland. The Dutch fleet was but half-manned, for a large part of their crews had had to be landed to assist the army. Meanwhile the English fleet, under the command of the Duke of York, took its station on the Dogger Bank. On the approach of the Dutch East Indies fleet, de Ruyter weighed from Blankenburgh, ' slid along the shoar, without being discovered by the English ', met the East Indiamen, and safely conducted them into Delfzey in the West Ems. Soon after the Duke of York was obliged to return to port through lack of supplies.

Though de Ruyter's recent victory in Sole Bay had dispelled the danger of an Allied invasion from the sea, the situation on land, where the Dutch were confronted by the overwhelming military force of France, now appeared almost hopeless. Their trade was in ruins; and the State securities and the East India Company's stock were ominously falling. On 20 June a band of French skirmishers entered Muyden, the key to Amsterdam. They were driven out again in the nick of time: shortly after this the dykes were cut; and the waters poured in, in ever-increasing volume, to relieve the hard-pressed defenders.

At this supreme crisis of their country's fortunes the Orangists had risen against the Republicans: the brothers de Witt were murdered in the streets of The Hague by an infuriated mob; and William of Orange—the great-grandson of William the Silent—was appointed Stadtholder. The young Prince, proclaiming his desperate resolve ' to die in the last dyke ', inspired his people with an indomitable spirit of resistance. This proved the turning-point of the war. Slowly but surely an impassable flood spread in a gigantic arc across the low-lying lands between the Zuyder Zee and the Maas. The French advance was thereby brought to a standstill. At the eleventh hour Amsterdam and the other cities of Holland were saved.

Charles II's hopes that the war would prove profitable for his exchequer were not realized. Moreover, Parliament became increasingly suspicious of his policy of toleration; some of the facts relating to the Secret Treaty of Dover were in danger of leaking out, and what his subjects did not know they suspected. Eventually the smouldering English hatred of all that was implicit in the cry of ' Popery and wooden shoes ' blazed up with such passion and fury as to occasion the dissolution of the Cabal and the passage of the Test Act. In consequence of this last measure, the Duke of York was succeeded in

command of the fleet by his cousin Rupert. Even then the House of
Commons continued to turn a deaf ear to Charles II's appeals for
money; and Rupert's failure to bring de Ruyter to decisive action in
the campaign of 1673 was in large measure due to the fact that the
government had not the wherewithal to send the fleet to sea adequately
manned, victualled, and equipped, or to maintain a sufficient reserve
of stores for refitting and repairs. Finance, as was so often the case
during the Stuart era, was the determining factor. The additional cost
of the war had brought the King's government, already heavily in
debt, to the verge of bankruptcy. The supplies voted by Parliament
actually fell short of the requisite amount by several hundred thousand
pounds.

As a result of the financial crisis in England, the Dutch fleet was
ready for sea before the English; and on 2 May the enemy entered the
Thames estuary with the design of blocking the narrow Swin channel
with sunken hulks filled with stones—a stratagem which, if successful,
would have immobilized a considerable part of the English fleet. The
enterprise all but succeeded; but at the last moment, as the Dutch
were about to escort the ' sinkers ' to the appointed place, a dense fog
closed down on the estuary, obliging them to sail slowly, with the
result that the English were warned in time. Then Rupert, by a daring
feat of seamanship, worked out through the shoals to the Nore and
took them by surprise; whereupon the Dutch retired to the Schooneveld.[1]

This year a great part of the Dutch fleet had to be laid up for lack
of ammunition; and with such ships as still remained in commission
de Ruyter, making good use of the natural strength of his country's
coast-line, pursued a brilliant defensive-offensive strategy. Though
the odds were heavily against him—76 of the line to 52; moreover, the
Allied ships were heavier gunned and better manned—he kept his
force intact. It was, perhaps, the most striking example in history of
the importance of a ' fleet in being '. Before the Allied squadrons
could either invade Holland or destroy her trade, it would first be
necessary to dispose of de Ruyter's fleet; and this they never succeeded in doing.[2]

---

[1] The anchorage in the Schooneveld, a long narrow basin, with good holding ground,
in depths of from 6 to 9 fathoms, is situated between the Rassen and Raan and
the outlying sands off the mouth of the Scheldt.

[2] An invaluable source of information for the campaign of 1673 is *Journals and*

The Dutch strategy was admirably adapted to the navigational conditions obtaining in this area of the North Sea. Here, in their home waters, all the advantage lay with the enemy. At this time the navigation of the intricate channels among the maze of banks and sands which fringe the Netherlands coast was but little known to the Allies. The latter, whenever they got within sight of the low flat Zeeland islands and the long monotonous coastline of Holland to the northward, were filled with disquiet and apprehension. To quote from a contemporary English *Life of de Ruyter*, in spring the Dutch admiral, ' not swerving from his former measures, thinking he gained enough when he did not lose, warily retired behinde the banks, those impregnable sea-ramparts, shunning at that time any engagement.' As in the two previous wars, the enemy turned their knowledge of the sands to good account: but this campaign of 1673 was their masterpiece. To observe the enemy, de Ruyter lay in the Schooneveld or, farther south, off Blankenburgh, where the heavier English ships dared not approach him. Throughout the campaign the Dutch pursued the same policy. When the Allies had the advantage of the wind, de Ruyter kept his fleet secure behind the islands and shoals; but, when an opportunity arose of taking his enemy at a disadvantage, he struck— and struck hard.

On 16 May the French under d'Estrées joined Rupert in the Channel; and while 8,000 English troops waited with their transports at Yarmouth ready to be ferried across the North Sea as soon as the way should be cleared, the Allied fleet sailed for the enemy's coast. On the 21st they sighted the Dutch lying in the Schooneveld, inside the labyrinth of submerged banks fringing the islands of Zeeland; in the midst of the encircling sands the enemy lay at anchor, as Rupert presently reported to the King, ' so that they may either go to sea or in, which the first opportunity of weather shall discover to us '.

From the 23rd to the 28th the Allies rode off the Oster bank, about a dozen miles from the land. Away to the eastward, beyond the Dutch fleet, lay the low-lying shores of Walcheren, with the spires and towers of Middelburg rising above the dunes. Between the Allies and this island, as well as for a good many miles in either direction,

Narratives of the Third Dutch War, ed. R. C. Anderson (1946). See also Brandt, *Leven van de Ruyter*, Colenbrander, *Bescheiden uit vreemde archieven omtrent de groote Nederlandsche Zeeoorlogen*, Warnsinck, *Admiraal de Ruyter: De Zeeslag op Schooneveld* (1930).

the distant coastline was fronted with dangerous and extensive banks—the immense triangular-shaped group of sands called the Raan, the shallow Rassen bank, the outlying Steen and Middel banks, and the treacherous Banjaard flats (steep-to to seaward)—obstructing the approach to the Flanders shore and the mouths of the Scheldt and Maas. Towards low water, tell-tale ripplings, significant streaks and circles of white, the discoloration of the water and the run of the seas, marked the hidden shoals; and closer inshore, an occasional wet brownish hump of sand rose above the working, heaving surface. It was a situation which tested the nerves of the English pilots to the limit.

Despite these dangers, as the Dutch showed no sign of emerging, ' but kept to their advantage riding within their sands at Schooneveld ' Rupert ' resolved to fight them in that very place, rather than permit them to wear away the summer with longer delays '. The attack was to have been made on the 24th, but a south-westerly gale sprang up. ' It blew so hard that we were fain to strike topmasts and yards,' Rupert declared, ' and all we could do was to keep some ketches under sail to sound the grounds about us. . . . During all this one of my afflictions was the contradictions of our ablest pilots.' There was considerable uncertainty as to the position of his own fleet. ' Where we ride is a great question among the learned,' wrote one of his followers. On the 28th Rupert sent in a detached division to draw the enemy out. But de Ruyter needed no such invitation. With a leading wind he emerged so swiftly that the Allies had scarcely time to form their line before he was upon them. In the long running fight which ensued, as is seen from Legge's narrative, the navigational conditions on that part of the Zeeland coast were a determining factor.

> Near one oclock our headmost ships came within shot of the enemy, and then we all hauled away N.E. fighting with our larboard tacks aboard till near 3 oclock. . . . Then we being in 8 fathom water and within a cable's length of the Banjaard sands we put our helm-a-lee and got our ship with much ado about, and then fought with our starboard tacks aboard till 6 oclock in the evening, and then tacked again and stood to the northward till 8, and then tacked again and stood to the southward till 10, still fighting the enemy. Then, being dark, we left off fighting, being little wind at N.N.E. . . . The place where we fought was very dangerous, for we feared more the losing of our ships upon the sands than we did losing our ships and lives in fight with the enemy.

The Allies extricated themselves with difficulty from the sands and anchored once again upon the Oster bank, 'the enemy . . . being at anchor just by their port behind their old and accustomed refuge, the banks and sands.' ' We have now very bad weather, wind at S.W. blowing hard,' wrote Haddock to the Navy Commissioners. ' I am glad we are out of the Schoon Veldt. I believe we shall not attack the Dutch in that narrow hole again.' During the next few days the rival fleets were engaged in repairing their damaged ships. Here the advantage lay with the Dutch, who had all the necessary stores close at hand, while the Allies were far from their home ports and began to run short of food and water. The latter, moreover, had to be constantly on their guard when the wind was favourable for another attack by de Ruyter.

Action was joined once more on 4 June. De Ruyter, having again secured the weather-gauge, bore down on the Allied fleet and fought an action which, though inconclusive, obliged his enemy to leave the Dutch coast to repair and refit. Once again Rupert's fleet was hamstrung through the breakdown of the administrative machinery and its refitting delayed through lack of the necessary stores.

It was not until the last half of July that the Allies were ready to renew their efforts to invade Holland from the sea; and once again de Ruyter's well-tried stratagem of dogging the Allied fleet, and at the same time avoiding close action, proved effective. ' While we stood to the northward ', Spragge observed on 22 July, ' the enemy followed. I tacked and stood to the southward; the enemy's van at the same time did the same.' The presence of de Ruyter's fleet on their flank made an Allied landing impossible. The Allied fleet then cruised off the mouth of the Maas and proceeded to threaten Scheveningen. But in vain. The Allies dared not attempt a landing with de Ruyter lying, within easy striking distance, in the Schooneveld. On the 28th the Dutch weighed from the Schooneveld and moved up to Scheveningen. For some time bad weather kept the rival fleets at anchor, de Ruyter to the south, and the Allies to the north-west, of the Texel. On the evening of 10 August the two fleets were steering a south-easterly course down the Dutch coast, the enemy several miles to leeward. That night de Ruyter, according to his custom, stood in close to the shore off Camperdown where the Allies feared to follow him. Soon after midnight the latter turned northward instead of southward; and this, combined with a slight shift of the wind, gave the enemy the weather-gauge.[1] At daybreak on the 11th the two fleets were to seaward of the Texel—the Dutch directly to windward of the Allies, and the wind at south-east.

The discipline and morale of the Dutch fleet had by now much improved; their shooting was rapid and accurate; and their great leader, Michael de Ruyter, was at the height of his powers. By skilful manœuvring de Ruyter managed to contain the Allied van, comprising some thirty French sail, while he concentrated his attack on part of the Allied centre. A desperate engagement then ensued between de Ruyter and Rupert in the centre, and another between the Dutch and English rear squadrons, commanded respectively by Cornelis Tromp and Sir Edward Spragge. Tromp and Spragge fought until the sea around was littered with wreckage and floating corpses; both admirals shifting their flags three times. ' In those three hours our mainstay was shot in pieces,' related an eye-witness in Spragge's flagship, the *Prince Royal*, ' and almost all the rigging, and our main and mizen masts disabled, a great part of the fine cabins beat into chips, and many valiant men sent into the other world without any ceremony besides peals of thundering ordnance.' Spragge was drowned while shifting his flag for the third time. Meanwhile Rupert in the centre was hard-pressed by de Ruyter's far stronger squadron. Most of the French being out of the fight, the ' whole burden and brunt of the battle ' fell on the Prince's squadron. ' If the French then lying within distance to windward had obeyed my signall, and borne downe upon the enemy according to their duty,' Rupert later complained, ' I must have routed and torne them all to pieces. It was the plainest and greatest opportunity ever lost at sea.' Eventually, after sustaining heavy casualties, Rupert extricated his squadron from this perilous situation. ' The enemy when darke night came stood off to their owne coast,' he wrote in his dispatch, ' which I had reason to be glad of,

---

[1] ' The Dutch by carrying all the sayle they could this night, and the French lying by keeping of an easy sayle (contrary to order), the wind then veering to the E. and E.B.S., the Dutch had the advantage to get the wind of us, by which we presently judged the Dutch had tacked soe that his H[ighness] thought it convenient to tack close, thinking it not safe to fall in amongst the enemyes fleet at night, doubting som disorder might happen, having soe many raw seamen under his comand; so his H[ighness] stood to the E.N.E., it being now about two of the clock in the morning, and the wind coming near to the S.E. the enemy had the wind, being close by the shoare under Camperdowne ' (Colenbrander, *Bescheiden uit vreemde archieven omtrent de groote Nederlandschen Zeeoorlogen, 1652–1676* (1919), **II**, p. 302).

resolving if I could avoyd it not to venture a new engagement the next day.'

Tactically this action, like the others in the Schooneveld, was indecisive; but de Ruyter's main object had been achieved. With greatly inferior forces he had held in check the combined fleets of England and France, successfully defended the coasts of Holland from invasion, and put an end to the blockade of the Dutch ports.

During the last few months of the war English merchant shipping was protected from the omnipresent Dutch capers by a force of frigates patrolling in the Soundings and Channel and by a system of convoys, organized with considerable skill and efficiency by Secretary Pepys, for the outgoing trade.

The apparent reluctance of our French Allies to engage the Dutch in the fight off the Texel had greatly increased their unpopularity in England, and the initial enthusiasm for the war was rapidly waning. The Navy Board was over £1 million in debt, and the seamen were unpaid. An angry clamour presently arose in the Commons against the Catholics, a Standing Army, the French alliance, and the King's ' evil counsellors '. Charles II bowed to the storm. Unable to secure the necessary funds from Parliament for fitting out the fleet, he was finally compelled to abandon the war and the French alliance. By the Treaty of Westminster, concluded in February 1674, the Dutch consented to pay a moderate indemnity and to concede the right of the flag, while colonial conquests were to be restored on both sides.

The struggle between England and Holland was marked by a growing controversy concerning the rights of belligerents and neutrals. While the English for the most part could effectively protect their trade against the enemy's frigates and privateers by convoys, the Dutch had been unable to find the necessary escort vessels. The bulk of their merchant shipping was in consequence laid up in port; and they were obliged to carry on their commerce, as far as possible, in neutral bottoms. The various methods they employed to disguise their goods in neutral shipping actually anticipated some of the ingenious stratagems and devices to which their descendants resorted, centuries later, in the war of 1914-18. The Dutch view of neutral rights, expressed in the maxim, *Free ships, free goods,* was embodied in the peace treaty of 1674, which declared, in effect, that neutral shipping was to be free in war as in peace, except with regard to contraband and blockades. The restriction of her maritime rights under this unfortunate treaty was destined to be a heavy handicap to Great Britain in future wars.

4

Following the passage of the Test Act in 1673, the Duke of York and the other Catholic officers of the Navy had been obliged to resign their commissions; though the influence of the King's brother was still strong behind the scenes: and for the next six years the office of the Lord High Admiral was executed, in part, by Charles II himself. Pepys was installed as secretary to the new Commission with the title of ' Secretary to the Office of Lord High Admiral of England '; during his thirteen years' apprenticeship as Clerk of the Acts he had familiarized himself with every detail of the day-to-day work of the administration; and in his new office he became, in Albemarle's famous words, ' the right hand of the Navy '. The Commissioners were, for the most part, capable and prudent men; while the Navy Board remained, as before, a body of technical experts. The period 1673 to 1679 witnessed a sustained improvement in the administration and discipline of the Service, and, towards its close, an energetic shipbuilding programme.

Though the war on the Continent continued for four years longer, the issue was scarcely in doubt. Maestricht fell to the invader early in the campaign of 1673; but Spain and Austria now ranged themselves against France, and many of the German States followed Austria. The Grand Monarch's designs on Holland had failed. By the Peace of Nijmegen, in 1678, the French restored all Dutch territory still in their possession.

Her great war effort, however, had fatally undermined the prosperity of Holland. She had preserved her independence, but at the cost of her maritime and commercial pre-eminence. The best days of the Republic were over. In the Third Dutch War the sea power of Holland had proved the decisive factor. Michael de Ruyter, the finest fighting admiral of his era, had by his superb defensive campaigns of 1672 and 1673 warded off the menace of seaborne invasion from her shores. It was through no fault of the Dutch seamen that from now onward the scales were weighted irrevocably against the small State which, through fortuitous and transient circumstances, had won a place for herself among the foremost Powers of Europe. The steady decline of the Dutch Republic during the ensuing decades furnishes a striking and convincing illustration of how indispensable a solid basis of territory is to a Sea Power. The drain on her limited resources had overtaxed her strength. The necessity of maintaining a large standing army to defend her long land frontiers obliged her to sacrifice her navy. During the period 1674-8 the Dutch fleet fought gallantly but unsuccessfully against the French in the Mediterranean, where the great de Ruyter died in battle.

One of the most significant developments in the international situation in the latter half of the seventeenth century was the sudden and dramatic expansion of French sea power. When Louis XIV took over the reins of government in 1661 there was only a handful of warships of any size belonging to the French Crown. Before the century was out the navy of France was of a size and strength to challenge the fleets of the Maritime Powers, England and Holland. The extension of French maritime, commercial, and colonial enterprise was steadily and systematically pursued under the aegis of Louis XIV's great minister, Colbert, who brought all these activities under the control of an efficient and highly centralized administration. It was then that the two Maritime Powers realized that a third and potentially formidable aspirant to naval power had entered the lists.

During the last four years of the war England profited greatly by her neutrality. Her commerce, especially in 1674 and 1675, was booming, and her mercantile shipping rapidly increasing. Much of the carrying trade formerly enjoyed by Holland was now lost to England. ' As to our stock in shipping,' wrote Davenant in 1698, ' old and experienc'd Merchants do all agree, that we had in 1688, near double the Tonnage of Trading Ships, to what we had *Anno* 1666.' In consequence of this expanding commerce, the yield of the Customs and Excise advanced by leaps and bounds, enabling Danby, the Lord Treasurer, to restore the national finances—paying off troops and seamen, settling long-standing debts, and reducing the rate of interest on government loans.

In 1677 an extensive shipbuilding programme, resulting in the addition of thirty fine ships of the line to the Fleet, arose from the increasing needs of the kingdom, and the better support now forthcoming from Parliament. The powerful navies of our neighbours,

Holland and France, the necessity for guarding the Mediterranean trade, our growing colonial commitments, all pointed the same way. In a great speech which Pepys made to the Commons on 21 February of that year the Secretary carried his point; and £600,000—a very considerable sum for those days—was voted by the House. The existence of this formidable English Fleet was one of the determining factors which led to the overthrow of Louis XIV's aggressive designs on the Rhine delta, and to the Peace of Nijmegen.

In the autumn of 1678 the mysterious and horrific circumstances attending the murder of a well-known London magistrate, Sir Edmund Godfrey, following swiftly upon the perjuries of Titus Oates, set off a politico-religious explosion of the first magnitude. The wildest alarms now spread like prairie-fire, and the populace was soon half-crazed with wrath and fear. In the face of the dangerous temper prevailing in Parliament and people alike Charles II strove patiently and with wonderful skill to preserve the Royal prerogative and the lawful succession. While this madness lasted the fate of the monarchy hung by a hair. For behind Oates and his lies was the strong Whig caucus headed by Lord Shaftesbury, who, from the party headquarters in the Green Ribbon Club at Temple Bar, dexterously controlled, organized, and directed the course of the Popish Terror.

The deterioration of the fine naval force which the Act of 1677 had called into being proved no less rapid than its rise. The conflagration of 1678-9 had led to the downfall both of the King's brother and of his servants, Samuel Pepys and Sir Anthony Deane. The Duke of York was now forced to leave England and Pepys was committed to the Tower, while the administration of the Navy was entrusted to a Commission of seven, who were for the most part entirely ignorant of sea affairs.

During the next five years the fighting efficiency of the Service was at its lowest ebb. The battle fleet had ceased to exist; there were only twenty frigates and a few fireships; the rest of the ships lay rotting at their moorings, and the state of the thirty fine new vessels laid down under the 1677 programme was even worse than that of the older ships. ' Their holds not cleaned nor aired, but (for want of gratings and opening their hatches and scuttles) suffered to heat and moulder, till I have with my own hands gathered toadstools growing in the most considerable of them, as big as my fists '—as Pepys later avowed.

' Noah's Ark ', observed the same authority, ' must needs be made of some extraordinary timber and plank, that could remain good after having been an hundred years in building, whereas our thirty new ships are some of them rotten within less than five.' The evils associated with ' land admirals ' and ' gentleman captains ' crept back into the Service, and a horde of rapacious underlings preyed on the dockyards. The naval debt had risen by over a quarter. Even the once honest and competent experts of the Navy Board had succumbed to what Pepys described as the ' general and habitual supineness, wastefulness and neglect of order '. Above all, the Service during this period was becoming increasingly split by faction, the opponents of the Duke of York being ranged against his adherents. The schism in the Navy was to have supremely important consequences in the crisis of 1688.

In all three Parliaments which followed the Popish Plot the Whigs had a majority. They clamoured for an Exclusion Bill to deprive the Duke of York of the succession to the throne. To this, however, Charles II resolutely refused to agree. Meanwhile the ambassador of Louis XIV contrived to keep the country divided by pouring oil on the flames of English party strife, to which end he bribed both sides impartially. For it was not only the King, but every one of the Whig leaders besides, that was in the pay of France at this time.

At the height of the uproar Charles II suddenly dissolved Parliament. He repeated this manœuvre when the Whigs continued to press forward their Exclusion Bill. By means of these Fabian tactics and with the aid of an annual subsidy from Louis XIV the King succeeded in baffling his opponents. The panic and fury engendered by the events of 1678–9 had time to subside, and eventually the tide of popular feeling turned. In 1682, after a final unsuccessful attempt to stir up the London mob to revolution on the anniversary of Queen Elizabeth's accession (17 November), Shaftesbury fled to Holland. The following year, on the disclosure of the Rye House Plot, the initiative returned to Charles II. The Whigs were now undone. Shaftesbury died in exile. Essex committed suicide, and Russell lost his head. Loyal addresses poured in from all parts of the kingdom and even from distant America. The King took advantage of the strong surge of Tory reaction which swept the country to undermine the Whigs' control of Parliament and the municipalities. At the same time he resolved to revoke the Admiralty Commission of 1679 and recalled his brother and Pepys to power—to save what was left of the Navy.

5

In 1683 the evacuation of Tangier[1], which had long been a serious drain on the Exchequer, was determined on. The acquisition of the port had enhanced English naval power and protected our commercial interests within the Straits against the depredations of the Moors. The place was strongly fortified and capable of holding out over a long period without support from the sea. But, however well situated Tangier was strategically, as a naval base it laboured under serious disadvantages; its harbour was exposed to westerly gales and could afford shelter to no more than a few frigates—even at the head of the mole there was a depth of only ten feet or so; moreover, the town was exposed to attack from the surrounding hills. Lord Dartmouth and Samuel Pepys were accordingly sent out with a squadron to arrange for its evacuation and demolition. The naval stores had already been removed to Gibraltar, then in Spanish possession. The garrison and other inhabitants of the town were taken on board the squadron. The houses were demolished, and the fortifications, town walls, and mole blown up. On 8 March 1684 the ruined fortress was abandoned to the Moors.

While the English power in the Mediterranean was thus declining, that of France was visibly advancing. Admiral Duquesne had effectively bombarded Algiers by means of the newly invented bomb ketches or ' bombs '. Year by year the great French arsenal at Toulon was becoming more formidable. ' Lord Dartmouth is mightily full of it,' observed Pepys on 29 March 1684, ' that the King of France designs, by his late and present dealings with Algiers, to make himself master of the Mediterranean, making the Turks his friends, and thereby enemies to us and others.'

Both the Tangier mission and the long holiday which he afterwards passed in Spain enabled Pepys to gauge the full measure of the laxity and corruption which had seeped into the Service during his period of exile from the Admiralty. He took careful notes in shorthand of all he saw. As will later appear, these observations were, in due season, to bear fruit an hundredfold.

[1] Tangier formed part of the dowry of Charles II's Queen, Catherine of Braganza.

On his return from Tangier in the spring of 1684 Pepys was invited by Charles II to resume his former duties with the title of ' Secretary for the Affairs of the Admiralty of England '. The King, with the assistance of his brother, now took over the control of the Navy. Though on account of the Test Act the Duke of York could not resume his former title of Lord High Admiral, the general direction of naval affairs was in his hands; and the credit is primarily due to James for the steady advance and consolidation of English sea power in the latter half of the seventeenth century.

Under the powerful protection of the Duke of York Pepys laboured to enforce the wise rules or ' Establishments ' for the governance of the Service, which, under the lax rule of the Commission, had fallen into desuetude; to extirpate venality and incompetence in high places, and, in a word, to restore ' the lost discipline of the Navy '. Pepys, in fact, had become, to all intents and purposes, the administrative head of the Admiralty: the authority that he exercised being roughly equivalent to that of a modern First Lord. It was in large measure due to Pepys's thorough-going devotion to duty, his ' indefatigable care and pains ' for the great Service over which he ruled, his boundless energy and determination, his tact and skill in handling men and affairs, his tireless inculcation of discipline and rule, that the fabric of administrative order and routine was established, during the two periods of his Secretaryship, on a firm and durable foundation.

The last few months of the reign of Charles II, together with the short but fateful reign of his brother and successor, James II, witnessed the restoration, in an astonishingly brief period, of the Royal Navy, and a sustained improvement in the organization, discipline, and morale of the Service. This was in the main due to the unremitting care and vigilance of Secretary Pepys. Nevertheless, it must be remembered that always behind the zealous Secretary was the King, who continued to retain in his own hands the office of Lord High Admiral.

On the accession of James II in 1685 and the easing of the financial situation, Pepys proposed that a Special Commission of experts should be appointed to repair and restore the Navy. The King approved; and an annual sum of £400,000 was allotted to the Service. The Special Commission got under way in the summer of 1686, and within two years and a half completed its work. In actual practice the brunt of the burden fell upon Pepys himself, and Will Hewer—formerly Pepys's confidential clerk—and Sir Anthony Deane, the great shipbuilder. By prudent and careful management Pepys contrived to pay off the greater part of the Navy's debts, which, amounting to £400,000 on the accession of James II, had by the beginning of 1687 been reduced to under £172,000. Thus at the eleventh hour the Navy of England was saved and restored.

The Special Commission did its work so thoroughly that, by the spring of 1688, the bulk of the battle fleet had been repaired. It was supported by well-equipped dockyards, storehouses, and magazines; and a fine new dry dock was in process of construction at Portsmouth. As his term of office approached its end, the Secretary regarded the result of his lifework and saw that it was good. ' The Navy ', Pepys was to declare in after years, ' will never be found to have been once in the good condition I have had the leaving of it twice, viz. in April 1679 and December 1688.'

In April 1686 the ' Establishment ' of May 1676, for Volunteers and Midshipmen Extraordinary was revived and enforced; and in the same year another important ' Establishment ' provided for the proper maintenance and issue of Boatswains' and Carpenters' Stores.

During the years following the Restoration the practice had grown up in the Royal Navy of carrying freight for the personal profit of the captains (euphemistically known as Good Voyages) to the neglect of the King's service. This was partly through the entry into the Navy of so many ' gentlemen captains ' with expensive tastes and partly through the inadequacy of their pay. The practice was particularly common in Spain and the Mediterranean. The commander-in-chief within the Straits, Vice-Admiral Arthur Herbert, actually drew a regular percentage of the profits made by his subordinates. Herbert had left the Mediterranean; but the evil continued. As a result of Pepys's observations during his mission to Tangier, the opportunities for making rapid fortunes by such methods were put a stop to; and to compensate captains for the loss of their irregular earnings a more liberal scale of pay and allowances was introduced. ' Were the profit of voyages taken away and captains' subsistence made large and constant,' Pepys observed shrewdly, ' it would oblige them to be and to continue good, for fear of forfeiting those settlements.' At the same time captains were ordered, at the conclusion of each voyage, to present 'a perfect journal thereof'. The new regulations, strictly enforced, put an end to the practice of Good Voyages; and far more effective control was thereby secured over ships on foreign service.

Another abuse, noted and later recorded by Pepys in his *Naval Minutes*, was the tendency of commanders to screen one another at the expense of subordinates. Pepys observed 'how certainly partial our courts martial are to commanders in any matter of difference between them and their under-officers, or in cases of miscarriage where it is possible to lay it upon any under-officer'; and he went on to record that at the court martial held after the loss of the *St. David* (where it appears that the carpenter was made the scapegoat), on the rising of the court one of the captains was overheard to say to the captain of the lost ship, ' God damme, Jack, we have made shift to bring you off, but by God you must remember to do the like by any of us when it comes to our turn.'

6

The seventeenth century witnessed important developments in naval architecture. The celebrated Pett dynasty, which sprang from a long line of Harwich shipbuilders, now established itself firmly in the royal dockyards, and there, throughout all the troubles and vicissitudes of the period—as David Hannay has drily remarked— ' served its successive masters with the undeviating loyalty of the Vicar of Bray '.

Under the patronage of the early Stuarts Phineas Pett turned out some of the finest warships which the world had yet seen. Among the most famous products of his skill were the *Prince Royal* (1610) and the *Sovereign of the Seas* (1637)—the latter being the first three-decker in the history of the Navy. The leading shipbuilders during the later Stuart era were Sir Phineas Pett and Sir Anthony Deane. The former was master shipwright at Woolwich in 1677 and commissioner at Chatham in 1686. The latter was chiefly responsible for the construction and restoration of the fine fleet with which this country entered the struggle against Louis XIV.

As may be seen from Van de Velde's sketches of late Commonwealth vessels like the *Naseby* and *London*, warships had altered greatly in appearance compared with those of the Elizabethan period. The brilliant paintwork of the previous century had been replaced by elaborate carving and gilding. In structure and design there were also major developments. The sheer was considerably less pronounced, the upper works at both bow and stern were reduced in height, and a rounded tuck was substituted for the older square stern. In the course of the Restoration era the galleon bow, with its long, low beak, gave place to the round bow, with a shorter, wider beak, and set at a much higher angle. To carry the increased weight of the armament it was necessary for the later Stuart ships to have their maximum beam on the water-line.

During the seventeenth century both the sail area and the number of sails continued to increase. One of the most important developments of this period was the great increase in the size of the fore and main topsails in relation to the courses. A natural result of this increase was the introduction of reef-points in the topsails, probably between the First and Second Dutch Wars. (However, in a gale a ship usually sailed under her courses, with furled topsails. In a hard blow she would lie a-try under her main course. To be ' blown into our courses ' meant, that the craft in question could no longer carry her topsails. This remained the common practice till well on in the seventeenth century.) Mizen-topsails were introduced early in James I's reign; by about the year 1640 the bonaventure mizen-mast had wholly disappeared. In good weather, fairly early in the century, studding-sails were set outside the courses and topsails. Topgallant-sails were set above the fore and main topsails. In the second decade of the century a spritsail topmast was fitted to the forward end of the bow-sprit, and on this was set a spritsail topsail, which served, of course, as an additional headsail. An even more important change was the gradual introduction of staysails between the masts, whereby the performance of a ship sailing on a wind was vastly improved.[1]

The majority of merchantmen built during this era were comparatively small ships. These continued to use the primitive six-sail rig of the sixteenth century. The East India Company, however, constructed in their yard at Blackwell a number of quite large vessels. In 1613 an East India fleet comprised the *New Year's Gift* (650 tons), *Hector* (500 tons), *Merchant's Hope* (300 tons), and *Solomon* (200 tons).

---

[1] ' Edward Battine's *Method of Building and Rigging Ships of War* of 1684 gives details of main and mizen staysails and of main and fore " topstaysails " ': see G. S. Laird Clowes, *Sailing Ships, Their History and Development* (1932), p. 80.

Shortly afterwards Phineas Pett built the *Trade's Increase* of 1,200 tons.

At this stage a word must be said about the timber problem which was beginning to exercise the Admiralty and which was to continue to do so at intervals during the next two hundred years. The immense shipbuilding programme of the Commonwealth government had made very heavy inroads on the national timber reserves. These, during the next few decades, were at a dangerously low level. The occasional and rather half-hearted attempts, in the second half of the seventeenth century, to restore the Crown forests were for the most part unsuccessful. But the plantations made on private estates after the Restoration—a development which may be attributed, at least in part, to the influence of John Evelyn's *Sylva*—together with such of the young growth as had escaped the wholesale felling of the Commonwealth era, matured in time to supply the needs of the Navy throughout most of the eighteenth century. It was not, in fact, until after the end of the Seven Years War that the timber problem once more became acute.

Another urgent problem was the provision of masts. It was from the coasts of the Baltic in general, and from the Riga district in particular, that the maritime States of Europe drew their largest and most important supply of masts. But, as we have seen, during the First Dutch War the English traffic with the Baltic had been cut off; and from 1653 onward the Navy Board began to draw unceasingly on the pine forests of New England for their great masts.

The white pine belt of North America covered the coast from Nova Scotia to New Hampshire, and extended westward to the upper reaches of the Connecticut and Hudson rivers. From Portsmouth at the mouth of the Piscataqua came most of the great masts required by the Navy down to the year of the Revolution. Falmouth, in Maine, was another important centre for the shipment of masts; and later on a certain quantity were exported from the forests of Pennsylvania. On account of the difficulties of land transport usually the ' great sticks ' growing near rivers were chosen: these were then floated downstream and brought round the coast to Portsmouth or Falmouth for export.

As is evidenced in the numerous manuals of navigation published during this period, the seventeenth century saw the increasing use of mathematics by English navigators. Much of the knowledge that formerly required long years of experience could now be gained, in a matter of months, by the diligent study of books on the subject and by careful tuition in the handling of the navigational instruments. The same era saw a gradual awakening of interest in ocean currents and wind systems. The influence of Trinity House continued to play an important part in these developments.

There remained, however, notable faults and deficiencies in current navigational practice. Judging from the shrewd observations made by Pepys during his passage to and from Tangier, in 1683-4, it appears that the navigation of the Navy itself even left much to be desired.

Pepys records in his journal how, three days before they sighted the Burlings, he ' did pray my Lord [Dartmouth] to cause a strict account to be demanded of all in the ship, and it appeared that they were very different. . . . So that had it not been for the calm we have had, or if we had come upon them in the night, the whole fleet probably would have been upon the Burlings.'[1] It is to be observed that not one of the twelve reckonings examined put the flagship within 75 miles of the danger; others made the distance from the Burlings at between 90 and 210 miles. Pepys discovered that the charts were hopelessly inaccurate. ' It is clear also that rather than show their differences, for fear of showing their mistakes, masters will conceal their differences and so let the charts for ever remain as they be. Their only care now being to lie off in the night and make in in the day, when they think themselves drawing in towards any shore . . . so that it is by God Almighty's providence and great chance ', Pepys commented grimly, ' and the wideness of the sea, that there are not many [more] misfortunes and ill chances in Navigation than there are.'

On the homeward passage, on entering the Soundings, there was the same uncertainty as to their position; and the slipshod navigation of the Service was again exposed. ' Strange the disagreements', observed Pepys, ' in so fair weather with so fair a wind immediately upon a fair observation and clear sounding at 65 fathoms and 49° 34' latitude, among our navigators about the entrance into our Channel, my lord and Mr Phillips being very positive that we were shot to the Eastward of Scilly, whilst Sir W. Booth and the Master and mates were of opinion that we were yet to the westward, and one part of them apprehensive of our running upon the French coast, and the

[1] *The Tangier Papers of Samuel Pepys*, ed. E. Chappell (1935), pp. 126-7.

other upon the English, some being for lying by all night, others for sailing boldly forwards, as we did, due East.'[1] In point of fact it was the Lizard that they sighted shortly afterwards.

In the Restoration era the art of marine surveying made considerable progress. The leading English cartographer was Captain Greenville Collins, whose coasting pilot was to remain in use for several generations. Sir John Narbrough's painstaking survey of the Magellan Straits and the coast of Patagonia must also be mentioned, and also the work of Captain Christopher Gunman, whose name is commemorated in the Gunman Sand off Dover.

7

The reigns of Charles II and James II marked an era of unexampled commercial and colonial expansion. After a long period of trade depression, business at last began to revive. Charles II's concern with commercial interests was seen in the substantial advantages secured for English trade to Portugal and her dependencies, following upon his marriage with Catherine of Braganza—an alliance which also brought us Tangier and Bombay. The King and his ministers were in close and constant touch with the city magnates directing the great commercial enterprises of the capital. ' Upon the King's first arrival in England ', his minister, Clarendon, recorded, ' he manifested a very great desire to improve the general traffick and trade of the kingdom, and upon all occasions conferred with the most active merchants upon it, and offered all he could contribute to the advancement thereof.' With the progressive recovery of the nation after the Civil and Dutch Wars, the dread visitations of 1665 and 1666, and the Peace of Breda, something like a trade boom set in. It was, to quote J. A. Williamson, ' a spontaneous outburst of national energy, comparable to that of the Elizabethans ': it was due for the most part to the sudden and rapid growth of the re-export trade, chiefly in produce of America and the East, and also to the exploitation of the African slave trade and the Newfoundland fishery.

In this unparalleled expansion the East Indian trade played a leading part. Under the aegis of Sir Josiah Child and other influential London merchants, the Company entered on a period of amazing

[1] *Ibid.*, p. 248.

prosperity. For a good many years its average annual dividend was about 25 per cent.; in 1683 a £100 share fetched £500 in the market. Its monopoly was rigorously enforced. Its trading posts extended from the Red Sea to the China coast. To handle this ever-growing traffic, there were, between 1675 and 1680, sixteen East Indiamen constructed with burdens rising to 1,200 tons.

On the other side of the globe, the Hudson's Bay Company (founded in 1670) also shared in the wave of prosperity which followed the restoration of peace with Holland in 1674. Year by year it sent out two or three vessels to load the pelts and furs which the Indians brought to the chain of posts set up around the bleak and inhospitable shores of Hudson's Bay. The company was encouraged by the success of its early ventures to increase its trade and to enlarge the scope of its operations. It made large profits during the twelve prosperous years which followed its inauguration, and in the 1680s began to pay handsome dividends. In the Mediterranean, the lucrative Levant trade was protected by our possession of Tangier and by a series of treaties with the piratical Barbary States. The Royal African Company was similarly very prosperous until 1687. The older regulated companies likewise shared in the general trade revival of the Restoration era; the Muscovy Company temporarily regaining a measure of its former prosperity.

The same period saw the completion along the North American seaboard of a continuous line of English settlements. From the southern colonies came an unceasing flow of cargoes of tobacco for home consumption and re-export. ' The Plantacon Trade ', wrote the Commissioners of the Customs in 1678, ' is one of the greatest Nurseries of the Shipping and Seamen of this Kingdome, and one of the greatest branches of its Trade.'[1] The Newfoundland fishery, another prolific training-ground of seamen, was worked by a fleet of well over two hundred vessels and manned by some thousand men; the majority of these came from our western ports and carried on an important triangular traffic between England, Newfoundland, and the Peninsula. The middle colonies, which could not supply the products or raw materials needed in England, were not so highly valued by the statesmen at home. New England, however, developed in isolation. Her fishing, lumbering, shipping, and shipbuilding industries were

---

[1] Q. Beer, *The Old Colonial System*, I, p. 17.

already well established and progressed rapidly during the following century. In the West Indies, about two hundred vessels, English-built, annually loaded the rich cargoes of sugar for home.

The inter-dependence of sea power, shipping, commerce, and colonies was well understood by the magnates of the city as well as by the King's ministers like Clarendon and statesmen like Downing and Shaftesbury. In the eyes of the mercantile school, sea power enabled this country to augment and to protect her overseas trade and this increased trade, in turn, enabled her to strengthen her Navy. Thus, on the adjournment of Charles II's first parliament, the Speaker remarked that the Navigation Act ' will enable your majesty to give the law to foreign princes abroad as your royal predecessors have done before you: and that is the only way to enlarge your majesty's dominions all over the world; for so long as your majesty is master at sea your merchants will be welcome wherever they come; and that is the easiest way of conquering.'[1] ' Only foreign Trade ', observed Charles Davenant, ' can maintain a great Fleet.' And elsewhere the same writer asserted: ' In a Trading Nation, the bent of all the Laws should tend to the encouragement of Commerce, and all Measures should be there taken, with a due regard to its Interest and Advancement.'

A generation later, in his *A New Discourse of Trade*, Sir Josiah Child declared that without the Navigation Act ' we had not been Owners of one half of the Shipping nor Trade, nor employed one half of the Sea-men which do we at present.' It is a fact that, between the Restoration and Revolution, the English merchant marine almost doubled its tonnage. The beginning of marine insurance in England likewise bore witness to the ever-increasing importance of merchant shipping in this era.[2]

One of the most important effects of the Navigation Act was to diminish the volume of trade to Scandinavia and the Baltic, but to increase the transatlantic traffic. Our east coast ports suffered in consequence; but Liverpool, Bristol, and Plymouth benefited considerably from the expanding trade with the American colonies. The general trend of English shipbuilding operated in the same direction. The fact is, English shipping could scarcely hope to compete with the Dutch in the bulk trades (' the lost trades ', as they were called) but was well adapted to the rich and hazardous trades for which the

---

[1] *Ibid.*, 4.   [2] See *infra*, p. 408.

strong, well-armed ships turned out by the English shipyards were a necessity. ' The East India, Turky & other rich Trades, will beare the employing of Ships with Guns,' wrote Sir George Downing in 1663, ' but the Norway and Eastland Trade can by noe means beare it.'

In the prosperous last years of Charles II's life, when the King was victorious over his enemies and parliament was in abeyance, England was able to store up strength and treasure for the coming duel with France. Even in the brief and troubled reign of his brother, James II, the rapid expansion of trade and colonial enterprise continued without a check.

8

Despite the Whigs and their Exclusion Bill James II had in the end succeeded to his brother's throne without question or opposition. A Tory parliament presently proceeded to vote him a larger revenue than any of his predecessors had ever enjoyed; Sedgemoor gave him, in the year of his accession, a standing army; the Whigs and Dissenters were, for the present, reduced to impotence; and by 1687 the restoration of the Navy was well under way.

All these advantages James II, in his headlong haste to abrogate the penal laws, successively cast away. Using the royal prerogative to override the Test Act, he published, in April 1687, the first Declaration of Indulgence ' for a general toleration of all religions '. Catholics were thereupon introduced, in fairly large numbers, into the Army and magistracy. Throughout the following summer the new policy was relentlessly pursued. The Tower of London was placed under a Catholic governor. The Catholic Duke of Berwick was appointed governor of Portsmouth. Next year another Catholic, Sir Roger Strickland, succeeded Herbert in command of the Channel Fleet. The Protestant Fellows of Magdalen College, Oxford, were evicted and replaced by Catholics. High Tories like Rochester were gradually ousted from office in favour of Catholics and the King's personal followers like the false-hearted Sunderland, who encouraged his master to press on with the rash and impolitic design which was to work his ruin. The whole trend of James II's policy was, in fact, calculated to exacerbate the most cherished national prejudices and to revive historic fears. Furthermore, these high-handed proceedings outraged, not merely the Whigs, his old opponents, but also the Tories, to whose loyal support he owed his throne.

At this stage events abroad seemed to point a moral. The revocation of the Edict of Nantes in 1685 and the barbarous cruelties of the *dragonnades* was followed by the wholesale exodus from France of the persecuted Huguenots. The story of their sufferings had inflamed English popular feeling against France and Catholicism in the highest degree. Collections were made in the parish churches all over the kingdom for the relief of the Huguenot refugees. The fear and loathing of the English ruling class centred on the King of France. ' I heare he stinckes alive,' declared Squire Verney of Louis XIV, ' and his cankers will stinck worse when he is dead, and so will his memory to all eternity.' The inhuman persecution of the French Protestants was one of the major contributory factors in the situation which produced the Revolution of 1688. In the end the deep-rooted English fear of ' Popery and wooden shoes ' turned the scales against, first, James II in England, and, later, Louis XIV in Europe.

In the decade of 1678–88 the Grand Monarch had reached the zenith of his power. There was no single State, nor, in the then condition of Europe, any combination of States, strong enough to resist him. But the disproportionate strength of France had at last aroused the Continent. The Catholic States of Austria and Spain looked to William of Orange to save them from a French hegemony. Together with the Papacy, they joined forces with the Protestant Powers of Holland and Prussia in defence of their common interests.

One thing, however, was yet lacking. It was the neutralization of England which had long enabled Louis XIV to defy the rest of Europe. Her formidable naval power and commercial wealth were essential to the success of the coalition against France. William of Orange, being both James II's nephew and his son-in-law, stood close to the succession. After the failure of Monmouth's rebellion and his subsequent execution, he became the Whig candidate for the throne. But now came a fresh development. The hope entertained by the English majority of a Protestant succession was suddenly shattered, on 10 June 1688, by the birth of a son to James II's Queen, Mary of Modena. It was at this juncture that the Whigs invented, and sedulously fostered, the legend of the Warming Pan. Its acceptance became a political necessity. Sinking their differences, the Whigs and Tories drew closer together in the face of the common peril.

That same summer events moved to a climax. James II made a

daring bid for the support of the Dissenters against the Tories, who were up in arms against his religious policy; he issued a second Declaration of Indulgence, which he ordered to be read in all the churches. The Primate and six other bishops publicly protested, and were in consequence prosecuted before the Court of the King's Bench. The proceedings against the seven broke down; and at the news of their acquittal the church-bells pealed for joy, the Pope was burned in effigy all over England, and even the King's army on Hounslow Heath broke out into tumultuous cheering.

Disguised as a common seaman, Herbert set off for The Hague with a letter bearing the signature of seven leading Whigs and Tories to William of Orange, inviting the Prince to invade England at the head of his troops and pledging their support. For a while the fate of England and Europe trembled in the balance. A French descent on Holland would have rendered the invasion project impossible. But in September Louis XIV declared war on the Empire and launched his armies against the Palatinate. For the winter, at least, Holland was safe. It was William's opportunity and he took it. To secure the adherence of England to the great alliance he determined to stake all on a desperate throw. Already that spring he had begun to prepare. An immense fleet of transports was gradually assembled in Holland in readiness to carry the Prince's great Protestant army of Dutchmen, Danes, Swedes, Swiss, Huguenots, Prussians, English, and Scots over to the opposite shore.

Early in August the naval and military preparations across the North Sea became so menacing that James II could no longer blind himself to his nephew's intentions. As the crisis approached, he resolved on a sudden change of policy. He issued a proclamation promising to summon a parliament from which Catholics should be excluded. Sunderland thereupon lost his office. The Catholic Lords-Lieutenant were dismissed. Catholic schools were ordered to close. The Protestant Fellows of Magdalen were reinstated. No pains were spared to appease the Tories. But these concessions to public opinion came too late. When James II attempted to bring over some regiments of Catholic Irish there was such an explosion of fury that the project had to be hurriedly abandoned. As the autumn wore on the tension steadily mounted. From end to end of England rose up the mocking strains of ' Lilliburlero '. ' The whole army, and at last the people, both in city and country, were singing it perpetually ', says Burnet. ' And perhaps never had so slight a thing so great an effect.'

> O, why does he stay so long behind?
> Ho! by my shoul, 'tis a Protestant wind.

> Lero, lero, lilliburlero!
> Lilliburlero, bullen-a-lah!

Meanwhile James II was preparing to defend his throne. Both by land and by sea measures were taken to resist the threatened invasion. The machinery of administration, under the aegis of Pepys and his colleagues on the Navy Board, operated on the whole smoothly and efficiently during the critical period of the mobilization—with the exception of a victualling crisis, brief but severe, in October. The mismanagement of the Ordnance Office was primarily responsible for the indifferent provision of guns, ammunition, and ordnance stores: but this Board was, in fact, outside the jurisdiction of the Admiralty, being a separate department which supplied guns and ordnance stores to both the Army and the Navy.[1] ' However matters may be represented to you from the [Ordnance] Office,' Pepys told Dartmouth on 20 October, ' there is not one shipp now behind you, from whose Commander I doe not daily hear of want of gunns, shot, carriages, or something else relating thereto, notwithstanding (as the captains averr) their gunners' daily attendance for them.'

On 1 October the fleet was ordered to rendezvous at the Buoy of the Nore. Sir Roger Strickland had been replaced by the Protestant Lord Dartmouth; a commander who, though personally upright and loyal, lacked nerve and resolution. One thing at least is certain: a fight at sea, whatever the outcome, must have ruined the Prince's plans: but Dartmouth failed to force that fight upon him. To meet the impending descent the English fleet lay off the Gunfleet, in the Thames estuary. In this ill-chosen anchorage Dartmouth remained inactive throughout the fateful autumn weeks when William's seventy warships and four hundred transports were held windbound in the Helvoetsluys. Exactly how far the Navy was disaffected to James II will probably

---

[1] ' From the sixteenth to the nineteenth century the Ordnance enjoyed an unbroken reputation for procrastination and corruption, attracting the attention of Marlborough as of Hawkins, and of Wellington as of Pepys ' (Ehrman, *The Navy in the War of William III*, p. 176).

never be known. That divided loyalties were a decisive factor in the situation, however, can scarcely be doubted.

At last, on 1 November, the wind came fair and William sailed on the evening tide. The Dutch fleet, under the command of the English Admiral Herbert, first steered a north-westerly course, and later, on the evening of the 2nd, altered course to the south-westward for the Channel. Dartmouth had lost his opportunity. On 30 October, with the wind at S.S.E., he had hoped, with the help of the afternoon ebb, to get clear of the Galloper before nightfall. Failing to do so, he anchored between the Sledway and the Longsand Head.

The wind now blew strongly from the east; and for several days the English fleet remained windbound. On Thursday, 1 November, Dartmouth wrote in his dispatch to the King, ' it blew so very hard that we were forced to strike all our yards and topmasts, and ridd with two cables and a halfe out, the winde fretting and never varying above one point either way.' At daybreak on the 3rd, one of the captains recorded, ' we espied several ships to windward, close-hauled under their low sails '; at that the English fleet prepared to give chase, ' but the ebb tide being almost spent, we could not weather the Longsand Head and the Kentish Knock.'

That same day the Dutch fleet, watched by huge crowds on either shore, passed through the Straits of Dover. The Prince's ship led the van. ' His flag was English colours ', observes Macaulay; ' and the motto impaled thereon was, " The Protestant Religion and the liberties of England "; and underneath, instead of " *Dieu et Mon Droit* " was " *Je maintiendrai* " '. While Dartmouth endeavoured vainly to clear the Thames estuary the ' Protestant wind " carried William triumphantly down the Channel to his destination. On 5 November the Prince's army disembarked in Torbay unopposed.

Early on the previous day the English fleet had at last got under sail and ran down Channel with the wind at E.S.E., ' a steady gale '; and then, the wind falling away, lay becalmed off Beachy Head. On the 6th they stood to the westward again. But on the 7th a south-westerly gale sprang up and drove them back past Beachy Head; a high grey Channel sea was running; as the wind increased, ' with thick rainy weather ', they bore away for the Downs, where they anchored. On the 19th, urged on by Pepys, Dartmouth stood towards Torbay and actually came within sight of the Dutch fleet; but even then he forebore to attack. Instead he retired towards the Isle of Wight, and, caught by a heavy gale at W.S.W., anchored in St. Helens.

There followed a long period of naval inactivity, while disaffection to the King swiftly spread through the fleet. James II, lying with his army at Salisbury, found himself suddenly betrayed, and by his oldest and most trusted followers. His nephew, the Duke of Grafton, and, above all, his commander, John Churchill, forsook him and went over to the Prince. His own daughter fled from him. Captain Matthew Aylmer and others were meanwhile engaged in winning over the officers of the fleet to the Prince's cause; and on 28 November Lieutenant George Byng met William at Sherborne, bringing with him assurances of support from the powerful Orangist faction. He was cordially received, and sent back with a letter of invitation to Dartmouth to join the Prince's party. Dartmouth, having by this time received news of the King's flight to France, on 12 December sent in his submission to William. Finally, on the 23rd, the French ambassador was ordered to quit the kingdom; England joined hands with the great European coalition which William of Orange had raised up against his implacable foe, Louis XIV; and the naval, military, and economic resources of the island State were cast into the scales against France.

VII

The Rhine Delta

I

On the eve of the long struggle between England and France, which occupied most of the period 1689–1815, it is useful and instructive briefly to examine the respective positions of those two kingdoms. The latter would at first sight have appeared to be admirably situated for the development of a great Sea Power. The population of France was far greater, and her territory larger and more fertile, than those of her rival. Her extensive forests furnished her with an abundance of timber for shipbuilding. Though her Channel ports were poor, she possessed excellent harbours on both her Atlantic and Mediterranean coasts. Her maritime population was already considerable. The Normans, Bretons, and Basques were first-rate seamen who were active in the Newfoundland fishery and carried on an extensive traffic with the French settlements overseas.

Under the wise and provident administration of Colbert, France had become a great maritime, commercial, and colonial Power. With the aid of lavish subsidies her shipbuilding industry had revived, and French merchant shipping penetrated to every quarter of the globe. Through an elaborate system of State regulation and supervision Colbert improved communications, promoted the formation of industrial and trading companies, and assisted the founding of colonies. The trading companies eventually decayed: but the colonies remained. By the end of the seventeenth century the number of French colonists settled in the immense territories held by France stretching southward from the St. Lawrence to the Mississippi had quadrupled, and the first French warships had appeared on Lakes Huron and Ontario.

At the same time the French navy had increased from almost nothing to a powerful fleet of two hundred sail, manned by a corps of 1,200 officers and more than 53,000 seamen. To this was added an auxiliary fleet of eighty privateers based on Dunkirk and other privateer ports. ' In the few years of Colbert's administration ', observes Mahan, ' is seen the whole theory of sea power put into practice in the systematic, centralizing French way; while the illustration of the same theory in English and Dutch history is spread over generations.' In 1662 and thereafter operations against pirates and the convoy of merchantmen and fishing craft became part of the regular duties of the French navy. Before his death Colbert had made France one of the leading sea powers of Europe. The manning of this huge force had presented a serious problem, which was solved in part by Colbert's system of maritime inscription. In the words of La Roncière, ' *Ce fut une révolution navale qui assura à la marine de Louis XIV les bénéfices de la conscription moderne.*'[1] To secure an adequate supply of trained officers for the fleet Colbert founded naval colleges at Saint-Malo, Toulon, Rochefort, and Brest. When the artillery school was established at Metz, in 1668, naval officers were sent to study there. Schools of hydrography were set up at Rochefort and Dieppe. Brest was made into a first-rate naval base defended by fortifications designed by Vauban; a large part of Toulon having been destroyed by a fire, the city was rebuilt on plans drawn by Vauban and approved of by Colbert, and provided with a fine dockyard and arsenal; and the harbours of Marseilles, Havre, Calais, Dunkirk, and many smaller places were also improved.

Colbert further endeavoured, despite many difficulties, to create and expand new supply industries. He established a number of State and private foundries for the supply of cannon for the fleet; and he encouraged—though with only limited success—the native production of tar and gunpowder. He promoted the manufacture of hemp in Brittany, Auvergne, and elsewhere; established rope-walks in a dozen different ports; increased considerably the output of sail-cloth; imported numbers of foreign shipwrights and carpenters: and though France still remained largely dependent on the Baltic for naval stores he nevertheless substantially reduced the proportion of such products that the kingdom had to purchase from abroad. As a result of Colbert's efforts, France became increasingly self-sufficient as regards supplies, particularly of ordnance and sail-cloth. In general, the French naval administration was decidedly superior to that of the Maritime Powers,

---

[1] It is to be noted, however, that after Colbert's death recourse had to be had to impressment.

and could fit out and man the fleet more quickly than the English and Dutch: this, during the first few years of the war, tended to counterbalance the numerical superiority of the Allied Navy. French shipbuilding, surveying and charts, and tactical studies were accounted the best in Europe. Between 1683 and 1690 the maritime expansion of France continued under Colbert's son and successor, Colbert de Seignelay.

In the early half of the reign of the Grand Monarch France had advanced from strength to strength. The matchless armies created by Louvois, led by some of the finest generals of the age, enforced her will upon Europe. Vauban's genius for fortification rendered her frontiers inviolable. The diplomacy of France proved no less potent than her arms. In organized power, in the numbers and intelligence of her population, in wealth, civilization, and culture, the French monarchy towered above all other States. The dazzling court presided over by the Sun King struck the imagination of the world. Friend and foe alike bowed to the cultural hegemony of France. Towards the close of the seventeenth century Louis XIV's great palace of Versailles, set in the midst of an immense expanse of magnificent gardens, parterres, avenues, colonnades, pavilions, lakes, and fountains, thronged with the most brilliant society in Europe, for whose daily and nightly diversion was put on an endless succession of fêtes, balls, masquerades, plays, and symphonies, presented a spectacle of elegance and splendour without parallel in the history of mankind. It was the golden age of the *ancien régime*.

In the second half of the century France stood at the crossroads of opportunity. Before her lay a choice of courses—the one leading to maritime, commercial, and colonial expansion, and the other to religious uniformity, military glory, and continental aggrandizement. Eventually she chose the latter. Faithful to the classical tradition of the French monarchy, Louis XIV endeavoured to extend the frontiers of modern France to the uttermost limits of ancient Gaul, and to gain possession of the left bank of the Rhine.

This policy raised up a host of formidable enemies on the Continent, while the threat to the Rhine delta excited the implacable hostility of England. It also entailed the sacrifice of Louis XIV's fleet to his army, and of his colonial empire to aggression on his eastern frontier. The French found themselves committed to a series of ruinously expensive wars, with the result that their peaceful commerce and mercantile shipping—with which alone a strong fighting navy could be sustained —speedily withered away.

Owing to her insular position, England had no need of a large standing army and could afford to concentrate her chief energies on her fleet. In this respect she had the advantage both of France, her enemy, and of Holland, her ally. Placed in a strategically strong situation on the trade-routes, with a sufficiency of good natural harbours on all her coasts, with a proportionately large seafaring population to minister to her world-wide commerce in peace, and to serve as an ample reserve of trained seamen in war, she was faced with no such dilemma as that which confronted her rival. Her rising sea power, which covered her commercial and colonial expansion, was equally her shield against the aggressions of France. With the wealth drawn from her world-wide commerce she could subsidize her allies on the Continent. Above all, the traditions of England were not military, but maritime; and the strength and efficiency of her fleet were the constant preoccupation of the politically powerful mercantile interest.

Towards the close of the seventeenth century England consciously strove for maritime supremacy. Halifax, in his *Rough Draught of a New Model at Sea* (1694), observed: 'As the importance of our being very strong at *Sea* was ever very great, so in our present circumstances it is known to be much greater: because, as formerly our force of shipping contributed greatly to our trade and safety, so now it is become indispensable necessary to our very being. It may be said now to England, "Martha, Martha, thou art busy about many things, but one thing is necessary." To the question, "What shall we do to be saved in this world?" there is no other answer but this—Look to your Moate. The first article of an Englishman's political creed must be, that he believeth in the sea.'

Lastly, a main and decisive factor in the long rivalry with France was the chronic weakness of our enemy in the Channel. During the age of sail navigational conditions in these waters were decidedly unfavourable to France. East of Brest there was no harbour for heavy ships, no port which could compare with Portsmouth or Plymouth— only tidal harbours which could take no more than a limited number of small craft. Consequently the French were at a serious disadvantage whenever operating against England, and, even when things went well for their navy, apt to be prevented from following up their success.

2

By 1686, as has already been explained, Louis XIV, by repeated acts of aggression, had aroused Europe against France; and a defensive alliance was finally formed under the leadership of William of Orange, who, by securing the English crown two years later, had cemented the alliance between England and Holland in the most effective way, and thereby gained control of the sea power which was destined to play a decisive part in circumventing the designs of the Grand Monarch. In the war which broke out in May 1689 and lasted until September 1697 Louis XIV fought to gain possession of the Spanish Netherlands and to restore James II to the English throne. The Whigs and Tories forthwith joined forces to secure the liberties of England from the domination of France and to defend the Protestant religion ' by law established '.

Once again the Rhine delta was seen to be in jeopardy. Since Louis XIV's policy aimed at the absorption of the southern half of the delta it must needs be by the destruction of the Dutch, who might be expected to resist to the death such an encroachment. At the same time the domination of this vital area by the French would revive that menace to our island security which was the abiding concern of the rulers of this country from the days of Queen Elizabeth to our own. Once again the eyes of our ministers turned anxiously on the cockpit of Europe, the Low Countries—on the long line of dunes and dykes fringing the coastlands of Holland and Flanders, the fertile Zeeland islands lying athwart the mouths of the Maas and Scheldt, and the great waterway winding majestically across the broad plains to the North Sea; on the chain of stout fortresses flanking the southern frontier and the endless trains of barges moving slowly down the straight and sluggish canals; on the floating forest of masts and yards by the crowded quays of Amsterdam and the rich and populous cities of the southern Netherlands; above all, on the ports looking out across the narrow seas on England, and on the great estuarine way to Ghent and Antwerp—that incomparable base for an invasionary army—the ' pistol pointed at England's heart '.

Danger threatened, too, from another quarter. The war with France and the existence at Brest of a first-class naval base flanking the Channel approaches rendered the establishment of a dockyard of our own well to the westward of Portsmouth a matter of pressing importance. After surveying and rejecting first Dartmouth and then Falmouth, the Admiralty finally decided on Plymouth as the site of this western base. In the 1690s work was accordingly started on a new dockyard on the Hamoaze; and a new town, called Dock, began to spring up outside the dockyard walls. One of the worst hazards in the approaches had been removed by the construction of a lighthouse on the Eddystone. But the Sound, which was then wholly open to the south-west, was a dangerous anchorage in heavy weather. For this reason Torbay, which afforded spacious and good anchorage in westerly weather, was often resorted to instead of Plymouth.

In the War of the English Succession the conditions under which hostilities at sea were conducted differed fundamentally from those which had obtained in the earlier conflicts with Spain and Holland. In the first place, our present adversary was nothing like so vulnerable at sea as our former enemies. The seaborne commerce of France was in any case less vital to her than the *flotas* were to Spain, or the trading fleets to Holland, and her trade-routes generally were less open to attack. The Dutch, who had hitherto followed the maxim *Free ships, free goods*, and had signed treaties on those lines with neighbouring states, now reversed their policy and joined forces with England in an attempt to throttle the enemy's commerce. In 1689, notwithstanding Swedish and Danish protests, it was proposed to bar the enemy from ' the trade of the North which supplies him with the material without which he cannot carry on the war '. But the Anglo-Dutch war on hostile trade proved wholly ineffective. Neutral States were naturally unwilling to subordinate their commercial interests to the naval and economic policy of the Maritime Powers, and it was some years before the latter were in a position to establish the necessary command of the sea-routes. Moreover, neither England nor Holland was able to prevent their own merchants from ignoring the restrictions on trade.

The continental campaign against Louis XIV was no sooner under way, in the spring of 1689, than William III found his position in the British Isles gravely imperilled. Before England could play her full part in the warfare in Flanders she had first to secure her own coasts. The danger from across St. George's Channel, which haunted our statesmen down to the beginning of the last century, suddenly materialized in its most alarming form. On 12 March a strong French squadron had landed the exiled James II, with an army of 5,000 men, at Kinsale in the south of Ireland; after which the squadron returned to France. Attempts were made to fit out a British force under Admiral Herbert, but, owing to the chronic shortage of supplies, it was some time before this force could be got to sea. Presently stores and ammunition were ferried over from Brest to southern Ireland by a fleet of twenty-four of the line commanded by the Comte de Château-Rénault, who on 10 May, in Bantry Bay, engaged an inferior force, under Herbert, which had been sent to drive him away. After a scrambling, inconclusive action fought at long range, Château-Rénault withdrew to Brest and Herbert returned to England. At the Revolution the bulk of the Irish regular army had declared for King James, and the peasantry were busily arming. The exiled king received an enthusiastic welcome from the Catholic Irish, and was soon in effective possession of the whole island except western Ulster. The dour Protestants of the north shut themselves up in Derry and Enniskillen. After many delays the Jacobite army set about their reduction. During the early part of the war the crucial theatre of operations was in Ireland. So far from being able to make a substantial contribution to the common cause, England fell back upon the defensive. Ireland independent and hostile would assuredly have been fatal to her security and prosperity. In 1689 the United Kingdom was in imminent peril of dissolution.

Here and now was France's opportunity. With an adequate military effort on her part, together with the vigorous use of her fleet, Ireland might well have been held for King James, and the Catholic Irish organized, armed, and drilled into a formidable army. As it was, the French failed to act in time or with sufficient strength during the critical months of 1689–90. Château-Rénault had failed to exploit his success in throwing a French army into Ireland and undermining the Revolution. In the long run, the Jacobite chances in Ireland depended upon command of the sea—but Château-Rénault, having achieved his immediate object, had been content to retire. Such an opportunity might never recur. At this juncture the French still further lessened their chances of obtaining superiority at sea by detaching forces to operate against the Dutch convoys. Though the Dutch losses in this respect were certainly severe, they did not appreciably influence the course of the war. Then, on 19 July 1689, the Toulon squadron of twenty sail under Tourville slipped past a superior English force under Herbert, in thick and stormy weather, and entered Brest. The united French fleet in Brest was now approximately equal in strength to that of the Allies.

In the face of these difficulties and dangers William III rashly divided his army into two forces, neither of which proved strong enough for the work that it had to do. He dispatched one of these forces, under Churchill, to Flanders, and the other, under Schomberg, to Ulster. In the next few months things went badly for the Revolution. The year 1689 closed with the Jacobites victorious in Ireland and Schomberg's army, ravaged by disease, forced back upon the defensive. As a result of these events, in the following year the chief resources of England had to be diverted from the continental theatre to the war in Ireland.

The struggle in Ulster centred on the defence of Derry and Enniskillen. The siege of the former constitutes one of the key events of Irish history. Half a century before, Derry had been a city of refuge for the Protestant settlers fleeing from the Irish Terror. Built on the slopes of a hill overlooking the Foyle, which encompassed it on the north, east, and south-west sides, and protected on the west and north-west by a marsh, the city was encircled by strong walls roughly a mile in circumference; crowded within those walls were some 30,000 men, women, and children, who, towards the end of July 1689, doggedly holding out against James II and a powerful Jacobite army, were at their last extremity. After a siege lasting for 111 days they had nothing ' left for their subsistence but nine lean horses and a pint of meal to each man '. A squadron under Commodore George Rooke sent to relieve the city had found the passage up the Foyle blocked at Culmore Point with a boom, which proved too strong to be forced, covered by formidable batteries on each bank. For weeks the relieving force lay inactive in the entrance to Lough Foyle. Within the city Captain Ash recorded in his diary on 27 July: 'Next Wednesday is our last, if relief does not arrive before it.'

In consequence of urgent orders from London, another attempt was then made to reach the city. Soon after sunset on the 28th the lookouts stationed on the cathedral tower distinguished the sails of three vessels standing up the Foyle on the flood. They were the store-ships

Mountjoy and *Phoenix*, escorted by Captain John Leake in the *Dart-mouth* frigate. 'The Enemy Fired most desperately upon them from the Fort of *Culmore*, and both Sides the River; and they made sufficient returns, and with the greatest bravery.'[1] While the *Dartmouth* engaged the shore batteries, the boats' crews swarmed out on the boom and hacked it asunder. The *Mountjoy* struck the boom and went aground, upon which a shout of triumph arose from the Jacobite ranks: the enemy 'Fired all their Guns upon her, and were preparing their Guns to Board her': but the *Phoenix* passed safely through and on. A well-directed broadside from the *Dartmouth* defeated the enemy's attempt to board the stranded *Mountjoy*, which, partly from the effect of the concussion, presently got afloat again. Shortly after her master, Micaiah Browning, a native of Derry, who had been standing with sword drawn upon the deck, was shot through the head with a bullet and killed. Just before dark the *Phoenix*, followed by the *Mountjoy*, came alongside Derry quay. While the cathedral bells broke out into joyful pealing the store-ships were quickly unloaded. Derry was saved. On the night of the 31st the Jacobite army fired their camp and broke up the siege. Later, with but exiguous means at his disposal, Rooke kept watch on the long Irish coast-line from Malin Head to Dublin and in August escorted the transports carrying Schomberg's army to Belfast Lough. In the meantime the defenders of Enniskillen had defeated a Jacobite army of 5,000 at Newtown Butler.

3

The supreme test for the Revolution settlement came in 1690. Throughout the winter months there had been the usual shortages and delays in refitting the fleet. 'For God's sake, my Lord,' observed Russell, writing to Nottingham in March, 'cast your eyes sometimes towards next summer's fleet. I dread the French being out before us. If they are we shall run the risk of being undone, which is no good prospect.' Russell's fears were justified in the event. A French fleet sailed from Brest early in the year before the English were at sea and disembarked a force of 7,000 troops under the Comte de Lauzan at Cork. Moreover, in response to the urgent appeals of the merchants, the Council had determined to dispatch a squadron under Killigrew

[1] Geo. Walker, *A True Account of the Siege* (1689).

to the Mediterranean to protect Allied commerce and to watch Château-Rénault in Toulon. Our forces in the main theatre were still further weakened by the detachment of a squadron of some eight sail under Sir Clowdisley Shovell[1] to cover the passage of an English army of 27,000 troops to northern Ireland.

Here was yet one more example of the incorrigibly weak and inept handling of their navy by the enemy. With so many of the Irish ports in their possession, the French might well have controlled the passages to Ireland until such time as the Maritime Powers had engaged, and decisively defeated, their fleet. Instead, they made no effort to command the Irish Sea and to impede the passage of William III and the pick of his forces to Ulster.

While the fate of Ireland remained uncertain, the French concentration of seventy-five sail of the line in the Channel that summer took the Allies by surprise. The Channel Fleet, under Torrington, found itself faced by a hostile force of nearly double its strength. Torrington's own proposal was that he should avoid action ' unless it may be upon equaller terms than for the present I can see any prospect of ', and to retire if necessary to the Gunfleet, ' the only place we can with any manner of probability make our party good with them in the condition we are in '. The Council, however, had other views; and Torrington received a letter from the Queen desiring him to fight ' upon any advantage of the Wind '. In consequence of these orders, on 30 June, being now to windward of the French, Torrington engaged the enemy. He was out-manœuvred and suffered a disastrous reverse. Tourville, however, instead of ordering a general chase, still kept the line of battle. By so doing he missed his opportunity of inflicting heavy losses on the beaten foe. Torrington retired to the Nore, burning several of his ships on the way to prevent them from falling into the enemy's hands, and for some time the French were masters of the Channel. Tourville's victory off Beachy Head was, in Mahan's opinion, ' the most conspicuous success the French have ever gained at sea over the English '. The news of the Allied defeat caused a panic in London. Trinity House was instructed by the Admiralty to take up the buoys in the Thames, and the militia was called out. Soon after this came the news of a great French victory at

---

[1] The Admiral's name is spelt variously. The form adopted here is, perhaps, to be preferred.

Fleurus in Flanders. Marlborough and such troops as were left in the country prepared to resist a hostile descent. 'As it was, most Men were in fear that the French would invade,' Torrington observed afterwards in the House of Commons; 'but I was always of another opinion . . . for I said, that whilst we had a Fleet in being, they would not dare to make an attempt.'

Following this defeat Torrington was superseded and court-martialled; he was acquitted, indeed, but was never employed again. It is worth noticing that from the disastrous campaign of 1690 arose the important strategic doctrine of the Fleet in Being.

In point of fact, the real danger lay not so much in a French invasion (since the necessary troops were not available for the attempt) as in an attack on the transports passing between England and Ireland. By the summer of 1690 the war had become general; French resources in man-power and organization were strained to the uttermost; French armies were then fighting in Flanders, Spain, Piedmont, and on the Rhine. A major invasion of the British Isles was out of the question. After Beachy Head Seignelay had counted on the appearance of Château-Rénault in the Irish Sea to destroy the hostile transports and thus to isolate the Orangist forces in Ireland. But Tourville's victory, to the disappointment of his countrymen, was not followed up; and, although England was unsettled and the Irish were still in revolt, nothing further was attempted during the critical period of William III's absence in Ireland. Through their failure to understand the true use of a navy, the enemy had let slip successive opportunities of striking a decisive blow before the Maritime Powers could develop their full fighting strength. Although Tourville cruised in the Channel for several weeks, all he did was to burn the small Devon fishing port of Teignmouth. Following these empty demonstrations the French fleet, stricken with disease and short of supplies, put back into Brest.

Meanwhile at the Boyne on 12 July [N.S.] William III had won the decisive action of the Irish campaign. The battle itself was really quite a small affair; the Orangists' successful forcing of the river was followed by the headlong flight of the Jacobite army: but its international significance was immense; it would be scarcely too much to say that the consequences of the Boyne cancelled out those of Beachy Head and Fleurus. James II now returned to France; and later in the year Lord Marlborough captured Cork and Kinsale. Before the summer was out the superior resources of the two Maritime Powers had had time to tell. Feverishly refitting their ships, their numbers increased by the arrival of Killigrew's squadron from Spain at the end of August, they again put to sea, about ninety strong. The Allies regained the command of the Channel, and French supplies to the Jacobite army in Ireland were almost completely cut off. Next year, notwithstanding the defeat and losses of Beachy Head, the Allied fleet, now under the command of Admiral Russell, numbered seventy-four sail of the line, while their adversary, Tourville, had only sixty-nine. To assist him Russell had Shovell, Rooke, and other experienced commanders. Aboard the Allied fleet were between 30,000 and 40,000 prime seamen of the two great Maritime Powers. No greater armament had ever appeared in the English Channel. The superior administration of the French fleet enabled them to be first at sea again in the season of 1691; the Allies being unable to concentrate off Brest in time to intercept them. With his inferior force Tourville, by skilful manœuvring, kept Russell far out in the ocean, always holding the weather-gauge and successfully avoiding action; while swarms of French privateers, ranging up and down the Channel, protected the various convoys dispatched to Ireland. Neither fleet succeeded in accomplishing its principal object: the French failed to catch the homeward-bound Smyrna convoy, and their opponents were unable to find Tourville.

Before the end of 1691 Jacobite resistance had been crushed in Ireland. After the battle of the Boyne, the Irish army had fallen back on the Shannon and had there made a stand. Reinforcements and supplies continued to arrive from France, but there were not enough of either to affect the issue of the campaign. In the autumn the Irish suffered a bloody defeat at the hands of Ginkel at Aughrim, and with the surrender of Limerick came the end. Their great leader, Patrick Sarsfield, left Ireland, never to return. The outcome of the Irish campaign was to seat William III at last firmly on the English throne and to enable him to use the resources of England in the war against Louis XIV.

For over a century there was profound peace in Ireland. The domination of the English government and their Protestant adherents was absolute. Generations were to pass by without one general insurrection. It is significant that during the critical months of 1745-6, when the greater part of Scotland was in open rebellion, the native Irish were so cowed and quiet that several regiments could safely be sent across St. George's Channel to reinforce the Duke of Cumberland's army in England.

4

When finally the French did attempt to invade, in 1692, the odds were heavily against them. The original plan had been to rush their transports across to Torbay, escorted by the Brest squadron, before the Allies were ready: after which the combined French fleets were to protect the army's communications. But the secret leaked out so that the essential element of surprise was lacking, and the Toulon squadron was delayed by contrary winds. Tourville was nevertheless ordered to make the attempt with but forty-four of the line. He gave battle to Russell off Barfleur and, largely owing to his seamanship and tactical skill, not a single vessel of the weaker French fleet was taken or sunk. The two fleets anchored at nightfall, and at midnight the French began to retire towards the Channel Islands. Part of Tourville's force escaped to the northward and eventually reached Brest. Twenty-two more of his ships got away through the perilous race of Alderney into St. Malo. But the remainder, caught by the flood-tide, were unable to anchor and, swept eastward on the stream, sought refuge in the open bays of Cherbourg and La Hougue. The English fleet followed them, and, during the next few days, cut out many of these vessels under the guns of the shore batteries. As a result of this action fifteen of the enemy's ships were destroyed, including the great *Soleil Royal*, together with the transports which were to have carried James II and the army of invasion to England. With the triumph of Barfleur ended the defensive phase of English strategy. For the rest of the wars of William III and Anne the French could no longer aspire to superiority at sea.

Though the French fleet remained a menace it was no longer the formidable force with which France had entered the war. This was due not so much to the losses she had actually suffered in battle as to the heavy cost of the continental war and the progressive exhaustion of the French nation which compelled Louis XIV to sacrifice his fleet to his army. Moreover, the navy of France was not based, like that of the Maritime Powers, on proportionately large resources of merchant shipping and overseas commerce, but was more an artificial creation of the State. The naval strength of France, in fact, rested on demonstrably inadequate foundations. It followed that French sea power showed none of the resilience which had enabled the Allied fleet to recover so quickly after its defeat at the hands of Tourville in 1690. Though the losses of Barfleur were made good and Tourville sailed out next year with a fleet of seventy ships, the effort was not sustained. The Brest fleet was laid up in port, and the French fell back on commerce raiding.

The year 1692 ushered in what might be described as the classic age of French privateering. Although France possessed comparatively little commerce, her seafaring population was still numerous. There was no lack of experienced mariners to man her privateers, a considerable number of them being taken out of the Brest fleet. At the same time a large number of warships were fitted out as privateers. Squadrons of from three to half a dozen of these raiders would be found operating under the orders of a single commander. The French government organized a system of special rewards for special captures, and naval rank was conferred on privateer officers. The geographical position of France greatly facilitated the activities of her privateers; inasmuch as, working from ports on the North Sea, the Channel, and the Atlantic, the French raiders sallied forth from bases which lay conveniently close to the focal areas of English trade. Under the leadership of such daring and resourceful commanders as Jean Bart, the French attack on Allied commerce speedily attained unprecedented dimensions.

Bart, the son of a Dunkirk fisherman, who had spent his early years in Dutch service, rose to be the greatest of all the French privateering commanders. Captured with the Comte de Forbin, in 1689, after a bloody fight against a superior English force off the Isle of Wight, Forbin and he succeeded in escaping, eleven days later, from Plymouth in a dense fog and returning to France in a rowing-boat. After again distinguishing himself by breaking out of Dunkirk in the face of a greatly superior blockading force, he was received in audience by Louis XIV. Bart—the roughest of rough old sea-dogs, with no Court manners and pronounced shipboard ones—caused a sensation at the palace by lighting up his pipe in the ante-room whilst awaiting his interview with the King.

'At . . . the kind reception given by the King to this remarkable man ', it is recorded, ' all the Courtiers were astounded; and gathering around him the moment he left the presence, asked him how he had contrived to get out of Dunkirk with his little squadron, while that port was blockaded by an enemy's fleet? He placed the noble inquirers in line, and then with punches of his elbows and thumps of his fists, broke through them, and returning, said, ' that's the method by which I did it.'[1] Bart enjoyed quite a vogue at Versailles. With him was another famous corsair commander, his old comrade Forbin; and it was a favourite diversion among the fine gentlemen of the Court to ' go and pay a visit to the Comte de Forbin and his *bear*.'

In 1693 Bart again broke out of Dunkirk with three frigates, seized a number of Allied merchantmen, and made a damaging raid on Newcastle, following this up with two further cruises in the North Sea. In the same year he played a leading part in the attack, off Lagos, on our Smyrna convoy. One of his most audacious exploits was his rescue from the Dutch, in 1694, of a grain convoy—of which commodity France then stood in the greatest need—off the Texel. Bart closed the enemy flagship, received a broadside, and replied with one at point-blank range: and ran her on board. Making straight for the Dutch admiral, Hides de Vries—a veritable giant of a man—Bart engaged him in desperate hand-to-hand combat until the Dutchman lay stretched at his feet. His squadron then took two more of the Dutch warships besides the flagship. In 1696 he once again slipped out of Dunkirk, past a blockading squadron under Benbow, and, shaking off his pursuers, cruised in the North Sea and attacked a large Dutch convoy off the Norwegian coast, capturing the entire escort and nearly half of the merchantmen. Shortly after Benbow sighted and pursued Bart's squadron; but the French ships were faster than the English, and once more he escaped.

' The name of Jean Bart was terrible to Englishmen, Dutchmen, and Spaniards,' declares a contemporary work. ' They knew his system to be—a determination to board, never to fire till at pistol-shot distance, and instantly to rush up the sides of the enemy's ships.'[2] Again and again he broke through the enemy squadrons stationed to intercept him, and successfully attacked the enemy convoys. Though Bart's

---

[1] *The Life of Jean Bart*, trans. Mangin, p. 50.
[2] *Ibid.*, p. 85.

hope of progressively wearing down the hostile battle-fleet by obliging the Allies to increase their escorts was never realized, none the less, in the final phase of the war, the *guerre de course* did considerable damage to Allied commerce.

Early in 1693 it was decided to resume the English traffic with the Mediterranean, which had been virtually suspended for nearly two years for want of ships to protect it against the enemy squadron in Toulon. Owing, however, to the deficiencies of the administration, the huge Smyrna trading fleet, comprising four hundred merchantmen, under convoy of an Allied squadron of twenty sail commanded by Rooke, and accompanied over the first lap of its passage by the Grand Fleet, did not leave until the end of May. The long delay proved fatal; for by this time the French fleet had slipped out of Brest and sailed down to the coast of Spain. On 6 June, when the convoy was believed to be well clear of the danger zone off Brest, Rooke was detached for the Mediterranean, while the Grand Fleet stood northward toward Ushant. Three weeks later, in Lagos Bay on the Portuguese coast, Rooke and his convoy suddenly encountered the main French fleet under Tourville. In the ensuing action some eighty of the merchant vessels and four of the Allied warships were taken and burnt, the remainder of the convoy being hopelessly scattered. The French attack on our Smyrna convoy constituted the most notable success achieved by the enemy in the *guerre de course*. It was a grievous blow to the Levant Company which, after a fleeting spell of prosperity in the Restoration era, had been going steadily downhill.

5

So far the Confederate fleet had contributed little towards winning the war. Its operations, indeed, had been mainly defensive—the defence of the British Isles against invasion, and commerce protection. The efforts of the Maritime Powers to isolate France from foreign trade had not been effective. The conjunct attempt on Brest, in 1694, had turned out a calamitous failure. The French depredations against Allied commerce were exacting a heavy and continuous toll. Since the chief part of our naval forces was occupied in containing the French fleet, there were never enough ships to protect our trade, which, in consequence, suffered severely.

The war in Flanders had also gone badly for the Allies, and it appeared to William III that there was little hope of successfully invading France from the north. It was with a view to assisting a flank attack in the south, as well as for the purpose of protecting the lucrative Levant trade, that he now urged the desirability of sending an Allied squadron to the Mediterranean. Following the disaster of Lagos Bay, a squadron under Commodore Wheeler in November 1693 was ordered to escort the outgoing trade to the Mediterranean, with instructions that an adequate force was later to be detached from this squadron to escort the homecoming convoy. The following year saw the main fleet, under the command of Admiral Russell, ordered out to the Mediterranean. The efficacy of the new strategy was immediately apparent. A French army, aided by Tourville's fleet, having lately invaded Spain, was then reducing the province of Catalonia. On the news of Russell's approach Tourville forthwith left his station before Barcelona and retired, with the French main fleet, to Toulon. The advance of the French army down the east coast of Spain was promptly halted. Barcelona was saved. Later, in spite of his protests, Russell was ordered to winter at Cadiz—a new departure in our naval policy. Material of all kinds and in considerable quantities now began to arrive from home, together with the necessary personnel; an English dockyard in miniature was, in fact, set up in this foreign town. In striking contrast to the general failure of naval administration in England, the refit of the main fleet at Cadiz, during the winter months of 1694–5, was a masterpiece of improvised and efficient organization.

Next year Russell sent home eighteen of his ships, which were in bad repair, and received eight fresh ships from England. At the end of that season the fleet, comprising thirty sail of the line, was sufficiently powerful to protect our Mediterranean trade and to render material assistance to our Spanish ally. The French fell back on the defensive, abandoning the control of the Mediterranean to the English and Dutch; and the French battle fleet, lying in Toulon, progressively deteriorated. It was not blockaded, but refused to come out. An attempt was later made to commission the first and second rates laid up in Brest harbour, for which purpose large numbers of seamen were sent overland from Toulon; but most of these deserted on the way and the project was abandoned.

It was therefore William III, with his deep insight into continental politics, who inaugurated the new strategy by which the Allied main fleet was employed in the Mediterranean—either wholly or in part—as the disposition of the enemy's forces required; thereby keeping a fleet interposed between the two principal centres of French maritime power, on the Atlantic and Mediterranean coasts. In the years to come this Mediterranean strategy was destined to be a potent and permanent factor in the politics of Europe.

The year 1695 saw English credit put on a modern basis. To the joint efforts of William Paterson and the Chancellor of the Exchequer, Charles Montagu, were due the Bank of England and the permanent National Debt. These developments had an immediate and enduring effect on naval policy; for it was the immense financial resources of the Bank of England which enabled our fleet to remain in the Mediterranean during the campaign of 1695 and similarly made possible the victories of Marlborough in the following reign.

In February 1696 Louis XIV, reverting to his former design of a surprise descent upon England, prepared to send over a force of some 12,000 men from the Channel ports at a time when most of our heavy ships were laid up in port. News of this project, however, reached London in time for a squadron which had been fitting out for the Mediterranean to be hurriedly diverted to the Downs, where it was presently joined by all the Allied ships which were available; and Rooke was recalled from the Mediterranean.

In 1696–7 the principal theatre of the war shifted from the Mediterranean to the Channel, where the Allied fleet contained the French main fleet in Brest. It was intermittently employed in a series of profitless attacks on French coastal towns, and was also diverted on an increasing scale, by the pressure of the mercantile interest, to the protection of trade. The Allied abandonment of the Mediterranean excited considerable dismay in Austria. But our ally was reminded that this decision was rendered inevitable through 'insurmountable difficulties about the victualling'. During the last few months of hostilities, while nothing of importance occurred at sea, the administration of the Navy was almost at a standstill.

The War of the English Succession ended in September 1697 with the Treaty of Ryswick, which virtually restored the *status quo ante bellum;* Louis XIV agreeing to give up all his conquests of the previous nineteen years (with the exception of Strasbourg), and to recognize William of Orange as King of England. The Treaty marked the close of the era of Louis XIV's successful aggressions on his eastern frontier.

VIII

The War of the Spanish Succession

I

After a few short years of peace, the struggle with France was renewed. The burning question of the Spanish Succession had finally come to a head, in 1700, with the death of the childless Charles II, King of Spain, leaving no heirs except in the Royal Houses of France and Austria. The various attempts at partition had failed and the whole of his immense dominions in Europe and overseas were at the last bequeathed to the French king's grandson, Philip of Anjou. Louis XIV accepted the will, and his grandson became Philip V of Spain.

By the accession of a French prince to the throne of Spain the vital maritime and commercial interests of this country, the Dutch carrying trade, and the safety and independence of Europe generally, were alike imperilled; for in the ensuing months Louis XIV proceeded, not only to occupy Italy, Spain, the Rhineland, and the former Spanish Netherlands, but also to exploit the Spanish Empire for the benefit of French commerce. The ' vent of English cloth '—a cardinal English interest—was in danger of being excluded from some of its most lucrative markets. Henceforth the Mediterranean, controlled by a strong French squadron based on Toulon, with the ports of Spain and Naples in enemy hands, would be closed to our shipping. English and Dutch merchants settled in Spanish sea-ports were directed to sell their wares at half price. The Spaniards were obliged to cede the *Asiento*, or contract, for supplying their American colonies with negro slaves to a French company. Public opinion in England was incensed by the exclusion of our merchants from the Spanish Indies. The Whig Opposition was clamorous for war.

Presently the French armies, having overrun the Spanish Netherlands, in the spring of 1701 seized the barrier fortresses in Flanders guaranteed by international treaty. The temper of the English Parliament at once stiffened. All that the Allies had so hardly won in the previous war vanished at the stroke of a pen. The occupation of the Spanish Netherlands by the troops of the Grand Monarch came as a direct threat to our national security. On the Continent, Catholic as well as Protestant Powers looked to William III to save them from the hegemony of France. Over and above all this Louis XIV had the ' Old Pretender ', the son of James II, solemnly proclaimed King of England at Versailles. In September 1701 the Treaty of Grand Alliance was signed by England, Holland, Austria, Prussia, and various lesser States for ' reducing the exorbitant power of France '.

When the War of the Spanish Succession broke out in the spring of 1702 the odds at first sight appeared to be overwhelmingly in France's favour, occupying as she did the strategic hub of Europe, and with the resources of the largest empire in the world added to her own. There was no necessity for Louis XIV to win any more victories: he had merely to avoid defeat in the next few years, and eventually the opposing coalition would be compelled, through the exhaustion of its resources, to accept the *fait accompli*. Conversely, if the Grand Alliance were to achieve its object it must speedily eject ' the man in possession ' and break up the hegemony of France over Europe before it hardened into permanency.

By a series of skilful manœuvres Marlborough expelled the French that summer from the valleys of the Maas and lower Rhine, which they had overrun during the previous year. He thus removed the threat to Holland of a French invasion, and prepared the way for his great campaign of 1704. But neither in this nor in the following campaign was he able, owing to the obstruction of the Dutch generals, to make any substantial progress in the Spanish Netherlands. Moreover, in September the foundations of the Grand Alliance were suddenly undermined by the entry of Bavaria into the war on the side of Louis XIV. The Allied German Princes of the Rhine found themselves taken in rear, and a hostile State separated the huge, sprawling mass of the Imperial territories from the rest of the Alliance. A yet more luring prospect now opened out before the Sun King. With the Bavarians as his allies, he could pass from the defensive to the offensive and launch his armies across central Europe to destroy that ancient rival of the French monarchy, the House of Habsburg. When in May Marshal Villars and his army arrived on the upper Danube it appeared as if the fall of Vienna could be only a matter of months. But

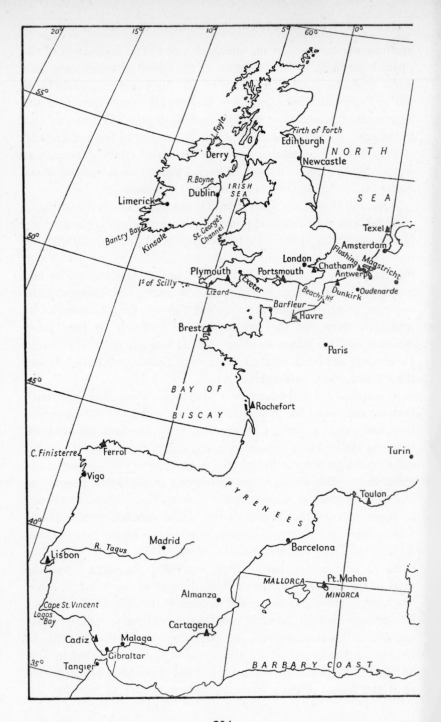

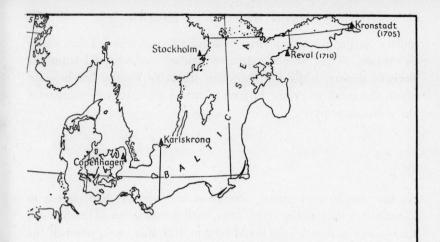

THE COASTS OF
EUROPE
IN 1700

.Blenheim

Vienna

Miles

| 0 | 100 | 200 | 300 | 400 |

Naval Bases ▲

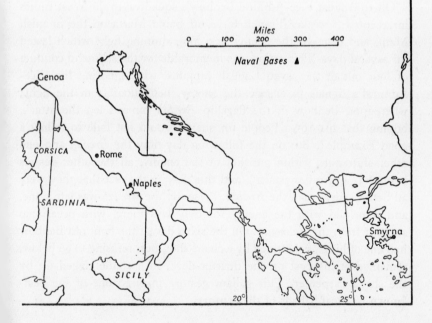

Villars, having quarrelled with the Bavarians, was replaced that winter by Marsin. Thus France's greatest soldier was removed from the decisive theatre, while the imminent threat to Vienna had brought about the recall of Prince Eugene of Savoy from Italy to reorganize the Austrian army.

2

As has already been stated, France in the late war had elected to sacrifice her navy to her army. Even with the adhesion of the Spanish fleet—such as it was—she could now muster only about one half the number of ships comprising the Confederate fleet. At the outbreak of the present war she had a squadron of thirty sail of the line in the West Indies, under the Comte de Château-Rénault, engaged in an abortive expedition against Barbados. In July 1702 the French Admiral with fifteen of the line left Havana for Europe, with the Spanish *flota*, or treasure-fleet, under his escort. Though the Mediterranean had become practically a French lake, the Allied control of the Channel and narrow seas was, from the outset, assured.

On 19 August Vice-Admiral Benbow's squadron in the West Indies intercepted a weaker French force off Santa Marta on the Spanish Main, and engaged the enemy in a long running fight which lasted for several days. This action was memorable for the shameful conduct of four out of the seven English captains, who, ignoring the Vice-Admiral's signals to engage the enemy, held aloof from the fight; whereupon Benbow in the flagship *Bredah* himself led the attack, hoping that his ' own People for shame would not faile to follow a good Example '. But on the following day only the *Bredah* and one other ship were within gunshot of the enemy, all the other vessels being ' 3, 4, 5 miles astern ', and this despite the fact that they were all better sailers than the *Bredah*. Presently the *Bredah* was left alone, and remained with the enemy for two days more, with occasional support from the *Falmouth*. On the sixth day of the fight old Benbow had one of his legs shattered by a chain-shot, but, refusing to go below, remained at his post on the quarter-deck, in a cradle rigged up by the ship's carpenter. This gallant gesture inspired one of the best-known nautical ballads of the century.

Brave Benbow lost his legs by chain shot, by chain shot,
Brave Benbow lost his legs by chain shot.
Brave Benbow lost his legs,
But on his stumps he begs,
   ' Fight on, my English lads, 'tis our lot, 'tis our lot.'

While the surgeon dressed his wounds, thus he said, thus he said,
While the surgeon dressed his wounds, thus he said:
' Let my cradle now in haste
On the quarter-deck be placed,
   That mine enemies I may face till I'm dead, till I'm dead.'

The action had to be broken off; and two of the offending captains were subsequently tried by court martial, condemned, and shot. Sad to relate, ' brave Benbow ' never recovered from his wound and died soon afterwards in the West Indies.

For Jamaica then at last he set sail, he set sail,
For Jamaica then at last he set sail,
Where Wentworth he did try,
And those cowards that did fly
   And from the French in fright turned tail, turned tail.

And those found most to blame, they were shot, they were shot,
And those found most to blame, they were shot.
Brave Benbow then at last,
For grief of what was past,
   In a fever died at last, by hard lot, by hard lot.

There was a similar case, in the same theatre, later in the war, when, in Admiral Wager's midnight action against the Spanish treasure-squadron off Porto Bello, in May 1708, the captains of most of the English vessels deserted their commander in the face of the enemy. Almost unsupported, Wager's flagship, the *Expedition*, proceeded to engage the enemy squadron of fourteen sail with such good effect that one large galleon blew up and sank with all her treasure, another great ship was captured with her rich lading, and a third was chased ashore and blown up. The destruction of the Spanish treasure-ships accelerated the financial exhaustion of the Bourbon Powers. ' This must in all probability prove a fatal blow to France,' wrote Sunderland to Marlborough, ' for I believe this was one of their last resources for carrying on the war.'

3

In the long-drawn-out struggle which ensued the naval dispositions of the Maritime Powers, England and Holland, were strictly subordinated to the grand strategy of the war. For on William III's death in 1702 John Churchill, Duke of Marlborough, inherited the great strategical designs of his master, including the decision to send the bulk of the Confederate fleet into the Mediterranean: to secure bases by the capture of Cadiz or Gibraltar, to command the Straits, to wrest the

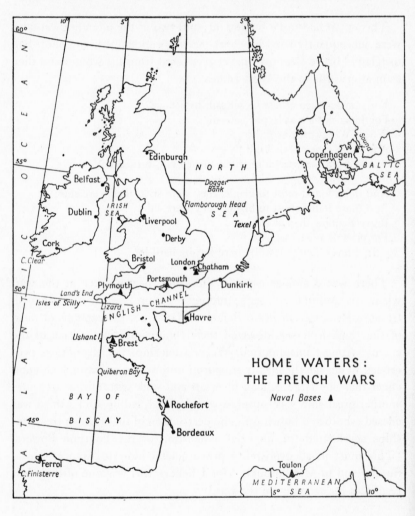

HOME WATERS:
THE FRENCH WARS

Naval Bases ▲

control of the great inland sea from the French, to strengthen and encourage our Allies on the contiguous shores, and—in the words of another and later Churchill—to strike at ' the soft under-belly ' of the Continent. The fleet could operate on the flank of the Allied forces, transporting not only troops but also supplies, munitions, and equipment, and at the same time denying similar support to the armies of the enemy. The sea route being thus closed to the French forces in the Mediterranean, they must move by land; and since this involved the use of larger forces, a considerable diversion would be created from the vital Flanders theatre.

To this end risks were run with the protection of our seaborne trade, as well as with the safety of our heavy ships, as never before or since. Notwithstanding the hazards of the winter passage and the alarmed protests of Rooke and other commanders, the Confederate fleet went out early and returned home late in the year[1]: to the lasting benefit of the Allied cause and the detriment of that of the enemy.

The result of this amphibious strategy, by means of which the overwhelming naval superiority of the Maritime Powers was brought to bear upon the furthest and most exposed frontiers of the enemy— namely, the Mediterranean seaboard, where it could, and did, operate with the maximum military effect—was to establish Great Britain, once and for all, as a Mediterranean Power. Marlborough was the first Englishman to grasp the true potentialities of fleet action in the Mediterranean. He possessed a really remarkable understanding—rare in a military commander—of the practical bearings of sea power upon the general strategy of the war; and he acted as exponent of these mysteries to our Allies in southern Europe, the Emperor and the Duke of Savoy. Marlborough and his colleagues had, however, also to reckon with the opponents of their Mediterranean strategy at home. For there was a strong party in England which believed that our main resources should be used against the enemy's shipping and colonies,

---

[1] ' Time is precious,' Rooke protested to Nottingham on 1 June 1702, ' so that I must repeat my opinion that no service can balance the hazard of bringing our great ships home in the winter season.' Later he expressed his hope that the Cabinet ' are very well assured of a southern winter port for our great ships, or I'm sure, I shall dread the consequences of their coming home in that season.' According to Horace Walpole, ' Sir Clowdlsey Shovell said that an admiral would deserve to be broke, who kept great ships out after the end of September, and to be shot if after October.' Admiral Van Almonde, the Netherlands commander, expressed the same opinion as Rooke and Shovell.

and not on the continent of Europe. This was the doctrine afterwards expounded by the formidable Dean Swift in his *Conduct of the Allies*.

Before the Confederate fleet could make its bid for the control of the Mediterranean, it had first to secure a base near the entrance to the Straits. Rooke was therefore instructed to take Cadiz, where Russell had based his fleet in the late war, when the Spaniards were our Allies. On 12 August 1702 he arrived before Cadiz with a powerful squadron, and a large landing force under the command of the Duke of Ormonde. But partly through the strength of the defences, partly through divided counsels, but principally through want of perseverance, the attempt failed and the expedition retired without fighting. The disgraceful conduct of Ormonde's troops on this occasion did much to antagonize the Spaniards and prejudice them against the Allied cause; when the expedition departed it was said that they ' left behind them such a filthy stench among the Spaniards that a whole age will hardly blot it out '.

On the homeward passage, however, Rooke received news that the Spanish treasure-fleet which Château-Rénault had brought home from the West Indies was unloading at Vigo. He thereupon sent in a strong squadron which broke through the boom that the enemy had laid across the bay, and attacked the *flota* and its French escorts. The French lost fifteen ships of the line and the Spaniards the whole of the *flota*, with a large quantity of treasure. The loss of so many of his warships, in the then state of Louis XIV's finances, was a crippling blow at the waning sea power of France. Moreover, the victory of Vigo Bay served to restore the prestige which the Allies had lost by their unsuccessful attack on Cadiz, and was a leading factor in securing the Portuguese alliance in the following year.

Though the year 1703 was barren of naval and military victories, it saw two highly important diplomatic successes scored by our government. In the summer the main fleet, under Sir Clowdisley Shovell, with Leake as his second-in-command, was dispatched to the Mediterranean, ' above all to induce the Duke of Savoy to declare for the House of Austria,' as the Secretary of State, the Earl of Nottingham, wrote to the Grand Pensionary of Holland; and also with the object of encouraging the Imperial party in the Italian States. Shovell's fleet in the event did little but ' show the flag ' in the western Mediterranean, unopposed by the French. But his cruise had one very important result. In October the Duke of Savoy forsook the Bourbon Powers and joined the Grand Alliance.

Earlier in the year we had gained an even more valuable ally. The negotiations patiently carried on by John Methuen and his son Paul, successive envoys at Lisbon, to persuade Portugal to throw in her lot with the Grand Alliance, were at last brought to fruition in May 1703 in the signature of the Treaties, commercial and political, which are known by their name. From the naval angle, the chief importance of the Methuen Treaties was that they secured the use of Lisbon's fine harbour as a base for the main fleet, which later made possible the capture and retention of Gibraltar and Minorca, and the English command of the Mediterranean. For more than a century to come, the Portuguese alliance remained the keystone of our Mediterranean strategy.

The naval campaign of 1703 closed with a grave disaster. The blind forces of nature suddenly showed themselves a far more dreadful adversary than the French and the Spaniards; and the Fleet was exposed to greater peril than in any action of the war. On 26–27 November the greatest storm in the recorded history of these islands raged for two days over the Channel and the south of England,[1] the wind veering from south-south-west to west-south-west, and finally to west by north, ' and still the more Northward it shifted, the harder it blew '. In the opinion of Defoe its greatest fury was experienced south of a line from the Bristol Channel to the Thames. What made the ordeal more appalling was the fact that the storm reached its height during the hours of darkness.

Winstanley's new lighthouse on the Eddystone was swept away and with it its unfortunate constructor. Shortly after the destruction of the lighthouse a homeward-bound Virginiaman ran on the un-lighted rock and instantly went to pieces, with the loss of most of her crew.

[1] ' The like not known in the memory of man,' writes Luttrell. ' This was such a storm as never was known before,' observes Defoe, ' and 'tis hoped the like may never be known again.' It was to the great storm of 1703 that Addison was referring in his famous comparison of Marlborough to an angel guiding the whirlwind.

So when an angel by Divine command
With rising tempests shakes a guilty land,
Such as of late o'er pale Britannia pass'd,
Calm and serene he drives the furious blast;
And pleas'd th' Almighty's orders to perform,
Rides in the whirlwind, and directs the storm.

A large part of the main fleet which had recently returned from the Mediterranean and was lying in the Downs and off the Gunfleet stood out to sea to avoid being driven ashore. Between three and eight in the morning of the 27th, according to the log of the *Prince George*, ' it blew a parfectt harrycane of wind att SW & SWbW.' It is related that, in the Downs, ' that place, which the evening before appeared like a goodly forest, in two hours was reduced to a desert, hardly an object being left to cheer the sight, had the darkness of the night permitted.' Throughout the night of the 27th and the day following these warships, together with thousands of merchant vessels from all parts of the coast, struggled to keep afloat. It is said that if the height of the storm had not coincided with full flood and a heavy spring tide many of the vessels which survived must infallibly have been lost on the shoals. Among the ships which escaped in this way was the *Association*, commanded by Sir Stafford Fairborne, which, about five o'clock in the morning of the 27th, ' passed over the tail of the Galloper in seven Fathom of Water ',[1] shipping at the same time ' a grate sea' and having so much water in her gun deck that her people were obliged to scuttle ' the same to lett it in to the hold '. About the same time the *Revenge*, likewise forced from her anchors, had a still narrower escape, being driven over the north end of the Galloper ' in less than four fathoms of water '. The *Mary, Restoration, Northumberland*, and *Stirling Castle* drove on the Goodwin and ' were all to pieces by ten o'clock '. Among the drowned was Rear-Admiral Beaumont, whose flag was flying in the *Mary*.

Sir Clowdisley Shovell in the flagship *Britannia*, with several other heavy ships, rode out the storm off the Gunfleet, ' tho' in great extremity, expecting death every minute '. The fact that these vessels survived the ordeal bears witness to their general seaworthiness and the remarkable strength of their ground-tackle.

At Yarmouth, most of the merchant vessels which found that they could not ride it out in the roadstead slipped their cables and stood out to sea. As they went away up the coast the wind moderated, and they found shelter under the high land north of Flamborough Head.

Even in the sheltered Thames the whole mass of shipping was

---

[1] In the same way most of the merchantmen in the Downs were driven out to sea, and, being comparatively small vessels, floated safely over the tops of the Goodwins. The *Resolution* and *Newcastle*, two of the men-of-war lying at St. Helens, were driven over the Owers.

forced from its moorings and driven inexorably to leeward: between Shadwell and Limehouse there were close on 700 sail piled up along the banks in indescribable confusion. ' From Execution Dock to Lime-house Hole ', according to one account, ' there was but 4 ships that rid it out.' London Bridge was jammed with wreckage. Innumerable wherries, lighters, galleys, and barges were smashed to splinters. An East Indiaman was cast away near Blackwall. The *Royal Catherine* was driven ashore and sunk in the Medway. Ashore folk cowered within their tottering dwellings, ' for whatever the Danger was within doors, 'twas worse without; the Bricks, Tiles, and Stones, from the Tops of the Houses, flew with such force, and so thick in the Streets, that no one thought fit to venture out, tho' their Houses were near demolish'd within.' The total damage was immense. Houses were blown down by the hundred, and the leads on the City churches were rolled up like scrolls. Defoe estimated that property valued at £1 million was destroyed in London alone.

Approximately 1,500 seamen and thirteen warships were lost in the Great Storm—representing a material loss nearly equal to that of Beachy Head—besides an unknown number of merchantmen. (It was actually believed at Versailles that our entire Fleet had been lost.) The losses, indeed, would have been far heavier but for the courage and fine seamanship of the crews. As it was, the dockyards worked rapidly to repair the damage and the Fleet was brought up to strength again before the winter was over.

4

The Allied naval operations in 1704 began badly with a project for seizing Toulon, which had to be given up, a fruitless demonstration by the fleet before Barcelona, and Rooke's failure to prevent the junction of the Brest and Toulon squadrons in the Mediterranean. For a time the French main fleet was stronger than the English; but in mid-June the timely arrival in the Straits of another squadron from England, under Shovell, who had been watching the French in Brest, established numerical equality with the enemy, and the initiative returned to Rooke.

At a council of war held aboard his flagship in the Straits a proposal for making another attempt on Cadiz, agreeable to the wishes of the

' two Kings ' (Pedro II of Portugal and ' Charles III ', the Habsburg candidate for the Spanish throne), was rejected, owing to lack of troops: instead it was decided to seize Gibraltar. The idea of taking and holding the Rock, ' the key to the Levant ', had long been entertained in England. ' Major Beckmann,' Pepys had noted during the expedition to Tangier, ' do speak to me greatly in commendation of Gibraltar as the place which above all others our King ought to have for keeping an entire command in the Straits.'

The old stronghold was weakly held and in no condition to withstand a determined assault. There were scarcely fifty regular troops and about three times as many militia, together with a force of volunteer townsmen, to defend what was potentially one of the key fortresses of Europe. The strength of the Allied fleet was overwhelming—forty-five heavy ships, as well as frigates, fire-ships, and bomb-vessels. Rooke sent in a squadron of sixteen English vessels and six Dutch, under Byng's command, which, early in the morning of Sunday, 23 July, opened fire on the dilapidated defences of Gibraltar, until the smoke of the cannonade hid the crumbling walls and forts from the gunners' view, and a considerable number of the civilian defenders fled away up the mountain-side; meanwhile a force of 1,800 marines occupied the low-lying isthmus to the north. At noon the cannonade ceased, and in the afternoon large landing-parties of seamen under Captain Edward Whitaker of the *Dorsetshire* occupied the hostile batteries. The following morning the Spanish governor, Don Diego de Salines, surrendered; and later in the day the marines marched into the town. After the capitulation a large number of private houses and every church except one in Gibraltar were sacked; and, despite the Allies' guarantee of rights of religion and property, nearly all the civilian inhabitants elected to leave their homes and to begin life anew in the interior.

The defence of the Rock was entrusted to 1,900 marines and 400 Dutchmen, under the command of Prince George of Hesse; and sixty great guns and their gunners were landed from the fleet. A few months after the marines were joined by a substantial force of English regular troops. Efforts were later made to get our Allies to contribute to the defence of Gibraltar; but these failed, and the fortress continued to be garrisoned by English troops at the cost of the English government. From the standpoint of Allied strategy, the capture of the Rock

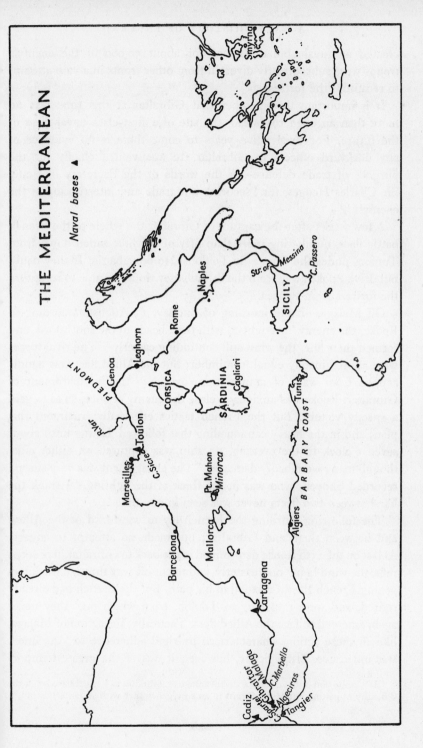

THE MEDITERRANEAN

Naval bases ▲

Smyrna

Str. of Messina
C. Passero
SICILY

Naples
Rome
Leghorn
Genoa
PIEDMONT
CORSICA
SARDINIA
Cagliari
Tunis
BARBARY COAST

River Var
Toulon
C. Sicie
Marseilles
Pt. Mahon
Minorca
Mallorca
Barcelona
Algiers
Cartagena
C. Marbella
Malaga
Gibraltar
Cadiz
C. de Gata
Algeciras
C. Tangier

created an invaluable diversion: for about 50,000 of the enemy's troops were subsequently diverted from other fronts in a vain attempt to recapture the fortress.

It is important to remember that Gibraltar at this time was no more than an open roadstead, the site of a first-class naval base of the future. For twenty-five years to come there is no evidence of any dockyard officers in Gibraltar. It was valued chiefly for the purpose of trade defence—in the words of the Secretary of State, Sir Charles Hedges, for ' securing our trade and interrupting of the enemy's '.[1]

A few weeks after the capture of Gibraltar the whole of the French battle fleet, numbering more than fifty of the line, sailed down from Toulon, under the Comte de Toulouse, to offer battle. If they could but drive Rooke away from the Straits, they would be able to recapture the fortress from the sea.

Off Malaga, on the morning of Sunday, 13 August, according to Rooke, the enemy ' brought-to with their heads to the southward, and formed their line, the wind still continuing easterly '. The rival forces were approximately equal in number; but the Allied fleet was handicapped from want of ammunition, owing to the bombardment of Gibraltar. Rooke was anxious to close the enemy at once, so as to gain a speedy victory. But the French tactics effectually frustrated this plan; and in the heavy cannonading that followed, lasting until about seven o'clock in the evening, no ship was captured on either side, though many were badly damaged. ' The engagement was very sharp,' recorded Shovell, who was in the thick of the fighting, ' I think the like between two fleets never was seen in any time.'

The following morning the French lay to windward of the Allies, and between them and Gibraltar; but made no attempt to engage. At last on the 15th Rooke determined to get back to Gibraltar in order to refit, the wind being now easterly, and to cut his way through the intervening French fleet if it stood in his path. But the French had already retired, and were returning to Toulon, from which port they never again emerged to face the Allied fleet. Tactically, the action of Malaga, like all those actions characterized by rigid adherence to ' the line ', was indecisive. Strategically, however, it was of the greatest impor-

---

[1] It is to be noted that a serious disadvantage of Gibraltar as a naval base lay in the difficulty of getting out of the Straits in an emergency save with an easterly wind.

tance; for it saved Gibraltar, and left the Allies in control of the Mediterranean, and all that that entailed.

After Malaga Rooke sailed home with the bulk of the fleet, leaving a small squadron under Leake to winter at Lisbon. The value of the Portuguese alliance was now made manifest. Without Lisbon as a base, the Rock could never have been held. Drafts, stores, and ammunition were hurriedly dispatched from England to the Tagus, and thence convoyed to Gibraltar. Throughout the following winter and spring the Spaniards and French made strenuous efforts by land and sea to recover the fortress. Spain relinquished her operations against Portugal and sent 9,000 men under Marshal Tessé to assail Gibraltar. France's contribution to the siege was a smaller army of 3,000 men and a squadron of twelve of the line and seven frigates under Admiral Pointis. But the huge grey rock—on its eastern, or Mediterranean, side a sheer precipice; on its western, or Atlantic, side a tangled, scree-covered slope; joined to Spain, at its northern extremity, by no more than a narrow sandy isthmus—was virtually impregnable from the land. A naval brigade had been landed to defend the new mole, and cannon and mortar hauled up to the heights and trained on the enemy positions below; while the boats of Leake's force kept the hostile camp at Algeciras in a constant state of alarm. ' Whole armies could not take Gibraltar from the north ', observes Trevelyan, ' so long as the friends of the garrison held the sea.' It was in large measure owing to the superior seamanship of his squadron that Leake thrice drove off the enemy squadron and relieved the hard-pressed garrison.

The final and decisive engagement occurred at the end of February 1705. In response to peremptory orders from Madrid, Pointis arrived in the bay with his squadron, and preparations were set in train for the grand assault. Then, before Tessé was ready, a westerly gale drove most of Pointis's force away to leeward, while the admiral with only five ships lay under Cape Cabrita. Leake appearing suddenly out of the mist just before daybreak on the 28th took the French by surprise and conclusively defeated them. Of Pointis's five three-deckers, three were taken and the others driven ashore and burnt. The ships which had been forced up the Straits made sail at the sound of the firing and got safely away to Toulon.

As a result of Pointis's defeat, Tessé immediately raised the siege and returned to the languishing war in Portugal; and England's hold upon the Straits was finally assured.

5

Louis XIV never came nearer to achieving his purpose than in the spring of 1704. Spain, Italy, and the Netherlands were still held by his armies, and the French hegemony of Europe was an accomplished fact. Dejected and demoralized, the Grand Alliance was in imminent peril of disintegration. Our Dutch Ally showed ominous signs of cracking beneath the strain. Austria, ravaged by her Hungarian rebels to the eastward, and assailed by the French and Bavarians to the westward, was appealing urgently for aid. Savoy also was in desperate straits. It was apparent to Marlborough that only by a resounding victory could the Alliance be saved and the grip of the Grand Monarch on Europe be loosened. The opening years of the war had brought no such military success. Such was the unpromising situation when Marlborough evolved the grand strategical design which was fated to be the turning-point of the war.

Marlborough's plan, in essence, was suddenly and swiftly to switch his whole army from the Netherlands to Central Europe, to overthrow Bavaria, and to force the French back from the Imperial frontier. Meanwhile, at the other end of Europe, an Allied force with the support of Rooke's fleet was to invade Spain on behalf of the Austrian claimant, Charles III; by May some 4,000 troops were actually engaged along the Portuguese frontier.

There were further projects, indeed, which were to have been set in train in southern Europe, illustrating in their turn the ' incalculable power of strategical disturbance that lies open to a Mediterranean fleet ';[1] but these never materialized. Nevertheless, Rooke's fleet played its part in the grand strategy of the campaign in preventing support from being sent from the Mediterranean theatre to the decisive battle-ground in Central Europe. ' The operations of the Fleet ', observed Sir Charles Hedges, the Secretary of State, ' can nowhere be so useful as in the Mediterranean.'

Marlborough's long and hazardous march from the Rhine to the Danube had been rendered possible by his seizure of the Rhine and

[1] Corbett, *England in the Mediterranean*, II, p. 224.

Maas valleys in the campaigns of 1702-3. As day after day the scarlet columns wound on tirelessly through the forests and mountains of High Germany the eyes of Europe followed them with wonder and expectation. Louis XIV's generals waited to see what he would do. Only when he was actually approaching the Danube did they realize that his purpose was to strike down Bavaria and succour Vienna. At the hard-fought battle of the Schellenberg, on 21 June, the Allied army gained a bridge-head over the Danube and proceeded systematically to lay waste Bavaria. On 31 July Marlborough joined forces with Prince Eugène, and on the following day, in one of the great decisive battles of world history, routed the French and Bavarians under Marshal Tallard at Blenheim. Vienna was saved. The French army, with its morale severely shaken, was driven out of southern Germany. The German princes rallied to the support of the Emperor, who now gained control of Bavaria. Savoy was reprieved. In the same year, as has already been related, the Allied fleet secured the control of the Mediterranean and wrested the Rock of Gibraltar from Spain.

In 1705 our principal naval effort was again in the Mediterranean; and again there was a diversion of the enemy's force from the Northern theatre. In the summer a powerful expedition, under the joint command of Sir Clowdisley Shovell and Lord Peterborough, was launched against Barcelona, the chief commercial centre of Spain. With the co-operation of the fleet (comprising on this occasion fifty-seven of the line, besides frigates and bomb vessels) the Allied troops besieged the city, which capitulated on 28 September. Shortly after Charles III was crowned and set up his court in Barcelona. In the ensuing campaign for the conquest of Spain the Allies were severely handicapped by the lack of a suitable naval base: Gibraltar being without stores or other means for refitting the fleet. Throughout the summer Byng, with the Channel Squadron, was engaged in trade protection in the Western Approaches.

The years following Blenheim and Malaga saw the waning of the fortunes of France, while England advanced to the leadership of Europe. Marlborough's second great victory at Ramillies, in 1706, was followed by the general retreat of the French forces in Flanders. Cities, towns, and fortresses were surrendered, one after the other, to the Allies. Not only were the Spanish Netherlands thereby lost to France but, in his anxiety to restore the army of Flanders, Louis XIV forfeited his chances of final success in Italy. Outside the walls of Turin Prince Eugène overthrew the French army and saved Savoy; thereafter he drove the enemy out of northern Italy: and the hegemony of France was ended. Though the war dragged on for six years longer and Marlborough was to win two more major victories, it is not too much to say that the campaign of 1706 determined the main outlines of the Peace of Utrecht.

In the spring of the same year Vice-Admiral Sir John Leake had successfully carried out yet another of his brilliant relieving operations. In the absence of the Confederate fleet from the Mediterranean, the French had invested Barcelona by land and sea. On 26 April, when the fortifications had been breached and the enemy was preparing to storm the city, the French squadron blockading Barcelona suddenly learned of the approach of the Allied fleet; upon which they immediately left the bay and sailed for Toulon. Next morning Leake appeared with a powerful fleet comprising some fifty sail of the line and a large number of transports carrying a force of 5,000 troops. The troops were landed on the quay and at once marched off to fill the breach; whereupon the French raised the siege. Once again Leake had arrived on the scene in the nick of time and saved a city.

During the year 1707 the project of a grand conjunct expedition against Toulon was revived. The plan was Marlborough's, and the funds were supplied by the British government. The object of this—one of the greatest combined operations in history—was to destroy the enemy's fleet, to secure the principal naval arsenal of France, and to invade that country from the south. The capture of Toulon had, indeed, been the prime objective in the naval war since Savoy joined the Allies in 1703. Such a design, if successful, must spell the ruin of French sea power in the Mediterranean, and thus liberate a large part of the Confederate fleet for the protection of trade. Moreover, with Toulon in Allied hands, the urgent problem of a base within the Straits for the Confederate fleet would at last be solved. The moment appeared propitious for attack. While Marlborough contained the main French army, weakened by the heavy losses of the Ramillies campaign, on the Flanders front, the Austrians and Piedmontese, crossing the Alps, moved westward along the Mediterranean coast. Throughout that summer the Confederate fleet, under the command of Sir Clowdisley Shovell, assisted by Sir George Byng and Sir John Norris, co-operated energetically with the Imperial forces, led by the Duke of Savoy and his brother, Prince Eugène.

As always in war, everything now turned on the time factor; and the Allies were too slow. Prince Eugène's heart, indeed, appears not to have been wholly in this enterprise. ' Eugène was a land animal', as Churchill has observed. ' He never liked a plan which depended upon the sea.'[1] Not until the end of June did the army reach the Var. The Confederate fleet, comprising about fifty sail of the line, anchored near the mouth of the river; and presently four of these vessels stood in and bombarded in flank the enemy's positions. On the withdrawal of the defenders some six hundred seamen and marines landed and occupied the French defences; at the same time Eugène's troops forced a passage higher up the river. ' We are about to march now straight for Toulon ', Eugène declared in a letter to Marlborough on 3 July, ' with the intention of besieging it unless we meet such obstacles as will make the enterprise completely impracticable, leaving in our rear all the other strong places.'

From the Var to Toulon was only some seventy miles; but, notwithstanding that their artillery and supplies were carried by the fleet, the Allied army was a full fortnight on the march. When at last they arrived before Toulon Shovell urged an immediate assault on the city's defences before strong reinforcements could reach the place. In view of Eugène's reluctance, however, the Allied leaders compromised with a series of bombardments and local assaults. On 19 July the Imperial troops, at the cost of heavy casualties, stormed the heights of St. Catherine's. To aid the attack (there was never really a siege of Toulon) Shovell disembarked several thousands of seamen and marines and hundreds of cannon: for days and weeks the doubtful battle raged under and around the outworks of Toulon: but large reinforcements were already reaching the city and, on 4 August, a French counterattack drove out the Allies from St. Catherine's. On the following day when a squadron under Byng attempted to bombard Fort St. Louis the wind blew so hard that most of the ships could not get in and the attack failed. Prince Eugène and his brother thereupon determined to raise the siege. The Allied fleet embarked the sick and wounded, as well as the artillery, in its transports. But while the enemy troops retreated in five long columns along the coast Shovell resolved to

[1] W. S. Churchill, *A History of the English-Speaking Peoples*, III, 57.

attack their fleet in the dockyard basins. Soon after daybreak on 10 August, the weather having by now moderated, a flotilla of bomb ketches under Rear-Admiral Sir Thomas Dilkes anchored near the shore and flung their shells into the dockyard over an intervening strip of land, destroying or damaging a number of ships and store-houses. The bombardment continued throughout the night and the first part of the following day. ' I would we had had more time,' Shovell observed to Byng, ' but they brought guns to the water side and mauled our bomb vessels.'

Toulon after all had proved too hard a nut for the Allies to crack. But the attempt was not wholly in vain. ' This diversion ', Marl-borough presently informed Shovell, ' has been of great use to the King of Spain, and likewise put a stop to the successes of the French in Germany by the detachments they were obliged to make from all parts to Provence.' At sea, the attempt on Toulon had produced a result of decisive and lasting importance; for it led to the ' half-sinking ' of the enemy fleet in Toulon harbour. To save their ships from the Allied bombardment, the French had scuttled them in shallow water, in consequence of which the greater part were ruined. The enemy's main fleet was virtually destroyed.

This was Shovell's last service. The Allied fleet, having covered the retreat of the Imperial forces until they were safely back across the Var, sailed for Gibraltar. There the fleet divided: part of the ships were left behind for various duties, the remainder—fifteen sail of the line and five lesser vessels—sailed, on 29 September, for England with Shovell, Byng and Norris. On this passage Shovell met his end in the kind of disaster which English commanders of that era had so often apprehended.[1]

On the morning of 21 October the squadron came into the sound-ings. At noon good observations of latitude were obtained, which, taken in conjunction with the soundings, would place the squadron perhaps some 200 miles S.S.W. of the Lizard. It was squally, and some of the ships took in reefs in their topsails. On the 22nd no sights were possible. Nor, for various reasons, could any clear guidance be expected from the depth and nature of the ground brought up on the arming. The squadron was steering E.N.E.—a risky course, as ex-

[1] For a detailed account of Sir Clowdisley Shovell's last passage, see the present writer in the R.U.S.I. *Journal*, CII, 542–8.

perience has often shown, in weather not allowing of good sights for latitude. Since the previous day the wind had been south-westerly, and freshening. It now blew a strong south-westerly gale, with rain and thick weather.

The passage had been a long one, and Shovell was steering much the same course as in 1703 and in 1705, when his fleet had made a good landfall. This, and a fair wind up Channel, appears to have dispelled a sense of caution. At four o'clock in the afternoon the squadron brought-to and sounded. It was thick and blowing weather, and night was approaching; the squadron was coming within the 60-fathom line, and under the worst possible conditions. None the less, relying on their dead reckoning and the apparent corroboration of the soundings, the Admiral took the fatal decision and determined to sail on. It is presumed, as was later reported, he believed he had the Channel open. Order was given to make sail. Shortly after six the squadron bore away.

The flagship *Association* stood away under her courses, steering E. by N., until at about eight o'clock she and several of the other vessels suddenly found themselves among breakers and rocks and made the signal of danger. Soon after, a number of them were caught on the rocky ledges projecting to the south-westward of St. Agnes. The *Association* struck on one of the group of rocks known as the Bishop and Clerks and immediately went to pieces.[1] Sir Clowdisley Shovell and all the ship's company were lost. The *Eagle* and *Romney*, sailing inshore of the flagship, were wrecked about the same time. Except for one man saved out of the *Romney*, all hands were drowned. The *Firebrand* fireship was also lost; but most of her people got safely ashore. Sir George Byng in the *Royal Anne* and Lord Dursley in the *St. George* all but shared the fate of their Admiral. ' The *Royal Anne* was sav'd by great presence of mind in both officers and men, who in a minute's time set her top-sails, one of the rocks not being a ship's length to leeward of her, and the other, on which Sir Cloudsley Shovel was lost, as near, and in a breach of the sea.'[2] ' Nor had the Lord Dursley, Commander of the *St. George*, a less miraculous escape; for his ship was dash'd on the same ridge of rocks with the

---

[1] The place where the *Association* actually struck was Gilstone Ledges, which was for long known in the Scillies as the Shovell Rock.
[2] *London Gazette*, 3 November 1707.

Association, and the same wave which he saw beat out all Sir Cloudesly's light, set his own ship afloat.'[1]

Of the six vessels which struck on the rocks that night, four—the *Association*, *Romney*, *Eagle*, and *Firebrand*—had gone down, and two —the *Royal Anne* and *Phoenix*—had got off again. Most of the other ships appear to have been further out to sea. In the course of the next few days they arrived at Spithead.

The news of the loss of Sir Clowdisley Shovell and so many of his men, coming as it did on top of Du Guay-Trouin's recent success against our Lisbon convoy, struck dismay into the hearts of Englishmen. ' The news of Sir Cloudsley Shovel, and the *Association's* being lost,' was the *Observator's* comment, ' has quite sunk my spirits.' Contemporary criticism centred upon the unfortunate Admiral. ' It was very unhappy ', the *Spectator* declared, ' for an Admiral, reputed one of the greatest sea commanders we ever had, to die by an error in his profession; which could not have happened, if a proper care had not been wanting.' ' It cannot be imagined but that this sad accident occasioned a very great surprize at home,' observed Burchett, the Secretary of the Admiralty, ' especially since so experienced a seaman, and so good an officer, as Sir Cloudesley Shovell was had the conducting of the Fleet, and there were other Flags, as well as private captains, with him of undoubted knowledge. As I cannot undertake to give the true cause of this unhappy miscarriage, I shall leave it with this common observation, that upon approaching land after so long a run, the best Looker-out is the best Sailor, and consequently the lying by in the night time, and making sail in the day, is the most safe, which I think this unhappy Gentleman did not do.'[2]

As a result of Shovell's untimely end, the command of the Fleet devolved upon Sir John Leake.

Towards the end of 1707 conflicting reports reached the British government of an expedition preparing in the northern French ports.

---

[1] A. Boyer, *The History of the Reign of Queen Anne* (1708).   ..

[2] The disaster of 1707, although certainly the most memorable of its kind, was but one among many which must be attributed to the same cause; namely, an error in reckoning *due to the variable northerly set across the entrance to the Channel*. ' I am surprized to find my ship so far to the northward,' the captain of the *Lenox* later declared. ' We were much to the northward of what was expected,' said the captain of the *Torbay*, ' and likewise more to the eastward.' Towards the end of the century, the hydrographer James Rennell cited a number of revealing instances in his paper, *Observations on a Current*, etc. (1793).

Early in the following spring the French dispatched a squadron of five frigates from Dunkirk, under the Chevalier de Forbin, with a force of 6,000 troops carried in fast-sailing privateers, to land Prince James Stuart, the ' Old Pretender ', in Scotland, to support a Jacobite rising. Vice-Admiral Sir George Byng, who was blockading Dunkirk, was forced off his station by a north-easterly gale and obliged to shelter under Dungeness; and the French got away to sea. But Byng gave chase and eventually arrived in the Firth of Forth only a few hours behind Forbin; the latter only just managed to escape in time and to return to Dunkirk with the loss of one frigate and six of the transports.

As a result of the apprehension excited by the Alarm from Dunkirk, as it was called, a plan was propounded for blocking up the approaches to Dunkirk by sinking ships filled with stones and ballast. The proposal proved impracticable, however, and was abandoned.[1]

6

As the ill-fated project to seize and hold Toulon had fallen through, it was necessary to secure some other port within the Straits on which the Allied fleet might be based the whole year round; for want of such a base Marlborough's Mediterranean strategy had compelled the fleet to run grievous risks going out early and coming home late in the season. In the previous reign Rooke had warned the government of the extreme danger of bringing our heavy ships home late in the winter. The disaster of 1707 had underlined that warning. Again, Barcelona might well have been lost in the winter of 1705–6 after the Confederate fleet had left the Mediterranean. Hitherto our winter squadron had been obliged to withdraw every year to Lisbon to refit; and apart from the deficiencies of Lisbon as a base there was always the possibility that contrary winds or currents might hinder its return through the Straits in the event of a sudden emergency.

It was the earnest desire of Marlborough and the Cabinet to maintain a strong squadron inside the Straits during the winter months. Accordingly, in 1708, the capture of Minorca, with its deep, land-locked harbour of Port Mahon, was decided upon. ' All our seamen ', observed Stanhope, the commander-in-chief of the British forces in Spain, ' agree that it is in all respect the most convenient harbour in

[1] See J. H. Owen, *The War at Sea Under Queen Anne* (1938), pp. 238–70.

Europe.' ' I am so entirely convinced that nothing can be done effectually without the fleet ', Marlborough wrote to Stanhope only two days after Oudenarde, ' that I conjure you, if possible, to take Port Mahon.'

At Barcelona Stanhope, hard at work assembling troops, guns, and transports for the expedition, wrote to apprise the Admiral of his impending departure. Leake at this time lay off the Sardinian coast, having lately reduced Cagliari to submission to our Ally, King Charles III, with his bomb-vessels and a landing-party of marines, seamen, and Spaniards; he replied briefly to Stanhope on 18 August: ' I received yours of the 24th instant, N.S., this morning and believe I shall be at Port Mahon as soon as you.' The same evening he sailed for Minorca.

Leake was as good as his word, arriving off the island on the 25th, about a week before Stanhope; the rest of the men-of-war and transports, with a mixed force of some 2,000 men on board, arrived two days later. On Stanhope's arrival, the whole island surrendered to the Allies with the exception of Fort St. Philip, commanding the harbour entrance. To cover the landing of the heavy cannon Leake ordered the *Dunkirk*, *York*, and *Centurion* to anchor off the south-east point of the island. Batteries were then erected on the south side of the harbour to bombard the fort. On the 28th, leaving Rear-Admiral Whitaker with seventeen sail to assist in the reduction of Port Mahon and to perform the other winter services, Leake, in pursuance of his orders, left Minorca with seven English and eight Dutch sail of the line in order to water in Mallorca and thence proceed to England.

This was the last service rendered by the Main fleet in the Mediterranean. Once again the enemy force in Toulon had made no attempt to face the Confederate fleet. About a week later, before Leake had cleared the Straits on his homeward passage, the garrison of Fort St. Philip had surrendered to an offer of good terms.

' I heard from General Stanhope on the 30th of last month to the effect that the fortress of Mahon surrendered to him the day before,' Marlborough wrote at the end of October. ' . . . There is no doubt that we shall now be able to keep a good squadron in the Mediterranean throughout the winter.'

Port Mahon was speedily occupied by a squadron of eighteen ships ordered out in mid-winter from Lisbon and arrangements were set in train by Leake's successor, Admiral Sir George Byng, for the transference of naval stores and dockyard gear from that port to Minorca. Port Mahon thenceforward took the place of Lisbon as a base where our squadrons could winter and refit. ' England ought never to part with this Island ', Stanhope declared, ' which will give the law to the Mediterranean in time of war and peace.' Strategically, Port Mahon was ideally situated for masking Toulon and controlling trade in the western Mediterranean and, in conjunction with Gibraltar, made Great Britain the undisputed mistress of the inland sea.

The following year Byng had a powerful fleet at his disposal as well as a first-class naval base inside the Straits. But at this juncture the war in the Mediterranean was approaching stalemate. Just as Toulon was impregnable to the Allies, so was Barcelona to the French. The Confederate fleet, henceforth reduced in strength, was restricted to minor operations, such as harassing French commerce and protecting Barcelona's food supply.

7

Colonial operations in this war were on a relatively small scale. They were essentially strategical measures undertaken for the protection of our colonists' interests and possessions and in response to urgent appeals from the colonial authorities.

In the North American theatre, Port Royal, the capital of Nova Scotia, was in 1710 the objective of a combined naval and military force, comprising three 50s and two frigates and a bomb, under the command of Captain George Martin, and five provincial regiments, led by Colonel Francis Nicholson, which was one of the best planned conjunct expeditions of the century. The naval and military commanders co-operated loyally and harmoniously, and all went well. On 24 September Martin's squadron anchored off Port Royal. Next day the troops were landed, and the hostile positions bombarded; the attack was pressed home, and the French governor capitulated. The town thereupon received the new name of Annapolis Royal. In the meantime another small squadron under Captain John Aldred had been engaged in destroying the French settlements on the Newfoundland coast and in burning or capturing their shipping. But another conjunct expedition, comprising a strong squadron under Rear-

Admiral Sir Hovenden Walker and 5,000 troops under Brigadier John Hill, dispatched against Quebec in 1711, ended in total failure, largely owing to the want of proper planning and preparation. The ships were short of provisions; and such pilots as had been obtained for the passage did not know their business. Soon after entering the St. Lawrence, in an easterly gale accompanied by fog, the whole fleet narrowly escaped running aground; and eight of the transports were wrecked, with a loss of nearly 900 men. Following on this disaster, it was resolved at a council of war to abandon the attempt; and the squadron and its convoy returned to England.

Throughout the war of 1702–13 the protection of the seaborne trade upon which the prosperity of the Maritime Powers depended was a prime charge laid upon the Confederate Fleet. It was the wealth derived from their immense commerce that enabled England and Holland to assist their German and Italian allies with lavish supplies of money and munitions of war. But owing to the heavy demands of the Main fleet in the Mediterranean there was a chronic shortage of ships and men for the defence of the trade-routes and the provision of convoys. In the very first year of the war Newcastle colliers had been kept waiting in harbour for convoys which were not ready at the appointed time; and the price of coals in London rose to unprecedented heights. The outcry of English merchants against the defects of the convoy system were not without foundation. There were some particularly glaring examples, especially on foreign stations.[1] In home waters, English shipping was subject to attack, not only by swarms of privateers working from the Channel and Biscay ports, but also by whole squadrons of warships led by such resourceful and experienced commanders as Jean Forbin, Saint-Pol, and Du Guay-Trouin. After Malaga the French laid up most of their heavy ships and devoted all their resources to a systematic attack on Allied commerce. From now onward massed assaults were to be made on our merchantmen by squadrons of some half a dozen sail of the line, accompanied by lesser vessels. As the Lord High Admiral declared in 1708, ' the enemy hath ever since the battle of Malaga totally altered their methods of carrying on their naval war. And instead of sending forth great fleets, they fill

---

[1] ' On the West Indian station, Commodore Kerr was in the habit of exacting blackmail from merchants before he would grant them protection, and ships had been lost that could not afford to pay his nefarious charges.' (Trevelyan, *England Under Queen Anne*, II, p. 322).

the seas with privateers and with squadrons of their nimble ships; and by that means watch all opportunities of seizing upon our trade, for which the situation of their ports gives them but too good opportunities.' In spite of the great superiority enjoyed by the Allies at sea our trade losses had become so heavy that, in 1707, a parliamentary inquiry was ordered to be held.

As a result of the increasing depredations the reign of Anne saw a gradual but substantial improvement in the organization of the convoy system. The protection of commerce was now organized on a three-fold basis. First, cruisers were stationed around the coasts of the British Isles, and of the colonies. Second, convoys were provided for the overseas trades, and also for the more important coastwise traffic (e.g., the coal trade between Newcastle and London). Third, squadrons were disposed to cover the departures and arrivals of foreign-going trade in focal areas like the Channel Soundings. The trade bound for North America and the West Indies was generally convoyed by two or three cruisers with additional protection while passing through the Channel. East Indiamen were provided with convoys as far as St. Helena or the Cape of Good Hope. The trade bound for Portugal and the Mediterranean required a stronger convoy, passing as it did so near the Atlantic ports of France. Inside the Straits the lucrative Levant trade enjoyed the powerful protection of the main fleet, and its losses were comparatively light. In the Western Approaches the cruisers of the Channel Fleet, based on Plymouth, protected the trade in the danger area. The ships were stationed well to the westward of a line from Ushant to Scilly. They cruised on this post for several weeks at a stretch, periodically returning to Plymouth in turn to refit. There was a strong squadron in the narrow seas, based on Harwich and the Downs, for covering the important North German, Baltic, and Russian trades. Protection was also given to the principal fishing fleets in the Channel and North Sea. In the North Sea, as well as in other trades, the English and the Dutch often provided convoy for each other's mercantile shipping. As a result of the strengthening of commerce protection in the Channel and Soundings, more of the enemy raiders transferred their operations to the further side of the ocean. ' It is very reasonable to believe ', observed Colonel Jennings in Virginia, ' that we shall be much more infested with the privateers than formerly . . . since the interruption they have found in the Channel by the prudent disposition of the cruisers obliges them to come in greater numbers to America.'

In this war Du Guay-Trouin proved himself a worthy successor of the great Jean Bart, who had died a few weeks before the outbreak of hostilities in 1702. In 1703 Du Guay-Trouin destroyed a considerable number of Dutch whalers off Spitzbergen, while Saint-Pol attacked Allied shipping in the North Sea. In 1704 damaging attacks were made on our trade in the Channel and Soundings by small French squadrons led by Du Guay-Trouin from Brest and Saint-Pol from Dunkirk, and several of the English men-of-war on convoy duty were thereby lost to the enemy. It was usually our smaller convoys and the 'runners' which suffered. In October 1705, a number of English merchantmen homeward-bound from the Baltic were intercepted by a superior force under Saint-Pol from Dunkirk, with the result that all the three escorts and nearly all the merchantmen were captured, together with a badly needed supply of naval stores. Later in the same month Saint-Pol died gloriously in destroying the Dutch Baltic convoy. The following year Forbin, cruising in the North Sea, attacked the Dutch Muscovy convoy of 100 sail; the convoy got away, but most of the escorts were taken or destroyed. In 1707 the squadronal attack became more threatening. Our naval forces stationed in home waters proved insufficient to protect the trade, which was severely attacked in the Bay, the Channel, and the North Sea by squadrons and privateers from Brest and Dunkirk. In February a strong force under Du Quesne-Mosnier fell upon a convoy of victuallers for our army in the Peninsula in the Bay of Biscay and captured nearly every vessel. In May Forbin fell upon a coastwise convoy off Brighthelmstone and captured two of the escorts and more than half of the merchantmen. Later he attacked the trade bound for Russia, then returned north-about and successfully eluded Sir Thomas Hardy in the Channel Soundings. Du Guay-Trouin worked the Soundings for a few weeks without success and then returned to port to refit and refresh his ships' companies. Later he returned to the attack. In the early morning of 10 October the combined squadrons of Forbin and Du Guay-Trouin were cruising about midway between Ushant and Scilly when their look-outs sighted a large English convoy. It was a fine sunny autumn day, with a fresh breeze at north-east and a good deal of western sea. Both French squadrons bore up and ran down towards the English, who presently formed a line of battle. Du Guay-Trouin bore the brunt of the fighting in the early part of the action, but was later joined by Forbin, capturing some dozen of the merchant-men and accounting for four out of the five escorting warships, which sacrificed themselves to give the merchantmen the better opportunity to escape. This was the outstanding success achieved by the enemy in the *guerre de course* of 1702–13. The chief importance of the squad-ronal attacks, however, was that they tended to draw off the English cruisers in pursuit, thereby clearing the field for the French privateers, which actually did most of the damage. There were sometimes as many as one hundred privateers at sea from Dunkirk alone. The last great privateering operation of the war was the capture of Rio de Janeiro by a strong expedition commanded by Du Guay-Trouin in 1711.

In the later years of the war more ships were forthcoming on our side for the essential service of trade protection. In the Cruisers and Convoys Act of 1708 it was established that ' at least 43 ships of war be employed as cruisers in proper stations ' and the ' aforesaid men-of-war to be careened at least three times a year, or oftener if there shall be occasion.' The course of the war at sea re-emphasized the important lesson that far greater strength was needed to protect sea communications than to attack them. For the enemy was always free to choose his time and point of attack: British cruisers could not be everywhere; periodically they must return to port to clean and refit. Moreover, France had the advantage of geographical position. As it was, a full two-thirds of our warships were constantly engaged in the protection of trade.

Side by side with the work of commerce protection went that of commerce destruction. The war on the enemy's trade was carried on, not only by English cruisers on their stations engaged in protecting our own,[1] but also by considerable numbers of English privateers. Parliament, indeed, passed new laws to encourage privateering, which played an important part in clearing the seas of enemy commerce. One of the best-known of these privateersmen was the redoubtable Woodes Rogers, of Bristol, who later wrote an account of his experi-ences. By the Navy, however, privateering was not regarded as an

---

[1] An important feature of the Cruisers and Convoys Act was the provisions relating to prize money. It was laid down in the Act that the value of the prizes taken was to be awarded to the Navy ' for the better and more effectual encouragement of the Sea Service'.

unmixed blessing. 'The privateers which are commissioned by the government', observed Admiral Whetstone, who was then commanding on the West Indian station, 'have slockstered away several of our men, notwithstanding we use all the care we can to prevent it.'

France in 1709 was in such straits, owing to the failure of the harvest of 1707 and the hard winter of 1708, that she was obliged to import grain. 'Her Majesty judging it to be of the highest importance to her affairs as well as those of all her allys to distress the enemy as much as possible by taking the most effectual methods for preventing them from receiving such supplies at this juncture,' it was determined to cut off the food imports to France and to this end all kinds of corn were declared contraband. To intercept the grain ships from the Baltic a squadron under Norris cruised in the Sound; another under Leake lay off the ports of Flanders; and another under Dursley guarded the Soundings; at the same time one of the chief duties of the Mediterranean Fleet was to prevent the corn ships from North Africa, the Levant, and Genoa from entering the southern ports of France.

8

Despite the increasing exhaustion of France, the war continued for several years longer. For the Portuguese alliance which had given the Maritime Powers entry to the Mediterranean had at the same time committed them to the long-drawn-out Peninsular War in support of the Habsburg candidate for the Spanish succession. In this phase of the war the Allies, advancing on Madrid from Catalonia to the eastward and from Portugal to the westward, with the support of the fleet, endeavoured to expel the Bourbon from Spain. But national sentiment in Spain for the most part favoured the cause of Philip V. Twice—in 1706 and again in 1710—the Allied army entered the Spanish capital, from which it was twice forced to retire. The struggle in the Peninsula dragged on for eight years, ending in December 1710 with the capitulation of Stanhope's army at Brihuega.

During this final phase of the war the supremacy of the Allied fleet —which was becoming more and more the Navy of Great Britain alone: since Holland, impoverished in the long struggle, found herself increasingly in arrears with the quota of ships she had agreed to supply —was unchallenged by the enemy; and the silent, invisible pressure of sea power progressively throttled the seaborne trade of France, ruined her prosperity, and turned the scales of relative strength decisively against her. The brilliant victories of Marlborough on land: the sustained success of his Mediterranean strategy; the mounting prosperity of our industry and commerce; the continuous expansion of our merchant marine; the decline at sea alike of our enemy, France, and of our ally, Holland, all served to establish the naval supremacy of Great Britain on a basis where it was to remain for more than two centuries to come.

The war ended in 1713 with the Peace of Utrecht, the principal provisions of which, in so far as they related to Great Britain, may thus be summarized. It was laid down in this treaty that France and Spain were never to be united under the same crown: that the Spanish Netherlands were to be annexed to Austria (which was not a maritime Power): that Naples and Sardinia were also to be ceded to Austria, and Sicily was to be handed over to the Duke of Savoy—in consequence of which neither France nor Spain would be able to block the narrows of the Mediterranean: that the French port of Dunkirk, whose ' nimble privateers ' had so often sallied forth to prey on British commerce, was to be dismantled: that Gibraltar and Minorca were to be retained at the peace by Great Britain, which thus became a Mediterranean, as well as an Atlantic, Power: that the territory around Hudson's Bay, Newfoundland, and Acadia, or Nova Scotia, were to be transferred to the British Crown: that Great Britain was to be granted the *Asiento*, and also the right to send one ship every year to Spanish America to trade with the colonists. Moreover, Louis XIV was obliged to recognize the Protestant Succession in England and to abandon the cause of the Pretender.

Above all, as Mahan has declared, ' The demands made by England, as conditions of peace in 1711, showed her to have become a sea power in the purest sense of the word, not only in fact, but also in her own consciousness.'[1] Our old rival, Holland, gained nothing of maritime value or importance by the war. She had badly overtaxed her powers by her efforts to maintain an army which reached a maximum strength of 80,000 men; and in so doing she had had to sacrifice the claims of her navy. The Dutch fleet had shrunk by more than 25 per cent. Naval shipbuilding in Holland had practically ceased. Her fishery had

[1] A. T. Mahan, *The Influence of Sea Power upon History* (1890), p. 217.

been hard hit by the late war, from which it never really recovered. The days of Holland as a Great Power were ended. Meanwhile, the numerical strength of the British Navy had continued to increase, together with that of the mercantile marine: in 1712 the seaborne trade of Great Britain was actually greater than it had been before the war. Finally, in the all-important element of bases Great Britain was now well provided.

IX

The War of 1739-48

I

The relatively peaceful interlude which followed the Peace of Utrecht witnessed an immense expansion of Great Britain's industry, commerce, and merchant shipping, and the vigilant preservation of her naval interests. It witnessed also the revival of the royal navy of France, the phenomenal increase of her mercantile marine, the preponderance of French merchants in the West Indies and the Levant, and the steady growth of French influence and commerce in India. The influential mercantile interest of this country watched with jealous and suspicious eye the resurgent power and prosperity of our ancient rival; and although for a generation, under the pacific rule of Sir Robert Walpole in England and Cardinal Fleury in France, peace was maintained between the two kingdoms, that peace was at best a precarious one, owing to the ultimate clash of national interests.

As the century advanced, Holland was gradually but surely losing her old pre-eminence in the world's carrying trade. Great Britain enjoyed one decisive advantage over her rival, in that she had abundant manufactures of her own to sell abroad—in particular, cloth—while the Dutch had little to export but herrings. In Walpole's England a substantial proportion of the population lived by industry and commerce. That proportion continued to increase. The mercantile tonnage of Great Britain which, as previously stated, had practically doubled during the Restoration era, was destined to treble during the first three-quarters of the eighteenth century. Between the powerful fighting Fleet and the immense seaborne trade of Great Britain there existed, as Mahan has truly asserted, a most intimate connection. ' It was in the union of the two, carefully fostered, that England made the gain of sea power over and beyond all other states.' And Mahan adds that this gain was associated with, and dated from, the War of the Spanish Succession: ' Before that war England was one of the sea powers; after it she was *the* sea power, without any second.'[1]

Just as it was the expanding industry and commerce of Great Britain which enabled her to maintain a powerful Navy, so it was the protection of that Navy which preserved her industry and commerce, in time of war, from the disasters which overtook those of her rivals. ' Your trade is the mother and nurse of your seamen,' Lord Haversham had declared in 1707; ' your seamen are the life of your fleet, and your fleet is the security and protection of your trade, and both together are the wealth, strength and security of Britain.'

Both the home and the overseas trade of this country were largely controlled from the capital. ' London, which sucks the vitals of trade in this island to itself,' as Defoe had declared in his *Tour through Great Britain*, had by now supplanted Amsterdam as the chief centre of the world's commerce. And besides being an unrivalled entrepôt, London was also a great manufacturing centre, whose innumerable crafts and industries attracted a wide range of commodities from near and far—iron, copper, timber, hides, tallow, wax, paints, indigo, kaolin, hemp, wool, silk, linen, cotton, calico, and other stuffs. London River was the busiest, most crowded highway in the kingdom. ' The whole River, in a Word, from *London Bridge* to *Blackwall*, is one great *Arsenal*, nothing in the World can be like it,' wrote Defoe; adding that, in the Pool of London, ' I have had the Curiosity to count the Ships as well as I could, *en passant*, and have found above Two Thousand Sail of all Sorts, not reckoning Barges, Lighters or Pleasure-Boats, and Yachts; but of Vessels that really go to sea.' It is recorded that in 1728 no less than 1,839 foreign-going British merchant vessels entered the Port of London, as well as 6,837 British coasters. For unloading the incoming, and loading the outgoing, vessels, there were about 140 wharves and 2,000 lighters, barges, billy-boys, and other small craft.

Of the total imports of Great Britain, London's share amounted to upwards of 80 per cent; and of the total exports, to nearly 74 per cent. Incomparably the greatest port in the kingdom, London now practically monopolized the trade with India and China, as well as controlling most of that with Europe and the Mediterranean, and sharing the

[1] *Op. cit.*, p. 225.

American trade with Bristol and, to a lesser degree, with Liverpool. A high proportion of the commerce with the Port of London was carried on by the great trading companies—the East India Company, the Russian Company, the Levant Company, the South Sea Company, the Hudson's Bay Company.

The swarming coastal traffic of the kingdom was likewise dominated by London. To the Thames were carried three-quarters of the coals exported from Newcastle; vast quantities of corn from East Anglia and the southern counties; herring and cod from Lowestoft and Yarmouth; Norwich woollens; Cromer lobsters; butter and cheese from Ipswich; oysters from Queenborough and Faversham; Kentish hops, pippins, runnets, and cherries by the hoyload; Folkestone mackerel; Purbeck flags and marble, and the white Portland stone that had been used for the building of the new St. Paul's; Dorset ale; woollens, serges, and cider from Exeter and Topsham; Cheddar, and other West Country cheeses; Cornish tin, lead, and copper; druggets, cantaloons, mixed cloths, and other stuffs from Bristol; Welsh oats; Cheshire cheese and salt; hides and wool from Cumberland; Scottish salmon. From innumerable ports, great and small, up and down the coast, came the unending stream of ships, supplying London with food, fuel, and raw material. In this busy coastwise traffic, which, in the days before railways, canals, or macadamized highways, was of immense economic importance, the largest type of vessel engaged was the Newcastle collier. The coal industry throughout the period under review was continually expanding. ' This trade is so considerable ', Defoe observed ' that it is esteemed the great Nursery for our best Seamen.'

Meanwhile, as the history of this period will show, the maintenance and extension of our maritime interests were the constant care of the British government. Some striking illustrations of this policy will be briefly recorded.

Five years after the Treaty of Utrecht, the peace of Europe was threatened by the aggressive designs of the Spanish government in the Mediterranean. Under the strong and efficient rule of Cardinal Alberoni Spain had recently undergone a national revival which bordered on the miraculous; the Cardinal's reforms extended to every branch of the administration; the army and navy, finance and taxation, were systematically overhauled; Alberoni was resolved to make his country a great naval Power, and for a time the fleet he maintained in the Mediterranean was, in fact, far stronger than the British. In pursuance of these far-reaching designs, the Spaniards proceeded to occupy first Mallorca and presently Sardinia.

In the hope of recovering Spain's lost Italian provinces and of defeating any British counter-action, the Cardinal, by his skilful diplomacy, quickly raised up a formidable coalition against Great Britain. The crux of Alberoni's enterprise was that the Jacobites should make another bid for the throne, supported by the Swedes and Russians, while our fleet was tied down in the south. The danger was very real. The Hanoverian succession was by no means firmly established. With the object of persuading Spain to forego her ambitions in Italy, our ambassador at Madrid actually offered Alberoni Gibraltar. The offer, however, was turned down; and the Cardinal, in defiance of the provisions of Utrecht, prepared to occupy Sicily.

On New Year's Day, 1717, a large Spanish squadron, escorting a convoy carrying 30,000 troops, appeared before Palermo; with the result that the Savoyards presently evacuated the greater part of the island. Great Britain and France then intervened to prevent a general war. On 30 July a greatly superior British fleet under the command of Vice-Admiral Sir George Byng sighted a Spanish squadron in the Straits of Messina. His opponent retiring in a long, straggling line, Byng instructed the four best sailers in his fleet—the *Kent*, *Superbe*, *Grafton*, and *Oxford*—to make all the sail they could to overhaul him. The chase continued throughout the night. Next morning, off Cape Passaro, the leading British ships came up with the sternmost Spaniards, which thereupon opened fire. The long running action which ensued resolved itself into a series of single combats, in which the Spaniards were one by one overpowered by greatly superior force; the Spanish commander-in-chief was made a prisoner, and his squadron was practically annihilated. It is to be noted that this action marks ' the first occasion on which " the chase " was used as the main tactical feature of a battle, and it was a complete success'.[1]

Byng followed up this stroke by convoying an Austrian army to Sicily and co-operating with them in the war until, in 1720, the Spaniards abandoned their attempt to conquer the island and withdrew. Meanwhile in the north Alberoni's principal ally, Charles XII of Sweden, had been killed in battle; soon after, his whole grandiose

[1] M. A. Lewis, *The Navy of Britain*, pp. 522–3.

scheme having collapsed like a pack of cards, the Cardinal was dismissed from office.

To protect her vital naval interests Great Britain similarly intervened in the north. The protracted struggle around the shores of the Baltic between Sweden and a coalition comprising Denmark, Poland, and Russia had resulted in the prostration of the former, which was in danger of being overrun by Peter the Great's victorious troops. Now the destruction of the balance of power in this region would have endangered not only our commercial interests, which were very considerable, but also the bulk of the Baltic spars, hemp, timber, and tar without which our Navy could not move. Though the supply of New England masts and heavy spars had been developed during the past fifty years, Great Britain still relied on the Baltic trade for the major part of her naval stores. Already in the War of the Spanish Succession the supply of Swedish masts and naval stores from Russia had been cut off through the war between Sweden and the Tsar.

By 1716 the stocks of naval stores were running dangerously low, and Townshend (then the Secretary of State) declared that, ' It is our misfortune at this juncture, by the knavery of the Muscovites in imposing on our merchants last year, to have our magazines so ill provided with stores, particularly with hemp, that if the fleet of merchant ships now loading in the Baltick should by accident miscarry, it will be impossible for His Majesty to fit out any ships of war for the next year, by which means the whole navy will be rendered perfectly useless.'

Great Britain acted with energy and promptitude. She concluded a treaty of mutual assistance with Sweden and sent an Anglo-Dutch squadron to the Baltic to support Sweden against the Danish fleet. The intervention of the British Navy in the Great Northern War, as Mahan has remarked, produced ' another effectual illustration of the sea power of England, manifested alike in the north and south with a slightness of exertion which calls to mind the stories of the tap of a tiger's paw '. When peace was eventually restored it was the settled policy of the British government to prevent any one Power from establishing a hegemony of the Baltic States, and to ' preserve the tranquility in the North '. To this end, throughout the eighteenth and early nineteenth centuries British squadrons were repeatedly sent out to the Baltic in order to keep open the Sound and to secure the safe passage of the annual fleets of merchantmen from our East Coast ports to the Baltic markets.

During the late war, owing to the difficulty experienced in procuring supplies of pitch and tar from Sweden, an attempt had been made to foster the introduction of naval stores on the other side of the Atlantic, by an Act ' for encouraging the importation of naval stores from Her Majesty's plantations in America '; which, according to the Act, might ' commodiously afford great quantities of all sorts of naval stores, if due encouragement be given '. A certain amount of pitch and tar was now forthcoming from our American colonies, which broke the monopoly of the Swedish Tar Company and freed us from total dependence upon the Baltic. For spars and hemp, however, the latter remained the principal source of supply.

Finally, a word must be said about the Ostend Company. In 1718 a series of trading voyages had been started from Ostend to India and China, and in 1722 the Ostend Company received its charter from the Emperor Charles VI, who granted it a thirty years' monopoly of trade with Africa and the East and West Indies—the Spanish ports of South America being thrown open to the Company's ships by treaty three years afterwards. It was apprehended in this country that the new company not only threatened British trading interests, but might conceivably lead to the foundation of a naval base endangering our national security. ' Should the Ostend Company go on with success ', it was observed, ' by the natural course of things the Emperor will in time have a naval force on the coast of Flanders, which may prove much more inconvenient to us than a fleet in the Mediterranean or Adriatic Seas.' In response to the alarmed protests of the British commercial community the government took action; and a general war was averted only by the timely compliance of the Emperor, who first suspended, and later abolished, the Ostend Company.

2

Sir Robert Walpole, the son of a Norfolk squire, who was destined to be the first of the illustrious roll of British finance ministers, became leader of the re-united Whig Party, in April 1721, following upon the collapse of the South Sea Bubble. Enjoying the firm support of the first two Georges, he successfully resisted the attacks of an Opposition group styling themselves ' the Patriots ', and retained the reins or government throughout the next two decades. The prime object of Walpole's policy was the furtherance of his country's economic interests; and it is significant that the King's Speech in 1721 referred to the desirability of making ' the exportation of our own manufactures, and the importation of the commodities used in the manufacturing of them, as practicable and easy as may be '. It was essentially on these lines that Walpole proceeded to overhaul the national fiscal system, substituting order for chaos. It had been said with justice that he found our tariff the worst in the world, and left it the best.

The general advance in British industrial and commercial activity which characterized the third and fourth decades of the eighteenth century; the development of our great joint-stock Companies; the significant increase of our merchant shipping; the rapid expansion of our trade with the colonies—all these may, in large measure, be attributed to Walpole's enlightened fiscal policy. At the same time his strong and able administration effectually promoted the gradual reconciliation between the old landed and the new moneyed interest, and firmly established the House of Hanover on the throne.

Peace was indispensable to the success of his policy; and for twenty-one years he managed to steer Great Britain clear of European wars and entanglements. When the War of the Polish Succession broke out in 1733, Walpole remained faithful to his friendship with France, and, notwithstanding George II's desire to support the Emperor, succeeded in keeping this country out of the struggle. ' Madam,' he observed complacently to Queen Caroline one day in 1734, ' there are fifty thousand men slain this year in Europe, and not one Englishman.' Towards the close of the same decade, however, a graver crisis arose.

According to the provisions of the Peace of Utrecht a single British ship was permitted to trade annually with Spanish America. The yearly sailing became the cover for an extensive contraband traffic. The quarrel between British smugglers on the one side and Spanish *guarda-costas* on the other gave rise to a series of violent encounters, the best known of which was the affair of Jenkins' Ear. According to a contemporary version of the incident, Jenkins, the master of the brig *Rebecca*, was boarded by a gang of *guarda-costas* in the Caribbean. After first hanging their prisoner and cutting him down again alive, one of the Spaniards ' took hold of his left ear, and with his cutlass slit it down, and another took hold of it and tore it off, but gave him the piece, bidding him carry it to His Majesty King George.' Several years afterwards, brought to the bar of the House of Commons by an Opposition clamorous for war, the victim of this outrage is reported to have declared, in reply to a question as to what were his feelings in this extremity, ' *I commended my soul to God and my cause to my country.*' A howl of execration immediately rose throughout the land. It was in vain that Walpole strove to bring about a peaceful settlement with Spain: the Opposition, supported by popular feeling, would not have it. Though ostensibly the affair of Jenkins' Ear and similar clashes were the cause of the ensuing struggle, the true and underlying motive was, in fact, the desire of the British mercantile interest for conquest and loot. Excitement rose to fever-heat in the course of 1739; and on 19 October war was declared against Spain, to the savage joy of the British populace.

3

Owing to the failure of the British government to maintain the Navy during the long years of peace in a reasonable state of efficiency, and also through the lack of an adequate system of manning the ships, the outcome of naval operations in the early years of the war was in no way commensurate with the actual and potential strength of Great Britain at sea. Thus the blockade of Cadiz by Haddock was wholly ineffective. His force was based on Gibraltar, where there were neither sufficient stores nor facilities for refitting; the enemy's squadrons sailed in and out of their ports more or less as they pleased. The enemy was able to reinforce both his garrison and his squadron in the West Indies. Haddock's cruisers being too few for the task of trade protection, the enemy's privateers were snapping up British merchantmen in increasing numbers. It was not long before he was obliged to leave his station for Port Mahon; and during his absence the Spanish force in Cadiz harbour slipped out to Ferrol. In the meantime Vice-Admiral Sir John Balchen failed to intercept a squadron under the command of Admiral Pizarro on its way home from America with the treasure fleet.

In November a small squadron under Vice-Admiral Edward Vernon captured Porto Bello on the Darien coast. Vernon in consequence became a national hero. The news of his victory was received at home

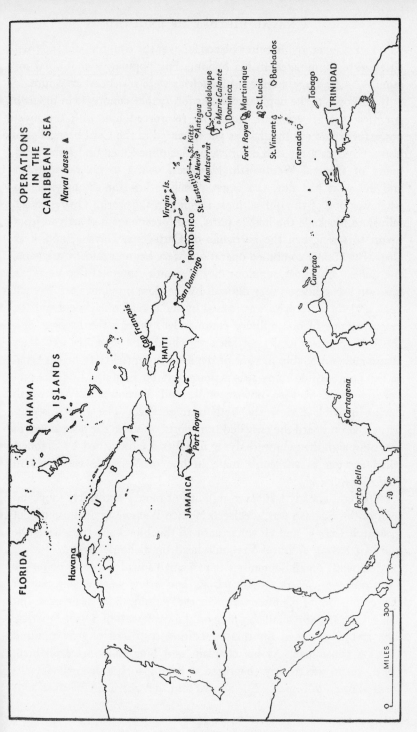

OPERATIONS
IN THE
CARIBBEAN SEA

Naval bases ▲

FLORIDA

BAHAMA ISLANDS

Havana

C U B A

JAMAICA
▲ Port Royal

HAITI
Cap Français

San Domingo

PORTO RICO

Virgin Is.

St. Eustatius — St. Kitts
St. Nevis — Antigua
Montserrat Guadeloupe
Marie Galante
Dominica
Fort Royal ▲ Martinique
St. Lucia
St. Vincent Barbados
Grenada
Tobago
TRINIDAD

Curaçao

Cartagena

Porto Bello

MILES
0   300

253

with extravagant joy. Bonfires blazed all over the country, and the chief cities were illuminated in his honour. His popularity continued for months, and a large number of hostelries were re-named after him.

In response to the popular clamour for further conquests in Spanish America, the government eventually reinforced him with the most powerful armament that had as yet appeared in the Caribbean. There also arrived an army of 8,000 raw, undisciplined men under the command of General Wentworth. However, owing to mismanagement and delay, it was now the worst possible time for campaigning in what was one of the unhealthiest regions in the world. Owing to the failure to blockade the hostile ports, reinforcements had arrived from Spain to strengthen the garrisons of Cartagena, Havana, and Vera Cruz. Eventually combined operations were begun against Cartagena, the richest and most populous city of South America: but Vernon's position was rendered very difficult by the close proximity of a French fleet, and the enterprise was ruined by the spread of sickness and the incompetence of our military commander; though the harbour and the forts commanding its entrance were held for a time they were later abandoned—probably in view of the soaring mortality to be expected in the approaching rainy season; attempts on Santiago in Cuba and Panama were likewise unsuccessful; and Vernon and Wentworth having quarrelled violently, both were recalled. The ghastly scenes witnessed on board the crowded transports where in the later stages of the campaign the men were dying like flies are described by Smollett (then serving as surgeon's mate in one of Vernon's warships) in *Roderick Random*.

' We have already lost seven millions of money and thirty thousand men in the Spanish war,' declared Horace Walpole in disillusionment in March 1744—' and all the fruit of all this blood and treasure is the glory of having Admiral Vernon's head on alehouse signs.'

Meanwhile on 18 September 1740 a small squadron, comprising the *Centurion*, 60, *Severn*, 50, *Pearl*, 40, and a few smaller ships under the command of Commodore George Anson, had been sent out against the sea-ports and shipping on the west coast of South America. The troops provided for this expedition consisted of five hundred Chelsea pensioners. As his chaplain and biographer later testified, ' Mr. Anson was greatly chagrined at having such a decrepit detachment allotted to him . . . but he was told that persons who were supposed to be better judges of soldiers than he thought them the properest men that could be employed on this occasion.' The majority of these pensioners deserted at Portsmouth; and of the 259 cripples and invalids who actually embarked not a single man ever saw England again. Owing to the interminable discussions and delays which preceded its departure the Spaniards had received ample warning of the expedition and its proposed objective and sent out a stronger squadron, under Admiral Pizarro, to intercept it. On passage to the Horn the two squadrons all but met. Off the stormy cape that season the weather was terrific. The *Severn* and *Pearl* parted company, and a smaller vessel was wrecked. Struggling for months in mountainous seas and under sullen skies to make westing, Anson at last got round. After enduring appalling hardships and losing more than 600 of their ships' companies the *Centurion* and two other vessels at last reached their rendezvous at the island of Juan Fernandez and remained there for several weeks to refresh.

Anson then sailed northward up the west coast of South America and took several prizes. After missing the treasure-ship at Acapulco, he sailed on 28 April 1742 for China. To recruit the health of his men, he remained for two months in the Ladrone Islands. Early in November he reached Macao, where he refitted; then the following summer he sailed for the Philippines and, on 20 June 1743, captured the Manila galleon with a lading worth half a million. On 15 October the *Centurion* —now the only vessel left to Anson—stood westward across the Indian Ocean, reaching the Cape in March 1744: whence she sailed for England, arriving on 14 June at St. Helens, after an almost miraculous escape from a French squadron cruising in the Soundings (through the midst of which the Commodore had steered in a fog). Their treasure, which was valued at £1¼ millions, was disembarked at Portsmouth and taken up to London, where it was paraded through the city streets with the ship's company marching with colours flying and band playing.

Though the material achievement of the voyage was comparatively small, Anson's circumnavigation of the globe was an epic of heroism, resolution, and resource: the ravages of the scurvy had lost him no less than three-quarters of his men; with but indifferent means at his disposal he had overcome all obstacles and successfully fulfilled his mission: and it is not without significance that a number of the young officers of the squadron, notably Saunders, Saumarez, Denis, Brett, Keppel, Hyde Parker, and Howe, afterwards became distinguished commanders.

In 1740 the quarrel over the Habsburg inheritance brought about the War of the Austrian Succession (1740–8), in the course of which Austria, Holland, and Great Britain were finally ranged against Prussia, France, and Spain. In 1743 the Bourbon Powers renewed the Family Compact made ten years earlier, and relations between Great Britain and France rapidly deteriorated. As between this country and France, maritime and commercial rivalry lay at the root of the matter. The British objects were, first, to prevent the Rhine delta from falling under hostile domination; second, to defend the Electorate of Hanover against the French and the Prussians; third, to check the expansion of the French settlements in North America and in India. Eventually the War of Jenkins' Ear merged in the War of the Austrian Succession; Great Britain being officially at war with France from 1744 onwards.

During the earlier stages of the war British naval operations were characterized by strategic and tactical weakness and accompanied by recurrent dissensions among the Board of Admiralty and senior flag officers. It was for lack of any clear strategical policy—such as was later represented by the growth of the Western Squadron—that the Navy at this juncture so often failed to intercept enemy convoys, and that our overseas possessions were exposed to the risk of attack. Moreover, the general strategy of the war was not infrequently deflected by commercial and financial considerations. In spite of these handicaps, however, the British Navy successfully defended this country against invasion during the critical months of 1744–5; transported the small British army to Flanders, and co-operated in the Mediterranean with the Allied armies; protected the seaborne trade of Great Britain, and assailed that of the enemy: and, if the direction of the Navy was defective and its administration chaotic, the conduct of the war by our opponents was even worse. France and Spain made no attempt to co-operate at sea, or to employ their fleets in pursuit of a definite strategical objective—instead they frittered away their naval strength in small detachments for convoying their merchant shipping.

During the years 1742–4 the British fleet in the Mediterranean, under the command of Admiral Thomas Mathews, was by no means strong enough for the multifarious duties imposed on it by the government; and further to complicate matters, there was the ever-present possibility that the French might join forces with our enemy, Spain, who was threatening the Austrian possessions in Italy. While the attitude of France was still uncertain, a Spanish squadron of twelve of the line was chased by Mathews into Toulon and blockaded by him there.

Four months later, on 19 February 1744, the Spaniards came out in company with the French Toulon fleet. After pursuing for three days Mathews came up with the enemy. At daybreak on the 22nd there was a light easterly wind, with a heavy swell. Mathews had the advantage of the wind; but the enemy's ships were cleaner and faster than his, and his rear division lay several miles to windward and astern. Realizing that his van could not hope to get up with the enemy's van, Mathews intended to pit his headmost ships against the enemy's centre. While leaving the signal for the line of battle still flying, therefore, the Admiral abandoned the line himself and bore down on the enemy's rear. The ships of his own division stationed immediately ahead and astern followed his example; but the majority of the others fell into a state of utter and irredeemable confusion, and the battle went to pieces. For this the rigidity of the Fighting Instructions and the inadequacy of the signalling system then in use, combined with quarrels and dissensions among the senior officers (between Mathews and his second-in-command, Vice-Admiral Richard Lestock, there was bitter animosity), was largely responsible. During the heavy cannonading between the two fleets Mathew's flag-captain lost his arm, which, as the Admiral later observed, ' was a great misfortune to me, as the whole conduct of the ship fell to my share '. The action, which continued for six hours, was inconclusive; the fighting was actually between a few vessels, rather than between fleets; but the Spanish squadron received a good deal of damage, and one of their ships was taken by Captain Edward Hawke. For two days more the opposing fleets remained in sight of each other. Mathews, however, abandoned the pursuit, fearing to be drawn towards the Straits, and the coast of Italy thus left unprotected. Both the Admiral and Vice-Admiral were subsequently court-martialled. Lestock was acquitted, but Mathews found ' guilty of divers notorious breaches of his duty ' and cashiered.

This verdict perplexed as well as astonished public opinion in the Service. It was ascribed, by no means justly, to political animus. For, when all is said and done, it was the imperative duty of the commander-in-chief on the Mediterranean station to destroy the enemy force. By breaking off the pursuit as he did, Mathews had cast away his opportunity of gaining a signal and decisive victory which would have assured us the control of the Mediterranean and thereby secured our communications in the Channel and Western Approaches against the threat of a superior concentration. Apprehensive, like Byng and Calder in similar case, of the consequences of failure, Mathews had not done his utmost, as was his duty, to destroy the enemy. And Richmond's comment is worth recalling here: ' The admiral who has the enemy's fleet in sight and for thought of what will happen if he be defeated fails to bring about a decision will share the fate of those unfortunate officers.'[1]

In the autumn of 1743 the French government had resolved to annex the Austrian Netherlands. Knowing that such an attempt would mean open war with England, they determined to launch a sudden descent on this country without any declaration of war. It was calculated that 10,000 men would be sufficient to deal with such forces as might be expected to oppose them on this side of the water. Early in 1744 an army was assembled at Dunkirk under the great French commander, Marshal Saxe; and while these preparations went forward the grandson of James II, Prince Charles Edward Stuart, the ' Young Pretender ', lay secretly at Gravelines. The Brest fleet under the Marquis de Roquefeuil sailed up the Channel to cover the passage of the army. Most of the troops were then embarked. But the veteran Sir John Norris, one of the ablest of our earlier strategists, then in command of the Channel Fleet, had sailed out of Portsmouth, and, making the enemy's transports his main objective, appeared off Dunkirk on the 25th, intending, if they should elude him, to pursue and destroy them.[2] In the afternoon, when within eight miles of

[1] *The Navy in the War of 1739–48*, II, p. 56.
[2] ' But if they should unfortunately get out and pass us in the night and go north-ward,' Norris stated in his dispatch, ' I intend to detach a superior force to endeavour to overtake and destroy them; and with the remainder of my squadron either to fight the French fleet now in the Channel, or observe them and cover the country as our circumstances will admit of; or I shall pursue the embarkation with all my strength.' Norris's strategy obliged the Brest fleet to come up the Channel in order to clear the army's line of passage. Now, as always, the hostile *army* was the primary objective, from which Norris did not intend to be lured away by the advent of the French battle fleet.

Roquefeuil's fleet, Norris was obliged with the turn of the tide to come to anchor. Late that evening there fell a flat calm; the French fleet weighed or cut its cables, and, with no lights showing drifted down-Channel on the ebb unobserved. At midnight it began to blow from the north-east and rapidly freshened to gale force. During the night the British fleet was dispersed. The gale continued throughout the 26th. It drove Roquefeuil's fleet to the westward; during the next few days his ships arrived back at Brest by two's and three's. At Dunkirk a number of Saxe's transports were wrecked by the gale, and several other vessels ran ashore. The invasion project was given up, and the Marshal appointed to the command in Flanders. Once again the weakness of the French in the Channel had been made manifest. Because no port of refuge existed east of Brest, the French battle fleet usually came into the Channel with reluctance, and hastened to leave it again when things went wrong.

With the return of the Channel Fleet, now under Sir John Balchen,[1] from convoying the victuallers to Gibraltar, the campaign in the Channel came to an end. The French strategy was now principally concentrated on commerce destruction and the interception of Allied supplies to the Mediterranean. In both cases the vital theatre was the Channel approaches. Next year the Western Squadron was reconstituted and ordered to cruise to the westward, with Plymouth as its base, under the command of Admiral William Martin.

With the entry of France into the struggle, the war entered upon a new phase. On this side of the Channel there still remained sufficient affection for the exiled Stuarts—more especially in the northern parts of the island—to constitute a serious threat to the House of Hanover.[2] In the spring of 1745 Saxe's army overran Flanders, and on 30 April decisively defeated the British and their Allies, under the command of the Duke of Cumberland, at Fontenoy. Tournai, Ghent, Bruges, and Oudenarde successively surrendered; Saxe laid siege to Ostend, and the Allies fell back endeavouring to cover Antwerp. The advance of Saxe's greatly superior army caused consternation in England.

---

[1] In a heavy gale on 3 October 1744 Balchen was lost with all hands in the *Victory*. It is believed that the ship ran on the Casquets.

[2] Less than thirty years before, in the summer of 1715, the ' Old Pretender ' had landed in the north, and was supported by a number of the Scottish chieftains. But a squadron under Vice-Admiral Sir George Byng patrolled the Channel and prevented reinforcements and arms from being ferried over from France; and the rising was speedily suppressed.

The British Government had already supplied its full contingent of troops for the defence of this vital area. It was feared that the French successes in Flanders would be followed by a descent on this side of the water. ' As we have now lost Flanders ', the Duke of Newcastle wrote despondently to Lord Hardwicke, ' we may soon lose England and Holland too, for I don't know what can stop that victorious army. I am sure our's in Flanders cannot.'

With most of the seasoned British troops thus absent on the Continent, the Jacobite peril suddenly came to a head. On 11 August Prince Charles, voyaging from France with a handful of followers in a single frigate, landed at Moidart in the west of Scotland. Fired by the gallant personality of the young Prince, some of the principal clans of the Highlands marched to his standard set up at Glenfinnan. For a while the insurgents carried all before them. Sir John Cope and his troops, advancing across the Corriearrick, from fear of an ambush retired hurriedly into Inverness, and afterwards took ship from Aberdeen for Leith. After capturing Dundee, Perth, and Edinburgh, the Jacobite army on 21 September routed a large force of regulars— the veterans of Dettingen and Fontenoy—at Prestonpans in something less than six minutes. This made Prince Charles virtually the master of Scotland, and in London a French descent was expected daily. ' The alarm in this city is very great ', wrote Beauclerk to Vernon on 25 September, ' and a run upon the Bank.' Prince Charles army, by this time some 5,000 strong, now crossed the Border into England, following the western route by Carlisle in order to evade Marshal Wade's large army at Newcastle, and presently slipping past another formidable force, commanded by the Duke of Cumberland, which had been hastily brought over from the Low Countries, in the Midlands.

On ' Black Friday ', 6 December, the news reached London that the Prince's army lay at Derby, with no regular force remaining between that town and the capital. The City was seized with panic. Jacobite proclamations appeared on the walls overnight; George II was actually contemplating flight to Hanover; and there was a run on the banks, which was to some extent countered by the ingenious stratagem of paying out red-hot coin. But the English Jacobites proved unresponsive; and, alarmed at the strength of the forces which were concentrating against them, the insurgent army retreated northward and recrossed the border.

As in the 'Fifteen, the crucial factor in the situation was the control of sea communications. ' Sire,' the Maréchal de Noailles had observed to Louis XV, ' if Your Majesty truly wishes the Mass to be said in London, you will have to send 30,000 men to serve it.' That autumn an invasion flotilla was assembled in the French Channel ports; a force of about 15,000 troops under the command of the Duc de Richelieu was encamped at Dunkirk; and once more the French pressed forward their preparations for a descent. The small Jacobite army had indeed achieved an almost miraculous success; but vastly superior forces were now gathering to overwhelm it and, the situation as it was, everything turned on the arrival of reinforcements and supplies from France. If Richelieu landed on these shores with his large army or any considerable part of it, the fortunes of the British Isles would once more be in the melting pot.

For several weeks the fate of the Hanoverian Succession rested uncertain. It was in large measure owing to the naval dispositions pressed by Vernon on a sluggish and reluctant Admiralty that the rising of the 'Forty-five ended as it did. It was Vernon's policy to maintain a strong squadron of heavy ships under Martin in the western entrance of the Channel and a smaller force under his own command in the Downs; and he occasionally detached squadrons under the command of Commodores Smith, Knowles, and Townshend, which were the means of intercepting many vessels carrying troops and ammunition, destined for the Jacobite army in Scotland. He rightly insisted on the importance of having the right kind of ships for each of these squadrons. ' It was always my opinion ', as he later declared, ' that a strong squadron kept at sea to the Westward, and a squadron of smaller ships in the North Seas, were the only secure Guardians to these His Majesty's Kingdoms against Invasions.' The watch kept by our flotillas cruising in the Channel and the narrow seas became increasingly vigilant. The small Dover privateers engaged by Vernon himself were admirably adapted to this kind of service.

' The best of our situation is our strength at sea,' recorded Horace Walpole in the middle of September, ' the Channel is well guarded, and 12 men-of-war more are arrived from Rowley. Vernon, that simple noisy creature, has hit upon a scheme that is of great service; he has laid Folkestone cutters all round the coast, which are continually relieved and bring constant notice of everything that stirs.'

Vernon also succeeded in persuading the Admiralty to maintain a squadron under Byng off the Scottish coast to intercept any French force that was endeavouring to get reinforcements and supplies through to the Jacobite army, with the result that such reinforcements and supplies were largely cut off. Moreover, this squadron also served to disrupt the Jacobite communications across the lochs and firths of the north; and, under Byng's successor, Commodore Smith, it materially assisted the Hanoverian army during the final stages of the campaign. Lastly, the Admiralty agreed to Vernon's proposal to station a mobile light squadron off the East Anglian coast as an additional precaution in the event of a sudden landing at some unexpected point. If the landing took place to the *south* of this station, the mobile squadron was to reinforce Vernon; if to the *north*, it was to join hands with Byng.

Vernon's uncontrollable pen and temper having finally alienated his superiors at the Admiralty, his proffered resignation at Christmas, 1745, was accepted with alacrity; and after a further act of indiscretion on the part of the old Admiral, his name was struck out of the list of flag officers. Nevertheless the dispositions that he had initiated were followed by his successor; and it is significant that, only a few weeks later, the French abandoned all idea of invading England.

Following upon this frustration of their plans and the inconclusive action off Toulon, the French, as has already been said, abandoned the attempt to secure a decision by fleet action and fell back on the strategy of the *guerre de course*. They fitted out several squadrons of battleships to attack Allied communications in the Mediterranean and the Atlantic.

4

The generation following the Peace of Utrecht had witnessed the steady extension of French influence through the Carnatic and the rise of French sea power in Indian seas. In 1742 Dupleix was appointed governor-general of French India and in the next few years developed his plans for building up a great French principality, with Pondicherry as its capital, in southern India. Meanwhile La Bourdonnais, governor of the Isle of France (Mauritius) and Bourbon Isle since 1735, was converting Port Louis into an important naval base with a fine dockyard, well-furnished storehouses, and a fortified harbour. This was the more advantageous in view of the fact that the Coromandel coast, where the principal French settlements were situated, was exposed to the full force of the monsoon; and that on the approach of the north-east monsoon in the autumn French ships were accustomed to run for shelter to Mauritius, just as our own vessels would seek refuge in

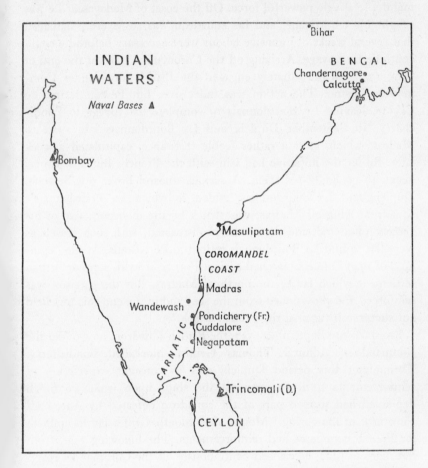

INDIAN
WATERS

Naval Bases ▲

Bombay

°Bihar

BENGAL
Chandernagore●
Calcutta●

●Masulipatam

COROMANDEL
COAST

Madras

Wandewash ●

●Pondicherry (Fr.)
Cuddalore

Negapatam

CARNATIC

Trincomali (D.)

CEYLON

Bombay. There was nothing visionary or impracticable about Dupleix's dreams of empire. So far as the native powers and principalities of the Deccan were concerned his plans were eminently feasible. But in the end they were defeated by one insuperable obstacle. This was the presence in India of the rival British Company and the superiority of British sea power.

When the news of the outbreak of war between France and Great Britain reached La Bourdonnais in the autumn of 1744 he arrested and armed every French Indiaman calling at Port Louis and trained their crews for war. He was later joined by a French ship of the line, so that when finally he sailed for Pondicherry he had under his command a relatively powerful force. Off the coast of Madagascar he was caught by a hurricane, and his squadron was so severely damaged that several weeks of intensive labour were necessary before he could continue his voyage. Arriving off the Coromandel coast at the end of June 1746, he immediately engaged the British force under Commodore Peyton. The action was indecisive; but Peyton retired to Ceylon, leaving La Bourdonnais to complete his voyage to Pondicherry. In September Dupleix and La Bourdonnais laid siege to Madras, which, after a rather feeble resistance, capitulated a week later. So far the initiative had lain with the French. But now things began to go badly for them. A serious quarrel broke out between Dupleix and La Bourdonnais, added to which La Bourdonnais's squadron, lying off Madras, was struck by the monsoon: two of his vessels foundered, and the rest were dismasted; with such vessels as were left to him La Bourdonnais retired to Port Louis. At the beginning of 1747 Dupleix marched against Fort St. David, a minor British settlement which lay to the north of Madras. But the garrison was reinforced and provisioned from the sea; and in the end this fort held out successfully against the French attack.

From May to September 1747, the British squadron, now under the command of Admiral Thomas Griffin, blockaded Pondicherry. Throughout this period Dupleix was in constant expectation of reinforcements from France: but the ships upon which so much depended had formed part of the squadron defeated by Anson off Finisterre in the spring.[1] Month after month Griffin lay in ambush for French commerce and reinforcements. The following year, from February to June, he cruised continuously off the Coromandel coast.

With the rapid increase of our naval strength during 1747 it became possible to send out substantial reinforcements to India. On 4 November Rear-Admiral Boscawen left St. Helens with a squadron of six of the line and four smaller vessels and a fleet of transports and East Indiamen under his convoy. At the end of the following July he

[1] See *infra*, pp. 270–1.

arrived off the Coromandel coast with the strongest squadron that had as yet appeared in Eastern seas. Added to the vessels already stationed on the coast, the total force under his command amounted to thirteen of the line and some twenty smaller craft. Pondicherry was now closely invested by land and sea: but the French garrison, under the able leadership of Dupleix, put up a stubborn resistance; and the imminent approach of the monsoon having obliged Boscawen to retire, the siege was broken up in October. Hostilities were ended by the arrival of news from Europe that a peace treaty had been signed.

On the other side of the globe the British had enjoyed better fortune. Early in 1745 it had been resolved to attempt the capture of Louisbourg, the great French naval base on Cape Breton Island at the entrance to the St. Lawrence, the strongest arsenal in North America, and the ' key to Canada '. This was fundamentally a defensive measure; it was designed to secure our American colonies against hostile attacks from Canada, and also to strengthen British sea power in American waters. In the words of the Governor of Massachusetts, who had initiated and launched this project, the capture of Louisbourg might be expected to ensure ' the preservation of Nova Scotia and gaining Canada as well as Cape Breton which would secure to His Majesty the whole Northern Continent, gaining the whole fishery exclusive of the French, increasing greatly the nursery of seamen for the Royal Navy, and securing the navigation of Great Britain to and from the Northern Colonies as far as Virginia '.

The enterprise was entrusted to a well-organized amphibious expedition which comprised a colonial army from New England and a naval squadron under the command of Commodore Peter Warren. With a careful regard to the time factor, the convoy got under way as soon as the ice cleared. To prevent supplies from reaching the garrison, Warren blockaded the harbour of Louisbourg, while the troops from New England invested the fortress. The turning-point in the siege was a naval engagement fought on 19 May. In a long running action the *Mermaid*, 40, commanded by Captain James Douglas, assisted by a privateer snow, engaged the far more powerful *Vigilant*, 64, which was laden with drafts, guns, and stores for the beleagured garrison. The *Vigilant* had narrowly escaped running into the midst of Warren's squadron in a fog-bank. She then stood to the south-westward under a press of sail, with the *Mermaid* clinging to her starboard quarter and yawing to give her a broadside whenever occasion offered. The attack was skilfully sustained. In the evening the *Superbe* and the *Eltham* came to Douglas' support; and an hour later the *Vigilant* surrendered. Her capture marked the beginning of the end. On 17 June Louisbourg surrendered after a siege which had lasted for six weeks.

The conquest of Cape Breton Island was a convincing illustration of the important contribution made by the American colonies to the sea power of Great Britain. For the successful outcome of the siege of Louisbourg was very largely due to the 4,000 New England fishermen forming the colonial army.

Following the capture of Louisbourg and the withdrawal of the Jacobite army from England, towards the end of 1745, our government resolved to take the offensive in continental America. The general plan of operations was similar to that adopted by Pitt in the following decade: that is, an assault was to be made on Quebec both by way of the St. Lawrence and overland. The decision, however, was taken too hastily, and there was a total lack of the necessary planning and preparation. Admiral Martin, then in command of the Western Squadron, was not given sufficient force to prevent the enemy from getting out of the Biscay ports, with the result that a squadron and convoy commanded by Admiral d'Anville presently put out from Rochefort unobserved.

The First Lord of the Admiralty, Lord Sandwich, completely failing to comprehend the true strategy of the Western Squadron, had erroneously assumed that the function of that force was purely defensive—namely, to hold the entrance to the Channel: had a strong Western Squadron been then on its station and the ocean ports of France vigilantly watched by our cruisers, d'Anville's squadron would scarcely have escaped into the Atlantic in this manner. As it was, Martin, under the impression that the hostile squadron was greatly superior to his own, retired on Ushant to await reinforcements. Anson, on succeeding to the command of the Western Squadron, strongly criticized the system which had permitted d'Anville to get away, and subsequently to return to Brest in safety.

D'Anville's arrival on the other side of the Atlantic broke the blockade of the St. Lawrence, and Quebec was reinforced with men and supplies. Our expedition against Quebec was in consequence first postponed and later abandoned. The defences of Louisbourg, however, had by this time been completed and the place was in little danger from d'Anville. ' I am under very little apprehension ', wrote the Governor, Sir Charles Knowles, on 19 September, ' about their attacking this place while we have the squadron here and can keep them out of the harbour.' It was believed, too, that the long passage made by d'Anville must have resulted in much sickness in his squadron; as, indeed, was the case. ' Could they have arrived timely and brought their people in good health I think they would have succeeded without any great resistance ', Knowles observed, ' . . as, if they had got here in August or before, only five or six guns were mounted to the land [side] and the breach not yet repaired.'

5

By 1746 the Navy had clearly established its ascendancy over the combined fleets of the Bourbon Powers. Great Britain was able to maintain strong squadrons both in the Atlantic and in the Mediterranean. It at last became possible for her to take the offensive. The strategical and tactical weaknesses that had been manifest at an earlier period were now effectually remedied.

As Richmond has declared, ' A navy, however well conducted, officered and manned, can do nothing in the shadow of inefficient strategical direction; the best manned fleet will be impotent if its tactical government embodies a wrong doctrine.'[1] It had been for lack of a sound strategical conception that, until the later years of the war, the British possessions in North America and the West Indies had been inadequately covered and the French had been able to carry on their trade without serious interference. Again and again hostile convoys had crossed the ocean unimpeded. France could as yet reinforce her land and sea forces operating in the colonial theatres of the war; at the same time raw materials were still reaching her factories at home and her manufactures could still find markets. Hitherto the most serious deficiency of British naval dispositions had been the failure to provide for a squadron in the soundings strong enough to deal with the main forces of the enemy in the Atlantic.

' Look back to the latter end of the Reign of Queen Anne ', Vernon had said in 1745, ' when we had well-conducted Western Squadrons

[1] *The Navy in the War of 1739-1748*, I, xi.

under the direction of experienced Admirals, with a proper latitude in their orders, and it will be found that the Trade was well protected by them, the enemy's privateers suppressed, and some detached to proper stations that distressed the enemy's trade at the same time; and were in the best stations with the Main Body, or protecting all these Kingdoms from invasions.'[1]

In the War of Jenkins' Ear Norris had urged this strategy upon the government, but without success; it had been revived, however, by Vernon; and from 1746 onwards the Western Squadron, which was at first concerned merely with the protection of British trade and the interception of hostile convoys, was gradually reorganized by Anson as the keystone of our naval strategy.

Appointed to command the Western Squadron in succession to Martin in August 1746, Anson had been given a far stronger force—seventeen sail of the line, six 50s, four frigates, and two sloops—and, what was equally important, far greater freedom to dispose it. Its functions were both defensive and offensive. It was strong enough to face any fleet, division, or convoy sent out by the enemy: it could hold the entrance of the Channel against a hostile fleet, and detach a flying squadron to deal with any special task that the situation demanded. Further, it provided protection for British merchantmen outward or homeward bound in the focal area, and served as a decisive factor in the attack on the enemy's trade.

In the later stages of the struggle, as the naval strength of the Bourbon Powers steadily declined, it became possible to reduce our Mediterranean fleet and to strengthen that in the Western Approaches. At the same time more ships were gradually being fitted out. When, towards the close of 1747, the Western Squadron was fully established and maintained on its station by a system of reliefs, the naval superiority of Great Britain over her opponents became increasingly pronounced.

The efficacy of these improved dispositions was revealed in the decisive actions of May and October 1747. Early in the year it had become known at the Admiralty that the French were fitting out expeditions to India and North America, and preparations were made to intercept them. In April Anson, with Rear-Admiral Peter Warren as his second-in-command, cruised off Cape Finisterre, with fourteen ships of the line, diligently exercising his squadron. It was during these

[1] Vernon, *Some Seasonable Advice from an Honest Sailor* (1746).

WESTERN
APPROACHES

60°

15°   10°   5°   0°

Færoe Is.

Shetland Is.

Orkney Is.

• Rockall

N O R T H

Glasgow

55°

S E A

O C E A N

IRISH
SEA

Slyne Hd.

Dublin   Liverpool

Cork

Kinsale St. George's
C. Clear   Channel   Bristol   London

50°

Plymouth   Portsmouth
Falmouth   Downs
Land's End   Torbay   CHANNEL   Calais
Isles of Scilly Lizard Start Pt.   Boulogne
S O U N D I N G S   ENGLISH Cherbourg
Channel Is.   Havre

A T L A N T I C

Ushant I. Brest   St. Malo   Paris

Lorient
I. de Groix Quiberon Bay
Belleisle   R. Loire

B A Y

O F   I. de Rhé   Rochefort

45°

B I S C A Y   Bordeaux

C. Ortegal

C. Finisterre   Ferrol

Miles

Vigo   0   100   200   300

269

weeks that, continuing the work done by Vernon, he introduced important reforms in tactics. The care taken by Anson to practise his captains in forming line of battle, bearing down together, and the evolutions of the attack, won the warm approval of his subordinate. ' Sir, how necessary 'tis to exercise the fleet!' Warren wrote to Anson that spring. ' 'Tis pretty difficult to keep a good line close by the wind; and I think you next please to exercise the fleet in separate divisions, and abreast, the line should be formed at a distance one division to windward of the other, as you shall judge proper, and the windward one to go down on the leeward in order of battle so near as you would have them engage an enemy.' Anson had disposed his cruisers in this campaign in lines which made it virtually impossible for the French to evade him.

On the morning of 3 May, with the wind at N.N.E., moderate and fair weather, the French fleet was at last sighted, comprising nine sail of the line under Admiral de la Jonquière. Anson formed his ships in line of battle and steered for the enemy's centre; whereupon the French admiral, who had covered his convoy up to the last moment, broke his line and bore away; ' the enemy ', observed Captain Boscawen of the *Namur*, ' crowding all the sail they could set ' to the west-south-westward. Anson, hauling down the signal for the line and hoisting that for the general chase, then shook out his reefs and made sail. Seeing it was the intention of the French to escape, if possible, under cover of the night, he ordered each of his leading ships to attack the first enemy ship which it could reach, and, having crippled her, to press on in pursuit of the enemy ships ahead, leaving her to be finished off by the other British ships coming up from astern.

The *Centurion*, Captain Peter Denis, having got up with the rear-most ships of the enemy at about four o'clock, boldly engaged the *Sérieux* and *Invincible*. ' The *Namur*, *Defiance*, and *Windsor* being the headmost ships,' wrote Anson in his dispatch, ' soon enter'd into the action, and after having disabled these ships in such a manner that the ships astern must come up with them, they made sail ahead to prevent the van of the enemy making an escape, as did also several other ships of the fleet.' Late in the afternoon the remainder of the British squadron began to come up. ' The *Yarmouth* and *Devonshire* having got up and engaged the enemy,' Anson went on, ' and the *Prince George* [his flagship] being near the *Invincible* & going to fire into her, all the ships in the enemy's rear struck their colours betwixt six and seven o'clock, as did all those that were in the line, before night.' The prizes totalled six men-of-war and several Indiamen.

'To do justice to the French officers', Anson observed, 'they did their duty well, and lost their ships with honour; scarce any of them striking their colours, till their ships were dismasted.' He attributed Jonquière's defeat in large measure to the superiority of British gunnery and discipline. 'The fire on our side was much greater,' Anson declared, 'and more regular than theirs; and it is very evident our shott were better placed.' Two of the prizes, the *Sérieux* and the *Diamant*, were so badly damaged that they were with great difficulty kept from sinking. The defence, however, was sufficiently strong to enable the greater part of the convoy to escape.

Anson's victory of 3 May prevented the succour so badly needed from reaching the French colonies. It was the first decisive naval success of the war. Tactically, it marked an important development of the 'chase' technique, and paved the way for the great decisive victories of the following decade. On the 16th Anson arrived in St. Helen's with his prizes. He was rewarded with a peerage; and Warren was made a K.B. Anson now returned to the Admiralty, leaving Warren in command of the Western Squadron.

In the meantime, a small force under Captain Fox, cruising in the Western Approaches, on 20 June sighted a large French convoy under M. de la Motte homeward-bound from San Domingo; and in the course of the next two days, in a south-westerly gale, succeeded in taking thirteen of these merchantmen—the great majority, however, reached port in safety.

Later in the summer Warren went down with the scurvy, and Rear-Admiral Hawke succeeded to the command. About the same time intelligence reached London that a large armament was preparing at Brest, which our Admiralty was determined to intercept. Warren recommended that everything should be done to strengthen Hawke, who on 8 September received orders ' to cruise with the said squadron or the major part thereof between Ushant and Cape Finisterre, keeping 20 leagues to the westward of each cape, and to make the land of the former every 14 days '. Here, despite the spread of sickness, stinking beer, and the fact that a number of his ships badly needed cleaning, Hawke contrived to keep together fourteen sail; and on 12 October he was able to assure the Admiralty that ' the situation we are now in seems very well calculated for intercepting both the Eastward and homeward-bound trade of the enemy. I shall do everything in my power to keep the ships out with me as long as possible, and intend staying out myself while I can keep any number of them together.'

At daybreak on the 14th, with the wind south-easterly and fair weather, Hawke's squadron was somewhat scattered when his lookouts suddenly sighted strange sails to the south-westward. Soon the mastheads of an immense fleet rose above the horizon: it was the long-awaited West India convoy, escorted by Admiral de l'Étanduère with eight of the line and a 60-gun East Indiaman. Reefs were quickly shaken out, as Hawke signalled a general chase. There was a six-knot breeze blowing, the wind backing to S.S.E., and the sky clouding over; and his squadron rapidly overhauled the enemy. When within four miles of the French escorts, Hawke made the signal for the line of battle. In order to give the convoy an opportunity to disperse, Étanduère lay-to for a while and then attempted to escape likewise: upon which Hawke discarded the line of battle and signalled general chase. As he related in his dispatch, ' Soon after I perceived the enemy's convoy to crowd away with all the sail they could set, while their ships of war were endeavouring to form in a line astern of them, and hauled near the wind, under their topsails and foresails, and some with topgallant-sails set. Finding we lost time in forming our line, while the enemy was standing away from us, at 11 made the signal for the whole squadron to chase.'

In the second battle off Finisterre much the same method of attack was employed as in the earlier action. Each of Hawke's leading ships engaged whichever ship of Étanduère's she first overhauled; and then, as a fresh ship came up from astern, stood up the enemy line to engage the next ahead. At 11.30, according to the log of the *Lion*, ' began to engage enemy being the headmost ship: received and returned the fire of the whole squadron '. Close astern of the *Lion* came the *Princess Louisa*. As soon as the other British ships began to come up, the *Princess Louisa* made sail and, like the *Lion*, passed up the enemy line; tacked and stood to windward, and presently stationed herself on the weather bow of Étanduère's leading ship, the *Terrible*. ' The enemy having the weather-gage of us,' Hawke observed, ' and a smart and constant fire being kept on both sides, the smoke prevented my seeing the number of the enemy, or what happened on either side for some time. In passing on to the first ship we could get near, we received many fires at a distance, till we came close to the *Severn* of 50 guns, which we soon silenced, and left to be taken up by the frigates astern.' After two hours of desperate fighting the resistance of the French rear began to slacken. The manner in which several of Étanduère's ships stood up to the lengthening odds was as admirable as anything in the history of the French navy. It was not until half-past three when, dismasted and their decks piled with dead and wounded, having received the fire of nearly the whole of the British squadron, the *Neptune* and *Monarque* finally struck their colours. While Hawke was engaging the enemy flagship, the *Tonnant*, 80, the lower-deck guns of his own flagship, the *Devonshire*, carried away their breechings, with the result that ' the guns flew fore and aft, which obliged us to shoot ahead.' Later he engaged successively the *Trident*, 64, and the *Terrible*, 74, and compelled both these ships to strike. ' As the enemy's ships were very large ', declared Hawke, ' except the *Severn*, they took a great deal of drubbing, and lost all their masts, excepting two, who had their foremasts left.' By about five o'clock, according to the captain of the *Defiance*, ' the French Admiral had bore away before the wind in a very shattered condition, having lost his main and mizen topmasts.' The result of the action was that before nightfall every French warship except the flagship and her second had struck;[1] but, under cover of darkness, the convoy escaped. The *Tonnant*, which a few hours earlier had been in the thick of the fighting, got away in the night with the assistance of the *Intrépide*.

' Having observed that six of the enemy's ships had struck, and it being very dark, and our own ships dispersed, I thought it best to bring-to for that night. . . . As to the French convoys escaping,' Hawke concluded, ' it was not possible for me to detach any ship after them at first, or during the action, except the frigates, and that I thought would have been imprudent, as I observed several large ships of war among them.' Next morning he discovered that his ships were in ' so shattered a condition ' that he was still unable to pursue them. However, by his promptitude in dispatching the *Weazle* sloop to the Leeward Islands with warning of their approach, Hawke also ensured the capture of the greater part of the convoy.

---

[1] Three 74s, two 64s, and a 50.

The destruction of Étanduère's squadron on 14 October was a far more considerable achievement than that of Jonquière's in the spring; for the former was stronger and more homogeneous. As Hawke had observed in his dispatch, Étanduère's ships 'took a great deal of drubbing'. To Captain Pocock's 'steady and systematic cruising' on his post was due the successful mopping-up of so many of the enemy merchantmen as they dropped in on the Leeward Islands. It was one of the most serious reverses which French commerce had sustained during the war; and the capture of 900 prime seamen was an even heavier blow to French shipping, especially to the privateers fitting out in Martinique. Last but not least, the experience gained by Hawke in this second action off Finisterre was an invaluable preparation for his operations in the next war and the crowning triumph of 1759.

The effect of these two victories was both to safeguard our overseas possessions from attack and to speed up the destruction of the enemy's trade. The loss of their two squadrons made it extremely difficult for the French to find escort vessels for their convoys. At the same time the British dockyards laboured hard throughout the winter, under Anson's vigorous supervision, to refit the Western Squadron for the campaign of 1748.

In December 1747 Warren urged the Admiralty to fit out two strong divisions under one command, the first to cruise in the Bay and the second off Cadiz. By this means it became possible next year to operate against the enemy's commerce on the two principal trade-routes to France and Spain. The squadron in the Bay was under the command of Admiral Warren, and Hawke commanded the division off Cadiz.

6

In the opening phase of the war the Spaniards had concentrated their chief energies on the attack on trade. In the vital area of the Channel Soundings there were not nearly enough ships at this stage to protect British commerce; and both here and elsewhere serious losses were sustained through the activities of the Spanish privateers. Soon after the failure of their invasion project, the French also had recourse to the *guerre de course*. In reply to our merchants' continual complaints of lack of protection, the Admiralty was obliged to remind the government that it was no easy matter to get the merchantmen to obey the commanders of convoys, when convoys were in fact provided.

> Nothing is more frequent than the complaints from the commanders of convoys of the obstinacy or folly of several masters of merchant ships who refuse to obey their signals or directions for the better keeping company together; but disregarding all order and government desert their convoys from impatience of getting sooner into Port.

And the memorandum continued:

> If the trade could be brought under regulation, as was practised in the late wars, when those concerned in the same branches of commerce advised together, and conformed to the rules agreed upon between them and the Government, for sending out their ships at times settled and fixed for the departure of their respective convoys, fewer cruisers would have sufficed for all the purposes of our foreign trade, than have been employed in this war on that service; but the greatest part of our trade is at present under no sort of order or method, which we presume proceeds from the great increase of the practice of insuring ships, beyond what was known formerly.[1]

Despite these difficulties, the war of 1739–48 saw the further development of the convoy system. The importance attached to the proper protection of our shipping was reflected in the orders given to the convoy commanders, who were instructed to make the safety of the merchantmen they were escorting their first and principal care; thus they were strictly forbidden to chase out of sight of their convoys, but were to be ' watchful in defending them from any Attack or Surprize '; they were to deliver to ' all the masters of merchantmen ... printed books of instructions ', and were ' strictly forbid to receive any Money, or other Gratification ', from any masters of vessels under their convoy. Though Great Britain lost more than three thousand ships in the war (which was nearly as many, in fact, as those lost by the Bourbon Powers), these figures represented a far smaller proportion of her total tonnage.

While the mercantile shipping of Great Britain was effectually protected, that of the enemy was vigorously assailed. Owing to the victories of Anson and Hawke in 1747, the activities of Pocock in the West Indies, the blockade of the Coromandel coast by Griffin, and the progressive improvement, in these last years of the war, in British

---

[1] *The Navy in the War of 1739–1748*, I, pp. 183–4.

naval dispositions and administration, the enemy's convoys were now exposed to continual attack, and his shipping was driven off the seas.[1] The consequence was that, whereas British imports and exports had actually increased since the beginning of the war, the once flourishing seaborne trade of France was virtually ruined. Her manufactories were starved of the raw materials needed for production, and her financial position was well-nigh desperate. Though victorious on the Continent she was faced with the destruction of her industry and commerce and the probable loss of her overseas possessions. Through the capture of Louisbourg she had lost the Newfoundland fisheries; and her West Indian islands were in such distress for lack of food that they could not have held out much longer when peace was signed in 1748.

In the attack on enemy commerce during the war of 1739–48 the Navy was seriously embarrassed by the concessions made under the Anglo-Dutch treaty of 1674. For their part the British developed the argument that a neutral must not in time of war engage in any trade closed to him in peace (e.g., Spain's trade with her American colonies), while the Dutch found strong support for their claim of *Free ships, free goods* in the treaty previously mentioned. In 1746 the Admiralty had occasion to complain of the Dutch ' covering the seas with their ships carrying supplies of provisions and naval stores to our enemies, and furnishing them with every destructive means of ruining our commerce, and even endangering our common safety '; and next year the Earl of Chesterfield similarly complained of the ' great inconveniences which we have long so sensibly experienced from the latitude given to the Dutch by the 8th article of the Marine Treaty '. It is to be noted that though neutrals were in this war prevented from trading with Spain, no such veto was applied to neutrals trading with France.

Though finally triumphant at sea Great Britain was obliged to consent to terms of peace which left the principal causes of dispute in America and India still undecided. For the sea power of Great Britain was offset by the land power of France, with the result that

---

[1] ' Though there was no blockade in the sense it is now understood there was so great a stoppage of French trade, once the fighting fleet was disabled by two very complete victories in 1747, that the results were almost equivalent to those of blockade. For though neutrals could reach French ports, there were no neutrals of sufficient maritime importance to assist her. Captures at sea raised insurance rates to such a height—35 per cent. is quoted—that trade could not stand it and died ' (H. W. Richmond, *Imperial Defence and Capture at Sea*, 1932, p. 213).

the war ended in something like stalemate. In June 1746 the great city of Antwerp had been lost to the enemy. Not only was practically the whole of what is now Belgium in hostile hands, but Dutch Brabant also was overrun by the French, and the strong fortress of Bergen-op-Zoom had been taken; while Maestricht (the fall of which would have laid the United Provinces open to attack from the rear) was in imminent danger of capture by Marshal Saxe. Great Britain, moreover, had reached the limit of her resources. Since the outbreak of the war the National Debt had increased from £46 millions to £77½ millions. ' Money ', it was said, ' was never so scarce in the city, and cannot be had at twelve per cent.' The financial plight of our ally Holland was even worse.

Louisbourg had to be handed back to France in order to secure the restitution of the Austrian Netherlands and Madras; and as for the original cause of the war with Spain, namely, the right of search by *guarda-costas* on the South American coast, it was not so much as mentioned in the treaty. In these circumstances the peace signed at Aix-la-Chapelle in April 1748 held out small prospect of a lasting settlement.

X

The Seven Years War

I

The Peace of Aix-la-Chapelle, like the Treaty of Ryswick half a century earlier, proved no more than a breathing-space consequent upon the mutual exhaustion of the belligerents. The real matters at issue between Great Britain and France were, after all, not European, but colonial; and these remained outstanding. In the West Indies, in India, and, above all, in North America there was a clash of national interests which was certain, sooner or later, to lead to war. The future of four disputed West Indian islands—St. Lucia, Dominica, St. Vincent, and Tobago—was still uncertain. In India the French, under the leadership of the brilliant Dupleix, had resumed the offensive. It was their intention to establish a vast French empire in the south and, with the aid of native allies, to eject the rival British Company. On the other side of the world also the French were advancing. From their first discovery of the Mississippi they had aimed at linking Canada with the Mississippi delta by a continuous zone traversed by this great waterway and its effluents, the Ohio and Allegheny. Under the aegis of the Marquis Duquesne they began to occupy the Ohio country in strength and to erect forts. At the same time the British colonies on the Atlantic coast were expanding westward into the interior. Shortly after the Peace of Aix-la-Chapelle, the British Ohio Company was formed. British and French traders and settlers were rapidly converging on the Ohio.

Within a few years of the cessation of hostilities in Europe the smouldering antagonism between the two races in North America had flared up into something like regular warfare. Things were brought to a head by a frontier skirmish, fought by a colonial regiment led by Colonel George Washington, in which the British were disastrously repulsed. It was a small enough affair in all conscience: but British pride and prestige were involved. ' We begin to think ', Horace Walpole wrote on 6 October 1754, ' that the world may be roused again, and that an East Indian war and a West Indian war may beget such a thing as an European war.' In the same year each government

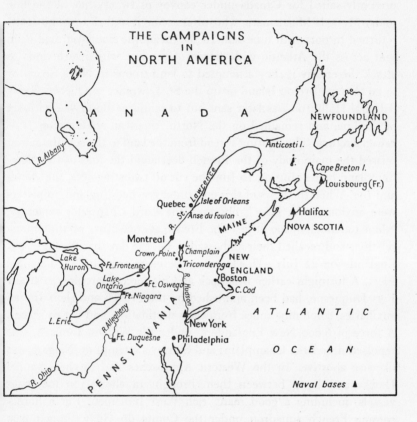

THE CAMPAIGNS
IN
NORTH AMERICA

reinforced its colonial troops contending for the possession of the Ohio valley. Early in 1755 the British Cabinet sent out two regiments of regulars to form part of the forces which General Braddock was to lead against the French on the Ohio.

The Navy was put on a war footing: on 12 February 1755 Hawke hoisted his flag in the *Terrible* at Spithead, and two days later thirty-five of the line were commissioned; bounties were offered for seamen and able-bodied landsmen, and a hot press swept the streets of each of the principal ports. Nevertheless, there was no attempt to blockade the enemy's coast; and between January and March 1755 no less than three squadrons got away from Brest to the West Indies or Canada. On hearing of Braddock's expedition, the French at once assembled a force of 3,000 regulars at Brest and Rochefort, which presently sailed for Canada under convoy of twenty-five of the line under M. de la Macnamara, who, after seeing it well clear of the coast, returned to port with nine sail. In the meantime Boscawen had been sent across the Atlantic with eleven of the line with instructions to attack the enemy if they attempted to land troops in Nova Scotia or to go to Cape Breton Island or up the St. Lawrence to Quebec. Rear-Admiral Holburne was later sent out to reinforce Boscawen with six of the line, and remained on the North American station after Boscawen's return. The fighting spread from the land to the sea. Boscawen missed the main body of the French fleet amid the fogs of the Newfoundland banks: but on 10 June he cut off two stragglers, the *Alcide* and *Lys*. When the news of this encounter reached England, ministers were anxious. ' We have ', observed the Lord Chancellor sapiently, ' done too much or too little.' The French at once broke off diplomatic relations and recalled their ambassador. On the day that the latter left England—on 22 July—Hawke was ordered to sea with the Channel Fleet. A fortnight earlier Braddock and his force, marching to attack Fort Duquesne, had been ambushed by the French and their Indian auxiliaries, some nine miles from their destination, and cut to pieces. A force of 6,000 New Englanders, under Sir William Johnson, was repulsed near Lake Champlain; and Shirley's attempt on Niagara was likewise abortive. In the Western Approaches and in the Channel Hawke and Byng between them brought in about 300 merchant vessels, including a good many rich West Indiamen. But a home-coming French squadron under the Comte du Guay slipped past Hawke and got safely into Brest; and the latter's cruise was brought to a premature end by the spread of sickness which wrought havoc on the crowded mess-decks. ' Had I staid out a week longer ', Hawke informed the Admiralty, ' there would not have been men enough to have worked the large ships; they fell down so fast.' On the other side of the Atlantic M. de la Motte, after disembarking his reinforcements, got away again from Louisbourg through a storm which dispersed and seriously damaged Holburne's blockading squadron. In the summer of 1756 war was formally declared between Great Britain and France.

The Seven Years War opened badly for Great Britain with a series of reverses in North America, a Franco-Austrian alliance, and a threatened invasion of England. Early in April 1756 the Marquis de Montcalm, the new commander-in-chief in Canada, slipped out of Brest past Hawke and crossed the Atlantic with six of the line and about 1,000 troops. He was accompanied by de Lévis, his second-in-command, and Bougainville, his aide-de-camp. Montcalm arrived in Canada about the middle of May and at once began to reorganize the colony's defences. Throughout the summer the French continued to dispatch troops in single ships to Canada. Following on the destruction of Braddock's army, their Indian allies swept over the frontier, and ravaged, burnt, and slaughtered in Pennsylvania, Maryland, and Virginia, while Montcalm captured Oswego, the British station on Lake Ontario. With Oswego was lost its port and its flotilla—whereupon the control of the Great Lakes passed to France. In August the fateful compact was signed between Maria Theresa and Louis XV which precipitated the war. Some 50,000 troops were encamped on the northern coast of France under Marshal Belleisle, and cannon and transports assembled for the descent. The squadrons at Brest and Rochefort were to combine and come round into the Channel to cover the passage of the French army, and at the same time feints were to be made at Scotland and Ireland. Further to confuse and disperse the British defence, an expedition was fitted out against Minorca.

The British naval dispositions, however, made it impossible for the enemy to secure even a temporary command of the Channel. The experience of the previous war—particularly the campaign of 1747—had demonstrated the crucial importance of the Western Squadron. The enemy's transports could not get out until our flotilla forces had been driven off. The French battleships lying in Brest and Rochefort were continually watched by our cruisers; and the Western Squadron, based on Portsmouth and Plymouth, effectually prevented a hostile concentration in the Channel. Belleisle's invasion project was for the present abandoned.

Meanwhile, under cover of demonstrations in the Channel, the French had fitted out at Toulon a squadron of twelve of the line which, under the command of Admiral de la Galissonière, convoyed a fleet of transports, with 15,000 troops on board, to Minorca. A week later this force was safely disembarked at the western end of the island while Galissonière blockaded Port Mahon.

For the disaster which followed Anson's faulty distribution of our forces is largely to blame. The situation was in any case difficult and uncertain. The naval resources of Great Britain were strained to the utmost during those critical spring weeks by the necessity of securing the Western Approaches and of protecting the trade-routes. ' The truth was ', Walpole declared, ' the clamours of the merchants, sometimes reasonable, always self-interested, terrified the Duke of Newcastle; and while to prevent their outcries in the city of London he minced the navy of England into cruisers and convoys, every other service was neglected.' Early in 1756 Anson had ordered Osborne, who with thirteen of the line had been escorting a convoy to the southward, to return home instead of proceeding to the Mediterranean; had dispatched a battle squadron under Hawke to attack the enemy's trade; and had, moreover, twice strengthened Boscawen's fleet off Brest when it was already superior to the hostile force he was watching. In order to keep as many vessels as possible in home waters, he failed to send sufficient reinforcements to the Mediterranean or to send them there in time.

Galissonière's expedition was already on the point of sailing when Rear-Admiral John Byng, on 5 April 1756, left England with a force of only ten of the line. He arrived off Minorca on 19 May, whereupon Galissonière stood out to meet him and to cover the entrance to the harbour. Action was joined on the 21st; and in a confused, indecisive engagement the French had rather the better of it. Soon after noon a sudden shift of the wind had given Byng the weather-gauge and, while the French line was in momentary confusion, an opportunity to bear down and attack the enemy. But Byng, with his mind full of the action off Toulon in 1744 and its sequel, was determined to carry down his whole fleet together, or not at all. ' You would not have me, as admiral of the fleet, run down as if I were going to engage a single ship', he observed to his flag-captain. ' It was Mr. Mathews's misfortune to be prejudiced by not carrying down his force together, which I shall endeavour to avoid.' He accordingly held on in line ahead, while the enemy re-formed his line. In the course of the engagement the British van, under Byng, was separated from the rear, under

Temple West, and bore the brunt of the fighting. Late in the afternoon the action ceased and was not renewed. ' There appeared to me no further possibility ', Byng afterwards declared, ' of bringing the enemy to action again, as they declined it, without I had a sufficient force and superiority to enable me to make the general signal to chase.'

It was not, in fact, the action of the 21st, but Byng's proceedings following the action, which eventually wrought his ruin. Had he resolutely pursued a defensive strategy in waters of which he had had long experience,[1] the menace of a fleet ' in being ' must have interrupted the passage of the reinforcements and supplies on which the hostile forces in Minorca depended. Instead of which he retired, after a council of war, to Gibraltar. On the news of Byng's retreat becoming known to the enemy in Minorca, it at first could scarcely be believed by them. Throughout the month following the sea was open to the French; and on 28 June the small garrison besieged in Port Mahon surrendered.

The British public was roused to fury at the news. ' Our disgrace in the Mediterranean has so filled my spirits that I could not sleep all night,' Boscawen informed his wife a few weeks later. ' What shall we come to?' ' The clamour is extreme,' Walpole wrote in July, ' we are humbled, disgraced, angry.' ' Never ', recorded Thomas Turner, a Sussex shopkeeper, in his diary, ' did the English nation suffer a greater blot.' The City was well aware of the importance of Port Mahon as a naval base. The support of the merchants was indispensable to the government; this was now in jeopardy; already, in fact, there were threats of denying supplies unless an example were made of ' the authors of our late losses '.

The prime minister, the Duke of Newcastle, alarmed at the frantic chorus of denunciation, declared that Anson must order ' the immediate trial and condemnation of Byng, if, as I think, there can be no doubt he deserves it.' Sir Edward Hawke was at once sent out to supersede Byng; and the unfortunate Admiral was brought home under close arrest. On his arrival at Portsmouth an enraged crowd was with difficulty restrained from tearing him limb from limb. With popular excitement rising to fever heat throughout the kingdom, the ministry's one object was to divert the coming storm from their own heads. Byng was burnt in effigy in almost every town and village in England;

[1] Byng had commanded on the Mediterranean station in the late war.

the merchants clamoured for his execution; papers were posted up on the Exchange with the words, ' Shoot Byng, or take care of your King '; Westminster resounded with the ' song of a hundred ballad-singers, the burthen of which was " to the block with Newcastle, and the yard-arm with Byng " ' ; the mob was encouraged to enact mock trials of the Admiral in London and certain sea-ports, and ' to haul along a log of wood in a lace coat ', and petitions poured in from all sides urging his immediate condemnation. Finally, after several months' imprisonment in Greenwich Hospital, Byng was court-martialled, found guilty of neglect of duty, sentenced to death under the new 12th Article of War, and executed on the quarter-deck of the flagship *Monarque* in Portsmouth Harbour.

In the Mediterranean, Hawke's instructions were to protect Gibraltar, cover British commerce, destroy the enemy's privateers, and clean and refit his ships in Gibraltar or some Sardinian port. Though superior in numbers to the British, the French squadron did not venture out of Toulon. In January 1757 Hawke returned to England.

During the opening phase of the war, all was weakness and confusion. The Duke of Newcastle was an experienced party manager, but one wholly unfitted to conduct a war. Despite George II's dislike of Pitt, he was obliged by the pressure of events to admit him to office in the late autumn of 1756, with the Duke of Devonshire as the titular head of the government. During his first short-lived ministry (10 November 1756 – 6 April 1757) Pitt began to develop his great strategic designs of the future: but as yet his personal following in the House of Commons was small, and he was severely handicapped by the distrust of the great Whig families and the implacable hostility of the Court. On Pitt's dismissal by the King in the following spring it was speedily apparent that neither Newcastle nor anyone else could form a ministry without him; and for nearly three months the ship of state drifted helplessly in the trough without a helmsman.

The year 1757 looked like being no better than 1756. The truth was that the Navy had by no means established the ascendancy over the Western Approaches that it had enjoyed ten years earlier in the previous war. Reinforcements and supplies still continued to reach the French possessions overseas. British seaborne trade suffered severely; for the seas swarmed with enemy privateers, and there were not enough of our cruisers to cope with them. The maritime neutrals were becoming increasingly restive at the restraints on their trade resulting from the belligerent rights claimed and enforced by Great Britain.

On land also things went badly for Great Britain. With the fate of Prussia—our one European ally—was linked that of George II's Electorate of Hanover; Austria, France, Russia, and Sweden had now combined against Frederick the Great, whose army had suffered appalling losses and had been heavily defeated at Kollin. The Duke of Cumberland was soundly beaten by the Duc d'Estrées at Hastenbeck and the French were fast overrunning Westphalia, Hesse, and Hanover. On 2 July they had captured Emden, thereby jeopardizing Cumberland's communications with England. In the meantime a formidable French army threatened to descend on this country from Ostend and Nieuport. In India, the Nawab of Bengal had captured the British stronghold of Fort William at Calcutta and thrown his prisoners into the Black Hole.

In North America, our attempt to seize Louisbourg had miscarried; and Fort William Henry on Lake George had surrendered to Montcalm. After four years of almost uninterrupted failure and defeat the British cause seemed nearly desperate. Notwithstanding that they outnumbered the French ten to one, our colonists, divided as they were by sectional interests and jealousies, were quite unable to make headway against them. The French acted promptly and decisively while the British deliberated and postponed. Moreover, the enemy enjoyed all the advantage of position. Between Canada and the nearest British military headquarters lay a vast wilderness of forest, for the most part impenetrable to an army. Louisbourg firmly secured the entrance to the St. Lawrence. Quebec, the citadel of the whole hostile system, was so strong as to appear virtually unassailable. The Ohio and the approaches to Canada were still held by the French. Along the frontier the Indians were rapidly deserting a losing cause and going over to the enemy.

At this stage of the struggle perhaps the best that could be hoped for was some sort of stalemate such as that which had brought the Austrian Succession war to a close. At worst this country might even be forced to accept an unfavourable peace. If the government itself had little confidence in the outcome of the war, it was scarcely to be wondered at that a good many others shared these misgivings.

' Could any object of attack ', Newcastle had inquired in dejection earlier in the year, ' either in the Mediterranean, the West Indies or North America be agreed upon, that would keep up people's spirits and divert their resentment?' ' It is time for England to slip her own cables ', wrote Walpole in the autumn, ' and float away into some unknown ocean.' About the same time Lord Chesterfield observed: ' This winter, I take for granted, must produce a peace, of some kind or another; a bad one for us, no doubt, and yet perhaps better than we shall get the year after.'

2

The situation demanded a leader, and the nation's call was for Pitt. The pressure of popular opinion finally became too strong to be resisted; and after prolonged negotiations by the Earl of Hardwicke there was formed on 29 June 1757 the Pitt–Newcastle ministry, which, in its four years of power, won the war. The combination was amazingly successful. ' The Duke of Newcastle and Mr. Pitt ', Lord Chesterfield observed, ' jog on like man and wife; that is, seldom agreeing, often quarrelling; but by mutual interest upon the whole, not parting.' Or, as Horace Walpole declared, ' Pitt *does* everything, the Duke of Newcastle gives everything. As long as they can agree in this partition they may do what they will.' Newcastle, First Lord of the Treasury and nominal head of the government, managed Parliament and finance, whilst Pitt, Principal Secretary of State, with virtual control of the Navy, Army, and foreign affairs, directed the war. Anson (Hardwicke's son-in-law)—one of the greatest administrators and strategists in our history—became, for the second time, First Lord in the new ministry, and Pitt's trusted adviser in sea affairs. Hardwicke himself sat in the Cabinet, though he held no office.

Relations between George II and Pitt, which at the outset had been strained, gradually improved. Under the inspired direction of the Great Commoner the British war effort was given a cohesion and driving-force which it had hitherto lacked. ' I am sure I can save this country, and nobody else can,' had been Pitt's memorable words when entering on his second term of office. The next few years saw this claim triumphantly justified. It was said that no man ever went into his closet ' who did not feel himself, if possible, braver at his return than when he went in.' ' Your country ', observed Frederick II to the British minister in Berlin, ' has been long in labour, and has suffered much, but at last she has produced a man.' Pitt made use of the wide powers belonging to a Secretary of State in order to secure for himself the personal supervision of naval and military operations. Under his so-called ' system ' admirals and generals frequently received their orders direct from the minister himself. ' Mr. Pitt's spirit, vigour, and perseverance ', Grafton declared in his autobiography, ' seemed to instil itself into the hearts of every individual, as well as those employed in both services, in a manner more than natural, and this in every quarter of the globe. The consequences were security at home, and as complete success by sea and land as Britain has to boast.'

It was Pitt's policy to contain the French in Europe, on land, by the Prussian and Hanoverian armies, and, at sea, by the blockading fleets which formed a covering force for our main offensive in North America. These dispositions served to secure the British Isles against invasion and also to prevent reinforcements from reaching the hard-pressed French settlements across the ocean. The result was that Great Britain, with an army small in comparison with those of other States, was able successfully to protect her own shores and to strike hard at the territories and trade of her enemy beyond the sea. For the supreme direction of our fleets and armies was now in the hands of a master of world strategy; and within a few months of Pitt's accession to office, France—for all her formidable military strength—found herself powerless to succour the vital North American front. At Louisbourg, Quebec, and Montreal successively the enemy were confronted with superior forces. The determining factor in the struggle for Canada was, after all, the control of sea-communications; and the French fleets, penned in their ports by Anson's blockading squadrons, had ceased to dispute the command of the sea.

When Pitt began his second term of office the war in Germany was rapidly approaching a crisis. It seemed that Frederick II must finally succumb to the united power of Austria, France, and Russia. In the eyes of Pitt, the continental side of the war was wholly subsidiary. Nevertheless, the French attack must be held if Prussia were not to be overwhelmed; and he accordingly supported Frederick II first with subsidies and later also with troops, to enable him to hold out against his many enemies and so to keep the French tied down in Europe, while Great Britain concentrated on the naval war and the North American offensive.

In early November the situation improved. Marching swiftly westwards into Saxony, Frederick II took the French under the Prince de Soubise by surprise, and on 5 November decisively defeated them at Rossbach. He thereupon hastened back to Silesia, and overthrew a much superior Austrian army under Marshal Daun at Leuthen; as a result of which Silesia was reconquered by the Prussians. Most of Hanover was now recovered by Prince Ferdinand of Brunswick. Next spring, while Ferdinand held the French in check on his western front, Frederick II turned on the Russians, who had already penetrated deep into his realm, and inflicted a bloody defeat upon them at Zorndorf near Frankfort-on-Oder. 'In the short space of three quarters of a year', observes Macaulay, 'he had won three great battles over the armies of three mighty and warlike monarchies, France, Austria, and Russia.' Enthusiasm for the 'Protestant Hero' ran high in England; and his victories were celebrated with bonfires and popular rejoicings. Portraits of Frederick II, with his cocked hat and long queue, were to be seen in every home; at many a rural hostelry the sign-painters were set to work touching up Admiral Vernon into the King of Prussia; and on our ally's birthday the streets of London were ablaze with illuminations.

Following upon these successes, co-operation between our government and Frederick II became much closer; in April 1758 a second treaty was concluded between Great Britain and Prussia, whereby the latter was to receive further British and Hanoverian support; with the result that France was obliged to exhaust her principal energies across the Rhine. A minor part in these covering operations was played by the amphibious expeditions organized by Pitt—at the urgent request of Prussia—against Rochefort, St. Malo, Cherbourg, and Belleisle, which had the effect of lessening the pressure on Frederick II's western flank.

British commerce also was recovering. 'At the beginning of that war,' says Burke at a later date, '(as in the commencement of every war), traders were struck with a sort of panick. Many went out of the freighting business. But by degrees, as the war continued, the terror wore off; the danger came to be better appreciated, and better provided against; our trade was carried on in large fleets, under regular conduct, and with great safety. The freighting business revived.'[1]

Pitt took office too late in the campaigning season to effect much in 1757. Several long months, indeed, were to pass before his strategy began to bear fruit. One of his earliest measures was greatly to improve his colonial intelligence service; to which much of our later success was due. The first of the conjunct expeditions against the French ports was a complete fiasco: it left England on 8 September and arrived off Rochefort on the 19th; the place was weakly held, and the conditions of weather and tide were ideal for attack; nevertheless the commanders could come to no decision about landing their troops, and so a great chance was thrown away. ' The famous council sat from morning till late at night,' declared Wolfe afterwards, ' and the result of the debates was unanimously not to attack the place they were ordered to attack, and for reasons that no soldier will allow to be sufficient.'

As has already been said, during 1757 there were not enough ships to maintain an effective blockade of the French ports; moreover, the weather favoured the enemy. In January the Chevalier de Bauffremont slipped out of Brest and sailed, by way of the West Indies, for Louisbourg with five of the line; in May M. de la Motte left Brest for the same destination with nine more and several transports, and the Comte d'Aché sailed for the East Indies with six ships. Meanwhile in April du Reveste had got out of Toulon with five of the line and, slipping past Saunders' squadron at Gibraltar, also reached Louisbourg. Our containing operations had, in fact, completely broken down. As in 1755 and 1756, reinforcements continued to reach Louisbourg; and in July a powerful conjunct expedition under the command of Rear-Admiral Holburne and General Loudon was abandoned owing to the presence in Louisbourg of a numerically superior French fleet (which was, however, rotten with typhus) and a reprehensible lack of enterprise on the part of the British commanders. On 20 September a violent storm dispersed and almost destroyed Holburne's squadron: upon which M. de la Motte once again ran the blockade; and, on his arrival in the Soundings, was again favoured by the weather—for Boscawen's blockading force was driven into port by the same gale which brought the French safely into Brest.

[1] Burke, *Observations on a Late State of the Nation* (1790).

In the Mediterranean a powerful squadron under the command of Osborne and Saunders attacked the enemy's commerce and protected our own. In the autumn Osborne retired to his winter quarters at Gibraltar. Early in November M. de la Clue sailed from Toulon, intent, like Bauffremont ten months earlier, on reaching the West Indies and Louisbourg. Approaching the Straits, he learned that Osborne was awaiting him there with a much superior force and at once put into Cartagena. Osborne accordingly remained in the Straits with his battleships, while his cruisers kept a close and constant watch on Clue in Cartagena.

In 1758 the grip of the blockade tightened. Early in the year the government received news that the French were preparing a large relief force for Louisbourg in their Atlantic ports. In March Hawke, now in command of the Channel Fleet, was ordered to cruise in the Bay with a small squadron, comprising seven of the line and three frigates. He discovered the Rochefort squadron and its convoy, which were on the point of sailing for the relief of Louisbourg, in the Basque roads, and on 4 April drove the whole force ashore on the mud-flats. ' At 5 next morning I saw them all aground,' observed Hawke in his dispatch, ' almost dry, about 5 or 6 miles distance from us . . . many of the merchants and several of the ships of war, were on their broadsides.' Cruising off Ushant, a powerful Western Squadron secured the entrance of the Channel against an enemy fleet, and prevented the French squadrons from concentrating at Brest. Admiral Anson, who had succeeded Hawke in the command of the Channel Fleet, was a strong advocate of this strategy. ' The best defence for our colonies,' he declared, ' as well as our coasts, is to have a squadron always to the westward as may in all probability either keep the French in port, or give them battle with advantage if they come out.' Anson kept the sea all the summer, handing over the squadron to Saunders in September. At one point only was the Navy unable to prevent reinforcements from slipping past its guard. In 1758 it failed to close Brest. Several small divisions got out this year, carrying troops and stores to the French possessions in North America.

Meanwhile in the Mediterranean a squadron under the command of Rear-Admiral Sir Henry Osborne, based on Gibraltar, held the Straits and prevented the Toulon fleet from getting across the Atlantic to the relief of Louisbourg. But Osborne's position was one of great difficulty; since the bulk of the enemy fleet, under Clue, still remained in Cartagena—a neutral port; and, early in February, a reinforcement from Toulon, under Duquesne, was expected to join him there. To prevent the threatened junction Osborne sailed with a westerly wind for Cartagena, expecting to be off that port before Duquesne, and knowing that, if the wind came easterly, he could still get back to Gibraltar well in advance of Clue. On the 28th Osborne fell in with Duquesne's squadron in the vicinity of Cartagena. While Osborne with most of his force blockaded Clue, ships were detached to pursue Duquesne. By the evening the *Orphée*, 64, had been made a prize, and the *Oriflamme*, 50, driven ashore under a Spanish battery. By a singular coincidence it happened that Duquesne's flag was flying in the *Foudroyant*, 80, which had been the flagship of Galissonière in the fateful action off Port Mahon; and that one of the vessels sent in pursuit of Duquesne, the *Monmouth*, 64, was commanded by Captain Arthur Gardiner, who had been Byng's flag-captain in the same action. In the gathering dusk the *Foudroyant* stood out to sea with the *Monmouth* hot on her heels. At about four o'clock the *Foudroyant* began to fire at the *Monmouth* with her stern-chase. A long running action ensued, in the course of which Gardiner was killed. Under her first lieutenant, Robert Carkett, the *Monmouth* continued the unequal fight, until her masts were shattered, her rigging and sails cut to pieces, and more than a hundred of her crew dead or dying. As for the *Foudroyant*, her decks were a shambles and her fire was almost silenced. By one o'clock in the following morning both ships were crippled and lay side by side in the darkness. It was then that the *Swiftsure* and *Hampton Court* arrived on the scene; whereupon the *Foudroyant* struck to the *Monmouth*—and Port Mahon was avenged. The consequence was that Clue had no longer any chance of forcing Osborne's position in the Straits; within a month he was back in Toulon, and his fleet dismantled. Before the year was out the British Mediterranean squadron was overwhelmingly superior to the French and the enemy's trade within the Straits had almost ceased to exist.

The British offensive in North America planned by Pitt for 1758 was to be launched on three main lines: first, an army under Brigadier John Forbes was to strike up the valley of the Ohio; second, a force of 6,000 regular and 9,000 colonial troops, under General James Abercromby, was to advance along the line of Lakes George and

Champlain, and then, with the assistance of a strong flotilla commanded by Commodore Loring, to capture Crown Point and Ticonderoga and to recover the control of the lakes which had been lost in 1756; third, the attack on Louisbourg which had failed the year before was to be renewed by a powerful battle fleet and a force of 11,000 regulars commanded by General Amherst.

Under cover of Anson's blockade a fleet of transports was dispatched to North America with no more than a trade defence convoy, while Boscawen, unhampered by escort duties, took the battle fleet across the ocean and arrived off Cape Breton Island in overwhelming force. His squadron numbered twenty-three sail of the line, besides a division of frigates, as opposed to five French battleships lying in Louisbourg harbour. On board his transports was Amherst's powerful army. On 7 June the first of the troops, led by Colonel James Wolfe, got ashore in a heavy surf in Gabarus Bay. During the next few weeks Amherst's siege-train closed in on the doomed fortress. On the night of 25 July 'Old Dreadnought'[1] sent a cutting-out expedition into the harbour, which managed to burn one of the enemy's battleships and drove another ashore under the guns of a British battery. On the following day Louisbourg surrendered. The French squadron in the harbour was destroyed and the fortress dismantled. The fall of Louisbourg opened the way up the St. Lawrence to Quebec and Montreal.

Durrell was left on the station with ten of the line on Boscawen's return to England. A small French squadron under du Chaffault later got past Durrell out of Quebec, and, eluding both Boscawen and Hawke in the Soundings, reached Brest in safety. Towards the end of October, there was considerable alarm in England, following the escape of du Chaffault's squadron, for the safety of our West Indies convoy—most of which, however, had sought shelter in Cork.

Abercromby's expedition against Ticonderoga failed as to its main object; but part of his force, an American contingent led by Lieut.-Colonel John Bradstreet, one of the ablest of the provincial leaders,

---

[1] Boscawen was nicknamed ' Old Dreadnought ' after the ship which he commanded in 1744. A story used to be told of him that, while he was in the *Dreadnought*, 60, the officer of the watch one night hurried down into Boscawen's cabin crying, ' Sir, there are two large ships, which look like Frenchmen, bearing down on us; what are we to do? ' ' Do? ' retorted Boscawen, turning out and going on deck in his nightshirt—' Do? damn 'em, fight 'em! '

on 27 August surprised and seized Fort Frontenac, situated at the north-east end of Lake Ontario. The loss of this great stronghold, from which were supplied all the forts of Upper Canada and the Ohio valley, severed the line of French communication between the St. Lawrence and the Ohio; moreover, in its harbour lay the flotilla with which the French had controlled the lakes since they overthrew the rival British station at Oswego in 1756. Fort Frontenac was now razed to the ground, and most of the hostile flotilla taken or destroyed. Bradstreet's success had opened the line of advance into Canada by way of Lake Ontario; the command of the Great Lakes returned to the British; and the loss of the fort was one of the principal contributory factors which brought about the evacuation of the Ohio valley by the French later in the year. Meanwhile General Forbes' expedition, marching slowly and warily through the forests of Pennsylvania, had at last arrived safely before Fort Duquesne. Finding the place burnt and abandoned, they presently built a new fort, which they named Fort Pitt, at the Forks of the Ohio.

With the turn of the year the struggle approached its climax. During 1758, as we have seen, the French had been forced back on the Great Lakes and the St. Lawrence. The British control of the sea-routes had virtually cut off all reinforcements and supplies from France. In 1759 both sides prepared to seek a decision.

Before the end of December 1758 Pitt had completed his plans for the final offensive against Canada. After Abercromby's failure against Ticonderoga in the previous campaign he was recalled and replaced by Amherst, who now received instructions to advance overland from Albany towards either Montreal or Quebec. Forbes' successful operations on the Ohio were to be completed by driving the French out of their remaining posts at Niagara and on Lake Erie. For the main operation of the campaign of 1759, a direct attack upon Quebec up the St. Lawrence, Amherst was ordered to embark 12,000 men from New York to Louisbourg: the command of the fleet being entrusted by Pitt to Rear-Admiral Charles Saunders, who had been one of the brilliant band of young officers who served under Anson in the great voyage of 1740–4 and who had distinguished himself a few years later in the second action off Finisterre; and the command of the troops to Lieut.-General James Wolfe, who was undoubtedly the finest soldier this country had produced since Marlborough and another of Pitt's inspired selections. Canada, therefore, was to be assailed both from the sea and the St. Lawrence and also overland.

On 14 February 1759, in pursuance of Pitt's plan, the vanguard of the greatest fleet which had ever left Europe for America weighed and sailed from Spithead under the command of Admiral Holmes, bound for the great conjoint expedition assembling at Louisbourg that was destined to be the decisive enterprise of the North American war. Through head-winds and heavy seas Holmes' fleet made a long and tedious passage of it; and it was not until May that they eventually sighted the coast of Nova Scotia. Louisbourg harbour being still blocked with ice, they then had to stand southward to Halifax, where Wolfe found a large part of his troops awaiting him.

Meanwhile instructions were dispatched to the Channel Fleet to tighten the blockade of the French ports to prevent help from being sent to Canada. Durrell was moreover ordered to sail from Halifax as early in 1759 as the ice-conditions would allow and to proceed some two hundred miles up the St. Lawrence to prevent reinforcements and provisions from reaching Quebec.

3

In 1759, while the issue of the North American campaign was still uncertain, events in Europe moved to a crisis. Towards the end of 1758 a rival to Pitt had appeared in France in the person of the Duc de Choiseul, who now took over the direction of the war, and, to relieve the pressure on Canada, revived Belleisle's project for the invasion of England. It was originally proposed to collect a large flotilla of flat-bottomed craft between Boulogne and Ambleteuse to ferry 50,000 men across the Channel. This project, however, was soon abandoned in favour of another and far more elaborate one. Thanks to the Austrian alliance, the French were able to base an army of invasion on the Flanders coast, opposite the Thames estuary. The later proposal was to station a force of 20,000 men at Ostend and to launch them suddenly against the Essex coast. The problem as to how this expedition was to be passed across the intervening forty miles of water was to be solved in a novel and ingenious manner. A second army, also of 20,000 men, assembling in Brittany under the Duc d'Aiguillon, was to be landed up the Firth of Clyde; it was to be convoyed to its

destination by the combined Brest and Toulon squadrons, totalling
between thirty-five and forty of the line; after disembarking d'Aiguillon
and his army, the fleet was to proceed north-about round Scotland
and down through the North Sea to cover the passage of the Flanders
force to the mouth of the Blackwater. At the same time Captain
François Thurot, the distinguished privateer commander, was to lead
out his cruiser squadron from Dunkirk for a diversionary raid on
Ireland. In other words, the enemy's main expedition against a vulnerable and almost unguarded part of our coastline, within easy
striking distance of London, was to be supported by formidable
diversionary attacks against Scotland and Ireland in the hope that
this sudden descent on our hitherto inviolate island realm would
disrupt the national economy, occasion a general panic, and compel
our government to make peace.[1]

Choiseul at the outset had hoped for the active assistance of neutral
States exasperated at British interference with their trade. He was
anxious to foment and exploit this exasperation with a view to organizing a coalition of maritime neutrals against Great Britain. The threat
of such a coalition was, in Pitt's judgment, far more dangerous than
the French invasion project.

It seemed to Pitt that there was a likelihood of the Dutch and
Danish fleets suddenly arriving in the Channel and joining forces with
the enemy to avenge their injuries. As Newcastle had declared in a
memorial to the King on 22 November 1758: ' Mr. Pitt's apprehension,
that the Dutch, and the Danes, may come into our Channel, without
our having any certain knowledge of their object; and, if the Court of
France should have any design to disturb us, those very ships may
join, & assist, in it. And therefore some care should be taken to man
the Fleet, and to have a sufficient force at home, & a certain means
of making up a certain number of ships in all events.'

It had originally been part of Choiseul's scheme that the Russians
and Swedes should assist in the descent on Great Britain and that the
Dutch navy should join forces with the French. Relations between
this country and the Northern States were already sufficiently strained:
but Pitt's conciliatory approach to the matters at issue successfully
countered Choiseul's diplomacy and at the prospect of an open breach

---

[1] For a critical survey of the French invasion plans, see Lacour-Gayet, *La marine
militaire de la France sous le règne de Louis XV.*

with Great Britain, Russia and Sweden drew back. It was apparent that the co-operation of the maritime neutrals would not be forth-coming; and France was left to attempt the descent alone.

At the outset the more pressing peril was from Toulon, where the French preparations were further advanced. To make sure that the enemy squadron there did not reach Brest, Boscawen was sent out in April with a reinforcement to take over the command of the Mediterranean Fleet.

On 16 May he joined forces with Vice-Admiral Brodrick off Cape Sicie and assumed command of the augmented squadron, comprising fifteen of the line and a number of cruisers. Throughout the early summer of 1759 he kept a vigilant watch on Toulon and Marseilles. By standing close in every day he compelled the Toulon fleet, numbering thirteen of the line and a few frigates, under the command of Clue, to retire into the inner roadstead under the protection of the batteries. ' I have ', he declared in a dispatch to the Admiralty on 1 July, ' continued on this station as long as the water & provisions of the ships under my command would permit me, and have almost every day since my being here seen the French squadron in the inner road in Toulon.' An important part of Boscawen's duties on this station was to provide escorts for British convoys in the Mediterranean and to gain intelligence of enemy privateers. The health of the ships' companies was, as usual, his constant care. From time to time he sent one of his ships into port to clean and to refit. Owing to the exigencies of the war a good many of these ships were in a bad state of repair. With the object of enticing Clue from his refuge, Boscawen had in June dispatched three ships to attack a couple of the enemy's frigates which were then lying in a bay outside the port. The attempt was energetically repelled by the shore batteries; and Boscawen's three vessels, which had suffered a good deal of damage in the fighting, had to be towed out again. It was found necessary for them to go to Gibraltar to refit; and, as the whole fleet was in urgent need of water and fresh victuals (since, owing to the loss of Minorca, there was no nearer base available), Boscawen was obliged to proceed there also.

' We arrived here the 3rd instant,' he wrote from Gibraltar on 8 August, ' and are fitting with all expedition for sea.' But Boscawen's absence from his blockading station had in the meantime become known to the enemy. He was still lying at Gibraltar when Clue, under orders to sail for Brest to join the squadron intended to cover the invasion of England, attempted to slip through the Straits under cover of night. Clue's force was, however, sighted at eight o'clock in the evening of the 17th by a British frigate stationed in the Gut.[1] When the alarm was given Boscawen and some of his principal officers were several miles off dining with the Spanish governor of San Roque. Nevertheless, in rather less than three hours, most of the squadron were at sea and in pursuit of the French. In the words of an eye-witness, ' A signal for the fleet to *cut* or *slip* was immediately made on the Admiral's return and great was the hurry and confusion which ensued: some ships having their sails unbent, and their yards newly tarred; others, I think, with their yards and top-masts struck, over-hauling their rigging; and almost all having seamen and officers on shore, either on pleasure or on the several duties of the fleet; little expecting at that moment the approach of an enemy.' At ten o'clock Boscawen got under way with his flagship, the *Namur*, and seven others of his division. An hour later, off Cabrita Point, the *Namur* brought to and hoisted in the boats. At 1 a.m. she shook out reefs and set topgallant-sails. ' On the morning of the 17th, some ships were seen a-head. The wind was strong at east; the weather fine, the water smooth; and we soon perceived that we gained exceedingly fast upon the enemy; which were now plainly discovered to be seven large ships of the line, and one of them carrying a French Admiral's flag.'

Five of Clue's battleships and all his frigates, in accordance with their instructions, had proceeded to Cadiz. Clue himself had determined to press on up the coast; but owing to the deficiencies of the French book of signals was unable to make his intentions known to all his ships. Mistaking Boscawen's leading ships for his own vessels, he was actually waiting for them to come up. When he realized his error it was too late to escape. At 10 a.m. Boscawen made the signal for battle, ' the ships to engage as they came up, without regard to the line of battle. The enemy's ships were formed in a line a-head, and crowding away from us under a press of sail. . . . We had a fresh gale and came

---

[1] This is a striking example of the immense strategic importance of the Rock. A significant passage in a letter, addressed twenty-three years later by John Sinclair to Lord Shelburne, then prime minister, puts the whole matter in a nutshell: ' Gibraltar has been described as that happy spot, which in the possession of Great Britain, divides France from France, and Spain from Spain, and consequently as a place which ought not on any account to be relinquished.'

up with them very fast,' continued the Admiral. 'About half-past two, some of the headmost ships began to engage: but I could not get up to the *Océan* [the French flagship] till near four.' In the running fight which followed, the *Namur*, engaged for half an hour with Clue's flagship, and losing her mizen mast and both topsail yards, was disabled and fell astern. 'The enemy then made all the sail they could,' observed Boscawen. 'I shifted my flag to the *Newark*.' The brunt of the battle fell on the enemy's rearmost vessel, the *Centaure*, 74. She fought desperately for three hours and more, and struck her colours only when the *Centaure* herself was a wreck, and the captain and nearly half the ship's company had been killed.

With the surrender of the *Centaure* the action ceased and the pursuit began. During the night, under cover of the darkness and haze, the *Souverain* and *Guerrier* altered course and escaped. 'I pursued all night,' went on the Admiral, 'and in the morning of the 19th saw only four Sail standing in for the land *of Lagos*. . . . About 9 the *Océan* ran in among the breakers, and the three others anchored *close to the shore*.' The *Océan* ran on shore with all her sails set—on touching 'every mast went by the board and fell over the bows'; the other vessels had anchored under the guns of a Portuguese battery in Lagos Bay. Regardless of neutral rights, Boscawen at once went in after them. The *Océan* and *Redoutable* were burned, and the *Téméraire* and *Modeste* brought off as prizes.[1]

All hopes of a combination of the Brest and Toulon fleets had now to be abandoned. Boscawen detached part of his fleet to reinforce the Western Squadron, which, now as ever, formed the pivot of the British defence. When he presently returned to England Brodrick blockaded the enemy squadron in Cadiz so closely that the Spaniards are said to have exhibited a notice with the inscription, 'For sale, eight French men-of-war. For particulars apply to Vice-Admiral Brodrick.' The French warships did not in fact stir out of Cadiz until a gale of wind forced Brodrick to retire to Gibraltar.

4

It was not until the spring of 1759 that the state of the enemy fleet at Brest gave any serious cause for alarm. During all this time the

[1] 'I flatter myself', Boscawen wrote to Pitt, 'that my conduct in this affair will be approved by you. It is easier to satisfy that Court [Portugal] than for the French to build four men-of-war.' *Q.* Tunstall, *William Pitt, Earl of Chatham* (1938), p. 233.

formidable preparations going on at Havre and the other Channel ports had become known to the government through intercepted letters and the reports of spies; and Newcastle's agitation increased apace. 'You know, I suppose', he wrote at the beginning of April, 'that flat-bottomed boats are preparing all along the French coasts.' There was a powerful faction in the Cabinet which saw little hope in the outcome of Pitt's grand strategy, which in any case drained the kingdom of troops that might be desperately needed to repel an invasion. The Duke's fears of a French descent early in the war had contributed in no small degree to the Mediterranean débâcle of 1756 and the loss of Minorca. Had it been left to Newcastle, indeed, he would in all likelihood have abandoned Pitt's overseas expeditions and appeased the enemy at almost any price.

Nor were these apprehensions confined to the Duke and his followers. By May the alarm had become general. 'Ten thousand workmen', the *Annual Register* announced, 'are employed at Havre de Grace, in building 150 flat-bottomed boats, 100 feet long, 24 broad, and 10 deep. 100,000 livres are paid to them weekly. These boats are to have a deck, and to carry two pieces of cannon each, and to use either sails or oars, as occasion may require. Some will carry 300 men, with their baggage, and others 150 horse with their riders; 150 more are building at Brest, St. Maloes, Nantes, Port L'Orient, Morlaix and other ports of Brittany.' 'We talk of nothing here but the French Invasion,' wrote Lord Lyttleton some weeks later in London; 'they are certainly making such preparations as have never been made to invade this Island since the Spanish Armada; but I trust in God and Lord Anson.'

It was not to be wondered at that an invasion scare now gripped the country. After all, apart from our Fleet, we had not much in the way of formal defences. There was in this island no well-planned system of formidable fortresses such as Vauban had bequeathed to France. The odds, on paper, were overwhelming. To all outward appearance France was still *la grande nation*, whose power and prestige overshadowed the Continent. The population of England was then barely eight millions, that of France nearly twenty millions. It was an alarming thought that, if ever the enemy should land here in force, the havoc wrought by such a stroke might well be so great as to oblige our government to come to terms.

But Pitt stood firm. Notwithstanding the Duke's agitation and his demand for stronger forces at home, he stoutly refused to recall a single ship or regiment from any of his expeditions overseas, relying upon the existing system of home defence. He stationed a strong corps of regular troops in the Isle of Wight and ordered a large fleet of transports to be held in readiness at the Nore to carry them to any part of the British Isles which might be threatened with invasion. He further ordered thirty-four sail of the line to be put into commission at the earliest moment; and, before the summer was over, had increased the total number of seamen in home waters from 18,000 to 25,000. Another important measure taken at this time was the calling out of the militia, which, being assigned for the most part to garrison duties, released a corresponding number of regular troops. But, first, last, and all the time, the main bulwark upon which Pitt relied was a Channel Fleet stronger than anything which the enemy could send against it.

The underlying principle of Anson's dispositions was so sound that Pitt's confidence in our naval defensive was entirely justified. The French found themselves faced by the same dilemma which had confronted them in 1756. So long as the blockade held, our continental foes—actual and potential—were powerless to strike at us. Anson's prompt and vigorous action had secured the effective control of home waters. The flotilla forces massing in the French Channel ports were blockaded by stronger British flotillas and supporting cruiser squadrons. Since the French had no heavy ships in their Channel ports it was impossible for their transports to cross until their battle fleet came up into those waters and cleared the way for the passage of their army. But the Brest and Toulon fleets were held in check by superior British forces; and the possibility of an enemy concentration at Brest became increasingly remote.

On 13 May Sir Edward Hawke, who had once again been appointed to the command of the Channel Fleet, hoisted his flag at Plymouth and a week later sailed from Torbay. In his next dispatches to the Admiralty he enunciated an important new departure in naval strategy.

Throughout the first three years of the war—1756, 1757, and 1758 —the Admiralty had relied on the time-honoured system of watching Brest from one of our western ports. Anson's present instructions to Hawke had, indeed, been framed on these lines. But the situation confronting him was, in the Admiral's judgment, too critical for him to retire with the squadron from the vital post off Ushant; and in the campaign of 1759 he abandoned the old policy altogether in favour of the new strategy of the close blockade.[1]

Arriving off Brest on the 24th and discovering eleven sail in the roads, he informed the Admiralty of his intention of remaining where he was, unless he were recalled, or strong westerly winds obliged him to seek shelter. ' Upon the whole I do not think it prudent ', he

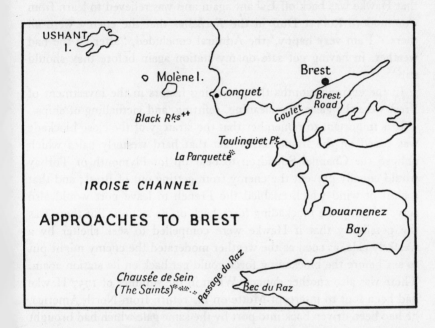

observed in his dispatch, ' as they [the eleven sail] may be soon joined by more from Brest Harbour, to leave them at liberty to come out, by returning to Torbay. . . . I have detached the *Rochester* and *Melampe* to keep a constant watch over their motions, and the *Prince Edward* cutter to run between us with intelligence.' On 4 June he reported that there were now seventeen sail in the roads and reaffirmed his intention of remaining off Brest till further orders.

On the following day, however, with the wind backing to the south-west, it blew a heavy gale; ' a great swell from the S.W.' set in; the

[1] For a comprehensive and detailed survey of the close blockade of Brest, see the present writer's *Quiberon Bay* (1960).

wind and sea continued to increase, with rain and heavy squalls; and on the 6th he was obliged to bear up for Torbay. Attempting to regain their station on the 11th, ' turning down Channel at Noon under close reeft topsails ', Hawke's squadron was on the 12th, off the Lizard, ' surprized by a violent storm ', which did not abate until late in the evening, and in the course of which the *Hero* lost all her masts, the *Torbay* her main course and other sails, and the *Temple* had her foremast and bowsprit very much sprung. It was not until the 21st that Hawke was back off Ushant again and was relieved to learn from Commodore Robert Duff in the *Rochester* that the enemy were all there. ' I am very happy,' the Admiral concluded, ' after all the bad weather, in having got safe on my station again before they should stir.'

In the ensuing months the governing factors in the investment of Brest were the gales, the cleaning, refitting, and victualling of ships.

It is important to remember that the strategy of the close blockade was based on the fundamental fact that hard westerly gales which obliged the Channel Squadron to bear up for Plymouth or Torbay would equally prevent the enemy from getting out of Brest; and that a shift of wind which enabled the French to leave port would also serve to bring the blockading force back on its station. But there was the possibility that if Hawke were compelled to seek shelter by a westerly gale, as soon as the weather moderated the enemy might put to sea before the blockading force could get back on its station again. There was also another danger. When in the summer of 1757 Hawke had been sent to intercept Motte on his return from North America, he had been driven back into port by the same gale which had brought the enemy squadron safely into Brest. The same mischance could—and, in point of fact, did—recur during the blockade of 1759.

From time to time it would become urgently necessary for Hawke to send in some of the ships—which were not yet coppered—' to clean and refit for Channel service ': thus weakening the squadron with which he was blockading the enemy in Brest. The difficulties inseparable from cleaning and refitting must be expected to increase when, on the approach of the Equinox, strong westerly winds were to be apprehended.

The health of the ships' companies was a prime factor in the block-ade. It will be remembered that Hawke's ten-weeks' cruise in the

Channel in 1755 had been cut short by the outbreak of a virulent epidemic. Already remonstrances had been passing between the Admiral and Whitehall on the subject of pressed men and bad beer; already he was appealing for regular and adequate supplies of good beer ' as the best preservative of health among new-raised men '.

During the whole course of the blockade Hawke waged a stubborn and on the whole successful struggle against the lethargy and incompetence of the dockyard, victualling, medical, and other authorities. As his biographer, the late Captain Montagu Burrows, R.N., has truly observed, ' The least weakness in giving way to the traditions of bureaucracy on the questions of victualling, cleaning, and dispatching back again his ships, would have left Hawke powerless on the day of battle, with sick crews, ships that would not sail, and officers worn out with the endless fatigues of cruising in gales of wind and on a lee shore.'[1]

From the reports of the inshore squadron it was apparent that the French were unlikely to leave port for some time. ' The operations of the enemy indicate a long cruize for the squadron,' Hawke wrote on 3 July. ' In order to preserve it in a condition to keep the sea, I propose to send in two ships of the line to clean at Plymouth every spring [tide].' The difficulties of cleaning presented a perennial problem. ' If ships take up a month by cleaning ', he observed three weeks later, ' from the time they leave me to their return, it will be impossible for me to keep up the squadron. The only practicable way is to heel, &c., and confine them to ten days in port, for the refreshment of their companies.' He stressed the importance of this latter point.

Their Lordships will give me leave to observe that the relief of the squadron depends more on the refreshment of the Ships' Companies than on cleaning the ships. By the hurry the latter must be performed in (unless the ship continues a month or five weeks in port, which the present exigency will by no means admit of) the men would be so harassed and fatigued that they would return to me in a worse condition than when they left me.

The Secretary of the Admiralty replied, on 13 August, to the effect that, since Hawke was of the opinion that cleaning the ships would be prejudicial to the health of the men, ' which must be particularly

---

[1] Montagu Burrows, *The Life of Admiral Lord Hawke* (1883).

attended to ', and that giving them boot-hose-tops[1] would answer the purposes, their Lordships would leave it to him to give such to the ships he might from time to time send in, ' as he should judge best for the Service '.

Like Boscawen, Hawke spared no pains to promote the health and well-being of his ships' companies. In his dispatch to the Admiralty on 23 July he observed:

> I have not yet received the supplies of butter and cheese, beef, pork, etc., insomuch that I cannot help regretting the want of a commanding officer at Plymouth to see all orders executed with the expedition and punctuality necessary. As I shall not now have it in my power to relieve the whole squadron, and must in all probability remain here a considerable time, will their Lordships give me leave to recommend to their consideration the sending out live cattle now and then, under such regulations as shall be thought proper.

Complaints concerning the beer and the victualling arrangements at Plymouth continued to recur in the Admiral's official correspondence. ' Our daily employment is condemning the beer from Plymouth, insomuch as that article is becoming very scarce in the squadron. Give me leave therefore to repeat my entreaties for beer being sent with the utmost expedition from the Eastward.' Some weeks earlier the *London Evening Post* had published a letter written by an officer on board the *Bellerophon*.

> We have a fine Fleet, all in high Spirits, and well. I am a little surprized that you lazy, idle Fellows don't make a Motion for supplying the Fleet with fresh Beef, from Ireland, which would keep all Englishmen in good Health: They send us Beer and Water enough, but no fresh provision nor Greens for our People. If the French don't chuse to come out, we shall have a Four-month Cruize, and consequently the Scurvy will prevail amongst the Seamen, whom I look upon as the strength of the Nation. I wonder how a Parcel of Landdrones can see poor Jacks suffer so.

Hawke's remonstrances had not gone unheeded. That summer and autumn the letters passing between the Admiralty and the various port authorities exuded an altogether unprecedented promptitude,

---

[1] ' The meaning of the word " boot-hose-top ", which is of frequent occurrence in letters of those times, is to heel over the ship as far as possible, to scrape or burn off the grass, slime, shells, barnacles, etc., which adhere to the bottom of a wooden vessel long out at sea, and to daub it over with a mixture of tallow, sulphur, and resin, as a temporary protection ' (Burrows, *Ibid.*, p. 376).

energy, and drive. The Admiralty on 29 June gave orders for a supply of butter and cheese to be sent to Plymouth, whence a convoy would transport them to the fleet. Live bullocks for the sick were also to be provided, Hawke was informed on 19 July. To and fro between the squadron and the southern naval ports, as regularly as the weather allowed, sailed the well-laden fleets of victuallers under convoy of the *Swallow* and the other sloops of war. ' No fleet employed on similar service ', observes Laird Clowes, ' had ever before been so amply supplied with beer, provisions, or vegetables.'[1]

Though the French overtures to Sweden had been coolly received, Choiseul continued to develop his scheme of invasion. Early in July the Marquis de Conflans arrived to assume command of the Brest fleet. Newcastle, who had small confidence in the efficacy of Hawke's blockade, was once again a prey to nervous fears. The situation on the Continent in the summer of 1759 appeared to favour the French design. Since the spring the Allied forces in Germany had been steadily giving ground to the French. It seemed unlikely that Ferdinand of Brunswick would be able to retain even the line of the Weser. A ring of hostile armies closed in on the dwindling forces of the King of Prussia; the Austrians overran Saxony and threatened Berlin; the Prussians were heavily defeated by the Russians on 23 July at Züllichau, and on 12 August at Kunersdorf. Frederick II's plight had now become so desperate that he was contemplating suicide. But the Austrians and Russians failed to follow up this victory and by their inactivity left the King of Prussia to reorganize his forces, which he did with astonishing celerity and dispatch. Frederick II's recovery after Kunersdorf is one of the marvels of military history.

Meanwhile in England there was growing alarm at the threat from across the Channel. By far the greatest part of our regular army was out of the country: there were 27,000 of our men in America, 10,000 in Germany, 5,000 at Gibraltar, and 4,000 in Africa. That summer the London newspapers were full of the threatened French invasion. Presently, as half a century later, during the Revolutionary and Napoleonic Wars, there arose disturbing but groundless rumours of the enemy having actually landed. ' This day ', recorded the Sussex diarist, Thomas Turner, on 7 July, ' received by post the disagreeable news of the French being landed at Dover.' ' Nothing ', wrote Horace

[1] W. Laird Clowes, *The Royal Navy*, III p. 223.

Walpole on 1st August, 'is talked of here, as you may imagine, but the invasion.'[1]

On the other hand, the apprehension excited by the French preparations to invade us must not be exaggerated. Though Choiseul's design was taken very seriously by the Dutch and other continental newspapers, and though it succeeded in arousing from time to time waves of alarm on this side of the Channel, it never became a deciding factor in the British counsels. If, indeed, through illness or other cause Pitt had been removed from the political arena, it might well have become so. Dread of the French flat-bottoms was strong in the breasts of Newcastle and his following. But while Pitt continued at the helm the ordinary life of town and country went on much as usual, in spite of the calling-out of the militia and the recurrent alarums and excursions.

After the destruction of Clue's squadron by Boscawen, the French had resolved to press on with the invasion scheme with the Brest fleet alone. Conflans was instructed to escort d'Aiguillon's transports, assembling in the Morbihan, with the main French fleet. He hoped, perhaps, to avoid Hawke's squadron; yet nothing was more certain than this, that the British Channel Fleet would continue to make the hostile flotillas their primary objective.

So long as the blockade of the French arsenals held, the chances of successful evasion were slender indeed. Blocking in the enemy's principal fleet at Brest was the Western Squadron, or Channel Fleet —then, as always, the pivot of the British strategic system—whose main and ultimate function was to hold the approaches to the Channel, and to prevent a hostile concentration at Brest. When the wind was easterly, the main body of Hawke's fleet occasionally stood in to St. Mathieu Point. In hard westerly weather, the rendezvous was some 15 leagues W. ½ S. of Ushant. The advanced squadron—the strength of which varied from time to time—lay for long periods off St. Mathieu Point or to the southward of the Black Rocks. Frigates kept a vigilant

---

[1] There is an allusion to the invasion alarm in David Garrick's immortal 'Heart of Oak,' which was set to music by William Boyce. This air was first heard in the winter of 1759.

> They swear they'll invade us, these terrible foes;
> They frighten our women, our children, and beaus;
> But should their flat-bottoms in darkness get o'er,
> Still Britons they'll find, to receive them on shore.
>
> Heart of oak are our ships, etc.

watch on the Passage du Four and the Passage du Raz. At the same time the second division of the French invasion forces, stationed in Flanders, was blockaded by a cruiser squadron under Commodore Boys. A third division lying at Havre, where there were only flat-bottomed craft, was held by the British flotilla; while a supporting cruiser squadron, under Sir Piercy Brett, lay in the Downs.

In consequence of the rigorous investment Brest was virtually starved of provisions and naval stores. ' As I have cruisers off Brest road, the Passage de Raz & du Four,' Hawke informed the Admiralty on 16 July, ' I considered Brest as blocked up in the strictest sense; so that I gave Capt. Hervey orders not to suffer a neutral vessel of any nation whatever to enter that port, but direct them to stand off the coast.' Later he sent similar instructions to Captain Reynolds who was in command of another detached squadron further down the coast. Intelligence reached the Admiralty from our agents across the Channel of the straitening effect of Hawke's blockade on the enemy's main naval arsenal; and towards the end of the month the master of a Dutch dogger which had just come out of Brest reported that ' 'twas surprizing the price of everything, and no white bread to be had.'

The bombardment of Havre and the destruction of the flotilla there by Rodney in early July further disorganized the enemy's plans. Havre remained blockaded during the rest of the year. On 1 August a British victory at Minden on the Weser saved Hanover from the French and largely restored the continental part of Pitt's defensive system.

The failure of the enemy's forces at Havre to achieve anything had resulted in increased activity in the Brittany ports. As the summer advanced, therefore, Hawke extended his blockade to the transports and troops which were assembling at Port Louis, Vannes, and other towns to the southward. On 15 August Captain Roddam was directed to cruise with a small squadron as far south as L'Orient, and instructed to make the destruction of the enemy's transports, rather than his warships, his principal object. On the 22nd the Admiralty, acting on intelligence from abroad concerning the French preparations at Port Louis, Vannes, and Auray, ' where a considerable number of trans-ports are collected together under convoy of several frigates of war ', ordered Hawke to do everything in his power to counter these plans by taking or destroying the enemy's shipping, and further suggested that Duff, who had already shown himself ' very active on this station ', should be entrusted with the mission, for which purpose they were sending out reinforcements. On the 26th the Admiral ordered Reynolds to cruise with a squadron between Port Louis and Nantes.

In the middle of September, in accordance with the Admiralty's instructions, Hawke resolved to attempt the destruction of the enemy's transports. Duff was accordingly directed to cruise with a squadron between Port Louis and Nantes and to take Reynolds' division under his command. But before the new orders could take effect Reynolds reported that the transports at Nantes had slipped out of the Loire with three frigates and sailed northward to join those at Vannes; that he had pursued them in Quiberon Bay, and that they had taken refuge in the Auray.

To get at the transports where they lay, in the Vannes and in the Auray, presented almost insuperable difficulties. The Morbihan, an extensive inlet, was on the north-east side of Quiberon Bay. Its shores were much indented and encumbered by numerous islets and shoals, between which were intricate narrow channels leading to Vannes and Auray. To pass up these channels with their many dangers, above-water and sunken, and strong, swirling tides, demanded the co-operation of pilots intimately acquainted with their intricacies: such pilots were not available.

Leaving most of his squadron in Quiberon Bay to watch the enemy's invasion forces in the Vannes and Auray, Duff took up his station with the *Rochester* and a few frigates off the Île de Groix to blockade Port Louis.

' As to Morbian,' Hawke informed the Admiralty, ' I beg leave, that in my opinion, the enemy cannot stir from thence, and that should they attempt it, Capt. Duff has sufficient force to destroy them in the entrance of the river, from whence such a number of ships cannot pass with safety, in face of an enemy determined to attack them.'

As autumn approached the hard blockading service began to tell, with ever-increasing effect, on both the captains and their ships. Hervey[1] was warned that he must on no account send in any of the inshore squadron to refit without consulting the Admiral. ' As I have but 17 sail of the line ', Hawke wrote, ' I desire you will not send any

[1] The Hon. Augustus Hervey had succeeded Duff on the advanced station on 3rd July.

ships in without giving their Captains positive orders to join me first, as I must be left to judge of the necessity of their going in.' Like Nelson forty years later he begged for more frigates. ' I am ', he had written some time before, ' in the utmost distress for want of frigates.' Several of the captains were presently laid up, and a number of the ships were reporting more or less serious defects.

The days grew shorter, and the winds and sea rose; a succession of westerly gales scourged the perilous lee shore; and finally Hawke was compelled to let go.

' Yesterday and this day the gale rather increasing,' he reported on 13 October, ' I thought it better to bear up for Plymouth than the risk of being scattered and driven farther to the Eastward. While this wind shall continue it is impossible for the enemy to stir. I shall keep the ships employed night and day in completing their water and provisions to three months; for at this season there can be no dependence on victuallers coming to sea. The instant it shall moderate I shall sail again.' In his following dispatch he reassured the Admiralty about the threatened descent. ' I shall not stir out of the *Ramillies* myself, and I hope to be at sea again in a few days in a condition to keep there without depending on victuallers. . . . Their Lordships may rest assured there is little foundation for the present alarms. While the wind is fair for the enemy's coming out, it is also favourable for our keeping them in; and while we are obliged to keep off, they cannot stir.' ' If their Lordships ', he added on the 17th, ' will consider how necessary it is not to alter any rendezvous, on which I must always keep the Channel open, and that consequently in strong Westerly gales I cannot keep the sea, they will readily lay their account with my putting often into this port. At the same time they may depend upon my keeping the strictest guard over the motions of the enemy that the weather will permit.'

That the weather will permit. That—first, last, and all the time— was the root of the matter. Always there was the danger that, as soon as the weather moderated, the French might put to sea before Hawke could get back on his station; and, a few weeks later, that was what actually happened.

5

Pitt's well-laid plans for following up the capture of Louisbourg with an early descent on Quebec had fallen through owing to the inactivity of Vice-Admiral Durrell, who had allowed a small French squadron under Bougainville to slip past him up the St. Lawrence to Quebec, bearing with them the copy of a letter intercepted from Amherst, disclosing the secret plan of campaign. Otherwise the city might well have fallen to a surprise attack with hardly a struggle—for both Montcalm and de Lévis, his second-in-command, were away at Montreal organizing the French defences against Amherst's expected thrust up Lake Champlain and there had been practically no attempt to fortify the river banks below Quebec. Cut off from reinforcements and supplies from home, the French had been concentrating their chief energies on the defence of their southern front. Now they suddenly had to meet a direct attack upon the citadel itself. Bougainville reached Quebec on 10 May. As soon as he learned of the formidable preparations which were being made for the attack up the St. Lawrence, Montcalm returned at once with Bougainville to Quebec, just in time to organize the strong defences which made it impossible for Wolfe to carry out the original plan of a surprise attack. The French strategy was to hold on grimly to the positions covering Quebec until the opposing forces were compelled by the approach of winter to retire.

Such was the position when, on 4 June 1759, a powerful conjunct expedition under the command of Admiral Saunders and General Wolfe sailed from Louisbourg and on the 21st entered the St. Lawrence.

The passage of Saunders' fleet—comprising twenty-two sail of the line, besides frigates and sloops, and the two hundred transports carrying Wolfe and his army up the St. Lawrence to Quebec—may well be accounted one of the finest feats of seamanship in our history. For three hundred miles of uncharted tidal waters, unlighted and unbuoyed; despite fogs, squalls, rocks, shoals, foul winds, tide-ripples, and conflicting currents; through the hazards of the Traverse Passage, where Durrell's mark-boats lay out along the fairway, and where the old tough transport skippers—complete masters of their calling—piloted their craft by the ripple and colour of the water[1] (so confident

[1] Captain John Knox, who was present in one of the transports, has described how the master piloted his vessel through the Traverse: ' He gave his orders with great unconcern, joked with the sounding-boats who lay off on each side, with different coloured flags for guidance; and, when any of them called to him, and pointed to the deepest water, he answered, " Ay, ay, my dear, chalk it down—a d—d dangerous navigation, eh? If you don't make a splutter about it, you'll get no credit for it in England, etc." After we had cleared this remarkable place, where the channel forms

were the French that this feat was impossible that they had neglected all measures for blocking the channel until it was too late): sailed the huge and heterogeneous force, divided into three squadrons, each led by a frigate, arriving in the Basin of Quebec, on the evening of the 26th, without the loss of a single ship.

High above the St. Lawrence rose the great rocky plateau on which the city of Quebec was built, its encircling walls guarded by batteries which swept the river to the eastward, and which were themselves raised so high above the waterway (at this point just over a mile wide) as to be beyond the elevation of the British guns. To the north-west Quebec was protected by the tributary St. Charles. The city's front was amply secured by cliffs falling almost sheer for three hundred feet to the lower town, and stretching away for miles to the westward up the river: they formed a virtually impassable barrier to the plateau above. On the further side of the great basin the ground rose by stages to a range of thickly wooded mountains. Everywhere the assailant was faced with cliffs and escarpments and commanding heights.

For the next few weeks the opposing armies faced each other across the water. Wolfe had originally proposed to invest Quebec from the rear: but this had been found to be impossible owing to the enemy's dispositions. Montcalm, with forces a good deal superior in number but inferior in quality to those led by Wolfe, occupied a strong defensive position along the north bank of the basin, denying all access to the city from the Beaufort shore. His right flank rested on the St. Charles and his left on the rocky gorge of the Montmorenci. For several miles above Quebec the plateau was watched by a strong detachment under Bougainville. Until the French field army was disposed of, the city itself was unassailable. A desperate attempt against Montcalm's left on 31 July was repulsed with heavy losses. Considering the natural strength of the country and the approach of winter, it became at length doubtful whether the fate of Canada would be decided in the course of the present campaign. Notwithstanding all that Wolfe could do to threaten his communications or to separate his forces, Montcalm refused to be drawn away from the decisive positions he held on the north side of the water. ' The enemy puts

a complete zig-zag, the Master called to his Mate to give the helm to somebody else, saying, " D— me if there are not a thousand places in the Thames more hazardous than this; I am ashamed that Englishmen should make such a rout about it !" ' (*Historical Journal of the Campaigns in North America,* 1757–60).

nothing to risk,' Wolfe wrote to his mother on 31st August, ' and I can't in conscience put the whole army to risk. My antagonist has wisely shut himself up in inaccessible entrenchments, so that I can't get at him without spilling a torrent of blood, and that perhaps to little purpose.' ' We have almost the whole force of Canada to oppose,' he declared in a dispatch to Pitt on 2 September. ' In this situation, there is such a choice of difficulties that I own myself at a loss how to determine.' On the day before the French Governor-General, the Marquis de Vaudreuil, had observed confidently, ' Everything proves that the grand design of the English has failed.' A week later Wolfe wrote even more pessimistically to Pitt. The sands of time were running out, and, as has already been said, the campaign must be ended before the St. Lawrence froze.

But several weeks before Rear-Admiral Charles Holmes had led part of the fleet past the guns of Quebec and pushed high up the river, forcing the enemy to extend his right flank. Eventually the French detachments were strung out for as much as fifty miles up the St. Lawrence; and Wolfe, enjoying all the advantages of amphibious warfare, endeavoured, by skilful manœuvring, to outwit and exhaust his opponent. On the night of 8 August Holmes attempted a landing at Pointe aux Trembles, some thirty-five miles above Quebec, but was beaten off by Bougainville. On the 16th, however, he landed at Deschambault, fifteen miles further up the St. Lawrence, and burnt a great quantity of military stores. For weeks on end the scattered French forces were kept wearily marching and counter-marching to meet the impending descent while the British moved freely up and down the St. Lawrence.

As a result of these operations a gap developed in the French centre, into which Wolfe determined to thrust the whole strength of his army. Anticipating a landing ten or fifteen miles above the city, the French had left the high ground immediately above Quebec virtually un-defended. Under cover of a naval demonstration by Saunders in the Basin of Quebec, causing Montcalm to mass his forces to repel an expected landing, the real attack was made by Holmes' squadron at a point just above Quebec. On the night of 12 September the squadron was anchored about three leagues above the intended landing-place. At the appointed signal—two lanterns hoisted to the main-top shrouds of the *Sutherland*—Wolfe with about one-half of his men dropped downstream on the ebb in the ships' boats, and, landing at an un-guarded approach to the high ground above Quebec, scaled the precipitous hanging woods above the St. Lawrence in pitch darkness. Holmes' ships followed about three-quarters of an hour later and put the rest of the force ashore.[1] Large numbers of seamen landed with them and hauled the guns up to the heights. At dawn on the 13th Wolfe had between 4,500 and 5,000 of his finest troops drawn up in line of battle on the Plains of Abraham; what time Saunders with the heavy ships continued by a feint attack to threaten the French positions above Quebec, thereby holding back large numbers of the enemy from the vital theatre on the heights. While Bougainville was hastening from upstream to his support, Montcalm was marching his troops from the Basin up to the Plains of Abraham, where drawn up in perfect order, silent and collected, Wolfe's men awaited the French attack. Reserving their fire until the enemy was within point-blank range, the British fired three steady and shattering volleys: after which they charged—and the French army was swept away like chaff, part of it taking refuge in Quebec, and part making for Montreal. Both Wolfe and Montcalm lost their lives in this fight, which decided the issue of the campaign. Bougainville's relieving force was beaten off; and by the end of the week more than a hundred guns and mortars had been hauled up to the heights. On the 17th Saunders brought his battleships into the Basin within range of the Lower Town, and on the 28th the garrison surrendered. The redcoats marched into the Upper Town, while the seamen occupied the Lower. From beginning to end the campaign had been a perfect example of loyal and har-monious co-operation between the Services.

In the meantime Amherst's forces had been advancing slowly along Lake George; while a contingent under Prideaux ascended the Mo-hawk river to capture Fort Niagara. Arriving at the foot of Lake Champlain, Amherst set to work to construct a flotilla which eventually destroyed all the enemy shipping on the lake. But by now it was

---

[1] Holmes subsequently described the operation as 'the most hazardous and difficult task I was ever engaged in. . . . For the distance of the landing place; the impetuosity of the Tide; the darkness of the Night; and the great chance of exactly hitting the very Spot intended, without discovery or alarm: made the whole ex-tremely difficult: and the failing in any part of my Disposition, as it might overset the General's Plan would have brought upon me an imputation of being the cause of the Miscarriage of the Attack, and all the misfortune that might happen to the Troops attempting it.'

October, and he was unable to reach the St. Lawrence. The Marquis de Vaudreuil still held out in Montreal, threatening the British garrison in Quebec. During the winter of 1759–60 the latter lost more than half their numbers through scurvy and starvation, and in the following spring were defeated by a French force under General de Lévis advancing from Montreal. Once again everything turned on the arrival of convoys from across the ocean. It was now the turn of the French to lay siege to Quebec. Then, in the nick of time, a British squadron with transports and supply ships sailed up the St. Lawrence and relieved the city. About the same time an enemy convoy with reinforcements and stores arrived off the entrance to the St. Lawrence, only to discover that the British were several days ahead of them. The French convoy thereupon put into La Chaleur Bay, where it was presently caught and destroyed by two small British squadrons under Byron and Colville. The last service performed by the Navy in the great offensive against Canada was to co-operate in the march on Montreal. Finally Montreal capitulated to the British forces advancing from all sides, and Canada passed under the British flag.

Meanwhile, under cover of the naval blockade of France, expeditions had been sent against the French African colonies of Senegal and Goree. Senegal was conquered in 1758 and Goree in 1759. Owing to the British command of the sea these successes were achieved with an amazing economy of force. Amphibious attacks were similarly made on French possessions on the other side of the Atlantic, in the West Indies. In 1759 a strong force seized Guadeloupe, the richest of the French sugar islands.

6

On the approach of winter Hawke warned the Admiralty that with the worsening conditions he might be forced to run for Torbay. ' Single ships may struggle with a hard gale of wind when a squadron cannot,' he wrote on 5 November ' it must always, by wearing, lose ground in working against a strong Westerly wind in the [Iroise] Channel, where it cannot make very long stretches, but more especially if it should blow as to put it past carrying sail. If for the future this should happen I shall put into Torbay, as I cannot be induced to think there is sufficient room for so large a squadron, or water, for the three-decked ships in Plymouth Sound at this season of the year.'

The crisis of the campaign was now approaching. Once again the copy of an intercepted letter of Choiseul's had reached the British government, containing the vital information that d'Aiguillon and his army were to sail immediately and that Conflans had been ordered to cover their passage ' au risque d'un combat '. Duff's squadron blockading the transports in the Morbihan was to be driven off or destroyed. The French battle fleet and its convoy were then to shape course for Scotland. Anson had therefore directed all the ships that could possibly be got ready to join Hawke ' with the utmost expedition '.

Early in November Hawke, as he had feared, was again forced off his station by a westerly gale and obliged to bear up for Torbay, leaving frigates to watch in his stead. ' After several efforts,' he reported in his dispatch of the 10th ' not being able to get to the westward of the island [Ushant] with the squadron, I was obliged on the 7th to carry all the sail I could to the northward. The gale continued very hard between the N. by W. & N.W. by N., and at noon of the 8th the Start bore N. by W., distant 9 leagues. Moderated a little in the evening, I worked under the Start by 8 in the morning of the 9th and till afternoon entertained some hopes of being able to keep the sea, and get to the westward. But the wind increasing at W. by N., I was obliged and lucky enough to get in here last night.'

The whereabouts of a hostile squadron under Bompart, whose arrival from the West Indies at some French port was almost hourly expected, was at this time causing the Admiral considerable concern. ' It blows a mere frett of wind [i.e. a heavy gale] from the N.W.,' he concluded. ' Bompart if near may get in, but no ship can stir from any port of the enemy in the Bay. The instant the weather will admit of it, I shall get to sea again.'

Hawke sailed again at last on the 12th, but was driven back to Torbay on the 13th by the violence of the gale, which had now backed to the south-west. He was obliged to shift his flag from the *Ramillies*, which ' having for some time past complained greatly, & been water log'd whenever it blow'd hard ', to the *Royal George*; and on the following day he once again sailed for Ushant.

On 7 November Bompart's sudden arrival off Brest, on the wings of the same gale which drove Hawke off his station, had revealed to Conflans the absence of the blockading squadron. The latter immediately ordered Bompart's seasoned crews on board his own ships.

When on the 14th Hawke's fleet again stood down Channel towards their station off Ushant it was already too late: the birds were flown. ' The same wind which carried us from Torbay,' the Admiral later declared, ' carried Conflans from Brest.' On the same day the enemy had got away to sea with a north-westerly breeze and shaped a course for the Morbihan, a hundred miles or so to the south-eastward. By midday on the 16th the fleet was half-way to its destination, having reached a point about twenty-three leagues west of Belleisle. That afternoon, however, the wind came easterly and rapidly freshened to a gale, with heavy seas. The French were obliged to bear up and run; and it was not until the afternoon of the 19th that they were again on their course and within seventy miles of the island. Towards the evening the wind dropped and they lay becalmed. Then, shortly after midnight, it began to blow fresh from the W.N.W. Conflans signalled the fleet to proceed under short canvas, so that they should not make the land before daylight; and, just before dawn, he hove-to. He was by this time about seven leagues west of Belleisle.

In the meantime Hawke had received secret intelligence from London of Conflans' plan to sail from Brest to pick up the transports which were lying in the Morbihan. This intelligence was confirmed by some of our victuallers which Hawke had encountered on the 16th on his way to the blockading rendezvous off Ushant. From the master of one of them, the *Love and Unity*, he learned that on the day before, about seventy miles west of Belleisle, they had sighted Conflans' fleet, comprising eighteen sail of the line and two frigates, standing to the south-east. The frigates were pursuing one of our own vessels, the *Juno*, which was on her way to warn Duff's squadron in Quiberon Bay of the enemy's approach. Hawke at once hurried in pursuit. ' I have carried a press of sail all night ', he declared in a dispatch to the Admiralty the next morning, ' with a hard gale at south-south-west, in pursuit of the enemy, and make no doubt of coming up with them at sea or in Quiberon Bay.'[1]

[1] The following account of the pursuit and defeat of the French fleet by Sir Edward Hawke is based principally upon the Admiralty Papers preserved in the Public Record Office, the Hawke Papers, and the Archives de la Marine at Paris; supplemented by Thompson, *A Sailor's Letters;* Beatson, *Naval and Military Memoirs of Great Britain from 1727 to 1783;* Locker, *Memoirs of Celebrated Naval Commanders;* Corbett, *England in the Seven Years War;* Hannay, *Short History of the Royal Navy;* Guérin, *Histoire maritime de France;* Troude, *Batailles navales de la France;* Lacour-Gayet, *La marine militaire de la France sous le règne de Louis XV.*

At first the wind drove his fleet considerably to the westward; but on the 18th and 19th, though variable, it proved more favourable; and Hawke stood to the south-east. Having been joined in the meantime by the frigates *Maidstone* and *Coventry*, Hawke instructed their commanders to keep ahead of the squadron, the one on the starboard and the other on the larboard bow. The position of the fleet at noon on the 19th was about seventy miles W. by N. of Belleisle. That night, which began with light south-westerly breezes and fine weather, ended with strong westerly winds freshening to gale force, heavy squalls, cloudy skies, and double-reefed topsails; at three o'clock in the morning Hawke's squadron backed their topsails and lay-to until seven. Then, the wind having shifted to the northward ' in a hazy squall ', all the ships made sail and sent up topgallant-masts, and bore away. The *Magnanime*, which had been signalled to come within hailing distance of the Admiral, was ordered to go ahead in order to make the land and the enemy. At noon it was blowing hard from the W.N.W.; already the *Royal George* had been obliged to take in two reefs in her topsails.

At half-past eight the *Maidstone* suddenly let fly her topgallant sheets—the signal for discovering a fleet—which the *Magnanime* repeated. Soon after this, according to the captain of the *Swiftsure*, the Admiral ordered the fleet ' to draw into a line of Battle a breast at the distance of 2 cables asunder '. About an hour later the *Magnanime* made the signal for the fleet ahead to be that of the enemy. ' We ascertained them to be the French squadron of 21 ships of the line and 3 smaller ships,' observed a chaplain on board the British fleet, ' and that they were then chasing Captain Duff's frigates and bombs, the destruction of which was one object of their destination. Upon their having a distincter view of our ships, they gave over the chase.' Hawke's prediction of the 17th was thus fulfilled. ' In a short time after ', declared the captain of the *Swiftsure*, ' Sir Edward Hawke changed the signal for the line to one for a general chace, the enemy's ships (who were now within sight of our whole fleet) not being formed into any regular order, and by their motions seemingly confused. The whole English fleet gave chace accordingly, and at noon nine of our best ships were in the pursuit advanced abreast of Belle Isle, the west end of that Island bearing N., distant 3 leagues.'

For his part Conflans ordered his ships to stop chasing Duff's force and to close on the flag. Then, taking a swift decision, he made the signal for order of sailing in single line ahead and wore and stood towards the entrance of Quiberon Bay. In the open, his squadron would be no match for Hawke's far stronger fleet and well-trained, seasoned crews: in a good defensive position in Quiberon Bay it would be another matter; and, as he later declared in his dispatch to the King of France, Conflans believed he could get all his ships inside the bay before the British could enter.

'All the day we had very fresh gales at N.W. and W.N.W., with heavy squalls,' observed Hawke. 'Monsieur Conflans kept going off under such sail as all his squadron could carry, and at the same time keep together; while we crowded after him with every sail our ships could bear.'

At about ten o'clock the *Royal George* shook out the second reef in her topsails and set her studding-sails; and soon after her look-outs sighted land ahead, which they took to be Belleisle. The Admiral made the signal for the headmost ships to form in a line as they came up with the enemy;[1] and at the same time he hoisted his colours. The enemy continued standing in for the land. Despite the threatening weather the *Royal George*, and presently the *Magnanime*, set their topgallant-sails.

By midday Hawke's fleet was standing in towards the southward of Belleisle, along the foot of whose high steep cliffs the western swell was breaking heavily. Far in the distance loomed the scattered sprays cascading over the rocks off Haedic, and the group known as the Grand Cardinals standing out of surf and broken water. The southern entrance to Quiberon Bay lay between these Cardinals and the Four shoal, a dangerous rocky bank about seven miles to the east-south-eastward. A heavy breaking sea was rising over the Guérin and other rocky banks flanking the approach.

The wind increased, and the *Royal George* was obliged to take in her topgallant-sails, though half an hour later she was able to set them again. It was now blowing hard from the W.N.W., with frequent showers of rain and heavy squalls; and the British, led by Lord Howe

---

[1] ' Observing, on my discovering them, that they made off, I threw out the signal for the seven ships nearest them to chase, and draw into a line of battle ahead of me, and endeavour to stop them till the rest of the squadron should come up, who were also, to form as they chased, that no time might be lost in the pursuit ' (Hawke's *Dispatch*, 24 November 1759).

in the *Magnanime*, gained fast upon the enemy. Conflans, who had thought to get safely inside the bay, and then, hauling his wind, to form line of battle under shelter of the western shore, had reckoned without the headlong speed of Hawke's advance. Despite the rising gale, the heavy sea, and a lee shore bristling with rocks and shoals, the British ships came on, with their spars buckling to overstrain, shaking out their topsail reefs—both the *Royal George* and *Magnanime*, as we

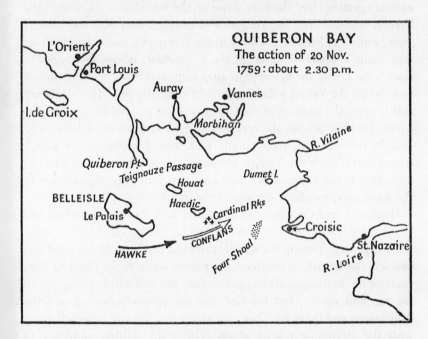

QUIBERON BAY
The action of 20 Nov.
1759: about 2.30 p.m.

L'Orient
Port Louis
Auray
Vannes
I. de Groix
Morbihan
R. Vilaine
Quiberon Pt.
Teignouze Passage
Houat
Dumet I.
BELLEISLE
Haedic
Le Palais
Cardinal Rks
CONFLANS
Croisic
HAWKE
Four Shoal
St. Nazaire
R. Loire

have seen, had even set their topgallant-sails. The severe training of the blockade was now bearing fruit. The fact that, notwithstanding all the factors favouring Conflans' plan, the enemy was brought to action that afternoon was due in the last resort to the overwhelming superiority of British seamanship.

Soon after half-past two the rear of the French and the van of the British squadron began to engage. ' We were then to the southward of Belleisle,' Hawke wrote, ' and the French Admiral headmost soon after led round the Cardinals.' In the first phase of the action a heavy rain-squall struck the opposing fleets. The *Temple* was obliged to double-reef her topsails. The *Dorsetshire*, with her lee ports under water, had to luff in order to clear the water between decks. 'At this time we received so much water in at the lee ports ' the master of the *Torbay* recorded, ' we were obliged to bring the ship up in the wind.' Three of the foremost British vessels—the *Magnanime, Montague*, and *Warspite*—collided in the squall and carried away their jib-booms and spritsail yards. This accident momentarily delayed the pursuit, while the enemy stretched ahead and to windward of them. On the *Magnanime*'s getting clear she bore down on the *Formidable*, flagship of the French rear-admiral, du Verger, and engaged her. She was shortly after ' joined by Sir John Bentley in the *Warspight*, and in half an hour they made a dreadful havoc in the *Formidable*, whose fire began to slack '. Receiving the fire of ship after ship, and being reduced almost to a wreck, du Verger's flagship fought doggedly on. ' Her starboard side ', wrote the surgeon of the *Coventry*, ' was pierced like a cullender by the number of shot she received in the course of the action.' The French rear-admiral, flag-captain, and second captain were killed. About four o'clock the *Torbay*, coming alongside the stricken Frenchman, gave her two broadsides with which to silence her, then left her to the *Resolution*, to whom she soon after struck.

Hauling round the Cardinals soon after half-past two, Conflans had heard the sound of distant gunfire; but he had no clear idea of what was happening. During the squalls the wind had gone higher, and this enabled the British to overhaul the enemy more rapidly and to concentrate on their rearmost ships. Conflans got well within the bay with his van and centre: but his line was not properly formed and the *Magnanime* and those with her now swept into the bay pell-mell along with the sternmost enemy ships. The wind shifting suddenly to north-west had thrown Conflans' line into utter disorder. ' The confusion was awful,' wrote a French officer, ' when the van, in which I was, tried to go about. Part could not do it. We were in a funnel, as it were, all on the top of each other, with rocks on one side of us and ships on the other.'[1] Into an area scarcely five miles long and six and a half miles broad, hemmed in by islands and shoals, crowded two large squadrons, totalling not far short of fifty of the line. In these narrow waters there was no room for manœuvring. Under the fast-darkening, grey November sky and drifting clouds of smoke, individual British and French ships, rolling heavily in the great ocean

[1] Q. Corbett, *England in the Seven Years War*, II, p. 66.

swell, contended furiously during the brief remainder of the day, watched by many thousands of spectators who had run out from Croisic and the surrounding villages. Such an action, under such conditions of weather and sea, had never been fought before. The wild moaning of the gale, accompanied by the unending rattle of blocks, creaking of yards, slatting of canvas, clatter of sheets, and thrumming of backstays, mingled with the louder roar of the guns and crash of falling spars. To add to the confusion, another hard squall came down. The *Thésée*, a new 74, which had been in action with the *Torbay*, was quickly laid on her beam ends and, her lee ports being open, instantly filled and sank. Her captain, Kersaint de Coëtnempren, and six hundred of his men went to their doom. It would appear that the *Torbay* narrowly escaped a similar fate. On the sinking of the *Thésée*, her opponent immediately hoisted out all her boats and sent them to the wreck to endeavour to save as many of her people as they could: but there were only twenty-two survivors. About the same time the *Magnanime*, being disengaged, stood away with the *Chatham* after the *Héros*, 74, which had been in the thick of the fighting and ' had lost her fore and mizen topmast ', and was now making off to the southward. Swiftly overhauling the *Héros*, the *Magnanime* ' bore down close under her stern and raked her '; soon after, as the *Chatham* came up, the *Héros*, which in a quarter of an hour had ' lost every officer on board down to a midshipman, and had near 400 killed and wounded ', with her helm shot away and her decks encumbered with wreckage, struck; ' and she came to anchor,' as Hawke observed in his dispatch, ' but it blowing hard, no boat could be sent on board her '.

Conflans' attempt to form line inside the bay and get into his station in the centre having failed, he endeavoured to lead the fleet out to sea again and, followed by two other vessels, bore up for the entrance. Several of the British ships now found themselves between two fires. Meanwhile, the *Royal George* had got round the Cardinals shortly before four o'clock and was making all the sail that she could bear in order to overhaul the French flagship, which was then steering for the entrance of the bay. In the fast-failing light and rising wind and sea Hawke ordered his ship to be laid alongside the *Soleil Royal*. To the remonstrations of the master concerning the danger of this proceeding, the Admiral replied, ' You have done your duty in this remonstrance; now obey my orders, and lay me alongside the French

Admiral.' 'The French Admiral seemed to have the same ambition on his part,' observed the naval chaplain, who was an eye-witness of this phase of the engagement, 'and it was a glorious sight to behold the blue and white flags, both at the maintopmast-head, bearing down to each other.' The *Royal George* passed by the *Torbay*, which was then closely engaged with the *Thésée*; while on the other side the *Magnanime* was engaging the *Héros*. 'At 35 minutes after 4,' wrote Hawke's flag-captain, 'we got up with 4 sail of the enemy ships who all wore and gave us their broadsides; we then began to engage.' The rival flagships were now very near; and the *Soleil Royal* gave the *Royal George* her broadside, which the latter promptly returned. Several other French ships in succession engaged the *Royal George*; but the last of these fared not so well. 'At 41 minutes after 4'—the time is precisely recorded in her captain's journal—the *Royal George* poured two broadsides into the *Superbe*; after which the latter suddenly foundered. The sea ran so high that no assistance could be rendered to the poor wretches struggling in the water. 'The *Royal George's* gave a cheer,' declared the naval chaplain, 'but it was a faint one; the honest sailors were touched at the miserable state of so many hundreds of poor creatures.' Astern of the *Royal George*, Sir Charles Hardy in the *Union*, 90, with the *Mars*, *Hero*, and several other ships, was pressing on to support the Admiral. At this moment the *Intrépide*, 70, one of the French vessels which were following in the wake of the *Soleil Royal*, steered between the two flagships. Nevertheless, Conflans' plan had been effectually frustrated: manœuvring to avoid being raked by the *Royal George*, the *Soleil Royal* fell to leeward, and in trying to tack, fell aboard two of the ships following her; with the result that she was unable to weather the Four and had to run back and anchor off Croisic.

It was now five o'clock of a winter's evening, and nearly dark; ahead lay the foam-lashed shores of Dumet Island, close to leeward were the rocks and shoals of Croisic; to the southward a roaring chaos of breakers and broken water marked the dangerous Four shoal, which this same night was to claim one victim and early the following morning a second; round about were various imperfectly known reefs and shoals; the gale was still increasing. In the final phase of the action the wind coming again more northerly obliged the French fleet to wear; and as more and more of the British vessels continued to pour into the bay the action became more general. The *Royal George* drawing very near the enemy, they made what sail they could to avoid her; but several of the French were nevertheless ' very warmly engaged by the *Royal George* and some others of His Majesty's ships ', till the evening closed. Seven of the enemy, led by Villars de la Brosse in the *Glorieux*, tacking to avoid the rocks and shoals which encompassed them, fell deeper and deeper into the bight towards the estuary of the Vilaine. The ebb was now running out against the wind, and a terrific sea was rising. As the pall of advancing night descended upon the heaving, foam-flecked surface of the bay all fighting ceased.

' Night was now come,' wrote Hawke in his dispatch, ' and being on a part of the coast of which we were totally ignorant, without a pilot, as was the the greatest part of the squadron, and blowing hard on a lee shore, I made the signal to anchor, and came-to in 15-fathom water, the Island of Dumet bearing E. by N. between 2 and 3 miles, the Cardinals W.½S., and the steeples of Crozie S.E., as we found next morning.'

It was now the turn of the British to suffer a reverse. When nightfall had put an end to the fighting, though a number of his ships were severely damaged, Hawke's force remained intact. About ten o'clock, however, while standing towards the main body of the fleet, the *Resolution* ran on the Four shoal. Notwithstanding that her people did all they could to save her, she struck twice again ' very hard ' and was bulged. Later during the night a number of the enemy ships, under Bauffremont, losing sight of the *Soleil Royal*, and fearful of the reefs and shoals which encircled them, reached to windward and stood out to sea.

All this was, of course, unknown to Hawke and Conflans. The former did not know that the *Resolution* was aground; the latter was unaware that half his force was missing. During the hours of darkness considerable uncertainty prevailed as to the state of the rival fleets. Though the fighting had gone in Hawke's favour, the first light of dawn might reveal a calamitous change of fortune. ' In the night ', the Admiral observed, ' we heard many guns fired, but, blowing hard, want of knowledge of the coast, and whether they were fired by a friend or enemy, prevented all means of relief.'

At daybreak on the morrow it still blew hard and a heavy sea was running. Bauffremont and his division having got safely out of the bay were well on the way to the shelter of the Basque roads.[1] Their departure had left Conflans with only eight sail. For his part Hawke was about to suffer a further loss. The *Resolution* was seen to be aground on the Four shoal, ' with all her masts gone and firing guns of distress '. The *Héros* also, and the *Soleil Royal*, which in the darkness of the night had chanced to anchor in the midst of the British fleet, presently cut and ran ashore to the westward of Croisic.

The *Essex* being ordered to slip and pursue the enemy, likewise got on the Four. Soon after Hawke made the signal to weigh in order to work up and attack seven French ships which were anchored between Penris Point and the mouth of the Vilaine. ' But it blowed so hard from the N.W.,' the Admiral declared, ' that, instead of daring to cast the squadron loose, I was obliged to strike topgallant-masts.' Hawke signalled all the boats to go to the assistance of the ships in distress. But because of the weather nothing could be done to save the *Resolution* and *Essex*, though most of their people were taken off safely. The gale continued throughout the whole of the 21st. In the course of the day five of the French vessels, after jettisoning all their guns and gear, escaped with a favouring wind over the bar into the river in two tides— a feat which had never before been accomplished.

On the 22nd the weather moderated and Hawke sent in three of Duff's vessels to burn the *Soleil Royal* and *Héros*. The crew of the *Soleil Royal* thereupon set fire to the flagship, while the British destroyed the *Héros*. The remaining French vessels succeeded in getting into the Vilaine on the flood.

The British losses in the action of Quiberon Bay were the two ships wrecked on the Four and between three and four hundred men; while the enemy had lost five ships, including the two flagships, the *Soleil Royal* and *Formidable* (another four of their vessels were destined to break their backs on the mud in the Vilaine),[2] and about 2,500 men, the great majority of whom were drowned.

Hawke's victory was the prize of consummate seamanship and a resolute acceptance of all risks to attain a supreme objective of naval warfare—viz. the destruction of the enemy's fighting fleet. ' When I consider the season of the year, the hard gales on the day of action, a

[1] The *Juste* ran aground when entering the mouth of the Loire and soon after broke up.

[2] Hawke's plan for destroying the enemy's ships in the river by means of fire-boats had eventually to be abandoned as impracticable.

flying enemy, the shortness of the day, and the coast they were on, I can boldly affirm that all that could possibly be done has been done. As to the loss we have sustained,' the Admiral concluded, ' let it be placed to the necessity I was under of running all risks to break this strong force of the enemy.'

Quiberon Bay has been justly described by Professor Lewis as ' the greatest of all " chace " victories '. The Brest squadron and the whole elaborate organization for the invasion of Britain—' their last desperate effort to turn the tide of an unfortunate war ', as the surgeon of the *Coventry* observed—had been swept off the board at a single stroke. ' It not only defeated the projected invasion, which had hung menacingly so long over the apprehensions of Great Britain,' Smollett wrote in his *History of England*, ' but it gave the finishing blow to the naval power of France.' The verdict of another eighteenth-century historian, Frederick Hervey, is also worthy of notice. ' Thus was the last hope of the French marine frustrated. The long-threatened invasion which was to repair their losses in every part of the world, was rendered impracticable, and their national greatness annihilated.' The situation at home was greatly eased. As a result of Conflans' defeat, Pitt was able to dispatch some 20,000 regulars to reinforce Prince Ferdinand in Germany. Quiberon Bay once and for all extinguished the waning hopes of the Jacobites. ' Th' illustrious House of Hanover, and Protestant Succession ' was thereby rendered unchallengeably secure. For generations to come this island was to remain staunchly and truculently Protestant.

In 1759 the Navy played a far more important part in the Seven Years War than at any other time, before or after. All our defensive and offensive operations throughout that year had turned, in the last resort, on Anson's dispositions. The blockading squadrons off the enemy's arsenals and the fleet which carried Wolfe and his army to their final triumph on the Plains of Abraham all made part of the same strategic plan.

The action of 20 November came as a triumphant climax to the Year of Victories. Month by month the good tidings had come pouring in—Goree, Guadeloupe, Ticonderoga, Niagara, Minden, Lagos Bay, Quebec, and finally, Quiberon Bay. ' Oh, what pleasure it is to every true Briton,' wrote Thomas Turner, the Sussex diarist, ' to see what success it pleases Almighty God to bless his Majestie's arms; they having success at this time in Europe, Asia, Africa, and America!' Not within living memory had there been such bell-ringing, such drinking of loyal toasts, such blaze of bonfires and illuminations. The rich autumnal tints of the English countryside that year formed a fitting background to the crescendo of rejoicing; for the fine summer weather lingered on until long after Michaelmas. ' It is still all gold,' recorded Walpole on 21 October. ' I have not dined or gone to bed by a fire till the day before yesterday. Instead of the glorious and ever-memorable year of 1759, as the newspapers call it, I call it this ever-warm and victorious year. We have not had more conquest than fine weather: one would think we had plundered the East and West Indies of sunshine. Our bells are worn threadbare with ringing for victories.' And on 30 November, at the news of Hawke's victory over Conflans, he remarked exultantly, ' Thus we wind up this wonderful year.'

7

Naval operations in the West Indies in the earlier stages of the war, as in the East Indies from first to last, were essentially a matter of commerce protection. As soon as Pitt took office in 1756 he strengthened the squadron on the West Indian station; and in the ensuing years he was under continual pressure to provide better protection for our commerce with these islands. The West Indian trade was at that time the richest and most important that Great Britain possessed. Immense convoys were accustomed to sail each year for home laden with sugar, rum, molasses, coffee, syrup, cotton, ginger, and tobacco. Upon the safe passage of these convoys depended the wealth and credit of the City merchants who financed the day-to-day war expenditure of the government.

The protection of the West Indian trade presented considerable difficulties. The French enjoyed a major advantage in the position of their bases. In Fort Royal (Martinique) they had a first-class windward base, and in Cap François (Haïti) a base which lay to windward of the principal British base in Jamaica. The enemy bases in Martinique and Haïti were watched by squadrons of heavy ships; large frigates were stationed in the chief trade focals, and smaller cruisers in the coastal tracks where French privateers were most active. The majority of our convoys reached their destination in safety; but much of the trade could not sail in convoy, and, owing to the superiority of the enemy's position in the West Indies, proved most awkward to protect. The enemy exploited these natural advantages with so much success that they retained the control of the Caribbean throughout the early half of the war.

In 1759 the war in the West Indies entered on a new phase. Though the overthrow of the French power in North America remained the ultimate object of the war, it was decided in that year to launch an offensive in the West Indian theatre with a view to securing a pledge for the eventual recovery of Minorca. An expedition consisting of about 6,000 troops, escorted by ten sail of the line and several frigates, sailed in November 1758. Finding the great French naval base at Fort Royal too strong to attack, the expedition crossed to Guadeloupe and, after a hard and protracted struggle, succeeded in capturing the island. In June 1761 a force dispatched from British North America captured the island of Dominica, and later, with the help of reinforcements, attacked Martinique, which surrendered in February 1762. The French power in the Caribbean was now broken. The fall of several other French islands followed later in the same year. It is significant of the high commercial importance of the West Indian islands in the eighteenth century that both Great Britain and France allotted for these operations in the Caribbean naval forces roughly three times as great as those employed in the Indian Ocean.

8

The years 1760–1 witnessed the culmination of Pitt's triumph in both hemispheres. In 1760 the campaigns in Canada and India were brought to a victorious conclusion. The destruction of Clue's and Conflan's squadrons in 1759 had made it impossible for the enemy effectively to reinforce his overseas possessions. From Dunkirk to Marseilles the French naval ports in which were lying the scattered fragments of the enemy's fleet were held fast in the grip of the blockade. Rodney cruised in the Channel, and Brett in the North Sea. Hawke and Boscawen relieved each other in Quiberon Bay. Quiberon Bay and the Basque Roads had become in fact British anchorages; their islets were actually worked as vegetable gardens for the refreshment of the ships' companies. A number of the enemy's homecoming men-of-war were intercepted and taken, together with a good many of his merchantmen and privateers; the coastwise traffic of France was almost completely paralysed. Saunders, commanding on the Mediterranean station, kept the Barbary pirates in check, protected British commerce, and virtually annihilated that of the enemy. ' The diligence of Admiral Saunders was such ', declared Beatson, ' that from the time he made his appearance in these seas the enemy's trade was reduced to a state of stagnation.'[1] Meanwhile a squadron under Colville cruised in North American waters, and another under Holmes in the West Indies; Pocock commanded on the East Indian station. In the summer of 1761 a conjunct expedition under Commodore Keppel and General Hodgson captured the island of Belleisle off the mouth of the Loire. In the autumn Pitt prepared the plans for the reduction of Martinique, Grenada, and St. Lucia, and appointed Rodney to command on the West Indian station.

What Pitt was now aiming at was nothing less than the total destruction of the enemy's sea power. His intention was to put it out of France's power ever again to challenge us either at sea or in the colonies. The present impotence of the French fleet left little doubt of the success of the measures he had in mind. The Royal Navy had at this stage attained to the unprecedented strength of 100 sail of the line and rather more than as many frigates, while the French fleet numbered scarcely half this total and was immeasurably inferior in seamanship and morale. Pitt's colleagues, however, were becoming increasingly restive at the prodigious cost of these world-wide campaigns and mistrustful of his schemes of national aggrandizement. ' To drive France entirely out of any naval power ', observed Bedford, who was strongly opposed to Pitt's design, ' is fighting against nature, and can tend to no good to this country; but, on the contrary, must excite all the naval powers of Europe against us, as adopting a system, viz.: that of a monopoly of all naval power, which would be at least as dangerous to the liberties of Europe as that of Louis XIV was, which drew all Europe upon his back.'[2] The whole controversy centred eventually on the Newfoundland fishery. Choiseul was firmly resolved on no account to give up the French fishing rights. On his side Pitt

---

[1] *Naval and Military Memoirs of Great Britain from 1727 to 1783* (1790), II, p. 426.
[2] Q. Tunstall, *William Pitt, Earl of Chatham* (1938), pp. 293-4.

was no less determined to strip the enemy of all his fisheries in North
American waters.

9

The concluding phase of the Seven Years War was marked by the
long-threatened intervention of Spain. On the accession, in 1761, of
her new sovereign, Charles III, an inveterate enemy of Great Britain,
she joined France under the terms of the Family Compact between
the two Courts, and added her fleet, which in point of numbers was
still formidable, though decidedly inferior in quality, to what was left
of the navy of France. Apprised of Spain's hostile intentions, Pitt
expressed the opinion that ' this was the moment for humbling the
whole House of Bourbon.' He had intended to anticipate the imminent
attack by seizing the Spanish treasure fleet, on which the Spanish
government depended to pay its army and navy, before the actual
declaration of war; Keppel with a force of sixty sail lay off Cape
Finisterre, and could have secured the treasure before the Spaniards
had any inkling of the danger; but Pitt was overruled in the Cabinet,
and resigned on 5 October.

Notwithstanding the change of ministry, the grand strategy of the
war, of which Pitt was the author, rolled irresistibly forward. ' The
single eloquence of Mr. Pitt ', declared Horace Walpole, ' can, like an
annihilated star, shine many months after it has set.' Towards the end
of the war the Pope observed that, so great was our national glory and
reputation all over the world, he esteemed it the greatest honour to be
born an Englishman. As soon as it was perceived that a rupture with
Spain was unavoidable, a large reinforcement of ships, under the command of Sir Piercy Brett, was sent out to strengthen Saunders in the
Mediterranean. Early in 1762 a conjunct expedition under Rear-
Admiral Rodney and General Monckton took possession of Martinique,
St. Lucia, Grenada, and St. Vincent. Meanwhile the Bourbon States,
having attempted without success to persuade Portugal to join their
alliance, declared war and sent an army against her. The Portuguese
were obliged to fall back before the superior hostile forces; but in response to their appeal the British government presently prepared to send
an army of 8,000 men to their assistance; and Anson warned the new
Prime Minister, Lord Bute, that the Channel Fleet must immediately

be got to sea to secure the safe passage of these troops to Lisbon. While in July 1762 Hawke cruised between Ortegal and Finisterre, with a chain of cruisers thrown out to watch the enemy in Ferrol, and Saunders moved out of the Straits to blockade the Cadiz squadron, the fleet of transports passed safely up the Tagus in time to stiffen the Portuguese defence. With the help of these reinforcements and the naval co-operation of Saunders in the south of Portugal, the Portuguese were able to hold out against their enemies. In the end the Spaniards were driven out of Portugal; and our army invaded Spain. The naval defensive system organized by Anson in the last months of his life covered the whole Channel and Atlantic coasts of the Bourbon Powers; Choiseul's project for a victorious counterstroke came to nothing; and, under cover of the blockade, the British war machine— now geared up to the highest pitch of efficiency and power—was swiftly set in motion against the outlying possessions of Spain, as well as those of her exhausted ally. On 14 August 1762, a powerful naval and military force under Admiral Sir George Pocock and General Albemarle captured Havana, the capital city of the Spanish possessions in the West Indies, together with one-fifth of the entire Spanish navy, and nearly a hundred merchantmen. The total prize money accruing from this conquest amounted to close on £$\frac{3}{4}$ million. The loss of Havana was a crippling blow to Spain; the port was of the highest strategical and commercial importance, commanding as it did the passage of the treasure fleets on which the Spanish finances depended. On 6 October an expedition sent out from India under the command of Rear-Admiral Cornish and Colonel Draper captured Manila, the capital of the Philippines. The subjugation of the whole island-group followed soon after. The capture of Manila dried up the source of Spanish wealth in the East as effectively as the conquest of Havana had destroyed that in the West. About the same time Cornish's squadron captured the Acapulco galleon with some three million dollars on board; and in the North Atlantic the Spanish treasure-ship *Hermione* was taken about one day's run from Cadiz by two of Saunders' cruisers. ' No nation ever paid dearer for a ten months' war than Spain did,' Beatson declared, ' and she well deserved it for her temerity.'

Well under a year after her declaration of war against Great Britain, Spain, in fact, had been knocked out.

As has already been stated, from the strategical point of view the campaign in Indian waters was once more a question of simple commerce protection. It was the object of the French to destroy the British trade and coastal settlements; while the British endeavoured to protect them. The Admiralty accordingly maintained in those waters a small squadron, under the command of Rear-Admiral Charles Watson, for the purpose of commerce defence. When the French squadron on the East Indian station was strengthened by a small reinforcement under Admiral d'Aché, the Admiralty replied by sending out a squadron of four of the line, under Commodore Steevens, which was sufficient to bring our naval forces in Indian waters up to an approximate equality with those of the enemy. From first to last no attempt was ever made by the Admiralty to maintain, in the East Indian theatre, naval forces of such preponderance as would have been required for a general offensive, such as that about to be launched against Canada.

After the seizure of Calcutta by the Nawab of Bengal in 1756 Watson and his squadron co-operated with the military force led by Robert Clive, and on New Year's Day 1757 recaptured the city. They followed up this success with a well-organized expedition against Chandernagore, the headquarters of French trade in Bengal, situated about fifty miles above Calcutta. Watson pushed up the river with his squadron and supported Clive with the devastating fire of his ships' guns. Chandernagore capitulated on 15 March. Then, judging that his force was too small to defend the Company's possessions on the Coromandel coast as well as in Bengal, he elected to leave Madras to take its chance while he co-operated with Clive in the operations which terminated in the decisive victory of Plassey. This made the Company the virtual rulers of all Bengal and Bihar. Watson died of fever and was succeeded by his second-in-command, Rear-Admiral George Pocock. Pocock remained in Bengal till the defences of Calcutta were completed, and then, early in 1758, sailed for Madras to join forces with Steevens and his squadron.

Meanwhile Bussy, the disciple whom Dupleix had left behind in the Carnatic, had completed the chain of French coastal settlements by capturing Masulipatam, a British port lying to the north of Madras.

But what had been gained by Clive and Watson in Bengal far out-balanced these losses in Madras. Moreover, the situation in India was such that the future of French power there depended, in the last resort, on their gaining the command of the sea. Despite his superiority in strength over Pocock, the Comte d'Aché fell back on a cautious, defensive strategy which necessarily proved fatal to the prospects of France. On the British side, though Pocock and his successor were unable ever to bring d'Aché to decisive action, they nevertheless prevented the French from destroying our commerce or counter-attacking in Bengal. In an inconclusive action between Pocock and d'Aché off Fort St. David on the Coromandel coast, the enemy had recourse to his usual manœuvre of retiring in succession and reform-ing his line to leeward; by firing langridge at his opponent's rigging, he rendered the British squadron unable either to manœuvre or to pursue. There was another engagement on the same lines off Pondi-cherry on 3 August. On the approach of the monsoon that autumn d'Aché sailed for Mauritius to shelter and refit, while his adversary retired to Bombay. The French military commander, the Comte de Lally, deprived of d'Aché's squadron, for the present turned inland instead of against Madras. It was not until towards the end of 1758 that the French, who had already taken the British station at Fort St. David, at last laid seige to Madras. Clive, however, had no misgivings as to the outcome of the struggle. ' Notwithstanding the extraordinary effort made by the French in sending out M. Lally with a consider-able force last year', he wrote to Pitt the following January ' I am confident before the end of this [1759] they will be near their last gasp in the Carnatic unless some very unforseen event interpose in their favour. The superiority of our squadron and the plenty of money and supplies of all kinds which our friends on that coast will be furnished with from this province [Bengal], while the enemy are in total want of everything, without any means of redress, are such advantages, as if properly attended to, cannot fail of wholly effecting their ruin in that as well as in every other part of India.'

Clive's confidence was justified in the outcome. The opportune arrival of Captain Kempenfelt with two frigates and half a dozen trans-ports off Madras on 16 February caused Lally to break up the seige and retire to Pondicherry. In April Masulipatam was recaptured from the French. In September d'Aché returned to the Coromandel coast with a squadron superior both in numbers and power to that of Pocock. The latter, however, did not hesitate to attack. In this third and final engagement between the two admirals, which was fought off Pondicherry on 10 September, the French had the worst of it; but, because the British rigging was as usual badly cut up, Pocock was unable to pursue and d'Aché got safely into port. At the end of the month d'Aché retired to Mauritius. This, as Lally perfectly well understood, spelt the ruin of French hopes in India. The end was now only a matter of time. With the British in permanent control of Indian waters their ultimate triumph was assured.

Pocock at this point returned to England and was succeeded by Rear-Admiral Charles Steevens. On 22 January 1760 Lally was soundly beaten by Colonel Eyre Coote at Wandewash. The British spent the next few months in reducing all the lesser French settlements in the Carnatic and in assembling strong forces for an expedition against the enemy's capital. Once again the squadron co-operated harmoniously with the troops. Pondicherry was besieged by Coote and blockaded by Steevens. Only d'Aché's return and energetic intervention could save the great French stronghold. But d'Aché had received peremptory orders from his home government, which was apprehensive of a British attempt against Mauritius, forbidding him to return to the Coromandel coast. Pondicherry was accordingly left to its fate. Under Lally's leadership it put up a fine defence; but the decisive factor was the fine seamanship of Steevens and his men. For on New Year's Day, 1761, the British squadron was struck by a cyclone. ' I found myself under an absolute necessity of cutting my cable and making the signal for the squadron to do the same,' related Steevens, ' driving off under a reef'd mizen.' As a result of this disaster, four of Steevens' eight battleships were dismantled, while two other ships foundered, and one was driven ashore. The lesser vessels fared no better. ' The English Squadron is no more,' Lally wrote triumphantly from Pondicherry on 2 January. ' Sir, out of the twelve ships they had in our road, seven are lost crews and all, the four others dismasted, and it appears there is no more than one frigate that hath escaped.' Steevens' flagship, however, got safely out to sea and later returned to her post off Pondicherry. Here, joined by welcome reinforcements, Steevens resumed the blockade. On 15 January Pondicherry, now the sole remaining centre of French power in India, surrendered with 600 guns and an immense quantity of gunpowder and other military stores.

II

It has elsewhere been observed that the maritime supremacy of Great Britain rested upon her immense mercantile marine no less than upon her fighting fleet. The Seven Years War furnishes a striking illustration of this fact. Every year, in spite of the war, British trade was increasing. The merchants of London, Bristol, Norwich, Glasgow and other great commercial and manufacturing towns had never been more prosperous. The City was the centre of the world's finance. Its steadily increasing prosperity was reflected in the multiplication of banks and joint-stock companies. The proud inscription on Pitt's monument in the Guildhall records the fact that, under his administration, commerce had been ' united and made to flourish by war '. ' No such circumstances of glory and advantage,' declared Burke, ' ever attended upon a war.'[1] Year by year the forest of masts in the Thames grew wider and deeper; to and from the Port of London came shipping from every quarter of the globe. For the first time, too, there was, other than in the capital, a considerable urban population: some nine or ten provincial towns had each a population of more than 20,000; Bristol, the second city of the kingdom, possessed 100,000 inhabitants. British exports rose from £11¾ millions before the outbreak of the Seven Years War to £14½ millions in 1761; during the same period British mercantile tonnage had increased by over 32,000.

' Thus our trade encreased nearly a fifth,' observed Burke; ' our British navigation had encreased likewise with this astonishing encrease of trade, but was not able to keep pace with it; and we added about 60,000 ton more of foreign shipping than had been employed in the last year of peace.'

The total mercantile tonnage of these islands was now reckoned at well over 500,000, or about one-third of that of all Europe. It has even been claimed, by an amazing paradox, that the prosperity of Great Britain was evidenced by the very magnitude of her losses, which considerably exceeded, indeed, those of the enemy.[2] For while the

---

[1] *Observations . . . on the Present State of the Nation* (1769).

[2] ' The enemy's trade being in a great measure annihilated, the captures made this year [1760] were consequently few. They amounted to only one hundred and ten vessels. On the contrary, our trade flourished in every part of the globe; and the

merchant shipping of this country increased and multiplied under the shield of the Navy, that of the enemy rapidly declined. In the final phase of the struggle Great Britain had no less than 8,000 merchantmen at sea and the supply of seamen appeared almost inexhaustible: the Navy alone employed 70,000 of them. The long columns of captured ships and cargoes which appeared in *Lloyd's List* were, in fact, no true index to the realities of the situation. From her ubiquitous commerce Great Britain was able to build up a battle fleet of overwhelming superiority to all other navies, and to subsidize the continental ally whose skilful and heroic defence compelled France to expend her principal energies in Europe instead of on the decisive battle-ground across the Atlantic.

In home waters, and particularly in the great trade focal of the English Channel, commerce protection was provided by patrolling cruisers. The Channel Squadron, cruising off Ushant, covered the passage of British merchant shipping entering or leaving the danger zone of the Western Approaches, while the eastern end of the Channel was held by the North Sea Squadron, which was based as a rule on the Downs. For the principal trades convoys were organized with escorting warships. At the terminal ports overseas, e.g. in the East and West Indies, protection was provided by the local British squadrons. In a word, the terminals and principal trade focals, where the traffic was busiest and most likely to attract raiding squadrons, were strongly defended areas; while on the ocean, where it was unprofitable for such squadrons to operate, the convoy escorts were sufficient protection. These measures served to secure the safe passage of the bulk of our seaborne trade during the Seven Years War. Most of the damage, in fact, appears to have been done, not to the convoys, but to the coastal craft and small vessels generally, by the enemy's privateers.

The Channel Squadron was the mainspring of our attack on the enemy's trade in the Western Approaches, just as it was of the protection of our own. British cruisers preyed on enemy merchantmen entering the focal between Ushant and Scilly, and so starved the northern ports of France. At the same time the Channel Squadron

enemy, having swarms of small privateers at sea, captured no less than three hundred and thirty of the British ships' (Beatson, *Naval and Military Memoirs of Great Britain from 1727 to 1783* (1790), II, p. 426).

served to cover our cruiser forces operating against the busy coastwise traffic of France. In the latter stages of the war the enemy's overseas trade was seriously damaged by the loss of such important entrepôts as Louisbourg, Guadeloupe, and Martinique. The wholesale destruction of the once thriving commerce of France was significantly reflected in the ruin of her credit.

Inevitably all this was not achieved without considerable interference with neutral trade. It was not that the rules laid down by Great Britain were so much harsher than those of other States, that made the enforcement of her maritime rights more grievous to neutrals; it was because her naval power was incomparably greater. The geographical position of Great Britain was also a factor of prime importance. The trade of Holland, Denmark, Sweden, Russia, and northern Germany all passed through the Channel close to her ports: for in the days of sail ships hugged the English coast.[1]

Throughout the war the carrying trade of neutrals was vitally important to France and Spain (it has been estimated that no less than two-thirds of the trade of France in the eighteenth century was carried in neutral bottoms); and neutral shipowners, particularly those of Holland, were not slow to exploit the situation. Thus in the latter stages of the war our cruisers based on the Downs found more employment from Dutch, than from French or Spanish shipping. ' The sea is full of ships,' wrote Boscawen in the spring of 1756, ' but all Dutch. These rogues carry on a swinging trade while the English and French languish in port, and laugh at us both.'

These differences were aggravated by the fact that France, to preserve her West Indian trade, had suspended her navigation laws and opened that formerly exclusive traffic to neutrals. Here, however, they encountered the strong and uncompromising resistance of British statesmen and judges, who now developed the Rule of the War of 1756, which had already been applied, in the War of 1739–48, in the

---

[1] Since a fair wind up-Channel—that is, at south-west—was always liable to fly to the northward, should such a change occur vessels standing along the south side would find themselves immediately on a dead lee shore. On the French side of the Channel, too, from Ushant to Alderney, there were numerous islands, rocks, and outlying dangers; and along this shore, and among the islands and rocks, the flood-tide, at a distance of some thirty miles off the land, set to the south-east, while the ebb did not set north-west, but west: with the result that vessels driven on this coast with north-westerly gales would not have the tide to help them off, and would be most liable to be driven on shore.

case of Spain. The Rule of the War of 1756, which was strongly up-held by Pitt and Anson, was summarized as follows by Lord Mansfield, the Solicitor-General:

> All the European nations exclude foreigners from their American colonies, and so things stood at the time of the treaty of 1674. It is the general rule still, and cannot possibly be varied, except as a new invention fraudulently to screen French effects from capture, and the question is whether England shall suffer them to trade thither in time of war, without seizure, when the French themselves will not suffer them to trade thither, in time of peace, on that very account.[1]

With the Rule of the War of 1756 was linked the doctrine of Continuous Voyage. In the British view, whether a voyage had originated in a neutral or an enemy port, it made no difference if the neutral were engaged in a traffic closed to him in time of peace. What was in fact at issue were two conflicting interpretations of international law: for while the Dutch and certain others claimed that enemy goods in neutral ships were immune from capture, the British maintained that enemy goods were lawful prize everywhere at sea.[2] The more pressing grievances of the neutrals centred on the increasingly lawless and violent activities of the British privateers: some of which, indeed, were little better than pirates. The Swedes had shown themselves hostile to Great Britain from the outbreak of the war. The Danes and Dutch were naturally unwilling to relinquish the lucrative West Indian traffic. Russia was already at war with our ally, Frederick II, and protested bitterly at the piracies committed by our privateers against her merchantmen. It was not only the Northern Powers that were growing restive. The Spanish protests at the depredations of our privateers became more insistent; while Choiseul was labouring to revive the Family Compact between the two Bourbon States.

In the years 1757–8 the blockade in the Channel became increasingly effective. Following upon the seizure of large numbers of Dutch and Danish merchantmen, intense indignation arose among those neutrals who had hoped to profit by the war: the traditional alliance with Holland became a dead letter and there was talk in Copenhagen of a

---

[1] Q. Pares, *Colonial Blockade and Neutral Rights, 1739–1763*, p. 180.

[2] The *Monitor* in January, 1759, put the matter in a nutshell: 'If Holland and France have a right by the laws of nature and nations to prescribe rules for the commerce of neutral states, *flagrante bello*, in time of war; what shall debar Britain from the same right?'

maritime league of neutrals. Fortunately for Great Britain, these out-bursts of neutral resentment were not simultaneous. First the Danes and the Swedes, then the Dutch, and lastly the Spaniards fulminated against our interference with their trade. The object of French dip-lomacy in the meantime was to bring about a maritime union against Great Britain; but the attempt failed. When the danger was at its height —between August 1758 and August 1759—Spain was paralysed by her home politics; and the Dutch claim of *Free ships, free goods* was strongly and successfully resisted by Great Britain. Pitt's treatment of this most difficult question was a triumph of tactful but resolute statecraft. To the Russian Vice-Chancellor, Woronzow, our envoy expressed profound regret for the excesses of the privateers, but explained, ' that they were the consequences of a maritime war, where the giving of commissions to privateers was necessary; and must unavoidably now and then fall into bad hands, as the persons who follow that trade were often not the people in the world of the best morals and strictest discipline; but that the Government were doing everything in their power to put a stop to these licentious proceed-ings.'[1]

Pitt stood firm on our traditional maritime rights, including the right of search; at the same time he brought pressure to bear upon the prize courts to release as many captured neutral ships as possible and did his utmost to restrain the worst excesses of the privateers by administrative and legislative action. ' England the mistress of the Ocean should not act despotically there,' he told the House of Com-mons. ' . . . The misfortunes accruing to this country from the rob-beries committed by privateers are such that, unless a step is timely made, the neutral nations would all be offended.' The Admiralty offered a reward of £500 for the discovery of the culprits, a number of whom were subsequently arrested, condemned, and executed for their crimes. The Bill which Pitt introduced in May 1759 to curb these abuses gave satisfaction to the maritime neutrals generally. ' I cannot think that the King of Denmark will take a part in the present war,' he had observed earlier in the year, ' which he cannot do without great possible danger; and he is well paid by France for his neutrality; is safe, let what will turn out; and, in the meantime, carries on his com-merce with great advantage and security.' The event showed that Pitt

[1] Q. Hotblack, *Chatham's Colonial Policy* (1917), pp. 142–3.

was right. The Danish government soon abandoned their claim to trade directly with the French West Indian islands. Sweden, though hostile, was not strong enough to act alone; and Great Britain carried on her Baltic trade without hindrance. Nevertheless, the resentment of the maritime neutrals at Great Britain's enforcement of her belligerent rights was a leading factor in the re-alignment of States and paved the way for the Armed Neutralities of 1780 and 1801.

In the last phase of the war Frederick II, now almost at the end of his resources, continued to fight against overwhelming odds. The misery of Prussia was extreme: her once flourishing provinces had been mercilessly plundered and impoverished; in 1760 Berlin had once again been occupied by the enemy. Although Frederick II was able to defeat the Austrians at Leignitz in Silesia in August, and at Torgau in Saxony in November 1760 the campaign of 1761 was on the whole disastrous to the Prussians. The fall of Pitt had deprived the king of his only friend in Europe. Once again hostile armies were closing in on the remnant of his forces. Prussia had by now lost not less than one-ninth of her entire population. At the eleventh hour Frederick II was saved by the death of his implacable foe, Catherine the Great, in January 1762, and the exhaustion of France. Unable to carry on the war alone, Austria was finally forced to relinquish Silesia; and peace was signed at Hubertusburg on 15 February 1763.

The Seven Years War was brought to a close on 10 February 1763 by the Treaty of Paris, whereby Great Britain, renouncing once and for all the prospect of world supremacy, restored to her enemies a considerable part of the colonial possessions which she had acquired by conquest. Her gains at the peace were nevertheless immense. She acquired at the expense of France, the whole of Canada, Nova Scotia, and Cape Breton Island: Grenada, St. Vincent, Dominica, and Tobago: Senegal in West Africa, and Minorca. She received from Spain Florida and certain rights in Honduras. The other possessions of the Bourbon States were restored to them. France for her part gave up Louisiana to her ally as a measure of compensation for the losses Spain had incurred on her behalf during the war.

XI

Sea life under the Georges

I

Throughout the greater part of the eighteenth century British naval construction was usually inferior to that of France and Spain. Compared with ours, the enemy's ships were large in tonnage, and correspondingly large in scantling, with massive frame-timbers and stout oaken sides not easily pierced by shot. Outside the Service, however, this was not properly understood. ' The unthinking populace are too free to censure without inquiry into the reasons of things', Admiral Knowles remarked during the war of 1739–48, ' and imagine it strange that an English ship of war of 70 guns cannot take a French ship of the same force, whereas it is pretty apparent that our 70-gun ships are little superior to their ships of 52-guns.' Shortly before the first action off Finisterre, in the spring of 1747, Admiral Warren observed in similar terms to Anson: ' I am greatly pleased to hear it has been proposed, with a prospect of success, to augment the number of ships and weight of metal in all the different classes of our ships, to put them on a par with those of the French.' ' The Spanish men-of-war we have taken ', Rodney informed his wife after the Moonlight victory in 1780, ' are much superior to ours.' The French vessels in particular were faster, better-proportioned, and, class for class, larger and more powerful than their British opponents. The French frigate *Aurore*, captured in 1758, was considered markedly superior to the best of our British frigates. The *Tonnant*, *Malta*, and *Canopus*, all 80-gun ships, taken at the battle of the Nile, were declared to be the ' finest on two decks ever seen in the British navy; their ports were generally seven feet a-midships, and their qualities in sailing and carrying sail have rarely, if ever been surpassed '; and the *Egyptienne*, taken at Alexandria in 1800, ' the finest ship on one deck we ever had '. The excellence of French shipbuilding was, however, in general much more than counter-balanced by the superior strategy, seamanship, and discipline of the British Navy.[1]

The truth was that the art of naval construction was studied far more carefully across the Channel than over here, where the rule-of-thumb methods of shipwrights, rather than scientific principles, usually prevailed. ' It is a bare act of justice to the fame of the French ship-builders ', Charnock declared, ' that to their studious exertions and experiments is primarily owing the energetical improvement made in modern times on the form, dimensions, and general contour of vessels, be the purpose to which it was intended they should be applied whatsoever it might.'[2]

According to Charnock, the several deficiencies of British ship-building ' which had long been discovered ' were, at last, generally admitted as facts at the beginning of 1746. ' The first attempt towards emancipation from the former servitude ', he went on, ' was the construction of the Royal George. . . . The services rendered by this ship to the public were of the most important kind. Her force nominally exceeded that of any vessel then possessed either by France, Spain, or any other country in the universe.' The Royal George was laid down at Woolwich in 1749 and launched in 1756. Altogether forty ships of the line were added to the Navy during the Seven Years War, representing a substantial improvement on previous construction.

Under Anson's administration a new class of 74-gun ships was introduced in place of the old 70s, and of 64-gun ships in place of the old 60s: these were of 1,500 and 1,200 tons respectively. Later, in 1758, two 74s of still larger design were laid down on the lines of the French prizes captured by Anson and Hawke in the two victories off Finisterre in 1747. ' The advancement of more than three hundred tons at one stroke ', says Charnock, ' in vessels of the same rate, was undoubtedly a grand stroke of mechanics.'

Arising out of the experience of the Austrian Succession and the Seven Years War, important innovations were made in the organization

[1] As Captain John Creswell, R.N., has pointed out in his *Naval Warfare* (1942), despite the fact that individual British vessels might be slower than the French, ' the speed of our squadrons was considerably higher than anything the enemy could accomplish ' owing to the fact that ' the skilful handling of ships and squadrons more than made up for our comparative clumsiness of design.'

[2] John Charnock, *History of Marine Architecture* (1802).

of the Fleet. Hitherto no clear line of demarcation had existed between the line-of-battle ships and cruisers, and there had been a considerable proportion of hybrid types, which were not strong enough to lie in the line of battle or sufficiently fast to serve as cruisers, but now the tendency was towards a classification of ships according to function, and, generally speaking, a simplification and specialization of the three main types of fighting ships. The fire power of the battleships was increased; the cruisers became faster and more seaworthy; and, for inshore work and subsidiary services, large numbers of flotilla craft were constructed.

The first and second rates were three-deckers of 90 guns and upwards. The third and fourth rates, comprising the bulk of the Fleet, were two-deckers, usually of 74 and 64 guns. Altogether ten 74s were constructed during the Seven Years War; and, towards the close of the century, this was to become the standard line-of-battle ship. Anson's term of office also saw the development of the fast-sailing, single-decker frigate, which amply proved its value in the actions of the Seven Years War. Twenty-two new 28-gun frigates were laid down; and there was a numerous class of 32-gun frigates. In 1757, under the superintendence of Sir Thomas Slade, a new class of 36-gun frigates was begun. According to Charnock :

A new class of vessels was introduced into the British navy. They carried 36 guns, and were of about 730 tons burden. They were constructed with every possible attention to their being swift sailers. The endeavours of the builders proving by no means unsuccessful, the few that were built by way of experiment, became regarded with an admiration bordering almost on enthusiasm, so that the command of them was coveted as highly as that of the most powerful and complete ships in the British service.[1]

Between the frigates, and the sloops and lesser flotilla craft, a wide gap was forming, as between the line-of-battle ships and the frigates. At the same time Anson set to work to eliminate a number of intermediate classes, such as the small battleships and slow cruisers. Again to quote Charnock:

The superior class of ships in the fifth rate mounted 44 guns, on two decks, and certainly were the worst vessels which, at that time, composed

[1] The first of the 900-ton, 38-gun frigates, the *Minerva*, appeared in 1780 ; during the French Revolutionary War these were regarded as the finest frigates in the Service. During the American War of 1812-4 there was a further advance in the size and gun-power of British frigates.

any part of the British navy. Long use had caused the continuance of their construction, and experience of their manifold defects proved scarcely sufficient to abolish the ridiculous and absurd custom.

It is worth noting that no less than twelve 60s, eight 50s, and ten 40s were broken up during the Seven Years War.

The practice of sheathing a ship's bottom with copper to obviate the need of frequent cleaning was first tried, on Anson's orders, with the *Alarm* frigate in 1761. The experiment proved so successful that, during the next twenty-five years or so, almost every ship in the Navy was ' coppered '. ' For God's sake, and our country's ', observed Captain Young to Sir Charles Middleton in 1779, ' send out copper-bottomed ships to relieve the foul and crippled ones.' ' I perceive you cry out loudly for coppered ships ', Sandwich wrote to Rodney after the Moonlight action; ' and I am therefore determined to stop your mouth. You shall have copper enough.' It was found by experience that copper-sheathing not only preserved the bottom planking of a vessel, but also materially improved her sailing qualities, especially in light airs. Despite its high cost, the practice before long spread to all large merchantmen sailing to the tropics.

Among the various inventions and improvements which increased the material efficiency of the Georgian Navy must be mentioned the chain pump introduced by William Cole in 1764. It was discovered by experiment that whereas the old pump required seven men to pump out a ton of water in 76 seconds, the new pump would pump out the same quantity of water with but four men in not much more than half this time. Cole's pump was soon in common use throughout the Service. For steering large vessels the wheel was now generally re-placed by the tiller. Lightning conductors were fitted to warships, at Anson's instance, in the early 1760s. Stills for producing fresh water from salt were introduced, on a small scale, in the last half of the century. During the same period an increasing number of our ships were equipped with ventilating apparatus. The method invented by Samuel Sutton of extracting the foul air out of ships by means of pipes and a furnace was the one in general use; though a rival method of ventilation, through a system of fans operated by windmills, which was developed by the Rev. Stephen Hales, also had its advocates, among whom was Admiral Boscawen.

Internally the sides of British men-of-war were painted scarlet. A uniform scheme of external painting was long in arriving. On the eve of Trafalgar the ' Nelson chequer ' of black and yellow bands, with black port-lids, became common, though by no means universal. The familiar black and white chequer was introduced during the final phase of the Napoleonic War.

During the period under survey there were also very important developments in rigging and sail-plan. Early in the eighteenth century the bowsprit was lengthened by the addition of a jib-boom to carry the new triangular jib, which, with the foretopmast staysail, gradually superseded the old spritsail-topsail. To hold the bowsprit down to the stem a bobstay was fitted. The introduction of jibs into the three-masted ship constituted an innovation of the highest importance. Such a feat as Anson's beat down Channel in the face of a strong head-wind in the autumn of 1740, and, still more, his westward beat round the Horn several months later, would have been quite impossible with the old spritsails and spritsail-topsails.[1] Staysails between the masts were fully developed by the middle of the eighteenth century. The ensuing decades witnessed the evolution of the spanker, or driver, from the old lateen mizen. Towards the close of the century the mizen-mast was prolonged by a topgallant-mast in order to carry a topgallant-sail; royals were introduced on all three masts, and studding-sails were set on the fore-mast and main-mast. ' An ocean-going ship,' Laird Clowes has observed, ' with her masts and sails was incomparably the most elaborate structure and the most complicated mechanism which the mind of man had yet evolved.'

As the eighteenth century advanced the timber problem came increasingly to the fore. It was an article of faith among British shipwrights that oak was immeasurably superior to all other timbers for shipbuilding. Our shipwrights firmly believed that the best oak was English oak, and, moreover, that the best of this timber came from Sussex. It was quite usual for naval contracts to specify ' good, sound

---

[1] It was long, however, before the spritsail was finally supplanted. The value of this sail was convincingly demonstrated at the action of the ' Glorious First ', 1794, when the *Ramillies* wore by means of her spritsail and spritsail-topsail only. The only living seaman who has had actual experience of the spritsail—Commander Alan Villiers, R.N.R., who in 1957 sailed the ' new *Mayflower* ' across to America —made these observations in a lecture to the Society for Nautical Research: ' The spritsail proved itself a most useful manœuvring and balancing sail, though the spritsail yard was always a " bit of a brute to handle ". . . . On a wind, the spritsail set and pulled very well, for the yard could be braced up.'

Sussex oak '. Earlier in the century Daniel Defoe had discoursed confidently of the oak-groves of south-eastern England as ' an inexhaustible Store-house of Timber '; and he went on rashly to assert, ' nor can all the Ship-building the whole Kingdom are able to build, ever exhaust those Counties '. However, it became apparent that the new growth of oak had by no means kept pace with the ever-increasing demand. An oak-tree took about one hundred years to attain maturity. Nearly two thousand oak-trees had to be felled for the construction of a 74. The produce of the royal forests being altogether inadequate to meet the requirements of the Navy, the mainstay of the supply was the timber raised on private estates.

By the end of the Austrian Succession and Seven Years War the oak plantations of the southern counties had been stripped nearly bare of timber suited for shipbuilding. ' Indeed, so great has the consumption been ', wrote a contemporary authority, Roger Fisher, ' that one of the most eminent timber dealers of the county of Sussex now living, has declared to me, that there is not now, as he verily believes, more than one tenth part of the full grown timber, standing or growing, as there was when he entered into business, forty-five years ago.' In the county of Hampshire the ' great decrease in large oak ' was visible to everybody; and it was estimated that there was not a quarter of the quantity standing, ' fitting for the Navy ', that there was forty years before. He added that a number of leading timber merchants in the south of England were agreed that, ' in another century they do not know where timber will be got to keep up our navy, and that there is no provision made by planting '. It was supposed that the decrease on the east coast was not so great; ' yet an ancient shipwright of Hull, who has lately retired from business, apprehends that near three-fourths of all the full-grown timber on that side of the Kingdom have been cut down since the time he commenced a builder.'[1]

At the same time the increasing use of oak timber and plank from the American colonies helped to some extent to relieve the demand on English oak. American oak, it is true, never found favour with the Navy Board; but it was imported in considerable quantities for mercantile shipbuilding and was also used on a large scale in domestic architecture. Soft woods, such as white pine and spruce from the forests of New Hampshire and Maine, also provided timber admirably

[1] Roger Fisher, *Heart of Oak, the British Bulwark* (1763).

suited to shipbuilding. Early in the eighteenth century the New Englanders had built up an extensive shipbuilding industry of their own and exported large numbers of vessels annually to England. Close to the water's edge were most of the raw materials for shipbuilding. ' Masts of white pine or fir, logs of oak fifty feet long, clear of knots, and straight-grained for ship timbers and planks, pitch pine for tar and turpentine, and hemp for cordage furnished almost all the materials needed in the construction of a wooden sailing vessel.'[1] Towards the end of the colonial period American-built ships comprised no less than one-third of the total British registry.

Because of the continued dependence of Great Britain on the Baltic for timber and naval stores, it was an object of cardinal importance to the Admiralty to keep open the Sound to British shipping, and to prevent the Baltic from falling under the domination of any one Power. The supply of Swedish iron was another important consideration. ' The Baltic remained the Achilles heel of British strategy, the one area where a trade vital to British defence was wide open to foreign attack.'[2] The timber problem, together with the whole matter of naval stores, was destined to become one of the crucial factors in the War of American Independence.[3] On the outbreak of hostilities in 1775 it was out of the question for Great Britain to restore her lost ' two-power ' standard. The Admiralty in fact experienced the greatest difficulty in preparing and maintaining as many as 100 sail of the line. The Bourbon States had at least half as many again in commission.

By the turn of the century there was not enough English oak to meet more than a fraction of the Navy's requirements.[4] The most

---

[1] Bogart, *Economic History of the American People* (1942), p. 22.
[2] Charles Wilson in *Economic History Review*, 2nd Ser., II, p. 155.
[3] An interesting report was made to the Earl of Shelburne by Lieut. John Blankett, who visited Russia between the wars, on the outbreak of the American revolt. ' I must premise that almost all those stores we were used in better times to take from America, we must now take from Russia, such as Pitch, Tar, Rosin, Turpentine, Tallow, Masts, Yards, Spars, Compass Timber, Fir Timber & a variety of other articles used in Ship building. When it is said that Denmark & Sweden can supply those articles, it is true only in part. Sweden can export a great quantity of Pitch & Tar, but the connections of Sweden are too well known to place much dependence on a supply of Naval Stores from thence. We can only depend on Denmark for the Norway timber, some turpentine, & Rosin. But we must owe our Naval existence to Russia for a supply of Hemp, Sail Cloth, Masts & some other articles which no other Country can furnish us.'
[4] ' The increasing scarcity of English oak is reflected in the rising cost per ton of a 3rd-rate: 1600, £5 10s.; 1675, £9; 1693, £11 5s.; 1719–41, £12 to £13; Seven Years

pressing scarcity was that of curved or compass timbers. The cost of stern-posts, rudder pieces, wing transoms, common knees, and wing transom knees rose to unprecedented heights during the timber crisis of 1804. ' If the country gentlemen do not make it a point to plant oaks wherever they will grow ', Collingwood prophesied, ' the time will not be very distant when, to keep our Navy, we must depend entirely on captures from the enemy. . . . I wish everybody thought on this subject as I do; they would not walk through their farms without a pocketful of acorns to drop in the hedge-sides, and then let them take their chance.'

In the matter of masts the British during most of this period enjoyed a substantial advantage over the French.[1] The great sticks which they regularly imported, first, from the virgin pine forests of New England and, latterly, after the revolt of the American colonies, from Canada, were superior in practically all respects to the ' made masts ' on which the French relied.[2] In the Revolutionary War the convoying of the masts ships was one of the most important tasks laid upon the Halifax squadron.

2

The striking progress in gunnery made by the British Navy in the last two decades of the eighteenth century was due in the main to important improvements introduced by Sir Charles Douglas, Rodney's Captain of the Fleet. Douglas substituted flannel for silk as a cartridge-casing and utilized steel springs to control the recoil of the guns. He was similarly responsible for the invention of the gun-lock. As a result of these and other improvements in serving the guns the gunners were able to fire as many as two rounds in three minutes; and, by means of a system of blocks and tackles, it became possible for the first time to employ oblique fire. The improvements were officially approved by the Admiralty early in 1781 and introduced in the West Indies squadron at Rodney's special request. The efficacy of these new methods was apparent at the action of The Saints, in 1782, when more men

War, £16 to £17; 1775–1802, £20 to £21; 1803, £34 10s.; and 1805, during the great shortage, £36 ' (Albion, Forests and Sea Power (1924)).

[1] The War of American Independence was a notable exception. See *infra*, p. 417.

[2] ' The made masts customarily used by the French, however expertly assembled, were distinctly second-rate compared to the great masts taken from New England and Canada by the British, or channelled to them from the Baltic market ' (Bamford, *Forests and French Sea Power, 1660–1789*, pp. 207–8).

were killed in the French flagship, the *Ville de Paris*, than in the entire British fleet. ' I can aver from my own observation that the French fire slackens as we approach,' wrote Dr. Gilbert Blane, who was present at this action, ' and is totally silent when we are close alongside.' The carronade,[1] which was a short piece with a large bore, light and easy to handle in close-range fighting, was first introduced into the Navy in 1779. It was destined to play a leading part at The Saints (the first great carronade action), the Glorious First, Camperdown, St. Vincent, Nile, Copenhagen, and Trafalgar; all of which actions were fought at close range. Throughout this period the carronade substantially increased the fire-power of the battle fleet under such conditions and contributed to an important degree to the great roll of British victories in the Revolutionary and Napoleonic Wars. In the last two decades of the century the majority of British frigates were fitted with carronades. The carronade gradually became larger in calibre and, in the smaller British cruisers, often comprised the entire armament of the vessel with the exception of a pair of bow-chasers.

3

Throughout the first half of the eighteenth century the Fighting Instructions issued by Russell in 1691 and Rooke in 1703 were supplemented by a series of Additional Fighting Instructions. Vernon seems to have been the first commander to perceive the inadequacy of the old system of Fighting Instructions and to supplement it by the Additional Fighting Instructions. The evidence for this is contained in a pamphlet written about 1744, in which the following passage appears:

> Mr. V[ernon], that provident, great admiral, who never suffered any useful precaution to escape him, concerted some signals for so good a purpose, widely foreseeing their use and necessity, giving them to the captains of the squadron under his command. And lest his vigilance should be some time or other surprised by an enemy, or the exigencies of his master's service, should require him to attack or repulse by night,

---

[1] The carronade, first cast in the Carron foundry in Stirlingshire, was described by Laird Clowes as ' a quick-firer of large calibre but very short range '. On 4 September 1782, the French frigate *Hébé* was attacked by the British frigate *Rainbow* off the Île de Batz: such was the force of the *Rainbow's* carronade that the captain of the *Hébé*, believing his opponent to be a ship of the line, immediately hauled down his colours.

he appointed signals for the line of battle, engaging, chasing, leaving off chase, with many others altogether new, excellent, and serviceable.[1]

The work of Vernon was afterwards carried on by Anson, who, as First Lord, issued the best of Vernon's additions throughout the Fleet, and added a few of his own. Although this admiral was never to fulfil the hopes that his disciples had entertained of his effecting a general improvement in tactics, the effect of Anson's additions—and of the later Additional Fighting Instructions evolved successively by Hawke, Boscawen, Rodney, and Hood—was to make tactics a great deal more flexible and elastic.

In the scientific study of naval tactics our writers, indeed, lagged far behind the French. The marked improvement of battle tactics was not the least important aspect of the French naval renaissance which took place between the American and French Revolutionary Wars. Nothing like Morogues' *Tactique Navale* (1763) or de Villehuet's *Le Manœuvrier* (1765) was published on this side of the Channel until a generation later.[2]

Our commanders throughout this period were faced with a twofold problem. In the first place, the proficiency of British and French alike in forming and maintaining the close-hauled line of battle ahead almost invariably led to stalemate. Secondly, the unwillingness of the French commanders to accept decisive action presented our own with the tactical problem of fixing the enemy. The problem seemed to Jervis in 1778—as will later appear—virtually insoluble.

The method by which the British eventually forced the French to continue an action once begun was by breaking the enemy's line. In the action off The Saints in 1782, Rodney, as the result of a sudden shift of the wind, succeeded in doing this from the leeward position —and though the main body of the enemy's fleet got away, individual groups of French vessels were effectually fixed. In 1783 the manœuvre of breaking the enemy's line, now fully understood, was given a corresponding signal by Hood.[3] The usual procedure, however, was

---

[1] *Navy Records Society*, XXIX, p. 206.

[2] The first important original work on tactics to appear in English was Clerk of Eldin's *An Essay on Naval Tactics* (1797). This made no major contribution to the subject, but did much to propagate the hard-bought lessons of experience among naval officers. Nelson is said frequently to have ' expressed his approbation ' of Clerk's work.

[3] ' The latest Additional Fighting Instructions will reveal to us how ripe and sound a system of tactics had been reached. The idea of crushing part of the enemy by

for a British fleet to attack from to windward. In spite of the grave risks of this mode of attack against an opposing fleet of approximately equal strength and efficiency and willing to fight it out, the tactic of breaking the enemy's line became a virtual necessity if British commanders were to obtain a decision in face of the elusive tactics developed by the French. It was this procedure—a completely new manœuvre—which Howe adopted on the Glorious First of June.

The advance of tactics was closely bound up with the system of signals. The restrictions imposed by the inadequacy of the old signal book had for long been a drag upon tactical progress. Our signal code, in fact, formed part of the Fighting Instructions issued by Russell and Rooke, which, even with the Additional Instructions already mentioned, seriously circumscribed a commander's tactical control in action. The signal book allowed of only a strictly limited number of signals, and was, moreover, easily put out of commission by damage to masts and rigging.

The French were actually first in the field with the highly efficient method of signalling invented by Mahé de la Bourdonnais. It was not, however, the French but their British adversaries who profited chiefly by these new developments. To Howe in collaboration with Kempenfelt belongs most of the credit for the revolutionary improvement in our system of signalling towards the close of the eighteenth century. In 1781 there appeared ' *General Instructions for the conduct of the ships of war, explanatory of, and relative to the signals contained in the signal-book herewith delivered by Rear-Admiral Richard Kempenfelt* '. It was not enough to devise an efficient method of signalling; it was also necessary to get it generally adopted. ' I therefore followed in great measure Lord Howe's mode,' observed Kempenfelt, ' he being a popular character.' In 1782 Howe brought out his early Signal Book, somewhat on the lines of the numerary system already devised by the

concentration had replaced the primitive intention of crowding him into a confusion; a swift and vigorous attack had replaced the watchful defensive, and above all the true method of concentration had been established; for although a concentration on the van was still permissible in exceptional circumstances, the chief of the new articles are devoted to concentration on the rear. Thus our tacticians had worked out the fundamental principles on which Nelson's system rested, even to breaking up the line into two divisions. " Containing " alone was not yet clearly enunciated, but by Hood's signals for breaking the line, the best method of effecting it was made possible. Everything indeed lay ready for the hands of Howe and Nelson to strike into life' (Corbett, *Fighting Instructions, 1530–1816*).

French, entitled *Primer of Speech for Fighting Ships*; in 1790, when he resumed command of the Channel Fleet, there appeared his *Signal Book for Ships of War*, embodying various improvements, which was generally adopted throughout the Service.[1] Howe's first and second Signal Books superseded the old rigid system of Fighting Instructions, thereby giving the admiral, for the first time, full tactical control of his fleet. The new system of signals went far towards solving the main tactical problem of the eighteenth century, namely, that of 'fixing' the enemy and forcing him to close action. The year 1799 saw the official Signal Book on the new system printed and issued by the Admiralty. By this means elasticity in naval tactics was at last achieved. A year later Sir Home Popham's *Telegraphic Signals or Marine Vocabulary* marked a further step forward. For the first time the Commander-in-Chief was able to say exactly what he pleased by signal. The new code came rapidly into general use. Nelson's immortal signal at Trafalgar, *England expects that every man will do his duty*, was made with Popham's code.

In 1796 a system of semaphore signalling was adopted by the Admiralty for communicating with Portsmouth and Chatham, the signals being passed on by a chain of signal stations erected on hill-tops within sight of each other. In London, the semaphore apparatus was erected on the roof of Admiralty House, the residence of the First Lord. The sites of the signal stations on the Portsmouth line were as follows: Admiralty – Royal Hospital, Chelsea – The Highland, Putney – Netley Heath – Hascombe – Blackdown – Beacon Hill, Harting – Portsdown Hill – The Glacis, Portsmouth; on the Chatham line: Admiralty – 36, West Square, Southwark – New Cross Gate, Nunhead – Shooter's Hill – Swanscombe – Gad's Hill, Shorne – Chatham Yard. The system was later extended to Plymouth and Yarmouth. It has been said that in clear weather a signal could be transmitted by this means from Whitehall to Portsmouth in about ten minutes. In fog, of course, the manual telegraph could not operate.[2]

---

[1] The later edition of the Signal Book was used on the Glorious First, and also in the actions of St. Vincent and the Nile.

[2] It will be remembered how in Marryat's naval novel, *Peter Simple*, the hero's friend Terence O'Brien, having recently been promoted to post-rank, hurried down to Portsmouth to read himself in before his commission could be cancelled as the result of an intrigue—' I looked up at the sky as soon as I left the Admiralty portico, and was glad to see that the weather was so thick and the telegraph not at work, or I might have been too late.'

4

Though the French on numerous occasions displayed fine seamanship—particularly in the war of 1778–83—they scarcely attained to the same high level of excellence as the British. Still less did the Spaniards, whose efforts our own officers were accustomed to regard with tolerant contempt. In the summer of 1793 Nelson noted how our Spanish Allies were unable, after several hours of manœuvring, ' to form anything which could be called a Line of Battle ahead '. In the same year Gardner observed how, when he was in the *Berwick*, they fell in with a dismasted Spanish frigate, to whose crew they were able to render some much-needed assistance; ' as they appeared to be deficient in nautical knowledge,' was the British officer's acid comment, ' or, in other words, the vilest set of lubbers that ever were seen. They positively did not know how to get a jury mast up.' But Gardner was no less severe on his own countrymen when, owing to the negligence of the pilots, the *Blonde* frigate narrowly escaped disaster on the Shipwash sand in the winter of 1799, arriving (as he observed) at Sheerness the following evening:

> Ragged, and shabby, and all forlorn,
> By wind and weather tattered and torn,
> Occasioned by pilots who treated with scorn
> The good advice that was given that morn;
> For which a rope their necks should adorn,
> The damnedest lubbers that ever were born.[1]

The British superiority in seamanship revealed itself over and over again in the long struggle with France. The *Mermaid*, 40, manœuvring in pursuit of the *Vigilant*, 64, off Louisbourg in 1745; the high standard of disciplined skill necessitated by Anson's evolutions, two years later, in the first action off Finisterre; the passage of the Traverse by Saunders' fleet and the landing of Wolfe's troops in the ships' boats under the Heights of Abraham; Boscawen's squadron clearing from Gibraltar only four hours after the signal ' Enemy in sight ' had been received; the *Royal George* and the *Magnanime* sweeping into Quiberon Bay in a rising gale under topgallant-sails, in headlong pursuit of Conflans; the outmanœuvring of a superior French squadron by

---

[1] Captain Keats once declared in a letter to St. Vincent that ' whoever trusts implicitly to a Pilot is *sure* to lose his vessel.'

Howe, in the summer of 1778, off the North American coast; Rodney's fleet running before a fresh westerly gale between the Spaniards and a dead lee shore, and then, during the day and night following the Moonlight action, clawing off the shoals of San Lucar; Hood steering under the enemy's guns into the anchorage off St. Kitts vacated by de Grasse; Kempenfelt cutting in between de Guichen and his convoy; the rounding of Ushant by the *Formidable* and eleven more of Rodney's squadron in a January gale in 1782; Howe working between his convoy and a superior Spanish squadron lying in Algeciras Bay at the third relief of Gibraltar; Fremantle in the *Inconstant* frigate manœuvring in pursuit of the huge *Ça Ira*; Pellew in the *Indefatigable* frigate weathering the Penmarck, after forcing a French battleship ashore; St. Vincent's infinite capacity for improvisation while on the Mediterranean station, and the matchless sail-drill of the squadron under his command; the *Alexander* towing the dismasted *Vanguard* into St. Pierre's anchorage, off Sardinia, and the refitting of the latter vessel within four days; Blackwood in the *Penelope* frigate pursuing the *Guillaume Tell*, 80, and severely damaging her in the long night action of 30 March 1800; the passage of the Hollænder Deep by Nelson's division before the battle of Copenhagen; Sir Charles Pole, in the following spring, steering a British squadron for the first time through the winding channels of the Great Belt and against contrary winds; the landing of Abercromby's troops in Aboukir Bay in the face of strong enemy resistance; Nelson's fleet beating through the Straits of Messina in chase of Villeneuve; the rapid pursuit of the Combined Fleet from Lagos Bay to the West Indies, and back again to Gibraltar; the conduct throughout the war of 1793–1815 of innumerable convoys, landing-parties, and cutting-out expeditions—are all examples of that superb seamanship which so often had a decisive influence on the course of operations.

Above all, the masterly handling of British ships and squadrons was made manifest in the investment of the enemy's coasts and ports—in the close blockade of Brest by Hawke in 1759; revived, at the turn of the century, by St. Vincent and later continued by Cornwallis: in the investment of Cadiz by St. Vincent, Keith, and Collingwood; of Ferrol, by Pellew, Cochrane, and Calder; of Toulon, by Nelson, Collingwood, Cotton, and Pellew, in the Revolutionary and Napoleonic Wars. On the advanced station, close in with the iron-bound Brittany coast, the arduous, grim blockading duty was a rigorous test of seamanship. Well might Cornwallis declare that, ' The officer in charge of those ships [the inshore squadron] should have a particular turn for that kind of service.' It took a cool and resourceful seaman to discover the passage off Béniguete, whereby the batteries near Conquet might be avoided. It took a bold seaman to run for Douarnenez Bay in a rising gale, with mortar batteries crossing each other from the Bec du Chevre and the Bec du Raz, and with a shoal in the middle of the entrance. The day-to-day routine of the inshore squadron—perpetually on the alert for the vagaries of the weather, currents, and tidal streams; their watchful care of their anchors and cables; the countless risks they ran to watch the motions of the enemy in Brest, to cut out gun-boats and *chasse-marées*, and to prevent timber- and other supply-ships from getting into Brest—bred up an incomparable race of seamen. How often, on the other hand, in the course of these wars, was a French squadron, on leaving port, incapacitated or even obliged to return to harbour again, through stress of weather.

The handling of British frigates was responsible for some remarkable feats of seamanship. Edward Pellew (later Lord Exmouth), of whom Mahan justly writes, ' a seaman inbred, if ever there was one,' was, perhaps, the frigate captain *par excellence*.[1] A midshipman who had served under his command on the Newfoundland station between the American and Revolutionary Wars records the following anecdote.

Wherever there was exertion required aloft, ' to preserve a sail or a mast, the captain was foremost in the work, apparently as a mere matter of amusement, and there was not a man in the ship that could equal him in personal activity. He appeared to play among the elements in the hardest storms. I remember once, in close-reefing the main topsail, the captain had given his orders from the quarter-deck and sent us aloft. On gaining the topsail yard, the most active and daring of our party hesitated to go upon it, as the sail was flapping violently, making it a service of great danger; but a voice was heard from the extreme end of the yard, calling upon us to exert ourselves to save the sail, which would otherwise beat to pieces. A man said, " Why, that's the captain! How the — did he get there?" He had followed us up, and, clambering over the backs of the sailors, had reached the topmast head, above the yard, and thence descended by the lift,'—a feat unfortunately not easy to be explained to

[1] 'Pellew possessed to a very remarkable extent that delicate art of seamanship which consists in so handling a ship as to make her do just what you want, and to put her just where she should be ' (Mahan, *Types of Naval Officers* (1901)).

354

landsmen, but which will be allowed by seamen to demand great hardi-hood and address.[1]

Another celebrated frigate captain, who greatly distinguished him-self in the Mediterranean during the Napoleonic War, was Patrick Campbell of the *Unité*. Under his command, it was claimed, the *Unité* became ' the smartest ship in the sea.'

In the *Unité*, so ready was every individual to his station, and so confident was the First Lieutenant of everyone's abilities and exertion, that, instead of saying, hoist away this, that and the other, sail, he had only to say two words—' Make sail '—and in a few moments the ship from appearance as a naked tree would be as a cloud, in so short a time that a landsman would hardly credit his own sight, was he to be a spectator.

After Trafalgar, the ports of Napoleon's far-flung empire were held fast in the grip of the blockading squadrons until the end of the war. For the future most of the fighting was done by single ships of the line or by cruisers. Captain Lord Cochrane—under whose command was the young midshipman, Frederick Marryat—distinguished him-self during the famous cruise of the frigate *Impérieuse*, in 1808, by innumerable feats of daring and initiative. Years after, Marryat was to draw on this memorable experience of his youth in describing the club-hauling of the *Diomede* by Captain Savage in *Peter Simple*.

The ship continued to hold her course good; and we were within half a mile of the point, and fully expected to weather it, when again the wet and heavy sails flapped in the wind, and the ship broke off two points as before. The officers and seamen were aghast, for the ship's head was right on to the breakers. ' Luff now, all you can, quartermaster,' cried the captain. ' Send the men aft directly. My lads, there is no time for words—I am going to *club-haul* the ship, for there is no time to wear. The only chance you have of safety is to be cool, watch my eye, and execute my orders with precision. Away to your stations for tacking ship. Hands by the best bower anchor. Mr. Wilson, attend below with the carpenter and his mates, ready to cut away the cable at the moment that I give the order. Silence, there, fore and aft. Quarter-master, keep her full again for stays. Mind you ease the helm down when I tell you.' About a minute passed before the captain gave any further orders. The ship had closed—to within a quarter of a mile of the beach, and the waves curled and topped around us, bearing us down upon the shore, which presented one continued surface of foam, extending to within half

---

[1] Q. Mahan, *op cit.*, pp. 444–5.

a cable's length of our position. The captain waved his hand in silence to the quarter-master at the wheel, and the helm was put down. The ship turned slowly to the wind, pitching and chopping as the sails were spilling. When she had lost her way, the captain gave the order, ' Let go the anchor. We will haul all at once, Mr. Falcon,' said the captain. Not a word was spoken, the men went to the fore brace, which had not been manned; most of them knew, although I did not, that if the ship's head did not go round the other way, we should be on shore, and among the breakers in half a minute. . . . At last the ship was head to wind, and the captain gave the signal. The yards flew round with such a creaking noise, that I thought the masts had gone over the side, and the next moment the wind had caught the sails, and the ship, which for a moment or two had been on an even keel, careened over to her gunnel with its force. The captain, who stood upon the weather-hammock rails, holding by the main-rigging, ordered the helm amidships, looked full at the sails, and then at the cable, which grew broad upon the weather bow, and held the ship from nearing the shore. At last he cried, ' Cut away the cable!' A few strokes of the axes were heard, and then the cable flew out of the hawse-hole in a blaze of fire, from the violence of the friction, and disappeared under a huge wave, which struck us on the chess-tree, and deluged us with water fore and aft. But we were now on the other tack, and the ship regained her way and we had evidently increased our distance from the land.

The crucial importance of seamanship as a factor in naval strategy can be gauged from the significant fact that, during the period under survey, by far the greater part of the casualties suffered by the Navy were due, not to enemy action, but to the ' dangers of the sea '. The gravest disasters were those caused by severe weather, like the great storm of 1703, the West Indian hurricane of 1780, and the violent gale off Newfoundland in 1782 which sank so many of the prizes taken at The Saints; to errors of judgment like those made by Sir Clowdisley Shovell in 1707 and the master of the *Ramillies* in 1760; above all, to the exigencies of the blockading service, which put so heavy a strain upon men and gear. Again and again the preservation of our ships and squadrons from imminent disaster was due to the superiority of British seamanship.

From the works of Falconer, Steel, Darcy Lever, and others it is possible to gain some insight into the elaborate minutiæ of rigging and seamanship, the different evolutions under sail, and all the other old lore of ' sailorizing ': of setting up the rigging; of weighing anchor; of catting and fishing the anchors; of setting and taking in sails; of staying and wearing; of box-hauling and club-hauling; of lying-to under different sails; of sending down spars in blowing weather; of working off a lee shore in a gale; of sudden shifting squalls; of sounding; of warping along shore in chase; of using an anchor on a dark night; of anchoring in a crowded roadstead in blowing weather; of hoisting out boats; of taking in water, etc.

5

The eighteenth century witnessed various developments of outstanding importance which ushered in a new era in navigation. To this fact, indeed, was largely due the remarkable accuracy of Captain Cook's observations during his voyages of exploration in the South Pacific. It is worth noting that the principal contributions to the new nautical science were all British.

In 1731 there appeared John Hadley's reflecting quadrant, from which the modern sextant was evolved by John Campbell in 1757. Hadley's instrument was in point of fact a measure of ninety degrees: the principle of construction remained the same in Campbell's instrument, but the latter extended the circular arc so as to be able to measure up to one hundred and twenty degrees.

With the swift expansion of British merchant shipping in the opening years of the eighteenth century the need to discover a solution to the problem of longitude determination became so urgent that, in 1714, an Act of Parliament was passed setting up the Board of Longitude and providing for a reward of £20,000 to be paid to any person or persons who should devise a sufficiently accurate method of calculating a ship's longitude. Various attempts to use the variation of the compass as a basis for ascertaining longitude at sea had indeed been made for centuries; but this procedure had been proved unreliable. The ingenious method evolved by the astronomer-royal, Dr. Nevil Maskelyne, of determining the longitude by lunar observations, involving as it did certain complicated mathematical calculations, was scarcely practicable in the ordinary way. Still it was a distinct improvement on dead reckoning and was used by a number of enterprising masters. James Cook on his first voyage to the South Pacific (1768–71) employed the lunar method with remarkably accurate results. No really practical method existed of determining longitude at sea until well on in the eighteenth century:[1] the vast majority of mariners continued to trust to their dead reckoning, or calculation of course and distance run; and, since this at best was extremely uncertain, recourse was had to latitude sailing. At last came the solution of the problem. For centuries it had been known that if a clock could be constructed which would accurately keep the time of the port of departure throughout a long voyage, it would become possible to ascertain the longitude: but this knowledge was in fact of no more than academic interest, seeing that, not until the fourth decade of the century, did any such time-piece exist. The first chronometer was invented and constructed, in 1735, by a village carpenter, John Harrison—' Longitude Harrison ', as he was called. Harrison constructed a second in 1739 and a third ten years later. Duplicates of this third chronometer were carried by Captain Cook on his second and third voyages. The marvellous accuracy of Harrison's instruments marked a revolutionary advance upon anything that had hitherto been achieved. By the close of the eighteenth century his time-keeper had virtually superseded all other methods of getting Greenwich time. In the last two decades of the century chronometers were being produced commercially. Their cost, however, was high; and it was not until many years later that they came into general use.

As a result of an inquiry following the disaster of 1707, the Admiralty decided that brass instead of wooden compass bowls should be used in future. In the later half of the eighteenth century the compasses manufactured by Dr. Gowin Knight, which were fitted with very strongly magnetized needles and proved considerably more accurate than the others then available, were adopted by the Navy and a number of merchantmen. Knight's method of manufacturing artificial magnets was so successful that they speedily replaced the lodestones formerly used for re-magnetizing compass needles. Towards the close of the century his compasses, however, were being superseded by those made by Ralph Walker, which marked a further advance.

Among the more important navigational works of this period were Joshua Kelly's *The Modern Navigator's Compleat Tutor* (1724), Captain Daniel Newhouse's *The Whole Art of Navigation* (1727), N.

[1] How extremely baffling this problem appeared in the eyes of the contemporary world may be gauged from a significant observation of young Marlow's in Goldsmith's comedy, *She Stoops To Conquer*—' Zounds, man! we could as soon find out the longitude.'

Colson's *The Mariner's New Kalendar* (1746), John Robertson's *Elements of Navigation* (1754), Dr. Nevil Maskelyne's *The British Mariner's Guide* (1763), and Norie's *Epitome of Practical Navigation* (1805)—this last ran through numerous editions in the course of the nineteenth century. An outstanding contribution to the advance of modern scientific navigation was the publication, in 1767, of the first number of Maskelyne's *Nautical Almanac*—a work of amazing and unprecedented accuracy. Maskelyne continued to compile the *Nautical Almanac* during the rest of the century.

By the middle of the eighteenth century considerable progress had been made in the lighting and buoying of the coasts of the British Isles, while a number of Acts of Parliament had been passed for improving the harbours. In Queen Anne's reign the Gilkicker mark, near Gosport, was erected, and the Horse buoy laid at Spithead. The hazardous passage into the Hamoaze from Plymouth Sound was buoyed by about 1730. The lightship at the Nore (1731) was the first to be moored off the English coast. It was followed, in 1736, by another off the Dudgeon shoal, in Norfolk. The earliest lightship at the Goodwin sands dates from 1795. A lighthouse was built on the Lizard in 1751. Smeaton's new tower on the Eddystone, constructed entirely of stone, was completed in 1759. It remained in use for well over a century. Light was provided from twenty-four tallow candles which were replaced in 1810 by oil lamps and reflectors. Other notable lighthouses constructed during this period were those on the Skerries (1730), Smalls Rock (1778), Needles and St. Catherine's (1780), Portland (1789), Longships (1793), and Beachy Head (1802).

Starting with the publication of Captain Collins' charts of Home Waters towards the close of the seventeenth century, there was a striking and sustained advance in hydrography throughout the eighteenth century. With the aid of sextant, station pointer, and other instruments fitted for marine surveying, the position of rocks, banks, and shoals could be fixed with far greater precision; and in the latter half of the eighteenth century a series of admirable surveys were carried out by Murdoch Mackenzie and his nephew, and later by Graeme Spence[1] and Captain William Bligh.

[1] One of Graeme Spence's early achievements was an accurate survey of the Isles of Scilly. ' Although lying close to a much frequented shipping route, the position of the islands previously to 1791 had been in error by as much as 26½' of longitude ' (A. H. W. Robinson in *Empire Survey Review*, XI, p. 64).

In the Georgian era exploration and discovery were recognized as an integral part of the functions of the Royal Navy. It is significant that, in their instructions to Captain John Byron, who was appointed to command a small expedition which they had dispatched on a voyage of discovery in 1764, the Lords of the Admiralty declared that ' nothing can redound more to the honour of this nation as a maritime power, to the dignity of the Crown of Great Britain, and to the advancement of the trade and navigation thereof, than to make discoveries of countries hitherto unknown.' Byron sailed across the Atlantic and, after taking formal possession of the Falkland Islands, rounded Cape Horn and crossed the Pacific. He returned home by way of the Cape of Good Hope and anchored in the Downs in May 1766. The expedition of Wallis and Carteret in the *Dolphin* and *Swallow* (1766–8) resulted in the discovery of Pitcairn and various other islands. The latter half of the century also witnessed a great advance in the work of surveying and charting. In these activities Cook, Vancouver, Puget, Flinders, and Bass were prominent: but the greatest of all was Cook.

James Cook, a native of Whitby, who had served his apprenticeship in the coasting trade, entered the Navy in 1755 and was shortly after rated master's mate. In the North American campaign which ended in the conquest of Canada Cook made his name as a navigator and hydrographer. His work was so highly esteemed at the Admiralty that, in 1768, he received a lieutenant's commission and was sent out to Tahiti in the *Endeavour*, in command of a well-equipped expedition, ostensibly to observe the transit of Venus, actually to forestall the French in the search for *Terra Australis Incognita*, the great southern continent which was believed to lie somewhere to the south of the tracks of former explorers. Cook sailed from Tahiti to the Society Islands, and then stood southward in the direction of the alleged continent. He charted the coasts of New Zealand and the eastern seaboard of Australia, and established beyond doubt the fact that there could be no continental land north of latitude 40° S. between New Zealand and Cape Horn. Shortly after his return to England in 1771 Cook was promoted to the rank of commander and appointed to lead a second expedition of discovery in the Pacific. On his voyage of 1772–5 Cook completed the exploration of the southern hemisphere. He sailed further south than man had ever penetrated before, until, in latitude 71° 10′ S., his progress was stopped by ice. Sandwich

Land was discovered in latitude 60° S.; but the theory of a vast southern continent was now finally disproved. Cook rapidly surveyed and charted the coasts of Tasmania, the Friendly Islands, and a number of other island groups, and also corrected his survey of New Zealand. The extraordinary accuracy of his charts, no less than his meticulous attention to detail, entitles him to be regarded as the father of modern hydrography. He explored many thousands of miles of hitherto unknown coastline. He established a new standard in chart-making; some of Cook's surveys were still in use at the end of the nineteenth century. On his return he was promoted to post-rank, and elected a Fellow of the Royal Society. The object of his third voyage to the Pacific (1776–9) was to settle once and for all the question of a north-west passage from the Pacific to the Atlantic Ocean. No such passage was in fact discovered; but he surveyed and charted the Pacific coast of North America from latitude 44° N. to latitude 70° 44' N., as well as both sides of the Behring Straits. As a result of Cook's voyages Australia and New Zealand passed into British keeping.

Some time later George Vancouver, assisted by Peter Puget, made an admirable survey of the intricate channels and inlets along the west coast of North America, and he also charted the south-west coast of Australia. Matthew Flinders, with the assistance of George Bass, surveyed the coast of New South Wales and later charted the Gulf of Carpentaria.

In the latter half of the eighteenth century the foundations of the science of oceanography were laid by Major James Rennell (1742–1830), an authority of European reputation on winds and currents, who was offered, but declined, the post of Hydrographer at the Admiralty. As an example of the kind of work he did mention may be made of two papers read by Rennell before the Royal Society, in 1793 and 1815 respectively, on the subject of the variable northerly set off the entrance to the English Channel, subsequently known as Rennell's Current.[1] Throughout his long life Rennell devoted much of his time to the systematic study of winds and currents; he brought together an enormous mass of materials, patiently collected from the logs of his friends and correspondents; and the publication in 1832 of his posthumous *Investigation of the Currents of the Atlantic*

---

[1] *Observations on a Current*, etc. (1793).

Ocean marked a milestone in the progress of modern scientific navigation.[1]

6

It cannot be too strongly emphasized that the naval superiority of Great Britain depended upon the excellence of the personnel, rather than that of the matériel. Numerical superiority, in fact, did not always rest with the British; and, as has already been said, not only the French, but also the Spaniards, not infrequently built better ships than we did. Perhaps the greatest and most decisive factor of all was the British superiority in the quality of the officers. It would scarcely be too much to say that these officers *were* the Navy—i.e. the regular, continuous-service Navy. The crews were paid off after every commission—the officers remained. They formed the permanent, effective *cadre* of the Service; they were imbued with the strongest sense of professional pride and *esprit de corps*: even in time of peace there were large numbers of them continuously at sea—far more than was the case with the Bourbon navies.

The year 1748 saw the establishment of a regular uniform for certain officers of the Royal Navy—namely, admiral, captain, commander, lieutenant, and midshipman. Hitherto these officers had been accustomed to dress more or less as they pleased. In his *Roderick Random* Smollett thus described the appearance of Lieutenant Bowling:

> He was a strong built man, somewhat bandy-legged, with a neck like that of a bull, and a face which, you might easily perceive, had withstood the most obstinate assaults of the weather. His dress consisted of a soldier's coat, altered for him by the ship's tailor, a striped flannel jacket, a pair of red breeches, japanned with pitch, clean grey worsted stockings, large silver buckles, that covered three-fourths of his shoes, a silver-laced hat, a black bob wig in buckle, a check shirt, a silk handkerchief, a hanger with brass handle, girded to his thigh by a tarnished laced belt, and a good oak plant under his arm.

According to tradition, the original uniform of the British naval officer was modelled on the riding habit worn by the Duchess of Bedford, which had happened to take the King's fancy. It would appear that uniform was but slowly and gradually adopted in the

---

[1] The work of Rennell was continued and amplified by Lieutenant M. F. Maury of the United States Navy, who published in the middle of the nineteenth century his celebrated *Wind and Current Charts*.

Service. The Lords Commissioners of the Admiralty were obliged to point out to the three commanders-in-chief at the home ports: ' As example is on these occasions extremely necessary, you are to cause every captain under your command to appear in the said dress, and we do expect that you yourselves shall constantly appear in the same.' It is said that when uniforms were first provided for lieutenants, there was but one uniform coat kept in the wardroom for the use of these officers, when sent on duty to other ships, or on shore. As the century advanced, uniform was generally worn by all officers: though from time to time, as may be seen from the *Recollections of James Anthony Gardner*, considerable liberties might be taken by individuals.

> Our first lieutenant was a very droll and strange personage, in dress as well as in manners. When he commissioned the *Edgar* he had on a uniform coat made in days of yore, with sleeves that reached to his hips, a very low collar, huge white lappels and cuffs, the buttons behind at a good fighting distance, and the skirts and pockets an enormous size. A red waistcoat, nankin breeches, and black worsted stockings, with great yellow buckles on round-toed shoes, a hat that had been cocked, but cut round, with a very low crown, so that he was obliged to keep his hand to his head to prevent its blowing off in the lightest breeze.

But these variations on the regulation theme were becoming rarer towards the end of the century. Gardner observed that about 1788 Captain Charles Thompson of the *Edgar*, whom he described as ' gruff as the devil' and ' very particular concerning dress', issued the following order: ' If any officer shall so far forget himself as to appear when on shore without his uniform, I shall regard it as a mark of his being ashamed of his profession and discharge him from the ship accordingly.' In Gardner's next ship, the *Barfleur*, Captain Robert Calder was no less strict in the matter of dress. ' We dared not appear on deck without our full uniform,' said Gardner, ' and a round hat was never allowed; our side arms always on the quarter-deck ready for duty, and when exercising sails the midshipmen in the tops were to be in full dress.' Captain Thomas Hardy once cured his ' young gentlemen ' of strolling round the deck with their hands in their pockets by having their pockets *sewn* up.

The century saw a gradual but sustained improvement in the manners and status of the British sea-officer. ' The last war ', wrote Edward Thompson in 1756, ' a chaw of tobacco, a rattan, and a rope of oaths were sufficient qualifications to constitute a lieutenant; but now, education and good manners are the study of all.' ' I will venture to say ', the same writer went on to observe, ' that the gentlemen of the navy will bring more laurels to their country than were ever brought in any former time.'[1] In the latter half of the century this prediction was fulfilled in full measure.

The influence of Anson had much to do with this improvement. Between the Austrian Succession and the Seven Years War he had doggedly resisted the efforts of the Duke of Newcastle to draw the Navy within the orbit of his all-embracing system of patronage. ' He withstood recommendations of interest or favor more than any First Lord of the Admiralty was ever known to do,' the second Earl of Hardwicke wrote long afterwards. ' I must ', observed Anson on 15 June 1759, to the Duke, ' now beg your Grace will seriously consider what must be the condition of your Fleet if these borrough recommendations, which must be frequent are to be complyed with. . . . My constant method, since I have had the honour of serving the King in the station I am in, has been to promote the lieutenants to command, whose ships have been successfully engaged upon equal terms with the enemy, without having any friend or recommendation; and in preference to all others, and this I would recommend to my successors if they would have a Fleet to depend on.'[2]

The appointment of Anson to the Board of Admiralty in 1745 marked an era in naval administration. It would be difficult, indeed, to exaggerate the debt which the Georgian Navy owed to this great officer. In 1751 he became First Lord and continued to hold that office, with but one brief interval, until 1762. He was unquestionably the ablest, strongest, and most responsible administrator since Pepys. The revision of the method of promotion to flag rank; the introduction of a new code of articles of war; the establishment of a uniform for the officers of the Service; the reorganization of the corps of marines, were all due to Anson. Another important reform for which he was responsible was a measure providing for the punctual payment of the men and allowing them to assign part of their pay to their families. He overhauled the dockyards and other shore establishments of the Navy, and materially improved the whole administration of supply.

---

[1] Edward Thompson, *A Sailor's Letters* (1767).
[2] *Q.* L. B. Namier, *Structure of Politics at the Accession of George III*, I, pp. 43–4.

Even though these reforms cannot be said to have extirpated the variegated and deep-rooted abuses of the dockyards, they nevertheless did much to put down idleness, incompetence, waste, and embezzlement. It was from Anson that some of the finest officers of their day had procured preferment. Hawke, Boscawen, Rodney, and Howe were his selections. Jervis received both his nomination and his commission from Anson.

Hawke also did much to improve the manners and deportment of the British sea-officer. A protégé of his, the future Captain William Locker, declared many years afterwards that he considered him ' as the founder of that more gentlemanly spirit, which has since been gradually gaining ground in the Navy. At the period when he first went to sea, a man of war was characterized by all the coarseness so graphically described in the novels of Smollett. Tobacco and a checked shirt were associated with lace and a cockade; and the manners of a British Admiral partook of the language and demeanour of a boatswain's mate. . . . His gentlemanly deportment and propriety of conversation effected a salutary improvement among his officers. He steadily discountenanced the coarseness of language and demeanour which disfigured too many of the old school, and still clings to some of the present more enlightened age.'[1]

That this general improvement was rapid in later years is evidenced in the correspondence of St. Vincent, Nelson, Collingwood, and their contemporaries and also in the novels of Jane Austen and Captain Marryat.

Socially the officers of the Royal Navy were a mixed lot.[2] The middle class was strongly represented, and promotion from the lower-deck to the quarter-deck (not always with the happiest results) was by no means uncommon. In the latter part of the period under survey the increasing popularity of the Navy as a career for young men of family was regarded as a not unmixed blessing by the other serving officers.

[1] E. H. Locker, *Memoirs of Celebrated Naval Commanders* (1830).
[2] It will be recollected that Jane Austen's Sir Walter Elliot, Bt., had two strong grounds of objection to the Service: ' First, as being the means of bringing persons of obscure birth into undue distinction, and raising men to honours which their fathers and grandfathers never dreamt of; and, secondly, as it cuts up a man's youth and vigour most horribly; a sailor grows old sooner than any other man. I have observed it all my life. A man is in greater danger in the navy of being insulted by the rise of one whose father his father might have disdained to speak to, and of becoming prematurely an object of disgust himself, than in any other line.'

In a letter of St. Vincent's, dated 9 July 1806, there is a significant reference to the ' idle, licentious aristocrats who are taking away all the first-fruits of the Service, to the utter exclusion of friendless merit '. In Marryat's *Peter Simple* the hero overhears the First Lieutenant observe to the Captain:

> The Service is going to the devil. As long as it was not popular, if we had not much education, we at least had the chance that natural abilities gave us; but now that great people send their sons for a provision into the navy, we have all the refuse of their families, as if anything was good enough to make a captain of a man-of-war, who has occasionally more responsibility on his shoulders, and is placed in situations requiring more judgment, than any other people in existence. Here's another of the fools of the family made a present to the country—another cub for me to lick into shape. Where's Mr. Simple? . . .

In his earliest novel, *Frank Mildmay*, a work which is to a great extent autobiographical, Marryat vividly records his first impressions of the midshipmen's berth. ' I followed my new friend down the ladder, under the half deck, where sat a woman, selling bread and butter and red herrings to the sailors; she had also cherries and clotted cream, and a cask of strong beer, which seemed to be in great demand. We passed her, and descended another ladder, which brought us to the 'tween decks, and into the steerage, in the forepart of which, on the larboard side, abreast of the mainmast, was my future residence—a small hole, which they called a berth; it was ten feet long by six, and about five feet four inches high; a small aperture, about nine inches square, admitted a very scanty portion of what we most needed, namely, fresh air and daylight. A deal table occupied a considerable extent of this small apartment, and on it stood a brass candlestick, with a dip candle, and a wick like a full blown carnation. The table cloth was spread and stains of port wine and gravy too visibly indicated the near approach of Sunday. The black servant was preparing for dinner, and I was shown the seat I was to occupy. " Good heaven! " thought I, as I squeezed myself between the ship's side and the mess-table, " and is this to be my future residence?—better go back to school; there, at least, is fresh air and clean linen." '

One of Marryat's messmates briefly catalogued the appointments of the midshipmen's berth as follows: ' One battered, spoutless, handleless japanned tin jug that did not contain water, for it leaked; some tin mugs; seven or eight pewter plates; an excellent old iron tureen which contained our cocoa in the morning, our pea soup at noon and performed the character of wash basin whenever the midshipmen's fag condescended to cleanse his hands. It is a fact that when we sailed from England, of crockery ware we had not a single article. We had no other provisions than the ship's allowance. Bread, it is well re-marked, is the staff of life; but ' the writer added drily, ' it is not quite so pleasant to find it life itself, and to have the powers of loco-motion.'

The early impressions of Admiral the Hon. Sir George Elliot were more favourable.

' These were happy days ' he remarked, ' though not luxurious ones. When I first went to sea, midshipmen had no servants, they cooked for themselves, made and washed their own things, but kept up a tolerable appearance; we had little beyond the ship's allowance of provision, and only a tin pot or two to drink out of. . . . I never slept on shore as a midshipman except between paying off the *Goliath* and commissioning the *Elephant* early in 1800; and I had not probably been in port, on an average a fortnight in the year, unless attacking or defending some place.'

When on a visit to Plymouth in 1789 Fanny Burney was shown over the *Bombay Castle*, 74, by Captain Duckworth, she also remarked upon the Spartan simplicity of the ' young gentlemen's ' quarters. ' In going over the ship,' she observed, ' we came to the midship-men's mess, and those young officers were at dinner, but we were taken in: they were lighted by a few candles fastened to the wall in sockets. Involuntarily I exclaimed, " Dining by candle-light at noon-day!" A midshipman, starting forward, said, " Yes, ma'am, and Admiral Lord Hood did the same for seven years following!" '

It was by no means an unheard-of thing for youngsters to be borne upon the ship's books who were still at school, or even in the nursery. False certificates of age were usually winked at. Peter Parker (grandson of Nelson's patron) passed for lieutenant at the age of sixteen, being officially reported as ' upwards of twenty-one '. Nelson himself was certified as over twenty when he was actually under nineteen. In the same way Nelson got his stepson, Josiah Nisbet, promoted to com-mander by flouting the regulations. It was related by Admiral Elliot that, in 1800, when he and a number of other youngsters went to pass for lieutenants' commissions: ' Our examinations before the old Commissioners of the Navy were not severe; but we were called on to produce certificates that we were all twenty-one years of age—I was sixteen and four days. The old porter in the hall furnished them at 5s. apiece, which, no doubt, the old Commissioners knew; for, on our return with them, they remarked that the ink had not dried in twenty-one years.'[1]

In a good many families successive generations entered the Navy as a matter of course; a boy would follow in his father's footsteps, or, perhaps, in those of an uncle; in the Navy List the old familiar names constantly recur. A naval historian of the early nineteen-hundreds, discoursing of Rodney's action off The Saints, makes this point amply clear.

It is an interesting instance of hereditary inclination—of how the naval spirit runs in families. Two-thirds of Rodney's captains, practically, are represented at the present hour in the Royal Navy by direct descendants. One has only to turn over the pages of the current Navy List to find Hoods and Inglefields and Parrys, and Graveses and Gardners, Fanshawes and Dumaresqs, a Buckner, a Blair, a Burnett, a Balfour, a Savage, a Symons, a Charrington, an Inglis, a Wallace, a Byron, a Cornish, a Truscott, a Saumarez, Knights and Wilsons, and Williamses and Wilkinsons and Thomsons, besides others, who either trace their descent directly from Rodney's captains or come of the same stock.[2]

Early inured to the hardships of their calling, many of these young officers attained to an astonishingly high level of professional skill and capability. Progressing for the most part by practical experience rather than by study, they acquired a thorough knowledge of the science of seamanship, rose promptly and coolly to an emergency, and learned to pit their strength and skill against every vagary of weather, wind, and sea. As has already been said, midshipmen would frequently pass for lieutenants while still in their teens. Frederick Marryat was not quite twenty when he led a party to cut away the main-yard of the *Aeolus*, when that ship had been laid on her beam ends in a heavy gale off the New England coast in September 1811. It is always to be remembered that the strength of the Navy lay not so much in a comparatively few very famous seamen like Blackwood, Broke, Hoste, or Riou, as in a whole multitude of obscure officers of the type of Gardner and his

[1] *Q.* W. Laird Clowes, *The Royal Navy* (1903), IV, p. 160.
[2] E. Fraser, *Famous Fighters of the Fleet* (1904), p. 78.

associates, men who seldom rose to post-rank, but whose patient labours helped to form the fleets and squadrons which the great Admirals were later to lead to victory.

The quality of the post-captains varied greatly. There is ample evidence to show that the majority of them were good enough seamen; but in other respects they were often found wanting. ' We are likewise to recollect, that all commanders of men of war are not gentlemen or men of education,'[1] observed that keen observer, Captain Edward Thompson: ' I know a great part are brave men, but a much greater seamen.'

' I expect a great deal from you,' wrote Captain Curtis Barnett, when Anson was appointed to the Admiralty in 1745. ' I am stupid enough to think that we are worse officers though better seamen than our neighbours; that our young men get wrong notions early, and are led to imagine that he is the greatest officer who has the least blocks in his rigging. I hope you will give a new turn to our affairs and form a society for the propagation of sea-military knowledge.' Much the same opinions are expressed in a paper, which has been attributed to Vernon, early in 1747.

> It is certainly necessary that a sea officer should have some natural courage; but it is equally just that he should have a good share of sense, be perfect master of his business, and have some taste for honour; which last is usually the result of *a happy education, moderate reading, and good company, rarely found in men raised on the mere credit of being seamen.* . . . The general notion about sea officers is that they should have the courage of brutes, without any regard to the fine qualities of men, which is an error themselves too often fall into. This levels the officer with the common seaman, gives us a stark wrong idea of the nature, design, and end of the employment, and makes no distinction between the judgement, skill, and address of a Blake, and a mere fighting blockhead without ten grains of common sense.[2]

There was a remarkably high proportion of first-rate commanders in the squadrons led by Boscawen and Hawke in 1759. Moreover, as

[1] Nor, judging from the following excerpt from a letter written by Admiral Thomas Pye to Lord Sandwich, would it appear that all gentlemen were men of education. ' Give me leave my Lord to make one Observation More and I have Don—and that is When You peruse Admiral Pyes Letters you will please not to Scrutinize too Close either to the speling or the Grammatical Part as I allow my Self to be no proficient in either. I had the Mortification to be neglected in my education, went to sea at 14 without any, and a Man of War was my University.' (*Sandwich Papers*, I, p. 35.)
[2] Q. *The Navy in the War of 1739-48*, I, p. xii.

the century advanced, it is evident from the observations of Gardner and others, the proportion of commanders who were good captains as well as fine seamen steadily rose. The advantage that our officers enjoyed over their opponents in point of practical skill and experience was increased by the British policy that obtained in the latter half of the century of rigorously blockading the enemy's naval ports.

It is noteworthy that at least two of the commanders who served under Hawke during the campaign of 1759 had ' come up through the hawse-hole'. Captain John Campbell of the *Ramillies* had been one of the petty officers of the *Centurion* in the voyage of 1740–4. He first went to sea in the coasting trade. While serving his apprenticeship, his coaster had been overtaken by the press-gang, and the entire crew, with the exception of the master and himself (who was exempt by his indentures) had been pressed into the Navy. The mate burst into tears at the prospect of being thus torn from his family, and young Campbell had asked if he might take his place. ' Ay, my lad,' was the gruff rejoinder; ' I would rather have a lad of spirit than a blubbering man.' Campbell had risen in the Service and had become Hawke's flag-captain shortly before the action of Quiberon Bay. Another of them was Captain John Bentley of the *Warspite*, who served during the early half of the campaign with Boscawen in the Mediterranean and during the second with the Channel Fleet. These are well-known names; but there were many other such cases of officers in the Georgian Navy who had successfully worked their way up in the Service. There was in fact no such unbridgeable gulf between the lower- and the quarter-deck as existed a hundred years later.[1]

In the *Recollections of James Anthony Gardner* the Old Navy lives for ever. ' His book ', observes Dr. David Mathew, ' is in fact the classic account of the life of a sea officer of the late eighteenth century.' Though it is clear from these memoirs that Gardner's messmates were all too frequently addicted to hard drinking, and occasionally to puerile and brutal horseplay, the general impression to be gained from the *Recollections* is one of good fellowship and abounding high spirits. Incidentally the account serves to show that Marryat's description of some of the amazing characters in his naval

---

[1] The life-story of Captain Robert Carkett, who, as first of the *Monmouth*, had so greatly distinguished himself in the ' Moonlight Action ' of 28 February 1758, illustrates both the pros and cons of promotion from the lower-deck.

novels, such as ' Gentleman Chucks ' the boatswain and ' Mr. Muddle ' the carpenter, are in no way exaggerated. ' As I have said before,' remarked the author of the *Recollections*, ' every ship has its strange characters.'[1] In the unrivalled gallery of originals, cranks, and eccentrics portrayed by Gardner, particular mention must be made of the famous Billy Culmer, who prided himself on being the oldest midshipman in the Navy and looked upon young captains and lieutenants with contempt. ' Billy in person was about five feet eight or nine,' wrote Gardner, ' and stooped; hard features marked with the smallpox; blind in an eye, and a wen nearly the size of an egg under his cheek bone. . . . He had a custom, when half seas over, of sounding a horn like a huntsman and calling the hounds, and used to swear he would be in at the death.' Another of Gardner's messmates in the midshipmen's berth was ' old Collier, who drank like a fish, and when drunk used to sing the Thirty-fourth Psalm and prognosticate that the ship would founder with all hands'. Another of his shipmates was Johnny Bone, boatswain of the *Edgar*. ' This Johnny Bone was a devil of a fellow at Cap-a-bar,[2] and would stick at nothing. It is related that the late Lord Duncan, when he commanded the *Edgar*, once said to him, " Whatever you do, Mr. Bone, I hope and trust you will not take the anchors from the bows ".' Of John Stiles, lieutenant of the *Salisbury*, Gardner wrote briefly, ' Fond of mastheading for little or nothing '; of John Roskruge, master of the *Edgar*, ' one that was better acquainted with rope-yarns and bilge-water than with Homer or Virgil. He said a man's ideas should go no further than the jibboom end '; of John Watson, mate of the same vessel, ' sickly and crabbed as the devil. Cato the Censor never ended a speech without saying " Delenda est Carthago," and this man never ended his without saying " Damn your whistle " '; of Henry Foularton, midshipman, also of the *Edgar*, ' drank very hard, and died regretting that a keg of gin (along side of him) should see him out '; of Billy Chantrell, first lieutenant of the *Barfleur*, who on turning in at night used to say, ' Call me at six, and don't come bothering me about blowing and raining and all that damned nonsense '; of Jackson Dowsing, lieuten-

---

[1] In one of Boscawen's letters, dated 4 June 1756, there is a similar observation regarding the ' many odd personages jumbled into a ship, the history of them would be entertaining '.

[2] Misappropriation of Government stores.

ant of the same ship, ' all jaw and singing from morn till night '; of Love Constable, first lieutenant of the *Queen*, ' the devil on board, but an angel on shore '; of Joseph Kemble, boatswain of the *Berwick*, ' a snappish cur '; of Alexander Mackenzie, midshipman of the same vessel, ' This man, when he was a midshipman, used to sneak after the lieutenants; when made a lieutenant, sneaking after the captains, and when made a captain, was at his old tricks, sneaking after the admirals. Had he lived to be made a flag officer, he would have sneaked after the devil.'

7

The peace-time strength of the Royal Navy was no more than a fraction of what it became in time of war. It was not, in fact, until the middle of the nineteenth century that seamen were recruited on a continuous-service basis. Moreover, throughout the period under review the Navy's demands rose higher and higher. In 1756 some 50,000 men sufficed for the needs of the Fleet. The following year the number was increased to 55,000; in 1759, to 60,000; in 1760, to 70,000. Just before the outbreak of hostilities with the American colonists the total strength of the Navy stood at 18,000 men. In 1776 it was increased to 28,000; in 1779, to 70,000; in 1781, to 90,000; in 1783, to 110,000. But in 1784 it had fallen to 26,000, and more than 80,000 men were paid off and turned adrift. In 1792, on the eve of the long-drawn-out Revolutionary and Napoleonic Wars, the total personnel of the Navy amounted to only 16,000 men. In 1802 it stood at the unprecedented figure of 135,000. In 1812 it reached a total of 145,000.

The outbreak of hostilities invariably found a large part of the Fleet paralysed for lack of men; and it became necessary to draw heavily on the immense maritime reserves of the realm in the shape of merchant seamen, fishermen, bargemen, boatmen, lightermen, and longshoremen generally. The absence of any effective, organized system of recruitment was a perennial and serious weakness. Though from time to time suggestions were made by various writers, from Defoe in the seventeenth century to Marryat in the nineteenth, for manning the Fleet, the Admiralty continued to rely on the time-honoured expedients of bounties and impressment.

Certain cities and corporations, as well as the government, offered bounties for enlistment. At the time of the ' Spanish Armament ' in 1770, for example, Edinburgh and Montrose offered a bounty of 42s. a head for prime seamen, London 40s., Aberdeen 21s., and Bristol 20s.; while the government offered 30s. But the expedient was only partly successful.

Prime seamen constituted the effective nucleus of the crews, of which only about one-fifth were volunteers. The rest were conscripts of various sorts. Press gangs swept the streets and alleys of the dock-yard towns and boarded the homecoming trades, or merchant fleets, as well as colliers and fishing vessels. From these two main sources— the mercantile marine and the fisheries—came the pool of trained seamen from which, in war-time, were drawn most of the crews for the Navy. The majority as well as the best of the pressed men came out of the merchant vessels—for the most part those homeward-bound —in the Channel and North Sea.[1]

As the Navy continued to expand, the supply of prime seamen was no longer adequate; and a considerable number of landsmen were swept up by the all-embracing net of the press gang, which gradually extended the range of its activities up and down the coasts of the United Kingdom. In London, according to J. R. Hutchinson, the historian of the press gang, ' the streets, and especially the water-side streets, were infested with gangs. At times it was unsafe for any able-bodied man to venture abroad unless he had on him an undeniable protection or wore a dress that unmistakably proclaimed the gentle-man.'[2]

The marked prejudice against service in the Navy that formerly existed in certain of our fishing ports may not infrequently be traced back to distant memories of the press. In this connection ' The Press'd Man's Lamentation ' is worth recalling:

> Now the bloody war's beginning,
> Many thousands will be slain,
> And it is more than ten to one
> If any of us return again.

---

[1] ' Everbody knows that our fleets cannot be fitted out,' wrote Lord North in 1770, ' except when our trade is at home or just coming home, because sailors are at no other time to be had ' (Q. Oswyn Murray in *Mariner's Mirror*, XXIV, p. 217).

[2] And not always then. It is on record that on one occasion John Wesley was impressed.

To hear the cries in every City
Likewise in every seaport town,
'Twill make your heart to bleed with pity,
For to hear the press'd men moan.[1]

Occasionally the men would put up a stubborn fight, and sometimes the gangs were beaten off. Certain stretches of the coast were notoriously too strong for the gangs to tackle; others were too difficult: for instance, the Cornish peninsula was largely forbidden ground to the press gang. Portland, again, offered unrivalled facilities for concealment. Often the men received warning in time and managed to get away. The great press of 1755 offered many examples of successful evasion. To escape capture, seamen would sometimes disguise themselves as labourers, stablemen, etc.; and their employers would assist them to evade the press by concealing them in their houses, and even in their bed-chambers. Strictly speaking, only seafaring men could lawfully be taken by the press gang, and there was an Act which exempted from the press every male under eighteen and over fifty-five. But in any serious crisis the law was simply ignored, and then would be enacted scenes such as Rowlandson depicted and Smollett described. As an American visitor to this country observed, ' Englishmen would rise in arms, should the military impress for the army, citizens of every rank, from the fields, the streets, and public roads; but, one particular class of men seem to be abandoned by society, and relinquished to perpetual imprisonment, and a slavery, which, though honourable, cuts them off from most things which men hold dear.'[2]

' After a seaman,' Pitt observed to the House of Commons in 1755, ' by hard service for many years at sea, has earned and saved as much as may establish him in a quiet retreat at land, he does not know but that in six months, or a less time, he may be torn from his wife and family, and forced again to undergo all the fatigues and perils of a common seaman, without any certainty of ever being released, whilst he is fit for serving in that situation.'

It would appear that the press was generally regarded as a great but necessary evil. There was never anything in the nature of large-scale agitation for its abolition. The whole problem was, in fact, thus

[1] Q. David Mathew, *The Naval Heritage* (1944), p. 98.
[2] Silliman, *Journal of Travels in England, Holland, and Scotland* (1806).

pithily summed up: 'You may talk o' the hardships of pressing—your man-hunting—and the likes of such lubberly prate; but if there's no ent'ring, how the h–ll can you help it? Men-o'-war must be manned. . . . '[1] *Men-o'-war must be manned.* That was the crux of the matter.

The machinery of impressment was materially improved, on the eve of the French Revolutionary War, through the inauguration of the Impress Service. For this the Comptroller, Sir Thomas Middleton, was mainly responsible. For the future individual captains were no longer saddled with the onerous burden of finding and pressing their own crews, which was taken over by the new organization. Further, the activities of the press were to some degree supplemented by the operation of Pitt's two Quota Acts of March and April 1795, in accordance with which the various counties, cities, and towns of Great Britain were required to furnish an additional quota—in proportion roughly to their population—for the King's service. This new intake, which included some very dubious material, duly received the bounty. According to a contemporary authority, Captain Brenton, 'The quota-bounty given in 1795, 1796, and 1797, we conceive to have been the most ill-advised fatal measure ever adopted by the government for manning the Fleet. The seamen who voluntarily entered in 1793, and fought some of the most glorious of our battles, received the comparatively small bounty of £5. These brave fellows saw men, totally ignorant of the profession, the very refuse and outcasts of society, flying from justice and the vengeance of the law, come on board with bounty to the amount of £70. One of these objects, on coming on board a ship of war with £70 bounty, was seized by a boatswain's mate, who, holding him up with one hand by the waist-band of his trousers, humorously exclaimed, " Here's a fellow that cost a guinea a pound." '

The proportion of landsmen among the crews of Nelson's ships in the campaign of 1805 has, perhaps, been somewhat exaggerated. But such was the scarcity of seamen during the Revolutionary and Napoleonic Wars that eventually all sorts and conditions of men were gathered in. Since the crews of merchantmen were racially very mixed, and it was from the mercantile marine that the Navy was principally recruited, it followed that many different nationalities were represented

[1] *The Naval Sketch Book.* By an Officer of Rank (London, 1826).

in the Service. Vagrants, debtors, fugitives from justice, felons even, were often to be met with on the lower deck; the worst elements of which were once referred to by Collingwood as ' the refuse of the gallows and the purgings of a gaol '. Those of the landsmen who could not well be trained as seamen were employed as swabbers, scavengers, etc., in the waist.

In port the seamen were accustomed to supplement the ship's allowance with fresh supplies brought out to them by the local dealers. A vessel would be scarcely anchored at Spithead before she was surrounded by a fleet of wherries, laden with legs of mutton, pounds of butter, quartern loaves, beef sausages, casks of porter, vegetables, and other delicacies, jostling and manœuvring to obtain the preference. Some of these bumboat-men and bumboat-women were well-known characters. Such a one was Mrs. Cary of Portsmouth, who, when the *Ville de Paris* arrived off Spithead for a refit in July 1804, was there in her boat to meet the flagship, and presently sent up a letter to Cornwallis couched in brief terms: ' Mrs. Cary presents her respects to Admiral. She is alongside the *Ville de Paris* with a bottle of *Gin*, a Brown loaf, a pot of Fresh Butter, a Basket of garden stuff and a pint of rich cream. If the Commander-in-Chief will not receive her and Party, she will immediately dash off to some of the young Captains.'

In Marryat's *Peter Simple* there is a lively description of a ship in harbour being paid off before going to sea:

The ship was now in a state of confusion and uproar; there were Jews trying to sell clothes, or to obtain money for clothes which they had sold; bumboat-men and bumboat-women showing their long bills, and demanding or coaxing for payment; other people from the shore, with hundreds of small debts; and the sailors' wives, sticking close to them, and disputing every bill presented, as an extortion or a robbery. There was such bawling and threatening, laughing and crying—for the women were all to quit the ship before sunset—at one moment a Jew was upset, and all his hamper of clothes tossed into the hold; at another, a sailor was seen hunting everywhere for a Jew who had cheated him—all squabbling or skylarking, and many of them very drunk. . . . About five o'clock the orders were given for the ship to be cleared. All disputed points were settled by the sergeant of marines with a party, who divided their antagonists from the Jews; and every description of persons not belonging to the ship, whether male or female, was dismissed over the side. The hammocks were piped down, those who were intoxicated were put to bed, and the ship was once more quiet. Nobody was punished for having been tipsy, as pay-day is considered, on board a man-of-war, as the winding-up of all incorrect behaviour, and from that day the sailors turn over a new leaf; for, although some latitude is permitted, and the seamen are seldom flogged in harbour, yet the moment that the anchor is at the bows, strict discipline is exacted, and intoxication must no longer hope to be forgiven.

In harbour the seamen's wives were generally allowed to come on board. 'Where and when they were married was never inquired,' wrote a naval surgeon, 'the simple declaration was considered as sufficient to constitute a nautical and temporary union and which was authorized by long established custom as practised from time immemorial in His Majesty's Navy.' Down to the peace of 1815 considerable numbers of women accompanied the crews to sea and used to assist the boys at quarters. When in 1806 the Princess of Wales was being shown over the *Caesar*, Sir Richard Strachan's flagship, all the women then on board, numbering several hundreds, received strict instructions to keep out of sight on the orlop deck until the Princess had left the ship. Earlier it is recorded that Jervis seized every opportunity to get rid of what he regarded as an intolerable abuse, complaining that 'the women, who still infest His Majesty's ships in great numbers, will have water to wash, that they and their reputed husbands may get drunk with the earnings, and where these vermin abound, the crews are so much addicted to drinking at sea as in port, and the hold is continually damp and a vapour arising from it highly pernicious to health.'[1] Captain Edward Berry, Nelson's friend and his flag-captain in the *Vanguard* in the campaign of the Nile, held similar views. 'There are 300 women on board,' he observed in March 1798, 'and not less than 150 supernumeraries besides the ship's company. All the females go on shore to-morrow if we are paid. At all events I have set my face against taking *one* to sea.' Collingwood, too, was strongly opposed to the custom of permitting women to accompany the crews to sea. 'I have heard there was a woman in the *Pickle*,' he observed in August 1808. 'I never knew a woman brought to sea in a ship that some mischief did not befall the vessel.' 'Captain Carden had given permission for a number of women to come in this ship' [the *Ville de Paris*], he complained the following year. 'I have reproved him for this irregularity and considering the mischief they

[1] See 'Journal of a Naval Surgeon', *Naval Yarns*, ed. W. H. Long, p. 63.

never fail to create wherever they are, I have ordered them all on board the *Ocean* to be conveyed to England again.'[1]

There was yet no uniform for seamen, but the dress which had gradually become customary among them consisted of white trousers, blue jacket, and tarpaulin hat. Pig-tails were still commonly worn on the lower deck, though abandoned by the officers. The men at quarters would wear their black silk handkerchiefs tied round their heads. The time-honoured belief that these handkerchiefs were introduced into the Navy as a mark of mourning for Nelson is without foundation; they were in fact used by our seamen many years before Trafalgar.

When the drums beat to quarters to the familiar double-double-double beat of 'Heart of Oak', the crews would hail the prospect of a fight with the keenest relish and satisfaction. ' When everything was cleared,' remarked an eye-witness of the battle of Cape St. Vincent, ' the ports open, the matches lighted, the guns run out, then we gave them three such cheers as are only to be heard in a British man-of-war.' ' We were all ready,' declared old Swinburne in Marryat's *Peter Simple*, recalling the same action, ' bulk-heads down, screens up, guns shotted, tackles rove, yards slung, powder filled, shot on deck, and fire out.' Gardner tells of the strong impression that these businesslike preparations made on a certain Spanish officer who visited his ship, the *Berwick*, 74, when she was cleared for action. ' The officer seemed astonished when he saw our men at quarters,' Gardner observed, ' their black silk handkerchiefs tied round their heads, their shirt-sleeves tucked up, the crows and handspikes in their hands and the boarders all ready with their cutlasses and tomahawks, that he told Sir John Collins that they put him in mind of so many devils.' In *Frank Mildmay* Marryat has sketched for us an unforgettable description of a smart frigate's crew at quarters, recalling the 'noble tier of guns in a line gently curving out towards the centre: the tackle laid across the deck; the shots and wads prepared in ample store (round shot and canister); the powder boys each with his box full, seated on it, with perfect apparent indifference as to the approaching conflict. The captains of guns, with their priming boxes buckled round their waists; the locks fixed upon the guns; the lanyards laid around them; the officers, with their swords drawn, standing by their respective divisions.'

[1] *The Private Correspondence of Admiral Lord Collingwood*, ed. E. Hughes (1957), p. 251.

8

The prospect of prize money bulked large in the imagination of the Old Navy, quarter-deck and lower-deck alike. Though the spoil was always very inequitably divided, all felt they had a stake in the great lottery of war. 'If these French gentry do not escape me this time, they will pay for the house and furniture too,' wrote Boscawen to his wife in May 1756, 'besides something to save hereafter for all our dear children.' 'You can't think how keen our men are,' he observed in a later letter; 'the hope of prize money makes them happy [and] a signal for a sail brings them all on deck.'[1] The abiding attraction of prize money is well brought out in many a contemporary ballad. After Kempenfelt's victory over de Guichen in 1781, Gardner, then a pupil at the Naval Academy, happened to be standing on Gosport beach when some of the French prisoners taken in the engagement were landed under escort of the military, accompanied by a naval lieutenant and several midshipmen; and a crowd of women came running out of a neighbouring alley chorusing:

> Don't you see the ships a-coming?
>   Don't you see them in full sail?
> Don't you see the ships a-coming
>   With the prizes at their tail?
> Oh! my little rolling sailor,
>   Oh! my little rolling he;
> I do love a jolly sailor,
>   Blithe and merry might he be.
>
> Sailors, they get all the money,
>   Soldiers they get none but brass;
> I do love a jolly sailor,
>   Soldiers they may kiss ——
> Oh! my little rolling sailor,
>   Oh! my little rolling he;
> I do love a jolly sailor,
>   Soldiers may be damned for me.

Captain William Parker of the *Amazon* frigate kept a journal in which he was accustomed carefully to record the various amounts of prize money to which he was entitled. 'When he finally paid off the *Amazon*

[1] *Navy Records Society*, XCII, p. 225.

in 1812 he had received no less than £40,000 in prize, which was not bad going for a man then just under thirty years of age. . . . A considerable number of promising young officers were lost to the Navy because, having made a quick fortune in prize money, they retired from the Service to live ashore on their gains.'[1] The more spectacular hauls were sometimes made the occasion of a naval triumph. Anson's victory over the French in 1747 was celebrated by a grand military procession through the streets of London, with the wagon-loads of captured treasure as the principal show-piece; the houses were illuminated and there were bonfires in every street. The capture of the Spanish *Hermione* by a couple of British cruisers outside Cadiz, in 1762, brought in a haul of about half a million pounds. According to Beatson:

> The treasure was conveyed from Portsmouth to London in twenty waggons, escorted by a party of sailors. The waggons were decorated with the British colours flying, having those of Spain underneath them. . . . On their coming to London, they were joined by a troop of light dragoons, with a band of music, consisting of kettle-drums, French-horns, trumpets and hautboys: and in this manner did they march on through the city to the Tower, amid the acclamations of a prodigious concourse of people.[2]

After the storming of Havana, also in 1762, the Admiral received nearly £122,700 as his share of the prize money, while each seaman secured £3 14s. 10d.

Prize money brought many a fortunate commander-in-chief a splendid fortune. Anson and Saunders, in particular, amassed enormous sums out of prize money. Boscawen, Hawke, Rodney, and later St. Vincent, Hyde Parker, Keith, Rainier, and Pellew were among those who also did very well for themselves. In the words of David Hannay,

> When the man got a few pounds, just enough to keep him drunk for a fortnight, the lieutenant gained a few score, the captain a few hundreds, the admiral gained thousands, for he shared in all the prizes taken on his station, whether he had been present at the capture or not. It is therefore easy to see what an important matter prize-money was to a flag-officer. To get a rich station, and to keep it free from the intrusion of a superior, was the ideal of luck.

[1] P. K. Kemp, *Prize Money* (1946).
[2] Beatson, *Naval and Military Memoirs of Great Britain*, II, p. 588.

For those few, who, surviving the hazards of battle and tempest, rose to the summit of their profession, there was the compelling lure of honour and glory. It is said that in his years of retirement St. Vincent invariably wore the star of the Order of the Bath; and to a small boy who one day asked him what it was and where he found it, the old Admiral replied, ' I found it upon the sea; and if you become a sailor, and search diligently, perhaps you may find just such another.'

9

' Hygiene and supply,' the late Sir Herbert Richmond declared, ' are fundamental elements affecting both strategy and tactics.' In the Royal Navy, during the period under survey, the proportion of deaths due to sickness was far in excess of the number of those who died in battle. It is clear from a study of the evidence that one of the principal factors which limited the sea-keeping of ships and squadrons was this prevalence of disease. The evil was rampant, not only on unhealthy foreign stations, but also in temperate climates and in home waters.

In the blockade of Puerto Bello in 1727 no less than 5,000 men had died of disease, including the commander-in-chief and eight of his captains.[1] During the great voyage of 1740–4 Anson's squadron had suffered appalling losses through sickness; and a large number of those who survived owed their lives to the vigilance and forethought of the Commodore rather than to any medical provision made by the authorities.

On board the *Grafton*, 70, during a cruise which lasted from 12 May to early September 1755, 21 men died at sea, and 112 sick were landed at Halifax—many of whom appear to have died also. ' In 1756,' Captain Edward Thompson related, ' . . . when she had been on no long cruise, and had been exposed only to the hardships of a few months of service in the Channel, the *Stirling Castle*, 64, Captain Samuel Cornish, arrived in Portsmouth with four hundred and eighty men, of whom two hundred and twenty-five were the pressed refuse of gaols and scum of streets. She was full of fever and other sicknesses, and when the diseased had been sent ashore, but one hundred and

---

[1] ' The fact that the Admiral's body was buried in the gravel ballast of his flagship is a sufficient reason for the sickness not abating and provides useful evidence of the state of contemporary naval hygiene ' (Brian Tunstall, *Realities of Naval History*, p. 109).

sixty remained for duty.' Less than three months later, when, having filled up her complement in England, the *Stirling Castle* had proceeded to New York, Thompson wrote, ' We have now one hundred and fifty-nine people ill in fluxes, scurvies, and fevers.'

The number of seamen and marines killed in action during the Seven Years War was rather more than 1,500; but no less than 133,708 are said to have died of sickness or deserted.[1] In the next war, of some 175,990 raised between 1774 and 1780, only 1,243 were killed; but 18,541 died of disease and 42,069 deserted. ' Of the thousands and tens of thousands that perished in our late contests with France and Spain ', wrote Dr. Johnson in 1771, ' a very small part ever felt the stroke of an enemy; the rest languished in tents and ships, amidst damps and putrefaction. . . . By incommodious encampments and unwholesome stations, where courage is useless, and enterprise impracticable, fleets are silently dispeopled and armies sluggishly melted away.'

Scurvy was still the bane of the Service. Down to the latter half of the eighteenth century little progress had been made in combating the disease. This was mainly due to the apathy of the authorities, for the causes had long been known.

Two other dread diseases which periodically ravaged our squadrons were typhus and ' Yellow Jack '; the latter was the particular scourge of the West Indies.

Much of the sickness which decimated the Service is to be attributed to the poor quality of the provisions supplied to the Navy. Many an admiral had occasion to complain of insufficient and bad supplies. Incompetence, neglect, and at times corruption, on the part of those responsible for the victualling of the Service lay at the bottom of these evils. Contemporary pamphlets contain such illuminating items as the following:

> That seamen in the King's Ships have made buttons for their Jackets and Trowsers with the Cheese they were served with, having preferred it, by reason of its tough and durable quality, to buttons made of common metal; and that Carpenters in the Navy-Service have made Trucks to their Ships' flagstaffs with whole Cheeses, which have stood the weather equally with any timber. . . . That their bread has been so full of large

[1] These figures are taken from the *Annual Register* for 1763. Though they are certainly exaggerated the losses due to disease and desertion must none the less have been enormous.

black-headed maggots and that they have so nauseated the thoughts of it, as to be obliged to shut their eyes to confine that sense from being offended before they could bring their minds into a resolution of consuming it. That their beer has stunk as abominably as the foul stagnant water which is pumped out of many cellars in London at midnight hour; and that they were under a necessity of shutting their eyes, and stopping their breath by holding of their noses before they could conquer their aversion, so as to prevail upon themselves in their extreme necessities to drink it. . . . That the pork, which the Fleet under the command of the late Admiral Boscawen was served with, was so rotten, that when boiled it wasted away to mere rags and crumbs, so that it could be eaten with a spoon, and that when the liquor it had been boiled in was drawn off, it flowed out of the cock of the ship's boiler like curds and whey: it was also so nauseous that it made the men sick who did eat of it; and therefore resolving to fast rather than eat any more of it, they have thrown it privately out of their ship's port-holes to prevent being discovered by the officers of their ship.[1]

The author of the observations quoted above was William Thompson, who was systematically victimized and vilified and at last driven out of the public service on account of the embarrassment he had caused to those in authority by these revelations. In a later work he goes on to illustrate with telling effect the intimate connection, in naval warfare, between hygiene and supply and strategy and tactics.

But one instance of the corrupt victualling of the Royal Navy, occur'd whilst I was there, and this too extraordinary to be forgot, was the late Admiral *Martin's* bringing into *Plymouth* Hospital and Sick Quarters, such an incredible number of sick men, as can best be verified by the books of the sick and dead List, if not falsified, at his return from a six weeks cruize, to intercept Mons. *D'Anville*, who then commanded the *Brest* squadron. The sickness by the report of the Admiral, and unanimous opinion of all, both officers and common men, was owing to the badness of their provisions; if so, it will be easy for a common capacity to determine what must have become of Admiral *Martin's* whole squadron, if Mons. *D'Anville* had given him battle.[2]

Shortly before the outbreak of the Seven Years War Hawke embarked on a protracted struggle with the victualling department regarding the quality of the beer supplied to his squadron. Anson had experienced the same difficulty in the war of 1739–48. Since water had to be stored in casks it could not be kept sweet for any length of

---

[1] William Thompson, *The Royal-Navy Man's Advocate* (1757).
[2] *An Appeal to the Public* (1761).

time. Ships then took to sea nearly as much beer as they did water: consequently a supply of good beer was of prime importance if a squadron was to keep at sea. In the autumn of 1755 Hawke observed:

> The beer which came off in the two tenders from Plymouth was very bad; so that I was obliged to direct it to be expended immediately: and if what is now coming should prove to be the same, the squadron will be greatly distressed, as good beer is the best preservative of health among new-raised men. Notwithstanding the promise of the contractors for slops to supply better, I find what were issued to the ships at their coming out to be of the same quality with those complained of: and yet our wants oblige us to make use of them, which I beg their Lordships will please to give directions for effectually remedying hereafter.

Bad ventilation was another prolific source of sickness. It was related by the surgeon of the *Cambridge* that during a cruise in the Bay of Biscay in 1758 the weather was so wet and stormy as to prevent the gunports on the middle deck being opened to ventilate the ship. ' The consequence was a putrid fever,' observed the writer, ' which spread rapidly amongst the seamen and marines, so that in six weeks we had 300 men upon the sick-list—almost half the complement.'

A most important measure for improving the health of the seamen was due to Vernon, who, on 14 August 1740, issued his famous order for the watering of the rum ration to all the captains of his squadron. ' You are . . . hereby required and directed as you tender both the Spiritual & Temporal Welfare of His Majesty's Service, to take particular care that Rum be no more served in Specie to any of the Ship's Company under your Command, but that the respective daily allowance of Half-a-Pint a man for all your Officers & Ship's Company be every day mixed with the proportion of a Quart of Water to every Half-Pint of Rum.'

In 1749 a celebrated London physician, Dr. Richard Mead, produced his *A Discourse on Scurvy*, which treated mainly of that disease as it was observed on board Anson's squadron during his voyage round the world. In the following decade James Lind, one of the most knowledgeable of the naval surgeons of his day, published, whilst engaged in private practice in Edinburgh, two highly important works, *A Treatise on the Scurvy* (1753) and *An Essay on Preserving the Health of Seamen in the Royal Navy* (1757). In the first of these works, which he dedicated to Anson, Lind suggested vegetables, fresh fruit, and lemon juice as anti-scorbutics. The publication of this book marked a milestone in the progress of naval hygiene. ' *A Treatise on the Scurvy* ', writes Dr. Roddis of the United States Navy, ' is one of the great classics of medicine. . . . As has been pointed out, many others had used the citrus fruit juices, both as a preventative measure and in the treatment of scurvy, but it was Lind who most clearly and convincingly proved their value.' More than forty years, however, were to pass before Lind's recommendations about the use of lemon juice as an anti-scorbutic were officially adopted.

The introduction in the middle of the century of artificial ventilation between decks was a revolutionary improvement[1] brought about largely through the strong advocacy and great professional prestige of Dr. Mead. Frequent mention is now made in the captains' logs of the ventilators at work, notably in the campaigns of the Seven Years War.

Both Boscawen and Hawke were renowned for their persistent efforts to improve the health and comfort of the seamen under their command. It was Boscawen who was responsible for introducing Hales' ventilators, first in his flagship, the *Namur*, in 1747, and in later years in the Navy generally. The inscription on the Admiral's monument justly testifies to his ' concern for the interest, and unwearied attention to the health, of all under his command '. The care of the sick and the supply of medical necessaries were somewhat improved as a result of Hawke's protests in 1755. In the crucial year of the Seven Years War his insistence on the regular and adequate provision of beef, beer, and other supplies for his squadron proved, as we have seen, a factor of prime importance in the long blockade of Brest.

A still more important figure than those already mentioned was Captain Cook. As a result of his meticulous attention to the health of his men, Cook, on his second voyage to the Pacific in 1772-5—after remaining at sea for longer than anyone else in history—had lost only one man through sickness. ' The method which he discovered ', observed one of his officers, Lieutenant King, ' and so successfully pursued, of preserving the health of seamen, forms a new era in navigation, and will transmit his name to future ages amongst the friends and benefactors of mankind.'[2]

[1] See *supra*, p. 343.
[2] ' His great contribution to the subject was his realization that what was needed was

In 1781 Rodney secured the appointment of Gilbert Blane, who in the previous campaign had sailed with him as his own private doctor, as Physician of the Fleet. Dr. (afterwards Sir Gilbert) Blane was not only a very skilful physician, but also a first-class administrator. Enjoying the firm support of his Admiral, he made a number of recommendations for improving the general health of the fleet, which were embodied in an official report and eventually carried into effect. He laid particular stress on preventive measures.

> I hardly ever knew a ship's company become sickly which was well regulated in point of cleanliness and dryness. It is the custom in some ships to divide the crew into squads or divisions under the inspection of respective officers, who make a weekly review of their persons and clothing, and are answerable for the cleanliness and regularity of their several allotments. This ought to be an indispensable duty in ships of two or three decks; and when it has been practised, and at the same time ventilation, cleanliness, and dryness below and between decks have been attended to, I have never known seamen more unhealthy than any other men. The neglect of such attentions is a never-failing cause of sickness. . . . It would certainly be for the benefit of the service that a uniform should be established for the common men as well as for the officers. This would oblige them at all times to have in their possession a quantity of decent apparel, subject to the inspection of their superiors. . . . The greatest evil connected with clothing is the infection generated by wearing it too long without shifting, for the jail, hospital, or ship fever seems to be more owing to this than to close air.[1]

The reforms recommended by Blane concerned such vital matters as these, also regulations for the prevention of scurvy, a more adequate supply of medical necessities, the avoidance of ' filth, crowding, and mixture of diseases ' in naval hospitals ashore, and the provision of hospital ships. Special attention was paid to the provisioning of ships on foreign stations, with the result that scurvy was slowly but surely eradicated from the Royal Navy and mercantile marine. In consequence of these medical and sanitary reforms advocated by Blane, the health of the squadron was greatly improved during the latter part of Rodney's command, and, whereas in the year ending on 13 October 1781 one

---

fresh food in general, and clean water, and, as a counter to depression, variety of food; and, as another contribution, cleanliness of person, clothes and quarters; and, as an aid to that, a dry and disinfected ship ' (J. C. Beaglehole in *The Geographical Journal*, CXXII, p. 425).

[1] Blane, *Observations on the Diseases incident to Seamen* (1785).

man out of every seven had perished from disease on the West India station, in the same period ending on 16 July 1782 the loss had been reduced to only one in twenty. In 1785 there appeared the first edition of Blane's classic work, *Observations on the Diseases incident to Seamen*.

It was in large measure due to Blane's powerful support that, in 1795, the general use of lemon juice as a specific was enjoined by the Admiralty: with effects that were almost magical. When two years afterwards Lord Spencer, then First Lord, in the course of a visit to Haslar wished to see something of the scurvy, there was not a single case then in the hospital. Dr. Andrew Baird, who played something of the same role under St. Vincent's command as Blane had under Rodney's, was also a strong advocate of the provision of lemon juice as an anti-scorbutic.

Another important figure in the naval medical service was Dr. Thomas Trotter. Trotter, who rose from surgeon's mate to be Physician of the Channel Fleet (1794–1802), did much to raise professional standards in the service, to overhaul the discipline and administration of Haslar hospital, and generally to improve the diet and conditions on the lower deck.

The Commissioners of the Sick and Hurt Board, upon whom fell the main responsibility for the medical service of the Fleet, on the whole discharged their duties conscientiously and well. The Commissioners were usually doctors, some of them highly distinguished ones. Both Blane and Baird served, in their time, on the Board. Blane during his term of office continued to promote the improvement of the diet and hygiene of the seamen. Baird was an indefatigable visitor of ships and hospitals (it was largely due to his representations that pig-sties were eventually shifted from the vicinity of the sick berths). Though down to the close of the Napoleonic War there was never a sufficient number either of surgeons or of office-workers in the service, the period was one of steady progress. A notable improvement was the provision, on the recommendation of Dr. Lind, of slop-ships for the examination, cleansing, and clothing of new recruits; and another most important measure, due to Dr. Trotter while Physician of the Channel Fleet, was the introduction of inoculation against small-pox. The supply of medicines was much improved; stoves and better methods of ventilation were installed; and a more adequate provision of fresh meat, vegetables, and fruit was ordered. Last but not least, the status and emoluments of the surgeons were materially improved.

These and other reforms inaugurated a new era in naval hygiene and immeasurably improved the health of the Navy. It may safely be said that, without these measures, it would have been impossible to maintain on their stations the large squadrons of the Revolutionary and Napoleonic Wars.

10

In 1731 there appeared the first issue of King's Regulations and Admiralty Instructions. Hitherto every commander-in-chief had issued his own code of instructions to the squadron under his command. For the future K.R. and A.I. were to be the permanent disciplinary code of the Fleet.

In 1755 the corps of marines passed under Admiralty control and was organized in three divisions, which were stationed respectively at Chatham, Portsmouth, and Plymouth. As the years went by they came to be regarded by the authorities as the king-pins of naval discipline and established their reputation for unswerving loyalty and complete trustworthiness in the troubled era of the 1790s; it was in recognition of these loyal services that, in 1802, they were given the appellation of ' Royal Marines'. ' I never knew an appeal made to them for honour, courage, or loyalty ', wrote St. Vincent, who was mainly responsible for this measure, ' that they did not more than realize my expectations. If ever the real hour of danger should come to England, they will be found the country's sheet-anchor.'

One of the shrewdest and most influential disciplinarians of his day was Richard Kempenfelt, who, in the early years of the American War, was responsible for the general introduction of ' Divisions'[1] in the Service. In a long letter to Sir Charles Middleton, the Comptroller of the Navy, Kempenfelt outlined his project.

The only way to keep large bodies of men in order is by dividing and subdividing of them, with officers over each, to inspect into and regulate their conduct, to discipline and form them. Let the ship's company be divided into as many companies as there are lieutenants—except the first lieutenant, whose care should extend over the whole. Each lieutenant's

[1] The origin of Divisions may be traced back to certain orders issued by Vice-Admiral Thomas Smith, then commanding the squadron in the Downs, in 1755. See *Select Naval Documents*, ed. Hodges and Hughes (1936), pp. 147–8.

company should be formed of the men who are under his command at quarters for action. These companies should be reviewed every day by their lieutenants, when the men are to appear tight and clean. He is to see that the raw men are daily exercised at arms, and the sails and rigging. The captain should review them himself at least once a week. When it can be done, the men should always have the full time for their meals and for repose, and certain portions of time in the week allotted for washing and mending; but at all other times they should be kept constantly employed; and whatever they are exercised about, be particularly careful that they do it with attention and alertness, and perfect. Labour to bring them to a habit of this, and suffer nothing to be done negligently and awkwardly. The adage that idleness is the root of evil is with no people more strongly verified than with sailors and soldiers. In what order is a military corps kept on shore, when well officered! Certainly the situation of a ship's crew is more favourable to sustain order and regularity than that of a corps ashore, confined within narrow limits, without tippling houses to debauch in, and under the constant eye of their officers. But if six, seven, or eight hundred men are left in a mass together, without divisions, and the officers assigned no particular charge over any part of them, who only give orders from the quarter-deck or gangways—such a crew must remain a disorderly mob, business will be done awkwardly or tumultuously, without order or despatch, and the raw men put into no train of improvement. The officers, having no particular charge appointed them, the conduct and behaviour of the men are not inspected into; they know nothing of their proceedings; and the people, thus left to themselves, become sottish, slovenly and lazy, form cabals, and spirit each other up to insolence and mutiny.[1]

There can be no question that there was a marked increase in severity throughout the Service as the century advanced; particularly after the outbreak, in 1793, of the Revolutionary War. As Captain Owen has said, ' a normal sentence awarded by court martial for a serious offence would be two or three hundred lashes with a cat-of-nine tails under George III, whereas the punishment for the same offence under Anne would be fifty lashes.'[2] The forms of corporal punishment commonly in use were flogging, ' running the gauntlet ', ' starting ', and ' gagging '. Of these flogging with the cat-o'-nine tails —a whip with nine lashes made of knotted cords—was by far the severest. According to a contemporary witness, *Jack Nasty Face*[3]:

[1] *Navy Records Society*, XXXII, p. 355.
[2] J. H. Owen, *The War at Sea under Queen Anne* (1938).
[3] The evidence of *Jack Nasty Face* is not always to be relied upon: but in this case it is fully confirmed by other sources.

The Captain orders this punishment for anything that himself or any of his officers may consider a crime. The prisoner is made to strip to the waist; he is then seized by his wrists and knees to a grating or ladder; the Boatswain's Mate is then ordered to cut him with the cat-o'-nine tails; and after six or twelve lashes are given another Boatswain's Mate is called to continue the exercise; and so they go on, until the Captain gives the word to stop.[1]

The same authority gives a detailed description of the terrible punishment known as ' flogging through the fleet ', which was commonly inflicted for desertion and other serious crimes. By the men it was regarded almost as the equivalent of a death sentence; and often, indeed, resulted in the death of the victim.

Whilst lying at Spithead, in the year 1809 or 1810, four impressed seamen attempted to make their escape from a frigate then lying there: one of their shipmates, a Dutchman to whom they had entrusted the secret, betrayed their intention, and informed the commanding officer of their designs. They were tried by a court-martial, and sentenced to receive three hundred lashes each, through the fleet. On the first day after the trial that the weather was moderate enough to permit, the signal was made for a boat from each ship, with a guard of Marines, to attend the punishment. The man is placed in a launch, *i.e.*, the largest ship's boat, under the care of the Master-at-Arms and a doctor. There is a capstan bar rigged fore and aft, to which this poor fellow is lashed by his wrists; and for fear of hurting him—humane creatures—there is a stocking put over each, to prevent him from tearing the flesh off in his agonies. When all is ready, the prisoner is stript and seized to the capstan bar. Punishment commences by the officer, after reading the sentence of the court-martial, ordering the Boatswain's Mates to do their duty. The cat-o'-nine tails is applied to the bare back, and at about every six lashes a fresh Boatswain's Mate is ordered to relieve the executioner of this duty, until the prisoner has received, perhaps, twenty-five lashes. He is then cast loose, and, allowed to sit down with a blanket rolled round him, is conveyed to the next ship, escorted by this vast number of armed boats, accompanied by that doleful music, ' The Rogues' March '. In this manner he is conveyed from ship to ship, receiving alongside of each a similar number of stripes with the cat, until the sentence is completed. It often, nay generally, happens that nature is unable to sustain it, and the poor fellow faints and sinks under it, although every kind method is

---

[1] ' As many as 500 lashes were sometimes awarded. The Boatswain's Mates were drilled to flog effectively, by being made to practise on a cask, under the superintendence of the Boatswain ' (Laird Clowes, *The Royal Navy*, V, p. 28).

made use of to enable him to bear it, by pouring wine down his throat. The doctor will then feel his pulse, and often pronounces that the man is unable to bear more. He is then taken, most usually insensible, to what is termed the ' sick bay '; and, if he recovers, he is told he will have to receive the remainder of his punishment. When there are many ships in the fleet at the time of the court-martial, this ceremony, if the prisoner can sustain it, will last nearly half the day.[1]

' Running the gauntlet ' was a punishment commonly inflicted for petty theft. The culprit, stripped to the waist, was made to sit in a tub which was hauled on a grating around the deck, to be belaboured in turn by the bosun and his mates with a cat-o'-nine tails, and by each member of the crew with a knotted rope yarn. ' This punishment is inflicted by the Captain's orders ', says Jack Nasty Face, ' without the formal inquiry by a court-martial.' ' Starting ', or beating by a bosun's mate with a rope's end, was such an every-day occurrence in many ships that no mention of it was made in the log. For ' answering back ', ' gagging ' was a common penalty. The procedure was for the offender to be seated with both his legs in irons and his hands bound behind his back; and his jaws being then forced open, an iron bar was placed in his mouth much as a bit is fixed in a horse's mouth.

All this was strictly according to regulation. Not so were such appalling cases of abuse of power by sadistic tyrants like Captain Pigot of the *Hermione*. It would appear that some of the complaints against individual officers which found utterance during the mutinous outbreaks of 1797 were by no means unfounded. ' The ill-usage we have on board this ship ', the crew of the *Winchelsea* had protested to the Admiralty early in the Revolutionary War, ' forced us to fly to Your Lordships the same as a child to its father.' ' Our first Lieutenant,' ran a similar complaint, ' he is a most Cruel and Barberous man, Beating some at times, untill they are not able to stand, and not allowing them the satisfaction to cry out.' Captain Pigot (whose maddened crew at last rose and murdered him, together with his officers) was accustomed to flog the last man down from aloft. Sometimes, but not very often, a guilty officer would be court-martialled

---

[1] From the *Naval Chronicle*, 5 January 1804: ' This morning, at ten o'clock, a signal was made from the *Royal William* at Spithead for a boat from each ship, manned and armed, to attend the punishment of a marine, who was flogged through the fleet for desertion; after which he was sent on shore to Haslar Hospital.' This was the usual sentence for desertion.

and sentenced; there can be no doubt that the majority of such abuses went unpunished.

On the other hand, the influence of such humane and enlightened commanders as Boscawen, Hawke, Howe, Duncan, St. Vincent, Nelson, and Collingwood was gradually effecting a transformation. Howe as a young post-captain had initiated the custom of granting leave to his ship's company watch by watch and took the greatest care of his sick and wounded. Collingwood, who was renowned throughout the Service as a disciplinarian, came nearly to abolish flogging in the ships under his command.[1] He would not permit his officers to use coarse or abusive language when addressing the men; and he laid the foundations of a new and better tradition of relationship between the lower- and quarter-deck. Old Duncan was immensely and deservedly popular with his crews. Nelson's influence over officers and men alike was almost magical. ' He had ', declares Hannay, ' an extraordinary faculty for inspiring the men under his command, first with confidence in himself, and then with a desire to emulate him. The real Nelson Touch was the torch of fire with which he lit up the souls of men.' In the early months of 1797 the *Theseus*, Captain John Aylmer, had been, according to St. Vincent, ' an abomination '. But the latter at last got Aylmer to transfer to the *Captain*; and one night, early in June, a paper was dropped on the quarter-deck of the *Theseus*, now the flagship of Rear-Admiral Sir Horatio Nelson:

> Success attend Admiral Nelson! God bless Captain Miller! We thank them for the Officers they have placed over us. We are happy and comfortable, and will shed every drop of blood in our veins, and the name of *Theseus* shall be immortalized as high as the *Captain's*.

A by no means unimportant factor in the relationship between officers and men at this time was that of common territorial ties. Nelson, Collingwood, Hardy, Saumarez, and Pellew could reckon upon a substantial following of volunteers from Norfolk, Northumberland,

---

[1] ' The punishments which he substituted for the lash were of many kinds. Among the rest was one which the men particularly dreaded. It was the ordering any offender to be excluded from his mess, and be employed in every sort of extra duty; so that he was every moment liable to be called up on deck for the meanest service, amid the laughter and jeers of the men and boys. Such an effect had this upon the sailors, that they have often declared that they would much prefer having three dozen lashes: and to avoid the recurrence of this punishment, the worst characters never failed to become attentive and orderly ' (G. L. Newnham Collingwood, *A Selection from the Public and Private Correspondence of Vice-Admiral Lord Collingwood*, I, p. 72).

Dorset, Guernsey, and Cornwall respectively; and there were numerous other local attachments. ' In consequence of the great war establishment ', observes Dr. Mathew in *The Naval Heritage*, ' naval officers who had links with a countryside would often place the sons of neighbouring farmers or gamekeepers or bailiffs on board the different line-of-battleships. This, with Nelson's example, fostered the growth of that penetrating individual care for the members of the ship's company which was to prove so clear a characteristic of the naval captain '.

A dashing frigate captain had little difficulty in securing crews. When the *Impérieuse* was commissioned in 1806 every man of the ship's company who had served under Cochrane in the *Pallas* at once turned over to his new command. Another important factor in the gradually improving situation was the good influence of the ' blue lights ', as they were called—commanders of firm Evangelical convictions, who were prepared to put their precepts into practice.

Although it was not until late in the nineteenth century that the cat was finally abolished in the Service (strictly speaking, it was only *suspended*), the ordering of tyrannical and excessive punishments was gradually discontinued. The punishment of running the gauntlet was abolished in 1806 and that of starting three years later. In Captain Cumby's private order book of 1811 it was explicitly ruled that, ' The highly improper practice of what is called starting the men is most peremptorily forbidden.'

II

Our three naval bases—Portsmouth, Chatham, and Plymouth—were all situated in the south of England, whence most of the personnel of the Service, then and for generations afterwards, were drawn. Its unique strategical location had made Portsmouth—to quote the words of a contemporary authority—' the grand naval arsenal of England ' and ' the rendezvous and headquarters of the British Navy '.

The town, which stands on a narrow peninsula, was then encircled by formidable ramparts guarded by batteries, and also enclosed by a deep and wide ditch. On these ramparts the inhabitants of Portsmouth were accustomed to promenade of a fine evening to listen to the military bands and to observe the mass of shipping at Spithead and in the harbour. Several miles to the northward, behind the town, rose the smooth grey undulations of Portsdown Hill.

Portsmouth was bisected by its long High Street, in which were situated most of the principal inns, shops, banks, libraries, and offices of the various naval departments. The George, to which the senior officers of the Navy usually resorted and where Nelson spent his last hours in England, stood on the south side of the High Street almost opposite the port admiral's office. The Fountain, a hostelry chiefly favoured by the lieutenants, lay further down the street. Portsmouth theatre, of which mention is made in Marryat's naval novels and other contemporary works, was situated at the upper end of the High Street. Meredith the tailor (father of the great Victorian novelist), who was the leading naval outfitter of his day, resided at No. 73, opposite the Parade Coffee House; in this house Hardy and a number of other officers used to lodge when in Portsmouth. Opposite the Fountain, at No. 85, was the establishment of one Morgan, displaying a sign which notified the passer-by: *Sailors rigged complete from stem to stern*. Between the High Street and the shingle beach, divided from the rest of the town by a drawbridge, was Portsmouth Point, a picturesque, heterogeneous assemblage of taverns, cook-shops, tailors, drapers, and pawnbrokers, backed by a warren of mean streets and alleys. In Portsmouth Point, next to the coach office,[1] stood a famous hostelry fronted by two large blue posts, much frequented by the ' young gentlemen ' of the Service. This, as the coachman informed Marryat's Peter Simple at the end of their drive down from London, was ' the Blue Postesses, where the midshipmen leave their chestesses, call for tea and toastesses, and sometimes forget to pay for their breakfastesses '. Of hostelries there was a wide choice at the Point —these for the most part called after well-known fighting ships or famous victories. In the main street were the Royal George, the Arethusa, the Worcester, and the Neptune and Mars; in Bathing House Square were the Quebec and the Roving Sailor; and in Capstan Square, besides the Blue Posts, there was the Lord Hood. A turning off the main street, on the left-hand side, led down to the sally port.

Across The Hard from Portsmouth Point was the main entrance to

---

[1] In 1805, both the number and speed of the coaches were considerably augmented. At this time the coaches for London were, the ' Royal Mail ' and the ' Regulator ', which both started from the George; the ' Hero ', from the Fountain, the ' Nelson ', from the Blue Posts, and the ' Rocket ', from the Quebec.

the dockyard. Thence the visitor was conducted through two great gates and along the carriage road skirting the wharves, past the mast-houses and mast-pond, the rope-houses, the Commissioner's House, the mould and sail lofts, the offices, workshops, and store-houses, the officers' quarters, the boat-houses, docks, and building slips, the mills, and the anchor-forge. The dockyard lay on the eastern side of the broad, bottle-shaped harbour, which was, according to Henry Slight, ' capacious enough to receive the whole British Navy, affording most excellent anchorage, with a depth of water at any time of tide, for a first-rate ship to enter, or ride in security therein '.[1] On the further side of the harbour was Haslar hospital.

Dr. George Pinckard, writing of Portsmouth in 1795, describes ' the crowd and confusion of the picture ' which accompanied the departure of Grey's expedition for the West Indies: ' such as multitudes passing into and overflowing the shops; people running against or tumbling over each other upon the streets; loud disputes and quarrelling; the sadness of parting; greetings of friends unexpectedly met and as suddenly about to separate; sailors quitting their trolls; drunkards reeling; boatmen wrangling; boats overloaded or upset; the tide beating in heavy spray upon the shore; persons running or hurrying in every direction for something new or something forgot; some cursing the boatman for not pushing off with more speed, and others beseeching and imploring them to stop a minute longer.

' Such was the state in which we left Portsmouth ', Pinckard observes, ' after a residence of three weeks, during which time we had regarded it as a dull, inanimate place; but the change was sudden and will be only transient; the hurry and tumult will vanish with the sailing of the fleet, and the town will relapse into its tranquil sameness until the recurrence of a similar occasion.'[2]

Similarly Colonel Landmann, who arrived in Portsmouth at the outbreak of hostilities against France in May 1803, many years later recalls in his reminiscences the scenes of unparalleled excitement and activity that attended ' the collecting here of vast fleets of merchant ships, seeking the protection of convoys, whose boats covered the landing-places, and whose thousands of sailors and passengers filled the streets, shops, and markets; the constant rattling of wheelbarrows

[1] Henry Slight, *The Royal Port . . . of Portsmouth* (1843).
[2] *Q*. W. G. Gates, *History of Portsmouth* (1900), p. 487.

full of luggage, the hallooing of porters accompanying them; the confusion created by the light carts passing to and fro from the landing-place at the Point engaged in the carriage of live stock, butcher's meat, vegetables, groceries, liquors, crockery, etc.; the crowds of officers of the navy and army about the doors and windows of the Crown and Fountain inns, and near the bank at the corner of the Parade, forming groups, actively discussing the news of the day, whilst others are shaking hands with old friends, just landed from abroad, and occasionally with a staff-officer, the bearer of important despatches, on his starting for London in a chaise-and-four, in faded uniform, having had no time to procure a plain suit. . . . Along the Point, and at the back of that celebrated thoroughfare, dozens of midshipmen were seen scudding about from drinking-shop to drinking-shop, and into all the dancing-houses, hunting up their boats' crews, and forcibly separating their dearly-beloved, but intoxicated sweethearts, in order that all might be right, on the Captain presenting himself, to be pulled to his ship.'

When Jack was ashore it was generally a case of *Tout aux tavernes et aux filles.* It would appear that the latter were only too willing to meet him more than half-way. ' In some quarters,' Pinckard remarks severely, ' Portsmouth is not only filthy, and crowded, but crowded with a class of low and abandoned beings, who seem to have declared open war against every habit of common decency and decorum.' Even during the few short weeks that the good doctor spent in the town he had seen enough of these ' Portsmouth Polls ', as they were called, to denounce, in no uncertain terms, their conduct, ' which puts the great orb of noon to the blush '.

Landmann describes in his *Adventures and Recollections* the inspiring spectacle of a regiment about to embark as it marched down Portsmouth High Street from Hilsea Barracks, 'with Colonel Mair riding at their head, the colours unfurled and flapping with the wind, dogs barking, women and children screaming, and a vast concourse following.

' In the contrary direction came trains of straggling recruits, just landed, some from Gosport, others from the Isle of Wight, or perhaps Southampton, with streaming blue, red, and white ribbons fastened to their hats, marching off to the depot, as merry as larks; and close on the heels of all followed gangs of *disinterested* Jews, pressing the sale of " sealing-wax made of brick-dust, and pencils mitout lead," warranted gold watches, at twenty shillings a-piece, gold wedding-rings at four-pence, silver pencil cases and penknives, all as cheap as dirt; lastly came fiddlers, mountebanks, fortune-tellers, pickpockets, and the never-failing two little brothers, offering, for the smallest trifle, to play you a tune on their chins.'

As a background to all the hubbub and excitement was heard the far-off clamour of the dockyard, the creak and splash of oars, the long-drawn-out rattle of waves on the shingle, the cries of sea-birds wheeling and circling above the crowded roof-tops.

'To these', writes Landmann ' may be added the frequent firing of salutes from the ships at Spithead, reechoed from the saluting-base on shore, then the huzzas of half-drunken sailors, parading through the streets on the tops of hired coaches, shouting and waving their hats and banners, and drinking and cheering at every corner, hailing one another from coach to coach with all the roughness and wit peculiar to their profession, and, in short, striving how to expend large sums of hardly-earned prize-money in the least possible time.'[1]

Nelson did not care for the town—' a dirty place ', he called it; though nowhere in the kingdom, in fact, was he acclaimed with greater ardour and affection, and Portsmouth's last farewell to Nelson, on 14 September 1805, was one of the most moving and memorable scenes in our history: an American visitor who was present on that occasion observed that the streets of Portsmouth were dirty and the town presented little that was pleasing or interesting ' beyond the means of war, of which ', he declared, ' it is little else than a great magazine '.[2] The annals of Portsmouth are indeed crowded with the alarums and excursions of war: of great armaments preparing at Spithead: of famous commanders arriving and departing: of historic courts-martial: of assembling of convoys, and blockades. In its teeming streets and alleys dwelt the families of the men who manned the wooden walls, as well as those of the thousands of dockyard ' mateys ' who built and maintained them. The eyes of the crowds strolling on the ramparts were constantly on the great ships anchored at Spithead. The dingy roads were daily a kaleidoscope of smart uniforms. The workaday life of the great naval arsenal was diversified by the periodical incursion of the press gang, by the fitting-out of fleets, by the return

[1] Landmann, *Adventures and Recollections* (1852), II, pp. 259-63.
[2] Silliman, *op. cit.*

of a victorious squadron with its prizes, by the paying-off of ships, and by such rowdy jollifications as Free Mart Fair.

Such was Portsmouth Town in ' Eighteen-hundred and war-time ', when Jane Austen's Fanny Price and her sailor brother, William, came down from Mansfield Park by post-chaise to visit their family.

12

The centre from which the world-wide ramifications of British sea power—squadrons, ships, commanders, ports, arsenals, dockyards, depots, and stores—were controlled was the unpretentious pile erected at the north end of Whitehall, in 1722–5, by Thomas Ripley. For thirty years and more the Admiralty was enclosed by a high brick wall with a single entrance. Adam's screen, facing the entrance from Whitehall, was added in 1760. Originally a large part of the building was reserved for the private apartments of the various members of the Board; then, as the business and numbers of the Admiralty staff continued to increase, further accommodation became necessary; and in 1785–8 a new wing was added, on the south or Horse Guards side, as the private residence of the First Lord.

A narrow cobbled courtyard led up to the tall portico below which was the entrance hall with its buff-coloured walls, plain pedimented doorways, and oaken doors. In the centre of the hall hung a handsome brass lamp, dating back to the end of the eighteenth century. The second door on the left gave access to the captains' waiting room, beneath whose fine arched ceiling Nelson's body lay, on the night of 8 January 1806, watched by Dr. Scott, before the burial next day in St. Paul's. According to tradition, it was over the chimney-piece of the Captain's Room that Marryat, in a moment of exasperated boredom, inscribed the following lines:

> In sore affliction, tried by God's commands,
> Of patience, Job, a great exemplar, stands;
> But in these days, a trial more severe
> Had been Job's lot, if God had sent him here.

Facing the head of the principal staircase, lighted by a dome, was the entrance to the Board Room. This was a large and nobly proportioned chamber with dark-oak panelling, elaborate carvings, and a high white ceiling. Along the east wall were three tall windows overlooking some mews. Opposite was the hearth (the grate still bearing the arms of Charles II), and above the chimney-piece was a set of charts wound round rollers. On the north wall were two book-cases; and between them was a globe, surmounted by a wind-dial, whose gilded pointer, geared to a vane erected on the roof of the Admiralty, showed at a glance which way the wind was blowing. Over in the corner stood a fine grandfather clock with a portentous tick, telling both time and date; it had been constructed, late in the reign of William III, by Langley Bradley, who had built the great clock of St. Paul's.

In the middle of this room where so much of England's history has been made was a long mahogany table around which the various members of the Board would take their seats. Beneath that lofty ceiling, each in his day, Wager, Anson, Hawke, Sandwich, Spencer, St. Vincent, and Barham presided over the deliberations of the Board of Admiralty. Here Anson evolved the great reforms that created the Navy which Jervis and Nelson knew. Here Sandwich held his agreeable dinner parties and considered the probable effects of Keppel's acquittal. Here Spencer heard the shameful news that Admiral Man had quitted his post, that our squadrons at Spithead and the Nore had mutinied, and that Bridport, watching Brest, had let Bruix slip through his fingers—and heard, too, in happier times, the joyful tidings of the Glorious First, St. Vincent, Camperdown, and the Nile. Here ' old Jarvie ', assisted by Troubridge and the faithful Tucker, applied himself to the herculean labour of reforming the dockyards. Here Barham set in train his dispositions for the crucial campaign of 1805 which culminated in the greatest sea-victory of all time.

And here on a November night Charles Marsden, the Secretary, was sitting late over his papers when suddenly in the small hours there was a rumble of wheels in the courtyard below and the door opened to admit Lieut. Lapenotiére of the *Pickle* schooner. ' Sir,' exclaimed the officer, who had come up post-haste from Falmouth with Collingwood's dispatches—' Sir, we have gained a great victory; but we have lost Lord Nelson!'

13

The eighteenth century witnessed the rapid and sustained expansion of British mercantile shipping. Our registered tonnage, which in 1702 had amounted to rather more than a quarter of a million tons had, by 1773, almost trebled; and by 1793 it had again practically doubled. It continued to expand throughout the Revolutionary and Napoleonic Wars. In 1814 it had risen from rather more than 1 million tons to 2½ million tons; the number of ships engaged in foreign trade had increased from 4,000 to 5,000—though many of the new vessels were transports and privateers. Much of the large carrying trade formerly possessed by the Dutch had by now passed into British hands. The development by our capitalists of the canal system and the turnpike roads served still further to increase the overseas trade of Great Britain. In the second half of the eighteenth century articles of general consumption, such as sugar and tea, began pouring into England, together with the raw materials of her steadily expanding industries, such as the Lancashire cotton manufacture. They were paid for by the increasing exports of coal and manufactured goods. In the final decade of the century there came a development of prime importance in the economic and maritime history of this country. In the course of the Revolutionary War Great Britain found herself no longer able to produce sufficient corn on her own soil to support her rapidly growing population; and from this time onward was obliged to import grain from abroad.

The Thames estuary was still the principal highway of the world's commerce. Three-quarters of the total imports of Great Britain and rather less of her exports passed through the Port of London. In 1799 the amount of floating property in the waterway was estimated at £70 millions. The wharves and quays having become totally inadequate for the wharfage and warehousing of all the goods landed and disembarked, the vessels had to moor in mid-stream, thus necessitating a fleet of lighters, barges, punts, billyboys, and other small craft, which materially added to the confusion. With each successive year it became more urgently necessary to relieve the congestion in the Thames; towards the turn of the century the forest of masts and yards extended almost without a break from the Pool to Greenwich, and, according to the Maritime Surveyor to the Admiralty in 1796, it was ' often so crowded between the Tower and Limehouse that a Wherry is scarcely able to pass with safety between the Tiers, much less a Vessel '. All this enormous mass of shipping was continually exposed to the depredations of innumerable gangs of water-thieves known by such picturesque appellations as Night Plunderers, Light Horsemen, Mudlarks, and Scuffle-Hunters, who are estimated to have cost the mercantile interest something like £1½ millions annually. The whole riverside, from St. Katherine's to Limehouse, was thick with thieves and their fences.

The period 1800–15 was marked by an enormous expansion of the dockyard accommodation of London. The progress of civil engineering had by now made possible the construction of docks on an unprecedented scale. In 1795 the West India merchants opened a subscription for funds to construct a dock and warehouse and in two days raised capital of £800,000. The West India Docks were opened in August 1802. There followed the construction of Brunswick Dock, in 1803; London Dock, in 1805; the East India Docks, in 1806; and the Commercial Docks at Rotherhithe, in 1813. The long lines of spacious quays branching off from the river vastly accelerated the loading and unloading of merchantmen. The Dock companies proceeded to erect extensive warehouses for the goods which they handled; for London was now the principal depot for colonial and tropical produce and carried on an immense entrepôt trade.

The same problem, though on a smaller scale, confronted our other leading ports. The Liverpool slave and cotton trade (the two interests were closely associated) expanded very rapidly after 1730. A lucrative triangular traffic was carried on between Liverpool, West Africa, and America. The slavers conveyed cargoes of Lancashire cottons to the west coast of Africa and exchanged them there for negroes, which they then carried to the West Indies and the American mainland and exchanged for sugar, cotton, and tobacco. In the prosperous decade 1783–93 Liverpool had become second only to London in point of tonnage and overseas trade. During the twenty years preceding its abolition in 1807 Liverpool succeeded in securing the lion's share of the slave trade; and in the last year of the trade owned 185 slavers which transported a total of 49,000 negroes across the Atlantic. During the French Revolutionary and Napoleonic Wars large fortunes were also made by Liverpool privateers. In the opening years of the eighteenth century the construction of the Mersey docks was begun, and before its close great progress had been made in the buoying and lighting of the river. The port of Liverpool was now equipped with first-rate warehouses, and its granite-walled docks were the finest in the kingdom.[1] Glasgow, which by the middle of the century had become the centre of the British tobacco trade, secured an outlet to the sea as a result of the progressive deepening of the Clyde through the scour of the current controlled by a system of jetties. The year 1790 saw the completion of the Forth and Clyde canal.

At this time the largest merchantmen afloat were the fine ships under charter to the East India Company, which, down to the year 1813, enjoyed a complete monopoly of British commerce with the East. ' John Company's ' fleet comprised some 100 vessels of various sizes, of which an average of about 75 were normally at sea. These East Indiamen could easily be mistaken for men-of-war, and their officers enjoyed a status very little inferior to those of the Navy. Towards the end of the eighteenth century a number of very large vessels were built for the eastern trade, including the *Marquis of Cornwallis*, 1,360 tons (1789), the *Nottingham*, 1,152 tons, and also the *Royal Charlotte*, 1,282 tons (1793). These larger vessels were engaged in the rich China tea trade. Sailing from the Thames in the spring, they would be home again by the midsummer of the following year. They docked at Blackwall, below the Pool. To the ocean commerce between London and the Asian ports must be added the Country Trade, or local traffic carried on in Indian-built ships. There were about 700 ships, averaging 250 tons, annually employed in the West India trade; by 1800 some of these vessels were of 500 tons, and gradually they became even larger. In the early years of the nineteenth century there were some 250 craft, averaging 230 tons, engaged in the trade to the United States; another 600 ships, averaging 250 tons, trading to Canada and our other North American colonies; and nearly 40 Falmouth packets, fast sailers, of some 200 tons, carrying the mails to the Peninsula, the West Indies, and certain other countries. About 1790 there were roughly 800 ships, averaging 150 tons, trading to the Baltic and the north; another 400, averaging 200 tons, to the Peninsula; and 200 more, of about the same size, to the Mediterranean. A very large number of vessels, averaging about 70 tons, were engaged in the coastal trade. This was the hard school in which so many skilled and experienced mariners, from the time of Chaucer's *Shipman* onward, had graduated. One of the most

[1] According to Defoe, writing in 1726, ' they have made a great wet dock, for laying up their ships, and which they greatly wanted. . . . This is the only work of its kind in England, except what is in the River Thames.'

prolific breeding-grounds of prime seamen was the Newcastle coal trade. Engaged in this traffic were about 500 vessels, averaging 200 tons. It was the coal trade which produced one of the finest seamen of the century, Captain James Cook.[1]

The Newfoundland cod fishery was regarded by contemporary statesmen and economists as being of fundamental importance to our naval supremacy and prosperity. It annually employed very large numbers of deep-sea fishermen, recruited principally from our western ports. Another important nursery of deep-watermen was the Arctic and South Sea whale fishery. The Greenland and South Pacific whaling annually employed from 100 to 150 ships, averaging 300 tons. The east coast ports still sent out their contingent, as of old, to the Iceland fishery.

The numerous inshore fisheries were for the most part worked by small, undecked craft from a multitude of fishing ports, large and small, situated all round the coasts of the British Isles. The East Anglian and other ports yearly assisted at the famous autumn herring fishery off Yarmouth. The Barking smacks, which were among our earliest trawlers, supplied the capital with fish; this being sent up to the market at Billingsgate in small boats. The fishermen of Ramsgate worked the banks off the Netherlands coast, the men of Rye and Hastings the flat-fish grounds in Rye Bay and the adjacent waters. Already a flourishing fishing centre, Brixham was during the 1770s to inaugurate the trawling industry which brought to its inhabitants nearly a century and a half of abounding prosperity. Notwithstanding the disadvantages of a shallow tidal harbour, it was far easier for local ' liners ' to work in and out of Brixham than for those which had to pass through the narrow entrance of the Dart. By the close of the Napoleonic Wars there were between 60 and 70 Brixham smacks working the southern part of the North Sea and landing their catches at Ramsgate to be hurried off to the London market in light vans. Herring, mackerel, and pilchard driving was extensively carried on in the West Country. All this was on a relatively small scale. The large-scale exploitation of the Scottish herring fishery was yet to come. As early as 1750, however, an Act had been passed for the encourage-

[1] ' Cook came to maturity on a lee-shore, as it were, with the leadline as one of his principal tools of navigation ' (J. C. Beaglehole in *The Geographical Journal*, CXXII, p. 420).

ment of the herring fishery: thirty years later there were more than 130 herring busses belonging to the eastern ports of Scotland; and, by the turn of the century, the herring buss fishery was firmly established. ' The places from whence this fishery is carried on,' observed an official report, ' have increased in wealth and numbers, and have not been backward, during the last war, in furnishing their quotas to the manning of the Navy.' Trawling was at the outset confined to certain bays and inshore grounds (even as late as 1835 there were only about 200 English trawling smacks). The distribution of fresh fish was mainly restricted to towns and villages on the coast, and to a limited area inland, by means of carts and pack-horses.

Mention must also be made of the illicit but lucrative smuggling industry, which flourished on many parts of the English coast, but more especially in the southern counties, which lay conveniently close to the Continent. (According to Edgar March, the historian of the British fisheries, by the middle of the eighteenth century ' it was a moot point whether many a fisherman on the South Coast was a smuggler in odd moments, or a smuggler who went fishing in his spare time.') In 1735 a letter appeared in the *Gentleman's Magazine* stating that ' in several parts of Kent the farmers are obliged to raise wages, and yet are distressed for want of hands to get in their harvest, which is attributed to the great numbers who employ themselves in smuggling along the coast.' The smugglers, many of whom were daring and resourceful seamen, were engaged in a perennial battle of wits with the revenue authorities both by land and sea. By the Navy they were usually regarded with suspicion and dislike. ' This smuggling has converted those employed in it,' wrote Vernon in 1745, ' first from honest industrious fishermen, to lazy, drunken, and profligate smugglers, and now to dangerous spies on all our proceedings, for the enemy's daily information.' Shortly before the younger Pitt dealt a damaging blow at this traffic by reducing the high excise duties, smuggling had increased to prodigious proportions, and the industry was organized as never before. The smugglers were adepts in every kind of stratagem and device for defeating the vigilance of the riding officers ashore and the revenue cutters at sea. The more important of these bands were led by such portentous and almost legendary figures as ' Black Jack ' Wenham of Hastings and ' Cruel Coppinger ' of West Country fame. The profits were enormous. The ' freetrader ' generally recouped himself if he saved but one cargo out of three. Whole fleets of luggers and other small craft, and whole armies of landsmen, were employed, by sea and land, in this smuggling traffic.[1]

The annual loss to the exchequer was estimated at £2 millions out of a total revenue of £12½ millions. In 1784 Pitt declared that only about 5½ million out of the 13 million pounds of tea consumed in the kingdom had paid duty to King George; and the House formally resolved that ' these enormities and great national losses well deserve the earliest and most serious attention of Parliament '. However, the smuggling interest also contributed its quota—unwillingly withal—to the Navy in time of war.

A factor which was of the greatest importance in the development of our sea power down to the end of the colonial period is to be found in the aggregate maritime resources of the British settlements on the North American seaboard—above all, in New England. On the long, deeply indented coast of the northern colonies, from Maine to Connecticut, was a chain of good, natural harbours; there had sprung up a great many ports and fishing villages, inhabited by a numerous seafaring population variously employed in coastal and overseas trade, the Newfoundland cod fisheries, whaling, and shipbuilding. The principal New England trade was with the British West Indian islands. There was also an important triangular traffic between the northern and middle colonies and England and southern Europe. Codfish, masts, boards, and naval stores from New England, flour, corn, salt beef, and pork from the middle colonies, tobacco, masts, and naval stores from the southern colonies, formed the chief exports. The leading seaports were Boston, Philadelphia, and New York; among the lesser, but still important, coastal towns were Falmouth, Portsmouth, Newport, Providence, New Haven, Baltimore, Charleston, and Savannah. One of the key industries of New England was lumbering. Another was

---

[1] From the *Sussex Advertiser*, September 1783: ' There is a most convenient port, about a mile from Seaford, for smugglers to land their goods, and so daring are they become, that a dozen or more cutters may frequently be seen lying-to in open day. On Tuesday evening, between two and three hundred smugglers on horseback came to Cookmere [Cuckmere], and received various kinds of goods from the boats, 'till at last the whole number were laden, when, in defiance of the king's officers, they went their way in great triumph. About a week before this, upwards of three hundred attended at the same place; and though the sea ran mountains high, the daring men in the cutters made good the landing, to the surprise of every body, and the men on horseback took all away.'

shipbuilding. The large-scale Puritan emigration of the seventeenth century had brought out to the northern colonies a host of shipwrights and master-builders who, together with the rope-makers, sail-makers, and other skilled artisans of the coast, had built up an extensive ship-building industry centred principally on Newburyport, Gloucester, Salem, and Boston. The Navigation Act of 1651 had given a powerful stimulus to this industry.

In the decade preceding the outbreak of the American Revolution, the fishing industry of New England reached the height of its prosperity. The great cod fishery off Newfoundland, together with the mackerel and other small fisheries, might, perhaps, be accounted the most important in the world. By 1765 there were close on 700 vessels and 4,000 fishermen employed in the cod fishery alone. The leading fishing ports at this time were Gloucester and Marblehead; but there were also a large number of lesser ports like Dorchester, Ipswich, Beverley, Scituate, and New Bedford. The industry was conducted on a share basis. The craft usually employed was the schooner, which was admirably adapted to the deep-sea fishery. Of almost equal importance to the fishery was the whaling industry, which employed 300 vessels and 4,000 men. The New Englanders were beyond comparison the most skilful, experienced, and enterprising whalers afloat. The principal whaling centre was Nantucket Island.

The tough Yankee stock bred some of the very finest seamen and shrewdest merchants of their day. The trading and fishing fleets of these northern colonies were manned by successive generations of hardy, adventurous youngsters attracted to the sea by the lure of high wages. The keener spirits among them made voyage after voyage; acquired skill and experience; studied, qualified, and became masters and mates in their turn. Navigation schools arose in almost every port of consequence on the New England coast. Resource and initiative were the leading characteristics of the able mercantile interest who directed the manifold business activities of the northern colonies.

During the latter half of the eighteenth century the rigs in common use in the British merchant service were those of the ship, barque, brig, snow, brigantine, pink, schooner, ketch, lugger, and dogger. The larger East Indiaman, which had increased from about 400 tons burden in 1708 to 1,200 at the end of the century, was of course ship-rigged and resembled externally a 64. It usually carried royals and staysails and was pierced for fifty-six 18-pounders. The West India-man, which was also ship-rigged, was a good deal smaller than the East Indiaman (even at the end of the century it did not exceed 500 tons); it was built for maximum carrying capacity, and was a slow sailer. Generally speaking, ship-rigged merchantmen of under 300 tons had by now been replaced by two-masters such as brigs, snows, pinks, schooners, and ketches. The majority of our colliers and Baltic traders were either brigs or snows. There were also a large number of single-masted vessels with gaff-sails like the sloop and the hoy. The lug-sail was *par excellence* the fisherman's rig—the great advantage of this being the facility with which sail could be shortened. The three-masted Yarmouth luggers were reputed the fastest of all our east coast fishing craft. But the cutter rig was also fairly common among the fishing fleets. The Barking, Brixham, and other trawlers were cutter-rigged, as were also most of the Isle of Man herring fleet.

The great Channel fairway was the principal trade focal of the world. Here, with a westerly wind, might be seen smart Falmouth packets standing in for the Lizard and St. Anthony Head; heavily sparred whalers from the South Seas conspicuous by the ' try-work ' on their decks; fast fruit schooners hurrying home from the Mediterranean for the London market; tall East Indiamen, with sterns sparkling with gilt and great cabin windows flashing in the sunlight, rolling majestic-ally on past the English headlands, nine months out from the Hoogli: closer inshore, was a host of small coastal craft—snows, brigs, brigan-tines, barquentines, hoys, and ketches—skilfully working the tides, and fleets of brown-sailed fishing luggers. Not a few of these merchant-men to be seen in the offing were foreigners—French brigs and Newfoundland schooners, Norwegian cats, Prussian snows and galliots, Dutch bilanders, busses, hoys, and schoots, and Danish West Indiamen; for in the days of sail, for navigational reasons, the traffic as a rule hugged the English coast,[1] standing in for the 'high blue western land ' and the line of sonorous-sounding promontories mentioned in 'Spanish Ladies'—a song that was already old in Nelson's boyhood:

> The first land we made was a point called the Dodman,
> Next Rame Head off Plymouth, Start, Portland, and Wight;
> We passed up by Beachy, by Farley,[2] and Dungeness,
> And we hove our ship to off the South Foreland Light.

[1] See *supra*, p. 336 n.   [2] Fairlight, near Hastings.

Here, too, in time of war passed and re-passed the vast convoys comprising the different trades: the East and West Indiamen, the Peninsular, Turkey, and Guinea ' fleets ', sometimes totalling several hundreds strong. Metternich has recalled how in his youth, early one morning in the summer of 1794, he watched from a hill-top in the Isle of Wight the Channel Fleet, under the command of Admiral Howe, escorting two great convoys of merchantmen to sea, and described it as the most beautiful sight that he had ever seen in his life. ' A fresh breeze sprang up ', observed Metternich, ' and this was the signal for the departure of more than four hundred ships. . . . At a signal from the admiral's ship the merchantmen unfurled their sails, the fleet for the West Indies turned to the west, the fleet for the East Indies passed to the east side of the island, each accompanied with a portion of the royal fleet. Hundreds of vessels and boats, filled with spectators, covered the two roads as far as the eye could reach, in the midst of which the great ships followed one another, in the same manner as we see great masses of troops moved on the parade ground. . . . In a few hours the two fleets met to the south of the island.'

14

In the reign of James II an enterprising coffee-house keeper called Edward Lloyd set to work to collect and post up information for the particular benefit of the shipping interest. By so doing he gradually built up a flourishing business. Six years later, in 1692, Lloyd's Coffee-House in Lombard Street, in the heart of mercantile London, had become a favourite rendezvous of merchants, shipowners, and ship-masters desirous of obtaining the latest intelligence concerning shipping and foreign trade. References to Lloyd's Coffee-House are to be found in the contemporary issues of the *Tatler* and *Spectator*; Steele mentions as one of the distinctive features of the establishment the pulpit from which auction sales were conducted and shipping news read out; and for a few months in the year 1697–8 the proprietor published a sheet known as *Lloyd's News* which contained shipping and other news. By experimenting with novel methods of signalling and other ingenious devices Lloyd endeavoured to secure for his clients prompt and accurate information of the shipping in the Thames, reports of casualties, and other marine intelligence. After his death, in 1713, the business continued to prosper under his successors. Sam's Coffee-House, which in the opening years of the century had been a rival to Lloyd's, gradually dropped out of the running. The fame and popularity of Lloyd's Coffee-House in Lombard Street steadily increased. Throughout the eighteenth century sales of ships were generally held at Lloyd's, which was now the recognized resort of ship-brokers.

At the outset, and for a good many years after, Lloyd's was not exclusively concerned with underwriting, but with ship-broking and foreign trade generally. It is in fact unknown when underwriting actually began at Lloyd's: but as the century advanced the business done in the crowded coffee room became more and more connected with purely maritime affairs, particularly marine insurance. Merchants who wished to insure their goods knew that at a certain hour they could count on meeting a wide choice of underwriters at Lloyd's. Somewhat later the underwriters frequenting the Coffee-House formed themselves into an association known as Lloyd's.

Owing to the steady increase of our overseas trade, the age of Walpole witnessed a progressive expansion in the volume of marine insurance undertaken, and in the number of marine underwriters, in this country. It was to satisfy the demand of the underwriting interest for shipping intelligence that in 1734 there appeared *Lloyd's List*, the precursor of the modern *Lloyd's Register*. The object of *Lloyd's List* was to publish all the arrivals and departures in overseas trade at the principal British ports. The important news service maintained by Lloyd's was, indeed, the essential clue to the remarkable popularity of the establishment among underwriters.

At other coffee-houses in the City they could no doubt get business accommodation free of rent. They need only frequent the places and spend a little money on food and drink to have a roof over their heads, pen ink and paper, a table to sit at and a fire to keep them warm. But at Lloyd's they got, as well, the best available news service about the world's shipping, messages from the Admiralty and from every British port, gossip brought by homeward-bound skippers from every part of the world in which they might be interested, and reports of casualties at the moment when they first reached London. With all these attractions to offer—negligible working expenses, the first cut at the news and the first show of the brokers' risks—it is not surprising that Lloyd's drew the underwriters like a magnet, and proved far too much for the cumbrous heavily capitalized chartered companies. The attractions were all considerable, but the greatest of the three was the news service. It was on that rock that Lloyd's was built.[1]

In the war of 1739–48 Lloyd's was sometimes able to send the first news of an important victory to the government. Thus the Coffee-House was first in this way with the tidings of Porto Bello in 1739 and of Anson's action off Finisterre in 1747. From this time onward there was that close and cordial co-operation between Lloyd's and the Admiralty which has continued down to the present day.

From 1771 onward Lloyd's was governed by a Committee elected by the subscribers. Three years later the corporation of underwriters established itself in the Royal Exchange, where it was to remain for over a century and a half. Thus, the Coffee-House had given to the underwriters who frequented it a collective name, which the underwriters now gave to their new quarters in the Royal Exchange. The increasing wealth and expanding organization of Lloyd's enabled it to stand the strain of the long years of war with France in the latter half of the eighteenth century.[2] It is hardly too much to say that, without such an organization, the continued expansion of British trade and shipping in those years would have been impossible. In the same way the French wars gave a tremendous impetus to the business done at Lloyd's. The security of a Lloyd's policy was very good. It attracted a large marine insurance business from all over the world.

The influence of Lloyd's was a leading factor in the development of the convoy system. It had been shown by experience that vessels which sailed and remained in convoy were a better risk than those which did not: with the result that premiums for the latter were from one-third to one-half higher. Similarly the requirements of the underwriters helped to enforce convoy discipline. By the Convoy Act of 1793 and the Compulsory Convoy Act of 1798 the organization of the convoy system was immeasurably improved and made obligatory, with only a few exceptions, for the entire British mercantile marine. Masters were required to furnish a written undertaking not to sail independ-

[1] D. E. W. Gibb, *Lloyd's of London* (1957), p. 38.
[2] Perhaps the blackest day in all the history of Lloyd's was that on which the news arrived of Cordova's seizure of almost the whole of the combined East and West Indies convoy, in August 1780, involving the then enormous total of £1½ millions. It has been described as the heaviest single blow that had fallen on British trade within living memory and led to widespread ruin.

ently and not to separate from the convoy; and owners were required to contribute towards the cost of their protection.

At the turn of the century the elected Committee of Lloyd's received the power of choosing the subscribers of whom it approved and refusing those to whom it objected. For the future the word ' members ' was used in place of ' subscribers '. In 1811 the Committee established a system of agents throughout the world which provided the underwriters with a continuous supply of news about ships' movements. The organization of this unique intelligence service was the lifework of John Bennett, who was appointed Secretary to the Committee of Lloyd's in 1804.

XII

The War of American Independence

I

The decade following the Treaty of Paris witnessed the apogee of the old mercantile empire of Great Britain and the exploitation of the immense gains—political, commercial, and colonial—secured for her by her sea power, which had been advancing from strength to strength, practically without a check, since the beginning of the century.

Yet, even in the hour of triumph, the situation was fraught with peril. With all fear of French attack from Canada removed the gulf between the mother country and her American colonies rapidly widened. Before the close of the Seven Years War a certain far-seeing observer had declared that the West Indian islands which we had taken ought to be retained, rather than North America, ' which cannot be prevented from rising to independency and Empire '. On the Continent, as a result of the stern enforcement of her belligerent rights by Great Britain in the late war, there was ever-increasing jealousy and hostility towards our naval supremacy, which neighbouring States were beginning to stigmatize as ' the tyrannical empire which England claims to maintain upon the ocean '. France and Spain drew closer together. Bute's policy, which cost us the Prussian alliance, had left us without a friend in Europe. In 1770 a quarrel over the Falkland Islands nearly led to war with Spain. Our former friendship with Holland was a thing of the past. The greatest danger of all came from France.

In vain had Pitt, rising from a sick-bed to criticize the preliminaries to the peace treaty, denounced the restitution to our historic enemy of ' all the valuable West India islands ' and our concessions in the Newfoundland fishery, since this had ' given her the means of recovering her prodigious losses and of becoming once more formidable to us at sea '. Pitt's counsel was rejected by the new administration, with the result that what George Meredith was long afterwards to describe as ' the Cod and Lobster question ' lingered on until the opening years of the present century. ' You leave to France the possibility of reviving her navy ', had been Pitt's warning; and events had proved him right. The conditions of peace to which France had perforce submitted in 1763, though not sufficiently severe to satisfy Pitt, were such as no proud State would willingly endure. Already, under the ministry of Choiseul, the enemy was plotting revenge. ' I would have you remember ', Pitt [now Earl of Chatham] exhorted the Lords in 1775, ' that France, like a vulture, is hovering over the British Empire, hungrily watching the prey that she is only waiting the right moment to pounce upon.'

At home, Great Britain was entering upon a period of internal dissension and instability which sapped the efficiency of her fighting forces and left her ill prepared to face the ordeal which lay ahead. Even the raw material of sea power, the home-grown ' heart of oak ' for the construction of her wooden walls, was beginning to fail. The abundant virgin woodlands of mediaeval and Tudor England were no more; the royal forests, which in the past had been shamefully neglected, yielded less and less; and the private oak-woods, on which the dockyards mainly depended for their timber supplies, were rapidly becoming exhausted.

So matters stood when, ten years after the Treaty of Paris, a serious crisis arose in the North American colonies. The increasing dis-affection of the settlers in recent years had originated in a series of grievances against the home government which largely centred on the latter's attempts to make the colonies contribute towards the cost of their own defence and to regulate their expansion to the westward. Another leading factor in the rapidly deteriorating situation was the resentment of the influential shipping interest in New England at the restrictions imposed on it by the Navigation Laws. The quarrel came to a head, during the ministry of Lord North, in the Boston Tea Party, which was followed by the closure and blockade of the port of Boston, the formation of the Congress in Philadelphia, the appointment of Washington to the chief command, the Battle of Bunker's Hill in 1775, and the Declaration of Independence in 1776. This country was now confronted with a national spirit as dogged and determined as its own. In the early days of the war the colonial army made little headway and owed its survival mainly to the genius of Washington. The Americans were in hard straits for war materials, particularly gunpowder; by hook or by crook, however, they managed to get their supplies from overseas in time. For their part the British Admiralty were confronted with a desperate shortage of spars and timber.

In 1771 the struggle for mastery between George III and the Whig magnates issued, after a succession of short-lived ministries, in the personal rule of the monarch carried on by a ministry headed by Lord North, with Sandwich as First Lord. The King's Friends were now in control of the whole machinery of parliamentary patronage; and the adherents of the defeated faction were thrust out into the, wilderness. The internecine strife of those years spread to the Navy, many of the senior officers being involved in parliamentary politics and on the losing side. A large number of these officers owed their appointments to previous Whig ministries, and, moreover, were strongly opposed to what Wilkes described as the ' unnatural and ruinous civil war '. ' What will become of us now Lord Chatham is gone? ' Jervis wrote to his sister in 1778. ' The very name of Pitt kept the House of Bourbon in awe. This wretched, pitiful scoundrel, North, will act his underpart to our destruction.' Many of these officers in fact resigned their commissions rather than serve against the colonists. The truth was, that few among the higher ranks of the Service belonged to the now all-powerful party of the King's Friends. The period that followed was marked by recurrent discord between the Board of Admiralty and Opposition flag-officers.

The naval side of the American War consisted, first, of combined operations against the insurgent forces undertaken by the British Army and Navy, and second, of privateering attacks on British trade carried on by the New England seamen. Owing to the lack of adequate land communications the co-operation of the Navy was essential for the support and provisioning of the British military forces. These troops were therefore supported by squadrons of battleships sailing up and down the coast, while a cordon of frigates and smaller vessels patrolled the long American seaboard. In 1775 Falmouth (Maine) was ruthlessly bombarded, and attacks were also made on Gloucester and New Bedford. The lucrative New England traffic with the West Indies was crippled, and the fisheries were almost destroyed. The great whaling centre of Nantucket Island lost 150 vessels by capture

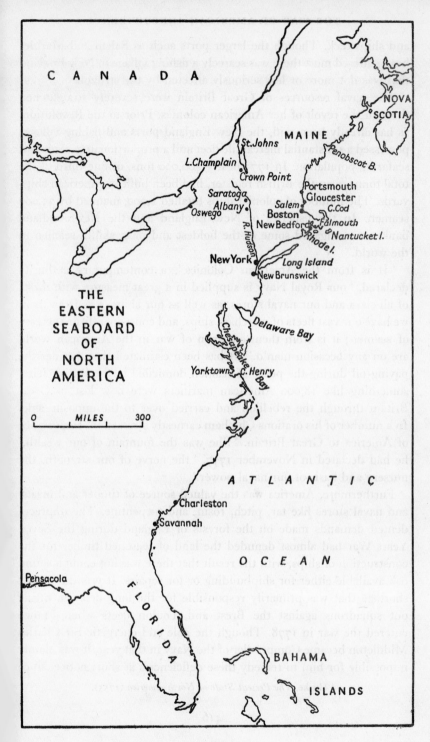

CANADA

NOVA
SCOTIA

MAINE

St.Johns

L.Champlain

Crown Point

Saratoga
Albany
Oswego

Portsmouth
Gloucester
C.Cod
Salem
Boston
New Bedford
Falmouth
Nantucket I.
Rhode I.

R. Hudson

Penobscot B.

New York

Long Island
New Brunswick

THE
EASTERN
SEABOARD
OF
NORTH
AMERICA

0   MILES   300

Chesapeake Bay

Delaware Bay

Yorktown   C. Henry

ATLANTIC

Charleston

Savannah

OCEAN

Pensacola

FLORIDA

BAHAMA

ISLANDS

and shipwreck. Though the larger ports such as Salem and Marblehead suffered most there was scarcely a fishing village in New England that was not more or less seriously affected by the struggle.

The naval resources of Great Britain were severely straightened through the revolt of her American colonies. Prior to the Revolution, as has already been said, the New England ports and fishing villages possessed a substantial mercantile fleet and a proportionately abundant seafaring population. In 1775 nearly 400,000 tons, or one-third of the total tonnage on the British register, had been built in American shipyards. The number of colonial ships totalled 2,000, manned by 33,000 seamen. In the fisheries of New England and the Newfoundland banks were engaged some of the boldest and most skilful seamen in the world.

' It is from the American Colonies ', a contemporary authority declared, ' our Royal Navy is supplied in a great measure with masts of all sizes and our naval stores, as well as our ships, it is from them we have our vast fleets of merchant ships, and consequently an increase of seamen; it is from them our men of war in the American world are on any occasion man'd.'[1] It has been estimated that, besides the paying-off during the peace of seamen domiciled in the British Isles, something like 18,000 American mariners were now lost to Great Britain through the rebellion and carried over to the opposite side. In a number of his orations Chatham earnestly stressed the importance of America to Great Britain. ' She was the fountain of our wealth,' he had declared in November 1777, ' the nerve of our strength, the nursery and basis of our naval power.'

Furthermore, America was the valued source of timber and masts, and naval stores like tar, pitch, rosin, and turpentine. The unprecedented demands made on the forests of England during the Seven Years War had almost denuded the land of seasoned timber for the construction of ships, with the result that there was not enough sound oak available either for shipbuilding or for repairs. It was the timber shortage that was primarily responsible for the long delay in fitting out squadrons against the Brest and Toulon fleets when France entered the war in 1778. Though the able and energetic Sir Charles Middleton became Comptroller of the Navy in that year, it was plainly impossible for him to remedy these deficiencies at short notice, since

[1] Huske, *The Present State of North America* (1755).

the roots of the trouble lay far back in the past—namely, in the failure of an earlier generation to replant after the heavy shipbuilding programme of the Commonwealth era, coupled with the mismanagement and neglect of our timber resources generally. Nor was that all. Another serious handicap was in the matter of masts. For well over a century past practically all the great masts needed for ships of the line had come from the virgin pine forests of New England. The Navy had in fact become largely dependent upon these American sticks. The fleets of Russell, Shovell, Leake, Norris, Anson, Boscawen, and Hawke all drew their great masts from the white pine belt of New England. But the supply of masts was cut off after 1775 and no adequate substitutes were to be found on the shores of the Baltic. The Navy Board was lethargic in taking action. The piecing together of composite masts had become a lost art and was not effectively revived until 1780. There was the usual three years' supply on hand, comprising some 400 great sticks in the British dockyards in 1775; but as Middleton observed, ' Although His Majesty's magazines are at present well supplied with masts, there are but few large masts due upon contract, and the present contractor apprehended difficulty in procuring further supplies.' As the war went on the mast-ponds of Portsmouth and Plymouth were gradually depleted of the ' great sticks ' so urgently required for the Fleet. For want of the tall New England masts and bowsprits many a vessel was to be crippled during the most critical phase of the struggle. These spars were normally due for replacement every ten years. Through the exhaustion of the mast-ponds, however, ships had to be fitted out with old sticks whose natural strength and resilience had long since departed. Eventually great masts began to be shipped from Riga; and, in the later stages of the war, masts from New Brunswick took the place of those from New England. But by that time the damage was done, and Great Britain had been worsted in the fight.

The colonists had, of course, no regular battle fleet (a 32-gun frigate was the largest ship which they had in commission); but more than 2,000 merchantmen were now fitted out as privateers, for the most part in the smaller ports of New England; and these, notwithstanding all counter-measures, continued to levy a severe toll on British shipping, not only in the West Indies, but even in home waters. ' The efficiency and determination of this new navy ', observes

James, ' forced the Admiralty to employ a large number of ships of the line on escorting duty, and the power of a well-handled mosquito fleet was never more clearly shown.'[1] It was because of the increasing scale of these attacks on our trade that, in March 1778, secret instructions were sent to Clinton ' to attack the ports on the Coast from New York to Nova Scotia ' together with shipping ' so as to incapacitate the Rebels from raising a Marine or continuing their Depredations upon the Trade of this Kingdom '. Most of the damage was done by American privateers cruising independently. In squadronal operations they were not so successful. It has been estimated that, by the end of 1778, no less than 1,000 British merchantmen had been taken by these American privateers. Before the war ended, this figure had been trebled. The losses of the Americans, however, were also very heavy; for their commerce had been increasing steadily during the course of the century.

Prominent among the American naval commanders was the renowned Paul Jones, who, cruising in the *Ranger* in the summer of 1778 in the Irish Sea, secured a number of prizes, including the British sloop *Drake*. Jones' raid on the shipping in Whitehaven harbour had only a limited success. But the moral effect was considerable: not since the Dutch attacked Sheerness, in 1667, had an English seaport suffered such an indignity. ' What was done,' Jones later observed, ' . . . is sufficient to show that not all their boasted navy can protect their own coasts, and that the scenes of distress which they have occasioned in America may soon be brought home to their own door.' On a second cruise in British waters, in 1779, Jones was appointed to command a squadron. On 23 September in a desperate moonlight action off Flamborough Head, in view of large numbers of people who had come flocking out on the cliffs from Scarborough and Bridlington, he defeated and captured a British frigate of superior force, the *Serapis*, 44. The fame of Paul Jones spread rapidly throughout the British Isles and the Continent. In vain the Admiralty now hastily sent ship after ship in search of him. ' Paul Jones resembles a *Jack o' Lantern*, to mislead our mariners and terrify our coasts,' declared the *Morning Post* on 1 October; ' he is no sooner seen than lost.'

Jones himself was of opinion that these guerrilla tactics were

[1] W. M. James, *The British Navy in Adversity* (1926), p. 38.

demanded by the circumstances of the war, and that it was 'the province of our Infant Navy to Surprise and spread Alarm, with fast-sailing ships'. War insurance rates rose to an unprecedented height and the coasts of the British Isles were harassed and alarmed as never before or since by the depredations of American cruisers and privateers.

'Privateers were of very little use in naval operations as the disastrous Penobscot expedition proved,'[1] observes Morison; 'but they were of the very greatest service in preying on the enemy's commerce, intercepting his communications with America, carrying terror and destruction into the very chops of the Channel, and supplying the patriot army with munitions, stores and clothing at Johnny Bull's expense.'[2]

Though by 1778 only four of the original thirteen frigates were left to the Continental Navy, a severe blow had been dealt at British commerce. It was even found necessary to provide convoy for the Belfast linen trade—a precaution never taken during the previous war. In particular, the war brought severe suffering to Liverpool, which declined both in tonnage and population. Meanwhile an active and regular traffic was kept up between the American colonists and continental Europe. Military stores continued to reach America from France, and numerous cargoes of American tobacco were safely transported to France.

The struggle between the British and Americans for the command of Lake Champlain, in 1775-6, is of considerable interest and importance. An offensive launched from Canada would have taken New York and the adjacent territories in the rear; but, owing to the impassable nature of the country surrounding its shores, Carleton's southward advance into American territory was impossible except across Lake Champlain. In the spring of 1775 the prompt and energetic action of Benedict Arnold secured the control of Lake Champlain for the Americans, who retained this superiority in the following season. 'We have happily such a naval superiority on Lake Champlain', observed their general, Schuyler, on 25 June 1776, 'that I have a confident hope the enemy will not appear upon it this campaign.'

---

[1] Apprised in the latter half of July 1779 of the sailing of a hostile force from Boston to assail the British post at Penobscot, Vice-Admiral Collier arrived in the nick of time to pursue and destroy the expedition.

[2] S. E. Morison, *The Maritime History of Massachusetts* (1941), p. 29.

Both sides—the Americans at Crown Point and the British at St. John's—had set to work that year to construct and equip a miniature fleet. Here the advantage clearly lay with the British, who had both the men and the materials to outbuild their opponents. The Americans finally constructed three schooners, a sloop, three galleys, and eight gondolas; the British, two schooners, twenty gun-boats, a number of lesser craft, and, above all, the 180-ton, ship-rigged *Inflexible*, which, carrying eighteen 12-pounder guns, was alone much more than a match for the opposing flotilla. ' By all these means ', observed Captain Charles Douglas, in July, ' our acquiring an absolute dominion over Lake Champlain is not doubted of.' The Americans successfully retained the control of the Lake until 11–13 October. In the action that then ensued the *Inflexible's* greatly superior armament proved a decisive factor. In the late afternoon she succeeded in manœuvring within point-blank range of the American flotilla, ' when five broadsides ', declared Douglas, ' silenced their whole line.' Though Arnold handled his command with consummate skill and courage, the little American navy on Lake Champlain was practically wiped out. Nevertheless, by this Lake campaign Arnold had succeeded in delaying the projected British invasion from Canada until the season was so far advanced that large-scale military operations were impossible; thereby saving Washington's hard-pressed army, retreating before Howe east of the Hudson, from being taken in the rear by Carleton. The latter now retired into winter quarters and Howe abandoned the campaign against Washington. In the words of G. W. Allen, ' American naval supremacy on Lake Champlain in the summer of 1776 had compelled the British to spend precious time in building a fleet strong enough to overcome it. The American defeat which followed was a victory. The obstruction to the British advance and a year's delay saved the American cause from almost certain ruin.'[1]

In 1777 Great Britain sustained a decisive reverse. After two seasons of inconclusive fighting the British forces attempted the subjugation of New England by securing the line of the Hudson and Champlain. But the intended junction of Burgoyne, marching south from Canada, with Clinton, ascending the Albany from New York, never materialized; and on 16 October Burgoyne was obliged to surrender to the colonists at Saratoga—an event which decided

[1] G. W. Allen, *A Naval History of the American Revolution* (1913), p. 179.

France's entry into the war on the side of the Americans. On 6 February 1778 she signed a secret treaty of alliance with the colonists. Thenceforward the character of the war changed entirely. The struggle in North America merged at last into a world-wide maritime war, in which Great Britain found herself striving grimly against the coalesced navies of France, Spain, and Holland.

2

The restoration of French sea power was primarily due to the energy and zeal of the Duc de Choiseul, who, in the last phase of the Seven Years War, had laboured to revive popular interest in the navy. From 1763 to 1771 it was Choiseul's endeavour to expand the fighting fleet and train it for war. A considerable number of new vessels were completed, many of them of improved design; on the eve of the next general war France had about eighty ships of the line afloat. The arsenals and dockyards were replenished, and large stocks of ship-timber laid up. To the existing arsenals of Brest, Rochefort, and Toulon, Choiseul added a fourth at Marseilles in 1762. A body of 67,000 prime seamen was enrolled under the well-tried system of maritime inscription; in 1767 the corps of highly skilled seamen gunners was formed; sea training in peace was provided by the form-ation of what was called ' Evolutionary Squadrons ', and an efficient code of signals was developed. The professional education of the French naval officers was admirably painstaking and thorough (though their discipline was adversely affected by class feeling)[1]; and in the scientific study of tactics they were far ahead of the British. The French crews were likewise highly trained and efficient. When Choiseul fell from power, his work was carried on by Sartine and de Castries.

In consequence of these various reforms both the French fleet and the arsenals and dockyard behind it were brought to a high state of efficiency. For a time, indeed, the Royal Navy of France became the first service of the realm. Treasure and credit were poured out without

[1] ' All these men too were so conscious that they were nobles as to somewhat forget the fact that they were officers. They thought little of their rank compared with their common nobility. They all messed together, they thee'd and thou'd one another in the friendly second person singular. This easy good-fellowship must have been socially more pleasant than the stern subordination of an English ship, on which the captain lived apart in solitary grandeur, and the midshipman looked up with awe to the lieutenants. But of the two, ours was the better system of discipline ' (David Hannay, *Rodney*, p. 114).

stint which enabled the fleet to be put into good repair and a vigorous shipbuilding policy to be carried on throughout the next decade. The American imbroglio gave France her opportunity. During the early phase of the struggle she made no move; but closely followed events across the ocean, biding her time.

Spain also had experienced something of a naval revival during these years; and a considerable number of new warships were laid down at Havana, Cartagena, and Ferrol.

On the French declaration of war in March 1778 the naval forces of Great Britain were in no fit state to meet the calls about to be made on them. Under Lord North's ministry repairs had been scamped, and the dockyards starved of essential stores. Although the nominal strength of the Fleet was about one hundred sail of the line, very few of these were actually at sea on any station. Burke's warning, in 1769, had fallen on deaf ears. ' Of all the public services ', he had declared, ' that of the Navy is the one which tampering may be of the greatest danger, which can worst be supplied in an emergency, and of which any failure draws after it the largest and heaviest train of consequences.' In vain likewise had Pitt, now Earl of Chatham, addressed the following prophetic words on the occasion of the Falkland Islands crisis in 1770. ' The first great and acknowledged object of naval defence in the country, is to maintain such a superior naval force at home, that even the united fleets of France and Spain may never be masters of the Channel. . . . The second naval object with an English minister should be to maintain at all times a powerful western squadron. In the profoundest peace it should be respectable; in war it should be formidable. Without it, the colonies, the commerce, the navigation of Great Britain lie at the mercy of the House of Bourbon. The third object, indispensable as I conceive, in the distribution of our navy, is to maintain such a force in the Bay of Gibraltar as may be sufficient to cover that garrison, to watch the motions of the Spaniards, and to keep open the communication with Minorca.'

The reductions in the Navy continued, and in September 1772 North observed complacently to Sandwich: ' I do not recollect to have seen a more pacific appearance of affairs than there is at this moment. This is the time, if ever there was a time, for a reasonable and judicious economy.' The majority of our heavy ships had been rotting in reserve during the past fifteen years and were unable to go to sea.

A good many of the battleships laid up in ' Rotten Row ' were mere stacks of decayed timber, consumed with dry rot and covered with toadstools. This was largely the result of building vessels with unseasoned timber during the Seven Years War and afterwards.

There were numerous cases of vessels foundering in the course of the American War. The most famous of these disasters was the dramatic sinking, on 29 August 1782, of the *Royal George* as she lay anchored at Spithead undergoing some repairs. The familiar lines of Cowper are in no way founded on fact. The truth of the matter was, that being ' slightly careened ', the vessel's frames were so rotten that the bottom simply dropped out of her—and down she went with nearly her entire crew, including ' brave Kempenfelt ', the most distinguished of our younger admirals. The findings of the ensuing court-martial were suppressed by the Admiralty.[1]

It was, moreover, impracticable speedily to increase the number of ships at sea, owing to the dearth of timber for shipbuilding, and the dispersion of trained personnel in the mercantile marine, and even in foreign service. The consequence was, that when Great Britain was committed to a maritime war with France and subsequently with Spain and Holland, her fleets were usually outnumbered by those of the enemy. In frigates and in privateers, as well as in capital ships, her forces were numerically inferior to those of the Bourbon Powers and their American allies. In European waters Great Britain stood strictly on the defensive. For the first time since the days of Tourville our sea power was faced with a most formidable challenge.

In the spring of 1778 France prepared a fleet at Toulon, under the Comte d'Estaing, to assist the American colonists, while at Brest she

---

[1] At the court-martial held on board the *Warspite* in Portsmouth Harbour on 9 September 1782, Vice-Admiral Milbank gave evidence as follows: ' When the *Royal George* was docked at Plymouth, I had the honour to command there, and during her being in dock I gave her very constant attendance, saw her opened, and asked many questions; and found her so bad that I do not recollect there was a sound timber in the opening. I asked several of the Officers of the Yard what they intended to do with her, and they said they should be able to make her last a summer, and very bad she was indeed, insomuch that they could scarce find fastenings for the repairs she underwent.' Sir John Jervis then confirmed what Vice-Admiral Milbank had related to the court, respecting the rottenness of the timbers that were exposed to view in her last docking. In the end the court found ' from the short Space of Time between the Alarm being given and the Sinking of the Ship, that some material part of her Frame gave way, which can only be accounted for by the general state of the Decay of her Timbers, as appears upon the Minutes ' (*Select Naval Documents*, ed. Hodges and Hughes (1936), pp. 151–2).

fitted out another, under the Comte d'Orvilliers, to threaten Great Britain with invasion. Thanks to her system of maritime inscription she was able at once to man fifty of the line.

On this side of the Channel everything was unprepared, and the dockyards were empty of stores. It was only with the greatest difficulty that the English dockyards presently patched up enough of the ships laid up in reserve to form two fleets. Admiral Keppel, who had been unwilling to serve against the American colonists, was appointed to command the Channel Fleet. When he went down to Portsmouth in March he complained that, instead of the ' thirty-five of the line, ready for service, and seven more in great readiness ', of which Sandwich had lately boasted in the House of Lords, he found only ' six ships fit to meet a seaman's eye '. He did not in fact get away to sea till June, and then with only twenty ships.

The first fleet action of the war, fought between Keppel and d'Orvilliers, on 27 July 1778, about seventy miles to the west of Ushant, was inconclusive. It began with the rival fleets sailing past each other on opposite tacks: the opposing lines were enveloped in smoke cloud, and each vessel fired as opportunity offered—the French, in accordance with their usual tactics, aiming at the masts and rigging of their opponents, with the result that Keppel's ships were so damaged that they were unable to tack; and when Keppel later wore his fleet to renew the action, Palliser, who commanded the rear, held his wind, and failed to wear with the others. Keppel was obliged to wait for him, and the opportunity was lost. By the time the Admiral had re-formed his line night was falling, and he did not renew the action. For his part, d'Orvilliers made no attempt to profit by the defection of the British rear and the damaged condition of the van and centre. No ship was taken or sunk on either side. At dawn on the following day the French fleet was out of sight and Keppel returned to Plymouth.

The enemy's tactics presented our commanders with a problem which was long to baffle them. Captain John Jervis went to the root of the matter when, four days after the battle, he informed the Secretary of the Admiralty, ' I have often told you that two fleets of equal force can never produce decisive events unless they are equally determined to fight it out, or the commander-in-chief of one of them so bitches it as to misconduct his line.'[1] Moreover, the high standard of French seamanship

[1] Q. O. A. Sherrard, *A Life of Lord St. Vincent* (1933), p. 56.

and discipline had come as a disagreeable surprise to their opponents.[1]

Public indignation at the outcome of the action immediately gave vent to a storm of political controversy. Relations between Keppel and Palliser had long been strained. At the close of October the quarrel suddenly came to a head. Palliser, finding himself anonymously attacked in the Press, replied with a counter-attack on Keppel in the *Morning Post*. The cleavage in the Service was complete. Palliser, who at the time was a member of the Board of Admiralty, was able to get his commander-in-chief tried by court-martial. Keppel's friends and followers, including a good many M.P.s, crowded into Portsmouth for the trial, which was held in the Governor's House. The case dragged on for five weeks amid scenes of wild excitement. The reports of the trial occupied the newspapers to the exclusion of other news. In the end, on 11 February, the court found the charge was ' malicious and ill-founded ' and that Keppel had behaved as ' a judicious, brave, and experienced officer '. On Keppel's acquittal a triumphal procession was formed, and the Admiral was chaired through the streets of Portsmouth to the strains of ' See the Conquering Hero Comes '.

This verdict was the signal for a stupendous anti-government demonstration. On the night when the news of Keppel's acquittal reached London pandemonium broke loose. ' The sentence arrived at half an hour after nine,' observed Horace Walpole, ' and in two hours the whole town was illuminated.' Palliser's house in Pall Mall was sacked and gutted by the mob, and his effigy burned on Tower Hill. The great gate of the Admiralty was torn off its hinges, and North had his windows broken. The next day votes of thanks to Keppel were passed in both Houses of Parliament, and the city of London voted him its freedom. The popular enthusiasm for Keppel and his cause was significantly reflected in the considerable number of hostelries named after him all over the kingdom.

---

[1] ' Enquire of those who were in the fleet with Mr. Keppel the summer before last,' Kempenfelt wrote to Sir Charles Middleton during the campaign of 1780, ' if the French did not manage their ships like seamen; and as to their frigates, they showed an alertness, I have been told, not equalled by any of ours. When their signals were at any time thrown out to make sail, they were in an instant under a cloud of canvas; when they returned to their admiral, or were called to him, they run close up to his stern with all sail set, when in a moment all disappeared but the topsails. If a ship was but at a small distance, if called to the admiral she immediately spread all her sail, even to stern [stun] sails if they would draw. This appears to be not only seamanship but the brilliancy of it ' (*Navy Records Society*, XXXII, p. 311).

The court-martial of Palliser followed; and he also was acquitted. Both Palliser and Keppel thereupon resigned. Palliser obtained the governorship of Greenwich Hospital, while Keppel continued the party fight from his place in Parliament. Feeling ran so high among the flag-officers that Howe and several others refused to accept commands so long as Sandwich remained at the Admiralty. During most of the war years the Channel Fleet was commanded by a succession of elderly, worn-out admirals who were appointed for political rather than for professional reasons. The resentment of the Whig officers focused upon the First Lord. It was openly avowed that ' out Twitcher must '.[1]

Recent research has disposed of the legend that the Sandwich regime was responsible for an orgy of incompetence and corruption. The truth is that Sandwich was a first-rate man of business, who had already been First Lord twice before and twice Secretary of State. He had been the friend and colleague of Anson, and he worked amicably with Rodney. ' No man in the Administration ', wrote Horace Walpole, ' was so much master of business, so quick, or so shrewd.' In 1749, when he first took his seat at the Board of Admiralty, one of his earliest measures had been to institute a strict and systematic visitation of the dockyards and other naval establishments. In later years he caused such visitations to be frequently made: as a result of which many abuses were brought to light and corrected. Among the most important of the other achievements of Sandwich's administration was the ' coppering ' of the entire Navy of Great Britain, ' from a first rate to the smallest cutter ', with the exception of a few ships that were not yet returned from foreign stations; he also took steps to improve the supply of timber for shipbuilding.

On 19 June 1779 Spain signed a treaty of alliance with France and entered the war against Great Britain in the hope of recovering Gibraltar and her other lost possessions. This accession of naval strength to the ranks of our enemies was, however, nominal rather than real: for, though the list of ships and guns which Spain could bring to the common cause was, on paper, sufficiently imposing, the personnel was of indifferent quality. Moreover, the allies were fighting with different objects and made little attempt to co-operate strategically.

[1] The allusion was to Jemmy Twitcher in *The Beggars' Opera*, who had 'peached ' upon Captain Macheath. It was Sandwich's betrayal of his former boon-companion, John Wilkes, that had gained for him this unsavoury nickname.

In the summer of 1779 the Bourbon Powers, in accordance with their pre-concerted plan, prepared to invade England. No effective blockade of Brest having been established, d'Orvilliers was able to join forces with the Spaniards in the Bay of Biscay; and finally the combined fleets, numbering sixty-six of the line, entered the Channel, where the British, now under the command of Sir Charles Hardy and Kempenfelt, could muster only thirty-five to oppose them. But the enemy fleet was superior in numbers rather than in fighting power. D'Orvilliers' allies had kept him waiting for seven weeks off Cape Finisterre—a delay which threw their whole plan of action out of gear; and when eventually the junction was made there was a further delay, while a uniform system of signals was arranged.

Hardy, who had been Norris's second-in-command in the campaign of 1744, prepared to take up his post some ten to twenty leagues W.S.W. of Scilly, ' which I am of opinion ', he observed, ' is the most proper station for the security of the trade expected from the East and West Indies, and for the meeting of the fleets of the enemy *should they attempt to come into the Channel.*' It was his declared intention to manœuvre them up the Channel, thereby forcing their battle fleet upon their transports.

There was great alarm in southern England, where a hostile descent was almost hourly expected. Two French divisions, each of them numbering 20,000 men, had been assembled for the invasion. Walpole trusted that the blow would fall on Ireland. ' I have no ill will to poor Ireland,' he remarked, ' but Ucalegon is at least one door farther off than one's own.' Orders were given that in the event of a hostile landing all horses, cattle, and provisions should be removed inland, and steps were taken to defend the coast. ' Even this quiet little village ', Walpole wrote later from Strawberry Hill, ' is grown a camp.' Fortunately two large convoys from the West Indies had arrived home shortly before the combined fleets appeared in the Channel; and an East Indies convoy was able to take refuge in the Shannon. It was to all appearances a moment of great peril. But the allied fleet missed its opportunity through a succession of delays, and a last-minute change of plan lost them what little chance of success remained. Meanwhile the weaker, but still formidable British force hovered somewhere to the westward, an ever-present threat, in the face of which d'Orvilliers dared not come far into the Channel or weaken himself by detaching a squadron to deal with the British cruiser force which was blockading the French invasion ports. The allied fleet was, moreover, seriously weakened through disease and lack of provisions, and labouring under the usual disadvantage of an enemy operating against Great Britain in the Channel.

' The British ', wrote d'Orvilliers to the Minister of Marine, ' whose harbours are all to leeward in Westerly or South-Westerly winds, can, without any risk, send their squadrons and fleet to sea; it is not the same for the combined forces of France and Spain. If this great collection of battleships has to withstand a Westerly gale, their only resource is to proceed up Channel and go to the Eastward; but if the gale is from the South, S.S.W. or even from the S.W., the greater number would not be able to round the most Southerly point of the English coast. . . . '[1]

As it was, the enemy cruised for several days within sight of the Lizard; becalmed and anchored, they lay off Plymouth on 16 August and on the 17th captured the *Ardent*, 64: on the latter day the wind came easterly, and d'Orvilliers was obliged to weigh: on the 18th the wind had increased to half a gale and swept the allied fleet out of the Channel. The same wind drove Hardy to the westward; a week later his fleet was 30 leagues to leeward of the Isles of Scilly. When d'Orvilliers learned of this, he decided to seek out the British fleet and not to attempt to re-enter the Channel.

On 31 August the enemy sighted Hardy's ships off the Scillies and pursued them for two days without success. On 1 September Hardy anchored off Plymouth. ' The Combined Fleet is now in the South East,' he observed in his dispatch. ' I shall do my utmost to draw them up-Channel.'

Kempenfelt also had no misgivings regarding the outcome of the campaign.[2] He was of opinion that ' twenty-five sail of the line, coppered, would be sufficient to hazard and tease this great, unwieldy, combined armada, so as to prevent their affecting anything . . . and if they attempted an invasion, to oblige their whole fleet to escort the transports, and even then it would be impossible to protect them entirely from so active and nimble a fleet.' About this time, in a letter

---

[1] *Q*. W. M. James, *The British Navy in Adversity* (1926), p. 180.

[2] Kempenfelt, now at the height of his powers, was Captain of the Fleet from April 1779 to September 1780 under Hardy, Geary, and Darby.

addressed to Sir Charles Middleton at the Admiralty, he outlined the general principles of British strategy:

> Much, I may say all, depends upon this fleet; 'tis an inferior against a superior fleet; therefore the greatest skill and address is requisite to counteract the designs of the enemy, to watch and seize the favourable opportunities for action, and to catch the advantage of making the effort at some or other feeble part of the enemy's line; or, if such opportunities don't offer, to hover near the enemy, keep him at bay, and prevent his attempting anything but at risk and hazard; to command their attention, and oblige them to think of nothing but being on their guard against your attack.[1]

In the middle of September the Combined Fleet returned to port, and d'Orvilliers resigned. The death-roll due to sickness had been heavy, and the number of sick landed at Brest totalled 7,000. As soon as certain information reached him that the enemy were back in Brest again, Hardy at once proceeded to provide escorts for the home-coming convoys and the East Indiamen which had been sheltering in the Shannon.

In May 1780 Hardy died of apoplexy and was succeeded by Admiral Sir Francis Geary, of whom Kempenfelt observed to Middleton: ' The present person is brave, generous and may, perhaps, have been a good officer, but he is wholly debilitated in his faculties, his memories and judgment lost, wavering and indetermined in everything.' In August 1780 Geary resigned his command.

The close blockade introduced by Hawke in the previous war was not continued by his successors. Kempenfelt and his school were strongly in favour of keeping the battle fleet in harbour during the winter months. In a letter addressed to Sir Charles Middleton from Torbay on 16 November 1779, Kempenfelt set out his reasons for this strategy

> I mentioned in my last my opinion of the improbability of the combined fleets coming out again this winter; for this reason, that it is morally impossible so numerous a fleet as theirs can keep the sea for any time at this season without receiving great damage. Long nights and heavy gales are formidable enemies to large fleets.
>
> But suppose the enemy should put to sea with their fleet—a thing much to be wished for by us. Let us act wiser, and keep ours in port; leave them to the mercy of long nights and hard gales. They'll do more in favour of you than your fleet can. A large fleet never tacks or wears when

[1] *Navy Records Society*, XXXII, p. 292.

it blows hard in a dark night without risking great damage. We have had occasion to do it three times since we have been out, and each time with narrow escapes.

Let us keep a stout squadron to the westward ready to attend the motions of the enemy. I don't mean to keep them at sea, disabling themselves in buffeting the winds, but at Torbay ready to act as intelligence may direct.[1]

Next summer, the combined fleets, numbering nearly fifty sail, returned to the attack. In point of numbers the French and Spaniards were overwhelmingly superior to any force that their opponents could scrape together, and again they entered the Channel unopposed. The Channel Fleet, numbering but thirty ships, under Admiral Darby, took refuge in Torbay. De Guichen, who on this occasion commanded the combined fleets, declared in favour of fighting; but he was overruled in a council of war by Cordova and most of the other Spaniards, together with some of his own officers. Once again the numerically superior allied fleet retired from the Channel and the invasion project was abandoned. The failure of the allies to make any use of their opportunities in 1779 and 1780 is an outstanding example of the chronic weakness of France in the Channel and the crucial importance of the Western Squadron. It had been proved up to the hilt that, even with a greatly superior force, no serious operation could be begun in these waters by an enemy until the Western Squadron had first been brought to action and conclusively defeated.

As the war dragged on the exasperation of neutrals at British interference with their trade progressively increased. To the Scandinavian peoples, in particular, the renewal of the struggle between Great Britain and France had brought a far larger share of the world's carrying trade and abounding prosperity. ' In the brilliant commercial period of 1775 to 1784 ', says Nathenson, ' the country [Denmark] and its people gathered their activities to an admirable degree. The nation was thereby enabled to obtain for the future a not inconsiderable rank among the great seafaring Powers.'[2] For her part France was no less anxious to secure the services of neutral shipping since her own was in danger of being driven off the seas. Once again she strove to bring about the maritime league of neutrals which she had endeavoured in vain to raise up in the last war. This time she succeeded.

[1] *Ibid*, p. 303.
[2] *Q.* Kulrud, *Maritime Neutrality to 1780* (1936), p. 323.

At the outset of hostilities France had formally adhered to the principle that property belonging to the subject of belligerents should be free on board neutral vessels, excepting merchandise of contraband. This had the designed effect on the Northern neutrals. An unending series of protests poured in against the belligerent rights claimed and enforced by Great Britain. Finally, in 1780, Russia, Denmark, and Sweden joined together in the 'Armed Neutrality' to resist the British practice of seizing enemy goods carried in neutral bottoms. Our seizure of Baltic timber and naval stores destined for the enemy's navies was a determining factor in this decision. Within a few months the Baltic States had close on eighty of the line in commission; and the British government, following in the steps of Pitt in the previous war, was constrained to submit to the curtailment of our historic rights. With the Navy already badly overstrained, Great Britain was in no position to resist the joint claims of the Northern Crowns, on whom she depended, moreover, for the greater part of her masts and naval stores. The example of the Baltic States was presently followed by all the maritime Powers of Europe, including Portugal. The isolation of Great Britain was thus complete. An important result of the Armed Neutrality was the partial replenishment of the French dockyards, which for long had been deprived of the vital Baltic stores.

In the same year the war spread to Holland. That country was involved in the contraband traffic to an even greater degree than the Baltic Powers and from her West Indian entrepôt of St. Eustatius the American colonies were drawing a large proportion of their munitions supply. In 1780 the Dutch leaders had been persuaded by the New England statesman, John Adams, to recognize American independence; and in December of the same year the British government declared war. The entry of Holland into the war, however, had but little effect upon the naval situation. The Dutch navy comprised only twenty sail of the line, and most of these were old and weak; and the British fleet occupying interior positions, the Dutch were unable to get down through the English Channel to join hands with the French and Spaniards. Before their fleet could be fitted out their trade had been driven off the seas, and their colonies captured. In 1780 more than two thousand Dutch vessels had passed through the Sound; in 1781 only eleven. The Dutch fishing fleets dared not quit their ports. On 5 August 1781 Vice-Admiral Sir Hyde Parker, who had lately escorted the trade for the Baltic and was homeward bound with a convoy of some two hundred merchantmen, encountered a Dutch squadron, which was likewise escorting a convoy on the Dogger Bank. The two squadrons were roughly equal in strength. Parker ordered his convoy to shape course for England, and then bore down on the enemy in line abreast, reserving his fire till his ships turned together just to windward of the Dutch, who had formed a well-ordered line of battle. Parker then had his ship laid alongside the enemy flagship, the *Admiraal de Ruyter*. After three hours' desperate fighting, in which both sides sustained very heavy loss, the Dutch bore away with their convoy to the Texel; but the British squadron was too badly damaged to follow them. On his return to England Parker severely criticized Sandwich for not having strengthened his force and insisted on resigning his commission. To the King he bluntly observed, ' Sire, you have need of younger men and newer ships.'

The following winter an opportunity was given to Kempenfelt to demonstrate the offensive potentialities of a flying squadron in the face of greatly superior hostile forces. On 14 December 1781 de Guichen, sailing from Brest with twenty-one of the line as escort for a large fleet of merchantmen and victuallers, was intercepted, about a hundred and fifty miles west of Ushant, by Kempenfelt in the *Victory* with eleven of the line. The wind was south-easterly and squally, with fog. A sudden lifting of the haze revealed the enemy to Kempenfelt; and as he approached the French squadron and observed that de Guichen was to leeward of his convoy he realized that he ' had a prospect of passing between the enemy's ships of war and a great part of their convoy '. Under a press of sail he thereupon passed astern of the enemy's line and attacked the merchantmen, many of which he managed to cut off.

Next morning the two fleets were still in sight of each other, but Kempenfelt, ' perceiving the force so much superior to my squadron, did not think it advisable to hazard an action,' and altered course for home with his prizes. Most of the French warships and merchant vessels then returned to Brest.

Later, in the House of Commons, the outcome of this action was severely criticized by Keppel, who rightly insisted that, had Kempenfelt only been given sufficient force, he might well have achieved a decisive, instead of only a limited, success.

Admiral Kempenfelt was a favourite with the Admiralty, and undoubtedly he deserved to be so; but still they had not given him a sufficient force. Upon the expedition from Brest to the West Indies depended the safety of our islands; and all concerns of an inferior nature ought to give way to the most pressing. The safety of our islands ought to be the principal object of our care; we should, therefore, have detached some of our force from the East to strengthen our commander before Brest, as the service he was upon was infinitely more important than was that for which our force in the Downs was stationed. . . . He, and he believed every man at all acquainted with the nature of a maritime war, held it to be indispensable, that where your force was inferior to that of your enemy, everything depended on the proper direction of it. It was no excuse to say, ' We sent so many ships here, and so many there,' enumerating a parcel of petty occasions. Lesser interests ought to sink before greater. . . . Admiral Kempenfelt's was a great enterprise; the object was more important than almost any other that had been attempted.[1]

3

After the failure of the allied operations in the Channel in 1779 and 1780, the war in European seas centred on the attack on British trade and the investment of Gibraltar and Minorca.

Throughout the war the vast and vulnerable seaborne commerce of the British Isles was exposed to continuous attack, which levied an ever-increasing toll on our shipping. These losses culminated, in August 1780, in the capture of almost the whole of the outward-bound East and West Indies convoy—valued at £1½ millions—by a Spanish squadron under Cordova. This was by far the worst disaster which had befallen British trade since the destruction of the Smyrna convoy in 1693. The total British shipping losses throughout this war were immense. It has been estimated that approximately one-third of our merchant marine was lost to the enemy.

Minorca, being relatively of small importance, was not assailed until towards the end of the war, when it fell after a six months' siege. Gibraltar, on the other hand, at once drew down the full fury of the enemy's attack. From July 1779 to January 1783 the fortress was heroically and skilfully defended by General Eliott.

Supplies ran short on the Rock; and, towards the close of 1779, Admiral Rodney, with twenty-two of the line and fourteen frigates,

[1] Q. Keppel, *The Life of Keppel*, II, p. 364.

was sent out to relieve the garrison, escorting a large convoy of victuallers, store-ships, and transports, and also the outward-bound trade of the East and West Indies, past the enemy's principal naval bases. Off Finisterre he chased and captured seven Spanish warships and sixteen merchantmen, and later, when off Cape St. Vincent, sighted a Spanish squadron of eleven of the line. Night was falling, and there was a heavy sea running: but Rodney at once made the signal for a general chase, and, running before a fresh westerly wind, cut in between the enemy and a lee shore: thereupon he made the signal for his ships to engage ' as they came up by rotation and to take the lee gage in order to prevent the enemy's retreat into their own ports '. By 4 p.m. Rodney's leading ships were engaging the enemy's rear. The action was continued throughout a dark and stormy night by the fitful light of the moon. Rodney succeeded in taking four of the enemy (including their flagship), and in destroying three more.

The ' Moonlight ' victory of 16–17 January 1780 was the reward of consummate seamanship, superior gunnery, and—last but not least —the speed of Rodney's coppered ships. On the aftermath of the action fine seamanship saved a number of Rodney's ships from imminent destruction on the Spanish shore. ' It continued very bad weather the next day ', the Admiral remarked in his dispatch, ' when the *Royal George*, *Prince George*, *Sandwich*, and several other ships, were in very great danger, and under the necessity of making sail to avoid the shoals of St. Lucar, nor did they get into deep water till the next morning.' After relieving Gibraltar, Rodney set out for the West Indies with four of the line, sending the rest of the fleet, with the prizes, back to England.

By the spring of 1781, it became known in London that the be-leaguered garrison of Gibraltar was once more within measurable distance of starvation. It was apparent that if the fortress were not speedily relieved it must fall: and the relieving force would have to run the gauntlet of the enemy's principal ports. A formidable French fleet lay in Brest, Cordova with over thirty of the line in Cadiz.

On 13 March Darby sailed from Spithead with twenty-eight of the line and a very great convoy; for in addition to nearly 100 victuallers and store-ships for the relief of Gibraltar the opportunity had to be taken to protect the large ' trades ', bound for the East and West Indies and North America, past the enemy's western bases. For the past several weeks Cordova's fleet had been cruising in the Atlantic; but it was now back in Cadiz and made no attempt to intercept Darby as he sailed past with the convoy.

'Nothing very material has happened during our passage', he observed on 11 April off Cape Spartel, 'which I may call a very good one: at the first we had some blowing weather, four or five of the heavy sailing colliers were obliged to put before the wind: but it moderated in the night, [and] we had the satisfaction of recovering them the next morning, so that I know of no vessel in the King's employ that is missing but a collier which may have followed other convoys as some have done before.'

The arrival on the 12th of the leading ships of Darby's fleet in the bay of Gibraltar was the signal for the Spaniards to open a terrific bombardment on the beleaguered fortress. At the same time the enemy's gunboats directed a harassing fire against our merchantmen while they were unloading: but, in spite of these attacks, the supplies and stores were safely landed within a week; and, the wind coming easterly, Darby's fleet weighed and shaped course to the westward.

As in former years, Great Britain in 1782 stood strictly on the defensive in home waters while she made her main effort in the West Indian theatre. 'The enemy I conceive at this time have two grand designs against us,' observed Kempenfelt in January. 'The one, the conquest of our West India Islands; the other, at home, not confined merely to the interception of our trade, but to favour, by their superiority, a formidable descent upon Great Britain and Ireland.'[1] 'As something must be left exposed,' added Middleton in a memorandum, 'it appears to me that Great Britain and Ireland are more capable of defending themselves than our colonies.' It was accordingly decided

[1] In the same letter, addressed by Kempenfelt to Middleton, are some highly important observations on the proper strategy to be followed in home waters: ' When inferior to the enemy, and you have only a squadron of observation to watch and attend upon their motions, such a squadron should be composed of two-decked ships only, so as to ensure its purpose. It must have the advantage of the enemy in sailing; else, under certain circumstances, it will be liable to be forced to battle, or to give up some of their heavy sailers. It is highly necessary to have such a flying squadron to hang on the enemy's large fleet, as it will prevent their dividing into separate squadrons for intercepting your trade, or spreading their ships for a more extensive view. You will be at hand to profit from any accidental separation or dispersion of their fleet from hard gales, fogs or other causes. You may intercept supplies, intelligence, etc., to them. In fine, such a squadron will be a check and restraint upon their motions, and prevent a good deal of the mischief they might otherways do' (*Navy Records Society*, XXXII, pp. 361-2).

to make certain of the area where the danger was greater, and to dispatch strong forces to the Caribbean.

The command of the Channel Fleet was entrusted to Lord Howe. It was his mission to protect the trade and coasts of the British Isles against the enemy; to prevent reinforcements from reaching the French in the West Indies from Brest, and to relieve Gibraltar; he was to engage the enemy only under favourable conditions. In May Kempenfelt cruised off Ushant with the main force while Howe controlled the North Sea and protected the homecoming Baltic trade against the Dutch; with the result that a convoy of nearly four hundred merchantmen presently reached England in safety. Later Howe sailed westward and joined Kempenfelt at Spithead on 5 June. He found, however, he was too late to prevent the junction of the Brest and Cadiz squadrons; and the combined fleets, comprising forty of the line (as against Howe's twenty-two), proceeded to cruise in the entrance of the Channel.

Howe's next task was to protect the homecoming Jamaica convoy, which was known to be then approaching these shores. Sailing from St. Helens on 2 July, ten days later he sighted the enemy fleet at daybreak. Supported by several of her consorts, his flagship, the *Victory*, stood towards the enemy, while the main body of the British fleet lay to leeward, formed ' in order of sailing ', i.e. in three parallel columns. The combined fleets made no attempt to engage, and some hours later bore away. Under cover of darkness Howe then carried his fleet between Scilly and the Land's End, disappearing before daybreak from the enemy's view. Continuing on its course, his fleet then secured both a favourable situation and the weather-gauge.

' As soon as their Force had been ascertained ', wrote Howe in his dispatch, ' I thought proper to avoid coming to battle with them as then circumstanced, and therefore steered to the north to pass between Scilly and the Land's End. My purpose therein was to get to the westward of the enemy, both for protecting the Jamaica convoy and to gain advantage of situation for bringing them to action which the difference in our numbers renders desirable.'

This strategy proved completely successful. With an inferior, but still formidable, British squadron lying somewhere to the westward, the enemy dared not venture into the Channel. Once again their crushing superiority in numbers had availed them little. They beat up and down seeking Howe in vain; presently they were forced to the southward by a gale; Howe and the Jamaica convoy entered the Channel without sighting a single enemy sail. Eventually the allies were obliged to return to port through lack of supplies; and Howe retired to Spithead to prepare for the relief of Gibraltar.[1] In the meantime the North Sea squadron was strengthened so that it might blockade the Texel again and cover the passage of our autumn convoys from the Baltic. This also was accomplished without the loss of a single ship.

The three years' siege of Gibraltar by the Bourbon Powers culminated in the grand combined assault by land and sea of 8–13 September 1782. At the close of July Cordova, the Spanish commander-in-chief, had received instructions to return home to assist in these operations. To support the attack nearly fifty of the line, together with a large number of frigates, lay in readiness in Algeciras Bay. Within 1,000 yards of the sea-wall of the beleaguered town were anchored ten floating batteries, to whose formidable fire was added that of numerous gunboats and bomb-vessels; on the isthmus joining Gibraltar to the mainland were mounted 300 pieces of artillery.

The British garrison of 7,000 were confronted by 30,000 troops on the land alone; in reply to more than 500 hostile guns they could fire only 96. But the red-hot shot fired by the defenders of Gibraltar accounted for nine out of ten of the floating batteries and effectually demoralized the assailants. When at last the bombardment began to slacken, Gibraltar presented a picture of unrelieved ruin and desolation: the forts that lined the shore opposite the floating batteries were beaten down to the water's edge; scarcely a house was left standing in the town, and the inhabitants were living in bomb-proof vaults— the only place of safety: but the British flag still floated over the summit of the Rock.

It was largely through the relentless pressure put upon the Admiralty by the prime minister, Lord Shelburne, that, at considerable risk to our other naval commitments, a supreme effort was made to succour the garrison.

On 11 September 1782 a convoy of fifty victuallers and the East Indies trading fleet, escorted by thirty-four of the line and a number of frigates, under the command of Admiral Howe, with his flag in the *Victory*, 110, left Portsmouth for Gibraltar. A number of other convoys

---

[1] It was during this concentration at Spithead that the *Royal George* was lost.

joined themselves to this armada, which stood down Channel under the protection of the Grand Fleet. ' There is something sublime ', recorded Horace Walpole, on the news of its departure, ' in this little island, beset with foes, calmly dispatching its own safeguard to maintain such a distant possession.' In the afternoon of the 12th, with a north-easterly breeze, they were off the Start; and by noon on the 13th they were past Land's End. Then the sky clouding over, the wind came westerly and freshened; on clearing the Channel Howe ran into heavy gales; but not one of the 186 ships comprising the fleet had parted company when they reached the latitude of Finisterre. On 11 October they all entered the Gut of Gibraltar. The Spaniards were anchored off Algeciras. The superiority of British seamanship was once more revealed as Howe's squadron proceeded to work between the convoy and the enemy; the unencumbered Spanish fleet, comprising forty-nine sail of the line, making no attempt to engage its weaker opponent.

By the 19th all the merchant vessels had unloaded and the Rock was made safe for another year with troops, ammunition, and supplies. After which, ' the wants of the Garrison provided for in every respect,' Howe wrote in his dispatch, ' I proposed taking advantage immediately, of the Easterly wind, which had prevailed the two or three preceding days, for returning thro' the Straits to the Westward.' Then, Cordova's fleet having retired, Howe returned home, arriving at Spithead on 14 November.

' The failure of the great siege of 1779–83,' a modern American historian has observed, ' established more firmly than ever the tradition of Gibraltar's invulnerability. Gibraltar, in short, became a symbol of British power and invincibility.'[1]

4

On the French intervention in 1778 the British made no attempt to hold the Straits of Gibraltar against the Comte d'Estaing, who sailed from Toulon with a strong squadron and, after an abnormally long passage, arrived off Delaware Bay on 8 July. Only ten days before Howe, apprised of his coming, had managed to get away with his weaker squadron and transports. The French next appeared off New

---

[1] Stetson Conn, *Gibraltar in British Diplomacy in the Eighteenth Century* (1942), p. 265.

York—the centre of British military power in North America—but Howe was ready for him there; and, after a half-hearted attempt to enter the Bay, d'Estaing retired. Meanwhile reinforcements from England were on their way out to North America. But this squadron, comprising thirteen sail of the line under the command of Admiral Byron, 'Foul-Weather Jack', ran into a gale in mid-Atlantic and suffered extensive damage. The old masts with which many of the ships were fitted were cracked or sprung. Byron's squadron was completely dispersed, and most of his vessels were dismasted. Howe's command was eventually reinforced by several of this squadron, although his force was still inferior to that of the enemy.

D'Estaing stood northward to Rhode Island; Howe sailed in pursuit; whereupon the French cut their cables, and, with the aid of a favouring wind, promptly abandoned the anchorage. Rhode Island was saved and, the winter being now at hand, d'Estaing sailed for the West Indies. With scarcely a shot fired, the stronger French squadron had been consistently out-manœuvred by its weaker opponent.

After Saratoga the British commanders made no further attempt to subjugate New England and concentrated their energies on the southern colonies, where a large proportion of the population was believed to be loyalist in sympathy. At the end of 1778 a British army under General Howe landed in Georgia and captured Savannah. In the first two months of 1779 the whole of Georgia was overrun. In 1780 Charleston, the capital of South Carolina, was besieged and taken by Sir Henry Clinton. The latter was succeeded by Lord Cornwallis, who temporarily subdued the Carolinas. During this phase of the struggle the insurgents received very little help from their French allies, whose fleet was mainly engaged in the West Indian theatre. The decisive importance which Washington attached to sea power is clearly revealed in this opening passage of his letter to Rochambeau, dated 15 July 1780: ' In any operations, and under all circumstances, a decisive naval superiority is to be considered as a fundamental principle, and the basis upon which every hope of success must ultimately depend.' At present this naval support was not forthcoming; and in 1781 the position of Washington and his army appeared almost desperate. His troops, ill-fed and ill-equipped, were deserting in thousands. A still more disquieting symptom was the apathy of Congress and the American public generally.

From the day that the British forces marched southward to the Chesapeake, everything had turned on the control of sea communications. The attempt to subjugate the Carolinas had involved a perilous division of the British army; and sea communications formed the vital link between the British southern army and their headquarters in New York. In the spring of 1781 it was decided to consolidate the British position in the south by the conquest of Virginia. Cornwallis marched northward into Virginia and entrenched himself at Yorktown, where he waited in vain for reinforcements.

At the end of August the Comte de Grasse arrived in Chesapeake Bay from the West Indies with a powerful fleet. The Americans and their French allies now closed in on Cornwallis' army in Virginia. In the end, penned in the Yorktown peninsula, where they hoped to be relieved by their fleet, the British faced greatly superior forces under Washington and the Comte de Rochambeau, while de Grasse, with twenty-four sail of the line, blockaded them from the sea. At the same time de Barras came south at Washington's request to join de Grasse: the French had thus effected an overwhelming concentration at the vital point. Their opponents were soon to add tactical, to strategical, failure. On 5 September Rear-Admiral Thomas Graves, with nineteen of the line, arrived off Cape Henry with a following wind. As soon as the British ships were sighted, de Grasse weighed and endeavoured to get out to sea around Cape Henry. But the wind was right in; and only the leading vessels of the French fleet had struggled round the cape when Graves came up. With most of the enemy's ships far astern, and downwind, the British had de Grasse's van completely at their mercy. But Graves took note of the enemy's numbers rather than of his situation. The fetish of ' the line ', which had for long exercised a paralysing effect on British naval initiative, lost him this heaven-sent opportunity of defeating de Grasse's fleet in detail and raising the blockade. Instead of ordering a General Chase he sailed on in line ahead and, after an indecisive action, the British squadron, outnumbered, retreated to New York. There, as Graves reported, there ' was scarcely a spar in the yard '. The result was that it was not until 19 October that his squadron was able to sail.[1] But on that same day

[1] A few weeks later Washington wrote to Lafayette once more stressing the importance of sea power—if only de Grasse had remained on the American coast a few weeks more, he observed, the British forces in the Southern States would have suffered ' total extirpation '. See Allen, *op. cit.*, p. 579.

Cornwallis, hemmed in by land and sea, had surrendered; and with the capitulation of Yorktown the war on land was virtually at an end. The decisive defeat of the British forces in North America spelt the ruin of George III's system of personal government. A few months after the surrender of Yorktown Lord North's ministry fell from power.

5

As has already been said, in European waters Great Britain stood continually on the defensive, reserving her main effort for the war in the Caribbean, which became, in the period under survey, the scene of large-scale naval operations.

In the West Indian theatre, naval strategy was in large measure determined by the constant factor of the easterly trade winds, which gave fleets or squadrons based on the Windward Islands a substantial advantage over those based on the islands to the leeward. Thus while a vessel would make the passage from Antigua to Jamaica in something over a week, it would take that vessel about three times as long to beat back again. In this respect the British, having no suitable station to the eastward, were at a serious disadvantage. Though there were facilities for a minor refit in Antigua and Barbados, for major repairs our vessels had to go to Jamaica, which lay 1,000 miles to leeward. The French, on the other hand, had a first-rate naval base in Fort Royal in Martinique as well as three other good depots in St. Lucia, Guadeloupe, and Cap François in Haïti; and their Spanish allies had a fine natural harbour at Havana with shipbuilding facilities. Another governing factor in naval operations in the West Indies was the incidence of the hurricane season in June, when the main fleets of the belligerents were accustomed to sail northward up the east coast of North America. In October, when winter conditions set in in North American waters, they would return to the West Indies. The North American and West Indian theatres of the war were therefore intimately connected.

It has also to be remembered that at this time the commercial importance of the West Indian islands was so great that purely military objectives had often to give place to the defence and prevention of trade. Behind the dazzling white beaches and tall green coconut-palms lay the extensive estates, controlled by whites and worked by slave labour, of the sugar and tobacco planters. Not a few of these plantations yielded fabulous fortunes for their European proprietors. Some of the leading planters, at the close of the century, were worth from £20,000 to £30,000 a year. They lived luxurious lives in fine country houses stocked with sumptuous furniture, fine china, costly silver plate, and rare wines. The term ' as rich as a West Indiaman ' had become proverbial. On the British side, the influence of West Indian planters and merchants in the city of London was always a paramount consideration with the government of the day. Our squadrons stationed in West Indian waters were obliged on occasion to escort the immensely rich convoys on whose safe passage the stability of the British economy largely depended. Thus the First Lord was beside himself with anxiety when, in the autumn of 1779, Admiral Rodney, who had been appointed to command on the West Indian station and was to escort the outgoing convoys, was delayed at Portsmouth. ' For God's sake,' Sandwich urged, ' go to sea without delay. You cannot conceive of what importance it is to yourself, to me and to the public that you should not lose this fair wind; if you do I shall not only hear of it in Parliament, but in places to which I pay more attention.'

The West Indian islands also bulked large in the eyes of the enemy. It has been estimated that the West Indian trade comprised some 30 per cent. of French imports and 35 per cent. of their exports. France might well hope by a successful war to add most of the British islands in this region to the territories which she already possessed. But she was destined to throw away her best opportunities of doing so. A fatal weakness in her naval strategy was the disposition to regard territorial conquests such as these as the primary, and the destruction of the opposing fleet as no more than a secondary, objective. The key to the situation lay, after all, in the fleets. The permanent occupation of the West Indian islands depended on naval superiority, not merely locally, but throughout the entire theatre of war. The reduction of these islands would have been an easy matter after the destruction of the hostile fleet.

At the outbreak of the war Admiral Barrington, commanding in the West Indies, revealed an energy and promptitude equal to Howe's. As soon as the expected transports arrived from New York, he sailed for St. Lucia and anchored there on 13 December 1778. He had landed about one-half of the troops on the island when a French squadron, under the Comte d'Estaing, arrived on the scene. The strength of d'Estaing's squadron was more than double that of the British. That night Barrington brought his transports inside his warships, which he anchored in a strong line across the entrance to the bay.[1] D'Estaing twice stood down along the British line, cannonading at long range: but made no attempt to force a decisive action. He then retired, and the French garrison on the island surrendered to the British. The seizure of St. Lucia—a fine base within thirty miles of the enemy's principal station in the West Indies, Fort Royal—to some extent neutralized the advantage hitherto enjoyed by the French in the matter of bases. Earlier in the same year, however, the French had captured the British island of Dominica.

Next year the British squadron in the West Indies was strengthened by the fleet of Byron, who now took over the command; but the French, having been reinforced by ten of the line, still remained superior in numbers. In the middle of June Byron saw the homeward-bound trade clear of the islands, while d'Estaing on the 16th seized St. Vincent, and on the 30th sailed with his whole force to attack Grenada. The French troops disembarked at Georgetown on 2 July, and two days later the British garrison surrendered. Byron then sailed with twenty-one of the line and a large convoy of transports for Grenada. Sighting the enemy fleet of twenty-five of the line off Georgetown and without waiting to form a proper line, he at once made the signal for a general chase and attacked the French from to windward as they were leaving the anchorage. Byron's bold but over-hasty assault on d'Estaing's stronger fleet failed; and four of the British ships were badly damaged. The French appear to have employed the same tactic on this occasion as off Port Mahon in 1756: namely, by taking up a good defensive position they obliged their opponents to run all the risks of attack; after which, by an adroit retirement, they compelled the latter to attack once more, and to run the same risks all over again. Content as usual with damaging the masts and rigging

---

[1] ' On shore, a defensive position is determined by the circumstances of the ground selected, improved by fortification; all which gives strength additional to the number of men. A sailing squadron anchored for defence similarly gained force by adapting its formation to the circumstance of the anchorage, and to known wind conditions, with careful preparations to turn the guns in any direction; deliberate precautions, not possible to the same extent to the assailant anchoring under fire. To this is to be added the release of the crew from working sails to manning the guns ' (Mahan, *Sea Power in its Relations to the War of 1812*, I, p. 376).

of their opponents, the French, after this preliminary success, neglected to follow up their advantage. D'Estaing thereby threw away a most promising chance of gaining a decisive victory and securing the command of the sea.

In October 1779 Rodney was appointed to command the British fleet in the West Indies. After relieving Gibraltar, he arrived on his station in the following spring and prepared to counter de Guichen's design for the capture of Barbados. On 17 April 1780 he intercepted the French fleet in the channel between Dominica and Martinique and engaged them from to windward. It was Rodney's intention, by reducing the gaps between his ships, to deliver a massed attack against the enemy's rear, before the van could come to its assistance. To that end he made the signal ' for every ship to bear down, and steer for her opposite in the enemy's line, agreeable to the 21st article of the Additional Fighting Instructions '. That the plan broke down was owing partly to the inadequacy of the signalling system then in use, and partly to misunderstanding between the Commander-in-Chief and his subordinates. Nelson's habit of taking his captains into his confidence was quite foreign to Rodney's nature; and the Admiral was unable to make his subordinates understand exactly what it was he wanted. Instead of bearing down in close order on the French rear, in accordance with Rodney's wish, Captain Carkett in the *Stirling Castle*, and several of the other captains attempted to fight ' ships for ships ', in the old way. The concentrated attack therefore never materialized. Rodney endeavoured for a while to secure the right position: but in vain. His flagship, the *Sandwich*, sailed through the enemy's line, practically unsupported. The manœuvre ended in complete confusion and the action was inconclusive.

Enraged at the miscarriage of his plan, Rodney laid the whole blame on his subordinates and mercilessly censured them in his dispatch. ' The French Admiral, who appeared to be a brave and gallant officer, had the honour to be nobly supported during the whole action,' he declared. ' 'Tis with concern inexpressible, mixt with indignation, that the duty I owe my sovereign and my country obliges me to acquaint Your Lordships that during the action with the French fleet on the 12th instant His Majesty's—the British flag—was not properly supported.' For some time after this abortive action off Martinique Rodney exercised the fleet in a frigate. ' My eye on them had more dread than the enemy's fire,' he wrote to his wife; ' and they knew it would be fatal. No regard was paid to rank; admirals as well as captains, if out of their station, were instantly reprimanded by signals, or messages sent by frigates; and, in spite of themselves, I taught them to be, what they had not been before—*officers*.' During the rest of the season Rodney was much occupied in protecting trade, and in August he sailed for Sandy Hook.

On Rodney's return to the West Indies in December 1780 he discovered that the Windward Islands had been swept by a severe hurricane, accompanied by an earthquake, as a result of which many vessels had been lost or injured, and enormous quantities of naval stores destroyed. ' Barbados ', wrote Rodney, ' has the appearance of a country laid waste by fire and sword. More than six thousand persons perished, and all the inhabitants are entirely ruined.' Furthermore, his own squadron had been severely damaged by another hurricane while on the passage from New York. ' What makes this distress the greater,' Rodney observed, ' no naval stores of any kind are to be got either at Barbadoes or St. Lucia, owing to the dire effects of the hurricane which happened on the 10th of October.'

Shortly after Rodney was joined by Rear-Admiral Sir Samuel Hood with eight of the line and four frigates; and in February 1781, on the arrival of news from home announcing that war had been declared against Holland, he captured the small Dutch island of St. Eustatius, which had hitherto profited vastly by the war and had become the centre of an immense contraband trade. Its whole harbour frontage was lined with miles of crowded warehouses let out at enormous rentals to merchants from the neighbouring belligerent islands anxious to take advantage of St. Eustatius's neutral status. It was from St. Eustatius, too, that de Guichen's squadron had been supplied with naval stores after the action of 17 April. All this rich booty, which was valued at £3 millions, now fell into Rodney's hands, involving him in much future litigation with the powerful commercial interests concerned. Moreover, his preoccupation with the spoils of St. Eustatius prevented him from taking the necessary steps to intercept a French fleet of twenty of the line, encumbered as it was by a large convoy, on its outward passage to Martinique. Had Rodney and his strong fleet been to windward of that island, the enemy would have been compelled to fight at a serious tactical disadvantage, or else

445

lose the convoy. On his arrival at Fort Royal, de Grasse embarked a strong force of troops, and then sailed south and captured Tobago; Rodney, whose health had broken down, remaining inactive. In July the latter returned to England in the *Sandwich*, convoying the trade, while Hood took the fleet to North America.

After the disastrous campaign which terminated in Cornwallis' surrender at Yorktown, Hood returned to the West Indies. In the meantime St. Eustatius had been retaken by the French, who then prepared to attack St. Kitts, Nevis, and Montserrat. About the same time a Spanish expedition occupied the Bahamas. While the French under de Grasse were engaged in investing St. Kitts Hood arrived with his squadron. On sighting the hostile squadron, de Grasse stood out to sea. By a consummate feat of seamanship Hood thereupon slipped under the enemy's guns into the anchorage lately vacated by his opponent. ' The taking possession of this road was well judged, well conducted, and well executed,' observed Captain Lord Robert Manners of the *Resolution*. ' . . . The van and centre divisions brought to an anchor under the fire of the rear, which was engaged with the enemy's centre; and then the centre, being at an anchor and properly placed, covered us while we anchored, making, I think, the most masterly manœuvre I ever saw.' Early next morning Hood re-formed his line in so strong a defensive position on the tail of the bank that de Grasse's successive attacks broke on it in vain. For want of troops Hood was unable to succour the British garrison hard-pressed by the enemy's forces on St. Kitts. A few weeks later the garrison capitulated; and de Grasse's squadron—which by this time had been strongly reinforced—sailed over to St. Nevis to revictual, preparatory to falling upon the British and destroying them. The same night Hood slipped his cables and silently decamped. Nevis and Montserrat likewise surrendered to the French.

On 10 January 1782 Rodney left Plymouth for Barbados. After struggling for a week against westerly gales, the flagship *Formidable* under a press of sail was just able to round Ushant in company with eleven other ships of the line. ' The fate of this Empire is in your hands,' wrote Sandwich on the eve of his departure, ' and I have no reason to wish it should be in any other.' Early in 1782 the French and Spanish forces in the West Indies had concerted a combined attack on Jamaica. It was proposed to concentrate at Cap François in

Haïti no less than fifty of the line and 20,000 troops. The command of the combined fleets was entrusted to de Grasse, who was to take on board all the troops and supplies assembled in Martinique and to convoy them to the allied rendezvous. At this moment of extreme peril for the British cause in the West Indies Rodney arrived once more on the scene with a squadron which brought our force up to a strength approximately equal to that of the French; it was his intention to intercept de Grasse before the latter could join hands with his Spanish allies in Haïti. The vital importance of Barrington's conquest of St. Lucia as a base close to Fort Royal was now made manifest.

There occurred at this stage yet another example of the incorrigible attachment of the French to ulterior objects. When Rodney at his anchorage in St. Lucia learned from his frigates watching off Fort Royal that the French were leaving port, he at once gave chase. On 9 April the British fleet was in pursuit of the enemy when it so happened that de Grasse had nine of Rodney's ships for several hours under his lee, while the main body of the fleet was lying becalmed under Dominica. ' Had de Grasse known his duty ', observed Hood a few days later, ' he might have cut us up, by pouring a succession of fresh ships upon us as long as he pleased; but being very roughly handled and to windward, he hauled off, and our fleet joined in the evening.' Though much superior to the detached division, de Grasse made no attempt to attack these nine ships except by a distant cannonade; and his action was upheld at the ensuing court-martial as ' an act of prudence on the part of the admiral, dictated to him by the ulterior projects of the cruise '. It was, always in short, the fixed and firm belief of the French that ulterior objects were of greater consequence than fighting the enemy's fleet.

' Time and again, in the four years prior to the battle of the Saintes, had the French held a British fleet in a position of numerical or tactical disadvantage: each time they had allowed it to escape. A fleet that persistently neglects its opportunities cannot expect its good fortune to last for ever. Sooner or later the enemy's turn must come.'[1] And, three days after de Grasse had let slip his supreme opportunity, his opponent's turn did come.

On the forenoon of 12 April the French fleet, encumbered as it was by a large convoy of merchantmen, transports, and store-ships, and

[1] Lieutenant N. Kemp, R.N., in the *Naval Review*, XXII, p. 727.

sailing in a ragged and disordered line, was brought to action by Rodney near The Saints, a group of small islands lying between Martinique and Gaudeloupe. The opening phase of the battle was on the lines of one of the usual inconclusive ' line ' actions: the two fleets slowly sliding past each other on opposite tacks, with the French holding the weather-gauge. But de Grasse, beating up the straits between Guadeloupe and Dominica against the easterly trade wind, was gradually approaching the becalmed area under the lee of Dominica, where he could no longer hope to frustrate his enemy's desire for close action. Twice he made the signal to wear in order to avoid

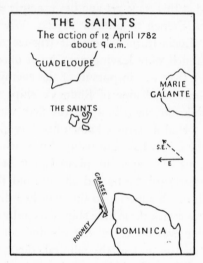

this windless zone: but this could not be done without colliding with the British to leeward. Then suddenly at 9.15 the wind veered to south-east at the southern end of the two fleets so that de Grasse's rearward vessels could not hold their course and were thrown into confusion, while the van held on its course.

It happened that at this juncture one of de Grasse's ships, the *Diadème*, was taken aback by the shift of wind and lost way just as the British flagship, the *Formidable*, approached on the opposite course; and Rodney, quickly seizing his opportunity, steered through the gap in the enemy's line, followed by the five ships next astern of him; while the *Duke*—next ahead of the *Formidable*—cut through the French line further down, and the *Bedford*—sixth astern of the *Formidable*—

broke through at yet another point. The *Bedford* was followed by all twelve ships of Hood's division.

The British manœuvre was brilliantly successful. ' This was the decisive act that crowned us with victory ', wrote Sir Gilbert Blane; ' and no sooner had the smoke cleared away, than we perceived the enemy separated, routed, and in flight.' Forging through the gap, the *Formidable* delivered a raking broadside to starboard through the stern windows of the *Glorieux* and another to larboard through the bows of the *Diadème*. As soon as he was through the gap, Rodney steered up the weather side of the French line, and, closely supported by the *Duke* and *Namur*, flung broadside after broadside into a group of the enemy's ships which lay hopelessly entangled astern of the *Diadème* under a heavy pall of smoke: ' Bore up,' recorded Rodney's flag-captain, ' and raked four of the Enemy's ships which had got foul of each other '; ' not a single shot missing ', wrote Douglas[1] later, ' and dreadful must have been the slaughter.'

The French line was thus cut at three different points and was never re-formed. The result was that a number of the enemy's ships were assailed by superior concentrations of British ships and heavily raked. Rodney's manœuvre, moreover, had brought these French vessels within reach of the British carronades, which played a decisive part in the short-range fighting which followed.[2] About noon the breeze freshened from the east, and twenty-five of the enemy's ships got away to leeward through the gaps left in the British line and escaped to the northward. Six disabled Frenchmen—including de Grasse's flagship, the *Ville de Paris*—were captured one by one as they dropped astern.

Jamaica was saved; and the long sequence of indecisive ' line ' actions was dramatically broken. But the outcome of the day's fighting was by no means to the satisfaction of Rodney's second-in-command, Sir Samuel Hood, who observed to Middleton:

After the glorious business of yesterday, I was most exceedingly dis-appointed and mortified in the commander-in-chief . . . for not making the signal for a general chase the moment he hauled that down for the line of battle, which was about one o'clock: had he so done, I am very confident we should have had twenty sail of the enemy's ships before dark. Instead of that, he pursued only under his topsails (sometimes his

[1] Rodney's Captain of the Fleet, and a gunnery expert. See *supra*, p. 347.
[2] The carronade was not as yet in use in the French navy.

foresail was set and at others his mizen topsail aback) the greatest part of the afternoon, though the *flying* enemy had all the sail set their very shattered state would allow.

On the morning of the 13th Hood went on board the *Formidable*, and expressed his regret that the Admiral had not continued to pursue the French, ' so as to keep sight of the enemy all night, to which he only answered, " Come, we have done very handsomely as it is." ' The truth was that Rodney, an ageing and infirm man, who had not slept for four nights, had reached the limit of his physical endurance and was incapable of further effort. Six days later, however, Hood captured four more of the enemy's ships off Porto Rico.

On his arrival at Port Royal in Jamaica Rodney was forced through lack of masts to send away nine of the damaged battleships (including the *Ville de Paris* and several other prizes), with a number of frigates, under the command of Sir Thomas Graves, to escort a home-going convoy of nearly a hundred merchantmen. Off the Grand Banks the convoy was caught in a heavy gale and five of the battleships were lost. Four 74s—the *Ramillies*, *Centaur*, *Hector*, and *Glorieux*—sank with most of their crews, and the *Ville de Paris* was abandoned and blown up. It is worth noticing that the number of lives lost on this occasion actually exceeded the total number of those killed in action throughout the entire American War.

Meanwhile the Rockingham ministry, which had succeeded North, without waiting to hear the results of the spring campaign had determined on Rodney's recall. His successor, Admiral Pigot, had already sailed when the news of the victory reached England.[1] The government thereupon changed its tune: for Rodney had become the hero of the hour. ' Till three in the morning ', wrote Walpole, ' there was no sleeping for rockets and squibs.' ' All London was in an uproar,' observed the Admiral's daughter Jane in exultation; ' the whole town was illuminated that night.' Both Houses of Parliament passed votes of thanks to Rodney ' for his able and gallant conduct '. Cities and boroughs showered their freedoms on him. He received a barony and a pension of £2,000 a year. Hood and the other subordinate admirals were likewise lavishly rewarded. When all was said and done, no such fleet action had been fought for nearly eighty years.

[1] Pigot achieved practically nothing in the West Indies. ' I believe ', observed Wraxall in his *Historical Memoirs*, ' he never captured any thing except a Spanish Polacre.'

6

During the Seven Years War and its aftermath Great Britain's hold on India had been greatly strengthened. Now her forces in the peninsula once again took the offensive. On the day that news of the outbreak of war reached India, 7 July 1778, Hastings instructed the governor of Madras to attack Pondicherry, while he himself seized Chandernagore. Pondicherry surrendered after a ten weeks' siege, and in March 1779, Mahé, the only remaining French settlement, also fell. About this time there arrived from England a squadron of six of the line under Vice-Admiral Sir Edward Hughes. Since the naval force of the enemy in Indian waters was insignificant during the first part of the war, Hughes, enjoying the undisputed command of the sea, was able in conjunction with the British troops to capture the trading-station of Negapatam and the vitally important port of Trincomali in Ceylon from the Dutch in January 1782.

Later in the war the state of affairs in the peninsula was unusually favourable to French intervention. The British power had recently been shaken by the combined assault of Hyder Ali and the warlike Mahratta confederation. The Company's treasury was nearly empty. In January 1781, a French force of six of the line and three frigates, under the command of the Comte d'Orves, had appeared on the Coromandel coast. But Hyder Ali's request that the French should assist him in an attack on Cuddalore was refused, and d'Orves returned to Mauritius, after which Hyder Ali was severely defeated by Sir Eyre Coote. Next year, however, there arrived a French commander of a very different kind. A squadron of five of the line—four of them coppered—under the Bailli de Suffren, had sailed with de Guichen from Brest on 22 March 1781. In company with this squadron were a number of transports destined for the defence of the Cape of Good Hope against an expected British attack. Suffren's immediate object was to save the Cape: without the food supplies furnished by the Dutch colony, Mauritius could scarcely be held by the French: and Mauritius was the key to India. Separating from the main body on the 29th, Suffren arrived on 16 April off Porto Praya in the Cape Verde Islands, where he surprised and attacked a weaker British squadron, under Commodore Johnstone, lying at anchor. Suffren was badly supported by his captains and the attack failed. He continued on his voyage and anchored off the Cape, where he proceeded to land his troops. The result was that Johnstone presently abandoned the proposed attempt on the Cape and returned to England. Then, with the first part of his mission accomplished, Suffren made sail for Mauritius, where he arrived on 25 October. Succeeding on the death of the Comte d'Orves to the command in Indian waters, he appeared off Madras on 15 February 1782.

Suffren's was the stronger of the rival squadrons; but he was without a port, either French or allied, as a base for his operations. He had arrived on the scene just too late to save the Dutch Indian possessions from capture; Trincomali had fallen only a month before. To the bulldog courage and determination of his British opponent were now opposed the ardour and tactical science of this brilliant Provençal. Suffren was no ' x-chaser ', no theoretician of the Père Hoste school. He relied mainly on experience—his own and that of others. In the early stages of the American War he had served with d'Estaing on the North American station and later in the West Indies. He had studied closely all d'Aché's campaigns in Indian waters, as well as those fought by de Ruyter. Animated with the offensive spirit to a degree unparalleled in any of his brother commanders, Suffren's one object throughout the following campaign was to seek out and destroy the enemy's fleet. Attack, not defence, was in his eyes the proper strategy. Alone among his contemporaries in the service, Suffren broke away from the trammels of a false and debilitating system and refused to be governed by those ulterior objects to which the strategy of the French navy had been continually subordinated. Twenty years afterwards Napoleon might well exclaim: ' Oh, why did he not live until my time, or why have I been unable to find a man of his stamp: I would have made him our Nelson and affairs would have taken a very different course.'[1]

As a tactician, Suffren was less successful. His tactical plan of concentrating in the rear was well devised and was communicated to his captains before action. It was attempted in the earlier, but not in the later, engagements of the campaign. But Suffren's skilful combinations demanded from his captains a degree of initiative which they unhappily did not possess. Moreover, the professional skill of most of the French captains was decidedly inferior to that of their

[1] Q. Richmond, *The Navy in India, 1763–1783*, p. 142.

opponents. These facts, considered in conjunction with Suffren's native impetuosity, amounting at times almost to rashness, and the good seamanship and dogged tenacity of Hughes and his captains, which repeatedly warded off defeat—serve to explain why, notwithstanding the superior numbers of the French at the outset of the campaign and the exceptional qualities of their commander, the British squadron, after five hard-fought actions, not only still existed, but had not lost a single vessel.

The actions between Hughes and Suffren were fought on 17 February, 12 April, 6 July, and 3 September 1782, and on 20 June 1783, off the eastern coast of the Deccan. In only one of these actions—that of 6 July 1782—was Hughes the assailant.

After the engagement of 12 April 1782 Suffren received orders from his government to return to Mauritius to refit. It was not thought possible in Paris, that the squadron could be maintained, in good fighting condition, off a hostile coast, without a port or supplies and so far from the nearest base. Nevertheless, Suffren resolved to remain on his station. He rightly considered that French interests in the East depended in the last resort upon the control of the sea, and, therefore, upon the continued presence of his squadron. In spite of every difficulty and disadvantage he returned to the attack and continually refitted his squadron on the spot, drawing his supplies from the storeships and commerce of the enemy. There was an outstanding example of the phenomenal energy and resource exhibited by Suffren in these operations after the action of 6 July 1782. In this engagement the French had suffered far heavier losses in men. But apparently the rigging of the British force was severely damaged; and on 18 July Hughes sailed off to Madras to complete his repairs, while Suffren—after refitting with almost incredible rapidity in the open roadstead off Cuddalore—was again ready for sea. On 21 August the French were strengthened by a reinforcement from home, and two days afterwards Suffren sailed, with fourteen of the line, for Trincomali, where he anchored on the 25th. On the following night he disembarked his troops and guns, and launched a vigorous attack. Five days later the British garrison surrendered; and Trincomali and its harbour passed into the hands of the French.

The loss of Trincomali was a severe blow for Hughes. On the Coromandel coast there was no harbour at all, the other anchorages being merely open roadsteads. On the approach of the north-east monsoon there was therefore no safe refuge on the eastern coast for the British squadron. After the autumnal equinox, when the monsoon, or trade-wind, changes its direction from south-west to north-east, throwing such a heavy surf upon the shore as to make landing often difficult or impossible, it was customary for the rival squadrons to retire to a secure harbour until the following spring. On the eastern coast Trincomali was the only such harbour; and its high strategic importance was further enhanced by the fact that, during the south-west monsoon, it lay to windward of the main theatre of war.

Up to this point Suffren had enjoyed a substantial superiority in numbers over his opponent. This advantage he was about to lose. As soon as news of the action of Porto Praya had reached England, the British government speedily fitted out a powerful squadron, under the command of Sir Richard Bickerton, to reinforce Hughes.

Leaving a large force to hold Trincomali, Suffren prepared to attack once more while the odds were still in his favour. He had fourteen vessels to Hughes' twelve. Action was joined on 3 September: the French ships were again handled so badly that their line fell into disorder, and the attack was a disastrous failure; Hughes succeeded in isolating the French centre and dismasting his opponent's flagship; and Suffren's squadron was worsted in the fight. To add to his embarrassments, Suffren shortly afterwards lost two of his ships through the mismanagement of their captains.

At this critical juncture the inadequacy of the reinforcements—both in ships and in troops—sent out by the home government seriously handicapped the French cause in India. When finally three of the line and a substantial body of troops did reach Trincomali, on 10 June 1783, after delaying over long in Mauritius, their commander, General de Bussy, had let slip an excellent opportunity of joining hands with Suffren and thereby effecting an overpowering concentration in the Carnatic before the arrival of Hughes' squadron from Bombay. Shortly afterwards de Bussy found himself shut up in Cuddalore, with a large British force from Madras encamped to the southward of the town, and Hughes' squadron blockading him from the sea. Suffren thereupon sailed up the coast from Trincomali to de Bussy's support. Hughes at once retired; and Suffren anchored off Cuddalore. In the late afternoon of 20 June Suffren, with fifteen of the line to Hughes' eighteen, bore down on the rival squadron. Fully supported on this occasion by his captains, the French commander attacked his enemy's stronger fleet *à l'anglaise*—' conterminously '. After a short but hard-fought action, in which the loss on both sides was nearly equal, the British, abandoning the battle-ground and their army, withdrew to Madras. At the end of March hostilities were terminated by the arrival of news from Europe of the conclusion of peace.

To sum up, it may be said that Hughes, though continually out-manœuvred and out-generalled and conclusively defeated in this final encounter, had conducted an admirably tenacious, and on the whole effective, campaign against one of the ablest, most original, and most brilliant naval commanders of all time. Together with Hastings and Coote he had effectually preserved the British possessions in India in a crisis of extreme peril.

7

The American Revolutionary War witnessed a number of celebrated frigate actions. Several of the most important of these were fought in the Channel approaches, while the enemy were trying to slip past our forces out of Brest.

On 17 June 1778 when France was on the verge of war with Great Britain, several French cruisers, including the *Belle Poule*, fell in with the Channel Fleet, under Keppel, cruising to the westward of the Lizard. There was a calm sea with little wind. Keppel made the signal for a general chase; but when the *Arethusa* came up with the *Belle Poule* at about six o'clock in the evening, the rest of the British squadron was still several miles astern of the *Arethusa* and could give her no assistance. The captain of the *Arethusa* requested the French captain to bring-to and to come with him to Keppel. Upon the latter's refusal, the British captain fired a shot which began the action. The two frigates fought broadside to broadside for two hours and more, as a result of which the *Arethusa* was so badly damaged that she was unable to manœuvre and the *Belle Poule* finally got away among the rocks of Plouascat. In the meantime the *Alert* cutter engaged and eventually boarded the French schooner *Coureur* which had been in company with the *Belle Poule*.

Several months later, on 6 October, the *Quebec*, 32, Captain George

Farmer, in company with the *Rambler*, 10, Lieutenant Rupert George, was cruising off Ushant on the look-out for an enemy force reported to be coming out of Brest. Next morning at daybreak they sighted the French frigate *Surveillante*, 32, Lieutenant Du Couëdic de Kergoualer, accompanied by the *Expédition* cutter. There was a heavy swell, and the wind at east was light and failing. It was not until 10 a.m. that the two frigates were within close range; and, lying broadside to broadside, began a furious action.[1] After an hour of this terrific cannonade, Farmer manœuvred so as to rake his opponent, but was prevented from doing so by Kergoualer's promptitude and judgment. The masts and rigging of both frigates were now in such a state that they could no longer sail to windward, but were forced to bear away. The murderous duel continued until Farmer himself was wounded, most of his officers were killed or injured, and there were scarcely men enough to work the guns. Kergoualer also had been wounded, but, like Farmer, refused to leave the deck. The *Surveillante's* masts went overboard; but, falling to port, did not mask her guns. Immediately after the *Quebec's* masts collapsed upon her deck, impeding the service of the forecastle and quarter-deck guns; moreover, the sails of her mizen-mast hung down on her engaged side and were soon afterwards set on fire by the flash of the guns. The fire spread to her quarter-deck. Kergoualer, who had been attempting to board, ordered fire to cease and had the *Surveillante's* bowsprit, which had become entangled with her opponent's wreckage, hurriedly cut away and the *Quebec* fended off with spars. At six o'clock the next morning the *Quebec*, her colours still flying, blew up. Only 68 of the *Quebec's* complement of 195 survived; among those who perished was her heroic commander. ' Thus died in the flower of his age a great and accomplished officer; and one of those who may be said to have made and moulded our Navy for the next French war. Under him Nelson and Troubridge served, and the master was worthy of his disciples.'[2] In recognition of the great gallantry Farmer had displayed throughout the action, and at the special request of the Board of Admiralty, a baronetcy was conferred on his eldest son and a substantial pension awarded to his widow.

[1] The *Quebec* was armed only with 9-pounders as against the *Surveillante's* 18-pounders, and the latter had nearly twice as many men.

[2] Clowes, *The Royal Navy*, IV, p. 42. Nelson as a midshipman had sailed with Farmer in the *Seahorse* frigate to the East Indies in 1773.

The famous action fought between the *Flora*, 36, and the *Nymphe*, 32, in the summer of 1780, demonstrated the value of the carronade, then recently introduced in the British Navy. The *Flora* was cruising in the vicinity of Ushant when, in the afternoon of 10 August, she sighted and chased a frigate and a cutter. The latter got away; but the former was overhauled and brought to action shortly after five o'clock. From 5.45 to 6.15 the two frigates fought yard-arm to yard-arm: the *Flora's* wheel was shot away, and her shrouds and rigging severely slashed; the French captain was mortally wounded, his vessel was twice on fire, and terrible execution wrought on deck by one of the *Flora's* 18-pounder forecastle carronades. At 6.15 the two ships fell on board each other. The French, abandoning their guns, endeavoured to carry the *Flora*. They were speedily driven back; and the British in turn boarded the *Nymphe*, which soon afterwards struck her colours. The *Nymphe's* casualties greatly exceeded those of her opponent. Though the former was the larger of the two ships and the better sailer, the *Flora's* heavier armament had given her the victory.

8

The defeat of de Grasse's fleet off The Saints had not only put new heart into the British people, but had correspondingly discouraged their principal adversary, France. Spain no longer hoped to retake Gibraltar. In the American States there was dissension and unrest. All this, and the mutual exhaustion of the belligerents, led, towards the close of 1782, to the opening of peace negotiations, culminating in the signing of the Peace of Versailles on 20 January 1783. Great Britain now formally recognized the independence of the United States, and ceded to France Senegal and Tobago, and to Spain, Minorca and Florida. France restored the British West Indian islands which she had seized during the war, Dominica, St. Vincent, and Grenada; while Great Britain gave back St. Lucia. That the British losses were no heavier, indeed, was mainly owing to the surrender of our claims respecting the American colonies and the fine fight which the Navy had put up against enemy forces which, in point of numbers, were overwhelmingly superior.

The Peace of Versailles actually left the British acquisitions in the Seven Years War—in North America as well as in the East and West

Indies—substantially intact. Not territorial, but maritime and commercial expansion, was the basis of Shelburne's shrewd and far-sighted design for the future. He aimed above all at the comprehensive development of our tropical trades and industries. On the ruins of the old mercantile empire arose the foundations of another and incomparably wider polity.

In conclusion, a word must be said about certain important lessons taught by the American War. On the British side, the great strategical failure lay in the dispersion of British naval strength throughout the various theatres of war instead of its concentration in the really vital areas. Thus the Admiralty made no attempt to blockade or mask the enemy's fleets in Brest or Toulon, with the result that the British control of sea communications on the North American and West Indian stations was continually being threatened by the arrival of reinforcements from Europe. ' In 1779 and 1781 ', as Mahan observes, ' . . . the English fleet was superior to that of the French alone; yet the allies joined unopposed, while in the latter year de Grasse got away to the West Indies, and Suffren to the East.' Perhaps the most glaring instance of our failure to blockade the enemy's fleet was in the latter year, when de Grasse was allowed to get out of Brest in the spring unopposed; for a British fleet of superior force was already at sea, but had been ordered by the Admiralty to the Irish coast—and again at the end of this year, when Kempenfelt was dispatched to intercept de Guichen with an inferior force, while sufficient ships to reverse the odds were kept at home.

Another very serious strategic error was to sail small convoys with weak escorts: in consequence of which a number had been successfully attacked by the enemy. This error was not repeated in the wars of 1793–1815, when large convoys and strong escorts were the rule.

On the other hand, the failure of the French and Spaniards to make the most of their opportunities was mainly due, first, to the fact that the allies were fighting with divergent aims, and, second, that they consistently dissipated their strength upon ulterior objects (in the case of France, it was the British West Indian islands: and in that of Spain, Gibraltar) instead of upon the true objective, namely, *the destruction of the enemy's fighting fleet*, which alone would have led to the realization of their hopes. The decisive theatre was in our home waters. Here lay the chief objective: the British Grand Fleet. Here, too, within easy striking distance of Brest, was the main British trade focal, through which passed the principal part of our seaborne commerce. Though the British fleet in home waters was greatly outnumbered by that of the Franco-Spanish combination, the latter never made any serious attempt to destroy it. In the significant words of Mahan, ' Neither in the greater strategic combinations, nor upon the battlefield, does there appear any serious purpose of using superior numbers to crush fractions of the enemy's fleet, to make the disparity of numbers yet greater, to put an end to the empire of the seas by the destruction of the organized force which sustained it. With the single brilliant exception of Suffren, the allied navies avoided or accepted action; they never imposed it.'[1]

Yet there is no principle more surely and securely established by all the history of sea warfare than that—first, last, and always—the primary objective of a navy is the annihilation of the enemy fleet: besides which ulterior objects, such as the capture of an island or the protection of a convoy, sink into insignificance.

In the field of tactics, it was mainly owing to their want of tactical skill and the inadequacy of their signalling system that the British as a rule failed to force the French to close action and so produce a mêlée, with the result that many an engagement degenerated into a mere artillery duel. In these encounters the French were accustomed to take the lee-gauge and, aiming at their opponent's masts and rigging, retire before the British could come near enough to resort to the rapid fire at point-blank range in which they excelled. ' They have formed a system of tactics ', observed Kempenfelt to Middleton, ' which are studied in their academies and practised in their squadrons.' In the later stages of the war, as has been seen in the previous chapter, Kempenfelt and Howe were experimenting with new and more flexible signalling systems.

On the other side, the tactical doctrine instilled in the French marine could not but be fatal to decisive action. The traditions of France were after all military, not naval. Her admirals were hampered by definite instructions to preserve their ships from injury. Over and over again the true function of a fleet would be subordinated to the success of some particular military operation. It is hardly surprising that the three principal French commanders, d'Estaing, de Guichen,

[1] Mahan, *The Influence of Sea Power upon History* (1890), p. 538.

and de Grasse, fought to cripple, rather than to destroy, the enemy. What they chiefly aimed at, indeed, was 'spar-wrecking'. Their hesitancy, excessive caution, and lack of the offensive spirit served for the most part to neutralize the advantage in numbers which they enjoyed over their opponents. Once more to quote Mahan, 'it must be noted as the supreme factor in the military conduct of the war, that, while the allied powers were on the offensive and England on the defensive, the attitude of the allied fleets in the presence of the English navy was habitually defensive.'[1]

The consequence was that the naval power of Great Britain, although substantially weakened by the loss of the American colonies, survived the ordeal; and continued to dominate the oceans of the world after the conclusion of peace.

9

The decade between the Peace of Versailles and the outbreak of the French Revolutionary War was an era of peace, retrenchment, and reform. The rapid recovery of British prosperity and prestige following the disastrous war of 1778–83 was largely due to the wise financial policy of the younger Pitt, one of the greatest peace ministers in our history, who combined the two offices of premier and chancellor of the exchequer. During the early years of his administration Pitt did much to bring the antiquated fiscal machinery of this country up to date by consolidating the different branches of excise, by systematically reducing indirect taxes (the duty on tea was cut down from 119 per cent. to 12 per cent.), and by reducing the cost of the collection of taxes and the temptation to fraud. By these measures and also by the 'Hovering Act', in 1784, which restricted the ownership of certain types of craft which had been commonly used for illicit purposes and instituted severer penalties, he effectually checked smuggling.

In the period under review British imports and exports increased by more than 50 per cent. In 1786 the national finances had been so far repaired that Pitt was able to establish a sinking fund for the redemption of the National Debt. With the increasing use of the new machinery evolved through the genius of Watt, Hargreaves, Arkwright, Crompton, and others, British industry was just then entering on a phase of

[1] *Ibid.*

progressive and unparalleled expansion. ' Our good old island,' wrote one member of the Government, ' now possesses an accumulation and completion of prosperity beyond any example in the history of the world.'[1] The rapidly rising revenue was largely derived from the growing customs yield on our continually expanding trade.

When at the close of 1783 he formed his first administration the kingdom had been faced with imminent bankruptcy. Nevertheless, out of a total revenue of £25 millions Pitt reserved £2½ millions for naval shipbuilding and raised the peace-time establishment of the Service from 15,000 to 18,000 men. The year 1789 saw a further increase of 2,000 men. Pitt defended this measure by arguing that ' the best economy that any country could practise in time of peace, was to keep up such a force, and take such measures of defence, as would be most likely to render the peace permanent, and insure its duration. It was with this view, that the additional 2,000 seamen had been proposed, because while the country kept up a moderate but a necessary force for its defence, it was the less likely that any other country would be tempted to disturb its tranquility.'

He firmly supported the Comptroller, Sir Charles Middleton, in his endeavours to effect certain much-needed reforms in the royal and private dockyards. ' It was no uncommon thing for Mr. Pitt to visit the Navy Office', observed Admiral Sir Byam Martin in after years, 'to discuss matters with the Comptroller, and to see the returns made from the yards of the progress in building and repairing the ships of the line.'

Under Middleton's administration the dockyard ' mateys ' were obliged to work longer hours (especially during the first two years of this period) than at any other time. ' The principle of our dockyards at present ' he informed Pitt in 1786 ' is a total disregard to public œconomy in all its branches; and it is so rooted in the professional officers that they cannot divest themselves of it when brought into higher stations. They have so many relatives and dependents, too, in the dockyards, that can only be served by countenancing and promoting improper expenses, that they can never lose an opportunity of supporting them when in their power, and on this account ought to have as small a voice as possible in creating them.'

Middleton was of opinion that more docks were required for repairing ships. ' In peace ', he declared, ' many ships that want repairs, and

[1] Q. C. E. Carrington, *The British Overseas* (1950), p. 234.

which might be done at no very great expense if taken in hand soon, become repairless from the length of time before they can go to work upon them through the paucity of docks.' At the same time he strongly condemned ' the many enormous abuses committed under the indulgence of chips ' and suggested that a sum of money might advantageously be substituted for these time-honoured perquisites. Largely as a result of Middleton's reforms the matériel of the Navy was effectively overhauled. When in 1789 Fanny Burney was shown round Plymouth dockyard—where a large number of ships of the line were laid up, and everything was kept in the most perfect order—she relates that she experienced ' a sort of sighing satisfaction to see such numerous stores of war's alarms!—ropes, sails, masts, and anchors—and all in the finest symmetry, divided and sub-divided, as if placed only for show.' An important innovation of Middleton's was the allocation of an adequate reserve of stores to each vessel, which greatly facilitated the fitting out of the Fleet. During this period no less than twenty-four of the line were laid down in the private yards, and another nine in the royal dockyards, which also rebuilt or largely repaired sixty more.

The ten years' peace was all but broken by three successive embroilments with France, Russia, and Spain. The first of these concerned the integrity of the Low Countries—that region of profound strategic significance to our island State. The internal dissensions of the United Provinces had, in 1787, given the French an apparently promising opportunity to intervene in favour of the republican opposition in that country with the intention of bringing about the political domination of Holland, which it had been for centuries the settled policy of Great Britain to prevent. Pitt joined forces with Prussia to oppose France: the rehabilitation of the Navy proved a factor of the utmost importance in the ensuing developments, since it served to hold Prussia firm to the alliance and ready to march into Holland to the support of the Stadholder. The almost bankrupt French monarchy dared not risk conclusions with both the Prussian army and the British fleet; and in the end France gave way without a fight.

Pitt's attempted intervention in the Black Sea region was by no means so successful. He found himself unable to prevent the annexation of Oczakoff by the Russians following on their defeat of the

Turkish fleet; but, in 1788, he intervened firmly in the north to prevent Sweden from a Danish invasion and to prevent the Baltic from becoming a Russian lake. The independence of Sweden was effectually assured; the Russian advance was brought to a halt and the political balance in the Baltic restored.

Yet another dangerous crisis arose in 1790 when Spain seized British merchant shipping lying in Nootka Sound and laid claim to the whole of what is now Vancouver Island. Great Britain immediately prepared for war. In the year of the Spanish Armament, as it was called, she had no less than ninety-three capital ships fit for service; on 4 May a general press was instituted all over the British Isles, and a fleet of forty sail of the line quickly placed in active commission. In August, it being reported that the Spanish fleet was at sea, Howe cruised for a month in the Channel Soundings with thirty-five sail of the line, which he exercised continually both in tactics and in the new code of signals on which he had been working during the past few years. Confronted with these formidable preparations, Spain abated her demands and a peaceful settlement followed.

On the eve of the next general war, in the early part of 1793, the British squadrons on foreign stations were numerically weak: in the Mediterranean, we had only one 50 and a couple of frigates; in the West Indies, three 50s and five frigates; on the North American station, one 50 and two frigates; on the coast of Africa, one 44; in the East Indies, one 50 and two frigates. But in home waters there was a substantial force in commission, comprising twenty-five sail of the line, nearly fifty frigates, and thirty lesser vessels. Three or four times as many capital ships were ready, or nearly ready, for service; for, in consequence of Middleton's measures for systematic stockpiling in the dockyards, large numbers of ships could be fitted out with extraordinary dispatch. To man the ships of the expanding wartime Fleet, and to keep the seaborne trade of this country flowing despite the heavy losses that must be expected from enemy attack, Great Britain possessed, in her immense mercantile marine and fisheries, well-nigh inexhaustible reserves of prime seamen. Notwithstanding the recent loss of her American ports and Minorca, she was still well provided with overseas bases. New York and Boston were gone but Halifax remained. Port Mahon was lost but Gibraltar still secured the entrance to the Mediterranean. Kingston in Jamaica also remained in our keeping for the defence of the rich sugar islands of the West Indies. The British squadron in Indian Waters was still based on Madras and Bombay. Most of the strategic points essential to the maintenance of our sea power were retained at the peace through Shelburne's skilful and successful conduct of the negotiations.

The national instinct and inclination for the sea ruled still as strong as ever. William Cobbett has related how in his youth he went, towards the autumn of 1782, to visit an uncle who resided in the vicinity of Portsmouth. From the top of Portsdown Hill this youngster from an inland village beheld, for the first time in his life, the sea—and, not only the sea, but the Channel Squadron riding at anchor at Spithead; and he declares, that no sooner did he behold this inspiring spectacle, than, like so many others of his generation, he longed to be a sailor. Large numbers of likely seamen still entered the Service as volunteers.

Above all, our country possessed a corps of sea officers that was unequalled in any other maritime Power in Europe, the veterans of Lagos and Quiberon Bay, of Finisterre and The Saints, under the leadership of seasoned flag officers who had distinguished themselves in the war of 1778–83: Lord Howe, Peter Parker, Edward Hughes, Thomas Graves, Sir Alexander Hood, Lord Hood, Sir John Jervis, Adam Duncan, the younger Sir Hyde Parker, and William Cornwallis. On the ample stores of experience laid up in many a former campaign these commanders were now to draw with telling effect. ' They were giants in those days,' Creswell declares, ' not necessarily because they were more favoured at birth than the men of our generation, but because many of them had experience of two or even three wars and each man was carrying a living tradition from the generation before him.'[1]

Thus the ' living tradition ' was handed on from Hawke to Locker, and from Locker in turn to the greatest fighting Admiral in the annals of the sea. One of Hawke's young officers, in the crucial campaign of 1759, had been Lieutenant William Locker of the *Sapphire* frigate; and one of Locker's lieutenants, towards the end of Hawke's life, was Horatio Nelson. It was to Locker, his old captain, that Nelson long afterwards, when at the zenith of his glory, wrote, ' To you, my dear friend, I owe much of my success. It was you who taught me,—" Lay a Frenchman close and you will beat him." '

[1] Captain John Creswell, *Naval Warfare* (1942).

Bibliography

GENERAL

By far the most important collection of manuscript sources consists of the Admiralty Papers now preserved in the Public Record Office, Chancery Lane, London. Other large collections which ought not to be neglected are housed in the British Museum and the National Maritime Museum, Greenwich.

The standard general naval history is Sir William Laird Clowes' *The Royal Navy*, 7 vols. (1903): but this work is now largely out of date and extends only to the death of Queen Victoria. David Hannay's *A Short History of the British Navy* (1909) finishes still earlier with the conclusion of the Napoleonic War. Captain A. T. Mahan's classic work *The Influence of Sea Power upon History* (1890) is indispensable. Among the more recent works are *The Navy of Britain* (1948) and *The History of the British Navy* (1957), both by M. A. Lewis, and *The Nation and the Navy* (1954) by C. C. Lloyd. Two admirable outline histories which may be mentioned are Hannay's *The Navy and Sea Power* (1913) and Brian Tunstall's *Realities of Naval History* (1936). A French authority of high importance is *La puissance navale dans l'histoire, I*, by L. Nicolas. The administrative side of naval history is exhaustively and accurately treated, throughout the mediaeval, Tudor, and early Stuart eras, in Michael Oppenheim's *History of the Administration of the Royal Navy, 1509–1660* (1896). Two highly important works on naval policy are Admiral Sir Herbert Richmond's *Statesmen and Sea Power* (1946) and *The Navy as an Instrument of Policy* (1953).

For the mercantile marine, seaborne trade, and colonial expansion, see *History of the World's Shipping* by W. S. Lindsay (1878), *Short History of the World's Shipping Industry* by C. E. Fayle (1933), *History of the Merchant Navy* by Moyse-Bartlett (1937), *Short History of British Expansion* (3rd ed., 1945) by J. A. Williamson, and *Empire of the North Atlantic* (2nd ed., 1958) by G. S. Graham.

The following are valuable monographs dealing with special subjects; R. G. Albion's *Forests and Sea Power* (1926), G. S. Laird Clowes' *Sailing Ships, their History and Development* (1936), G. Blake's *British Ships and Shipbuilders* (1946), F. L. Robertson's *The Evolution of Naval Gunnery*

(1921), and H. W. Richmond's *Invasion of Britain* (1941). *The Haven-Finding Art* by E. G. R. Taylor (1958) is much the best of the general histories of navigation: its contents are not, however, by any means of uniform value and accuracy; and unfortunately it is not documented. F. Marguet's *Histoire générale de la Navigation du XVe au XXe Siècle* (1931) may also be consulted, especially for the later centuries.

The inclusion of references to particular articles in historical journals would have expanded this bibliography to unmanageable proportions: but students would be well advised to go carefully through the files of the *English Historical Review, History, Economic History Review, Journal of the Royal United Service Institution*, the *Naval Review*, and, above all, *The Mariner's Mirror*, since these contain a mass of highly important material which is not to be found elsewhere.

CHAPTER I   The mediaeval prelude

There is at present no authoritative maritime history covering the mediaeval era; and, in the present writer's opinion, owing to the inherent difficulties of the subject it is very improbable that there ever will be. There are a number of first-rate monographs, and a few sketches of the whole period in outline; but a great deal of the ground is still practically unexplored.

The works of W. Laird Clowes and Hannay cited above are useful and important: but they should nevertheless be read with caution. The maritime sections in the *Victoria County History* and in the earlier volumes of *Social England*, 7 vols. (1904), ed. Traill and Mann, should also be studied. The standard authority on the administrative side is Oppenheim's *History of the Administration of the Royal Navy* (1896). Nicolas' *History of the Royal Navy*, 2 vols. (1847) is still a mine of useful information. Other important contributions to naval history in the period under review are as follows: *Sovereignty of the Seas* by T. W. Fulton (1911), *Prejudice and Promise in Fifteenth-Century England* by C. L. Kingsford (1925), *Constitutional History of the Cinque Ports* (1935) and the section on 'Shipping' in *Mediaeval England* (2nd ed., 1958), both by K. M. E. Murray.

A good deal of light is thrown on the trading systems of the Italian city states and of the Hanse by the following authorities: *Cambridge Economic History of Europe, II: Trade and Industry in the Middle Ages*, ed. Postan and Rich (1952), Schanz's *Englische Handelspolitik gegen Ende des Mittelalters* (1881), A. Ruddock's *Italian Merchants and Shipping in Southampton, 1270–1600* (1951), E. R. Daenell's *Die Blütezeit der deutschen Hanse* (1906), E. Baasch's *Die Islandfahrt der Deutschen* (1899), J. A. Gade's *The Hanseatic Control of Norwegian Commerce* (1951), J. Schreiner's *Hanseatene og Norges nedgang* (1938). For the growth of English trade during the later Middle Ages, see *English Merchant Shipping, 1460–1540* by D. Burwash (1947), *Studies in English Trade in the Fifteenth Century*, ed. Power and Postan (1933), *Commercial Relations of England and Portugal* by Shillington and Chapman (1907), *The Wool Trade in English Mediaeval History* by Eileen Power (1941), *Medieval Merchant Venturers* (1954) by E. M. Carus-Wilson, who also edited *The Overseas Trade of Bristol in the Later Middle Ages* (1937). For the English traffic with Iceland, the indispensable authority is *Diplomatarium Islandicum*, XVI, ed. Björn Thorsteinsson.

For ship-design and rigging, see G. S. Laird Clowes' *Sailing Ships, their History and Development* (1936) and Sir Alan Moore's *Rig in the North* (1956). For a detailed study of the subject, however, a careful search should be made through the files of *The Mariner's Mirror*.

CHAPTER II The early Tudor navy

For the religious, political, and commercial background, see Pollard's *Life of Thomas Cranmer* (1926 ed.), *Factors in Modern History* (1932 ed.), *Henry VIII* (1951 ed.), and *Wolsey* (1953 ed.), R. W. Chambers' *Thomas More* (1938), Garrett Mattingly's *Catherine of Aragon* (1942), Mackie's *The Early Tudors* (1952), and J. A. Williamson's *The Tudors* (1953).

The period is covered by the works of Sir William Laird Clowes and David Hannay cited above, but certain of their conclusions need to be revised in the light of recent knowledge. Oppenheim's monumental work, *The History of the Administration of the Royal Navy, 1509–1660* (1896), may be supplemented by his *Naval Accounts and Inventories of the Reign of Henry VII* (1896); see also *Papers relating to the War with France, 1512–1513*, ed. Spont (1897), and D. Burwash's *English Merchant Shipping* (1947).

Of the modern accounts of English maritime enterprise in the early Tudor period the most important are Connell-Smith's *Forerunners of Drake* (1947), A. L. Rowse's *Tudor Cornwall* (1951), J. A. Williamson's *The Ocean in English History* (1941) and *The Cabot Voyages and Bristol Discovery under Henry VIII* (1961).

The Art of Navigation in Elizabethan and Early Stuart Times by D. W. Waters (1958) is by far the most accurate and comprehensive work of its kind ever to be published: it casts an abundance of light in many dark places.

CHAPTER III The age of expansion

For the overseas expansion of the Peninsular States, see Fontoura da Costa's *A Marinharia dos Descobrimentos* (1933), *La Science nautique des portugais à l'époque des découvertes* (1935), and *A Arrojada viagem de Pedro Álvares Cabral* (1937), Prestage's *Portuguese Pioneers* (1933), A. P. Newton's *The Great Age of Discovery* (1932), Quirino da Fonseca's *Diarios da Navegação* (1938), C. R. Boxer's *Tragic History of the Sea, 1589–1622* (1953), R. B. Merriman's *The Rise of the Spanish Empire* (1918), B. Penrose's *Travel and Discovery in the Renaissance, 1420–1620* (1932), A. P. Newton's *European Nations in the West Indies* (1933), F. A. Kirkpatrick's *Spanish Conquistadores* (1934), C. Ibáñez de Ibero's *Historia de la Marina de Guerra Española* (2nd ed., 1943), S. Franco García's *Historia de Arte y Ciencia de Navegar* (1947), and S. E. Morison's *Christopher Columbus* (1957).

For English maritime enterprise in the sixteenth century, see D. W. Prowse's *History of Newfoundland* (1895), J. N. L. Baker's *Discovery of the Eastern Coast of America* (1937), *Three Voyages of Martin Frobisher*, ed. V. Stefánsson (1938), Sir William Foster's *England's Quest of Eastern Trade* (1933), A. C. Wood's *History of the Levant Company* (1935), A. L. Rowse's *Sir Richard Grenville of the Revenge* (1937), J. A. Williamson's *The Age of Drake* (1938), *The Ocean in English History* (1941), and *Hawkins of Plymouth* (1949), E. G. R. Taylor's *Tudor Geography, 1485–1583* (1930), G. D. Ramsay's *English Overseas Trade* (1957), T. S. Willan's *The Muscovy Merchants of 1555* (1953) and *Studies in Elizabethan Foreign Trade* (1959), and D. W. Waters' *The Art of Navigation in Elizabethan and Early Stuart Times* (1958).

An almost inexhaustible mine of information concerning the English traffics and discoveries during this era is Hakluyt's great work, *Principal Navigations of the English Nation*, 12 vols. (1903), while most of the original accounts of the foreign voyages and discoveries are to be found in the invaluable publications of the Hakluyt Society.

A short but extremely interesting and important work which may be consulted for this period is W. B. Whall's *Shakespeare's Sea Terms Explained* (1910).

CHAPTER IV The Spanish War

For the religious, political, and commercial background to the Spanish War, see *England and the Catholic Church under Elizabeth* by A. O. Meyer (1916), *Mr. Secretary Walsingham*, 3 vols., by Conyers Read (1925), *Queen Elizabeth* by Sir John Neale (1934), *The Reign of Queen Elizabeth* by J. B. Black, *The Tudor Age* by J. A. Williamson, *Mr Secretary Cecil and Queen Elizabeth* by Conyers Read, 2 vols. (1960), *King James VI of Scotland* by H. G. Stafford (1940), *Ireland under the Tudors*, 3 vols. (1890), by

R. Bagwell, *The Expansion of Elizabethan England* (1955) and *The Elizabethans and America* (1959), both by A. L. Rowse.

The standard authority for the Spanish War is Sir Julian Corbett, whose works on *The Spanish War, 1585–1587* (1898), *Drake and the Tudor Navy*, 2 vols. (1899), and *Successors of Drake* (1900) are indispensable for the detailed study of the period. The works of W. Laird Clowes and Hannay are also important. For the part played by Sir John Hawkins in the preparations for the war, see J. A. Williamson's *Sir John Hawkins* (1929) and *Hawkins of Plymouth* (1949). Hale's *The Great Armada* (1910), though to some extent superseded, is still useful, and Rodgers' *Naval Warfare under Oars* (1939) contains valuable information. An admirable recent account of the great 'climacteric year', 1588, is Garrett Mattingly's *The Defeat of the Spanish Armada* (1959). This is important for its vivid portrayal of the religious, political, and diplomatic background to the struggle, rather than for the naval war. Other important modern accounts of the campaign of 1588 are contained in J. A. Williamson's *The Age of Drake* and M. A. Lewis' *The Spanish Armada* (1959) and *The Armada Guns* (1960). *The Naval Tracts of Sir William Monson*, ed. with commentary by Oppenheim, should be consulted. An important contribution to the naval history of the post-Armada period is A. L. Rowse's *Sir Richard Granville of the Revenge*. For events in Ireland in 1588, including the Armada wrecks, see Cyril Falls' *Elizabeth's Irish Wars* (1950) and Bagwell's *Ireland under the Tudors*, III.

On the Spanish side see R. T. Davies' *The Golden Century of Spain* (1937), Altamira's *Felipe II, Hombre de Estado* (1950), Leon van der Essen's *Alexandre Farnese*, 5 vols. (1937), Thomazi's *Les flottes de l'or* (1937), Duque de Maura's *El designio de Felipe II* (1957), C. Ibáñez de Ibero's *Santa Cruz: Primer Marino de Espana* (1946), C. Fernández Duro's *La Armada Invencible* (1888) and *La Armada Española* (1895), E. Herrara Oria's *La Armada Invencible* (1929), and Froude's *Spanish Story of the Armada* (1892).

For the part played by the Netherlands, see P. J. Blok's *A History of the People of the Netherlands* (1900), G. Edmondson's *A History of Holland* (1922), Pieter Geyl's *The Revolt of the Netherlands, 1555–1609* (1932), J. de la Gravière's *Las Gueux de Mer* (1893), and Motley's *The United Provinces* (1904 ed.). The last-mentioned work treats the subject in full detail and is particularly informative concerning the vital strategic importance of the Flanders theatre. A recent and very valuable contribution to the subject is R. B. Wernham's essay in *Britain and the Netherlands*, ed. Bromley and Kossmann (1960): see also the same writer's contribution to *Elizabethan Government and Society: essays presented to Sir John Neale* (1961).

Much light is shed by the contemporary evidence contained in *New Light on Drake*, ed. Z. Nuttall (1914), *Sir Francis Drake's Voyage around the World* by H. R. Wagner (1926), *World Encompassed*, ed. by G. E. Hollingworth (1933), *Spanish Documents concerning English Voyages to the Caribbean, 1527–1568* (1929), *Documents concerning English Voyages to the Spanish Main, 1569–1580* (1932), and *Voyages to Spanish America 1583–1594* (1952), all ed. I. A. Wright, *English Privateering Voyages to the West Indies, 1588–1595*, ed. K. R. Andrews (1959), *Defeat of the Armada*, ed. J. K. Laughton (1895), and the *Calendar of State Papers*, especially *C. S. P.*, Spanish (1587–1603), ed. Martin Hume. To these must be added *The Spanish War, 1585–1587*, ed. J. S. Corbett cited above, and *The Observations of Sir Richard Hawkins*, ed. J. A. Williamson (1930).

CHAPTER V England and Holland

For the general political and commercial background, see G. M. Trevelyan's *England under the Stuarts* (19th ed., 1947), Pieter Geyl's *The Netherlands Divided, 1609–1648* (1936), G. J. Renier's *The Dutch Nation* (1944), Maurice Ashley's *The Seventeenth Century* (1952), and Davies' *The Early Stuarts* (2nd ed., 1957).

The early half of the seventeenth century is covered by the works of W. Laird Clowes, Hannay, and Oppenheim. For the administration of the Navy, *The Navy under the Early Stuarts* by C. D. Penn (1913) and *The Public Career of Lionel Cranfield* by R. C. Johnson (1956) should also be consulted. On the medical side see J. J. Keevil's *Medicine and the Navy: 1649–1714* (1957).

For the activities of the Barbary corsairs, see R. E. Weber's *De beveiliging van de zee tegen Europeesche en Barbarijsche zeeroovers, 1609–1621* (1936); a recent English work on the same subject, Sir Godfrey Fisher's *Barbary Legend* (1958), should be read with caution.

For English maritime, commercial, and colonial enterprise, see G. L. Beer's *Origins of the Old Colonial System, 1579–1660* (1908), Sir William Foster's *The English Factories in India, 1618–1629*, 3 vols. (1909) and *England's Quest of Eastern Trade* (1933), Cotton and Fawcett's *East Indiamen* (1949), A. P. Newton's *The Colonising Activities of the English Puritans* (1912), A. D. Innes' *Maritime and Colonial Expansion of England under the Stuarts* (1931), L. B. Wright's *The Colonial Civilisation of North America, 1607–1673* (1949), A. L. Rowse's *The Elizabethans and America* (1959), and R. W. Hinton's *Eastland Trade and the Common Weal in the Seventeenth Century* (1959).

For the Dutch expansion, see *Oorlogsinvloeden op de overzeese handel van*

Handel, 1551-1719 by F. Snapper (1959), *Jan Compagnie in Japan, 1600-1817* (1936) and *The Dutch in Brazil, 1624-1652* (1957), both by C. R. Boxer, *De Kapiteinsjaren van Maerten Harpertszoon Tromp* by F. Graafe (1936), *Jan Pieterz Coen* by W. P. Coolhaas (1953), *De Rotterdamse particuliere scheepsbouw in de tijd van de Republiek* by S. C. van Kampen (1953), and *Witte de With in Brazilie* by W. J. van Hoboken (1955). For the fight between the Spaniards and Dutch in the Downs in 1639, see *The Journal of Maarten Harpertszoon Tromp, Anno 1639*, ed, C. R. Boxer (1930).

A useful guide for the struggle with Holland is G. Edmondson's *Anglo-Dutch Rivalry during the first half of the Seventeenth Century* (1911). Primary authorities are represented by *Letters and Papers relating to the First Dutch War*, ed. Gardiner and Atkinson, 6 vols., the last of them appearing in 1930. The effect of the Navigation Act of 1651 can be studied in L. A. Harper's *The English Navigation Laws* (1939). An important monograph on the duel with Holland is Charles Wilson's *Profit and Power* (1957).

For the Baltic, in addition to R. W. Hinton's *Eastland Trade and the Common Weal in the Seventeenth Century* cited above, see R. C. Anderson's *Naval Wars in the Baltic in the Sailing Ship Epoch* (1910) and Kirchhoff's *Seemacht in der Ostsee*, 2 vols. (1917).

CHAPTER VI The Restoration Navy

For the political background, see G. N. Clark's *The Later Stuarts* (1934), A. S. Turberville's *Commonwealth and Restoration* (1936), Pieter Geyl's *Oranje en Stuart, 1641-1672* (1939), Maurice Ashley's *England in the Seventeenth Century* (1952), and David Ogg's *England in the Reign of Charles II* (1934) and *England in the Reigns of James II and William III* (1955).

This period is covered by the works of W. Laird Clowes and Hannay. More recent contributions to the naval history of the Restoration era are as follows: *The Navy of the Restoration* by A. W. Tedder (1916), *The Navy in the Revolution of 1688* by E. B. Powley (1928), *Memorials . . . of the professional life and times of Sir William Penn* by G. Penn (1833), *Edward Montagu, Earl of Sandwich* by Harris (1912), *Life of Sir John Narborough* by F. E. Dyer (1931), and *The Journals of Sir Thomas Allin* (1940) and *Journals and Narratives of the Third Dutch War* (1946), both ed. R. C. Anderson. For the administration of the Navy, see J. R. Tanner's *Samuel Pepys and the Royal Navy* (1920), and Sir Arthur Bryant's *Pepys*, 3 vols. (1938), as well as Pepys' *Diary* and *The Tangier Papers of Samuel Pepys*, ed. E. Chappell (1935).

The Mediterranean station is treated in W. F. Lord's *England and France in the Mediterranean, 1669–1830* (1901) and in Sir Julian Corbett's detailed and comprehensive study, *England in the Mediterranean, 1603–1703*, 2 vols. (1904).

On the Dutch side see G. Brandt's *Leven van de Ruyter* (1913 ed.), P. J. Blok's *Life of Admiral de Ruyter*, trans. G. J. Renier (1933), Colenbrander's *Bescheiden vreemde archieven omtrent de groote Nederlandsche Zeeoorlogen* (1919), and J. C. Warnsinck's *Admiraal de Ruyter: De Zeeslag op Schooneveld* (1930). The last-named work is an accurate and detailed study of de Ruyter's great defensive campaign of 1673.

On the French side see Guérin's *Histoire maritime de France* (1863), Troude's *Batailles de la France* (1867), Lacour-Gayet's *Le Marine militaire de la France sous les règnes de Louis XIII et de Louis XIV* (1911), and de la Roncière's *Histoire de la Marine française* (1932).

For seaborne trade, colonies, and exploration, see *Origins of the Colonial System* (1908) and *The Old Colonial System* (1912), both by G. L. Beer, *Cambridge History of the British Empire*, I (1929), *Short History of British Colonial Policy* by H. E. Egerton (9th ed., 1932), *Short History of British Expansion*, I (3rd ed., 1945) by J. A. Williamson, *The Great Chartered Companies* by David Hannay (1926), *Religion, Colonising and Trade: The Driving Forces of the Old Empire* by C. Lucas (1930), *Maritime and Colonial Expansion of England under the Stuarts* by A. D. Innes (1931), *Eastland Trade and the Common Weal in the Seventeenth Century* by R. W. Hinton (1959), *The East India Trade in the Seventeenth Century* by Khan (1930), *England's Quest of Eastern Trade* by W. Foster (1933), *Trader's Dream* by R. H. Mottram (1939), *Commerce and Conquest* by C. L. Reid (1947), *Explorers of North America* by J. B. Brebner (1933), *Colonial Civilisation of North America, 1607–1673* by L. B. Wright (1949), *Development of the Leeward Islands under the Restoration, 1660–1683* by C. Higham (1920), *European Nations in the West Indies, 1492–1688* by A. P. Newton (1933), *Merchants and Planters* by R. Pares (1960), *William Dampier* by C. Wilkinson (1929), and *Brethren of the Coast* by P. K. Kemp and C. C. Lloyd (1960).

CHAPTER VII The Rhine delta

For the political background, see G. N. Clark's *The Later Stuarts* (1934), Churchill's *Marlborough and his Times*, 4 vols. (1938), Bagwell's *Ireland under the Stuarts* (1916), P. Hume Brown's *History of Scotland* (1911), Ogg's *England in the Reigns of James II and William III* (1955), and Ashley's *Louis XIV and the Greatness of France* (1953).

The naval history of the reign of William and Mary is covered by both W. Laird Clowes and Hannay. A valuable work of recent date is John

Ehrman's *The Navy in the War of William III* (1953). This is chiefly important for the administration of the Fleet, in which respect it carries on Oppenheim's great work; for the war at sea it is somewhat inadequate.

For the Mediterranean, which begins to loom large in the naval scene, there are Lord's *England and France in the Mediterranean, 1669–1830* (1901) and Sir Julian Corbett's detailed and comprehensive study, *England in the Mediterranean, 1603–1713* (1904).

For the part played by the Dutch in the war, see *The Dutch Alliance and the War against French Trade, 1689–1697* by G. N. Clark (1923) and *De Vloot van den Stadhouder Koningk, 1689–1690* by J. C. Warnsinck (1935).

On the French side see Guérin, Lacour-Gayet, and de la Roncière as above, and also Troude's *Batailles navales de la France* (1867), Castex's *Les Idées militaires de la Marine du XVIIIᵉ Siècle: De Ruyter à Suffren* and *Théories Stratégiques* (1931), J. Tramond's *Manuel d'histoire maritime de la France* (2nd ed., 1927), C. W. Cole's *Colbert and a Century of French Mercantilism*, 2 vols, (1939), C. Farrère's *Jean-Baptiste Colbert* (1954), and G. S. Graham's *Empire of the North Atlantic* (1958). For the *guerre de course*, see *Life of Jean Bart*, trans. Mangin (1828), *La Grand Guerre des Corsaires* (1925) and *Jean Bart* (1947) by H. Malo, *Wolves of the Channel* by W. B. Johnson (1931), *Mémoires du comte de Forbin*, ed. Claude de Forbin (1934), *Jean Bart d'après des documents*, ed. A. Lesmaries (1935), and L. Haffner's *Jean Bart et la Marine de son temps* (1956). For the French colonies, see G. M. Wrong's *Rise and Fall of New France* (1928), L. P. May's *Histoire économique de la Martinique* (1930), J. B. Brebner's *Explorers of North America* (1933), and D. G. Creighton's *The Commercial Empire of the St. Lawrence*. For tactics, there is the very important *L'Art des Armées navales ou Traité des Evolutions navales* by Père Hoste (1697).

CHAPTER VIII   The War of the Spanish Succession

For the political and military background, see Ashley, Churchill, and Clark as above, and Trevelyan's *England under Queen Anne*, 3 vols. (1934).

For the maritime struggle, see W. Laird Clowes and Hannay as above. An admirable modern account of the war from 1702 to 1708 is *The War at Sea under Queen Anne* by J. H. Owen (1938). A useful contemporary record is Burchett's *Complete History of Remarkable Transactions at Sea* (1720), which may be supplemented by *The Naval History of England* by Lediard (1735), *Journal of Sir George Rooke*, ed. Browning (1897), *Life of Sir John Leake* by S. Martin-Leake (1920), and *The Byng Papers*, ed. Tunstall (1933).

For the Mediterranean, Lord's *England and France in the Mediterranean, 1669–1830* (1901) and Corbett's *England in the Mediterranean* (1904).

473

An interesting account of the Canadian expedition of 1711 is *The Walker Expedition to Quebec*, ed. G. S. Graham (1953), whose admirable *Empire of the North Atlantic* is useful for other operations in North American waters. For the West India station, see *Queen Anne's Navy in the West Indies* by R. Bourne (1939).

On the French side see Guérin, Troude, Lacour-Gayet, Castex, Tramond, and de la Roncière as above; and for the *guerre de course* consult the works of Malo, Forbin, and Le Nepvou de Carfort, also *Duguay-Trouin, corsaire et chef d'escadre* by H. Carré (1941).

CHAPTER IX The War of 1739–48

For the political and commercial background, see W. Basil Williams' *The Life of William Pitt, Earl of Chatham*, 2 vols. (1914) and *The Whig Supremacy* (1946), Simon Harcourt-Smith's *Alberoni* (1943), Paul Vaucher's *Walpole et la politique de Fleury* (1924) and *La Crise du ministère Walpole, 1733–4* (1925), A. McC. Wilson's *French Foreign Policy during the Administration of Cardinal Fleury* (1936), Sir Charles Petrie's *The Jacobite Movement* (1958), and J. H. Plumb's *Sir Robert Walpole*, 2 vols. (1960).

For operations at sea, W. Laird Clowes and Hannay as above. The main authority for the war at sea is *The Navy in the War of 1739–1748*, 3 vols. (1920) by Admiral Sir Herbert Richmond. This work is admittedly difficult to digest but it is indispensable to any thorough study of the subject. There is unfortunately no full-scale biography of either Vernon or Anson: for these two great commanders, see *Admiral Vernon and the Navy* by D. Ford (1901), *Angry Admiral* by C. H. Hartman (1955), *The Vernon Papers*, ed. B. Ranft (1958), *The Life of Anson* by Sir John Barrow (1839), and *The Life of Admiral Lord Anson* by W. V. Anson (1912). For the great voyage of circumnavigation, see Anson's *Voyage Round the World*, ed. G. S. Laird Clowes (1928) and *Commodore Anson's World Voyage* by Vice-Admiral Boyle Somerville (1934). For the combined operations of this war, see *Generals and Admirals* by John Creswell (1952).

On the French side see Guérin, Troude, Castex, Tramond, and de la Roncière as above; also Lacour-Gayet's *La marine militaire de la France sous le règne de Louis XV* (1902), J. S. McLennan's *Louisbourg from its Foundations to its Fall* (1918), Crepin's *Mahé de la Bourdonnais* (1922), G. M. Wrong's *The Rise and Fall of New France* (1928), L. P. May's *Histoire économique de Martinique* (1930), J. B. Brebner's *Explorers of North America* (1933), D. G. Creighton's *The Commercial Empire of the St. Lawrence* (1937), and Jouneau-Dubreuil's *Dupleix ou l'Inde conquise* (1942).

For seaborne trade and the colonies, see G. L. Beer's *The Old Colonial*

System, 1660–1754 (1917), H. Dodwell's *Dupleix and Clive* (1920), P. E. Roberts' *History of India under the Company and the Crown* (1923), R. H. Mottram's *Trader's Dream* (1939), J. B. Brebner's *New England's Outpost* (1927), R. G. Lounsbury's *British Fishery at Newfoundland, 1634–1763* (1934), R. Pares' *War and Trade in the West Indies, 1739–1763* (1936), C. Wilson's *Anglo-Dutch Commerce and Finance in the Eighteenth Century* (1941), and C. E. Carrington's *The British Overseas* (1950). Important primary sources are Josiah Gee's *Trade and Navigation of Great Britain* (4th ed., 1738) and also Defoe's *Plan of English Commerce* (1728) and *Tour through Great Britain* (ed. Cole, 1927).

For the Baltic, the following are important authorities: *History of the Russian Fleet during the Reign of Peter the Great*, ed. C. A. Bridge (1899), *George I and the Northern War* by J. F. Chance (1909), *Naval Wars in the Baltic in the Sailing Ship Epoch* by R. C. Anderson (1910), *Seemacht in der Ostsee* by H. Kirchhoff (2 vols., 1907), *Karl XII och den Ryska Sjömakten* by C. L. A. Munthe (3 vols., 1927), and *Svenska Flottans Historia*, II, ed. O. Lybeck (1943).

For the highly important factor of maritime rights, *Neutrality: I, The Origins* by Jessup and Deak (1935), *The Freedom of the Seas in History, Law, and Politics* by J. B. Potter (1936), and *Colonial Blockade and Neutral Rights, 1739–1763* by R. Pares (1938) are valuable.

CHAPTER X   The Seven Years War

For the general political and commercial background, see L. B. Namier's *England in the Age of the American Revolution* (1930), W. Basil Williams' *The Life of William Pitt, Earl of Chatham* (1914) and *The Whig Supremacy* (1946), Hall and Albion's *History of England and the Empire* (1937), G. P. Gooch's *The Monarchy in Decline* (1956), and Steven Watson's *The Reign of George III* (1960).

The standard British authority for the Seven Years War is Corbett's *England in the Seven Years War*, 2 vols. (1907), which contains a comprehensive and detailed exposition of Pitt's grand strategy both by land and sea. Mahan's *The Influence of Sea Power upon History* (1890) is still important. There is no modern authoritative study of any of the great fighting admirals, but *The Life of Anson* by Sir John Barrow (1834), *The Life of Lord Anson* by W. V. Anson (1912), and *The Life of Admiral Lord Hawke* by Montagu Burrows (1883) will be found useful. Other authorities which should be studied are Tunstall's *William Pitt, Earl of Chatham* (1938) and Sherrard's *Lord Chatham: Pitt and the Seven Years War* (1952).   For combined operations, see F. R. Hart's *The Siege of Havana* (1931) and R. H. Whitworth's *Field-Marshal Lord Ligonier* (1958). Beatson's *Naval and Military Memoirs of Great Britain from 1727 to 1783* (1790), compiled within a generation of the Seven Years War, contains a mass of useful material, and *Augustus Harvey's Journal*, ed. the Hon David Erskine (1953) is lively and enthralling as well as important. *Quiberon Bay* by G. J. Marcus (1960) is a survey of the campaign in home waters in the crucial year of the struggle, 1759.

For the Mediterranean, see W. F. Lord's *England and France in the Mediterranean, 1669–1830* (1901). Important contemporary evidence is contained in *Admiral Byng and the Loss of Minorca*, ed.Tunstall (1928).

For the North American theatre, see A. G. Bradley's *Fight with France for North America* (1900), Doughty and Parmelee's *Siege of Quebec*, 6 vols. (1901), W. Wood's *The Fight for Canada* (1905), *Logs of the Conquest of Canada*, ed. W. Wood (1909), John Knox's *An Historical Journal of the Campaigns in North America* (1916 ed.), J. S. McLennan's *Louisbourg from its Foundation to its Fall* (1918), G. M. Wrong's *Conquest of New France* (1921), and G. S. Graham's *Empire of the North Atlantic* (2nd ed., 1958). Two important recent accounts of the British offensive in North America are C. P. Stacey's *Quebec* (1959) and Robin Reilly's *The rest to fortune: The Life of Major-General James Wolfe.* (1959) For the West Indies, see Hart and Whitworth cited above, and also Smelser's *The Campaign for the Sugar Islands, 1759* (1955).

On the French side see Guérin, Troude, Lacour-Gayet, Castex, and Tramond as above, and also *Journal du Marquis de Montcalm, 1756–1759*, ed. H. R. Casgrain, (1895). A balanced and objective account of the whole struggle is Waddington's *La Guerre de Sept Ans*, 3 vols. (1904).

The vital issue of maritime rights is treated in Jessup and Deak's *Neutrality: I, The Origins* (1935), Kulrud's *Maritime Neutrality to 1780* (1936), R. Pares' *Colonial Blockade and Neutral Rights* (1938), and H. W. Richmond's *Imperial Defence and Capture at Sea in War* (1941).

CHAPTER XI Sea Life under the Georges

For ship-design and rigging, an important authority is John Charnock's *History of Marine Architecture*, 3 vols. (1802). Some useful modern studies are G. S. Laird Clowes' *Sailing Ships, their History and Development* (1936), G. Blake's *British Ships and Shipbuilders* (1946), Nepean Longridge's *The Anatomy of Nelson's Ships* (1955), and Sir Alan Moore's *Rig in Northern Europe* (1956). The maritime sections in *Social England*, ed. Traill and Mann (7 vols., 1904), should also be consulted. For the timber problem, which reached a crisis during this period, see R. G. Albion's *Forests and*

Sea Power (1926), Adler's *Englands Versorgung mit Schiffsbaumaterialien aus englischen und amerikanischen Quellen* (1937), Bamford's *Forests and French Sea Power, 1660–1789* (1956), and also, for contemporary evidence, Roger Fisher's *Heart of Oak, the British Bulwark* (1763).

For seamanship and navigation during the Georgian era, the following are standard authorities: T. R. Branckley's *A Naval Expositor* (1750), Falconer's *Universal Dictionary of the Marine* (1769), J. Hamilton Moore's *The New Practical Navigator* (1772), David Steel's *Elements and Practice of Rigging and Seamanship* (1794), John Norie's *A Complete Epitome of Practical Navigation* (1805), and Darcy Lever's *The Young Sea Officer's Sheet Anchor* (1808). See also James Rennell's *Observations on a Current*, etc. (1793) and *Investigation of the Currents of the Atlantic Ocean* (1832). A valuable monograph of more recent date is R. T. Gould's *The Marine Chronometer* (1923). The standard authority on lighthouses is D. Allan Stevenson, with his *English Lighthouse Tours, 1801, 1813, 1818* (1946) and *The World's Lighthouses before 1820* (1959).

Exploration and discovery are treated in *Pacific Horizons* by C. C. Lloyd (1946), *The Exploration of the Pacific* (3rd ed., 1947) by J. C. Beaglehole and *The Journals of Captain James Cook on his Voyages of Discovery* (1955), edited by the same author, *The Life of James Cook* (1939) by H. Carrington, who also edited *The Discovery of Tahiti* (1948), and *Voyages and Cruises of Commodore Walker*, ed. G. E. Manwaring.

For strategy and tactics, Corbett's *Some Principles of Maritime Strategy* (1911), Creswell's *Naval Warfare* (2nd ed., 1942), *Fighting Instructions, 1530–1816* (1905) and *Signals and Instructions* (1908), both ed. J. S. Corbett, and S. and M. Robinson's *A History of Naval Tactics from 1530 to 1930* (1942).

For hygiene and medicine, Tobias Smollett's *An Account of the Expedition against Cartagena* (1756), James Lind's *Essay on . . . the Health of Seamen* (1757) and *Treatise on Scurvy*, ed. C. P. Stuart and D. Guthrie (1953), Sir Gilbert Blane's *Observations on the Diseases incident to Seamen* (1785), W. Alison's *Sea Diseases* (1947), and Lloyd and Coulter's *Medicine and the Navy, 1714–1815* (1961).

For the social history of the Navy during this period there is an abundance of good material, among which the following choice may be made. Primary authorities: *Above and under Hatches* (Recollections of James Anthony Gardner), ed. C. C. Lloyd (1957), *Memoirs of Celebrated Naval Commanders* by E. H. Locker (1830), *Naval Yarns*, ed. W. H. Long (1899), *Letters of the English Seamen*, ed. H. Moorhouse (1900), *Landsman Hay*, ed. M. D. Hay (1953), *A Sailor's Letters* by E. Thompson (1767), and *The Barrington Papers*, ed. D. Bonner-Smith (1941). Secondary authorities: *Types of Naval*

Officers by A. T. Mahan (1901), *Famous Fighters of the Fleet* by E. Fraser (1904), *The British Tar in Fact and Fiction* by C. N. Robinson (1909), *Naval Courts-martial* by David Hannay (1910), *The Press Gang, Afloat and Ashore* by J. R. Hutchinson (1913), *Old Times Afloat* by C. Field (1932), *Young Gentlemen* by C. F. Walker (1938), *Captain Marryat and the Old Navy* by C. C. Lloyd (1939), *The Naval Heritage* by David Mathew (1944), *Prize Money* by P. K. Kemp (1946), also *England's Sea Officers* (1939) and *The Social History of the Royal Navy, 1793–1815*, both by M. A. Lewis.

For shipping, seaborne commerce, and the fisheries, the following are sound authorities: W. S. Lindsay's *The History of Merchant Shipping*, 4 vols. (1878), Moyse-Bartlett's *History of the Merchant Navy* (1937), C. E. Fayle's *Short History of the World's Shipping Industry* (1933), *Trade Winds*, ed. C. N. Parkinson (1948), Cotton and Fawcett's *East Indiaman* (1949), T. S. Willan's *Coasting Trade* (1938), Owen Rutter's *Red Ensign, A History of Convoy* (1947), D. Owen's *Ports and Docks, their History, Working and National Importance* (1904), E. Broodbank's *History of the Port of London* (1921), C. M. MacInnes' *A Gateway of Empire* (1939), C. N. Parkinson's *Rise of the Port of Liverpool* (1952), C. R. Fay's *Great Britain from Adam Smith to the Present Day* (1928) and *Imperial Economy* (1934), C. Lucas' *Religion, Colonising and Trade: The Driving Forces of the Old Empire* (1930), M. Q. Innis' *An Economic History of Canada* (1935), G. S. Graham's *Sea Power and British North America* (1941), Bogart's *Economic History of the American People* (1942), F. W. Pitman's *Development of the British West Indies* (1917), Pares' *A West India Fortune* (1950) and *Yankees and Creoles* (1956), Wright and Fayle's *A History of Lloyd's* (1928), D. E. W. Gibb's *Lloyd's of London* (1957), E. W. Holdsworth's *Deep-Sea Fishing and Fishing Boats* (1874), D. W. Prowse's *History of Newfoundland* (1896), G. S. Laird Clowes' *British Fishing and Coastal Craft* (1937), H. A. Innis' *The Cod Fisheries* (1951), also E. March's *Sailing Drifters* (1952) and *Sailing Trawlers* (1953).

CHAPTER XII   The War of American Independence

For the general background to the struggle, see Kate Hotblack's *The Peace of Paris, 1763* (1908), L. B. Namier's *Structure of Politics at the Accession of George III* (1929) and *England in the Age of the American Revolution* (1930), H. Butterfield's *George III, Lord North, and the People* (1949), R. Pares' *George III and the Politicians* (1953), I. R. Christie's *The End of North's Ministry* (1958), and Steven Watson's *The Reign of George III* (1960).

A detailed and comprehensive study of the whole struggle is G. O. Trevelyan's *The American Revolution* (1899). An indispensable authority is once again Mahan, whose *Major Operations of the Navies in the War of American Independence* (1913) may be supplemented by G. O. Paullin's *The Navy of the American Revolution*, 2 vols. (1906), G. W. Allen's *Naval History of the American Revolution*, 2 vols. (1913), W. M. James' *The British Navy in Adversity* (1926), and T. S. Anderson's *The Command of the Howe brothers during the American Revolution* (1926). There is no modern authoritative study of either Keppel, Rodney, or Howe. Keppel's *Life of Augustus, Viscount Keppel* (1842), G. B. Mundy's *Life of Admiral Lord Rodney* (1830), David Hannay's *Rodney* (1889), and Sir John Barrow's *Life of Howe* (1838) are still worth consulting. The part played by Paul Jones in the *guerre de course* is admirably portrayed in S. E. Morison's full-scale biography, *John Paul Jones* (1960). Other important studies are *The Maritime History of Massachusetts* (2nd ed., 1941), also by S. E. Morison, *The Empire of the North Atlantic* by G. S. Graham (1958), and *The Other Armada* (1961) by A. Temple Patterson. H. W. Richmond's *The Navy in India, 1763–1783* (1931) contains a clear and comprehensive survey of the struggle for mastery in Eastern waters – the importance of which is at last beginning to be properly understood; it may be supplemented by Sir William Hunter's *History of British India* (1899). *The Private Papers of John, Earl of Sandwich*, ed. G. R. Barnes and J. H. Owen (1938) serves to correct certain earlier misconceptions of the political and administrative background to the War of American Independence. Other important sources of evidence are Beatson's *Naval and Military Memoirs of Great Britain from 1727 to 1783* (1790), *Letters of Sir Samuel Hood*, ed. Hannay (1895), *Letters and Papers of Sir Thomas Byam Martin* (1901) and *Letters and Papers of Charles, Lord Barham* (1911), both ed. J. K. Laughton, T. Pasley's *Private Journals, 1778–1782* (1921), *The Letter-books and Orders of Sir G. B. Rodney*, ed. D. C. Barck (1932), and *The Barrington Papers*, ed. D. Bonner-Smith (1941).

For the Mediterranean, see Lord's *England and France in the Mediterranean, 1669–1830* (1901) and Stetson Conn's *Gibraltar in British Diplomacy in the Eighteenth Century* (1942).

On the French side see Guérin, Troude, Castex, Tramond, and Roncière as above; and also Lacour-Gayet's *La Marine militaire de la France sous le règne de Louis XVI* (1905), K. J. Tornquist's *Naval Campaigns of de Grasse*, trans. Johnson (1942), Calmon-Maison's *L'Amiral d'Estaing* (1910), C. L. Lewis' *De Grasse* (1946), E. Davin's *Suffren* (1947), and E. La Varende's *Suffren et ses ennemis* (1948).

For the part played by the Dutch, see *The Armed Neutralities* by Pigott and Omond (1914) and *La Crépuscule d'une puissance navale: la marine hollandaise de 1776 à 1783* by F. P. Renalut (1932).

The subject of maritime rights is treated in Jessup and Deak's *Neutrality: I, The Origins* (1935), Kulrud's *Maritime Neutrality to 1780* (1936), and Richmond's *Imperial Defence and Capture at Sea in War* (1941). For the Baltic background, see H. Kirchhoff's *Seemacht in der Ostsee*, 2 vols. (1907), C. L. A. Munthe's *Sjömaktens Inflytande på Sveriges Historia*, II (1922), *Svenska Flottans Historia*, II, ed. O. Lybeck (1943).

For the post-war reconstruction and revival of 1783–93, see J. Holland Rose's *William Pitt and the National Revival* (1914), P. Geyl's *De Patriottenbeweging, 1780–1787* (1947), J. T. Harlow's *Founding of the Second British Empire, 1763–93* (1951), and A. Cobban's *Ambassadors and Secret Agents* (1954).

Index